WITHDRAWN

POETRY
for Students

Advisors

Erik France: Adjunct Instructor of English, Macomb Community College, Warren, Michigan. B.A. and M.S.L.S. from University of North Carolina, Chapel Hill; Ph.D. from Temple University.

Kate Hamill: Grade 12 English Teacher, Catonsville High School, Catonsville, Maryland.

Joseph McGeary: English Teacher, Germantown Friends School, Philadelphia, Pennsylvania. Ph.D. in English from Duke University.

Timothy Showalter: English Department Chair, Franklin High School, Reisterstown, Maryland. Certified teacher by the Maryland State Department of Education. Member of the National Council of Teachers of English.

Amy Spade Silverman: English Department Chair, Kehillah Jewish High School, Palo Alto, California. Member of National Council of Teachers of English (NCTE), Teachers and Writers, and NCTE Opinion Panel. Exam Reader, Advanced Placement Literature and Composition. Poet, published in *North American Review, Nimrod,* and *Michigan Quarterly Review,* among other publications.

Jody Stefansson: Director of Boswell Library and Study Center and Upper School Learning Specialist, Polytechnic School, Pasadena, California. Board member, Children's Literature Council of Southern California. Member of American Library Association, Association of Independent School Librarians, and Association of Educational Therapists.

Laura Jean Waters: Certified School Library Media Specialist, Wilton High School, Wilton, Connecticut. B.A. from Fordham University; M.A. from Fairfield University.

POETRY
for Students

Presenting Analysis, Context, and Criticism
on Commonly Studied Poetry

VOLUME 34

Sara Constantakis, Project Editor

Foreword by David J. Kelly

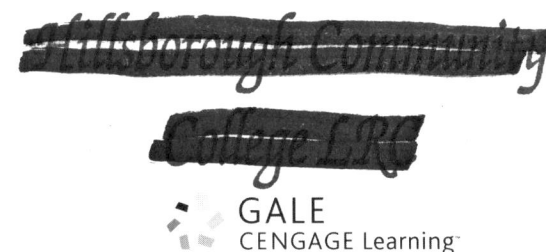

Detroit • New York • San Francisco • New Haven, Conn • Waterville, Maine • London

Poetry for Students, Volume 34

Project Editor: Sara Constantakis

Rights Acquisition and Management: Jennifer Altschul, Beth Beaufore, Kelly Quin, Robyn Young

Composition: Evi Abou-El-Seoud

Manufacturing: Drew Kalasky

Imaging: John Watkins

Product Design: Pamela A. E. Galbreath, Jennifer Wahi

Content Conversion: Katrina Coach

Product Manager: Meggin Condino

© 2010 Gale, Cengage Learning

ALL RIGHTS RESERVED. No part of this work covered by the copyright herein may be reproduced, transmitted, stored, or used in any form or by any means graphic, electronic, or mechanical, including but not limited to photocopying, recording, scanning, digitizing, taping, Web distribution, information networks, or information storage and retrieval systems, except as permitted under Section 107 or 108 of the 1976 United States Copyright Act, without the prior written permission of the publisher.

Since this page cannot legibly accommodate all copyright notices, the acknowledgments constitute an extension of the copyright notice.

For product information and technology assistance, contact us at
Gale Customer Support, 1-800-877-4253.
For permission to use material from this text or product,
submit all requests online at **www.cengage.com/permissions.**
Further permissions questions can be emailed to
permissionrequest@cengage.com

While every effort has been made to ensure the reliability of the information presented in this publication, Gale, a part of Cengage Learning, does not guarantee the accuracy of the data contained herein. Gale accepts no payment for listing; and inclusion in the publication of any organization, agency, institution, publication, service, or individual does not imply endorsement of the editors or publisher. Errors brought to the attention of the publisher and verified to the satisfaction of the publisher will be corrected in future editions.

Gale
27500 Drake Rd.
Farmington Hills, MI, 48331-3535

ISBN-13: 978-1-4144-4182-5
ISBN-10: 1-4144-4182-7

ISSN 1094-7019

This title is also available as an e-book.
ISBN-13: 978-1-4144-4955-5
ISBN-10: 1-4144-4955-0
Contact your Gale, a part of Cengage Learning sales representative for ordering information.

Printed in the United States of America
1 2 3 4 5 6 7 14 13 12 11 10

Table of Contents

ADVISORS ii

JUST A FEW LINES ON A PAGE
(by David J. Kelly) ix

INTRODUCTION xi

LITERARY CHRONOLOGY xv

ACKNOWLEDGMENTS xvii

CONTRIBUTORS xix

AUTOBIOGRAPHIA LITERARIA
(by Frank O'Hara) 1
    Author Biography 2
    Poem Text 2
    Poem Summary 2
    Themes 4
    Style 6
    Historical Context 7
    Critical Overview 9
    Criticism 10
    Sources 24
    Further Reading 24

THE BRIDEGROOM
(by Alexander Sergeyevich Pushkin) 25
    Author Biography 26
    Poem Text 26
    Poem Summary 28

Table of Contents

    Themes 30
    Style 33
    Historical Context 33
    Critical Overview. 35
    Criticism. 36
    Sources 42
    Further Reading 43

CONSCIENTIOUS OBJECTOR
(by Edna St. Vincent Millay) 44
    Author Biography 44
    Poem Text 46
    Poem Summary 46
    Themes 49
    Style 49
    Historical Context 50
    Critical Overview. 52
    Criticism. 53
    Sources 66
    Further Reading 67

THE FLY *(by William Blake)* 68
    Author Biography 69
    Poem Text 70
    Poem Summary 70
    Themes 72
    Style 74
    Historical Context 75
    Critical Overview. 77
    Criticism. 78
    Sources 91
    Further Reading 91

GRANDMOTHER *(by Valzhyna Mort)* 93
    Author Biography 94
    Poem Text 95
    Poem Summary 95
    Themes 96
    Style 98
    Historical Context 99
    Critical Overview. 100
    Criticism. 101
    Sources 110
    Further Reading 111

MIDSUMMER, TOBAGO
(by Derek Walcott) 112
    Author Biography 113
    Poem Summary 114
    Themes 115
    Style 116
    Historical Context 116
    Critical Overview. 118
    Criticism. 119
    Sources 129
    Further Reading 130

MY MOTHER COMBS MY HAIR
(by Chitra Banerjee Divakaruni) 131
    Author Biography 132
    Poem Text 132
    Poem Summary 133
    Themes 133
    Style 135
    Historical Context 136
    Critical Overview. 137
    Criticism. 138
    Sources 147
    Further Reading 148

POSSIBILITIES
(by Wisława Szymborska) 149
    Author Biography 150
    Poem Summary 150
    Themes 152
    Style 153
    Historical Context 153
    Critical Overview. 155
    Criticism. 156
    Sources 170
    Further Reading 170

SINCE FEELING IS FIRST
(by e. e. cummings) 171
    Author Biography 171
    Poem Text 172
    Poem Summary 172
    Themes 173
    Style 175
    Historical Context 175
    Critical Overview. 178
    Criticism. 178
    Sources 192
    Further Reading 192

THE SNOW-STORM
(by Ralph Waldo Emerson) 194
    Author Biography 195
    Poem Text 195
    Poem Summary 196
    Themes 197
    Style 198
    Historical Context 199
    Critical Overview. 202
    Criticism. 203
    Sources 213
    Further Reading 213

THE STOLEN CHILD
(by William Butler Yeats) 215
    Author Biography 216
    Poem Text 216

Poem Summary	217
Themes	219
Style	221
Historical Context	222
Critical Overview.	224
Criticism.	224
Sources	238
Further Reading	238

THIS IS JUST TO SAY
(by William Carlos Williams) 239
   Author Biography 240
   Poem Text 240
   Poem Summary 241
   Themes 242
   Style 244
   Historical Context 245
   Critical Overview. 246
   Criticism. 247
   Sources 252
   Further Reading 252

TO ALTHEA, FROM PRISON
(by Richard Lovelace) 253
   Author Biography 254
   Poem Text 254
   Poem Summary 255
   Themes 257
   Style 257
   Historical Context 258
   Critical Overview. 260
   Criticism. 261
   Sources 277
   Further Reading 277

UP-HILL *(by Christina Georgina Rossetti).* . . 278
   Author Biography 278
   Poem Text 279
   Poem Summary 280
   Themes 281

Style	282
Historical Context	283
Critical Overview.	285
Criticism.	286
Sources	291
Further Reading	292

THE WAKING *(by Theodore Roethke)* . . . 293
   Author Biography 293
   Poem Summary 294
   Themes 296
   Style 298
   Historical Context 299
   Critical Overview. 300
   Criticism. 300
   Sources 310
   Further Reading 311

WOMEN *(by Alice Walker)* 312
   Author Biography 312
   Poem Summary 314
   Themes 315
   Style 316
   Historical Context 317
   Critical Overview. 319
   Criticism. 320
   Sources 329
   Further Reading 330

GLOSSARY OF LITERARY TERMS. . . . 333

CUMULATIVE AUTHOR/TITLE INDEX . . 355

CUMULATIVE NATIONALITY/ETHNICITY INDEX. 367

SUBJECT/THEME INDEX 375

CUMULATIVE INDEX OF FIRST LINES . . 379

CUMULATIVE INDEX OF LAST LINES . . 387

Just a Few Lines on a Page

I have often thought that poets have the easiest job in the world. A poem, after all, is just a few lines on a page, usually not even extending margin to margin—how long would that take to write, about five minutes? Maybe ten at the most, if you wanted it to rhyme or have a repeating meter. Why, I could start in the morning and produce a book of poetry by dinnertime. But we all know that it isn't that easy. Anyone can come up with enough words, but the poet's job is about writing the *right* ones. The right words will change lives, making people see the world somewhat differently than they saw it just a few minutes earlier. The right words can make a reader who relies on the dictionary for meanings take a greater responsibility for his or her own personal understanding. A poem that is put on the page correctly can bear any amount of analysis, probing, defining, explaining, and interrogating, and something about it will still feel new the next time you read it.

It would be fine with me if I could talk about poetry without using the word "magical," because that word is overused these days to imply "a really good time," often with a certain sweetness about it, and a lot of poetry is neither of these. But if you stop and think about magic—whether it brings to mind sorcery, witchcraft, or bunnies pulled from top hats—it always seems to involve stretching reality to produce a result greater than the sum of its parts and pulling unexpected results out of thin air. This book provides ample cases where a few simple words conjure up whole worlds. We do not actually travel to different times and different cultures, but the poems get into our minds, they find what little we know about the places they are talking about, and then they make that little bit blossom into a bouquet of someone else's life. Poets make us think we are following simple, specific events, but then they leave ideas in our heads that cannot be found on the printed page. Abracadabra.

Sometimes when you finish a poem it doesn't feel as if it has left any supernatural effect on you, like it did not have any more to say beyond the actual words that it used. This happens to everybody, but most often to inexperienced readers: regardless of what is often said about young people's infinite capacity to be amazed, you have to understand what usually does happen, and what could have happened instead, if you are going to be moved by what someone has accomplished. In those cases in which you finish a poem with a "So what?" attitude, the information provided in *Poetry for Students* comes in handy. Readers can feel assured that the poems included here actually are potent magic, not just because a few (or a hundred or ten thousand) professors of literature say they are: they're significant because they can withstand close inspection and still amaze the very same people who have just finished taking them apart and seeing how they work. Turn them inside out, and they will still be able to come alive, again and again.

Poetry for Students gives readers of any age good practice in feeling the ways poems relate to both the reality of the time and place the poet lived in and the reality of our emotions. Practice is just another word for being a student. The information given here helps you understand the way to read poetry; what to look for, what to expect.

With all of this in mind, I really don't think I would actually like to have a poet's job at all. There are too many skills involved, including precision, honesty, taste, courage, linguistics, passion, compassion, and the ability to keep all sorts of people entertained at once. And that is just what they do with one hand, while the other hand pulls some sort of trick that most of us will never fully understand. I can't even pack all that I need for a weekend into one suitcase, so what would be my chances of stuffing so much life into a few lines? With all that *Poetry for Students* tells us about each poem, I am impressed that any poet can finish three or four poems a year. Read the inside stories of these poems, and you won't be able to approach any poem in the same way you did before.

David J. Kelly
College of Lake County

Introduction

Purpose of the Book

The purpose of *Poetry for Students* (*PfS*) is to provide readers with a guide to understanding, enjoying, and studying poems by giving them easy access to information about the work. Part of Gale's "For Students" Literature line, *PfS* is specifically designed to meet the curricular needs of high school and undergraduate college students and their teachers, as well as the interests of general readers and researchers considering specific poems. While each volume contains entries on "classic" poems frequently studied in classrooms, there are also entries containing hard-to-find information on contemporary poems, including works by multicultural, international, and women poets.

The information covered in each entry includes an introduction to the poem and the poem's author; the actual poem text (if possible); a poem summary, to help readers unravel and understand the meaning of the poem; analysis of important themes in the poem; and an explanation of important literary techniques and movements as they are demonstrated in the poem.

In addition to this material, which helps the readers analyze the poem itself, students are also provided with important information on the literary and historical background informing each work. This includes a historical context essay, a box comparing the time or place the poem was written to modern Western culture, a critical overview essay, and excerpts from critical essays on the poem. A unique feature of *PfS* is a specially commissioned critical essay on each poem, targeted toward the student reader.

To further help today's student in studying and enjoying each poem, information on audio recordings and other media adaptations is provided (if available), as well as reading suggestions for works of fiction and nonfiction on similar themes and topics. Classroom aids include ideas for research papers and lists of critical and reference sources that provide additional material on the poem.

Selection Criteria

The titles for each volume of *PfS* are selected by surveying numerous sources on notable literary works and analyzing course curricula for various schools, school districts, and states. Some of the sources surveyed include: high school and undergraduate literature anthologies and textbooks; lists of award-winners, and recommended titles, including the Young Adult Library Services Association (YALSA) list of best books for young adults.

Input solicited from our expert advisory board—consisting of educators and librarians—guides us to maintain a mix of "classic" and contemporary literary works, a mix of challenging and engaging works (including genre titles that are commonly studied) appropriate for different age levels, and a mix of international, multicultural and women authors. These advisors also consult on each volume's entry list, advising on which titles are most studied, most appropriate, and meet the broadest interests across secondary (grades 7–12) curricula and undergraduate literature studies.

How Each Entry Is Organized

Each entry, or chapter, in *PfS* focuses on one poem. Each entry heading lists the full name of the poem, the author's name, and the date of the poem's publication. The following elements are contained in each entry:

Introduction: a brief overview of the poem which provides information about its first appearance, its literary standing, any controversies surrounding the work, and major conflicts or themes within the work.

Author Biography: this section includes basic facts about the poet's life, and focuses on events and times in the author's life that inspired the poem in question.

Poem Text: when permission has been granted, the poem is reprinted, allowing for quick reference when reading the explication of the following section.

Poem Summary: a description of the major events in the poem. Summaries are broken down with subheads that indicate the lines being discussed.

Themes: a thorough overview of how the major topics, themes, and issues are addressed within the poem. Each theme discussed appears in a separate subhead.

Style: this section addresses important style elements of the poem, such as form, meter, and rhyme scheme; important literary devices used, such as imagery, foreshadowing, and symbolism; and, if applicable, genres to which the work might have belonged, such as Gothicism or Romanticism. Literary terms are explained within the entry, but can also be found in the Glossary.

Historical Context: this section outlines the social, political, and cultural climate in which the author lived and the poem was created. This section may include descriptions of related historical events, pertinent aspects of daily life in the culture, and the artistic and literary sensibilities of the time in which the work was written. If the poem is a historical work, information regarding the time in which the poem is set is also included. Each section is broken down with helpful subheads.

Critical Overview: this section provides background on the critical reputation of the poem, including bannings or any other public controversies surrounding the work. For older works, this section includes a history of how the poem was first received and how perceptions of it may have changed over the years; for more recent poems, direct quotes from early reviews may also be included.

Criticism: an essay commissioned by *PfS* which specifically deals with the poem and is written specifically for the student audience, as well as excerpts from previously published criticism on the work (if available).

Sources: an alphabetical list of critical material quoted in the entry, with full bibliographical information.

Further Reading: an alphabetical list of other critical sources which may prove useful for the student. Includes full bibliographical information and a brief annotation.

In addition, each entry contains the following highlighted sections, set apart from the main text as sidebars:

Media Adaptations: if available, a list of audio recordings as well as any film or television adaptations of the poem, including source information.

Topics for Further Study: a list of potential study questions or research topics dealing with the poem. This section includes questions related to other disciplines the student may be studying, such as American history, world history, science, math, government, business, geography, economics, psychology, etc.

Compare & Contrast: an "at-a-glance" comparison of the cultural and historical differences between the author's time and culture and late twentieth century or early twenty-first century Western culture. This box includes pertinent parallels between the major scientific, political, and cultural movements of the time or place the poem was written, the time or place the poem was set (if a historical work), and modern Western culture. Works written after 1990 may not have this box.

What Do I Read Next?: a list of works that might give a reader points of entry into a classic work (e.g., YA or multicultural titles) and/or complement the featured poem or serve as a contrast to it. This includes works by the same author and others, works from various genres, YA works, and works from various cultures and eras.

Other Features

PfS includes "Just a Few Lines on a Page," a foreword by David J. Kelly, an adjunct professor of English, College of Lake County, Illinois. This essay provides a straightforward, unpretentious explanation of why poetry should be marveled at and how *PfS* can help teachers show students how to enrich their own reading experiences.

A Cumulative Author/Title Index lists the authors and titles covered in each volume of the *PfS* series.

A Cumulative Nationality/Ethnicity Index breaks down the authors and titles covered in each volume of the *PfS* series by nationality and ethnicity.

A Subject/Theme Index, specific to each volume, provides easy reference for users who may be studying a particular subject or theme rather than a single work. Significant subjects from events to broad themes are included.

A Cumulative Index of First Lines (beginning in Vol. 10) provides easy reference for users who may be familiar with the first line of a poem but may not remember the actual title.

A Cumulative Index of Last Lines (beginning in Vol. 10) provides easy reference for users who may be familiar with the last line of a poem but may not remember the actual title.

Each entry may include illustrations, including photo of the author and other graphics related to the poem.

Citing Poetry for Students

When writing papers, students who quote directly from any volume of *PfS* may use the following general forms. These examples are based on MLA style; teachers may request that students adhere to a different style, so the following examples may be adapted as needed.

When citing text from *PfS* that is not attributed to a particular author (i.e., the Themes, Style, Historical Context sections, etc.), the following format should be used in the bibliography section:

"Angle of Geese." *Poetry for Students*. Ed. Marie Napierkowski and Mary Ruby. Vol. 2. Detroit: Gale, 1998. 8–9.

When quoting the specially commissioned essay from *PfS* (usually the first piece under the "Criticism" subhead), the following format should be used:

Velie, Alan. Critical Essay on "Angle of Geese." *Poetry for Students*. Ed. Marie Napierkowski and Mary Ruby. Vol. 2. Detroit: Gale, 1998. 7–10.

When quoting a journal or newspaper essay that is reprinted in a volume of *PfS*, the following form may be used:

Luscher, Robert M. "An Emersonian Context of Dickinson's 'The Soul Selects Her Own Society'." *ESQ: A Journal of American Renaissance* 30.2 (1984): 111–16. Excerpted and reprinted in *Poetry for Students*. Ed. Marie Napierkowski and Mary Ruby. Vol. 1 Detroit: Gale, 1998. 266–69.

When quoting material reprinted from a book that appears in a volume of *PfS*, the following form may be used:

Mootry, Maria K. "'Tell It Slant': Disguise and Discovery as Revisionist Poetic Discourse in 'The Bean Eaters'." *A Life Distilled: Gwendolyn Brooks, Her Poetry and Fiction*. Ed. Maria K. Mootry and Gary Smith. Urbana: University of Illinois Press, 1987. 177–80, 191. Excerpted and reprinted in *Poetry for Students*. Ed. Marie Napierkowski and Mary Ruby. Vol. 2. Detroit: Gale, 1998. 22–24.

We Welcome Your Suggestions

The editorial staff of *Poetry for Students* welcomes your comments and ideas. Readers who wish to suggest poems to appear in future volumes, or who have other suggestions, are cordially invited to contact the editor. You may contact the editor via E-mail at: **ForStudentsEditors@cengage.com.** Or write to the editor at:

Editor, *Poetry for Students*
Gale
27500 Drake Road
Farmington Hills, MI 48331-3535

Literary Chronology

1618: Richard Lovelace is born in Woolwich, Kent, England.

1649: Richard Lovelace's poem "To Althea, From Prison" is published.

c. 1658: Richard Lovelace dies in London, England.

1757: William Blake is born on November 28 in London, England.

1794: William Blake's poem "The Fly" is published.

1799: Alexander Pushkin is born on June 7 in Moscow, Russia.

1803: Ralph Waldo Emerson is born on May 25 in Boston, Massachusetts.

1825: Alexander Pushkin's poem *The Bridegroom* is published.

1827: William Blake dies on August 12 in London, England.

1830: Christina Rossetti is born in London, England.

1837: Alexander Pushkin dies of a gunshot wound on January 29 in St. Petersburg, Russia.

1847: Ralph Waldo Emerson's poem "The Snow-Storm" is published.

1861: Christina Rossetti's poem "Up-Hill" is published.

1865: William Butler Yeats is born on June 13 in Sandymount, County Dublin, Ireland.

1882: Ralph Waldo Emerson dies of pneumonia on April 27 in Concord, Massachusetts.

1883: William Carlos Williams is born on September 17 in Rutherford, New Jersey.

1886: William Butler Yeats's poem "The Stolen Child" is published.

1892: Edna St. Vincent Millay is born on February 22 in Rockland, Maine.

1894: e. e. cummings is born on October 14 in Cambridge, Massachusetts.

1894: Christina Rossetti dies of breast cancer on December 29 in London, England.

1908: Theodore Roethke is born on May 25 in Saginaw, Michigan.

1923: Edna St. Vincent Millay is awarded the Pulitzer Prize for Poetry for *A Few Figs from Thistles* and *The Harp-Weaver and Other Poems*.

1923: William Butler Yeats is awarded the Nobel Prize in Literature.

1923: Wisława Szymborska is born on July 2 in Prowent-Bnin, Poland.

1926: e. e. cummings's poem "since feeling is first" is published.

1926: Frank O'Hara is born on March 27 in Baltimore, Maryland.

1930: Derek Walcott is born on January 23 in Castries, St. Lucia, West Indies.

1934: Edna St. Vincent Millay's poem "Conscientious Objector" is published.

1934: William Carlos Williams's poem "This Is Just to Say" is published.

1939: William Butler Yeats dies on January 28 in France.

1944: Alice Walker is born on February 9 in Eatonton, Georgia.

1950: Frank O'Hara's poem "Autobiographia Literaria" is published.

1950: Edna St. Vincent Millay dies from a fall on October 19 in Austerlitz, New York.

1953: Theodore Roethke's poem "The Waking" is published.

1954: Theodore Roethke is awarded the Pulitzer Prize for Poetry for *The Waking*.

1956: Chitra Banerjee Divakaruni is born on July 29 in Calcutta, India.

1962: e. e. cummings dies of a stroke on September 3 in New Hampshire.

1963: William Carlos Williams dies on March 4 in Rutherford, New Jersey.

1963: Theodore Roethke dies of a heart attack on August 1 on Bainbridge Island, Washington.

1963: William Carlos Williams is posthumously awarded the Pulitzer Prize for Poetry for *Pictures from Brueghel and Other Poems*.

1966: Frank O'Hara dies of complications following an automobile accident on July 25 on Fire Island, New York.

1973: Alice Walker's poem "Women" is published.

1976: Derek Walcott's poem "Midsummer, Tobago" is published.

1981: Valzhyna Mort is born in Minsk, Belarus.

1983: Alice Walker is awarded the Pulitzer Prize in Fiction for her novel *The Color Purple*.

1986: Wisława Szymborska's poem "Possibilities" is published.

1991: Chitra Banerjee Divakaruni's poem "My Mother Combs My Hair" is published.

1992: Derek Walcott is awarded the Nobel Prize in Literature.

1996: Wisława Szymborska is awarded the Nobel Prize in Literature.

2008: Valzhyna Mort's poem "Grandmother" is published.

Acknowledgments

The editors wish to thank the copyright holders of the excerpted criticism included in this volume and the permissions managers of many book and magazine publishing companies for assisting us in securing reproduction rights. We are also grateful to the staffs of the Detroit Public Library, the Library of Congress, the University of Detroit Mercy Library, Wayne State University Purdy/Kresge Library Complex, and the University of Michigan Libraries for making their resources available to us. Following is a list of the copyright holders who have granted us permission to reproduce material in this volume of *PfS*. Every effort has been made to trace copyright, but if omissions have been made, please let us know.

COPYRIGHTED EXCERPTS IN *PfS*, VOLUME 34, WERE REPRODUCED FROM THE FOLLOWING PERIODICALS:

The American Poetry Review, v. 35, November/December, 2006 for "Frank O'Hara's Intimate Fictions," by Ira Sadoff. Reproduced by permission of the author.—*The Antioch Review*, v. 55, spring, 1997; v. 67, winter, 2009. Copyright © 1997, 2009 by the Antioch Review Inc. Reproduced by permission of the Editors.—*Criticism: A Quarterly for Literature and the Arts*, v. 37, spring, 1995. Copyright © 1995 Wayne State University Press. Reproduced with permission of the Wayne State University Press.—*The Dalhousie Review*, v. 50, summer, 1970. Copyright © 1970 Dalhousie University. Reproduced by permission.—*English*, v. 43, summer, 1994. Copyright © The English Association 1994. Reproduced by permission.—*The Explicator*, v. 65, fall, 2006. Copyright © 2006 by Helen Dwight Reid Educational Foundation. Reproduced with permission of the Helen Dwight Reid Educational Foundation, published by Heldref Publications, 1319 18th Street, NW, Washington, DC 20036-1802.—*The Kenyon Review*, v. 23, spring, 2001 for "Walcott, Poet and Painter," by T. J. Cribb. Reproduced by permission of the author.—*Liverpool Law Review*, v. 23, 2001 for "To Live Outside the Law: Frank O'Hara," by Joe Brooker. Copyright © 2001 Springer. Part of Springer Science + Business Media. Reproduced with kind permission from Springer Science and Business Media and the author.—*The Mississippi Quarterly*, v. 55, winter, 2001. Copyright © 2001 Mississippi State University. Reproduced by permission.—*Parnassus: Poetry in Review*, v. 28, 2005 for "'My Poet's Junk': Wislawa Szymborska in Retrospect," by Eva Badowska. Copyright © 2005 Poetry in Review Foundation, NY. Reproduced by permission of the publisher and the author.—*Poetry*, v. 193, January, 2009 for "In Persona," by Fiona Sampson. Reproduced by permission of the author.—*Poets & Writers*, v. 36, May-June, 2008. Copyright © 2008 Poets & Writers, Inc. Reprinted by permission of the publisher, Poets & Writers, Inc., 90 Broad St., Suite 2100, New York, NY, 10004, www.pw.org and Copper Canyon Press, www.coppercanyonpress.org.—*Publishers Weekly*, v. 248, May 14, 2001. Copyright © 2001 by Reed

Publishing USA. Reproduced from *Publishers Weekly*, published by the Bowker Magazine Group of Cahners Publishing Co., a division of Reed Publishing USA, by permission.—*Southern Cultures*, v. 10, spring, 2004. Reproduced by permission.—*The Southern Review*, v. 32, summer, 1996 for "Gentle Giant," by John Montague. Reproduced by permission of the author.—***Spring: The Journal of the E. E. Cummings Society***, October, 2000. Reproduced by permission. http://www.gusu.edu/english/cummings/cops.htm—*Style*, v. 30, summer, 1996. Copyright © *Style*, 1996. All rights reserved. Reproduced by permission of the publisher.—*World Literature Today*, v. 83, May-June, 2009. Copyright © 2009 by *World Literature Today*. Reproduced by permission of the publisher.

COPYRIGHTED EXCERPTS IN *PfS*, VOLUME 34, WERE REPRODUCED FROM THE FOLLOWING BOOKS:

Cummings, e. e. From "since feeling is first," from ***Complete Poems 1904-1962***. Edited by George Firmage. Copyright 1926, 1954, 1991 by the Trustees for the E. E. Cummings Trust. Copyright © 1985 by George James Firmage. All rights reserved. Used by permission of Liveright Publishing Corporation.—Divakaruni, Chitra Banerjee. From ***Black Candle: Poems about Women from India, Pakistan, and Bangladesh***. Calyx Books, 1991. Copyright © 1991, 2000 Chitra Banerjee Divakaruni. Reproduced by permission.—Emerson, Ralph Waldo. From "The Snow-Storm," in ***Anthology of American Literature, Vol. 1***. MS Am 1280H (136), Eighth Edition. Edited by George McMichael, James S. Leonard, Bill Lyne, Anne-Marie Mallon, and Verner D. Mitchell. Pearson Prentice Hall, 2004. Copyright © 2004, 2000, 1997, 1993, 1989, by Pearson Education, Inc. All rights reserved. Reproduced by permission of Ralph Waldo Emerson Memorial Association deposit, Houghton Library, Harvard University. Not to be reproduced in whole or in part without permission. — Millay, Edna St. Vincent. From ***Wine From These Grapes***. Harper & Brothers Publishers, 1934. Copyright © 1934, by Edna St. Vincent Millay. Copyright © 1962 by Norma Millay Ellis. Reprinted by permission of Elizabeth Barnett, Literary Executor, The Millay Society.—Mort, Valzhyna. From ***Factory of Tears***. Translated by Valzhyna Mort and Elizabeth and Franz Wright. Copper Canyon Press, 2008. Copyright 2008 by Valzhyna Mort. All rights reserved. Reproduced by permission.—O'Hara, Frank. From "Autobiographia Literaria," in ***Selected Poems of Frank O'Hara***. Edited by Donald Allan. Alfred A. Knopf, 1974. Copyright 1950, 1951, 1952, 1953, 1954, © 1955, 1956, 1957, 1958, 1959, 1960, 1961, 1962, 1964, 1965, 1966, 1967, 1968, 1969, 1970, 1971, 1972, 1973 by Maureen Granville-Smith, Administratrix of the Estate of Frank O'Hara. Reproduced by permission of Alfred A. Knopf, a division of Random House, Inc.—William Carlos Williams, from "This Is Just To Say," in ***The Collected Poems: Vol. 1, 1909-1939***, copyright © 1938 by New Directions Publishing Corp. All rights reserved. Reprinted by permission of New Directions Publishing Corp. and Carcanet Press Limited for UK/Commonwealth.

Contributors

Bryan Aubrey: Aubrey holds a Ph.D. in English and has published many articles on literature. Entry on "The Waking." Original essay on "The Waking."

Harriet Devine: Devine holds a Ph.D. in English literature and is emeritus professor in English literature at Edge Hill College, Lancashire, United Kingdom. Original essays on "The Stolen Child" and "Up-Hill."

David Kelly: Kelly is a writer who teaches creative writing and literature at Oakton Community College and College of Lake County in Illinois and has written for numerous scholarly publications. Entries on "Autobiographia Literaria," *The Bridegroom*, and "Midsummer, Tobago." Original essays on "Autobiographia Literaria," *The Bridegroom*, and "Midsummer, Tobago."

Sheri Karmiol: Karmiol teaches literature and drama at the University of New Mexico, where she is a lecturer in the University Honors Program. Entries on "Conscientious Objector," "Up-Hill," and "Women." Original essays on "Conscientious Objector," "Up-Hill," and "Women."

Lois Kerschen: Kerschen has a Ph.D. in English and is an educator and freelance writer. Entries on "The Fly," "The Stolen Child," "To Althea, From Prison," and "This Is Just to Say." Original essays on "The Fly," "The Stolen Child," "To Althea, From Prison," and "This Is Just to Say."

Melodie Monahan: Monahan holds a Ph.D. in English and operates an editing service, The Inkwell Works. Original essays on "My Mother Combs My Hair" and "This Is Just to Say."

Wendy Perkins: Perkins is a professor of English at Prince George's Community College in Maryland and has had several articles published on American and British literature. Entries on "Grandmother," "Possibilities," "since feeling is first," and "Snowstorm." Original essays on "Grandmother," "Possibilities," "since feeling is first," and "Snowstorm."

Claire Robinson: Robinson has an M.A. in English. She is a freelance writer and editor and a former teacher of English literature and creative writing. Entry on "My Mother Combs My Hair." Original essay on "My Mother Combs My Hair."

Autobiographia Literaria

**FRANK O'HARA
1950**

In "Autobiographia Literaria," Frank O'Hara describes a lonely child who hides from schoolmates on the playground, who feels no connection to other children or to the animals and birds around him. In the end, he explains, the suffering of his childhood is redeemed: He grows up to be a talented poet with the ability to create unprecedented beauty. The blossoming of the dejected child into a skilled artist is as unexpected as it is amazing, and the poet with a degree of self-mockery expresses awe at his own achievement.

Frank O'Hara wrote "Autobiographia Literaria" before 1950, when he was still a student at Harvard. Along with other New York writers who were closely connected to painters of the time, he became a founder and guiding force in the short-lived New York School of Poets. As an openly gay man living in a time when homosexuality was socially scorned, O'Hara was keenly aware of how it felt to be marginalized by the dominant culture; as an accomplished writer, though, he also knew how it felt to overcome that loneliness with the sense that he had something significant to offer.

Frank O'Hara died young, as the result of an accident. All of his poetry, including "Autobiographia Literaria," is available in one book, *The Collected Poems of Frank O'Hara*, published by University of California Press in 1995.

Frank O'Hara (John Jonas Gruen / Hulton Archive / Getty Images)

AUTHOR BIOGRAPHY

Francis Russell O'Hara was born on March 27, 1926, in Baltimore, Maryland. Throughout his life, he believed his stated birth date to be three months later than the actual one: His parents were strict Irish Catholics who wanted to conceal the fact that their child was conceived before they were married. O'Hara's father, Russell O'Hara, was an English teacher. He met Katherine Broderick on a bus ride and then later was her instructor at the Worcester (Massachusetts) Business Institute. He also worked part time at a haberdashery, which allowed him to move to Baltimore and take a job in a Baltimore hat shop to conceal Katherine's pregnancy. After Frank's birth, the family moved to Grafton, a Worcester suburb.

Frank O'Hara trained to be a pianist at the New England Conservatory. He served in the Pacific theater in World War II and then attended Harvard, studying classical piano. At Harvard he changed directions, focusing his attention on poetry, publishing his poetry in the *Harvard Review*. After graduation, he went to the University of Michigan, receiving his master's degree in 1951. After graduation, he moved to New York City, landing a job at the sales and information desk of the Metropolitan Museum of Art. He worked there until 1953 and then left to be an associate editor for *Art News*, where he frequently wrote columns and reviews. O'Hara returned to the Metropolitan Museum of Art in 1955, working as an assistant in the International Program. After a brief stint as the poet and playwright in residence at the Poet's Theater in Cambridge, Massachusetts, in 1956, he returned to the Metropolitan Museum, working his way up; by 1960, he was assistant curator in the Department of Painting and Sculpture. He was extremely social and had a wide circle of friends in the New York art and literary circles, many of them from friendships begun at Harvard. He was one of the most famous gay writers of his time.

In 1966, O'Hara was on vacation at Fire Island, a barrier island off the south shore of Long Island, New York, when he was accidentally run over by a dune buggy that was speeding in the dim light of sunrise. He died the next day, July 25, of injuries sustained in the crash.

POEM TEXT

> When I was a child
> I played by myself in a
> corner of the schoolyard
> all alone.
>
> I hated dolls and I   5
> hated games, animals were
> not friendly and birds
> flew away.
>
> If anyone was looking
> for me I hid behind a   10
> tree and cried out "I am
> an orphan."
>
> And here I am, the
> center of all beauty!
> writing these poems!   15
> Imagine!

POEM SUMMARY

Line 1

The first line of "Autobiographia Literaria" establishes a nostalgic tone: The speaker of the poem is looking back to some non-specific time in his past. Since readers do not know the

MEDIA ADAPTATIONS

- "Autobiographia Literaria," along with five other poems by Frank O'Hara, is set to music by Christopher Berg and sung by Paul Sperry on *Paul Sperry Sings American Cycles & Sets*, a compact disc released by Albany Records in 1990.
- A recording of Frank O'Hara reading his own poems is available on *Frank O'Hara*, a compact disc produced by Books on Tape as part of its "Voice of the Poet" series and released in 2005. It includes a book that contains a brief biography of the poet and texts of the poems read.

speaker's age, they do not know his relationship to the time being talked about. Still, these few words establish a weighty tone, showing that, even if the speaker is a relatively young person, childhood feels like a long time ago to him.

Line 2
The key point of this line is that the speaker is alone, which is not necessarily sad or pitiful. O'Hara might be characterizing a child who is highly imaginative, one who uses his time alone to devise fanciful dreams. This line ends in the middle of a thought, making readers wait to find out where the child played.

Line 3
Any hope that this poem is about a child who has made the most of his time alone is dashed when readers find out that the setting is a schoolyard, and more specifically the corner of a schoolyard. This is not a child who is making the best of solitary play; rather, it is a child who is isolated, even while other children are playing around him. The fact that he is in a corner shows that he is trying to avoid his environment, to make himself unnoticed in a place where other children are playing.

Line 4
If readers were not sure of the speaker's loneliness after reading about his situation, the short, direct two-word line that wraps up this stanza is a clear indicator. O'Hara affirms what is already clear, and he does it in an absolute way, using unsentimental, unequivocal language.

Line 5
The poet makes sure that the focus of the situation is on the isolated child by starting and ending line 5 with the word "I." He dispenses with any pity that readers might have by attributing to the child the strong negative emotion, hatred. He shows that, even though this might be a bad situation, the boy has made it worse by lashing out against the world.

Because the poet is male, readers are likely to assume that the speaker of the poem is male too. The word "Autobiographia" in the title affirms this connection. It is, therefore, notable that the first plaything mentioned in the poem is a doll, a toy commonly associated with girls. Since readers might assume a boy would be disinterested in dolls, the first thing the speaker says the boy hated is not as surprising as O'Hara could have made it.

Line 6
The poem's sixth line follows the boy's hatred of dolls with his hatred of games, indicating that these were the only forms of amusement available in the schoolyard. This line raises the subject of animals without making a clear, complete statement about them, leaving readers to wonder, if only for the brief millisecond that passes as they read on to line 7, what his relationship with animals actually was, whether he found the sort of companionship that humans denied him when he played with animals.

Line 7
The thought about animals is completed. Contrary to the commonplace expectation that lonely, alienated children are capable of forming emotional bonds with animals, as in many children's cartoons, for example, this speaker announces that no special relationship developed to save him. Once animals are eliminated as a source of companionship, though, this line goes on to mention birds, raising the reader's hope that the boy who could not relate to other children or animals might have been able to establish a relationship with birds.

Line 8

Like line 4, the poem's eighth line brings stops the narrative abruptly with two direct, flat words. In this instance, any hope readers might have that birds might befriend the lonely boy are dashed. The birds, he explains, showed their disinterest in him by flying away. This sudden stanza ending mimics the abrupt realization the boy must have felt when he saw that the birds had flown away and left him alone.

Line 9

The third stanza starts by giving readers some insight into the child's loneliness. The isolation that is described in the earlier lines is modified here by the information that sometimes people sought his company.

Line 10

When he was called, the boy hid. The reader's sympathy for the boy decreases as it becomes clear that his isolation is, at least to some degree, a choice.

Line 11

The fact that there were trees on the schoolyard says something about the time when O'Hara was young. Like the second stanza's mention of animals that could have been playmates, the tree suggests a natural environment in which children can play.

The child's actions are inconsistent, even irrational. At the same time that he hides from people, he also shouts out, assuring that he will be noticed. This ambivalence about socializing pervades the poem.

Line 12

The third stanza ends with words that summarize the insecurity, self-pity, fear, and anger that the boy has shown throughout the poem. Announcing that he is an orphan, even though no one has asked, shows the boy is desperate for sympathy and willing to blurt out a lie. If it is the lie that it appears to be, then shouting it out is a betrayal of his parents, denying their very existence just to make people feel sorry for him. If the speaker is actually orphaned, shouting out the fact as a way to avoid human contact is a misguided act of desperation.

Line 13

At the start of the fourth stanza, the poem's speaker brings the action into the present. No longer describing the situation of his childhood, he introduces readers to the results of that childhood, preparing them for a description of what the aforementioned shyness and rage and fear turned into as he has matured.

Line 14

Line 14 uses exaggeration to let readers know that the speaker of this poem is not serious, that he is mocking himself. If he were serious, he could say that his writing deals with beauty, but instead he overstates the case by saying that he is the "center" of "all" beauty.

Line 15

In the poem's second-to-last line, O'Hara gives readers some perspective for the beauty he refers to in line 14. The beauty, of which he is the center, is poetic beauty. In this sense, he is making fun of poets who inflate their own importance and locate themselves at the center of all that is beautiful. He uses the word "these" to show that the speaker's self-centered attitude refers not just to this particular poem, but to all of his poetry. He presents himself as a person who thinks that his artistic achievement is great, the sort of person who is impressed with himself because he is able to write so beautifully even with the handicap of an unhappy childhood.

Line 16

The last line of the previous three stanzas contains two words, but this stanza ends with just one word. This single word gives the end of the poem a feeling of mockery, undercutting the self-congratulation expressed throughout the fourth stanza. The poet takes the position that he is simply dumbstruck by his own tremendous accomplishment.

THEMES

Loneliness

The central focus of "Autobiographia Literaria" is the lonely child, who is presented to readers as the poem's author, Frank O'Hara, at a younger age. O'Hara uses the first two stanzas to describe a child who is removed from his surroundings, kept at a distance by those he should be near. He is physically isolated, lingering in a corner of the schoolyard while the other children are playing. He is emotionally isolated as well, lacking a

TOPICS FOR FURTHER STUDY

- Read the poems in Billy Merrell's collection *Talking in the Dark* that concern the poet coming to terms with his homosexuality in his early teens. Then write and present a two-person play showing a meeting between Merrell and Frank O'Hara, with each poet arguing his own view of life.

- Research the programs available for young poets in your area. After talking to the directors of the programs, report back to your class on whether you think poetry is a useful way to teach children social skills.

- Consider five or so lesser-known games that you think an alienated boy such as the one O'Hara depicts in his poem would like to play in the schoolyard. Present the games' instructions to your class, along with an explanation of why they might make a lonely child feel like participating.

- Do a color chalk, watercolor, or computer-generated picture that shows an isolated boy hiding behind a tree, done from the perspective of a person who thinks he is "the center of all beauty."

- In the poem, O'Hara says that "animals were not friendly," even though he describes how the little boy withdraws from people. Interview people who work at zoos, parks, and animal shelters about their experiences with animals that do not get along with certain people and create a chart that displays different theories about why this might occur.

common interest that would help him connect with other children. His disinterest in the games they play might seem to imply an aversion to competition, except that he does not like the non-aggressive outlet one could get from playing with dolls, either. His loneliness is so complete that even the birds and the animals shun him.

In the third stanza, readers find that the poet was not necessarily alienated when he was a boy, at least not entirely. To some degree, as he describes it, he brought his situation upon himself. He hid from people who tried to contact him, and he put emotional barriers between himself and others by claiming to be an orphan. O'Hara does not comment on these actions, so there is no way of knowing how much he takes responsibility for his loneliness or how much he feels that such actions were defense mechanisms of a child who had already been isolated. It is clear, though, that the poet feels both are to blame. The child who felt excluded from his social circle, possibly because of his sexual orientation, might choose to remove himself from society.

Art

This poem could not end effectively with the speaker making fun of his own artistic pretensions if people in general did not already have a preconceived notion about the role of the artist. O'Hara states that the poet is the "center of all beauty," which is only slightly more exaggerated than claiming for himself the same power that many people already attribute to poets. Though not claiming control over "all" beauty, poets, at least since the romantic movement in the early nineteenth century, have claimed that there is a link between beauty and their writing. Poets are typically assumed to be more sensitive to the human condition than other people, to have a special insight. This gift is believed by many to be the poet's source of creativity. As O'Hara describes the situation in the first three stanzas, though, this particular poet actually has less insight into the thoughts of others than more involved people might have. The poem does not deny that poets can create beauty, but it backs away from saying that this particular poet's artistry results from his suffering as a child.

Nature

While this poem does not explicitly state that the animals and birds the child encounters form opinions about him, it does link the animals to the other children in the poem. Like the children, the animals and birds are disinterested in him. The very fact that O'Hara is describing the animals' behavior indicates that he expects his readers to have some sort of expectation about them: He would not need to mention the ways that the animals behave toward the lonely boy if he were not setting out to correct some impression readers have of the animals. He is playing off other stories, such as those found in some Disney movies, that show children who are unable to socialize with other humans but who have an almost magical ability to communicate with animals and birds.

Such stories usually show the isolated individual forming a community with the animals, one that mirrors the kind of society that humans have with one another. They play together and explore the world together, and they understand each other's emotions. When human emotions and attributes are attributed to animals and birds, it is called *anthropomorphism*. While O'Hara depicts the animals in this poem realistically in that they are disinterested in the child or another species, he does hint slightly at anthropomorphism. The animals and birds' disinterest in the boy is similar to the disinterest shown by the other children, implying that the animals and birds have the same feelings toward the boy that the children have, as if the animals and children think alike.

Vanity

The last stanza expresses amazement at the poet's great ability to create beauty, but the exclamation points in the three final lines indicate that the speaker of the poem does not find his power all that amazing after all. The word "imagine," for example, could be a call to readers to join the poet in wondering at the unforeseen situation, but when it is punctuated with an exclamation point it reads like a call for attention, creating the impression that the speaker already knows he is a talented poet. He is not all that awestruck at his own accomplishments, but he wants the reader to pay attention to his talent.

The type of vanity displayed in the last stanza of "Autobiographia Literaria" is remarkable because O'Hara has already presented himself as a child who lacked self-esteem and was ignored by people and animals alike. In his youth he isolated himself by hiding from his classmates and pretending to them, and possibly also to himself, that his parents were dead. Readers expect such a shy child to grow up to be shy, not vain. But this poem presents a speaker who has exaggerated beliefs about his own artistic powers. At one time he might have believed himself unworthy of attention, but the speaker who is talking about himself in the present tense believes himself to be the center of all beauty.

Fire Island, off the coast of New York, was one of O'Hara's favorite retreats and where he had his fatal accident. (Image copyright Sylvana Rega, 2009. Used under license from Shutterstock.com)

STYLE

Hyperbole

O'Hara shocks his readers near the end of this poem by calling himself "the center of all beauty." This is the kind of exaggerated claim that no writer with a normal range of humility would make, the kind of statement that is so full of opinion that it can never be supported, just asserted. If readers were to take seriously what he says here, a claim like this would end up making the poet look foolish. O'Hara clearly knows that such an exaggeration will not ring true to any but the most gullible readers.

Exaggeration to the point of ridiculousness is a literary technique called *hyperbole*. Authors use hyperbole for the same reasons they use similes and metaphors: to make their readers think about the similarities and differences between two ideas.

In this instance of hyperbole, two subjects are compared. On one level, the paired subjects are the little boy who cowers on the playground and the grown man who is now a poet, writing in the center of beauty. On another level, the paired subjects may be understood as the authentic poet who may have overcome a difficult past and in the process developed the skill to create beautiful poetry and the egotistical artist who sees himself as the subject (the center) and his poem as peripheral. If O'Hara's exaggeration makes readers think about the legitimate relationship between the artist and his childhood and between the poet and his poem, then O'Hara's use of hyperbole is successful.

Archetype

Psychologist Carl Jung used the term *archetype* to describe images, characters, or plot types that recur in all cultures. According to Jung's theory, the archetype exists because all human beings share a *collective unconscious*, with memories that are transferred from one generation to the next.

The lonely child who grows up to be a great artist, which serves as the central image of this poem, is an image that might well be recognizable anywhere in the world. This universality may be explained by Jung's idea of the collective unconscious or it may be explained by certain sociological theories: Perhaps only lonely children have the time or inclination to refine their innate artistic skills to the level of greatness or perhaps children with inherent artistic temperaments are destined to have trouble relating to others. There can be various explanations for why the situation O'Hara describes is widely experienced and recognized, but the significant point is that it is: Readers see the isolated childhood described and the fact that the child grows up to be a poet, and they recognize a familiar relationship between a certain kind of childhood and becoming a successful artist in adulthood. The poem depends on readers' expectations, dramatizing the early isolation and exaggerating the later skill.

HISTORICAL CONTEXT

Modernism and Postmodernism

O'Hara arrived on the poetry scene just as artists around the world were in the process of evolving new theories about the arts. Just as World War I created the social fissures that led to modernism, World War II fueled a desire for change, for new ways of viewing the relationship between art and reality.

The men who served in World War I witnessed devastation unlike anything that had ever been previously experienced. Airplanes and trench warfare made war much more destructive and on a larger scale. Almost every major country in the West was pulled into the conflict by the end, including France, Italy, Germany, Russia, the United Kingdom, the United States. The borders of European countries were altered in a few years, as the Austro-Hungarian, German, Russian, and Ottoman empires were dissolved. The number of dead from the war is estimated at between 50 and 70 million, making it the deadliest war in history.

The artists of the postwar generation were disillusioned, and their despair showed in their work. Modernist writing revealed a clear break from the past: Many poets cast aside concerns about traditional forms, such as meter and rhyme, and tried to communicate raw experience directly to readers, writing to shatter readers' expectations just as the soldiers had been shocked themselves in the ravages of combat. Reassuring, familiar themes, such as love, nature, or the presence of God, were no longer considered serious poetical subjects; instead, modernist literature depicted a general loss of faith and expressed an amoral postwar worldview.

Modernism was new and compelling in the late 1910s and early 1920s. Over the years, however, its theories and styles lost popularity. To the generation of writers in the post–World War II era of the late 1940s, the modernists were no longer seen as brave trailblazers who took poetry in new directions; they were the standard bearers who were recognized with publications and awards. Out of the large-scale destruction of World War II arose a response to modernism that came to be called postmodernism.

Many critics have difficulty defining the term *postmodernism* and identifying when the movement began. The word itself was used as early as 1951, but what it means as a style was debated. Postmodern works tended to reject the modernist faith in the power of direct description. Faith in the power and importance of art was replaced with a cynicism that claimed faith itself is misguided. Postmodern poetry tended to be about

COMPARE & CONTRAST

- **1950:** Children have free time to spend on the playground, playing with no particular objective in mind.

  Today: Rising awareness of child predators and increased emphasis on structured after-school activities lead to more involvement by parents and teachers in children's recreational activities.

- **1950:** People play freely with cats and dogs that they encounter and even take strays to their homes.

  Today: Laws in the United States are strict about keeping pets confined or on a leash and having them wear identification. People learn from a young age to assume that an untagged stray might be carrying diseases.

- **1950:** A child claiming to be an orphan may be stigmatized and rejected by peers.

  Today: A child who feels estranged because he is an orphan has social services available to help him, whereas a child who claims to be an orphan in order to impress others may receive help from psychiatric services in identifying the cause of his social anxiety.

- **1950:** Readers are familiar with poetry that concerns itself with beauty, most of it written during the nineteenth century.

  Today: Contemporary poets focus less on creating beauty and more on capturing the emotional truth of a situation.

- **1950:** A poet such as Frank O'Hara can feign astonishment that someone like him can grow up to be a poet.

  Today: English teachers and poetry anthologies try to include perspectives from all different kinds of people; as a result, readers are introduced to poets who have various backgrounds.

- **1950:** An openly gay writer such as O'Hara makes some readers uncomfortable. The forthrightness in his poetry is unusual.

  Today: Anthologies that include gay writing only are in less demand, as readers care less about writers' sexual orientation and more about their talent.

---

poetry, and postmodern art tended to be about art; these writers and painters concentrated more on the context of the work and the relationship between the artist and the work. They considered these subjects the only knowable parts. Postmodernist works tend to be so unusual that oftentimes their audiences spend more time thinking about who made the work and why than about the philosophical issue the work seems to address. Postmodernism is a very broad term, encompassing a great number of divergent styles of art from the late twentieth century, including the New York School of Poets.

The New York School of Poets

Frank O'Hara is often identified with the New York School of Poets, the name of a loose association of writers that he and other poets began to promote around the year 1960.

The name *New York School of Poets*, commonly attributed to the critic John Bernard Myers, was derived from a similarly named movement among painters: In the 1950s, abstract expressionist artists Jackson Pollock and William de Kooning among others took the name New York School to describe their style, following the Paris School of art, which was itself begun with a sense of parody toward the revered School of Florence and the School of Venice in art. Like the members of the similarly named painting movement, the poets of the New York School brought together influences from surrealism, modernism, and an urban sensibility to create a style

Childhood loneliness is one of the themes of O'Hara's poem. (Image copyright Losevsky Pavel, 2009. Used under license from Shutterstock.com)

that reflected the time and place in which they worked. The poets who came to be associated with the New York School were familiar with the contemporary art scene: James Schulyer, like O'Hara, worked at the New York Museum of Modern Art, while O'Hara, Schulyer, John Ashbery, and Barbara Guest all wrote reviews of modern art for the magazine *Art News*.

The New York School of Poets was not really a school, then, so much as it was a gathering of like-minded friends. These writers were not interested in promoting particular political causes or in drawing attention to any specific social concerns. The only use they made of nature was when it could be used to highlight aspects of urban living in New York City. For the most part, the poets of the New York School avoided subjects having to do with mortality or loss or corruption. The central attitude or focus in their work is an urbane sense of humor and an interest in language, especially in the common speech that was used by city dwellers of their time.

CRITICAL OVERVIEW

Frank O'Hara was not famous poet during his short life, though he was known and well respected among his peers. He wrote much but did not publish collections of his poetry often. His most famous *Lunch Poems* was published in 1964, just two years before his accidental death. In New York City, he was a well-known literary figure, often giving readings at bookstores on the lower Eastside and spending nights carousing with artists and poets who were soon to become famous. Elsewhere in the United States, though, his reputation never took off during his lifetime.

After O'Hara's death, his reputation grew, in part because the people with whom he spent time, such as John Ashbery and Kenneth Koch, who remembered him fondly, became famous, and then spoke admiringly about Frank O'Hara's works, arousing public interest in them. Another contribution to his growing fame was the fact of his open homosexuality at a time when it was not accepted in the mainstream. Frank O'Hara wrote poems that revealed a person who was comfortable with himself. Writing in a 2008 review of *Selected Poems*, about the poems that O'Hara wrote at Harvard and just after, William Logan identified the exuberance in the poet's early style: "Jazzy, elated as an eel, a talent giddily in search of a manner, the poet scatters exclamation marks like penny candy. Posing as a wide-eyed innocent, O'Hara was drawn to the illogic and absurdity, to modes of presence and display far from poets like Yeats and Eliot and Lowell." In the years following his death, O'Hara was not often praised as one of the best poets of the mid-century, but he was constantly picked with interest by later generations of new readers. "Frank O'Hara's influence... is still abundant," wrote poet Ira Sadoff in the *American Poetry Review* in 2006: "you find traces of it in the work of John Ashbery, Kenneth Koch, in all of the second-generation New York School poets, in James Tate, Dean Young, Alice Notley, Arthur Vogelsang, David Lehman, many avant-garde younger poets, and a large cast of poets whose poems often seem so derivative that O'Hara's voice overwhelms theirs."

CRITICISM

David Kelly

Kelly is a writer and an instructor of creative writing and literature. In the following essay, he looks at the ways O'Hara establishes a sophisticated narrator in "Autobiographia Literaria" and then mocks the narrator's ego in the end.

To many readers, poet and playwright Frank O'Hara is the embodiment of New York City in the 1950s and 60s. During those years, the city reached a plateau as an urban center, having previously been considered throughout the world to be the center of U.S. sophistication. Soon, the urban decay of the 1970s saddled the city's image with the grim burden of despair, and then the information age eroded the relevance of large metropolitan centers in general. O'Hara's poetry conveyed an urbane quality associated with a world-class metropolis, a city of grit and glamour, panache and humor. He deliberately made his poems formless, using them to project an attitude toward art that a smart, busy city dweller might have. (For contrast, readers can compare the free verse ramblings of some of the Beat poets, O'Hara's peers, who often seemed so driven to eschew poetic form that their indifference

> IF THE NARRATIVE PORTION OF THE POEM ECHOES THE ROMANTIC TRADITION AND THE INTROSPECTION OF THE NEW YORK INTELLECTUAL, THE LAST STANZA SERVES TO REMIND READERS HOW CLOSE ALL OF THIS HAS COME TO BRAGGING, TO A RANK DISPLAY OF VANITY."

turned back on them, into self-consciousness.) O'Hara could name drop with ease, tossing off casual comments about great artists, musicians and writers, but he also proved that he was more than a show-off poet, that he actually lived within the New York art scene. He could tell pretense from foresight, hollow art worship from true art appreciation. Reading through his poetry, people often feel that they are riding with someone with the true ability to see around the next corner.

It is this fascination with the new and cool knowledge of whatever is next that creates the cultural split which fuels O'Hara's poem "Autobiographia Literaria". Written when he was still a Harvard student, in 1950 or a little before, the poem predicts the New York identity that he was soon to develop and sustain for the rest of his short life. In this poem, O'Hara builds a public persona anchored in the kind of psychological self-awareness that was popular at the time, but he then turns around and mocks it. He plays the intellectual for three stanzas and then, in the fourth, turns the sophisticated character he has been playing into the poetic equivalent of a gape-jawed rube from the sticks, a tourist who would walk down Fifth Avenue, exclaiming "Gee whiz," at all of the tall buildings.

This poem begins with O'Hara reflecting on an unhappy childhood, a cliché stance for poets throughout centuries. It is fair to think that self-absorption like this would have reached a peak in the middle of the century. Psychotherapy was at the peak of its popularity. Sigmund Freud had been dead for a decade, giving others their chance to develop ideas based on his, branching off in new directions without having

WHAT DO I READ NEXT?

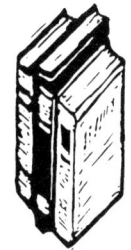

- O'Hara's title for "Autobiographia Literaria" is clearly based on the title of Samuel Taylor Coleridge's *Biographia Literaria*, a long essay about the nature of art with a few autobiographical bits included. Published in 1817 and available in a 2007 edition from Echo Library, Coleridge's primary work of literary criticism expresses the sense of artistic self-importance that O'Hara parodies in his poem.

- One of the most comprehensive books about the New York School of Poets is Geoff Ward's *Statutes of Liberty: The New York School of Poets*, published by Palgrave Macmillan in 2001.

- O'Hara worked closely with the poet John Ashbery. The two men were in college together and were co-founders of the New York School of Poets. Ashbery saved from obscurity one of O'Hara's most famous poems, "Memorial Day, 1950." It was not included among O'Hara's personal papers at the time of his death, and Ashbery found a copy he had typed out among his own papers. "Memorial Day, 1950" is included in *The Collected Poems of Frank O'Hara*, published by University of California Press in 1995.

- John Ashbery is one of the greatest and most celebrated poets of his generation, with a career that endured into the twenty-first century. His poem "Self-Portrait in a Convex Mirror," published in a 1975 collection with the same name, is generally considered to be one of the greatest poems written in the twentieth century. The collection is still in print.

- Gerard Wozek's poem "Song to Myself at Seventeen" examines the situation of a young man who feels alienated because of his sexual orientation and of the grown poet trying to understand the nature of that experience. The poem is included in *Bend, Don't Shatter: Poets on the Beginning of Desire*, a collection edited by T. Cole Rachel and Rita D. Costello and published in 2004 by Soft Skull Press.

- *Digressions on Some Poems by Frank O'Hara: A Memoir*, by Frank O'Hara's friend and sometime collaborator Joe LeSueur, gives a firsthand account of O'Hara's life during his most productive period (1955–1965), when the two men lived together. It was published by Farrar, Straus, and Giroux in 2003.

---

to worry that the old master himself might show up to prove them wrong. At the time, poets were working more and more with personal experience, especially traumatic personal experience, edging toward the emergence of a genre called confessional poetry, which became popular at the end of the 1950s. Confessional poets delved into their past with a level of self-disclosure that some readers found embarrassing, putting secrets and personal experiences into their poems as if daring the world to object. This approach to the poet's craft has something in common with "Autobiographia Literaria," only confessional poetry takes it to an extreme. O'Hara's point, at least at first, seems to be to make his readers pity the isolated boy he claims to have once been.

The confessional mode is a time-honored tradition going at least back to Coleridge, to whom O'Hara gives a tip of his hat with the poem's title, alluding to Samuel Coleridge's somewhat autobiographical theoretical essay *Biographia Literaria* and also to Coleridge's friend and associate William Wordsworth, whose poems about his own youth set the tone for generations of disaffected literary geniuses. From these late-eighteenth- and early-nineteenth-century writers sprung a belief that the artist is a person who develops out of or despite a miserable childhood. It makes sense. For one thing, the true artist stands apart from the rest. Also, having an unhappy childhood prompts certain people to understand suffering and transform it into art. Perhaps many artists have come to master their art only by transforming the difficulties of their youth, by finding a way to express the sense of estrangement that they once experienced. However, writers of all calibers have used the image of the solitary youth as a passkey for their admission into a select inner circle of artists.

After a few stanzas about the lonely child, a distinction develops between O'Hara the poet and the speaker in this poem. The alienated child, it turns out, is an active participant in the exclusion he experiences. He hides from those who reach out to him, and he lies about his parents being dead, in what appears to be a ploy to get sympathy from others. The ridiculous creeps in around the poem's third stanza, leaving readers unsure how to respond. Is the boy O'Hara has been describing really a troublemaker, a poseur who has brought loneliness upon himself because he fancies himself an artist? Or does his alienation take on a life of its own, so that, feeling freakish, the boy lies to make himself seem the freak that he sees in the mirror? At this point in the poem, there is still a bit of the same poignancy that heightens the traditional poet-with-a-bad-childhood tale. Given that the poem is in the first person and in past tense, readers can pick up the sense of self-analysis that was fashionable for intellectuals of the time in their weekly appointments on the psychologist's couch. The idea that the boy might be the agent of his own problems makes him even more pitiable, and the fact that the speaker of the poem is willing to confront his own role in his alienation shows him to be introspective. The pathos dissolves and the lingering suspicion of self-pity diminishes; an air of sophistication, of worldliness and honesty, emerges.

With admiration for the speaker, the reader goes into stanza four, which is where those ridiculous exclamation points show up, making a mockery of the self-restraint that the poem has shown so far. If the narrative portion of the poem echoes the romantic tradition and the introspection of the New York intellectual, the last stanza serves to remind readers how close all of this has come to bragging, to a rank display of vanity. It is here that the speaker shouts out his accomplishments: The dominant punctuation is, of course, those blaring, over-the-top exclamation points, but the basis of this stanza is the declaration, "I am." This is not a speaker who is amazed at the beauty of poetry so much as at the fact that he is the one who creates that beauty. The point he wants readers to take away from all this is not that a child from such a difficult background can accomplish what he does, but that it is he who accomplished it. If this were a study of the human condition, using the poet as the subject, its goal could be accomplished calmly, without exclamation marks. It is not a study, though; it is a declaration. The situation described in the early stanzas is eclipsed by this self-congratulation, and the budding poet who at one point seems to have grown into someone who can use his past to speak about human suffering has turned out to be the narcissistic type of writer who clumsily throws artistry out the window in his rush to talk about himself.

This poem accomplishes its end without any social context, but it also fits perfectly into the overall scope of Frank O'Hara's career. As one of the most urbane of poets from the mid-century, O'Hara knew where the romantic tradition met the psychoanalytic movement, and he was tough enough to create an unsentimental poem about the forlorn child. He was also realistic enough to admit that memories shrouded in fog could just be the tools that are misused by hack poets as a means of establishing that they are sensitive. The poet at the end of "Autobiographia Literaria," shouting about his artistic accomplishments, is not someone readers sympathize with, much as they might have wanted the lonely boy of the earlier stanzas to come out all right. He has found the self-esteem that the child he once was longed for, but he has overdone it. He has turned into a blowhard. There is a type of poet who fits this profile, and O'Hara, who surely went on to meet this type again and again, has captured that type perfectly.

Source: David Kelly, Critical Essay on "Autobiographia Literaria," in *Poetry for Students*, Gale, Cengage Learning, 2010.

Ira Sadoff

In the following excerpt, Sadoff asserts that the seeming spontaneity of Frank O'Hara's work is actually strategically planned. The digressions highlight themes within the poems.

"You do not always know what I am feeling," begins Frank O'Hara's "For Grace, After a Party." Implied in the richness of that rhetoric: a long-term closeness between the speaker and Grace, his peevishness about being misunderstood, at the same

> "O'HARA IS MOST ATTUNED TO THE SLIPPAGES OF SPEECH, THE WAY WORDS MEAN MORE THAN WE INTEND THEM TO MEAN."

time his implied disappointment that he can usually be "read" so easily. Like most of O'Hara's best work, the seamlessness of the statement, the charged conversational tone, might lead even a careful reader to believe in the lyric fiction of present tense invention—the whimsical, spontaneous, even the random. But O'Hara's apparent spontaneity is a strategic fiction. I'm not speaking of O'Hara's intentions here, nor how many drafts his poems went through (Mozart held virtually entire scores inside his head), nor his writing methods (he was a notorious fictionalizer about his work: according to James Schuyler's letters, O'Hara never wrote his famous *Lunch Poems* during his lunch hour but rather when he came back to work after lunch). I'm interested, rather, in the poem on the page, which in his best work is intricately structured and foreshadowed; even the digressions serve as metaphorical parallels and contrasts for the poems' obsessions, which in poem after poem reveal O'Hara's irresolvable romantic quest for both constancy and surprise.

Frank O'Hara's influence, even fifty years after he wrote his most adventurous poems, is still abundant: you find traces of it in the work of John Ashbery, Kenneth Koch, in all of the second-generation New York School poets, in James Tate, Dean Young, Alice Notley, Arthur Vogelsang, David Lehman, many avant-garde younger poets, and a large cast of poets whose poems often seem so derivative that O'Hara's voice overwhelms theirs: the resulting work is often clever but slight: the poems lack individuation of voice (diction and tone), necessity and shapeliness. For it is not an unmediated O'Hara we get in his poems: we get the full thrust of the passionate romantic (lover of Rachmaninoff), entangled with the cultured intelligence of the curator of MOMA who loved the way work was constructed in a Modernist, often impersonal and certainly not representational way. He was a Modernist too in his faith in art's capacity to supplant the religious impulse, to create an internal aesthetic order that would offer its own self-enclosed harmonies. Art wasn't necessarily in itself redemptive: O'Hara's redemption came through Eros, the linguistic and the lusty, as an adaptive strategy for a chaotic and irrational universe. (After all, in "On Personism" he disdained the moral impulse of poetry, proclaiming, "improve them for what, for death?") His romance with the irrational, his love of the dark ("you just let all the different bodies fall where they may, and they always do"), served as a primary trigger for his subjects.

For an ironic imagination like O'Hara's (whose stance often walks the thin line between playfulness and cleverness, sentimentality and posturing, openness and repression), tone drives the poems, the way music and story drive the ironies of a more formal poet like Philip Larkin. But O'Hara's Modernism and his connection with abstract expressionist painters and pop artists like Roy Lichtenstein (Marjorie Perloff's important early study of O'Hara, *A Poet Among Painters*, explores this connection) gave him license to translate painterly problems into poetry: so action paintings became poems in perpetual motion (accomplished by enjambments and long breathless sentences); tonal issues (dramatized by color in painting) were pursued with a broad range of dictions; and, like many postmodern texts and paintings that would follow him, O'Hara made use of Lichtenstein's comic book studies and Rothko's somber abstractions, blurring the lines between high and low culture. One O'Hara poem can include hamburgers and malteds and Genet and Verlaine. As he demonstrated ironically in "Why I am Not a Painter," he painted with words the way Mike Goldberg made words with paint. He enacted in his verbs the principles of action painting: "I go," time "goes by"; he dramatized and distorted the temporal (all action takes place in the eternal present, the same kind of space occupied in Pollock's paintings). In the processes of coming and going, of foregoing intention and subject for associative freedoms, O'Hara found mirrors in modern poetry and modern art. Those critics who think of O'Hara as a poet of personality (if that term means anything it reflects the diction and syntax of what some critics call "voice") fall for his jejune self-mythologizing as a spontaneous poet (he makes clear in his letters the limits of surrealist techniques like automatic writing) who reports and types up whatever comes into his head.

In O'Hara's signature poem, "The Day Lady Died," the almost breathless last four lines give the illusion that the reader and writer arrive at the closure at the same time. The poem ends with a flashback, though, so the present tense, insisted on from the first line, just like time itself, is a willful fiction. The speaker's passionate connection with Billie Holiday is ecstatic, transforming time and space while altering the self and the speaker's sense of identity. Art leaves us breathless: its intimate connections prove to be simultaneously exciting and dangerous: they not only bring us closer to feeling but also expose us to the danger of contingency and loss, expressed in the poem in terms of destabilizing time, space, and identity: intimacy touches and breaks the heart. The experience is both communal and isolating (consciousness attenuates and abstracts). All of these matters are foreshadowed in the speaker's restlessness: he thrives because of his friendships, his feeling for art and other artists. But the world of feeling is at odds with the counter desire of the poem: the speaker's attempts to thwart and defer uncertainty and contingency keep him dislocated and existentially alone. His anxiety is expressed in his exactitude about time and date, in specificity of book titles, and names. Every stanza begins with an assertion of these certainties (as it turns out, an evasion), and ends with those qualities effaced, diminished or dissolved. The stanzas end in strangeness and isolation because, in O'Hara's view, temporal experience by nature is always shifting, constantly moving. O'Hara, in his typically anti-effete fashion, talked about his "I do this I do that," poems because he was interested in action and gesture, but also, as a Modernist, he was keenly aware of movement. He was drawn to painters like Pollock, Klee and de Kooning because of their movement, color and composition. In most poems he embraced that movement as energetic and vitalizing, but in "The Day Lady Died," the loss of love and art takes away his capacity for sheer lightness and acceptance.

> The Day Lady Died
>
> It is 12:20 in New York a Friday
> three days after Bastille day, yes
> it is 1959 and I go get a shoeshine
> because I will get off the 4:19 in Easthampton
> at 7:15 and then go straight to dinner
> and I don't know the people who will feed me
>
> I walk up the muggy street beginning to sun
> and have a hamburger and a malted and buy
>
> an ugly NEW WORLD WRITING to see what the poets
> in Ghana are doing these days.
> I go on to the bank
> and Miss Stillwagon (first name Linda I once heard)
> doesn't even look up my balance for once in her life
> and in the GOLDEN GRIFFIN I get a little Verlaine
> for Patsy with drawings by Bonnard although I do
> think of Hesiod, trans. Richmond Lattimore or
> Brendan Behan's new play or *Le Balcon* or *Les Nègres*
> of Genet, but I don't, I stick with Verlaine
> after practically going to sleep with quandariness
>
> and for Mike I just stroll into the PARK LANE
> Liquor Store and ask for a bottle of Strega and
> then I go back where I came from to 6th Avenue
> and the tobacconist in the Ziegfeld Theatre and
> casually ask for a carton of Gauloises and a carton
> of Picayunes, and a NEW YORK POST with her face on it
>
> and I am sweating a lot by now and thinking of
> leaning on the john door in the 5 SPOT
> while she whispered a song along the keyboard
> to Mal Waldron and everyone and I stopped breathing

The poem begins with pronouncements about exact time and place. The opening lines of the stanza assert certainty or at least exactitude, but by the end of line 2 the word "yes" on the one hand suggests affirmation, but on the other serves as self-assurance. The gesture about Bastille Day, besides vaguely suggesting "independence," brings the relaxation of time—if summer and the speaker's about to venture out to "the country"; the celebration of the French holiday also foreshadows references to the foreign, which in later stanzas stand-in for movement away from consciousness and the here and now.

In the last line of the stanza—a formal strategy that's repeated in virtually every stanza—we come to understand the speaker's need for knowing where and when: he doesn't "know the people who will feed him." Lighthearted and casual as the voice in the poem begins, that line suggests loneliness and isolation: the speaker is a metaphorical orphan (dependent? hungry?), or at least a solitary wanderer. With that rhetorical and metaphorical flourish, the casual and seemingly superficial surfaces of the opening lines are transformed.

The second stanza uses the hunger association to feed the speaker and perhaps there's a little cheer in the "beginning to sun." Besides which, the speaker must move away from his anxiety, which he supplants with the distraction of distance and surface. His glib response, seemingly far from him and his vague dilemma, is to see what the poets of Ghana are doing. Later in the poem that distance is transformed by art, art as gift and celebration and sign of friendship.

Once again, though, when the speaker wants to turn away, the stiff and formal Miss Stillwagon suddenly trusts the speaker—miracle of miracles, a person momentarily supplants the pecuniary. So with the poets of Ghana on his mind, with the possibility of a human connection, the speaker chooses gifts to show friends his care for them, and in some way to suggest his alienation at this moment from American culture. He chooses foreign artwork for his friends (Genet and Verlaine and Behan—all proponents of the passionate and the irrational) and he chooses foreign pleasures for smoking and drinking. But, as in the closure of other stanzas, these strategies also fail both to enliven and to distance. So he "practically go(es) to steep with quandariness," an odd and elevated choice of diction. He's perplexed, uncertain, he seems almost paralyzed and depressed by so many choices: he's alienated and helpless. O'Hara intensifies this helplessness during the present tense climax of the poem, when the speaker sees the headlines about Billie Holiday's death. She becomes the emblem in the poem for the ecstatic: his love, his passion, the heart in art, in song.

All this repression and deferral fails (as the O'Hara of "An Image of Leda..." understands all too well), because he must face Holiday's death on his own. Time is odd and ambiguous in the poem: one way of looking at the poem is in terms of the tension between surface action and feeling, which suddenly shifts at the end of the poem. In this interpretation, the speaker's been all avoidance, preoccupied with errands: he's aimless until he sees the headline and is cast back into the past, where the immediacy of art crowds out everything else. But it's also possible that narrative time deceives here, and that the speaker from the beginning of the poem knows and feels lost and is withholding the knowledge of her death from himself as well as the reader. In either case we retrospectively look at the details and narrative in this poem and find that the daily contains both the pleasures of experience and ritualized bureaucratic boredom. The poem also reaches out, though in an attempt to both defeat and honor the daily: there's an osmotic relationship among friendships, human connections and art. In the final stanza time virtually stands still: the flashback is immediate and eternal, bringing the past back into the present with more vitality than any of the previous apparent "present tense" stanzas.

> and I am sweating a lot by now and thinking of
> leaning on the john door in the 5 SPOT
> while she whispered a song along the keyboard
> to Mal Waldron and everyone and I stopped breathing

The effect of this final stanza is breathtaking, but it also gathers up all the forces in the poem and transforms them. The intimate connections are assonant ("whispered a song along..."), the muggy sun motif is released in his sweating (but the sweating is also associated with his feelings of panic). Most of all, the tensions between the communal (earlier expressed as friendship) and alienation are kept in balance and released. So the syntax of the last line makes the speaker part of the community of art and simultaneously separate ("everyone and I"). The effect of Billie Holiday's song (most certainly tragic in the mid-Fifties when the poem's composed: her voice broken but her interpretations so richly and heartbreakingly dark) is "breathtaking" in both senses of the word: ecstatic and death-like. One thinks of Longinus' *Sublime*, which involves an encounter with God, Mastery, etc., that leaves one powerlessly transfixed with the need to reconstruct the self by returning to self-mastery. To live with such heightened emotional knowledge after such an encounter is impossible. The death of self implied in this poem both makes one feel more human and more alone, and most of all unavoidably conscious of our own deaths (metaphorical and otherwise).

It should be mentioned here too how much transgressive impulses in the Fifties, artistic and otherwise, almost always articulated that existential "aloneness," that alienation from the "normal" and the corporate, the conforming vacuity of American culture. The O'Hara poem was written too in the midst of the abstract threat of the Soviet Union, the Cold War and the A-bomb, all which suggested the possibility of instant annihilation. His need for escape and fantasy is demonstrated in his romanticization of Europe, particularly France; at the same time, the heroic stance of the speaker, represented by his "leaning against the john door," James Dean style, is all American alienation, being a spectator rather than a participant. That existential angst, that Romantic feeling of loneliness, was a response to a dominant culture that found increasingly less room for either art or pleasure...

"A Step Away From Them" is just as intricately structured and foreshadowed as the Billie Holiday poem. The poem's also obsessed with deferring knowledge of grief and loss and wrestles with art's capacity to transcend time set against the narrator's desire to live fully in the present tense. This concern is echoed in O'Hara's formal strategies throughout the poem. The ebullient present overflows with erotic energy, expressed in action, "hum-colored" synesthesia (often used by the poet as a vehicle of confusion, demonstrating the city's overload of sensation), lust, and the discomfiting—especially for readers now—exoticizing ethnicity...

At first the speaker glorifies the city's contradictions: he likes the combination of its dirt and its playful shine: "dirty / glistening torsos" and "cats playing in sawdust." He loves the earthly "down the sidewalk"; he likes the heavenly and the blending of the palpable and the impalpable "The sun is hot, but the / cabs stir up the air."...

> ...yellow helmets
> on. They protect them from falling
> bricks, I guess. Then onto the
> avenue where skirts are flipping
> above heels and blow up over
> grates.

And when "everything suddenly honks" though he's conscious of time, he's completely immersed in the present tense: "it is 12:40 of / a Thursday." This consciousness of time represents a turning point in the poem: it provides a moment of transformation.

The next stanza moves from timeless pleasure in all this excess (lights in daylight) to the sensory and associative pleasure of eating that triggers memory: Juliet hamburger stand reminds him of Giulietta Maina, and those lines are followed by his recognition of the unpleasantly absurd: a wealthy woman in furs taking her dog in a cab on a hot summer day. The speaker criticizes both the incongruous and ostentatious privilege and the woman's inability to take in the city's outdoor joys.

The moment is funny but also existentially absurd. Indeed, the whole question of function, which the speaker was casual about early on in the poem, begins to perplex. He tries to recover, noticing the Puerto Rican who makes the avenue "beautiful and warm." But the Puerto Rican is a stranger, unnamed, an objet d'art; all this consciousness of time and beauty and warmth brings him inextricably to his lost artist friends. These artists are not only named but nicknamed ("Bunny"): they provided the speaker's intimate connections; recollecting them shakes his confidence in the value of his impersonal pleasures. From this point on, all the preceding movements that served to give the speaker pleasure are problematized and developed further. "And one has eaten and one walks" is both impersonal and absurd: the meaning of "one's" life is no longer just the speaker's problem; the nudes then become associated with the dangers of bullfighting and finally a torn-down Manhattan storage warehouse (ruined by time). It used to hold, the speaker thinks, the important Armory Show of 1913, the adventurous exhibition of modern painters that included American painters strongly influenced by contemporary European painters just as the world used to hold his artists, just as the speaker was formerly able to accept the "dirt" with the erotic play, the memory of that art work is perplexing or fading from view.

On the one hand the ending of "A Step Away From Them," revisits Keats' "Ode to a Nightingale": life is short, art is long. But the context of the poem complicates the metaphor. In a poem about displacement of feeling, having one's heart in one's pocket seems less romantic, compartmentalized, outside the inhabited body.

Especially because that line is preceded by the casual "A glass of papaya juice / and back to work." Here the speaker cannot fully confront or inhabit the uncomfortable contradictions the poem raises: does death of loved ones, does the loss of those connections, diminish life's "fullness?"

> First
> Bunny died, then John Latouche,
> then Jackson Pollock. But is the
> earth as full of life was full, of them?

The complex syntax of those lines, like the inquiry of the poem, cannot be unwound or resolved. The earth seems to be as full of life as it always was—absurd, romantic, full of danger and lust—but at the same time the speaker sees diminishment in the change (the buildings being torn down). At this moment in the poem, being focused on the here and now both mediates and takes flight from the wreckage of time and history. But the closure brings us back to the title and the speaker's indeterminate feelings about time and the daily in the face of those losses. "A Step Away From Them" retrospectively asks the question, is he just one step from them (are they also in his metaphorical pocket), or is he moving a step away from them? If so, time as "sequence ("first Bunny, then") creates distance and the speaker's left with the fullness of his melancholy, which he can only defeat by "going back to work."

Because O'Hara's historically situated at the beginning of an age critical of the conservatism of new criticism—demonstrated in the resistance of Beat poets like Ginsberg—his biases are anti-intellectual and opposed to the snobbery of high culture. As Perloff underlined in her introduction, quoting from "Personal Poem," "we don't like Lionel Trilling / we decide, we like Don Allen we don't like / Henry James so much we like Herman Melville." In this way, as Mark Tursi also suggested in "Interrogating Culture: Critical Hermeneutics in the Poetry of Frank O'Hara" he was also situated on the edge of the postmodern, where judgments about cultural currency were shifting. Soon after O'Hara there would be Andy Warhol's Campbell's soup cans; but O'Hara was also titillated by hard-hats, Hollywood gossip ("Lana Turner please get up"), nuts and bolts, and in "On Rachmaninoff's Birthday," soup on the stove. What first appears to be a poem about madness turns out to be a Romance with deflating earnestness.

Perhaps few O'Hara poems seem more spontaneous and clever than "On Rachmaninoff's Birthday." His "Ode" to Rachmaninoff's music begins with the tumult of Romantic music and the speaker poised (in the enjambment) between going and going off his "rocker." The poem's mock suicide mirrors the melodrama he loves in Rachmaninoff's music (as he loves James Dean in "East of Eden," loving both the drama of the exaggerated romance while affectionately making fun of it). The poem then moves through a series of associative joke-y transformations: the onset of the mad scene becomes a town in Massachusetts. The shadow of Newton, Massachusetts, becomes the "fig-newton / playing the horn." The absurd surrealism here is both demented (dissociative) and associatively imaginative. Most of all every object transmutates. No thing can be held on to or stabilized. Everything, including the speaker, is on the edge, capable of "breaking "into powder."

> On Rachmaninoff's Birthday
>
> Quick! a last poem before I go
> off my rocker.
> Oh Rachmaninoff!
> Onset, Massachusetts. Is it the fig-newton
> playing the horn? Thundering windows
> of hell, will your tubes ever break
> into powder? Oh my palace of oranges
> junk shop, staples, umber, basalt;
> I'm a child again when I was really
> miserable, a grope pizzicato. My pocket,
> of rhinestone, yoyo, carpenter's pencil
> amethyst, hypo, campaign button,
> is the room full of smoke? Shit
> on the soup, let it burn. So it's back
> You'll never be mentally sober.

The Russian czars' palace becomes the speaker's random junk. The hinge lines of the poem are the surprising "I'm a child again when I was really / miserable." The powerless disordered ("grope pizzicato") child is far from, for the speaker, inhabiting that idealized Eden (here again, time past and time present is simultaneous). In fact, the objects he finds in his pocket break through the temporal: a yo-yo is next to a hypo, a cheap stone next to a campaign button. Are these the pockets of the syntactically aforementioned child? And just when the room is about to go up in smoke he declares "shit..." but he turns out not to be cursing the failure to order and control, but abandoning it: the association with childhood has in fact freed the speaker to "let it burn." Because of the vague antecedents, "So it's back," doesn't easily unpack: "it" simultaneously hovers over the madness, childhood, and/or some semblance of acceptance.

The closure of the poem releases all those forces: the diction of "You'll never be mentally sober," at first suggests madness becomes a permanent condition; but the word is not mad, it's "sober," and furthermore it's not the "I" of the poem, but the unnamed "you," which one assumes is the reader. In a modernist fashion O'Hara has been able to—thanks to snapped off perceptions and enjambments, a dream-like translation of Rachmaninoff's music—evoke the romance with madness and entropy itself. Its effect, though, becomes absurd, not horrifying. It becomes impossible to take the drama of madness seriously, as he blurs the boundaries between madness and imagination, anxiety and play. The poem resolves neither ironically nor straightforwardly the dilemma of the speaker going off his rocker: he's dramatized what it feels like, and in the process playfully "lets go" of his desire to control experience, resigning himself to the entropic irrational that seemed in the opening lines to drive him "mad."

The poem points to why O'Hara's poems seem more playful than clever. As much as the subject of cleverness has been discussed, no definitions suffice. One person's cleverness is another person's vitalizing play, or ironic/satiric revelation. The implication of the distinction suggests that cleverness is insubstantial, entertaining, a joke not to be returned to. O'Hara surely wrote, among his more than a thousand poems, a number of these kinds of poems (and what poet hasn't indulged him or herself in word play or jokes, or less self-consciously an inadequate or shallow approach to a serious subject?). What makes O'Hara's work compelling, I think, is what makes most poets compelling: an obsession, a poem written of personal necessity, coordinate with a tactile joy in the medium, the expression of that obsession. The way painters are in love with paint, O'Hara too is in love with his poetic materials. What this means is that he's capable both of surprising himself and the reader in mid-poem, but he's conscious enough to seize on the lived history of the poem (the preceding lines) and narrative (the lines that surround the present tense of the poem) and use that history to shape and transform. For it's hard to imagine a poet being successful more than a few times accidentally: every poet I know that I admire has a large dose of emotional intelligence, is attentive to the "suggestion" of gestures and the composition of experience. O'Hara is most attuned to the slippages of speech, the way words mean more than we intend them to mean. To the Freudian slip, to the half-conscious dialogue, to the gesture that demands more or less attention than a person may give it. That's why he's often an ironic poet, but not solely in the service of entertainment: his pleasure lies in bringing unconscious material up to the surface...

To return to "For Grace, After a Party," though the speaker claims, in arch diction that underscores the ironic exaggeration of the statement, that "it was love for you that set me / afire," in truth he's not only expressing his love, but pushing the absent Grace away. The speaker's ... gratification is betrayed by both his own unpredictable feelings and the way in which "odd(ly)" his feeling defended and anonymous allows him to feel ...

in rooms full of
strangers my most tender feelings
writhe and
bear the fruit of screaming.

These lyric lines, though providing the most iambic meters of the poem, mediate the speaker's satisfactions with jagged, anti-poetic line breaks and clotted syntax: fullness is followed by strangers, tender feelings "writhe" and only "bear the fruit" of screaming. No Fruit at all. Rage and frustration: the occasion that has made feeling possible has also rendered action impossible. The speaker's both safe and unsatisfied (there's no evidence of the speaker's being gay, but the emotional landscape of this poem would make an excellent "cover"). Grace doesn't know What he's feeling because his feelings are confused, surprising and uncontrollable, and are not always available to him when she's present. These lines allow him to pursue and advance the double-edge of desire and domesticity or friendship and closeness. The action of the poem moves away from an "other" being familiar enough to be able to predict his needs in advance; but the speaker also feels that to be known is to be predictable, subject to dull repetition. A perfect double-bind.

The unsatisfying closure of the poem moves further and further from Grace (Grace Hartigan the painter, but also the pun of grace itself). The warm spring air, which ironically brought forth a tirade instead of spring's usual promise of fruition, is transformed into warm weather "holding," implying stasis and the stale. Grace becomes "someone" and then disappears from the poem altogether. Under the guise of a "love" poem, O'Hara has written the poem as a defense of irrational surprise and his own unavailability, but it's a strategy in this poem that fails his speaker.

O'Hara's sensibility commands him to excess, as in the line "It was love for you that set me / afire," and he's fond of exclamation marks in many of his poems. Size and scope, of feelings and images, play a big role in O'Hara's discourse. Those excesses, feelings of grandiosity, his making master narratives of his momentary love affairs and mock manifestos, are mediated by his self-consciousness—his self-knowledge really. So often in poems he'll put forth those excessive sentiments and undermine them with irony, self-deprecation, or glibness. Although I described him as capable of the jejune, the open, boyish sensitive-soul O'Hara often appears in the voice of the self-consciousness naïf. It's most obvious in an early poem, pretentiously titled "Les Etiquettes Jaunes," one translation of which could be read as "Yellow Protocol":

> Leaf!
> You are so big!
> How can you change your
> color, then just fall!
> . . .
> Leaf! don't be neurotic
> like the small chameleon.

Here he playfully attaches himself to the yellow leaf in a child's voice: he asks the innocent question, undermined by "you are so big"—how big could a leaf be? He leaves us with the suggestion that we're residing in the world of metaphor: what bad manners of a leaf to "change your / color"; the enjambment makes us wait to consider what else might be changing, and then "just fall!" O'Hara's speaker both means this worry about mutability while he parodies the Romantic identification with nature and its recurrent parallels. The "joke" in the closure, characteristic of O'Hara's jokes, is only half-joking. To think of a leaf as neurotic is absurd. But the chameleon, that's a figure—as someone who changes feelings frequently and unpredictably, experienced most obviously in his enjambments— the speaker knows well. The big leaf becomes the small chameleon. The big chameleon: who could that be?

Few poets arouse such extreme responses as devotion or disdain as O'Hara. Attachment to O'Hara's sensibility depends to some extent on a reader's feelings about irony and tone. Nietzsche once said in Mixed Opinions and Maxims that "A joke is the epigram on the death of a feeling," but O'Hara, I think, teaches us otherwise. O'Hara's humor and irony is meant to reveal, with the qualifying knowledge that openness can lead to earnestness, self-aggrandizement and a vulnerability that must be turned away from to survive the "world" and "worldliness" of the New York landscape O'Hara loves and knows so intimately. Irony, as a sequence of revealing then concealing, expresses both O'Hara's stance toward the unconscious and his romance with darkness, Eros and the Unknown. The "Erotic zones" can only be seen reflected in others, as in "Poem" (I don't know if I get What D. H. Lawrence is talking about):

> and I suppose
> any part of us that can only be seen by
>   others
> is a dark part
> I feel that about the small of my back,
>   too and
> the nape of my neck
> they are dark
> they are erotic zones as in the tropics

One can see the tenderness expressed in those lines, and in the closure of the poem, and here the naive, unguarded voice of the speaker allows him to recognize both his own limited understanding of his own dark desires and the need for love and darkness to "urge us on and into the light."

> a coal miner has a kind of sexy
>   occupation
> though I'm sure it's painful down there
> but so is lust
> of light we can never have enough
> but how would we find it
> unless the dark urged us on and into it
> and I am dark
> except when now and then it all comes
>   clear
> and I can see myself
> as others luckily sometimes see me
> in a good light

The light-hearted pun at the end of the poem is not meant as a joke to entertain or make the

> "WHAT IS REAL MAY NOT BE RATIONAL, BUT WHAT IS ART, LIKE A COP, IS NOT TO BE ARGUED WITH."

reader laugh as in some comic poems. Here, as elsewhere, O'Hara manipulates tone, tries on voices and structures the movement of his poems to organize a vision that transgresses the puritan impulse. In the process he provides the rich multiple and mobile suggestions of poetry. Perhaps he wrote "you do not always know what I am feeling," not only because feeling is private and defended, but because the many poetic strategies of Frank O'Hara allowed him to feel many, often conflicting, feelings at once. That's at least how I see him "in a good light."

Source: Ira Sadoff, "Frank O'Hara's Intimate Fictions," in *American Poetry Review*, Vol. 35, No. 6, November–December 2006, pp. 49–52.

Joe Brooker

In the following essay, Brooker asserts that art and writing follow particular rules or laws and that Frank O'Hara chose to define his own set of poetic laws.

For Stephen Troussé

'Ride in a Studebaker, Jim', cooed Lou Reed, before unleashing his most banally memorable phrase: 'You know—those were different times': when

All the poets studied rules of verse
And the ladies / they whirled their eyes.

Lou learned at the feet of Delmore Schwartz, so he always told us ('Dedalus to your Bloom'): Schwartz, who wrote stony, reifying sentences: 'Consequently, his native gift for understanding other human beings was often annulled by his need to deny that other human beings were unlike himself; and thus he suspected everyone of everything because he suspected and convicted himself of many wrongs.' Not that Lou could write like that: 'It's my wife / And it's my life', indeed. He might have done well, all things considered, to have tried to learn from Frank O'Hara. But he might have failed.

Still: 'All the poets studied rules of verse'. When? In another country, a long time ago, perhaps, in the Academy; maybe even when Frank O'Hara was studying other poets' rules, reading William Carlos Williams or Gertrude Stein. Or Vladimir Mayakovsky, who wrote in 1926:

> The Revolution...has thrown up on to the streets the unpolished speech of the masses, the slang of the suburbs has flowed along the downtown boulevards...There is a new linguistic element. How can one make it poetic? The old rules about 'love and dove', 'moon and June' and alexandrines are no use. How can we introduce the spoken language into poetry, and extract poetry from this spoken language?

Lou Reed would say something similar, decades on: that after the Velvet Underground there would be no more moon in June. That was an overestimate not only of his influence but—less understandably—of his own work. But what Mayakovsky has to say about language here finds some echo in the O'Hara who wrote poems in his memory. A new linguistic element: how to make it poetic? How to get talk and poetry talking (and for that matter poeticizing) to each other?

Not through 'the old rules': on that much Mayakovsky is clear, writing of 'the provisionality of all rules about writing verse',

> In poetical work there are only a few general rules about how to begin. And these rules are a pure convention. Like in chess. The opening gambits are almost identical. But already from the next move you begin to think up a new attack. The most inspired move can't be repeated in any given situation in your next game. Only its unexpectedness defeats the opponent. Just like the unexpected rhymes in poetry.

You might start a poem predictably (but O'Hara didn't), but you'd better start surprising the reader soon enough. Books on how to write won't help much: they should be called How They Used to Write. The canons won't accept my lines, Mayakovsky cheerfully admits, which know nothing of metrical feet or consonance: 'But the Petersburg streets fathered these lines. Critics can investigate at leisure what rules underlie them.' What does this mean? That the rules are identical with the streets (which 'underlie' the poet), perhaps; notably, that the rules can be named *later*. 'I offer no rules to make anyone a poet', Mayakovsky insists, 'by following which he can write poetry. Such rules simply don't exist. A poet is a person who creates these very rules.'

So if you want to perform the unexpectedness, the knight's move (if only that was unexpected), the rules don't exist—yet. They might start to exist once you get going: you might make some of your own. Jean-François Lyotard would try at length to codify this principle of the uncodifiable: the really avant-garde work is one whose rules *will turn out to have been*—something or other; we don't yet know.

So some of the poets O'Hara studied said that you had better find your own rules of poetic functioning. As much as any writer's of his era, his work looks to be lawless: willfully undisciplined to a rare degree. In 1922 the reviewers wrote of Mr Joyce's 'great undisciplined talent', but that judgment came to seem misapplied: one thing we may feel about *Ulysses,* now, is that everything in the book needs to be in there, that details are placed to a plan. This may be one of the things that Art means: that unlike our lives, it's meant to be the way it is. Art combines law and lawlessness in extreme measures. Lawlessness? It can do whatever it likes: it's about fancy and whimsical rearrangement, like a child winning an actually lost battle with toy soldiers. It makes things up on the spot, drags us along with it, struggling to keep up the conviction that this feels real, that it matters and isn't so silly and irrelevant as to tumble ashamed to the ground. It reproduces things, not quite as they are, quite unnecessarily: it is superfluous. It's thus a realm of freedom, which is part of why it has figured as utopia for so many thinkers. 'By painting in the luminous colors of this world the beauty of men and things and transmundane happiness', writes Herbert Marcuse, art 'has planted real longing alongside poor consolation and false consecration in the soil of bourgeois life.' 'What counts as utopia, phantasy, and rebellion in the world of fact is allowed in art', he adds: 'There affirmative culture has displayed the forgotten truths over which 'realism' triumphs in daily life.'

Yet this realm of freedom is simultaneously a sphere of necessity: for what has become Art is necessary. The elements in a work of art—painting, novel, poem, film—*count.* They are not to be fiddled with by those of us not the artist: they're arranged the way they are because this is the way it must be. Those words in *Ulysses* only look undisciplined: seven iron years went in to plotting their order. The contemporary profusion of editions of the book testifies to the need to get it right, not the careless shrug that an extra comma here or there won't do any harm. Once a poem is finished, its license becomes compulsion—becomes, indeed, law, the rigorous internal law enforced in the country of the aesthetic. What is real may not be rational, but what is art, like a cop, is not to be argued with.

This is something that strikes the reader of Donald Allen's collections of O'Hara's verse. In a wry note at the front of the *Selected Poems* (1974), Allen writes of the *Collected* (1971) as a 'splendid place', whose erection took 'three years (five would have been even better)': this smaller anthology, he records, has eventually been sawed and hammered from that opus, a task that initially seemed 'impossible.' This makes the books into monuments—or rather, acknowledges their monumental quality, their monumentalizing activity. Anthologies and critical works give poets fame, we know: the publication of the *Collected Poems* is an act of canonization. What I'm more specifically thinking of is the way the *Selected Poems* makes you approach the poems themselves, as texts: all that blank cream in the square pages' margins, all O'Hara's creative uses of paper space and physical line lengths so rigorously, religiously maintained and done justice.

> Khruschev is coming on the right day!
>   the cool graced
> light
> is pushed off the enormous glass piers
>   by hard wind
> and everything is tossing, hurrying on up
>   this country
> has everything but *politesse,* a Puerto
>   Rican cab driver says
> and five different girls I see
>   look like Piedie Gimbel
> with her blonde hair tossing too,
>   as she looked when I
> pushed
> her little daughter on the swing on the
>   lawn it was also windy.

Just arranging that on the page is a task. One to relish, certainly, as it makes you savour his words anew, and notice for the first time the way that the first letter of 'Piedie' has to appear directly below the capital R of 'Rican', and that 'as' must start across the remains of the page two characters before the point where Ms Gimbel's forename begins. That's the law of art at work, one of the rules of the game of poetry: not merely the choice of words, line-breaks and punctuation are significant; the precise location of a word on the paper is to be reproduced following the specification of the official text. It won't look quite the same, pulled into a new context like this essay, surrounded by other words: but its internal organization as she looked when I pushed commands respect. But here is the incongruity. O'Hara's words demand proper care from us, loving attention (and doubtless they would love it, if they could—that's the kind of words they are) and faithful reproduction. They demand the status of poetry. Yet they frequently seem as unfitted for that status as any poetry we can think of. The reminiscence of Piedie Gimbel swings into view in the wake of the taxi driver's one-and-a-fifth line cameo, unannounced by punctuation ('and' is a fuller transition than O'Hara often grants the reader), and includes two synonymous adverbs—'tossing too', 'also windy'—which look dropped with carefree clumsiness. The particularity of the verbal arrangement fumbles against the raggedness of the writing. In fact, the status of the poem and the character of the words not merely stand in high tension but directly collide: it's *because* they are so deliberately cut and pasted this way that we see 'this country' and 'as she looked when I pushed' in hapless, ineloquent isolation.

And this is not to mention the unsuitability of the subject matter. Piedie Gimbel functions as a point of reference, a simile. What do those girls look like, on this windy day? Like swans—like flowers blown in the breeze—like angels? No: like Piedie Gimbel. But what does that mean? Frank alone knows. The metaphor is private, which means that it doesn't work as a metaphor in poetry should. Metaphors ought to do a work of translation, finding apt points of likeness: by extending the range of comparison, they should make it likelier that more people will get some feel for what's being mentioned. They should thus work outwards, generalizing, making available, even as they perhaps defamiliarize the given object. But O'Hara's 'Piedie Gimbel' is a dead metaphor in the sense that she is unavailable to us. Maybe we could dig up something on her with lengthy research: in that sense her quotidian obscurity is a parody of the classical and historical obscurity of the references, in *The Waste Land* or the *Cantos*. Failing that, what we can say is that 'Piedie Gimbel' is—the kind of woman who features in a Frank O'Hara poem. The simile is thus self-referential: the more such names are multiplied, the more they affirm not some other world of readerly comparison, but precisely the world of the poetry itself, O'Hara's proper domain.

That is to say that O'Hara's verse breaks laws—or simply disregards them—and in the same gesture makes laws of its own. To read him (and this is of course true, in different ways, of other distinctive literary voices) is to learn the ad hoc rules by which his writing works: how much he permits himself (it feels like—everything), how little he grants us ('too little' information on an occasion like this: too little, that is, by those old other people's rules which Mayakovsy said should be disregarded). His poetry is among other things a diary arranged in lines:

> last night we went to a movie and came
>   out,
> Ionesco is greater
> than Beckett, Vincent said, that's what I
>   think, blueberry blintzes
> and Khruschev was probably being
>   carped at
> in Washington, no *politesse*
> Vincent tells me about his mother's trip
>   to Sweden
> Hans tells us
> about his father's life in Sweden, it
>   sounds like Grace Hartigan's
> painting *Sweden*
> so I go home to bed and names drift
>   through my head
> Purgatorio Merchado, Gerhard Schwartz
>   and Gaspar Gonzales, all
> unknown figures of the early morning
>   as I go to work.

'I do this, I do that', O'Hara dubbed this branch of his work. Barrage of content, undetectable form: it's not so much that—as Mayakovsky's critical contemporaries might have said—the device is bared, more that the occasion is left hanging out. A listing of interpersonal, discursive events—'Vincent tells me', 'Hans tells us'; a showering of names which becomes almost self-parodically foregrounded as the content of the poet's thought ('and names drift through my head...all unknown figures'); a babble of asides and interruptions, signalled by the visual placing of the words—'Ionesco is greater', Vincent's insistence irrupts into the flow of the crowd. Associations are crucial, the impatient equations of the mind—'it sounds like Grace Hartigan's painting', though the reference may not be much more immediately available than Piedie Gimbel. Important, too, are *opinions*—not considered views or long perspectives, but prejudices and preferences which jerk to the surface: 'Ionesco is greater / than Beckett... that's what I think', or in another poem,

> we don't like Lionel Trilling
> we decide, we like Don Allen we don't
>   like
> Henry James so much we like Herman
>   Melville.

Memory is part of O'Hara's poetic business ('In Memory of My Feelings' is one of his better known titles), but he is not out to come to the judgment of posterity, not delaying in the name of wisdom. The past is about as undecided as the present, a mess of provisional evaluations delivered—inaptly enough—in no uncertain terms. Emotion is not recollected in tranquility, but re-enacted in effervescence, or lived through in surprise:

> where does the evil of the year go
> when September takes New York
> and turns it into ozone stalagmites
> deposits of light
> so I get back up
> make coffee, and read Francois Villon,
>   his life, so dark
> New York seems blinding and my tie is
>   blowing up the street
> I wish it would blow off
> though it is cold and somewhat warms
>   my neck.

Much of the effect is a rendition of 'experience', which looks raw and buffeted by the wind down the avenue, though like anything in art it's been selected and put in order according to some principle. But what principle? No criterion of objective 'importance' can explain O'Hara's poetic matter: large sleepless reflections on the metaphysical weather ('where does the evil of the year go') must coexist with small acts ('make coffee') and observations ('my tie is blowing up the street'), just as the public or world-historical ('Khruschev is coming') can only be experienced via the most personal terms (it was windy by the swing, on the lawn, too, that time). The principle of inclusion (we can hardly say, of 'order') appears in the end (or in the midst) to be an exultant subjectivity: a self defiantly making itself the measure of art, writing its own rulebook on the back of a napkin. The feeling of necessity which I've said seems to sanctify art is here just that—a *feeling*. And feelings being what they are, there'll be others along soon. What O'Hara raises to the legal status of the poetic is—whatever he likes: well, what else would he want to raise? Something of this comes over in his anti-manifesto, 'Personism' (1959), for which 'You just go on your nerve' and you could, if necessary, 'use the telephone instead of writing the poem.' Art and life—Frank O'Hara's life—become indistinguishable; or at least, the distance between them is only a short cab ride. This is to make a poetry out of the everyday—to *decree* that this stuff shall be poetry—but it is also to make the everyday into poetry. If those options sound the same, perhaps they are: perhaps even when O'Hara seems to be hitting a crescendo he hasn't really raised his register from the diary or his gaze from the shopfronts.

> as the train bears Khruschev on to
>   Pennsylvania Station
> and the light seems to be eternal
> and joy seems to be inexorable
> I am foolish enough always to find it in
>   wind:

maybe, but he's usually canny enough, too, to know that what feels eternal and inexorable (such strange words, amidst the blueberry blintzes) is the same scrappy stuff that feels fleeting and funny: transcendence ('joy') is this side of the street ('I don't believe in god, so I don't have to make elaborately sounded structures').

If the aesthetic conjoins freedom and necessity, O'Hara makes the most of both. He plays fast and loose with the bounds of the appropriate—he includes what he likes—and he makes that look as ineluctable as poetry. In that sense he is abusing—using at whim—the solemn category (Art) into which the posthumous collections will install him: sticking any old thing in the frame, then snickering when it's hung on the gallery wall. Then again, there is a kind of law, an inner necessity, guiding his verse: a principle of inclusion announced in *The Heart* 'you can't plan on the heart, but / the better part of it, my poetry', is open. As a 'diarist', he can't leave things out: he has to 'go by his nerve', to respond to the pressure of encounter and connection—to be ready to feel openly, and to register it all. And not—here's the hardest law in showbiz—to get boring and lose his audience, even if that audience is (as it no longer is) himself.

Two years after Frank O'Hara was hit by a beach buggy (at a distance his death sounds so sadly silly, it makes me think of Roland Barthes), a couple of years before Lou wrote about the vanished rules of verse, 'To live outside the *law,* you *must* be *honest*', sang another of Allen Ginsberg's many acquaintances, Bob Dylan. That line is trickier than it casually seems—it doesn't say that only those outside the (straight, bourgeois, repressive) law are honest, but lays down a challenge to those who would go beyond it. O'Hara seemed, as a writer, to stroll beyond the law ('and everything is tossing, hurrying on up'), or to make his own, founded on nothing more, or nothing less, than his life—his own sense, brief, blowing and scattered, of being alive. He seems, by that token, to have been honest; though that 'seems' perhaps holds his art ('As for measure and other technical apparatus, that's just common sense': but not common to everyone). His restless absence demands an addendum: and if you can't be honest, for gods sake be some fun.

Source: Joe Brooker, "To Live Outside the Law: Frank O'Hara," in *Liverpool Law Review*, Vol. 23, No. 3, 2001, pp. 263–67.

SOURCES

Gooch, Brad, *City Poet: The Life and Times of Frank O'Hara*, Alfred A. Knopf, 1993.

Hoover, Paul, "Introduction," in *Postmodern American Poetry*, Norton, 1994, pp. xxv–xxxix.

Logan, William, "Urban Poet," in *New York Times Book Review*, September 29, 2008, p. 1.

O'Hara, Frank, "Autobiographia Literaria," in *The Selected Poems of Frank O'Hara*, edited by Donald Allen, Alfred A. Knopf, 1974, p. 3.

Sadoff, Ira, "Frank O'Hara's Intimate Fictions." *American Poetry Review*, November–December, 2006 p. 49.

FURTHER READING

Feldman, Alan, "Humor," in *Frank O'Hara*, Twayne, 1979, pp. 134–53.

> Feldman discusses "Autobiographia Literaria" in his chapter about O'Hara's sense of humor, linking it to other, similarly themed works.

Ferguson, Russell, *In Memory of My Feelings: Frank O'Hara and American Art*, University of California Press, 1999.

> Much of O'Hara's life and poetry was wrapped up with contemporary art. In this book, Ferguson combines prints of postmodern paintings with O'Hara's poetry and prose, along with explanations about how his worldview was shaped by the art he saw.

Smith, Alexander, Jr., *Frank O'Hara: A Comprehensive Bibliography*, Garland, 1980.

> This work presents a complete list of all of the poems, plays, and essays that O'Hara composed in his short lifetime, along with information about where they can be found printed and reprinted.

Smith, Hazel, *Hyperscapes in the Poetry of Frank O'Hara: Difference/Homosexuality/Topography*, Liverpool University Press, 2000.

> Smith, a longtime admirer of O'Hara's work, argues that the locations in which the poet lived as he wrote influenced the themes and subjects he explored, even though O'Hara often tried to make such a connection seem irrelevant.

Watkin, William, *In the Process of Poetry: The New York School and the Avant-Garde*, Bucknell University Press, 2001.

> Watkin's survey of the brief movement of the 1960s gives readers a look at what it meant to be groundbreaking for O'Hara and the other New York poets, and the theories that defined and energized their approach.

The Bridegroom

ALEXANDER SERGEYEVICH PUSHKIN

1825

Alexander Pushkin's narrative poem "The Bridegroom" is a retelling of "The Robber Bridegroom," one of the German fairy tales compiled by the Jacob and Wilhelm Grimm in the early 1800s. In Pushkin's version, a young woman comes home after a three-day absence. She is obviously traumatized, but the poet does not tell his readers what has frightened her. At the end of the poem, she tells the assembled guests at her wedding feast about a strange dream that she had, and the details of her story cleverly draw out a confession to murder. Pushkin combines psychology, sociology, and the macabre in the form of a folk narrative, popular when this poem was published in 1825, to give a new twist to an old legend.

Alexander Pushkin is considered one of the greatest poets that Russia ever produced, if not alone the greatest. Part of his genius lies in his versatility: In addition to the folk narrative, which "The Bridegroom" illustrates, Pushkin also wrote ballads and plays, fiction and nonfiction, all with a commanding voice. Although a good English translation can capture the nuances of the story he tells, Russian literary experts confirm that the majesty of Pushkin's writing cannot be fully appreciated outside his native tongue. Still, the power of a tale such as "The Bridegroom" makes itself obvious in any language.

Alexander Pushkin (The Library of Congress)

AUTHOR BIOGRAPHY

Alexander Pushkin was born on June 6, 1799, in Moscow. His father, Sergey Lvovich Pushkin, who held a minor government job, came from a formerly rich, aristocratic landowning family, with a name reaching back six hundred years. His mother was a granddaughter of Abraham Hannibal, who had come to Russia as a slave in the early 1700s and was adopted by Peter the Great, eventually rising to be engineer-general of Russia.

Pushkin was an intelligent but unmotivated student, excelling only in Russian and French, which was the official language of the upper class at the time. Important literary figures often visited the Pushkin household. Pushkin was eleven when a new school, the Lyceum, opened on the estate of Tsar Alexander I Romanov (ruled 1801–1825) in St. Petersburg. His parents sent Pushkin there because tuition was free, and he stayed away from home for the next six years. At the Lyceum he came to the attention of the literary world by winning a poetry contest and having his work published; particular praise came from Vasily Zhukovsky (1783–1852), the leading Russian poet of the day. Pushkin also came to the attention of the government for associating with young men who supported constitutional reform and an end to serfdom, a popular cause among the lower classes.

Pushkin's adult life was tumultuous. He gambled and drank whenever he had any money. In 1820, Tsar Alexander I exiled Pushkin for his published political views; he was sent to Kishinev, a town in the remote south. His time in exile cut down on his raucous social life, but it gave him time to write. In 1823, he was allowed to move to Odessa, but an affair with the wife of the local governor general forced him to leave town soon thereafter. He went to the family estate in Mikhailovskoye, where he stayed from 1824 to 1826. During that time, Tsar Alexander I died, and the ascension of his second son, Nicholas I, triggered the Decembrist revolt, which involved several of Pushkin's friends, who were imprisoned or killed. Pushkin wrote "The Bridegroom" during this period.

Tsar Nicholas I pardoned Pushkin for his political leanings, making it possible for him to travel, but his works were still closely watched by a government censor. This made it difficult for Pushkin to publish much work, and he gambled away what little he did earn from writing. In 1831, he married Natalya Goncharova, a socialite. The couple spent their nights at parties in St. Petersburg, where Natalya was popular. Her extravagant lifestyle and his gambling kept the couple in debt. When the tsar gave Pushkin a minor government position—junior chamberlain, a position usually given to young men just starting out—Pushkin felt humiliated and assumed the position was a ploy by the tsar to keep Natalya in St. Petersburg.

In 1837, responding to rumors that his wife was having an affair, Pushkin challenged Baron Georges d'Anthès to a duel. Though he was experienced at dueling, this time Pushkin was injured. He died two days later, on January 29.

POEM TEXT

Three days Natasha'd been astray,
Who was a merchant's daughter,
When running home in wild dismay
At last the third night brought her.
Her mother and her father plied   5

The maid with questions, tried and tried;
She cannot hear for quaking,
All out of breath and shaking.

But fret and wonder as they did
And stubbornly insisted,   10
They could not fathom what she hid
And in the end desisted.
And soon Natasha grieved no more,
But flushed and merry as before
Went with her sisters walking   15
Beyond the gate and talking.

Once at the gate of shingled ash
The maidens sat together,
Natasha too, when in a flash
Past speeded, hell-for-leather,   20
A dashing troika with a youth;
And rug-clad cobs he drove, forsooth,
Drove standing up, bespattered
All in his path and scattered.

He, drawing closer, glanced upon   25
The maid; her glance replying,
He like the whirlwind galloped on,
The maid was nigh to dying.
And arrow-straight she homeward fled,
"It's he, I knew him well!" she said,   30
"Stop him, it's he, no other,
Oh, save me, friend and brother!"

Her kinfolk listened, grave and sad,
And shook their heads with ruing:
"Speak out, my lass," her father bade,   35
"And tell us how you knew him.
If something untoward occurred,
Speak openly, say just a word."
Natasha's back to crying,
No further word replying.   40

Next day a marriage-gossip came,
Came unexpected rather,
She spoke Natasha fair by name,
Fell talking to her father:
"You have the wares, we want to trade;   45
My buyer is a fine young blade,
Is lithely made and comely,
Not evil-famed or grumbly.

"Has wealth and wits, to never a man
In low obeisance bending,   50
But rather, like a nobleman
He lives with easy spending.
He's like to give his chosen girl
A fur of fox-skin and a pearl,
Gold hoops for golden tresses,   55
And stiff brocaded dresses.

"Last night he saw her on his ride
Out by the towngate linger;
Let's shake, take ikons and the bride
And to the altar bring her!"   60
There over tea and cake she sits
And hints and yarns and snares their wits,
While the poor bride's uneasy,
All fidgeting and queasy.

"So be it, then," her father said,   65
"Go forth, God speed you, dearie,
Take wreath, Natasha, and be wed,
Alone upstairs it's dreary.
Comes time for maids no more to flit,
For swallows, too, their chirps to quit,   70
It's time to nest, to nourish
Young bairns at home and cherish."

Natasha tried to have her say,
Her back to wall and rafter,
But all ashudder sobbed away,   75
Now racked with tears, now laughter.
The gossip in dismay runs up,
Makes her sip water from a cup,
And all the rest she dashes
And on her forehead splashes.   80

Natasha's kinfolk moaned and wept.
But she, back in her senses,
Announced: "I honor and accept
What your high will dispenses.
It's time that to the feast you bade   85
The groom, and many loaves were made,
Mead choice of brew and hearty,
The law bid to the party."

"Command, Natasha, angel child,
To please you, I am ready   90
To give my life!" A feast is piled,
Prodigious, rich, and heady.
Now worthy guests arrive apace,
They lead the bride to take her place;
As bridesmaids sing with weeping,   95
A sledge and team come leaping.

Here is the bridegroom—all sit down,
Cup touches cup with ringing,
The toasting bowl goes round and round
To drunken shouts and singing.   100

THE BRIDEGROOM

"I say, my merry friends, abide,
I say, why is my pretty bride
Not serving, eating, drinking,
All lost in mournful thinking?"

Said bride to groom: "I'll tell my plight   105
As best I may be able:
I find no rest by day or night,
I weep abed, at table.
A horrid nightmare wears me out."
Her father wonders: "What about?   110
Whatever kind it may be,
Tell us, my own dear baby!"

The maiden said: "I dream that I
Walk where the wood grows thickly,
It's late, and from a cloudy sky   115
The moonlight glimmers sickly.
I've lost my way; in pine and fir
No living creature is astir,
The trees alone are brushing
Their crowns with wispy rushing.   120

"But clear as day I now make out
Ahead a hut emerging;
I reach it, knock: no answer, shout:
No sound; I hail the Virgin,
I lift the latch, go in, advance,   125
Inside a candle burns; I glance—
All gleams with heaping measure
Of gold and Silver treasure."

THE BRIDEGROOM

"What is so bad about your dream?
It means you'll be in clover."   130

THE BRIDE

"I ask your leave, sir, it would seem
The dream is not yet over.
On gold and silver, rugs untrod,
Brocade and silks from Novgorod,
I stood in silence gazing   135
With wonder and amazing.

"Now hoofbeats clatter, voices roar,
Here someone comes a-riding;
I quickly up and slam the door,
Behind the chimney hiding.   140
Then voices swell in mingled din,
Twelve lusty lads come trooping in;
With them in modest duty
A fair and pure young beauty.

"Without a bow they throng the place,   145
The ikons never heeding,
Sit down to dine without a grace,
And, cap on head, start feeding.
The eldest brother at the head,
The youngest at his right hand fed,   150
At left in modest duty
There sat the pure young beauty.

"Hubbub and clink, guffaw and scream,
Exuberant carousal . . ."

THE BRIDEGROOM

"What is so bad about your dream?   155
It bodes a gay espousal."

THE BRIDE

"Your pardon, sir, it is not done.
The drunken din goes roaring on,
But as they cheer and riot,
The maid sits sad and quiet.   160

"Sat mute and neither ate nor sipped,
In bitter tears and fretting,
The eldest brother, whistling, gripped
His knife and fell to whetting;
The fiend glanced at the maiden fair,   165
And sprang and seized her by the hair:
I saw him kill and fling her
To chop off hand and finger."

"Sheer raving, fancy run amuck,
I would not let it grieve me!   170
Yet," said the groom, "it bodes good luck,
My tender maid, believe me!"
She gazed at him both hard and long:
"To whom, pray, did this ring belong?"
She asked, and, half-arising,   175
All stared with dread surmising.

The trinket, slipping, clinked and bounced,
The bridegroom blanched and trembled.
The guests stood awed. The law pronounced:
"Stop, bind him, all assembled!"   180
The fiend was tried, in fetters strung,
And shortly from the gallows hung.
Natasha rose to glory!
And therewith ends my story.

POEM SUMMARY

Stanza 1

The narrator gives the background of the story. Natasha, a merchant's daughter, has run away from home and is missing. On the third night she comes running home, so out of breath that she cannot even hear the questions being asked by her parents or her maid. She is so shaken that she cannot speak about what had frightened her.

Stanza 2

Her parents question Natasha about where she had been and what she has seen, but she cannot answer them, and eventually they let the matter drop. As time passes, Natasha forgets about her experience.

One day, cheerful as she was before her ordeal, Natasha goes with her sisters out beyond the gate of the village.

Stanza 3

While the sisters sit together outside the gate, a carriage, or *troika*, goes by. It moves along at a furious pace, with the driver, standing in his seat, forcing his short, muscular horses—cobs—to gallop at top speed.

Stanza 4

After a moment, Natasha recognizes the young man driving the carriage. A look passes between them. She fears him, turns and runs for home, crying out to those near her to save her from this fellow.

Stanza 5

At the house, her relatives gather to find out what is the matter. Her father asks Natasha

- "The Bridegroom" is one of the poems recorded on *Prentice Hall Literature*, a compact disc released in 2006 by Recording for the Blind & Dyslexic.

what is upsetting her, but she only cries and does not say a word.

Stanza 6
The following day, a marriage broker comes to the house. She has been approached by a wealthy young man who knows of Natasha, and she wants to discuss the possibility of a marriage between the two. The broker vouches for the man, saying that he is good looking, has a good reputation, and has a pleasing disposition.

Stanza 7
The marriage broker continues to describe the man who wants to marry Natasha. He is wealthy and confident enough in himself not to take orders from any man. He also is generous: In the broker's opinion, he is likely to give the woman who marries him dresses, jewels, and furs.

Stanza 8
The marriage broker explains that the young man saw Natasha by the town gate the previous evening. She tells stories and drops hints over tea and cakes, encouraging Natasha and her father to agree to the marriage. Natasha is uncomfortable with the idea but stays quiet.

Stanza 9
Natasha's father agrees to the marriage. He tells Natasha that the time has come for her to quit bouncing around like a sparrow, that she should leave her bland life at the family home and go into the world. She should start her own family, have her own children.

Stanza 10
Natasha responds strangely at the thought of marrying this man. First, she cries uncontrollably. The crying then gives way to a fit of uncontrollable laughter. To help her regain her composure, the marriage broker brings her a glass of water. She lets Natasha sip some and then splashes the rest on her head, hoping to shock her back to her senses.

Stanza 11
Natasha's irrational reaction distresses her family. Eventually, though, she calms down and agrees to the marriage. For the wedding, she says, she wants a feast, with bread and the best beer. She specifies that she wants the police invited to the reception.

Stanza 12
Natasha's father tells her that he is willing to give her the wedding that she wants, that he will arrange anything to please her. The poem then jumps forward in time to the day of the wedding. It is an extravagant affair. The guests are shown to their places, Natasha is ready, and her bridesmaids are singing and weeping. A carriage arrives.

Stanza 13
The groom steps from the carriage, and the feast begins. There are rounds of toasts for the happy couple, and people begin to feel drunk. Shouts and singing break out.

The second half of stanza 13 (lines 101–104) the bridegroom addresses the crowd, asking why, in the middle of all of this merriment, Natasha is not serving her guests and not eating or drinking. The bride is instead standing to the side, lost in thought.

Stanza 14
Natasha responds that she is never happy. She has had a nightmare that causes her to cry all of the time, leaving her exhausted. Her father implores her to tell everyone at the wedding about the nightmare.

Stanza 15
Natasha explains that in her dream she is walking in the woods at night. It is overcast, and the moon is hardly visible. She is lost. There are no animals moving. The wind is blowing through the treetops, creating a rustling sound.

Stanza 16
As she wanders through the woods, Natasha explains, she comes across a hut. She knocks on the door and calls out, but no one inside answers, so she opens the door and walks in. Inside, there are candles burning, an indication that someone has been there recently. The room is heaped with gold and silver.

Stanza 17
The bridegroom asks why this dream should upset Natasha so much. According to his interpretation, it should mean that she is going to be lucky.

Natasha asks him to just wait, as there is more to the dream. She describes the riches inside the hut in greater detail, including the fine silks and rugs.

Stanza 18
Natasha tells the people assembled for the wedding feast that as she stands in amazement, she hears horses approach. She hides behind the chimney. The door opens, and into the room step twelve boisterous young men, along with a "fair and pure" young woman.

Stanza 19
Natasha watches the twelve young men come in without giving the proper acknowledgement to the religious statues as they enter. Rudely, they sit down at the table to eat without removing their hats. The oldest of them sits at the head of the table, flanked by the youngest to his right and the fair young woman to his left.

Stanza 20
Stanza 20 includes lines 153 to 160, with several breaks. What identifies it as one continuous stanza is the poem's established pattern of eight-line stanzas.

Natasha describes the boisterous sounds made by the twelve young men as they eat. The bridegroom interrupts to ask why she considers this such a horrible dream, but she begs him to be patient, since there is more. The men are drunk and loud, she says, but the woman at the table with them sits quietly, feeling sad.

Stanza 21
As the woman sits crying, not eating or drinking, the eldest brother, beside her, begins sharpening his knife with a whetstone. He then jumps up, grabs the woman, and kills her with his knife. After that, he cuts off one of her hands.

Stanza 22
Natasha explains how she keeps herself quiet while watching this horrible scene. The bridegroom agrees, emphatically, that it was best for her to keep quiet. After staring at him for a moment, Natasha asks where the wedding ring he gave her is from and who owned it before she did. All of the people assembled for the feast fall quiet, and they come to understand what she is implying.

Stanza 23
Natasha lets the wedding ring drop. The bridegroom panics, trembling, but before he can make a move the sheriff calls out for the guests to hold him. The bridegroom is tried for the girl's murder, and he is convicted. He is hanged for the crime. Natasha, the narrator says, was recognized as a hero for bringing the murderer to justice.

THEMES

Fear
In "The Bridegroom" Natasha is filled with fear, so terrified that she cannot stop shaking and she cannot explain why. With the passage of time, her terror fades, only to flare up again when she sees the young man ride past and recognizes him. She runs home screaming for help, but she does not tell anyone what it is that has frightened her.

Although he withholds details, Pushkin makes it clear that Natasha recognizes the carriage-riding stranger and that she knows what he has done. The fact that she does not tell her family about him suggests trauma and fear of retaliation. She is first terrified about the prospect of marrying the man she saw commit murder, but she abruptly changes her mind, accepts the marriage proposal, and then laughs about it. She requests a large feast, specifying that the local police are invited. Clearly, gathering witnesses and police gives Natasha the confidence she needs to carry out her plan for entrapment. As soon as she starts planning the wedding feast, she no longer has trouble expressing herself. Having been isolated from her friends and family by her secret experience, she is able to overcome her fear by surrounding herself with those whom she can trust to protect her.

TOPICS FOR FURTHER STUDY

- Pushkin was an admirer of George Gordon, Lord Byron, the British poet associated with the early nineteenth-century romantic movement. Read one canto of Byron's masterpiece, the book-length poem *Don Juan*, and mark the similarities of style you notice between Pushkin's and Byron's work. Write an essay in which you compare and contrast these two poets' works and explain why you think one of them is a better poet than the other. Be sure to explain the criteria you used for evaluating the poets.

- Kathi Appelt's *The Underneath* is a contemporary novel with gothic elements similar to "The Bridegroom." Appelt's book weaves together stories about cats and dogs in danger. Read Appelt's book and then rewrite the story of "The Bridegroom," making it suitable for a younger audience, with animals instead of humans as the main characters, pointing out which aspects of their personalities you felt it was necessary to change.

- Illustrate a scene from the wedding or from the dream action Natasha describes. Bring your illustration to class to discuss with classmates.

- Write a short story that describes the thieves' crime spree before their arrival at the cottage and explains how the young woman came to be among the thieves. Make one member of their group a sympathetic character.

- Do some research in psychology, particularly about dream analysis, and write an essay that proposes a psychological diagnosis of Natasha that helps explain why she refrains from telling anyone about witnessing the murder or recognizing the killer on the road. Include psychological terms in your essay.

- The criminal band described in this poem have obviously been operating for some time, given the amassed stolen goods they have. Study stories from current news sources about criminal bands and how they were caught. Present the stories that you have compiled to your class and have them vote on whether Natasha's plan to trap the bridegroom is a good one.

Dream

At her wedding, Natasha narrates the event that traumatized her, but she tells it as a dream. Using the device of saying this is a dream buys her time and gives her a way through narrative of entrapping the murderer. The woman who enters with the thieves is so pale and frightened that she could easily be taken as a symbolic representation of Natasha herself. Overall, the fantastic elements of the story have the sort of exaggerated tone and incongruous details that one might expect to find in a dream.

It is difficult to tell how much of the related dream corresponds to the events Natasha actually witnessed in the forest. The bridegroom's interruptions seem intended to make Natasha quit talking, which suggests he may be uncomfortable about having this story related. However, the ploy that the story is only a dream keeps him listening. Perhaps he does not stop her completely because he does not recognize the details of Natasha's dream as leading to the murder he committed. If so, then disguising her actual experience in the lurid exaggerations of a dream turns out to be an effective way of revealing her account without the murderer realizing he is being accused until it is too late.

Patriarchy

In a patriarchal society, family decisions are made by the father, who is the head of the household. The most obvious evidence of this male-dominated society is that the "marriage-gossip" brings a proposal of marriage to Natasha's father, rather than to Natasha directly. The matchmaker talks about

Palace Square in St. Petersburg, Russia (Image copyright Sergey Borisov, 2009. Used under license from Shutterstock.com)

Natasha as if she were an object that can be traded for the dowry that the young man agrees to pay for her. While Natasha remains nervous about the offer, her father accepts, and then he talks to his daughter, trying to convince her of the wisdom of the course of action he has already arranged for her. Though the decision is the father's to make, her family does wait until Natasha agrees to be married before taking any steps toward arranging the wedding. The family members understand that the marriage arrangement is the father's business.

Another sign of the patriarchal society is that when she recognizes the murderer on the road, Natasha runs to the safety of home and the men who live there. She takes cover among her powerful male family members. Even the arrangement of the twelve brothers in the dream, with the oldest one taking the head of the table, reflects the patriarchal system in which the most importance is assigned to the oldest male present.

Marriage

The marriage broker's argument in favor of the marriage suggests some of the social assumptions about what makes a good marriage. The matchmaker claims that the prospective groom has a good personality and is generous. Though these traits do not prove to be true of the groom, they reveal what people value in a groom. The marriage broker must present her client in the most flattering light possible; after all, when the marriage occurs, the broker is paid for her services. The fact that the bridegroom expresses immediate interest in Natasha could be a sign of love at first sight, if it were not for the fact that she runs from him, shouting, "I know him well." His interruptions of her story could also be interpreted by wedding guests as his attempt to convince Natasha to look at the dream as a positive omen, not as a nightmare. Only later details indicate that he probably has been trying to stop her story before she can reveal too much.

Natasha is in a difficult situation when she comes home from the forest with eyewitness evidence of a murder, and her situation becomes even more complicated when she recognizes the murderer coming into her town. When she finds out that he seeks to marry her, Natasha knows she is doomed unless she can figure a way to entrap her suitor. She escapes because of her cunning plan for a public wedding celebration. Revealing the bridegroom's nature at the wedding allows her to escape her otherwise certain destiny of becoming his wife and living thereafter completely at his mercy.

STYLE

Narrative Poem
"The Bridegroom" is a narrative poem; it tells a story, beginning with Natasha's troubled three-day disappearance and ending with her successful entrapping of the murderer. Narrative poetry is one of the first forms of poetry, dating back to a time centuries before most people could read or write. Setting stories to fixed patters of rhythm and rhyme made them easy to remember and, therefore, easy to pass orally from one teller to another. As printed poetry became common some time in the Middle Ages, poets focused more and more on the poem's layout on the page.

One aspect common to narrative poems is that they have a narrator. In the case of this poem, the narrator makes himself conspicuous by omission. There are aspects of Natasha's story, such as where she was for three days or what she has in mind when she agrees to the marriage, that the narrator does not know. In this respect, the narrator knows no more than the townspeople or the members of Natasha's family know. In the last line of the poem, he refers to himself by calling the poem "my story," making the narrator a character within the poem and not just an omniscient viewer who is outside the action and knowledgeable of all of it.

Dialogue
Pushkin identifies speakers in several distinct ways in this poem. Sometimes dialogue is related directly and some comes indirectly through the narrator. This style occurs in the first stanza, where the words that Natasha's parents speak to the maid are not presented directly. Pushkin often uses direct quotations with the speaker identified within the text of the poem with such phrases as "she said" or "her father bade." One quotation, which spans lines 89 through 91, does not have a speaker directly identified: It appears to be Natasha's father speaking, but that is not made explicit. Throughout the poem, Pushkin uses ordinary identifiers that are common in plays. The words "The Bride" and "The Bridegroom" introduce speakers, sometimes breaking into the middle of a stanza to do so. This technique heightens the drama of the poem, giving it the feel of a play that is being presented before the reader's eyes.

Stanzas
Pushkin consistently uses an eight-line stanza in "The Bridegroom." The eight-line stanza is not common, but it is a variation of the four-line stanza, or quatrain, which is the most common stanza length. Even in cases in which only two or four lines are clustered together, they are followed by another group of lines that, added to them, make eight. In these cases, it is not that Pushkin has used a variant stanza length, but only that the stanza has been interrupted by a speaker identifier. The poem's stanzaic structure might be adjusted, but it is never broken.

HISTORICAL CONTEXT

The Romantic Movement
Pushkin is one of the Russian authors associated with the romantic movement in literature. The term romanticism designates a style and focus that characterizes literary, visual, and musical works produced from the late eighteenth century to the mid-nineteenth century. The romantic style and sensibility was, at least in part, a reaction against formalism and intellectualism of the previous period, called the Age of Enlightenment. During the late seventeenth and first half of the eighteenth century, writers, painters, and music composers were interested in logic and reason, symmetry and balance, and creative works reflected advances in science and in an hierarchical social order. The Enlightenment produced social thinkers such as Jean-Jacques Rousseau (1712–1778) and Thomas Paine (1737–1809), who promoted democracy through the recognition of the rights of individuals. By the end of the 1700s, Enlightenment ideals had led to revolutions against the established ruling order in North America, France, and Poland, which in turn raised questions about individualism in countries across the globe. Romanticism rose out of the social disorder that ensued.

In English literature, the beginning of the romantic movement is often pegged to the late eighteenth-century publication of *Lyrical Ballads*, a collection of poems by William Wordsworth

COMPARE & CONTRAST

- **1825:** An author basing his story on the relatively recent publication of the fairy tales recorded by the Brothers Grimm can expect his readers to know of the story's bizarre and violent twists.

  Today: The stories recorded by the Grimm brothers have been used as source material for countless children's stories and movies. Contemporary readers are accustomed to the more sanitized versions.

- **1825:** Marriages are routinely arranged by brokers, or "marriage-gossips," who coordinate the financial agreement of the two families involved.

  Today: Arranged marriages are rare in Western cultures. It is becoming less popular in those cultures where the practice is still followed.

- **1825:** A woman who has witnessed a crime risks not being believed by those to whom she reports it. She might do better to trap the culprit in a public setting.

  Today: Authorities understand how important it is to pay serious attention to anyone who reports a crime, even if it sounds hard to believe.

- **1825:** A dream, like the one Natasha relates in "The Bridegroom," is considered an interesting story with little real-life relevance.

  Today: Ever since Sigmund Freud made the connection between dreams and the subconscious in his 1900 essay *The Interpretation of Dreams*, people are inclined to find real-life meaning in a traumatized person's dream.

- **1825:** Revealing evidence like the ring that Natasha puts on the table at the end of this poem is good for making a criminal confess, but the link between the evidence and the accused person is not very solid.

  Today: Such a piece of material evidence would be key to making a case against a murderer, especially if the ring contained blood evidence or the victim's DNA.

- **1825:** A wedding is an occasion for the couple marrying to gather friends and family together for a festive celebration.

  Today: The tradition of the wedding feast continues, and in some cases, elaborate weddings cost tens of thousands of dollars.

---

and Samuel Taylor Coleridge. In the Preface to the second edition (1802), Wordsworth explained a new style of poetry, the literary equivalent of the basic political tenets of the romantic movement. These values were carried on in the next generation by Percy Bysshe Shelley and John Keats, who were Pushkin's contemporaries. In Germany, by contrast, the movement developed earlier, with Johann Wolfgang von Goethe's masterpiece *The Sorrows of Young Werther*, published in 1774, being considered a central text of German romanticism. The United States, a young country then, took a while to follow philosophical movements in Europe. American romantic writers include Edgar Alan Poe (whose greatest success "The Raven" was published in 1847) and Nathanial Hawthorne (who published *The Scarlet Letter* in 1850).

Given the social upheaval from which romanticism developed, romantic writers often focused on national identity. For some European writers, this meant taking ancient Greek and Roman stories as their own themes, to establish the connection between their countries and antiquity. For others, the focus on the past led to a revival of interest in folktales and fairy tales; thus, it was clearly within the scope of romanticism for the Brothers Grimm to record and publish their book of traditional folktales in 1812, providing Pushkin with his inspiration for "The Bridegroom."

Alexander I of Russia

The French Revolution spanned ten years of escalating tumult (1789–1799). In the end, the country came under the control of Napoleon Bonaparte (1769–1821), who seized power with a military coup. He then went about enacting a plan to take control of Europe, which involved invading countries across the continent, sometimes breaking treaties and alliances along the way. Between 1803 and 1812, France fought wars against Britain, Russia, Bavaria, Austria, Italy, Prussia, Saxony, and Sweden, among others. In 1812, a direct assault was made against Russia. Moscow was taken by French troops and troops that Napoleon had conscribed into his army from defeated countries, but the city had been evacuated, so the invaders were left to burn the city to the ground. The fight against Napoleon's troops as they retreated took all of Russia's resources and became the defining event for Pushkin's generation. Napoleon was defeated in 1814 and sent into exile; he returned to overcome the French king who had been returned to his throne and to mount another attack against his allies, losing a decisive battle in 1815 at Waterloo, Belgium.

In Russia, Tsar Alexander I (1777–1825) resisted both the encroachments of the Napoleonic empire and the movement for social reform that had fueled both the American Revolution and the French Revolution. The Russian social system was feudal in its structure, with a wide chasm between landowners and the serfs who worked on the land and had no legal rights. While European countries embraced equality and freed serfs from their de facto slavery, Russia still had tens of millions of serfs well into the 1850s.

Politically, the issue of serfdom was as divisive in Russia as the issue of slavery came to be in the United States. When Alexander died in 1825, his eldest son Constantine, next in line for the Russian throne, stepped aside for his younger brother, Nicholas I, to become the new tsar. Leftists who supported freedom of the serfs suspected that Constantine had been coerced, and in response, the Decembrist movement arose to try to take back the throne. Their battle was short lived. In just a few weeks at the end of 1825, the Decembrists were defeated. Among those who were jailed for being part of the conspiracy were several of Pushkin's closest associates and acquaintances going back to his school days.

Catherine's Palace, formerly the Pushkin Imperial estate, in St. Petersburg, Russia (Image copyright Bill Draven, 2009. Used under license from Shutterstock.com)

Pushkin himself was investigated as a possible conspirator, but set free.

CRITICAL OVERVIEW

Alexander Pushkin was considered one of Russia's greatest writers, although he struggled to make a living and died in debt. Nikolai Gogol, who was a friend of Pushkin, made the case while Pushkin was still alive that he should be viewed as a "national" poet, explaining that "there is not a single one of our poets who is superior to him and who has a greater right to be called national: it is a right which is decidedly his." One part of the problem was that some of his work was considered by the government to be subversive; therefore, Pushkin was prohibited from publishing much during his lifetime. In the decades after his death, moreover, he was often ignored by critics from both ends of the political spectrum. Those who thought that artists should be politically involved thought Pushkin was too much of a "pure" artist, concerned more with poetic structure than with the suffering of the underclass, whereas those who thought poetry should be free of the rules of this world felt that his anti-government stance weakened his artistry.

By the twentieth century, his supremacy in Russian literature was no longer questioned. In a 1924 essay, written nearly a hundred years after "The Bridegroom," Boris Eikhenbaum tracked the rise of the poet's reputation over the previous century and concluded, "Pushkin finally becomes our genuine, undeniable, if not our only tradition. ... No longer is Pushkin [a] plaster statuette. He has become an imposing monument." In 1960, Renato Poggioli specifically addressed Pushkin's fairy tale poems, such as "The Bridegroom," claiming that they revealed "a Mozart-like gift": "Certainly there is nothing to which they may be compared in the European letters of the epoch," Poggioli wrote, attributing to the Pushkin's fairy tales more than just entertainment value, but "the far more serious intention of amusing and pleasing the child within his and all men's hearts." As Thaïs S. Lindstrom put it in *A Concise History of Russian Literature*, "Ask a non-Russian to name the greatest among Russian writers, and he will at once think of Tolstoy, Dostoyevsky, or both. But a Russian will answer 'Pushkin,' as unhesitatingly as the English-speaking name Shakespeare sovereign of English literature."

CRITICISM

David Kelly

Kelly is a writer and an instructor of creative writing and literature. In the following essay, he discusses how Pushkin's poem varies in content and form from the Grimm version of the folktale.

Alexander Pushkin's 1825 poem "The Bridegroom" is clearly based on the story "The Robber Bridegroom" that the Brothers Grimm published in their 1812 collection *Children's and Household Tales.*. The Grimm version of the story bears resemblance to the story of Mr. Fox, an English folktale that had been passed down orally for at least a hundred years before then. The Brothers Grimm, in setting the tale down on paper, gave it details that made it uniquely theirs, and Pushkin took

"THE GRIMM VERSION TAKES READERS TO A STRANGE WORLD, BUT PUSHKIN GIVES HIS POEM THE PLAUSIBILITY OF REALITY."

their version and made changes in it in order to make it his own. It is worth looking at the changes that Pushkin chose to make. They bend the folk legend, a form that was much in vogue in the early nineteenth century, toward a sort of mystery/adventure story, one aimed at capturing and engaging readers' imaginations. Even more interesting is the fact that Pushkin's alterations can be seen as a natural result of his working in a closed poetic form.

"The Robber Bridegroom" has the sorts of nightmarish twists that one expects in a Grimm fairy tale. It is studded with blood, dismemberment, and sexual threat. The Grimm version, unlike Pushkin's, begins with the father of the bride-to-be making the decision that his daughter ought to be married and soon after being approached by a stranger who wants to marry her. The girl and the suitor are engaged for a while when he begins urging her to come to his house. It is out in the forest, and she is afraid she cannot find it, but he devises a plan to strew ashes along the pathway so that she can come the following Sunday, when he intends to have other guests visiting. The bride-to-be goes into the forest, following his markings and dropping peas and linseeds on the ground so that she will find her way back. Once at the house, she knocks and enters, and a bird in a cage warns her that she should leave with a chant that is repeated twice: She is in a murderer's house. In a cellar behind the house, the girl finds an old woman, who has been waiting a long time for her chance to escape. If she stays, the old woman explains, the bride will be cut to pieces, boiled, and eaten.

The two women hide behind a large cask as a band of men enters, dragging a young woman who is forced to drink wine and then stripped of her clothes, spread out on a table, and cut to pieces. Her finger, with a gold ring on it, bounces away and lands on the hidden girl's lap. The old woman tells the bandit to forget it while she

WHAT DO I READ NEXT?

- "The Robber Bridegroom" is number 40 in the standard collection of the stories first published in 1812 by Jacob and Wilhelm Grimm. There are many good versions of these stories, which are free of copyright laws, including the ones translated by Ralph Manheim in *Grimms' Tales for Young and Old: The Complete Stories*, published by Anchor Press in 1983.

- American author Eudora Welty adapted the Grimm brothers' story, setting it in Mississippi in the 1940s. Welty's novella, also called *The Robber Bridegroom*, was published by Harcourt Brace Jovanovich in 1978.

- *Eugene Onegin* (1837) is considered by many to be Pushkin's masterpiece, and it was one of the author's favorites. Written at the same time he wrote "The Bridegroom," it is a book-length poem, loosely plotted, following the lives of three men and three women. The Oxford University Press 1998 edition of *Eugene Onegin* is considered an excellent translation.

- Pushkin was a friend of Nikolai Gogol, considered to be one of Russia's greatest novelists. He is reputed to have given Gogol the idea for one of his most successful novels, *Dead Souls*, published in 1842. The novel is a political satire about land-owning Russians and the serfs whom they controlled. The 1997 Vintage Press edition is respected as one of the better translations.

- Robin Edmonds's 1994 biography *Pushkin: The Man and His Age* gives a contemporary look at the poet's life with the benefit of two hundred years' hindsight. Edmonds's prose reads like a historical novel as he describes Russia in the early nineteenth century.

- Tatyana Tolstaya's collection *Pushkin's Children: Writings on Russia and Russians*, published by Houghton Mifflin in 2003, seldom mentions Pushkin, despite the volume's title. The 20 essays are essentially a collection of reviews of recent books on the post-Soviet world. Still, they offer a useful perspective of how the issues that were current during Pushkin's life have turned into contemporary reality.

---

serves their supper, which she doses with a sleeping potion. She and the girl escape, following the trail of peas, which have begun to sprout. At home, the girl tells her father the whole story; he does nothing about it, and the next day the bridegroom arrives with a large wedding party.

The rest of the story unravels much like Pushkin's. At the wedding, stories are told. The girl tells of what she has witnessed as if it were a dream until she reaches the part about the lopped-off finger landing on her lap. Then she produces the finger, still wearing its ring, and places it on the table. The criminal gang is arrested and executed.

The differences that Pushkin chose to make are in some cases minor and in others relevant to the entire nature of the tale. The most important change is that Pushkin's Natasha does not know the murderer when she watches him assault another young woman whom, one can assume, she recognizes as being similar to herself. In Pushkin's version, Natasha was not invited to the house in the woods, she just happened upon it while she was lost. The Grimm version presents the bridegroom as a serial predator, proposing to the girl so he can lure her to his house and kill her; in Pushkin's "The Bridegroom," the predator sees the witness to his crime as he is riding down the road, and then he sends the marriage broker to ask for her hand in marriage, possibly to shut her up.

Moreover, in the Grimm version, the man is a cannibal; the old woman tells the bride-to-be directly that "he is a man and woman eater"). In the Pushkin version, he is a thief who has filled his hideout with wealth and attacks a girl when he is drunk. His behavior in the Pushkin version is no more excusable, but it is at least understandable in human terms.

Pushkin even gives the bridegroom some appeal. He presents quite a dashing figure when he rides past whipping his horses to gallop. At this point in the poem, readers have not been told about the criminal that he is, since Natasha's journey into the forest is kept secret from her family as well as from Pushkin's readers. All the Grimm brothers can say about him, by contrast, is that he "appeared to be very rich, and the miller could find nothing to say against him." The two versions divert in how they have Natasha involved with this stranger and in her culpability in his crime. In the Grimm version, she is skeptical about wandering into the woods (an act that is often used symbolically to signify facing the hidden aspects of human nature), and, once there, she has to watch her fiancé participate in symbolic gang rape and actual dismemberment. In Pushkin, the stranger's dashing figure is offset by the truth Natasha knows about him, but the reader does not know it. There is a specific moment when, after thinking over the situation, Natasha accepts the man's proposal and agrees to wear the ring she knows came from the murdered woman's severed finger, though clearly Natasha never accepts the bridegroom at all but instead plans to expose and entrap him.

Natasha, at the start of the Pushkin version, disappears for three days and does not reveal where she has been during that time. Her inability to speak implies she has witnessed something that has traumatized her. Later, when she sees the horseman gallop by, she panics: It is not clear what her panic is about, only that a look has been exchanged between them. Pushkin's audience cannot tell why Natasha is afraid of the horseman or if her fear is justified. In "The Robber Bridegroom," by contrast, the young woman's fear is absolutely justified: The caged bird tells her several times to flee for her life, and the old woman explains exactly what will happen if she stays. In both versions, at the wedding feast, she introduces the tale of adventure as a dream. In the Grimm version, readers have watched the events unfold, and so they know that what she says is no dream. But Pushkin's Natasha seems psychologically weak from the start. The idea that she might be relating something that has been generated by her traumatized mind is a possibility until the bridegroom confesses to his crime.

Pushkin's version of the story is a more tightly told tale. He keeps readers uncertain until the last line, when they can look back and feel they should have seen the inevitable conclusion coming. The Grimm version has a more haphazard structure, with the sorts of details that twentieth-century psychoanalysts learned to pick apart as possible clues to the human psyche, sometimes too enthusiastically. Certainly, the caged bird can be considered a foreshadowing of the bad marriage the girl is entering, and the girl who is molested and murdered by her fiancé is another form of Natasha, but are the scattered ashes and sprouting peas really significant or just quirky details? The Grimm version takes readers to a strange world, but Pushkin gives his poem the plausibility of reality.

As with all great art, form serves function in Pushkin's poem. He is able to remove some of the fantastical elements from his version precisely because he presents this tale in poetic form. He follows a closed structure of basically iambic tetrameter, which translators have trouble retaining, and eight-line stanzas, to which most translations adhere. The end result is that Pushkin's form takes on a life of its own. It exists in a world that is singularly its own, with a rhythm and feel that distinguish it from the real world. Pushkin does not need to include talking birds and plants that take root within hours or cabals of sinister men who feast on the meat of their victims just for the sake of doing evil. His poetic talent makes it possible for him to tell the story with just a few of the macabre details. The condensed poetic form brings his readers into the world of the work: He does not need many details to make readers realize how singular the place is he creates there.

Source: David Kelly, Critical Essay on "The Bridegroom," in *Poetry for Students*, Gale, Cengage Learning, 2010.

Kathleen M. Ahern

In the following excerpt, Ahern discusses the fact that Alexander Pushkin was of African descent and that this was significant to the poet, of significance in the newly formed Soviet Union, and a source of inspiration for African American intellectuals in the 1930s.

A shift in the discussion of Alexander Pushkin's African lineage during the early years of the

> WHILE THE PREVAILING SENTIMENT IN TSARIST RUSSIA MARKED PUSHKIN AS RUSSIAN, AS DID PUSHKIN HIMSELF, IN THE EARLIEST YEARS OF THE SOVIET ERA, THE SIGNIFICANCE OF PUSHKIN'S LINEAGE WAS INFLATED."

Soviet Union strengthened the bond between Russia and American blacks, a bond desired by both parties and seen as beneficial to each. The Soviets sought international recognition for their newly realized social experiment; African Americans sought a voice and a recognized identity within a larger cultural forum. Literary texts from a group of African American authors who visited the Soviet Union in the 1920s and 1930s reveal a general knowledge of Pushkin's African descent and a sense of inheritance through Pushkin that underpins their hope for literary acceptance. Allison Blakely, in his book, *Russia and the Negro*, calls these fellow travelers the black "pilgrims." The term is appropriate, as their role in pioneering this connection to the Soviet Union was significant. Their literary output leaves a clear understanding that, for them, Pushkin was as African as he was Russian and that this fact was not central to his greatness as a poet and literary figure.

Alexander Pushkin's Africaness (traced through his maternal great-grandfather, Abram Hannibal) has been the subject of commentary from Pushkin's own time to the present. Citations on Pushkin's lineage begin with the poet himself. In fact, the knowledge of Pushkin's heritage stemmed in large part from the poet's frequent mention of his African great-grandfather and the intellectual curiosity with which he examines the impact of his forefather on his own life. J. Thomas Shaw charts Pushkin's own citations within his published literary works, finding ten significant mentions of Hannibal, five in prose and five in poetry. The first of these allusions to heritage appears in a poem "To Lazykov," written in 1824:

> In the countryside, where Peter's foster-child,
> Favorite slave of tsars and tsarinas
> And their forgotten housemate,
> My Negro great-grandfather hid
> Where, having forgotten Elizabeth
> And the court and magnificent promise,
> Under the canopy of lime-blossom lanes
> He thought in cool summers
> About his distant Africa,
> I wait for you ... (Pushkin 133)

This reference, and many of Pushkin's mentions of Hannibal, can be traced to his period of exile at his family estate in Mikhailovskoe, in 1824 and 1825, which allowed him opportunity to gather and reflect on family history and lore. It is worth noting that Mikhailovskoe was one of the estates awarded to Hannibal for his service to the tsar. This exile at Mikhailovskoe coincides with the writing of the initial chapters of Pushkin's novel in verse, *Evengii Onegin*. Perhaps this delving into family lore spurred him to include, in the opening chapter, written in 1824, these lines in which the poet pines for his African skies: "Tis time to leave the dreary shore / of the element inimical to me, / and 'mid meridian ripples, / beneath the sky of my Africa, / to sigh for somber Russia, / where I suffered, where I loved, / where I buffed my heart." Pushkin footnotes this passage in the first edition of *Onegin*. He writes:

> The author, on his mother's side, is of African descent. His great-grandfather, Abram Petrovich Hannibal, was abducted at the age of eight from the shores of Africa and taken to Constantinople. The Russian envoy rescued him and sent him as a gift to Peter the Great, who had him christened at Wilno, standing godfather to him. [Here, Pushkin launches into a lengthy note about the education of Abram in France, and his distinguished service under Anna and Elizabeth and his retirement with the rank of General in chief and finally his death in 1781 at the age of 92].

In the poem, "To Lurev" (1829) Alexander Pushkin cites himself as the "ugly off-spring of Negroes" (Shaw, p. 129). This comment reveals the poet's self-deprecating humor, but Pushkin's references taken as a whole exhibit pride in his family's distinguishing feature.

Pushkin began "The Negro of Peter the Great," a historical tale based on the life of Abram Hannibal. It conveys a desire to represent his forefather as a man of intelligence, humility and a rational understanding of his unusual situation within Russian aristocratic society....

Pushkin's own references to his African heritage romanticize this somewhat vague and distant connection with Africa—a connection that comes to Pushkin largely through family lore.

Within the court society, and as a man of letters, Pushkin was a volatile figure. In at least one incident, his African forefather was used to ridicule the poet. The critic Fadej Bulgarin wrote a literary lampoon, published anonymously in 1830, stating that Pushkin's forefather was bought for a bottle of rum. Pushkin heatedly refuted this allegation in a two-part poem, "My Genealogy," but was dissuaded from publishing his rebuttal. Despite this stinging attack, Shaw concludes that Pushkin "did not cease to be proud of his black great-grandfather and great-uncle. His early comments about them are linked with feelings of exoticism, as well as with pride in their accomplishments in Russia" (Shaw, p. 133).

Pushkin's genius was abruptly silenced in a duel in 1837. Mythologized in death, Pushkin's life caught the attention of the critic P. Annenkov, who in 1855 began collecting biographical materials on the poet. In this first attempt to set down a comprehensive biography, he noted Pushkin's Africaness: "Pushkin often reflected on the founder of the family line, the black man, Abram Petrovich." Thus the poet's consideration of Hannibal's legacy was transferred and established within his official biography.

Prince D. S. Mirsky, too, cited these comments in his *History of Russian Literature* and in his *Pushkin*, relating the same information from Annenkov's volume with the addition that:

> Gannibal was not a Negro in the technical, anthropological sense of the word—he was an Abyssinian. He belonged to the race, which Deniker calls Ethiopian, and which is distinguished by the curliness rather than the frizziness of its hair. Though often jet-black, their features are rather like those of the Arabs. But on the other hand, the practice of slave hunting may have infused into them a certain proportion of purely Negro blood.

Mirsky added in his *History of Russian Literature* that "Pushkin was always proud of both his '600 year old nobility' and of his African blood." Mirsky's volumes were widely reviewed in U.S. periodicals, including its fledgling black press.

In academic circles in the U.S., certainly, Pushkin's Africaness was largely dismissed as a misunderstanding of fact. Ernest J. Simmons, a Harvard professor and leading Pushkin scholar of the 1930s, wrote at length on this subject in his critical volume *Pushkin*. He called the exploration of Pushkin's African lineage "treading on dangerous ground" and adds:

> Indeed, it would be profitable to dismiss here and now the whole muddled question of Negro blood. But Pushkin himself prevents this. If he had written his own biography, he would have devoted considerable space to the subject.... Pushkin took his African ancestry very seriously. On more than one occasion he referred poignantly to his Negro descent. He thought and dreamed about the black founder of his family in Russia, traced his physical appearance to him, and felt that this strain of African blood gave him a unique position in society.

... In 1896, Charles Chesnutt referred to Pushkin's lineage in a letter to S. Alice Halderman (whose financial backing of Emanuel Julius made possible the publication of the Socialist newspaper *Appeal to Reason*, in 1919). This citation is noteworthy in that it reflects a general knowledge outside of Russia of Pushkin's background well before the period of the black "pilgrims" and defends Pushkin's firmly established place as the premier poet within the Russian canon.

> Alexander Pushkin was the greatest of Russian poets. His grandfather was a full-blooded Negro, attached to the court of one of the Russia emperors. I ran across a beautiful translation of some of his shorter stories the other day. You will find his biography in any biographical dictionary, and if you don't find his pedigree or his African descent referred to in the first one you look at, you will probably find it in the next.

These citations from Chesnutt inform our understanding of Pushkin's Africaness in the nineteenth century. Pushkin's African lineage was known outside of his Russian context and did not, as in Chesnutt's case, create any sort of marginalization within the literary canon. The facts of his ancestry, according to Chesnutt, were readily available and did nothing to either enhance or detract from his stature within the same. This understanding was to undergo a marked shift after the Russian Revolution. While the prevailing sentiment in tsarist Russia marked Pushkin as Russian, as did Pushkin himself, in the earliest years of the Soviet era, the significance of Pushkin's lineage was inflated. A great deal of press was devoted to questions of race and ethnicity and the problems of incorporating, or subsuming, the Soviet Union's vast numbers of ethnic minorities into the emerging power structure. Additionally, the Soviet government sought to expand its base of support to further its initiatives around the world. The

Soviet press increasingly supported the movement to consider Pushkin a Negro.

Of what relevance was this information to the black community in the United States? What impact did Pushkin's own proclamations on his race and those of the Soviet press have? There was an active movement in the earliest years of the Soviet State to create an association between the Soviet Union and the American Negro. The Soviet government recognized the fact that broad-based support from minority populations around the world would aid in the effort to consolidate support of the Soviet's own ethnic minorities behind their newly established government. The situation of the American black in the first decades of the twentieth century virtually cried out for socialist intervention. The question first arose at the Second Comintern Congress in 1920, with Lenin's agenda item called "the Negro question." In 1925, the first five African Americans enrolled in the Far East University, created to educate international representatives of oppressed nations worldwide. These students were welcomed by Stalin. African Americans were representatives of an oppressed people to the Communist Party, who sought their support on two fronts. Considerable efforts were made to recruit and organize the largely uneducated, unskilled black workers and farmers in the South, with the organization of the American Negro Labor Congress founded in 1925. The Soviet government also extended invitations to prominent African American intellectuals, cultural figures and artists as it became clear that their greatest support in the spreading of communist ideology within the U.S. was to be found among black intellectuals.

The Soviet Union, with its espousal of a raceless, classless society, greatly appealed to the new black intellectual at a time of great disenfranchisement of blacks in the U.S. In addition, the open-arm policy of the new Soviet State towards blacks also appealed to a group largely segregated and shut out of economic opportunities, political and cultural life at home. The underwriting of travel to the Soviet Union by the Soviet government brought many African Americans to Russian soil to witness the unfolding social experiment. This group included such well-known individuals as W. E. B. Du Bois, Paul Robeson, Langston Hughes and others, less renowned, who sought out this experience for political reasons, as thrill seekers, and on the basis of economic need. Throughout the literature of this group, one thread binds this assorted group to their new Soviet experience, Pushkin's African heritage, which becomes a tacit statement of heritage, solidarity and promise.

The poet Claude McKay is perhaps the first black pilgrim. While his origins are in the Caribbean, his invitation to the Soviet Union came, nonetheless, out of the raising of the "Negro question" at the 1920 Second Comintern Congress. In an interview in *The Crisis* for December 1923, McKay gave perhaps the most precise statement of what the Soviet Union represented for blacks. "There is one great nation with an arm in Europe that is thinking intelligently on the Negro as it does about all international problems.... Russia is prepared and waiting to receive couriers and heralds of good will and interracial understanding from the Negro race." McKay's statements called for black pilgrims from every corner of the earth to come to Russia, and many of America's most promising black intellectuals took heed.

McKay also spoke of the impact of his 1922 Russian visit in his memoir, *A Long Way from Home*, published in 1937: "Never before had I experienced such an instinctive sentiment of affectionate feeling compelling me to the bosom of any people, white or colored. And I am certain I never will again" (p. 167). Later, again, "Never in my life did I feel prouder of being an African, a black, and no mistake about it" (p. 168). In Petrograd, during a visit with a literary scholar, McKay sees a book:

> There was a rare Pushkin book with a photograph of him as a boy which clearly showed his Negroid strain. (The Negroid strain is not so evident in the adult pictures of Pushkin.) I coveted the book, and told the Professor so. He said he was sorry that he could not make me a present of the volume. But he actually extracted that photograph of Pushkin and gave it to me. Mark you, that professor was no Bolshevik, contemptuous of bourgeois literature. He was an old classic scholar who worshiped his books and was worried about the future of literature and art under the Bolshevik regime. Yet he committed that sacrilege for me: "To show my appreciation of you as a poet," he said. "Our Pushkin was also a revolutionist...." Like Crystal Eastman's farewell note, that photograph of Pushkin is one of the few treasures I have (p. 170).

... Homer Smith (b. 1914) represents a different type of pilgrim. Unlike McKay, whose literary stature made him a desirable spokesperson,... Homer Smith sought an opportunity to engage in the type of meaningful work denied him in the U.S. Trained as a journalist but unable to secure a newspaper job at home, Smith made use of his experience as a postal worker and traveled to the Soviet Union to organize the Moscow postal system. In the seventh chapter of *Black Man in Red Russia*, he recounts:

> While reading Moscow's popular newspaper, *Evening Moscow*, on a white-night summer evening in 1936, I was brought up with a start. My eyes had fallen upon a story—surprising and intriguing to me—about Catherine Pushkin, great-granddaughter of the celebrated poet, Alexander Pushkin.
>
> Pushkin had always been one of my favorite men of letters and I had read just about all of his works that had been translated into English. I had even struggled with some of his untranslated works in Russian. But I had not the slightest idea that any of Pushkin's direct descendants were alive and living in Moscow, though I had already lived there for several years.

Smith's account documents the fact that, for him, Pushkin already holds a significant place in his literary heritage. Smith goes on to remark about the lack of Negroid characteristics in this descendant of Pushkin, who proves to be a rich resource for the young man. "She was steeped in Pushkin's life and activities and was well acquainted with the history of his African ancestry. My questions seemed endless, but she seemed to enjoy answering then" (p. 46). He particularly notes her parting words, "Alexander Sergeevich was dark-complexioned, a few shades lighter than you. I am so sorry that my color is so light. He would have been fond of you, I am sure" (p. 46). Pushkin's great-granddaughter, too, recognizes the significance of her forefather to this black stranger, and apologizes for her own light color. Homer Smith offers what is perhaps the most evenhanded treatment of the importance of Pushkin's African lineage. He recounts a thorough Pushkin genealogy and goes on to dispute America's leading Pushkinist, at the time E. J. Simmons, who had said that Pushkin had no African (black) blood. Smith reaffirms that Pushkin would have thought himself a Russian but does not deny that there were many who would like to claim Pushkin as a Negro and attribute his achievements to those bloodlines.

Perhaps the most well-known black pilgrim, Langston Hughes, contributed to this discussion with his memoir, *I Wonder as I Wander*. Hughes traveled with a group of young American intellectuals to the Soviet Union in 1932 to work on a race propaganda film, to be titled *Black and White*. The film was not made, but Hughes spent several months in Soviet Russia. After seeing a performance of *Eugene Onegin* in Moscow, Hughes remarked:

> Pushkin, a descendent of "the Negro of Peter the Great," is adored in Russia and his mulatto heritage was constantly played up in the press when I was there. His *Onegin* and *Boris Goudunov* are standard in all the Soviet schools. In the very heart of Moscow where the main trolley lines meet, there is a statue of Pushkin.

... Hughes's comments reiterate the underlying sentiments shared by all of his fellow black pilgrims. For whatever desired result, the Soviet Union was viewed as a place where blacks were not only warmly received but were deemed capable of the highest achievements and welcomed into the cultural dialogue.

... The great social critics and examiners of the human condition in Russian literature of the nineteenth century resonated with the situation of the African American. It is clear that to the African American intellectual, Pushkin was symbolic of that sense of welcome or acceptance found in Russia, espoused in Soviet rhetoric and so absent at home. This desire to hold Pushkin up as the greatest Russian poet, but also to claim him as a Negro, reflects the determined efforts of a small group of African American intellectuals to establish a literary lineage that superseded the constraints of the American cultural forum. In Pushkin, this emerging group sought and found a literary inheritance of greatness.

Source: Kathleen M. Ahern, "Images of Pushkin in the Works of the Black 'Pilgrims,'" in *Mississippi Quarterly*, Vol. 55, No. 1, Winter 2001, pp. 75–85.

SOURCES

Chaney, J. R., *Aleksandr Pushkin: Poet for the People*, Lerner, 1992.

Eikhenbaum, Boris, "Pushkin's Path to Prose," in *Alexander Pushkin*, edited by Harold Bloom, Chelsea House, 1987, p. 124; originally published in *Twentieth-Century Russian Literary Criticism*, edited by Victor Erlich, Yale University Press, 1975.

Gates, David, *The Napoleonic Wars, 1803–1815*, St. Martin's Press, 1997.

Gogol, Nikolai, "A Few Words on Pushkin," in *Russian Views on Pushkin*, edited by D. J. Richards and C. R. S. Cockbell, William E. Meeuws, 1976, p. 1.

Lindstrom, Thaï S., *A Concise History of Russian Literature, Vol. 1: From the Beginning to Chekhov*. New York University Press, 1966, pp. 90–91.

Owens, Lily, ed. "The Robber Bridegroom," in *The Complete Brothers Grimm Fairy Tales*, Avenel Books, 1981, pp. 167–68.

Poggioli, Renato, "The Master of the Past: Pushkin," in *Alexander Pushkin*, edited by Harold Bloom, Chelsea House, 1987, pp. 17–18; originally published in *The Poets of Russia, 1890–1930*, Harvard University Press, 1960.

Pushkin, Alexander. "The Bridegroom," in *Pushkin Threefold: Narrative, Lyric, Polemic, and Ribald Verse*, translated by Walter Arndt, Dutton, 1972, pp. 81–87.

Roberts, J. M., *The New Penguin History of the World*, Penguin Books, 2007.

FURTHER READING

Betha, David, *Realizing Metaphors: Alexander Pushkin and the Life of the Poet*, University of Wisconsin Press, 1998.

> Betha's approach to Pushkin's work is to examine the ways that various writers have viewed the poet's works throughout the past two centuries and comment on what this response indicates about the flexibility and appeal of his work.

Nabakov, Vladimir, "Notes on Prosody," in *Notes on Prosody and Abram Gannibal*, Princeton University Press, 1964, pp. 3–104.

> Nabakov, one of the greatest Russian writers in the twentieth century, examines Pushkin's *Eugene Onegin*, looking at formal elements and how Russian literature compares to English literature.

Pushkin, Alexander *Pushkin on Literature*, edited by Tatania Wolff, Northwestern University Press, 1986.

> This volume presents Pushkin's ideas about writing taken from various sources, including diaries and letters. It also includes a lengthy biographical introduction, and much background information on Pushkin's life.

Vickery, Walter N., *Alexander Pushkin*, Twayne, 1970.

> Written for students, this brief yet comprehensive overview of Pushkin's works serves as a good introduction.

Conscientious Objector

EDNA ST. VINCENT MILLAY

1934

Edna St. Vincent Millay's poem "Conscientious Objector" was included in her 1934 collection of poetry, *Wine From These Grapes*. "Conscientious Objector" is thirteen lines of free verse, loosely arranged in five uneven stanzas. This poem is a departure from pentameter, which Millay frequently used earlier in her career. The first few lines of "Conscientious Objector" personify Death as an aggressive man who mounts his horse and moves quickly to find his next victims. During the 1930s Millay engaged in social and political activism, and this poem expresses her pacifism through its personification of death, its condemnation of war and race hatred, and its depiction of victims of violence. "Conscientious Objector" is included in *Collected Poems of Edna St. Vincent Millay* (1956), which was reissued in 1992.

AUTHOR BIOGRAPHY

Edna St. Vincent Millay was born February 22, 1892, in Rockland, Maine, the oldest of three daughters born to Henry Dolman Millay, a school teacher and school superintendent, and his wife, Cora Buzzelle Millay. Her parents' marriage ended in 1899 when Cora Millay could no longer tolerate her husband's gambling. Although Mrs. Millay had been trained to be an opera singer, she began working as a

Edna St. Vincent Millay (The Library of Congress)

practical nurse to support her three daughters. While their mother worked, the three Millay girls were often left on their own. Although her childhood might be considered unconventional and was sometimes difficult, Millay occupied herself with reading and music. She took piano lessons and began to write poetry at age five. She had several of her poems published in a children's magazine, *St. Nicholas* between 1906 and 1910. Millay's mother encouraged her daughter to enter her poetry in a contest sponsored by *The Lyric Year*, a literary anthology. Although her poems did not win a prize, one poem, "Renascence" received much praise. After a school director offered to help pay for her education, Millay entered Vassar College, from which she graduated in 1917.

Millay's first collection of poetry, *Renascence and Other Poems*, was published in 1917. Other collections of poetry followed: *A Few Figs from Thistles: Poems and Four Sonnets* in 1920 and *Second April* in 1921. Millay received the Pulitzer Prize for Poetry in 1923, for these two earlier collections plus *The Ballad of the Harp-Weaver*, which was published in 1923. She was the first woman to receive a Pulitzer for poetry. By 1923, Millay had already received several offers of marriage, which she rejected. However, in July 1923, she married Eugen Jan Boissevain, a widowed coffee importer, who assumed responsibility for managing her career and paying for her medical costs, resulting from her frequent poor health. Although she was known for her poetry, Millay also wrote prose, drama, and even an opera libretto.

Millay and her husband purchased seven hundred acres and an old farmhouse in Austerlitz, New York. For several years, Millay worked at the farm, which the couple called Steepletop. In 1927, Millay was arrested for protesting the conviction and anticipated execution of Nicola Sacco and Bartolomeo Vanzetti, Italian immigrants convicted as anarchists. She wrote about her disillusionment with mankind in her next volume of poems, *The Buck in the Snow, and Other Poems*, published in 1928. Although many of her poems after this period focus on her political activism, many more were about romantic love, the subject of her 1931 collection, *Fatal Interview, Sonnets*. *Wine From These Grapes*, the collection in which "Conscientious Objector" appeared, was published in 1934. The manuscript for Millay's next collection of poetry, *Conversation at Midnight*, was destroyed in a hotel fire, and Millay reconstructed the poems from memory. Shortly after the 1936 publication of *Conversation at Midnight*, Millay was seriously injured in an automobile accident. Repeated surgeries and an addiction to prescription pain medication continued to affect Millay's health for the rest of her life.

Though Millay was a pacifist in the early 1930s, Hitler's march across Europe later in that decade and the Japanese attack on Pearl Harbor in December 1941 changed Millay's views about war. During World War II, she wrote propaganda for the Writers' War Board. Millay continued to write poetry for the rest of her life. Several more collections appeared, including *Huntsman, What Quarry? Poems* in 1939 and *Mine the Harvest* published posthumously in 1954. Millay's husband died in 1949. On October 19, 1950, a handyman discovered Millay, lying at the foot of the stairs, at her home at Steepletop. Some reports cited a heart attack as the cause of death, whereas others claimed that Millay died from the fall. In her 2001 biography, *Savage Beauty: The Life of Edna St. Vincent Millay*, Nancy Mitford includes a 1975 letter from Millay's doctor, in which he states that Millay died from breaking her neck in a fall down the stairs.

POEM TEXT

<pre>
  I shall die, but that is all that I shall do for
    Death.
  I hear him leading his horse out of the stall; I hear
    the clatter on the barn-floor.
  He is in haste; he has business in Cuba,
    business in   5
  the Balkans, many calls to make this morning.
  But I will not hold the bridle while he cinches the
    girth.
  And he may mount by himself: I will not give
    him a
  leg up.   10
  Though he flick my shoulders with his whip, I will
    not tell him which way the fox ran.
  With his hoof on my breast, I will not tell him
    where
  the black boy hides in the swamp.
  I shall die, but that is all that I shall do
    for Death;   15
  I am not on his pay-roll.
  I will not tell him the whereabouts of my friends
    nor of my enemies either.
  Though he promise me much, I will not map
    him
  the route to any man's door.   20
  Am I a spy in the land of the living, that I
    should
  deliver men to Death?
  Brother, the password and the plans of our city are
    safe with me; never through me
  Shall you be overcome.
</pre>

POEM SUMMARY

Stanza 1

The opening stanza of "Conscientious Objector", consisting of only one line, establishes the narrator's unwillingness to serve or help Death (which is capitalized), and in the very next line Death is identified as male. She knows she will die herself one day, but in the meantime she will not assist Death in his preparations to attack and murder others. The point is she acknowledges mortality but will not assist in the work Death must do in order for others to die.

MEDIA ADAPTATIONS

- *A Lovely Light* is an LP recording of the 1960 original Hudson Theatre performance of Dorothy Stickney reading several of Millay's poems. The recording is by Vanguard.

- *Edna St. Vincent Millay Reading Her Poetry* was released in 1961 and then re-released in 1986 by Harper Audio.

- *The Voice of the Poet: Five American Women: Gertrude Stein, Edna St. Vincent Millay, H. D., Louis Bogan, & Muriel Rukeyser* is a collection of audio cassettes of the poets reading some of their own works. Each of the audio cassettes includes a matching book of poems. Random House released an edition of these recordings in 2001.

- *Edna St. Vincent Millay—Journey Through Life* is a 2001 video tribute by Monterey Video, in which several celebrities read Millay's poetry.

- *Millay at Steepletop* is a 2002 video tribute to Millay. This video, which was directed by Kevin Brownlow and filmed by Milestone Video, includes footage of Millay reading her poems, interviews with family and friends, and images of her home.

Stanza 2

In the four lines of the second stanza, the narrator presents figuratively the position she states in the first stanza. In the first line of the second stanza, the narrator comments that she hears Death taking his horse out of its stall and walking it out the barn. Although Millay was writing this poem during a time when travel by automobile, train, and airplane is common and used in warfare, Death rides a horse to the places where people are dying in military conflict. Death is in a hurry to go to Cuba and to the Balkans. The reference to Cuba may be to the Spanish American War of 1898 between the United States and Spain over Cuban independence. The war lasted only four months, but the loss of life was high. The United

States and Spain together lost fewer than one thousand men; however, more than ten thousand Cubans died. There was plenty of work for Death in Cuba in the spring and summer of 1898.

In line two of the second stanza, the narrator also mentions that Death has much business in the Balkans. The narrator may be referring to World War I, which began with the assassination in Sarajevo on June 28, 1914, of Franz Ferdinand, the nephew and heir to the throne of the Austrian emperor, Franz Joseph. Shortly after this assassination, Austria declared war on Serbia, and World War I began. By 1918 when the war ended, both sides had suffered huge losses. There were nearly 38 million casualties, including the dead, wounded, and missing. As the narrator notes in "Conscientious Objector," Death needs to hurry, since there is much work for him to do. War causes Death to make many stops on his journey: The dead lie in trenches across Eastern and Western Europe; they include soldiers from Austria-Hungary, Germany, the Ottoman Empire, France, Belgium, Great Britain, the United States, and more than a dozen other countries.

In the final two lines of the second stanza, the narrator reaffirms that she will not help Death get ready for his journey. The narrator will not help Death saddle up or mount his horse. In truth, Death does not need any assistance. The narrator's unwillingness to help Death will not slow or halt his journey, and thus, her noncompliance is futile, as she no doubt recognizes.

Stanza 3

In the first line of the third stanza, the narrator speaks as if she is the horse Death rides. In this stanza, the expected journey is a hunt. At first it is a fox hunt. Fox hunting is a very old sport in England and Europe and is often associated with the British upper class and aristocracy, but fox hunting has also been a popular sport in the United States. Critics of fox hunting think it is a destructive and cruel activity. In fox hunting, scent hounds chase and quarry a fox, which is then killed, in the process fields are trampled, horses are placed at risk, and the fox if caught can be torn apart. Proponents argue that foxes are vermin and that the hunt is a sport. From her description of Death pursuing the fox, Millay seems to be an opponent of fox hunting.

In the second line of the third stanza, the narrator pairs the hunt of the fox with the hunt for a black boy in the swamps. Between 1882 and 1930, more than 2,300 African Americans were lynched. Lynching of blacks, almost all of whom were males, was openly tolerated in the southern United States. Just as the fox was hunted for entertainment and sport, so too was the black male hunted for entertainment and sport. The narrator-horse refuses to help Death as he seeks the victims of these two so-called sports. Although the narrator knows that Death comes and that Death will come calling for her, she will not assist Death in his wanton destruction. As the narrator notes in the last line of this stanza, she does not work for Death. He needs to work alone in his search for victims.

Stanza 4

The two lines of stanza four reiterate the earlier statements by the narrator that she will not assist Death in his search for victims. The narrator refuses to divulge the whereabouts of either friends or enemies. Although Death will continue his pursuit of those who are to die, whether from military action, crime, or violent sport, he will receive no assistance from the narrator. She ends this stanza with the promise that her help is not available at any price. No matter what Death might promise her, she will not help him find anyone; she will not give Death any directions.

Stanza 5

In the first line of the final stanza, the poet asks a rhetorical question about why Death should seek her help. She asks if Death thinks she is a spy, if she has information for sale, and she asserts that she will not give Death the information that he seeks.

The title of this poem, "Conscientious Objector," establishes that the poet is not a willing participant in bringing about the death of any other human being. She will not assist Death in claiming another life. Addressing all others as her brother, the narrator promises she will keep secret her knowledge of the surrounding area and the whereabouts of other people. This information is safe with her. The poet claims that Death cannot succeed through her assistance, but she recognizes that people die. The poet entreats people to remember that they are members of a single family, are brothers, and that if only they would stop killing one another, untimely and unnecessary deaths would occur much less often.

TOPICS FOR FURTHER STUDY

- One of the best ways to learn about poetic form is to write poetry. Imitate Millay's poetic style of free verse, using alliteration and personification. Using her poem as a guide, write one or two poems that imitate both her style, language use, and content. When you have completed your poems, write a brief evaluation of your work, comparing it to Millay's poem. In your written critique, discuss what you learned in the process of writing poetry about social and political issues.

- Millay is not the only poet to write poetry that protests injustice or that seeks change. *Revenge and Forgiveness*, edited by Patrice Vecchione, is a collection of poetry that expresses grief and anger. Study several of the poems in this collection, which is designed for young adults, and write your own poem about either a personal or national loss that touched you deeply.

- Poetry can create images or pictures in the reader's mind. Poetry uses language to create images that the reader can visualize while reading the poem. Draw or illustrate in some way one of the images that Millay's poem creates in your mind.

- Browse through art books in the library and select several pictures or illustrations that depict death as a person. Then, in a carefully worded essay, compare the art that you have selected to images in "Conscientious Objector," noting similarities and differences.

- Research the life of at least one of the following twentieth-century female poets, who were contemporaries of Millay: H. D., Louis Bogan, Vita Sackville-West, Stevie Smith, or Muriel Rukeyser. Write a research paper in which you discuss how the chosen poet's life, her experiences, and her political views are reflected in at least two of her poems.

- Research the history of conscientious objectors in the U.S. wars after 1898. Prepare a poster presentation in which you briefly describe each of the people you discover and how the American public and military confronted those who identified themselves as conscientious objectors.

- Millay pondered the widespread violence and murder that took place in many countries. With two or three other classmates, create a group presentation in which you report on the violence that gripped the world in the first third of the twentieth century. You might consider focusing on the Soviet Union, Ireland, Armenia, Greece, India, or perhaps one of the other areas of conflict. Divide the work by assigning different parts of the presentation to each member of the group. Good group presentations involve multimedia, so take the time to prepare graphs, timelines, and handouts that will help your classmates follow the presentation. Be sure to prepare a bibliography of your sources.

- One way to understand poetry better is to read it aloud. Read Millay's poem aloud to yourself and then read it aloud to an audience of friends or classmates. Ask one or two of your friends to read the poem aloud and listen carefully, noting how possible changes in tone affect meaning. What did you discover about the poem in each of these readings? Consider if the poem changes with subsequent readings and what you learn about poetry and then prepare a one-page reflection paper in which you discuss your observations.

THEMES

Brotherhood of Man

In "Conscientious Objector," the poet narrator refuses to participate in activity that may lead to someone else's death. Near the end of the poem, the narrator reassures a listener, an anonymous person, whom she calls "brother," that she will not divulge the map of their city. This commitment illustrates the trust and mutual protection that should exist between kin. The poet reassures her readers she will keep her brothers' secrets. Women are not mentioned in this poem, but there is no reason to think that Millay is excluding women when the speaker addresses the listener as a brother. Women helped in supportive war efforts, served in various roles during World War I, and civilian women were often victims of war.

Death

Millay personifies death in her poem, "Conscientious Objector." She makes death real, a person whom she describes. Death does not speak, but Death is present and active in the poem. The poet-narrator resists helping Death, while still acknowledging his power. Readers are able to imagine death in a new way, as a horseman. Millay's readers know death through personal loss and through news reports. But the poem describes Death differently, as busy man. The narrator refers to places where killing is happening and focuses on how the agents of Death murder animals and men, making no distinctions between slaying foxes and hunting down and lynching black boys. Both are hunted and slaughtered for sport. The poet makes clear that people have an obligation to refuse to participate in killing and to refuse to assist others in killing. The poem's title, "Conscientious Objector," provides the key for combating killing: People can object on moral grounds because their conscience tells them it is wrong.

Resistance

In "Conscientious Objector," the poet describes a way to reduce instances of dying, by refusing any activity that assists violent acts. Her resistance is passive, a steady refusal to assist or participate. The narrator repeats her position; recognizing the world is a violent place and killing occurs, she nonetheless remains steadfast. She will not help, she will not inform, and she will not facilitate. This passive resistance is a matter of holding

Edna St. Vincent Millay (left) and Doris Stevens in Washington, DC, 1923 (© Bettmann / Corbis)

steady in the face of others who surge ahead; it requires not engaging in any reaction that could itself be or become violent.

STYLE

Alliteration

Alliteration is the repetition of consonant sounds, particularly at the beginning of words. Alliteration can also be of repeated vowel sounds, except that the vowels are often embedded within the word. Millay uses both forms in "Conscientious Objector." The repetition of consonants in the second line of stanza two is a good example of how alliteration affects the sound and meaning of a poem and why it is so important to read a poem aloud. The alliteration of several consonants, including "h" and "b," creates a sound that suggests the sound of the horse walking across the barn floor. The repetition of vowels in that same line, especially the use of "u" adds to the aural impression of horse's movement. Alliteration is appreciated by hearing poetry read aloud.

Free Verse

Free verse has no prescribed structure, rhyme scheme, or meter. With free verse, the poet can fit the poetic line to the content of the poem. The poet is not restricted by a particular meter but can instead create rhythm and syntax to fit the purpose at hand. Free verse is not to be confused with blank verse, which is unrhymed iambic pentameter. In contrast, free verse relies on idiosyncratic line breaks to create the rhythm in the poem. Free verse is most often associated with modern poetry, as it is with Millay's poem. There is no pattern of rhyme or meter in "Conscientious Objector"; instead, the irregular meter and stanzas of different lengths allow the poet the freedom to express her ideas without the rigidity of a preset form.

Personification

Personification is a literary device that endows animals, inanimate objects, or abstract concepts with human qualities and/or human image. Personification can provide imaginary creatures with human-like qualities, personality, and intelligence. In "Conscientious Objector," Millay depicts death as a man, who saddles and rides a horse and is addressed as if he is interacting with the speaker. The personification of death is ancient, dating from the Hellenistic period, but even in contemporary society, many people speak of the Grim Reaper, thus imagining death as a hooded and cloaked figure carrying a scythe.

HISTORICAL CONTEXT

The Great Depression

While Millay was composing "Conscientious Objector" during the early 1930s, a widespread economic depression was causing increased unemployment, extreme poverty, and homelessness across the United States and throughout the world. Within a year of the stock market crash in October 1929, the unemployment rate in the United States was between 25 and 30 percent. Wages were depressed, banks and businesses failed, and many people lost their jobs and homes. People stood in bread lines and ate in soup kitchens. Unemployed men crowded into boxcars and rode the trains illegally looking for work away from home and family. Unemployment in Germany was at 25 percent by the beginning of 1932 and over 40 percent by the end of that year. Japan was also hit hard by the collapsing world economy. Fascist leaders in Germany and Japan used general discontent and hard times to gain influence.

In Italy and Portugal, new governments were also led by fascist dictators. In France, governments were replaced amid talk of a civil war. In India, Mohandas Gandhi urged civil disobedience as a means to resist and oust Great Britain. These non-violent protests were met with police brutality, and Gandhi was arrested several times. In the Soviet Union, Stalin sent millions of people to the gulag, a collection of political prisons and slave labor camps located in remote areas of Siberia. More than 60,000 slave laborers died building the Baltic-White Sea Canal. Stalin's efforts to establish collective farming resulted in a widespread famine in Russia and Ukraine, and an estimated 14 million people starved to death. In El Salvador, more than 30,000 people were executed after a failed uprising against the wealthy government. For Millay and other pacifists, reading newspapers back in the United States, the world must have seemed to be dissolving into chaos.

Rise of Nazism

Following the end of World War I, Germany faced economic depression. Its currency was seriously devalued. Many Germans resented the fact that their country was defeated in World War I. The Versailles Treaty, signed at the end of the war, strapped Germany with huge war debt and limited its future military development. The treaty established the League of Nations but excluded Germany from membership. Germany was required to forfeit more than 25,000 square miles of land, in which six million German citizens lived. Germany lost half of its coal and iron resources, which were badly needed for rebuilding after the war. The German army was limited to 100,000 men, the navy to

COMPARE & CONTRAST

- **1930s:** Between 1920 and 1925, there are 225 known lynching of African Americans. In 1922, the Senate fails to pass a proposed anti-lynching bill. The 1930 lynching of Thomas Shipp and Abram Smith in Marion, Indiana, is widely covered in newspapers and leads to more efforts to publicize and halt lynching in the United States.

    Today: In June 2005, the U.S. Senate apologizes for its failure to pass anti-lynching legislation.

- **1930s:** In December 1930, French workmen begin building a line of concrete forts along the French-German border. The hope is that heavy concrete forts and large guns will help to protect France from a possible German invasion.

    Today: In 2005, India begins building a 2,500-mile wall along the India-Bangladesh border. India hopes that the steel wall will halt illegal immigration from Bangladesh.

- **1930s:** In October 1931, the Japanese invade Manchuria in northeastern China. The Japanese military hopes that conquering China will provide cheap slave labor and other economic benefits that will help off-set the effects of a severe economic depression in Japan.

    Today: In August 2008, Russia invades South Ossetia, a contested area of Georgia that has been seeking its independence. A ceasefire is signed and Russian forces withdraw.

- **1930s:** In Scottsboro, Alabama, nine black teenage boys are tried and convicted on charges of raping two white women. Eight are sentenced to be executed. The jury deadlocks on executing the ninth teenager, a thirteen-year-old boy. After years of appeals, charges against four of the boys are dropped, and four others are pardoned. The last defendant escapes from jail and is never found.

    Today: In 2006, in Jena, Louisiana, five African American teenagers are charged with attempted murder after a series of confrontations between black and white high school students results in a white student being attacked by a group of black students. The student who is beaten suffers superficial injuries and is not hospitalized. After the case draws nationwide protests and charges of racism, the charges are reduced, and the conviction of one defendant is overturned. After repeated court filings, the removal of the judge for prejudice, and a three-year delay, the cases against the five teenagers are still pending. One of the charged teenagers attempts suicide in January 2009.

---

only a few small boats, and the air force was abolished. Allied armies would occupy Germany for ten years, and military and key governmental leaders were to be tried as war criminals. The reparations that Germany was ordered to pay, estimated at $40 billion, created such financial hardship that Germans felt unable to recover.

This post–World War I context provided a foothold for Adolph Hitler (1889–1945) to rise. He exploited German resentment of the Versailles Treaty in his campaign for a superior German Aryan race. He convinced Germans that their defeat was caused by Jews and Communists, and he advocated persecuting both groups. The breakdown of Germany's economy in 1930 made it easy for Hitler's Nazi Party to take control of the country. In 1926, the Nazi Party had 17,000 members; by 1931, it had more than a million members. Hitler claimed that the Jews were pacifists, who had refused to fight for their country, and that they controlled all the money and hence were responsible for the current economic depression.

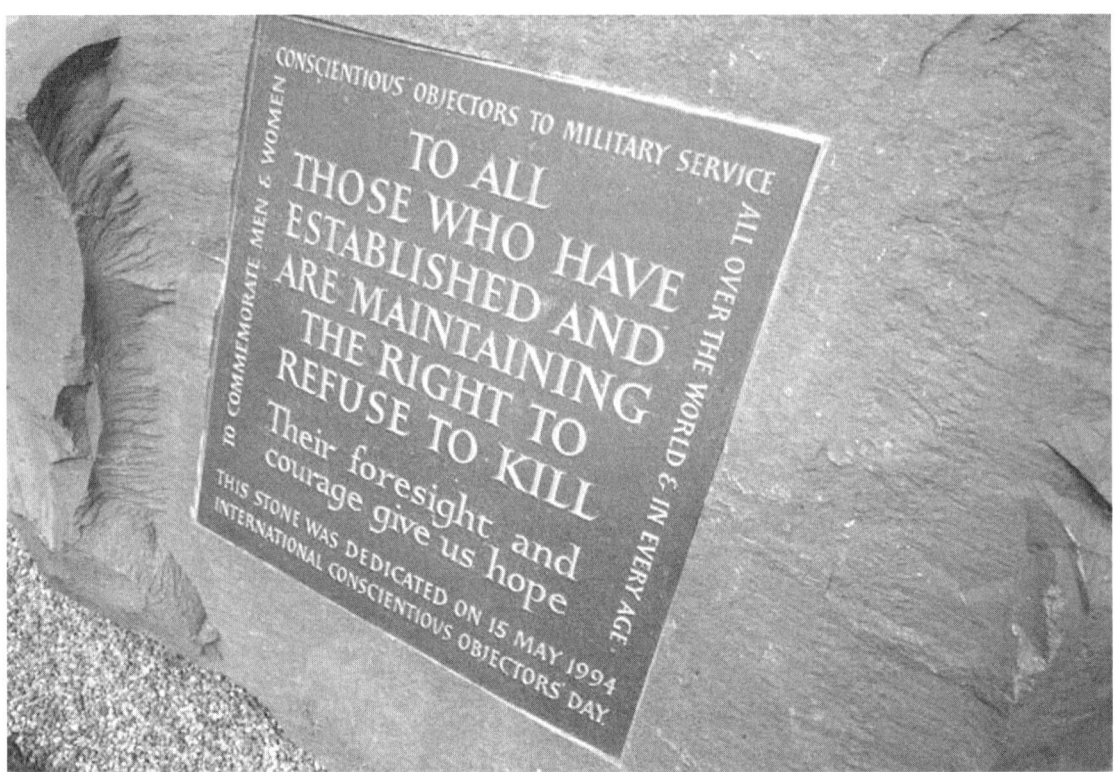

Memorial to conscientious objectors in London, U.K. (© Humphrey Evans; Cordaiy Photo Library Ltd. / Corbis)

By early 1933, Hitler had been elected chancellor of Germany, and within months, he seized all power as dictator. After that, he began targeting several groups for eradication, the euthanasia T-4 program, designed to wipe out those whom he considered non-productive members of German society. These included the elderly and those with physical and mental disabilities, along with intellectuals who opposed his racist platform. Eventually homosexuals and members of minority ethnic and religious groups, such as Gypsies, Jews, and Jehovah's Witnesses, were arrested and deported to various labor and extermination camps, and their assets were seized. By the time he died in 1945, Hitler was directly responsible for nearly 40 million deaths, occurring before and during World War II. Millay could not have known how many would die because of Hitler's reign, but even by 1934, when "Conscientious Objector" was published, it had become clear to many in Great Britain and the United States that Hitler's regime might be every bit as oppressive and violent as Stalin's had been in the Soviet Union.

CRITICAL OVERVIEW

When "Conscientious Objector" was published in the 1934 collection of poetry, *Wine From These Grapes*, Millay was already a well-known and popular poet. In 1923, she won the Pulitzer Prize for Poetry. By then, Millay's books were selling well, and she was making money writing poetry and short stories. "Conscientious Objector" is not mentioned by name in reviews of Millay's work. Critics of *Wine From These Grapes* tended to be mixed in their appreciation of the collection. Most reviewers focused on the sonnet sequence, which is generally considered the centerpiece of the collection.

Philip Blair Rice's review in the *Nation* is typical. Rice began by noting that this newest collection of poetry, the first in three years, shows evidence that Millay has matured as a poet. Rice noted that "there is evidence of a remarkable transformation, of a growth not only toward intellectual maturity but also toward poetic integrity." Rice described Millay's writing as tighter, with meter and rhythm that "shapes itself to the thought and mood." Although Rice wrote favorably of Millay's work in *Wine From These Grapes*, he took issue with the publisher's advertising claim that Millay is "*one of our great poets.*" Rice did not think Millay's poetry deserves such high praise. Her work is "not rich enough," nor is her work the "great poetry of ideas." Rather Millay's poetry "falls just short of that intensity which is found in the highest moments" in the poetry of some of Millay's contemporaries. However, Rice conceded that Millay shows in this collection her potential to develop into a great poet.

In another review of *Wine From These Grapes*, written for *Poetry* magazine, poet Louise Bogan asserted that in this collection Millay "at last gives evidence that she recognizes and is prepared to meet the task of becoming a mature and selfsuffing woman and artist." Bogan claimed that most of the poems in *Wine From These Grapes* show Millay's clarity of thought and her command of meter. In addition, Millay's "remarkable endowment" as a poet is more sustained in this collection. There are, Bogan stated, fewer "lapses into mere lyrical prettiness." Bogan lamented, however, the inclusion of experimental poems, which fill out the book.

Cleanth Brooks's review for *Southwest Review* is more negative, less willing to grant Millay's work has matured. In fact, Brooks denied the maturity that other reviewers observed. Brooks stated that the poems are failures. According to Brooks, Millay attempts satire unsuccessfully. Brooks insisted that Millay "is too conscious of her own superiority to Man's folly," and thus, her attempts at satire come across as immature. Brooks further suggested that tragic irony is needed for a collection of poems that primarily deal with death and the fate of mankind but that Millay "fails at major poetry," the kind of poetry that "makes predictions about life." What does work, though, Brooks added, is Millay's ability to state major themes "without evasions and without sentimentality." As a concession, Brooks assured his readers that there is not much poetry that can deal with themes, and so in this respect, the work succeeds.

A clearer picture of Millay's legacy as a poet is presented in a review of her last collection, *Mine the Harvest*, published four years after the poet's death. Robert Hillyer, writing for the *New York Times*, affirmed that in her final poems Millay achieved "a variety, spontaneity and depth that surpass all her previous collections." Hillyer cited the freshness of this collection, with poems that no longer rely upon propaganda and affectation to succeed. Instead, the poet is more thoughtful, contemplative, and focused. Hillyer stated that this final collection of poems contains "the essential heart and spirit" of Millay. These poems, according to Hillyer, are Millay's "strongest claim to immortality." In a 2006 review of the reissued collection *Selected Poems*, John Simon, writing for *New Criterion*, reminded readers that fashions in poetry often change, which accounts for the fact that feminists have not embraced Millay, as they have other twentieth-century female poets. For certain periods after her death, Millay was no longer trendy, her poetry was often characterized as archaic, and her topics were no longer seen as important. But Simon suggested that may change. Just as fashions in clothing or in decor change, fashions in literature also change, and so there is always the possibility, and certainly the hope, according to Simon, that with this new release, her poetry will once again be fashionable.

CRITICISM

Sheri Metzger Karmiol

Karmiol teaches literature and drama at the University of New Mexico, where she is a lecturer in the University Honors Program. In this essay, she discusses how Millay's poem conveys her resistance to human cruelty and her belief that all people need to stand together in opposition to war and violence.

Violent death can be frightening; it both repulses and fascinates, and while people can be personally sickened by violent death, they often seem unable to look away. They slow down for a close look at accident scenes, watch countless people murdered on screen at the theater, turn on the news to watch the latest crime report, and read about murder in the morning paper, as they eat breakfast. Violent death can transfix an audience. Violent death has always been present in human history, but in the twenty years prior to Millay's writing of "Conscientious Objector," violent deaths seemed especially prevalent. World War I alone caused more than eight million deaths. Perhaps a million or

WHAT DO I READ NEXT?

- Published by her sister after the poet's death, *Collected Poems* (1956) presents poems taken from each of Millay's poetry collections.
- Nancy Mitford's *Savage Beauty: The Life of Edna St. Vincent Millay* (2002) is a thoroughly researched biography of the poet.
- *Millay at 100: A Critical Reappraisal* (1995), by Diane Freedman, is a collection of twelve essays that reassess Millay's work and her legacy.
- *Selected Poems* (2006), edited by J. D. McClatchy, is the first book to be published in the Library of America, American Poets Project. The poems were selected to illustrate Millay's range of poetic forms and themes.
- *Poetry for Young People: Edna St. Vincent Millay* (1999), edited by Frances Schoonmaker and illustrated by Mike Bryce, is designed for children ages nine to twelve. This collection is beautifully illustrated.
- *Women's Poetry of the 1930s: A Critical Anthology* (1995), edited by Jane Dowson, is a collection of poetry written by Millay and some of her contemporaries.
- *Unsettling America: An Anthology of Contemporary Multicultural Poetry* (1994), edited by Maria Gazette Gillan and Jennifer Gillan, presents poetry that explores inequity, discrimination, and social injustice. This multi-cultural view of injustice pairs well with Millay's calls for social activism.
- W. H. Auden's *Selected Poems* (2007), edited by Edward Mendelson, provides readers with a selection from the poetry of one of Millay's most important contemporaries.

more people died from poison gas. In addition, aerial bombing was used for the first time in warfare and caused many civilian casualties. For Millay, the shocking manner of these deaths demanded a response, which poetry supplied.

Millay wrote poems as a way to illuminate political and social injustice. She understood that poetry which focuses on social issues can explore difficult topics, such as injustice and war. In writing poetry, Millay hoped to sway minds and create social change. Millay's poetry urges readers to consider their own views about war and whether pacifism is a response that might help to bring an end to the chaos and death war produces. For Millay, poetry can voice a call to protest and a call for change.

Most of the poems in *Wine From These Grapes* are focused on death and on the fate of people who seem unwilling to combat injustice and prevent violence and murder. The 1927 case of Nicola Sacco and Bartolomeo Vanzetti contributed to shaping Millay's chosen subject. Italian immigrants Sacco and Vanzetti were convicted and executed in 1927 for a 1920 robbery and murder. Many aspects of the trial were perceived then and later to be both political and prejudicial. The verdict was protested by many people, including Millay, who was arrested and jailed in 1927. Millay wrote several poems in response to the trial and execution, including "Justice Denied," which marked the beginning of her using political activism as a subject for poetry. In "The Woman as Political Poet: Edna St. Vincent Millay and the Mid-Century Canon," John Timberman Newcomb explores why Millay shifted from romantic subjects to political and social ones and how that shift affected her critical reputation. Newcomb claims that Millay's inability to intervene to save Sacco and Vanzetti "triggered a fundamental and permanent shift in the tone of her poetry." Newcomb suggests that because of their executions, Millay had "access to a subject matter of broader social scope." Her poetry became a way to "express her outrage at injustice and complacency." Subsequently, Millay's poetry became the vehicle of dissent and a call to her readers to join her in protesting the atrocities caused by intolerance.

In many ways, Millay was ahead of her time in using poetry to create political and social change. Twenty years after "Conscientious Objector" was published, Ezra Pound urged poets to play a social role by writing poetry that might change the world. In his *Literary Essays* (1954), Pound argues that it is the obligation of the poet to make people aware of their humanity. Poetry can inspire people to expose injustice and replace it with justice. According to Newcomb, it was Millay's "forceful coupling of a poetics of progressive political dissidence" with feminism that made her poetry seem threatening to many mid-century critics who saw political poetry coming from a woman as dangerous. Typically female poets wrote about domestic and family subjects. But Millay did not limit herself to women's topics. Newcomb points out that "Millay came to see one of the central social functions of poetry as that of protest and resistance." Newcomb argues that a re-evaluation of Millay's poetry is needed to appreciate Millay's role as a political poet. Rather than viewing Millay as a woman poet writing outside the accepted boundaries for female poets, Newcomb recommends seeing her as a poet who uses poetry to enlighten her readers and to motivate them to create change. Millay felt connected to the community of mankind and demanded change from that community. She used a poem, such as "Conscientious Objector," as a way to demand that her readers join her in changing the world. When the narrator refuses to help Death find more victims, the poet is urging all people join her in being conscientious objectors.

"Conscientious Objector" asks readers to recognize that violence is being perpetrated around the globe and to stop assisting in the carnage. Robert W. Blake argues in his essay, "Poets on Poetry: The Morality of Poetry," that poetry can help people to learn about themselves and the world. It informs about cultural values. Poetry is also a way to illuminate and explore social values. Blake points out: "Every culture has a code of actions, guides for behaving, criteria for judging right and wrong. Through poetry people learn the guides to personal and collective behavior." Millay's poetry works this way.

The world of "Conscientious Objector" is headed toward another war. The speaker knows what is coming and refuses to be a party to the destruction of human life. The speaker's warnings about Cuba and the Spanish American War and the many deaths of World War I are meant to remind readers that the war that appears on the horizon will be equally destructive. Blake sees poetry as a way "to reveal the human condition" and as a way to expose what people do not know or what they have not yet understood. Millay's poetry, in the 1930s and especially in "Conscientious Objector," with its focus on the recent past, reveals both the truth and the solution.

With "Conscientious Objector," Millay is using poetry to spur human resistance, which Pound argued was its essential role. When she links the Spanish American War of 1898 with an assassination in the Balkans and the start of World War I, she reminds readers of the terrors of the past and warns of the terrors of the future. In "Conscientious Objector," Death hovers over the soldiers in Cuba and watches hungrily in the Balkans as one murder quickly generates global conflict. In her poem, Millay confronts Death and refuses to assist. She uses her poetry to urge readers to do the same.

Source: Sheri Metzger Karmiol, Critical Essay on "Conscientious Objector," in *Poetry for Students*, Gale, Cengage Learning, 2010.

John Timberman Newcomb

In the following essay, Newcomb traces the politicization of Millay and her poetry and then examines how both the poet and her work were marginalized by New Critics such as Ransom and Ciardi in the mid-twentieth century.

For most of this century Edna St. Vincent Millay was among the most widely-known and read of all American literary figures. Yet at the peak of her popular reputation there began an intensive effort in certain critical circles to marginalize Millay's poetry, which by the time of her death in 1950 had succeeded in destroying much of her critical reputation. The widening disjunction between popular and critical evaluations of Millay mirrored a broader evaluative shift in the critical canons of modernist poetry during the mid-century period: away from communicative immediacy and social commentary, towards such qualifies as complexity, originality, and impersonality, and best exemplified by such poets as Eliot, Pound, and Yeats. Devastated by this canonical shift were the critical reputations of two groups of well-known writers: on the one hand, explicitly populist poets such as Vachel Lindsay, Carl Sandburg, Archibald MacLeish, and Stephen Vincent Benét; and on the other, female lyricists such as Amy Lowell, Sara Teasdale, Elinor Wylie, Grace Hazard Conkling, and numerous others. Millay is one of the few poets in both of these categories. In recent years feminist historians and critics of modernism have begun to reclaim Millay as a central figure in establishing and expanding the place of the female voice in American poetry; I hope to add a dimension to their portrayal of Millay by arguing that it was her forceful

> "THE POET THUS DEMANDED THAT HER AUDIENCE SEE HER AS NO FRIVOLOUS CAUSE-MONGER, BUT AS SOMEONE WRENCHING THE MOST PRIVATE OF PERSONAL RESPONSES INTO PUBLIC ACKNOWLEDGEMENT."

coupling of a poetics of progressive political dissidence with her longstanding feminism that made her especially threatening to the reactionary forces of mid-century criticism, whose efforts will remain in force until we can include in the critical reevaluation of Millay a serious, sympathetic consideration of her explicitly political poetry. In this two-part essay I will first trace the politicization of Millay's public persona and poetry, and will then offer an analytical sketch of the critical forces which have long obscured the potential value of her more explicitly political work in the academic canons of American poetry.

1

Millay was particularly well-positioned to have an impact on the politics of twentieth-century poetry because she was seen by many as a prototype of the "modern woman," especially in her assertion of the right to and need for female self-determination of body, mind, pocketbook, and voice. Virtually from the beginning of her career, critical discussion of Millay, favorable and unfavorable alike, had tended to treat her not merely as an individual writer but as an exemplary instance of "the woman as poet," as John Crowe Ransom put it. Thus her turn in the late 1920's towards poetry as an expression and potentially a form of political commitment was not merely an individual choice, but implied the potential for a broader scope for female poets at large.

The immediate external catalyst of Millay's politicization, of course, was the Sacco-Vanzetti case. In 1927, along with a number of other writers, she was arrested in the protests against the impending executions; unlike them, Millay commanded a renown which enabled her to arrange a meeting on the day before the executions with the Massachusetts governor, who apparently felt forced to sit and listen to her impassioned hour-long appeal. There is little question that the profound disillusionment she experienced from the failure to save Sacco and Vanzetti triggered a fundamental and permanent shift in the tone of her poetry, in which an aesthetic of "mature" bitterness superseded one of "immature" beauty. Millay came to see one of the central social functions of poetry as that of protest and resistance against the powerful forces of xenophobic paranoia and intolerance which appeared to control the American social establishment and system of justice. She was never able to muster much confidence in any specific political or social program; in this she shared an alienation from practical politics with most of the other bourgeois modernist poets of her generation. Unlike many of them, Millay refused to accept that alienation as a mandate to universalize or ignore the political. Instead she used her disillusionment to produce forceful, explicit expressions of protest against and critique of social injustice.

The first expression of her nascent agenda of progressive dissent emerged strikingly on August 22, 1927, the day before the executions, with the publication of her poem "Justice Denied in Massachusetts" in the *New York Times*. Here again Millay was able to use her prominence to open doors which would have been closed to less well-known poets. In this context, surrounded by reports of the worldwide protests and the preparations for the executions, "Justice Denied" functioned quite literally as news, as its title, modelled on a screaming newspaper headline, acknowledged. Indeed, the poem forcefully exploited the striking contrast between its title and its traditional conceptual structure of the allegorical landscape. The latter demanded that readers recognize that this was not just political sloganeering but was in fact a poem by a famous and revered poet, while the former refused to abstract or universalize the political dimension of existence to a comfortable distance, as poems so often tend to do. Millay's allegory mounted a critique of the forces of "quack and weed" which had choked the land's rich inheritance of social justice, leaving "a blighted earth to till/with a broken hoe." The detail of her allegorical arrangement implicitly presented Millay's vision of an ideal democracy and the current despoliation of American political freedoms: the land itself was sweet, bountiful and meant to be shared in common; the evil came from choking weeds, cancerous growths which interrupted the beneficent domestic processes of growing corn and larkspur. That not merely the ground but the present instruments of tending—hoes and hayrack—had been despoiled by increasingly impervious "stalks," suggested the urgent need for new and stronger methods of contemporary social reform.

The setting which framed the poem's description of the blighted land, "the sitting room"—traditional haven of the bourgeoisie—offered no comfort to the collective speaker, ironically becoming part of the poet's stinging rebuke to those who never committed themselves to the protest wholeheartedly, or who had given up too easily. Millay used persistent echoes of Eliot's "The Love Song of J. Alfred Prufrock" ("Let us abandon our gardens and go home / And sit in the sitting-room"; "Let us sit here, sit still, / Here in the sitting-room until we die"; "We shall not feel it again. / We shall die in darkness, and be buried in the rain") to mock the fashionably alienated stance towards contemporary society exemplified by Eliotic high modernism. The phrase which served as the refrain in these passages functioned not only as a conventional grammatical marker of future intention (as in "Let us go then, you and I"), but also as a plea from the enervated collective narrator for release from the exhausting burden of social responsibility ("let us go"). As her scornful portrayal of this persona suggested, the poet would not let her audience go with a clear conscience from the struggle for these gardens of America.

Those commentators unsympathetic to Millay's efforts to write poetry of explicit political critique have treated "Justice Denied in Massachusetts" as somewhat of a notorious fall from grace, the poet's first betrayal of her "natural lyric gift." In 1935, for example, Cleanth Brooks used the poem as a linchpin of his argument that Millay's "preoccupation with social and economic justice" had yielded "disappointing" results. In order to do so, however, Brooks had to contort the poem into offering the "advice" that "those who loved justice" should "'sit in the sitting room,' convinced that justice was truly dead and that no other effort in behalf of justice was worth making" (1), exhibiting a lack of sensitivity to the poet's irony which was downright astonishing in a critic who would later make irony a constitutive element of his theory of literature. Recognizing no difference between the poem's speaker and the poet, Brooks went on to patronize Millay as having the "attitude ... of a child whose latest and favorite project has been smashed" (1–2), evoking the stereotypical equation of woman—even woman writer—with child.

Not dissimilarly, in his 1938 "Tension in Poetry," one of the seminal essays of the nascent New Criticism, Allen Tate used "Justice Denied" as an example of "the fallacy of communication in poetry," which resulted not in genuine literary expression but in "patriotic poetry" which "you will find ... equally in a ladylike lyric and in much of the political poetry of our time." Like Brooks above, and Ransom below, Tate presented the image of a poetry tarnished by political zeal—whether patriotic or dissident does not seem to matter—quite gratuitously yoked to poetry exemplifying a female sensibility. Tate went on to use "Justice Denied" to develop another important tenet of New Criticism when he wondered ingenuously why "the execution of Sacco and Vanzetti should have anything to do with the rotting of the crops," or "How Massachusetts could cause a general desiccation" of the land (58). What the critic was doing here, of course, was attacking the whole notion of an allegorical method in poetry, making Millay's allegory seem absurd by taking it overly literally, and concluding (without justification) that "if you do not share those feelings" about social justice which the poet felt when she wrote the poem, "the lines and even the entire poem are impenetrably obscure" (58). Yet in the very same paragraph Tate had also objected to the allegorical system of Millay's poem as degraded "mass language" designed for (fallacious) communication. Tarred equally with ultrapersonal obscurity and meretricious communicability, the writer of "Justice Denied" was clearly being used to exercise a broad range of the bugaboos and prohibitions of the developing New Criticism—to which, apparently, female poets as a group were particularly susceptible.

Unlike these commentators, I would argue that "Justice Denied," like Millay's involvement in the Sacco-Vanzetti protests itself, was the catalyst in her reconstruction of her poetic persona into something more socially forceful. More than any other text, "Justice Denied" was central to the dissident poetics which Millay developed over the next decade, offering her access to a subject matter of broader social scope, and to a vocabulary of images upon which she could draw to express her outrage at injustice and complacency. The first descent of the poem in Millay's work emerged about two months after the executions, when her most significant prose essay, "Fear," appeared in *The Outlook*. "Fear" was a withering retrospective rebuke to those who, as in "Justice Denied," had shrunk before the painful struggle against injustice. It began, "There are two names you would not have me mention, for you are sick of the sound of them" (293), and drew again upon the central rhetorical gambit of "Justice Denied" in creating the wheedling, self-pitying voice of those who succumbed to fear and condoned the executions: "*Do* let us forget, you say; after all, what *does* it matter?" (293). Millay scornfully criticized those Americans who, while wrapping themselves in the noble concepts which supposedly govern the nation, were actually ruled by fear: "You do not know exactly what [honor and glory] are. For you do not live with them. They are not trees to shade you, water to quench your thirst. They are golden coins, hidden under the mattress in a very soiled wallet. The only pleasure they afford you is the rapturous dread lest some one may be taking them away" (294–95). Millay argued that indeed, "some one is taking them away. But not the one you think" (295). It was not anarchists, of course, but the paranoia and hypocrisy governing the parental generation which were turning their children into the very skeptics and unbelievers the parents feared. That Millay was willing to risk alienating a significant segment of her readership by putting her outrage into direct, unadorned prose speaks to its depth and sincerity. The effective transference of the thematic material of "Justice Denied" into the different context of "Fear" also indicates that unlike some of the critics who disparaged her willingness to abandon poetry for political polemic, Millay saw no contradiction, no barrier, between the two discourses. Not only were they not mutually exclusive, but they could draw upon the same organizing patterns of imagery, tone, and methods of address.

The development of Millay's new poetics, which we might call a dissident romanticism, was consolidated in the group of poems springing from the Sacco-Vanzetti experience, which she arranged together in her volume *The Buck in the Snow* (1928). The unavoidably political thrust of "Justice Denied in Massachusetts" lent the allegorical poems which surrounded it a level of political meaning which in other contexts it might have been possible to overlook. Collectively "The Anguish," "Justice Denied," "Hangman's Oak," "Wine From These Grapes," and "To Those Without Pity" formed a striking announcement to the poet's critics and readers that her previous poetic personal was insufficient to the task of facing ethnic bigotry and legalized political murder, and that she intended to follow permanently the stringent agenda of dissent she had expressed in "Fear."

The first of these texts, "The Anguish," acted as a foreboding prelude to the more direct and wrenching articulations of specific political situations in "Justice Denied" and "Hangman's Oak," which followed immediately. "The Anguish" expressed Millay's ambivalence at the new knowledge of self and world she had not asked for, but could not deny: though she "would to God" she could return to the "beauty" which had nourished her youth, "the anguish of the world is on [her] tongue," rendering her unable to swallow the easier nourishments of her earlier poetry. As well as the imagery of the Holy Eucharist, Millay was drawing upon the old Welsh custom of the sin-eater, an itinerant outcast who was fed a large meal over the bier of a dead person; the food represented the deceased's sins, which as they were consumed were removed from his or her soul. But what of the soul of the sin-eater? Though she accepted it, she did not relish this role of scapegoat; this speaker admitted that "there is more than I can eat," asking implicitly why her audience did not join her in trying to reduce the amount in her "bowl"—a figure of both earth and book. The final two lines extended this portrayal of the poet as a leader of a group of mature adults who, being the only ones not "toothless," must take the sober responsibility for digesting this anguish since they, and only they, could "rend this meat."

"Wine From These Grapes," following "Justice Denied" and "Hangman's Oak," framed those two poems with further exploration of the imagery of the Eucharist begun in "The Anguish" (and extended in "Hangman's Oak" through the links between the body of the lynching victim and the crucified Christ). Here the poet's irresistibly growing need to speak of social injustice was figured through a revision of the conventional portrayal of the Eucharist as a miraculous transubstantiation of the blood of

Christ into communion wine. Here, in contrast, the wine was created not by magic or prayer but by exhausting human labor:

> If you would speak with me on any matter,
> At any time, come where these grapes are grown;
> And you will find me treading them to must.
> Lean then above me sagely, lest I spatter
> Drops of the wine I tread from grapes and dust.
> Stained with these grapes I shall lie down to die.
> Three women come to wash me clean
> Shall not erase this stain.
> Nor leave me lying purely,
> Awaiting the black lover.
> Death, fumbling to uncover
> My body in his bed,
> Shall know
> There has been one
> Before him.

Millay figured her persona as a wine-presser charged with treading a wine of knowledge which, through the play on the word *must* (the juice, pulp, and skin of the crushed grapes before fermentation), became a pure, if bitter, distillation of the necessity for action according to moral principle. In an increasingly characteristic critique of the personal lyric genre in which she had made her reputation, Millay then turned from a personal beginning to address her readers directly on the subject of public debate. If they should seek to discuss any subject with her, she warned, they should stay well above "lest I spatter"; the poet's sense of outrage was thus seen as potentially communicable to the readers whom she invited into intellectual or emotional dialogue with her. Even her death and the cleansing ministrations of attending females would not eradicate these stains of knowledge. In the poem's final lines, Death itself was diminished into a "fumbling" cuckold by the force of her outrage, suggesting that her awareness of social injustice had been equal in impact to a sexual deflowering. The poet thus demanded that her audience see her as no frivolous cause-monger, but as someone wrenching the most private of personal responses into public acknowledgement. The character of these grapes made for a painfully bitter wine, yet Millay accepted that as her political eucharist; the more bitter the drink, the stronger the drinker able to make it her nourishment.

There is no question that Millay meant the argument of these poems to be an emblem of her arrival at a poetics of public dissent; she reinforced the assertion by reusing the title "Wine From These Grapes" in 1934, to name a whole book of her work. This volume was framed by two allegorical articulations of the nature and meaning of human existence examined through the fragile relationship between humans and the land which Millay had established as part of her political/poetic idiom in "Justice Denied." The first of these, "The Return," is an unsparingly grave meditation on the benevolent indifference of the earth. The wretched, defeated, self-absorbed man who "Has traded in his wife and friend" and who now "has no aim but to forget" was yet another portrayal of those who, as in "Justice Denied" and "Fear," shrank from the responsibilities and challenges of being human. Seeking to objectify the earth as a conventional maternal presence of consolation and forgiveness, this sniveling man found only a place to hibernate, or to lie down and die; all the earth afforded was a bleak "Comfort that does not comprehend." In effect, Millay rejected the conventional femaleness of the earth because the metaphor had too often been used to solace and reinforce the arrogance and self-absorption of patriarchal behavior. The volume ended with the important sonnet sequence *Epitaph for the Race of Man*, which sketched the history of the earth, including but not limited to the process of human evolution, from before our emergence from the primordial ooze until after our self-annihilation, at which time the unfazed earth would usher in another stage of life. The implicit demand made by these sober formulations was for her readers to stop relying on any outside agency, even the mothering bounty of the earth (which has sufficed for the poet in such earlier works as "Renascence"), to face instead the necessities and responsibilities of humanity.

Within the frame created by these two impressive texts, Millay arranged another cluster of works which extended her efforts to develop an outspoken poetry of progressive political critique. Perhaps the most striking single poem of the volume, "Apostrophe to Man," offered a frankly hortatory address conveying the poet's prescient outrage at the world's accelerating rearmament. Consisting rhetorically of a single twelve-line sentence of almost unbroken imperative statements, the poem combined a muscular rhythmic freshness with a dark wit to build to an ironic punchline, "Homo called Sapiens." By reducing the lofty concept of "Man" to a species which cannot even employ its supposedly distinguishing feature effectively enough to avoid self-slaughter, the poem functioned as a powerful anti-apostrophe to patriarchal complacency and escapism. Next came "Two Sonnets in Memory," addressed to the memory of Sacco and Vanzetti, the first of which identified the two dead men with the human heritage of "Justice" and "beauty," also now dead. While the second sonnet and the poem which followed, "My Spirit Sore From Marching," despairingly drifted away from a forceful political focus towards an abstract "beauty," the poem which ended the group, "Conscientious Objector," snapped back to a pithy engagement with contemporary events. Turning once again to the familiar technique of personifying Death, Millay did not treat it as a vague metaphysical abstraction but instead as a specific and all-too-familiar figure of the 1930's—invading army or secret police—with whom the speaker refused to cooperate under any circumstances. The forces of political tyranny initially inspired the speaker to significant, "conscientious" inaction; but notably, in the final lines—"Brother, the password and the plans of our city are safe with me; never through me / Shall you be overcome"—the objector began to merge into fellow resister, much as the poet had found herself drawn more and more actively into social causes.

As the 1930's continued, the stubborn Depression and the ominous rise of fascism gave Millay no reason to doubt her commitment to a poetics of public speech and, indeed, stimulated her to perhaps her most ambitious work of explicit political commentary, *Conversation at Midnight* (1937), which consists of dramatized exchanges among seven male New Yorkers who constituted a spectrum of the various political positions of the time, from Republican stockholder to communist intellectual. That Millay presumed to portray the contemporary male psyche, often satirically, would not naturally have endeared the work to conservative male critics. But its political aspect was perhaps even more problematic. By creating a quasi-public setting whose late-night aspect also allowed for intimately personal utterance, Millay's conversational form collapsed conventional divisions between public rhetoric and personal lyric. In representing the rhythms of prolonged conversation as a disjoined collage of subject matter and shifting emotional nuance, she demonstrated how some central formal attributes of high modernism could be appropriated for a poetry based not on alienated individualism but on social dialogue.

Although liberal and communist arguments carry more weight in the poem than others, Millay did not make a programmatic intervention on behalf of any political position. Indeed, the insufficiency of any single dogma was exactly the point. The poem rejects the analytical subject-object structure of the monolithic political assertion ("I have surveyed this situation and here is how it is"), and instead creates a space for political polyphony, in which everyone's argument is accorded a hearing, in which each character's often unreflective and self-satisfied opinions are repeatedly challenged and qualified, and through which readers might have the chance to examine the strengths and weaknesses of various points of view. Ultimately what the poem affirms most strongly is the process of public debate itself. Even more than Millay's previous 1930's volumes, *Conversation at Midnight* assertively transgresses the generic limitations of the personal lyric in the direction of social engagement, and deserves sympathetic attention by critics interested in reclaiming the politically progressive aspect of American modernism.

2

As Millay attempted quite consciously to shift her own position, and by extension, the position of women within American poetry, towards explicit social engagement, her efforts were by no means entirely unnoticed or unappreciated. That notion is a myth promulgated with substantial success by later denigrators. On the contrary, even some of the detractors of Millay's works of the 1930's tended to acknowledge that she was "one of the few poets of her generation who have continued to grow." To survey critical discourse on Millay through that decade is to discover a multitude of evaluative positions, sometimes existing contradictorily within individual pieces. The only consensus held about Millay was that of her enormous renown. As Atkins put it somewhat hyperbolically, "Everyone recognizes that Edna St. Vincent Millay represents our time to itself much as Tennyson or Byron the period of Romanticism."

Clearly, however, there were those who wished to dispute Atkins's estimate, which was itself obviously an attempt at canon-making. The attacks on Millay's work during the next two decades, even when couched in aesthetic terms, were therefore not just evaluations of a particular poet, but ideologically inflected sorties in a campaign to seize control of and homogenize the definitions and canons of "modern poetry" in two interdependent ways: by calling into question the ability of the female consciousness to deal with weighty, transpersonal subject matter; and by dismissing the propriety of seeing poetry as a form of political action. In sketching the critical marginalization of Millay I will focus on two representative attacks by influential poet-critics published at crucial junctures of the mid-century period. Though neither essay concentrated on Millay's explicitly political work, which is in itself revelatory, the structures of value they advanced were highly symptomatic of mid-century criticism's tendency to characterize major poetry as an activity which was both properly the province of males and which properly transcended politics.

As my references above to Tate and Brooks have suggested, the major figures of New Criticism largely concurred in their uneasiness at the idea that Millay was *the* exemplary modern poet. But while the remarks of these others, made in more casual or passing contexts, did grant Millay a measure of real distinction, John Crowe Ransom's essay on Millay, "The Woman as Poet," published in 1937 and reprinted the next year in one of the seminal texts of New Criticism, *The World's Body*, attempted a full-scale demolition of the notion of Millay's majority. Employing wholesale gender stereotyping in order to valorize a poetry of intellectual rigor and complexity which was strongly male in emphasis, "The Woman as Poet" has for good reason become a rather notorious example of anti-female criticism, referred to by Alicia Ostriker, William Drake, and Cary Nelson in their recent studies of modernist poetry, although a full-scale critique of the sexist assumptions and stereotypes employed by Ransom has still to be done. Here I will treat the essay primarily as an instance of reactionary canonical combat directed against the politically progressive—and female—aspects of modernist poetry represented by Millay.

It is worth noting the date of Ransom's essay, at the very beginnings of Agrarian-New Critical influence in American criticism. Prominent in the literary culture of 1937 was the "Popular Front" policy of accommodation between all left-of-center positions, which meant that the right-wing element of high modernism was to some extent on the defensive, by no means the hegemonic shaper of literary canons that it would be a dozen years later. Eliot and Pound were widely admired and influential, but then so was Millay. Ransom was thus engaged in an active canonical contest whose outcome was in much doubt. Under these circumstances, one strategy for devaluing Millay's engagement was to ignore it, by paying no attention to any of her explicitly political poetry. But what Ransom did reveal—his preconceptions of the limitations of female poets, and the ideals of poetic achievement he held up in contrast to Millay's—nonetheless constituted a prohibition against exactly the sort of social engagement that Millay was striving to establish for the modern female poet.

The scope of Ransom's decanonizing project was evident from its dual target, in that "The Woman as Poet" was conceived not only as an evaluation of Millay's work but as a review of Elizabeth Atkins's 1936 critical biography *Edna St. Vincent Millay and Her Times*. In other words, Ransom was scrutinizing the place of the woman as critic as well, remarking in his first paragraph that "To read [the biography] is to have a mounting inclination to try a little dialectic upon the poet's poetry and the critic's criticism" (76). Here Ransom portrayed himself as a sort of experimental scientist in a position to "try" various methods of analysis (including the wonder-drug "dialectic") "upon" the objects of analysis—poet and critic—both female. The possibility (or threat) of having female critics as competitors and peers helping to shape literary canons should not be underestimated as a factor forming Ransom's evaluation. Much of the essay's discussion is indeed devoted to Atkins's critical shortcomings. Ransom admitted being perhaps too harsh with Millay's work because he had been "teased by Miss Atkins's foolish admiration, and even ... by a vague sense that too much of that sort of thing has been going on" (102–103). If for Ransom Millay was the quintessential female poet, then Atkins's writing on Millay was equally representative of "that sort of thing": "a woman critic, satisfied with the effects of a woman poet, [who] almost ignores or almost resents the intellectual effects of other poets"

(79–80). This twinned portrayal of Millay and Atkins as equally exemplary of the nonintellectual female consciousness meant that when Ransom attacked the critic, it reinforced his attack on the poet, and vice versa.

The supposedly nonintellectual criticism of Atkins was itself a strategic characterization of Ransom's which needs closer examination. Though it was easy for Ransom to characterize it as silly by quoting one or two of its many undeniably florid passages, Atkins's book is actually a quite wide-ranging and authoritative work which was not written primarily for a popular audience, and which carried the imprimatur of the University of Chicago Press. Atkins's championing of Millay was placed in the context of a broader account of modern poetry which had little time for what she called the "nihilism" of Eliot and the obscurantism of such other canonical figures of high modernism as Hopkins and Pound. Though Ransom would have us believe otherwise by trivializing the critic's project as just more of "that sort of thing," Atkins was by no means just an irritatingly simple-minded celebrator of Millay, but was a threateningly learned critic attempting through interpretive, historical, and rhetorical means to demolish the high-modernist value structure Ransom had wholeheartedly adopted as his own.

In the body of his essay Ransom engaged in an ideologically potent counter-attack against those such as Atkins who resisted the elitist canons and values of high modernism. Eliot was only one of the high-modernist sacred cows Ransom defended by attacking Atkins's critical judgment and Millay's poetic achievement. Most notably, Ransom vehemently contested Atkins's attempt to appropriate the rising canonical status of John Donne. Ransom characterized the modernist recovery of Donne as "the way to identify [the] literary taste" of the age (78); but for Ransom Donne was exclusively and always "the poet of intellectualized persons" (78). By definition, then, the true taste of the age was an intellectual one, and it was nonsense to juxtapose Donne and Millay, as Atkins did, since Millay was "rarely and barely very intellectual, and I think everybody knows it" (78). The lesson Donne had taught modernists was the value of such qualities as "strength," "directness," "realism," and "unprettiness" (81). Donne and a living poet, Ezra Pound, had done the most to "purif[y] modern poetry of adventitious and meretricious decoration" (91). The purification inherent in Pound's "kind of preaching and teaching" was explicitly and exclusively a male activity: "an example of manly honesty rescued from a perishing tradition" (91).

Ironically and perhaps hypocritically, however, Ransom's admiration of the "manly honesty" and "directness" championed by Donne and Pound emphatically did not extend to approval of Millay's use of openly erotic imagery in one of her famous sonnets (85–86). Ransom rather prudishly called these lines "rude in substance," rashly assuming that Donne—no stranger himself to sexual imagery—would have been "revolted" by them as well. One cannot help but suspect that Ransom was particularly affronted at the spectacle of a *female* poet writing frankly about such subjects.

Of the many sexual stereotypes Ransom relied upon, the one which most strongly pertained to the issue of political engagement in poetry was the view which circumscribed the female consciousness to a subject matter of "personal moods" and "natural objects which call up love and pity" (104). The nonintellectuality of the female consciousness was supposedly compensated by a closeness to "the world of the simple senses" (77) in which she could remain comfortably "fixed in her famous attitudes ... indifferent to intellectuality" (78). In contrast, the male of the species "does not like to impeach his integrity and leave his business in order to recover" the simpler, immature world he had left behind (77). Even in the putatively anti-industrial Agrarian New Criticism, then, nature as a focus for poetic subject matter had been feminized (and thus, in Ransom's view, diminished) to a remarkable degree. Even certain male poets such as Wordsworth could be viewed as excessively "feminine" in their preoccupation with subjects of personal emotion and communion with nature: "the male reader feels some shame even at going with Wordsworth, feeling it monstrous that he should flee the humanized world which he actually inhabits and breathe exclusively the innocence of external nature" (99).

Against these anxieties over gender superiority and sexual potency Ransom buttressed "the Intellect," portrayed in an ultra-masculine, ultra-rationalist way which was highly relevant to the politics of the competing contemporary versions of modernism. Ransom explicitly identified "intellect" with "pure thought engaged in a series of technical or abstract processes" whose highest manifestation was "science" (100–101). One of the characterizing features of the "non-intellectual" female poet such as Millay was an ineptitude at handling poetic forms—since women's minds were insufficiently trained, and remained "not strict enough or expert enough to manage them" (103). In contrast, the male intellect worked by effectively "managing" and reshaping raw material into elegant, ordered form. This same picture of the intellect as a type of grasping tool which objectifies, dissects, and reconstructs an external Other undergirded the unwholesome view of the political which Millay had satirized in the male characters of *Conversation at Midnight*, who blindly made unequivocal political pronouncements, foolishly imagining they had achieved an Olympian vantage from which to grasp those situations fully and impartially. Ransom thus completely failed to comprehend the approach to political engagement Millay had presented in such poems as "Wine From These Grapes." There, as the persona is emotionally and physically marked with the force of her struggle against injustice, her consciousness/body encompasses both subject and object. In contrast to such holism, Ransom's crude dichotomizing of subject and object in his delineation of the creative intellect reveals a politically reactionary as well as a sexist aspect.

Ultimately, for Ransom, the extent of Millay's achievement was to have created "a distinguished objective record of a natural woman's mind" (104). His refusal even to acknowledge, much less to read sympathetically, any of Millay's explicitly political works was particularly outrageous, since in them she had done exactly what Ransom had said the female poet was uninterested in and incapable of doing: effectively working with subject matter not limited to the "personal," or to "innocent external nature." It was Ransom himself, and not Millay, who had enforced this prohibition.

Through an essay on Millay published twelve years after *The World's Body*, at the height of the postwar literary reaction against politics, we can view the results of the contest in which Ransom was actively engaged. John Ciardi's obituary consideration of Millay—subtitled "A Figure of Passionate Living"—operated within a canonical frame of reference completely dominated by New Critical values; the writers mentioned in his opening paragraph read as a New-Critical Who's Who, the first six being Pound, Eliot, Baudelaire, Yeats, Hopkins, and Joyce. In this context Ciardi treated Millay's career and value in an even more demeaning fashion than had Ransom as part of an immature stage of American modernist culture filtered through the critic's own intellectual and physical adolescence. While for Ransom Millay was "the woman as poet," for Ciardi she was equally quintessential, having "invented a decade" (9), the gay 20's. Thus Millay's primary role was not as a creator of poetic texts but as an exemplary persona, a fantasy female who embodied the exciting, liberating passions of youth: "It was not as a craftsman nor as an influence, but as the creator of her own legend that she was most alive for us" (77).

Despite his lip service to its achievements, Ciardi ultimately ridiculed Millay's decade, which was typified by such things as "a great deal of high-level small-talk by flat-chested girls in excruciating dresses," and which had left behind "stacks of unread little magazines" (8) (as if every decade of this century had not). In this world Millay was a "name for the kind of lyric to be imitated wherever the female heart beat fast" (8). Ciardi thus poured contempt upon those gullible, sentimental female readers excited by Millay's work; but as his essay makes clear, Millay was eminently capable of quickening the male heart as well. Her importance in Ciardi's adolescent modernism was quite literally as the object of the pubescent critic's desire. He described himself as "a happy prowler in the dark stacks" of his public library, who, having discovered in her works "grief, pride, curses, [and] whores," "began to read Millay avidly, to spout her endlessly" (9). "[W]hat an excitement it was then to curl up with [her work] in a corner of the stacks," anticipating the time "when you could recite it to a girl with the moon beside you, or, perhaps more accurately, to the moon with a girl beside you. Certainly the moon comes first" (97). Note Ciardi's discomfort, like Ransom's, with the sexual connotations of his system of figures. He could not bear to leave anyone with the impression that he used poetry as a direct sexual lure with his adolescent dating partners; therefore he had to show that, as a good mid-century New Critic, he understood that the symbol (the moon) was always richer, more meaningful, and somehow even more morally acceptable, than the actual girl. He thus managed to diminish not only Millay but his girlfriends as well, all of whom became mere props for the growth of his own imaginative capacity.

As Ciardi moved on to his college years we find him, even more bizarrely, blaming his devotion to the immature emotional melodrama of Millay's works for his falling in love "with our local Edna, or, more precisely, with the best of our local Ednas," of which he estimated two dozen even at his small college (9). It appears that to Ciardi women poets were not individuals but merely distillations of female consciousness, interchangeable members of a frivolous stereotype (call them Ednas), ultimately to be outgrown. (Of course even then Ciardi had the good taste to fall in love with the best his college had to offer.) Millay's feminist frankness regarding her own sexuality, and the exemplary position she occupied, were thus objectified and trivialized into a source of emotional titillation for the adolescent male mind, eventually to be discarded in embarrassment in one's more "mature" years.

This unenviable role was Millay's alone, and the critic flatly refused to let her grow beyond it. Ciardi felt that a sign of the maturity of his generation was that it had outgrown Millay's persona; but her own attempt to grow beyond that youthful persona he rejected out of hand. To Ciardi and his fellows Millay would forever be an embarrassing reminder of the "first fumblings and exaggerations" (9) of their own adolescence, both literary and sexual. By taking on such new and unsexy poetic subjects as social injustice and war, and in writing poems which sought to comprehend her own aging (such as the superb "The Fitting"), Millay had betrayed the critic's nostalgic fantasies of an idealized adolescent rebellion. The more serious forms of rebellion against unjust authority which Millay conveyed in her later work fell on totally deaf ears, works like *Conversation* [*Conversation at Midnight*] providing "no subject for her gift" (77). Indeed, Ciardi asserted, it became increasingly clear that "the one subject she could make exciting" was "her youth"—again, circumscribing the scope of the female poet's subject matter to her own range of personal emotional experience.

The biases of such mid-century critics as Ransom and Ciardi, and of course those of New Criticism more generally, created imposing obstacles to reading both poetry expressing female consciousness, and poetry of explicit political engagement, to the extent that when we turn to such poems as those I have discussed, we often feel the lack of a satisfactory vocabulary for sympathetically interpreting and evaluating them. In struggling against the outworn but still operative notion, itself highly political, that explicit political commitments in poetry are somehow inevitable violations of artistic integrity, there is much we can learn from Millay, and from other poets in the various (lyric, feminist, dissident) traditions to which she belongs. In our efforts to articulate responsible revisions of the ways poetic modernism can be portrayed and valued, Millay's work offers us precious access to such critical issues as the complex, potentially participatory relations between speakers and audiences; the relative benefits of explicit statement and specific topical reference as opposed to indirection and suggestion; the importance of alternative methods of constituting social identity through discourse, especially those which portray individuals as interdependent parts of an egalitarian collective rather than as masters of a hierarchical subject-object relationship; and the validity of the concept of belief and methods of expressing it in poetic discourse. Such questions are not merely of import to the canons of modernist poetry, but bear upon long-neglected debates on the function and potential of public discourse in our society.

Source: John Timberman Newcomb, "The Woman as Political Poet: Edna St. Vincent Millay and the Mid-Century Canon," in *Criticism*, Vol. 37, No. 2, Spring 1995, pp. 261–79.

Mary M. Colum

In the following excerpt, Colum discusses Millay's popularity as a poet and the unconventional views that she expressed in traditional forms of lyrical poetry.

In the 1920s Edna St. Vincent Millay was America's sweetheart. It was one of the rare periods when poetry, and especially lyrical poetry, was considered important. Now the fact is that this country has seldom been enthusiastic about lyrical poetry, and this largely explains the attitude to Edgar Allan Poe and to that troubadour, Vachel Lindsay. In a favored poet—Robert Frost—what gives him authority is not his lyrical but his narrative and meditative poetry. But Edna Millay struck a mood in American life when lyricism was being welcomed as something strange and moving. Then, what was called her philosophy roused to excitement not only the young men and women but their elders, too. Said philosophy was simply an attitude to life made familiar throughout the ages by the men poets—Herrick's "Gather ye rosebuds while ye may," Horace's "Carpe Diem," Catullus' "Vivamus mea Lesbia... Give me a thousand kisses, then another thousand... For when our brief life ends there is a never ending night and a never ending sleep." Edna Millay was probably the first woman in literature to back such ideas wholeheartedly, for women have been notoriously diffident in their support of hedonism. Her reputation for unconventionality caused her to be discussed by people for whom her poetic expression was not of first interest. It also caused W. B. Yeats, who was not overly impressed by her poetry, and Thomas Hardy, who was, to be excitedly interested in her personality.

When Edna Millay first began to be noticed, American women still could not smoke in restaurants or swim in such garb as the European *maillot* or without stockings to cover their legs; it was a time when people confused the regulations of *The Book of Etiquette* with the highest principles of ethics. She seemed to be the standard-bearer for the breakdown of futile conventions and of taboos. She advertised her love affairs and her sex affairs, and in her work she really made a differentiation between the two with a nicety that male poets seldom matched. Of her sex affairs:

I find this frenzy insufficient reason
For conversation when we meet again.

or:

What lips my lips have kissed, and where and why
I have forgotten, and what arms have lain
Under my head till morning...
I only know that summer sang in me
A little while that in me sings no more.

Then of her love:

Women have loved before as I love now;
At least in lively chronicles of the past,
Of Irish waters by a Cornish prow,
Or Trojan waters by a Spartan mast.

These unconventional emotions and ideas she expressed in that most conventional form of verse, the sonnet, which has such an attraction for American women poets. The form enticed her to go on and on, expressing the same emotions and ideas in an unceasing flow of sonnetry. Even people expert in knowing poetry by heart after a couple of readings find it difficult to distinguish one sonnet from another, though this can readily be done in the case of Elinor Wylie's love sonnets, where each reveals a distinct emotion and thought. But Elinor Wylie was a trained and disciplined artist in a sense that Edna Millay never was. She had the faculty to become an artist and a scholar, too; she never let her mind and emotions ramble as did Edna Millay.

The sort of mental and professional training that teaches poets how to say effectively what they have to say was not to be found in the New York of Millay's time. No one was there to show her, not so much the technique of writing verse, which she could learn for herself, but that higher technique of getting beyond one's private world, which would have prevented her repetitiousness. A woman admirer of hers, confusing artistic with conventional education, sent her to college after the publication of her first poems. In no country do people learn the essentials of the art of literature in colleges, but they learn even less of them in America than elsewhere. Edna Millay probably had a good time in college, but she learned little if anything of what might be useful to her as an artist. She could have learned more by staying at home and reading poetry with a few fellow writers, for as Yeats says, "There is no singing school but studying Monuments of its own magnificence." And, to put it in prose, there is this sentence of T. S. Eliot's: "It is important that the artist should be highly educated in his own art, but his education is one that is hindered rather than helped by the ordinary processes of society which constitute education for the ordinary man."

In this sense, Edna Millay, in her art, had not sufficient education to allow her to use effectively her poetic endowment, though occasionally, and especially in her earlier poems, she did so use it. This inadequacy of artistic education also injured her self-criticism: in spite of her interest in ideas, she could not cope with them in writing, and this is seen explicitly in her symposium, *Conversation at Midnight*, and her later work, [*The Murder at Lidice*]. She plunged into translating Baudelaire, for which she was not only linguistically but temperamentally unfitted. She could talk French fluently, but she was no French scholar and got confused by genders and difficult constructions. Then she was too feminine a poet to be able to deal with such a masculine, revolutionary, powerful mentality as that of Baudelaire, who could make an ugliness of nature—decrepit old men and women, a corpse rotting in a ditch—into a high beauty of art.

Edna Millay could only deal with the acceptedly beautiful. Death, however, did fascinate her, though in a romantic style. Most of the delighted readers of her poetry never noticed her concern in nearly every poem with death—her own personal death and her artistic death, the fear that her work might be forgotten. In "The Poet and His Book," one of her best poems, she wrote:

> Down, you mongrel Death,
> Back into your kennel...
> You shall scratch and you shall whine,
> Many a night, and you shall worry
> Many a bone before you bury
> One sweet bone of mine.
> Boys and girls that lie
> Whispering in the hedges,
> Do not let me die....

This was really the burthen of many of her poems, "Do not let me die." What aided her popularity in her heyday was her warmth of heart, her generosity, her compassion for the beaten, the downtrodden, and this not in the current way of an impersonal, generalized humanitarianism, but with a rich feeling that made her adherence a strong personal emotion. Few of her admirers realized her fundamental loneliness, her shyness, her sadness, which made her gladly leave the turmoil of New York for an isolated country house where she seldom saw anybody and where she died alone and lonely. As she has written:

> Lovers and thinkers, into the earth with you.
> Be one with the dull, the indiscriminate dust.
> A fragment of what you felt, of what you knew,
> A formula, a phrase remains—but the best is lost.

Source: Mary M. Colum, "Edna Millay and Her Time," in *New Republic*, Vol. 124, No. 11, March 12, 1951, pp. 17–18.

SOURCES

"About the Great Depression," http://www.english.illinois.edu/maps/depression/about.htm (accessed June 1, 2009).

Applebaum, Anne, "World Inaction," http://www.slate.com/id/2197155 (accessed June 1, 2009).

Blake, Robert W., "Poets on Poetry: The Morality of Poetry," in *English Journal*, Vol. 81, No. 1, January 1992, pp. 16–20.

Bogan, Louise, "Conversation into Self," in *Critical Essays on Edna St. Vincent Millay*, edited by William B. Thesing, G. K. Hall, 1993, pp. 67–68, originally published in *Poetry*, Vol. 45, February 1935, pp. 277–79.

Brooks, Cleanth, "Miss Millay's Maturity," in *Southwest Review*, Vol. 20, 1935, pp. 1–5.

Courtney-Thompson, Fiona, and Kate Phelps, eds., *The 20th Century Year by Year*, Barnes & Noble, 1998, pp. 106–16.

Drier, Peter, "Lynching Lessons," June 17, 2006, http://www.commondreams.org/views05/0617–23.htm (accessed June 1, 2009).

Glennon, Lorraine, ed., *The Twentieth Century*, Century Books, 1999, p. 136.

Goodwin, Wade, "Beating Charges Split La. Town Along Racial Lines," http://www.npr.org/templates/story/story.php?storyId=12353776 (accessed June 1, 2009).

Harmon, William, and Hugh Holman, *A Handbook to Literature*, 11th ed., Pearson Prentice Hall, 2009, pp. 14–15, 241, 412, 425–26.

Hillyer, Robert, "Of Her Essential Heart and Spirit," in the *New York Times*, April 25, 1954, p. BR5.

Humphries, Rolfe, "Edna St. Vincent Millay," obituary in the *Nation*, Vol. 171, No. 27, December 30, 1950, p. 704.

Jennings, Peter, and Todd Brewster, eds., *The Century*, Doubleday, 1998, pp. 147–78.

McCotter, Thaddeus G., "Russia's Invasion of Georgia," in the *Washington Times*, August 11, 2008.

Millay, Edna St. Vincent, "Conscientious Objector," in *Wine From These Grapes*, Harper & Brothers, 1934, pp. 47–48.

Mitford, Nancy, *Savage Beauty: The Life of Edna St. Vincent Millay*, Random House, 2001.

National Geographic Eyewitness to the 20th Century, National Geographic Society, 1998, pp. 125–41.

Newcomb, John Timberman, "The Woman as Political Poet: Edna St. Vincent Millay and the Mid-Century Canon," in *Criticism*, Vol. 37, No. 2, Spring 1995, pp. 261–79.

Parsed, Raekha, "India Builds a 2,500-mile Barrier to Rival the Great Wall of China," in the *Times* (London), December 28, 2005.

Pound, Ezra, *Literary Essays*, edited by T. S. Eliot, New Directions, 1954, p. 297.

Rice, Philip Blair, "Edna Millay's Maturity," in the *Nation*, Vol. 139, November 14, 1934, pp. 568, 570.

Simon, John, "All for Love," in *New Criterion*, Vol. 24, No. 8, April 2006, pp. 68–73.

Thomas-Lester, Avis, "A Senate Apology for History on Lynching," in the *Washington Post*, June 14, 2005, p. A12.

Tower, Samuel A., "She Was the Most Popular Poet of Her Time," in the *New York Times*, July 12, 1981, p. D33.

FURTHER READING

Anreus, Alejandro, Diane L. Linden, and Jonathan Weinberg, eds., *The Social and the Real: Political Art of the 1930s in the Western Hemisphere*, Pennsylvania State University Press, 2006.

> This anthology contains different representations of art created in the 1930s. The art includes paintings, sculpture, graphic arts, and photography.

Hapke, Laura, *Daughters of the Great Depression: Women, Work, and Fiction in the American 1930s*, University of Georgia Press, 1997.

> This study explores how women of the 1930s were depicted in literature and film and also discusses the reality of women's lives.

Hatt, Christine, *World War I, 1914–18*, Franklin Watts, 2001.

> This history of World War I is designed for middle-school readers and contains many photographs and maps.

Houghland, Mason, *Gone Away*, Derrydale Press, 2000.

> This small book is a how-to guide for fox hunting. The author also includes many stories about fox hunting.

Kyvig, David E., *Daily Life in the United States, 1920–1940: How Americans Lived Through the Roaring Twenties and the Great Depression*, Ivan R. Dee, 2004.

> This book is a social, cultural, and economic history of the period in which Millay wrote much of her poetry.

Strachan, Hew, ed., *The Oxford Illustrated History of the First World War*, Oxford University Press, 2001.

> This collection of essays and photographs examines several key issues that are necessary to understand regarding the events of World War I and their influence on the post-war world.

Trask, David F., *The War with Spain, 1898*, University of Nebraska Press, 1996.

> This book examines the political and military decisions that are important to understanding the Spanish American War.

Uschan, Michael V., *Lynching and Murder in the Deep South*, Lucent, 2006.

> This book is designed for middle-school readers. The author provides a history of events not often discussed with young readers.

The Fly

WILLIAM BLAKE

1794

"The Fly" is part of the *Songs of Experience*, a collection of poems that William Blake self-published in 1794 to accompany his 1789 *Songs of Innocence*. These two volumes contain nearly all of his short poems. After them, he wrote longer poems in a variety of styles, most of which are collectively referred to as the prophecies. Blake published his first volume of poetry in 1783 and was still working at his death in 1827. Few of Blake's works were read or appreciated, however, during his lifetime.

The meaning of "The Fly" has been widely debated, and division of opinion occurs on the question of whether there is one voice or two in the poem, that is, whether the first three stanzas come from the human and the last two from the fly. The latter may be the more likely interpretation according to many scholars because of the relationship of Blake's text to his illustration. The illustration of "The Fly" separates the two parts, thus seeming to indicate that there is a shift in narrator and perspective. As the title indicates, the subject of the poem is a fly that is swatted away by the hand of the narrator who then compares the value and vagaries of his life and those of the fly. It should be noted that in all of Blake's poetry, the noun *fly* signifies any winged insect. While not commonly found in anthologies of poetry, "The Fly" can be found in any number of editions of *Songs of Innocence and Experience, Shewing the Two Contrary States of the Human Soul*. The poem can also

William Blake

be found easily online, but not usually with the illustration that Blake created to illuminate the text.

AUTHOR BIOGRAPHY

William Blake was born on November 28, 1757, in London, England, the second of seven children born to James Blake, a hosier, and Catherine Harmitage. Their home was comfortable, financially secure, and loving. Blake did not attend school; rather, he worked as an errand boy for a haberdasher, which gave him the opportunity to observe the London of his times. As a child, Blake claimed to have spiritual visions that included glimpses of God's face in a window and angels perched in trees. His parents discouraged him from reporting these visions, assuming they were childish fantasies, yet throughout his long life, such visions spurred the poet's creative impulses and the ideals that infused both his poetry and visual artwork.

Although Blake was mostly educated at home, at age ten he was enrolled in a popular art school because he showed artistic talent. At age fourteen, he became an apprentice to a master engraver who often sent him to Westminster Abbey and other great churches to sketch. At twenty-one, Blake enrolled at the Royal Academy of Art where he made lifelong friendships with a few people who later became famous and supported his work. At this time, Blake sometimes would join the crowds who demonstrated for civil rights in the streets.

Blake began working full time as an engraver, and he then married Catherine Boucher on August 18, 1782. Catherine was initially illiterate, but Blake taught her to read and write, and she became his assistant. They had no children and endured financial difficulties all their lives. In 1784, the year his beloved brother Robert came to live with him, Blake opened his own print shop with another engraver, but the business soon collapsed, and Robert died in 1787.

In 1783, Blake published his first volume of poetry, *Poetical Sketches*, the only one of his works not self-published. By 1788, Blake had developed a method called *illuminated printing*, in which he would etch the illustration and text together onto a single copper plate. Blake used this laborious and time-consuming method in all his future publications. In 1789, Blake printed *Songs of Innocence*. He then combined the verses with *Songs of Experience* in 1794, in which "The Fly" appears, and titled the combined work *Songs of Innocence and Experience, Shewing the Two Contrary States of the Human Soul*.

Then Blake focused on his prophetic books: *The Book of Los* (1795), *Milton* (1795), and *Jerusalem* (1804–1820) among them. From 1800 to 1803, Blake and his wife lived in Sussex under the patronage of William Hayley, but he moved back to London when he realized he could not conform to Hayley's conventional expectations. Around 1818, a group of young artists known as the Ancients discovered Blake. Their admiration and friendship added to an active social life gave Blake a sense of being appreciated in his last years.

William Blake died on August 12, 1827. His poetry went largely unnoticed until Alexander Gilchrist published a biography of the poet in 1863. Since the 1920s, Blake has been regarded as one of the leading romantic poets and a major figure in literature and art.

POEM TEXT

Little Fly,
Thy summer's play
My thoughtless hand
Has brushed away.

Am not I   5
A fly like thee?
Or art not thou
A man like me?

For I dance
And drink, and sing,   10
Till some blind hand
Shall brush my wing.

If thought is life
And strength and breath
And the want   15
Of thought is death;

Then am I
A happy fly,
If I live,
Or if I die.   20

MEDIA ADAPTATIONS

- The Famous Authors series by Kultur Video includes the DVD *William Blake* (2006), a 30-minute discussion by scholars of the poet and his world, including images of archival materials and other memorabilia.
- The University of Michigan School of Music Symphony Orchestra, under the direction of Leonard Slatkin, recorded William Bolcom's version of *Songs of Innocence and Experience*, which uses the poems as lyrics set to music. The 2004 recording of three discs runs over two hours and is available from Naxos American Classics.

POEM SUMMARY

"The Fly" is about the brushing away of a fly by a human hand, a very simple action that takes on complex meaning as the narrator analyzes it.

Each of the five stanzas, with the exception of stanza four, begins with an anapestic line, that is, a foot with two unstressed syllables followed by a stressed syllable. An anapest usually gives a light, bouncy feel to a line, so an anapest is appropriate to convey the flitting of a butterfly. Then three four-syllable iambic lines follow, in most cases. An iamb is a foot of two syllables, the first unstressed, the second stressed, a rhythm common in spoken English. The exceptions to this pattern of three-syllable first lines followed by four-syllable second, third, and fourth lines, occur in the fourth and fifth stanzas, perhaps suggesting a change of speakers. Another oddity is that the first four stanzas have the ballad form of *abcb* rhyme scheme; however, the fifth stanza is a couplet quatrain with *aabb* rhyme scheme. The first three stanzas appear to be from one speaker, and each contains a single thought, whereas the last two stanzas reveal a shift in tone that suggests a new speaker and the two together make up one complete thought.

Not only are the lines in the poem short, but also the words are only one or two syllables and most contain only one to four letters. The short lines match the short bursts of movement of a butterfly, and the size of the words match the smallness of the insect. The shortness of everything in the poem may also suggest the brevity of life and the fact that death can come unexpectedly and quickly. Death is a theme in the poem. There are four references to death, two indirect and two direct: The indirect references occur in the phrase "brush'd away" in line 4, and "brush my wing" in line 12. The direct references occur in "And the want / of thought is death" in lines 15 and 16, and "if I die" in line 20. Each of these references to death appears in the final line of a stanza, just as death is metaphorically the final line of life.

Stanza 1

The first stanza begins with an apostrophe, a direct address to someone absent or some abstraction. In this case, the object of the direct address is the subject of the poem: "Little Fly." These three syllables constitute the whole first line. "Fly" is even capitalized as if it were a proper name. The second line, "Thy summer's play," starts the first statement to the fly and sets the season of the scene. The third and fourth lines, "My thoughtless hand / Has brush'd away," tells the reader that the speaker has just shooed away a fly. The use of the word "thoughtless" indicates that the speaker's movement against the fly was automatic, perhaps a reaction to the butterfly landing on the speaker's hand, and sets up the theme of vulnerability to sudden misfortune found in the next two stanzas. Lines 2, 3, and 4 are all four-syllable lines of two iambs.

Stanza 2

In the second stanza, the speaker contemplates what he has done by this thoughtless action. Again beginning with a three-syllable anapestic line, Blake combines the first and second lines to ask a question: "Am not I / a fly like thee?" Lines 3 and 4 ask a corollary question: "Or art not thou / A man like me?" In other words, the speaker wonders if he and the fly have similarly brief or vulnerable lives, so he compares the two with reverse similes. Lines 2, 3, and 4 are four-syllable lines of two iambs.

Stanza 3

The third stanza answers affirmatively the questions asked in the second stanza, by stating the similarities between the speaker and the fly. Once more beginning with a three-syllable anapestic line, the speaker likens his lifestyle and eventual death to that of the fly, "For I dance / And drink & sing: / Till some blind hand / Shall brush my wing." The speaker appears to be saying that he lives a carefree life ignoring what lies ahead, like the fly's "summer's play," but he recognizes he could just as easily meet his end by the blind hand of God or fate, by some thoughtless act like the one the fly encounters, even describing himself as having a wing. Here, *blind* and *thoughtless* are synonyms for behavior that is potentially destructive, and the carefree life does not include considering impending death.

Stanza 4

In this stanza, the third line is the anapest, and the fourth line returns to iambic meter. Breaking with the pattern of three-syllable first lines, stanza four seems to change moods or voices. It is the only stanza that does not use the first person. Many critics assert that the narrator is finished speaking, and the fly then gives a two-stanza response. Stanzas four and five present a syllogism, that is, the pattern used to reach a logical deduction: "If...then." The first two iambic lines define *thought*: "If thought is life / And strength & breath." The following two lines equate the absence of thought with being dead: "And the want / Of thought is death." If the want of thought is death, and the speaker in the first stanza is thoughtless in his action against the fly, then the reader can make the ironic connection that thoughtlessness can also cause someone else to die.

Stanza 5

The meter of the last stanza is anapest, iamb, anapest, iamb, befitting a couplet quatrain. The fifth stanza is the conclusion of the syllogism that began in the fourth stanza. If there is no thought in death, then in death a person cannot know unhappiness because the dead person knows nothing in a state of nonexistence. So, people might as well assume that individuals are happy in death because the dead do not know any difference. If the speaker is still the human, then the syllogism can be read as a way to rationalize his guilt over swatting the fly, that is, the fly is happy in life or death, so what is the harm? Or if the speaker is remorseless, the syllogism is an exercise in logic in lieu of thinking about the morality of the situation; thus Blake, who rejected the eighteenth-century philosophy of logic and physical nature, may be prodding the reader to question the value of logic if it means avoiding real life issues such as responsibility and spirituality.

Of the many interpretations of this poem, one is that if the fly is the speaker, its response indicates an indifference to matters of life and death. Blake believed that imagination can transcend mortality, so if thought is life, the fly is always happy because it is confident of the continuance of life through thought or imagination and, therefore, does not fear death. The message of the poem may then be that people should not neurotically worry about the injustice of random or reckless death but concentrate on the eternal divinity within each person. The poem can also be read as saying that since the fly is happy whether it lives or dies, the fly assures the speaker that there is no harm done. However, that interpretation seems to contradict Blake's worldview. It is more likely that Blake is pointing out that how people treat flies is an indication of how people treat other humans; the kinder people are to the other creatures, the more likely it is that they will be kind to each other.

A different interpretation is that if thought is life, then death is merely the cessation of thought, the difference between having awareness and not having awareness. If individuals are unaware, they cannot care whether they are alive or dead. Another interpretation is that the fly thinks the speaker is being presumptuous in comparing them. Further, the fly may have noted that the speaker asks these questions in a self-referential way rather than showing any sympathy for the fly. If the want of thought is death, then that thoughtless hand may be attached to someone whose soul, at least, is dead. Also, on the negative side, another interpretation is that the poem is saying there is nothing more significant in human life than there is in a fly's life. If the human's death comes in the midst of a trivial life of dancing, drinking, and singing, then how is that different from the fly's death during "summer's play"? However, there is room here to ask if there is value in human life that was lived with purpose. A life that has achieved nothing may not be mourned, but the end of a life rich with accomplishment causes great grief. Therefore, reading "The Fly" may cause individuals to reflect on what in people's lives is worthy enough to give individuals more value than a fly has.

THEMES

Mortality
Blake focused a lot on human vulnerability to death. In *Songs of Experience*, he reveals more about the difficulties of life than he does in *Songs of Innocence*. He asserts that the innocent imagination of childhood, which can transcend the negative aspects of life, should be sought for again to counter the disillusionment and temporal concerns of adulthood, including mortality.

Mortality as a theme in "The Fly" is seen in the four references to death in the poem: "brush'd away" and "brush my wing" as in the life of the fly is brushed away, "And the want / of thought is death" as a definition of death, and "if I die" as the beginning of a syllogism that tries to figure out logically what happens when one dies. The speaker is a person pondering the precariousness of human life and what death means or feels like.

Mistrust of authority figures and the power they wield is an important theme for the *Songs* as a whole. This mistrust is manifested in "The Fly" as a suspicion that the gods play with mortals. Blake may have recalled from *King Lear* a line comparing gods killing mortals for sport to naughty boys killing flies as a form of amusement. Since ancient times, the gods have been portrayed as unpredictable enough to kill humans on a whim, with no more forethought than that of the speaker in "The Fly" when he brushes away the insect. This correspondence with mythology underscores how human mortality makes people vulnerable, makes them likely to live in fear that the next instant could result in death from causes unknown and unexpected, from the unexpected motion of the speaker's hand or the vagaries of chance.

Imagination
Blake was a visionary, and he claimed to see God, angels, and other spirits. When his favorite brother, Robert, died, Blake said that he saw Robert's spirit rise, and until his own death, the poet continued to talk to his brother. Consequently, it was easy for Blake to believe in the power of the mind, in imagination, and in seeing beyond the temporal world. In "The Fly," the imagination that can transcend death is explained as the thought that is the essence of being alive.

In "The Fly," the human says he dances and sings, with an enjoyment of the bodily senses that Blake advocated, but he does so in a superficial, thoughtless way that does not invite the power of imagination. Only when he harms the fly does he stop to question an action and contemplate the role of thought. Although he was a mystic, Blake did not forget the realities of human existence. Instead, Blake found imagination to be inseparable from his humanity; thus, for him, thought is life. In fact, Blake believed that spirituality, even divinity, was part of humanity, an interwoven connectedness between God and humans that signifies being fully alive.

Blake hoped his poems would be read with the imagination, just as he used imagination

TOPICS FOR FURTHER STUDY

- Thomas Gray, in "Ode on the Spring," written in 1748, describes insect youth on the wing, and they, too, are "Brush'd by the hand of rough Mischance." Another poem titled "The Fly" was written by Ogden Nash (1902–1971) and is only two lines long. Compare Blake's poem "The Fly" to the poems by Gray and Nash in a class discussion. What are the similarities and differences among the three poems? Include tone, style, and theme in your discussion.
- Shakespeare wrote in *King Lear*, "As flies to wanton boys are we to the gods, / They kill us for their sport." Research mythology and write a report on an instance of a god making sport of killing a human. Does the attitude of the god in killing for sport correspond to that of the narrator in Blake's "The Fly"? You may incorporate images or drawings of the mythological characters involved in the report.
- Blake supported both the American Revolution and the French Revolution. Compare the two revolutions and comment on what new ideas and values were espoused in each. Make an outline of the key events in each revolution and explain these to your class in a PowerPoint presentation.
- During Blake's lifetime, the British Empire continued to expand, despite the loss of all the North American colonies except Canada. Britain's heavy involvement in the slave trade inspired Blake to write "Black Boy," and that involvement motivated others to organize the abolition movement. Form three groups in your class. Have one group research and report on the British slave trade, including the time period and extent of traffic. Another group may research and report on the abolition movement in Great Britain. The third group may research and report on how abolition of slavery put into effect by date and colony or commonwealth. As a class project, a film documentary could be made of the combined reports.

---

to write them. Blake rejected the empiricists of the eighteenth century who declared that all knowledge could be gained from the five senses and the rationalists who claimed that logic could produce answers to every question. Blake felt that the body sometimes confines and limits the intellectual eye, but it could not direct it. Therefore, using the imagination could help individuals transcend sense experiences and free them from the blinding limitations of the temporal and physical.

In like manner, there is no need to fear death because, just as the imagination can transcend sense experiences, it can transcend the limits of mortality. If thought is life, as Blake wrote in "The Fly," then the soul, the spirit that controls imagination, continues after death. Reality is not in the five senses, but in the mind. An unfettered imagination gives freedom to the spirit to live in a better world than the temporal one in which the body exists. With this belief that imagination can restore health to the mind, Blake developed a new value system based on the belief that freedom is necessary for the act of imagination that can create a better world. Blake was concerned about the politics, social issues, and theology of his time. Just as Thomas Paine and others used language to alter political thought, Blake saw language as it is used in literature as a vehicle for empowering the imagination to affect thought; he used his poetry to describe this process when the speaker in "The Fly" begins to contemplate the power of thought.

Overhead view of a common house fly (Image copyright Raymond Kasprzak, 2009. Used under license from Shutterstock.com)

STYLE

Lyric

In ancient Greece, a lyric was a song accompanied by the lyre. In the seventeenth century, lyric poetry was often set to music. In modern times, lyrics are the words to a song, and the lyric poem has a musical quality. It is defined as a short poem with a single speaker who, in solitude, muses over personal feelings or thoughts but does not tell a story. In a dramatic lyric, the speaker addresses someone else. The speaker is not the poet, and no biographical information is given about the speaker; the reader learns only about the speaker's state of mind and values. The dramatic lyric often contains metaphors and symbols, which can be interpreted in various ways.

"The Fly" is a lyric poem. It is written in deceptively simple language and has short lines that seem to match the erratic flight and soft landings of the fly or butterfly. It fits into the lyric category because of its length, its single speaker in solitude, and the speaker's self-absorption and thoughtfulness. The speaker is not the poet but the persona of the bard who speaks all the poems in *Songs of Experience*. The reader learns nothing personal about the speaker beyond his manner of self-analysis and his thoughts about life and death. The second stanza presents a pair of similes, asking "Am not I / A fly like thee? / Or art not thou / a man like me?"

In addition, "The Fly" has some features of the dramatic monologue. A dramatic monologue employs a lone speaker who addresses one or more others who do not speak but whose reactions are alluded to by the speaker, and the focus is on the character of the speaker as revealed by what is said. Usually, though, a dramatic monologue is a long poem. The form was used famously by Robert Browning in poems such as "My Last Duchess" and "The Bishop Orders His Tomb." It is not an exact fit to call "The Fly" a dramatic monologue, although some critics have, but it has some similarity to the form. The speaker in the poem addresses the fly, and the reader learns something about the speaker.

Simile

A simile is a comparison between two things using the words *like* or *as* to make the comparison obvious. In "The Fly" the speaker says "Am not I / a fly like thee?" What Blake does then is unusual in that he reverses the simile to ask "Or art not thou / A man like me?" This inversion of relationships between parallel and balanced phrases is called *chiasmus*. The point of the simile is to juxtapose the speaker whose life can be brushed away by a reckless deity with the fly whose life can be brushed away by a thoughtless person. The fly is to the person, as the person is to the deity.

HISTORICAL CONTEXT

Romanticism

The romantic period began in the late eighteenth century and continued until about 1850. The movement started in Germany and is considered to have been launched in England when William Wordsworth and Samuel Taylor Coleridge published the *Lyrical Ballads* in 1798. Other major British writers of the time include poets George Gordon, Lord Byron; Percy Bysshe Shelley; and John Keats; essayists Charles Lamb, William Hazlitt, and Thomas de Quincey; and novelist Charlotte Brontë.

Romanticism was a reaction against the rationalism of the Age of Enlightenment and the belief that pure intellect expressed through science could explain everything. This new philosophy and esthetic sensibility asserted that one could use the power of imagination to create visions of a better world and thus compensate for or escape rampant urban growth and pollution-causing industrialism. Characteristics of romantic literature include glorification of nature and country life; focus on the poor and rustic and on orphans and social outcasts; philosophical repugnance for the upper classes and the establishment; admiration of the ancient and exotic; belief in supernaturalism, idealism, intuition and feelings; indulgence in the senses; and a sense of carpe diem (seizing the day or living fully in the present). Romanticism was also a celebration of free, original artistic expression and the isolated free thinkers who can change society. According to Wordsworth in his preface to the 1802 edition of the *Lyrical Ballads*, poetry should use the language really spoken by common people and its subject matter should be the daily experience of ordinary people.

For the romantic writers, mortality was an important and intriguing subject. Thus Blake reflects the literary group to which he belongs in his exploration of death. Yet in many ways Blake's poetry is unlike the work of his contemporaries. Some critics see Blake not as much of the romantic period as anticipating it. These readers may see *Songs of Innocence and Experience* as more like late eighteenth-century children's poetry than the lyrical ballads Wordsworth wrote. Others emphasize Blake's uniqueness, stressing his dissimilarity to other artists of his time. Indeed, Blake asserted the importance of originality, of not being trapped by someone else's system of thought or artistic expression. Nonetheless, for most readers, Blake represents romanticism in its purest form. His visions and prophecies, his use of heightened states of emotion, his opposition to social oppression and to the hypocrisy of church and state, and his focus on ordinary low-class people and their experience, all of these align Blake with what literary scholars later called romanticism.

Engraving

Engraving is a technique of printmaking in which the reverse of the design to be printed is cut into a plate made of wood or metal. Blake's unique method used copper plates. When the plate is inked, the ink collects in the cut lines of the design; the rest of the plate is wiped clean before printing. The printing process itself requires intense pressure so that dampened paper can actually be forced into the inked incisions by a press roller. Once the ink has been transferred from the plate to the paper, the print will be a mirror image of the design drawn on the plate. Many prints can be pulled from a single plate. Engraving, which was first used in Germany in the fifteenth century, became an important technique for illustrating books and was widely practiced throughout Europe until the nineteenth century. Blake served an apprenticeship in order to become an engraver and remained in that profession his entire life. He was hired to illustrate other people's books, and he illustrated his own collections of poetry, engraving his words in mirror image and illustrating the subject matter with his engraved images.

COMPARE & CONTRAST

- **1780s–1790s:** Blake is interested in the American Revolution and, in 1789, the year Blake publishes the first half of the *Songs*, George Washington becomes the first president of the United States. In 1793, Blake prints *America: A Prophecy*, about the universal principles that can fuel a revolution.

  Today: The United States inaugurates its forty-fourth president, indicating that the American experiment in democracy is successful.

- **1780s–1790s:** Blake supports the French Revolution at first, but then is horrified by the violence that ensues. In 1891, Blake sets in type but never publishes *The French Revolution*, probably inhibited by the possibility of imprisonment for radical action.

  Today: France has a democratic political system, and its Fifth Republic has existed since 1958.

- **1780s–1790s:** Blake develops his own tedious method of copper-plate engraving for the printing of his poems and illustrations. In 1796, the Bavarian Alois Senefelder invents lithography, which uses simple chemical processes to create an image, and this process is the common commercial method until modern times.

  Today: Offset lithography, so called because the image is first transferred, or offset, to the rubber drum of the printing press, is the most common method used for book publishing. High-speed printers, print-on-demand books, and small printers for the home are available, making the task of printing documents and illustrations quick and easy.

- **1780s–1790s:** Although noted literary figure Samuel Johnson declares London to be an intellectual haven, Blake, who lives in London virtually all his life, describes in his poetry the darker side of London's political, social, and economic systems, particularly dirty streets, horrific prisons, and oppressive government. During the nineteenth century, London becomes the largest city in the world.

  Today: London has about 8 million residents, while the Greater London area has as many as 14 million. London is the most populous municipality in Europe and its greatest financial center. It has the busiest airport and the most extensive public transportation system in the world.

Eighteenth Century

While the eighteenth century was a time among the wealthy of elegance in furniture, architecture, art, and dress, it was also a time for the poor of extreme poverty, oppressive government, and widespread disease. Riots were not uncommon during the eighteenth century because that was the only means by which the disenfranchised could express their plight. It was a time of increasing freedoms, but the upper classes feared the effect such freedoms might have on well-established social institutions. Toward the end of the century, the American and French Revolutions asserted democratic values and denied despotic monarchical rule. These wars caused great bloodshed, particularly during the Reign of Terror in France: The births of democracies were painful and, in France at least, brought in a period of mob rule. The differences between Blake's *Songs of Innocence* and his *Songs of Experience* may reflect the conflicting aspects of his own tumultuous times.

Philosophy and science gained momentum during the eighteenth century with the development of geology and other physical sciences and the invention of various kinds of machinery, for example, the steam engine, which revolutionize the modes of manufacturing and initiated the huge social and economic upheaval called the Industrial Revolution. Toward the end of the eighteenth century and throughout the nineteenth century, a huge population shift from rural areas to manufacturing centers occurred, bringing with it the social and health problems associated with urban overcrowding and poverty. Literature and entertainment became available to the growing middle class, and literacy increased. For the colonial powers, including Spain and Portugal, settlement brought riches but also racial strife and the scourge of the slave trade, which then led to the abolition movement and the rise of humanitarianism. Blake's two poems entitled "Little Black Boy" in the *Songs of Innocence and Experience* show his concern for the 15,000 ex-slaves living in destitution in England after being abandoned by the system that brought them there.

Blake grew up near a workhouse and lived within the stench of a burial ground for the poor near his home. Exposure made him sensitive to social inequalities, and the blindness of wealthy people to the suffering of the poor bothered him all of his life and directed much of his poetic expression. He often used images of bondage and imprisonment to convey his sense of economic and political oppression. No other romantic writer expressed quite the same political insights that Blake did, but his dismal worldview held up a mirror for those who wanted to look in it. While Wordsworth described the poet as a person who speaks for nature, Blake saw the role as one of social protest and spiritual prophecy. Wordsworth believed that piety was inspired by nature, but Blake felt that nature proved the enmity between humans and God.

Blake met Mary Wollstonecraft, Thomas Paine, and other radical thinkers of his time, but he was not a political activist. Rather, he stated his protests in his revolutionary prophecies, *The French Revolution, Europe, America,* and *The Marriage of Heaven and Hell,* none of which was distributed to the public, but all of them were possibly more radical and prophetic than anything his contemporaries wrote. After his death, Blake's personal copies were made public, and they were later praised and studied. Unknown in his own time, these works were used in the twentieth century to justify his being appreciated as one of England's greatest and most intellectual poets.

Cover of Songs of Innocence and of Experience, *illustrated by William Blake* (© 1994 The Henry E. Huntington Library and Art Gallery)

CRITICAL OVERVIEW

In his lifetime, Blake was known as an engraver and artist, and even then by only a few. His poetry was virtually unknown, partly because, after his first book, he insisted on publishing them himself; thus, he was not known by any publishing houses, and he produced relatively few copies of his works. After a while, the requests for his books were more for the illustrations than for the poetry. In fact, customers demanded such highly colored plates that the text became somewhat obscured and some even requested prints without text.

Word did get around, though. In 1818, Samuel Taylor Coleridge, who is said to have called Blake a genius, listed some of the *Songs* according to his opinion of their merit, but his critiques were based on morality and doctrine, thus eliminating those poems that seemed to challenge accepted mores. Wordsworth made copies of some of the poems from the *Songs* even though he thought Blake was mad. Robert Southey, another famous literary figure, also thought Blake insane, but attended a Blake exhibition and included a Blake poem in one of his own publications. In the last decade of Blake's life, a group of talented young artists called the Ancients appreciated Blake for his genius and his visions, considered him a master, and gave him much joy with their frequent visits and discussions.

In March 1830, just three years after Blake's death, an anonymous critic in *London University Magazine* called the *Songs of Innocence and Experience* noble, quoted at length from the book, and declared that Blake's art and poetry show exceptional power. Nonetheless, Blake's poems were relegated to children's books and almost forgotten for several more decades.

When Alexander Gilchrist published his *Life of William Blake* in 1863, the poet caught the attention of notable literary critics such as A. C. Swinburne, Dante Gabriel Rossetti, and William Butler Yeats, who went on to edit a volume of Blake's poetry in 1893. In 1920, T. S. Eliot declared that Blake wrote with a "peculiar honesty" that "never exists without great technical accomplishment." Eliot added that the *Songs of Innocence and Experience* contain "poems of a man with a profound interest in human emotions, and a profound knowledge of them." Eliot also pointed out that "The emotions are presented in an extremely simplified, abstract form." In 1921, biographer Geoffrey Keynes set the standard for Blake criticism and established Blake as an appropriate topic for serious scholarship. The well-respected critic Northrop Frye published a book about Blake in 1947, and the acknowledgement of Blake as one of Britain's greatest poets continued for the rest of the twentieth century and into the twenty-first century.

Most criticism about the poems in *Songs of Innocence and Experience* are about the collection as a whole, not about individual poems, except for a few famous ones such as "The Tyger." Nonetheless, some analyses of the collection pay attention to each poem and some critics single out "The Fly." The criticism is seldom about the quality of style or techniques in the poem, but often focuses on whether the voice in the last two stanzas is that of the speaker or the fly and what the meaning of the poem is.

Regarding this matter of debate, G. S. Morris wrote in *The Explicator* about the apparent change of speaker in the first three stanzas from the human to the fly in the last two stanzas. It is Morris's opinion that the fly is upset with the human for comparing his action to that of the gods, thus giving himself the power of a god over the fly. The speaker has also disregarded the fly's activity as mere play. The fly is so contemptuous of the speaker that the answer to the question "Am not I a fly like thee?" is "Hardly." The fly, Morris asserted, "is a natural creature, and living or dying, thinking or not thinking, are all the same to it. The speaker, on the other hand, neurotically dreads the 'blind hand' of some greater power."

CRITICISM

Lois Kerschen

Kerschen is an English instructor and freelance writer. In this essay, she shows how the poem "The Fly" fits into the overall scheme of William Blake's illustrated collection Songs of Innocence and Experience.

"The Fly" is part of a group of poems called *Songs of Experience*, published in 1794 by William Blake. This collection was a sequel, so to speak, to the *Songs of Innocence*, which Blake published in 1789. In fact, he put the two works together thereafter and called them *Songs of Innocence and Experience: Shewing the Two Contrary States of the Human Soul*. The subtitle indicates that the two parts should be read together and compared.

Although there are a number of differences that can be pointed out, Blake discouraged reading the *Songs* "as a progression from a simplistic to a more sophisticated viewpoint, or a biographical shift from a youthful and naive attitude to an experienced and cynical one," according to Alan Richardson, a Blake scholar. Blake commented in *Marriage of Heaven and Hell* (1793) that "Without Contraries is no progression." Richardson reports that Blake meant that "neither an innocent nor an experienced perspective is in itself adequate to the complexities of human life. Each underscores and corrects the partialities and deficiencies of the other." The "contrary states" of innocence and experience can be found within lyrics in either group of songs.

WHAT DO I READ NEXT?

- *William Blake: The Complete Illuminated Books* (2000) is a paperback with 366 color and 30 black and white reproductions of Blake's illustrated poems, including *Songs of Innocence and Experience, America, Milton,* and *Jerusalem.* Also included is an introduction by David Bindman, a Blake expert, and essays by Peter Ackroyd and Marilyn Butler that provide an overview of Blake's life and times.

- *The Rime of the Ancient Mariner and Other Poems* (1817), by Samuel Taylor Coleridge, is a collection of well-known poems from a romantic writer and contemporary of Blake.

- *Favorite Poems*, a collection of 39 poems by William Wordsworth, gives a good sampling of the work of the poet laureate of England who died in 1850.

- A classic example of the romantic novel is *Jane Eyre* (1847), by Charlotte Brontë, which is a rags-to-riches story of a young woman on her own. The novel uses romantic elements such as natural elements, dreams, and mental telepathy to advance the plot.

- Thomas Paine's *Rights of Man* (1791) is a continuation of the political pamphlets that Paine wrote to incite the American Revolution by defining the role of government in terms of innate human rights.

- *Red Hot Salsa: Bilingual Poems on Being Young and Latino in the United States* (2005), by Lori Marie Carlson, is a collection of poetry by various poets, well-known and new, expressing in English and Spanish where and how they live their diverse lives.

- In 2008, Sterling Juvenile published *A Treasury of Poetry for Young People: Emily Dickinson, Robert Frost, Henry Wadsworth Longfellow, Edgar Allan Poe, Carl Sandberg, Walt Whitman,* which presents the works of these poets with illustrations, biographical information, and interpretations.

Among those who think that the significance of one poem depends on an understanding of the others is Nicholas Marsh, the author of a book on Blake's poems. In his examination of the two books, Marsh states that none of the conventional dualities about innocence and experience such as "ignorance and knowledge, illusion and disillusion, nature and society, optimism and pessimism, good and evil" actually fits Blake's intent. Rather, it might be more beneficial to consider the similarities than the differences between the two states. Marsh concludes that "the relationship between authority and the individual is fraught and ambiguous in both worlds, and both depend to some extent on fear." In "The Fly," the "blind hand," that is, the authority that can take away the speaker's life, is unidentified and may be frivolous, thereby leaving the person at risk, a threatening possibility.

When comparing the two books, one does not find heaven in innocence and hell in experience, just the different perspectives between the innocent joy of a child and the more experienced, less spontaneous response of an adult. Blake creates a dichotomy between wishes and desires, on the one hand, and duties and responsibilities, on the other, with an understanding that these states can be experienced by both children and adults. This type of dichotomy is apparent in "The Fly," between the human and the fly, between life and death, and between the responsibility for the fly's injury and the carefree attitude about present happiness in life.

Since "The Fly" appears in *Songs of Experience*, it is appropriate to point out the elements that are different in this second volume that are also noticeable in the poem. The *Songs of Experience* tend to be more dramatic as most of the characters are mired in a troubled mental state and are frustrated, feelings not seen in the harmony of innocence. The dialogues of the first volume become dramatic monologues in the second through which the speakers reveal their emotions and thoughts and tell readers more about themselves than even they understand. "The Fly" is a fitting example of this type of character because the lone speaker addresses the fly and reveals his sense that life is precarious and death may have no meaning, and then the solitary fly replies in its own monologue. In addition, in *Innocence* God is a presence; in *Experience* God is distant or absent. In "The

Fly," God becomes "gods" or "fate," too distant to care if its blind hand takes a life. Another element of *Experience* is that time changes from the seasonal renewal found in *Innocence* to a timeline leading from birth to the grave. In "The Fly," the discussion is of life and death as if those are the only concerns because one does not understand life and knows that death can come at any time. Therefore, one fills up one's time while waiting for death with the hedonistic pursuit of pleasure to make bearable the fact that each person's days are numbered.

Besides the two sets of poems belonging together, the poems are intertwined with their illustrations. Blake presented the text and illustration together as a single creation. By doing so, Blake created a complex situation in which the visual and the verbal interpret each other. Noted critic and Blake expert Northrup Frye explains: "The engraved poems of Blake are one of the few successful combinations of two arts by one master in the world, and one of the most startlingly and radically original productions of modern culture." The text of Blake's poems cannot be separated from the poet's illustrations of them. While many poems and stories have illustrations that match the descriptions of the scenes, Stanley Gardner states in his 1998 book on the times and circumstances surrounding *Songs of Innocence and Experience* that "Blake's illustrations 'out-do the text' with a visual statement which qualifies, amplifies or enriches the verse."

As a master engraver, Blake produced illustrations, so his commissions were for his artwork. His poetry was not known outside a small circle of readers and was so unappreciated that sometimes customers requested his illustrations without the accompanying poems. Modern readers who can understand that Blake was far ahead of his time in method and message can perhaps forgive his contemporaries for failing to appreciate his poetry. The text included on the back cover of *William Blake: The Complete Illuminated Books* states: "For Blake, religion and politics, intellect and emotion, mind and body were both unified and in conflict with each other: his work is expressive of his personal mythology, and his methods of conveying it were integral to its meaning."

The illustration for "The Fly" shows a mother or, more likely, a nanny standing between two children. The image of a taller child, a girl, is placed under the first three stanzas with her back to the reader. She is about to hit a shuttlecock with a badminton racquet. Considering her position, perhaps that is representative of the hand that brushes the fly. Under the last two stanzas, the image of the nanny is located, the figure bending down to hold the hands of a toddler about to take a step. Leafless trees frame the illustration, and their branches, or vines in the branches, unite at mid page and flow down to separate the first three stanzas from the other two. It is this physical separation in the illustration, not only by the vines but also by the nanny between the two children that causes many critics to believe that Blake was indicating that there are two speakers: the man in the first three stanzas and the fly in the last two.

What perhaps is most convincing about this argument is the fact that there is a butterfly drawn next to the last two lines. That butterfly may be Blake's clue that the "fly" is the speaker in those two stanzas. Critics may have missed this clue if they did not know that to Blake a fly was a butterfly. In fact, perhaps because the butterfly is all one color and looks more like a moth, some critics have identified it as just a "winged" creature or, like G. S. Morris in his article on "The Fly," as a bird in flight. Morris otherwise gives an interesting explanation of the illustration's toddler as the human speaker and the bird as the fly: "By infantilizing the philosopher and restoring the fly to health, the image confirms the fly's rhetorical triumph."

The use of images of vegetation to lend interpretation to the poems recurs in Blake's *Songs*. In *Innocence* leaves and trees add to the life in the pictures and their intertwining may symbolize marriage or harmony. In *Experience*, however, the trees are without leaves and the vines grow downward, as in "The Fly." The separation created by the vines represents divorce or lack of harmony. F. B. Beer, in an article for *British Writers*, notes the division created by the tendril that separates the last two stanzas from the first three in "The Fly". He comments on the sudden switch from the human to the fly, as if conjured "through a subterranean transformation of meaning that cannot easily be unraveled into ordered sense, but that has changed the terms of the discussion from the question of kindness to that of life and its significance."

Beer's analysis underlines the difficulty of interpreting "The Fly." That is why a knowledge of the context of the two parts of the *Songs* and consulting a copy of the illustrated poem are so helpful. Blake used recurring symbols and characters in the two books to create something akin to a continuous story. For example, the speaker throughout *Innocence* is the Piper, one who plays the pipe or the flute; the speaker in *Experience* is called the Bard, a term for poet. The nanny and children are also recurring figures. The use of landscapes, vegetation, and animals all add to the layered meaning of the poems that Blake never intended to be read just as text. It is tempting to study just the words as readers do with other poems, but it is worth the effort to find an illustrated copy of Blake's poems so that all the dimensions of his work are present and contribute to the reader's appreciation of Blake's work.

Source: Lois Kerschen, Critical Essay on "The Fly," in *Poetry for Students*, Gale, Cengage Learning, 2010.

G. S. Morris

In the following essay, Morris discusses the final two stanzas of "The Fly."

Blake's poem "The Fly" begins with an obvious apostrophe, human to fly: "Little Fly / Thy summer's play, / My thoughtless hand / Has brush'd away" (lines 1–4). Like the fly, this narrator considers, he plays his days away, until he too is struck by "some blind hand" (11)—God, fate, or circumstance. One may read (as many have) the last two stanzas as the continuation of this narrator's thought, as he explores his metaphorical fly-ness. Yet there is no logic in his musings: his conclusion, "Then am I / A happy fly" (17–18), does not follow from his Cartesian "thought is life" and "the want / Of thought is death" (13, 15–16). Instead of a moral, we have a non sequitur that becomes more absurd the more one considers it. However, as several commentators have realized, the illuminated text's arrangement—in which the last two stanzas are separated from the first three and closed off by vines and branches—offers another possibility: these final stanzas are a separate, parallel response to the initial narrator's philosophical speculation. Beyond the physical separation in the print, the text allows for a break between these sections. The first three stanzas certainly issue from one speaker, as they follow logically and sentimentally; likewise, the fourth and fifth stanzas are a unit, as they make up a single sentence. They are differentiated, however, by the fourth stanza's obscurity and tonal change: with its lack of first-person subject (present in all three previous stanzas) and its markedly impersonal tone, the fourth stanza simply reads as a break in voice. Although others (most recently Michael Simpson) have recognized the possibility of a second voice, none have admitted a strange, but illuminating, possibility: the second speaker could be the fly itself.

Given this reading, the ending stanzas take on a parodic quality that explains their logical fallacy. The fly confronts the first speaker's flabby, pretentious Romanticism with an incomprehensible parody of natural philosophy, pointing up the failure of both superficial romance and pure reason. In appropriating the first speaker's language in answer to his question ("Am not I / A fly like thee?" [5–6]), the fly undermines that speaker's magnanimous self-identification with nature. The fly picks up the first speaker's word "thoughtless" for its own parodic, pseudo-Cartesian thesis; the fly sets its terms as "If thought is life / And strength & breath; / And the want / Of thought is death" (16–19), calling ironic attention to the attitude embedded in the first speaker's language. Had the first speaker "thought," the fly would not be injured and possibly dying (because "thought is life" and "want of thought is death"), but his "thoughtless" hand has already caused the damage. The fly surreptitiously points out the first speaker's hypocrisy; in his self-regard the first speaker sees his injury to the fly only as an opportunity for self-reflection. His reflection offers no consolation to the fly, no sympathy, but only an abstract comparison and speculation: so the fly, in turn, replies with still more abstract speculation. Further, by positing that "want / Of thought is death," the fly cleverly implies the deadness in the thoughtless speaker's philosophy.

The fly's speech also punctures the first speaker's inflated self-image. The first speaker imagines that his life will end, like the fly's, by "some blind hand" (11) that strikes him down as carelessly as he struck down the fly. The first speaker makes the common mistake of imagining a god as thoughtless and careless as himself, and, by implication, makes himself the fly's god, undermining his superficial solidarity with the fly. The fly, however, denies the first speaker's power over it by declaring that it is "A happy fly, / If I live, / Or if I die" (18–20). The fly undercuts the standard of "thought" with the introduction of this new term, "happy": perhaps, the fly suggests, the first speaker's philosophy has omitted a point. Whether "happy" means "fortunate" or "joyful," the word contradicts the first speaker's speculation: the fly is no victim of circumstance, but fortunate; it is not suffering, but joyful. It is a natural creature, and living or dying, thinking or not thinking, are all the same to it. The speaker, on the other hand, neurotically dreads the "blind hand" of some greater power (one he creates in his own image), though he represses his dread. In asserting its equanimity, the fly points toward the contempt underlying the first speaker's words: if the speaker disregards the fly's occupation as "play," the fly will play "happy." Thus the fly answers the first speaker's question—"Am not I / A fly like thee?"—with a contemptuous "Hardly."

As the last two stanzas are a response to, not a continuation of, the first three, so Blake's illumination acts as a response to the poem. In the accompanying domestic scene a nurse and two children play beneath two trees. On the left, a young girl prepares to strike a shuttlecock with a racquet; on the right a toddler—too small to determine sex—stands, held up by the nurse, who separates the children. The image itself rhymes with the text above; the nurse separates the children as the vine separates the two columns of text, with the larger child on the left, below the longer block of text, and the smaller child below the shorter block. The circular position of the nurse's and toddler's arms echoes the encircling branches above. The first column of text opens out at the bottom with the shuttlecock just below it; this section has a strong downward movement as the tree branches point toward the girl and the shuttlecock falls—the lines "Till some blind hand / Shall brush my wing" seem to follow the feathered shuttlecock directly into the little girl's racquet. The visual rhyme extends to an ironic representation of the two narrators: the playing child takes the place of the philosophical narrator by becoming the "blind hand," while a flying bird directly beside the lines "If I live / Or if I die" stands in for the "happy fly." By infantilizing the philosopher and restoring the fly to health, the image confirms the fly's rhetorical triumph.

The coloring, however, presents a problem. In the earlier prints, the tree is imposingly dark and the background sky either a bleak dusk or a red and sulfur-yellow sunset; in these prints the tree would seem to clutch the words threateningly. The dark earlier prints call into question both the first narrator's transcendentalism and the fly's flippancy with their solemnity and

> NOT ONLY THE INTERNAL RELATIONS OF 'THE FLY,' BUT ALSO ITS EXTERNAL RELATIONS TO OTHER POEMS IN THE SEQUENCE ARE AT STAKE IN HOW THE POEM IS CONSTRUED."

repressed dread; the philosopher may be wise to fear a greater power, while the threatening branches trap the fly's speech even as he asserts his freedom. Significantly, in these prints, the nurse and toddler frown. But in later prints, as the tree lightens to a nut-brown and the sky becomes blue and white with the two stanzas against a white cloud, the encircling appears affectionate—an image of intimacy with nature. In these later prints the relative gentleness in the coloring adds a sense of peace to the scene; in these prints, the smiling nurse and child with their circling arms affirm the fly's natural wisdom. Although one can only speculate on the artist's reasons, the gradual alterations in color suggest an early cynicism evolving into an identification with his natural subject. Perhaps Blake's fly won over even Blake.

Source: G. S. Morris, "Blake's 'The Fly,'" in *Explicator*, Vol. 65, No. 1, Fall 2006, pp. 16–18.

Michael Simpson

In the following excerpt, Simpson argues that based on the grammar and word placement of "The Fly," differing interpretations are possible. Further, the graphic presentation in the original chapbook can be seen as suggesting a way to interpret the poem.

There is some critical consensus that Blake's "The Fly" has an ironic sting in its tail.... But I shall argue instead that it is we who are in danger in any encounter with the poem and that this danger originates not in the poem but in ourselves. I shall also propose, however, that the grammar of the poem, along with its formal identity as part of a chapbook, can enable us to recognize our destructive and ultimately self-destructive complicity in the text. It is in my emphasis on the agency of a reader, invoked by the poem, that the difference between my argument and the previous criticism consists.

I

There is, perhaps expectedly, more critical agreement about the poem's plot than there is about the consequences and significance of its "events": the fly always gets to die, and in the rest of the poem it is understood that the narrator's attempt to identify with his victim is variously complicated according to the degree of irony thus read into it. It is, however, this very stability, constituted by a critical consensus about the plot, that I shall challenge by the version of reader-response criticism that follows....

Despite the supposed stability of this poem's plot, the death of the fly and hence the narrator's culpability for it are highly contingent upon how we read the first stanza. What the narrator admits is that he has "brushed away" the fly's "summer's play." Either this admission is a soothing circumlocution for an act of destruction or it is an innocent account of how the narrator merely repelled, accidentally or otherwise, the fly's activity. To convict the narrator on the basis of his self-incrimination, we must first undergo a little jury selection. Virtually all the critics of this poem have established the murder by supplying the body themselves. But did they really get it from the text when the text itself does not definitively state that a death in fact occurred? In order to answer this question about whether the narrator or the reader is the dominant agent in this first stanza, we must, since the extent of the narrator's malefaction is suddenly at issue here, decide how much agency the narrator and the fly possess relative to one another.

However implausible the following scenario within a code of realism, the syntax of the first stanza allows "Thy summer's play" to be either object or subject of the verb "has brushed," and "My thoughtless hand" to be subject or object respectively. Depending on how we resolve the syntax, the narrator kills or repels the fly, or, inversely, the fly's impulsive activity successfully resists the encroaching hand. Whether the narrator or the fly is read as the subject of the verb, the sequence of the sentence, in both its variants, involves an inversion of the conventional word order of prose, so that no objection to the fly as subject can rest on an assumption about word order. Given that there is here no "normal" word order, because the poem is signaling its identity as poetry through the trope of syntactic inversion, we have no way to determine which of the two readings is more or less probable. Even if we suppose that the sequence "Little dog, your ready tooth the mailman's boot has damaged" would tend to be conventionally resolved so that the mailman's boot would be the subject of the sentence, and if we further suppose that this convention of prose syntax might govern the construing of Blake's stanza, installing the "mailman's boot" and the "thoughtless hand" as subject would nonetheless be only the most probable syntax in a range of plausible resolutions we might entertain until the sentence was read to its conclusion. That all critics who have written on the poem seem to understand the "thoughtless hand" as subject does not necessarily deny that there are no other possibilities that might finally be over-ridden at the end of the stanza.

Conditioning my alternative reading of the stanza are numerous instances within the scope of Blake's notoriously versatile syntax of such possible fluctuations of subject and object. In "The Sick Rose," for example, which is another "Song of Experience," the rose may be sick because its life is being destroyed by the worm's "dark secret love" or because this "dark secret love" is being destroyed by the rose's "life."

> O Rose thou art sick!
> The invisible worm,
> That flies in the night,
> In the howling storm,
> Has found out thy bed
> Of crimson joy;
> And his dark secret love
> Does thy life destroy.

The factor that specifically allows "his dark secret love" to be read as the object of "destroy" and "thy life" as the subject, is the rhetorical figure of syntactic inversion called "anastrophe."

What I am emphasizing in this focus on the possible transpositions of subject and object is how the plots of these brief lyrics can be easily and totally transformed and how considerable responsibility thus devolves onto a reader who can be seen to read among opposed options. What happens to the text determines what happens in the text (this continuity is incidentally signaled by the punning title of the poem, for it names an item within the text as well as the text itself). Despite the poem's apparent invocation of a reading subject, however, this subject will not be here elaborated into the familiar and less than sophisticated concept of the naive reader who, by recognizing his or her errors, is progressively educated to become a sophisticated reader. The reading subject I characterize will be such that we would be ingenuous to describe it as either naive or sophisticated. Invoked in the first instance by the polarized interpretive choices that the poem seems to offer, my reader is only as determinate as the choice that it finally makes within this dilemma. Since such a reader is figured by the dilemma only before it is resolved, the text itself provides no indication of which choice this reader must make, or, indeed, whether it must finally make a choice at all. This figured reader could choose either way, or might choose, agnostically, not to choose....

Helping to drive the prevailing interpretation of the poem, in which the fly dies and the narrator identifies with it, are some earlier literary texts that seem to be cited as prototypes by this account of the poem. Whether or not Blake is assumed to have been familiar with these texts, they are certainly available to be cited by the criticism of Blake's poem. One of these texts is William Oldys's lyric "On a Fly Drinking from his Cup":

> BUSY, curious, thirsty fly!
> Drink with me, and drink as I:
> Freely welcome to my cup,
> Couldst thou sip, and sip it up:
> Make the most of life you may,
> Life is short and wears away.
>
> Just alike, both mine and thine,
> Hasten quick to their decline:
> Thine's a summer, mine no more,
> Though repeated to three-score.
> Three-score summers, when they're gone,
> Will appear as short as one.

Oldys's lyric impinges specifically on Blake's text by rehearsing a plot in which the fly dies and thus becomes a determining or legitimating factor in later criticism of "The Fly." By advancing the following simile, the blind Gloucester in *King Lear* similarly establishes the death of a fly and one's consequent identification with it that later criticism of Blake's poem will quote specifically in the context of this passage.

> As flies to wanton boys, are we to th'Gods;
> They kill us for their sport. (2.1. 36–37)

...To quote this excerpt from *King Lear* as part of an account of Blake's poem is, of course, to presume that the fly dies. If, however, the fly is presumed to survive, an equally compelling literary antecedent might be invoked to corroborate this reading. In Chapman's *Iliad*, as the Greeks hesitate in their mission to recover Patroclus's body, Menelaus is said to have a special relation with Pallas:

> ...The king's so royall will
> Minerva joy'd to heare, since she did all the gods outgo
> In his remembrance. For which grace she kindly did bestow
> Strength on his shoulders and did fill his knees as liberally
> With swiftnesse, breathing in his breast the courage of a flie
> Which loves to bite so and doth beare man's bloud so
> much good will
> That still (though beaten from a man) she flies upon him still:
> With such a courage Pallas fild the blacke parts neare his
> hart. (17.485–92)

Unlike the Shakespearean "flies," and for that matter Donne's "flea," which also meets an unceremonious end, the Homeric fly is an epic emblem of action, "courage," and sheer survival. So resourceful is this Homeric fly that Pope, in his edition of the *Iliad*, denies that it can be a fly by effectively mis-translating the Greek word...as "hornet."

II

...Whether condemning the narrator from a vantage of moralistic superiority or approving of him from the perspective of a humane sympathy, the criticism has assumed a distance between itself and the text. This distance is, however, as fictional, or otherwise, as the fly's death, because it depends on the assumption that there is a standpoint from which this death can be confidently predicated. Once the poem's grammar is seen to be at issue, this death and its judicial consequences become just as uncertain as this grammar.

If there are crucial differences between the narrator and the fly, they are constituted, ironically, by the narrator's efforts to urge an identity between the two in order to override differences that otherwise would not be an issue. It is by staging a comparison that the narrator triggers contrasts that threaten to displace the initial comparisons between the two figures. The second stanza canvasses the possibility of this identity, and the next stanza can be read to provide the conditions for it. Apparently connecting the narrator with the fly is the dancing, drinking, and singing that is manifested not only as the thoughtlessness that impels the narrator to destroy, or dismiss, the fly, but also as the fly's "play" that enables the narrator to despatch it. Dancing, drinking, and singing here collapse thoughtlessness, "play," and blindness into an overall unity. The identification with the victim that this unity entails conveniently obviates any question about whether the fly's fate at the hands of the narrator was deliberate or accidental. Whether the narrator's hand was "thoughtless" in the sense of oblivious or whether it committed a deliberate but unreflective act are questions finessed by the supposed identification on the ground of a common impetuosity. If, however, this identification is questioned, either by the narrator or by the reader alone, this discrimination between different degrees of the narrator's motivation is considerably enhanced.

There is a similarly importunate effort to identify with an insect, first alive and then dead, in Donne's "The Flea." This poem entails a manipulative narrator who is about the usual business of seduction. He tries to achieve this goal by a synecdoche identifying the narrator and his potential lover within those "living walls of jet" that comprise a promiscuously blood-sucking flea. Since their bloods have already been mingled, the narrator asks, why not go the whole way? The related doctrines of incarnation, crucifixion, and communion, with which Donne's narrator dices, seem to stand behind Blake's poem too. It is these related doctrines that "The Fly" might be seen to resist as it interrogates the terms of the supposed identification between narrator and fly. All of these doctrines are predicated on a separation between God and Man that an act of sacrifice closes. Just as "The Fly" itself seems to disrupt this formulation, so other works by Blake, such as the first stanza of "The Human Abstract," deny both this separation and the necessity of sacrifice.

The fourth and fifth stanzas can be understood to continue the attempted identification between the narrator and the fly on further grounds. Correlating "thought" and its absence with "life" and "death," and then suggesting that his happiness, as a fly, is already secure, the narrator may be arguing that just as he assures a continued life to the absent fly by thinking about it in the poem, so also is he supplying a perpetuity for himself by thinking of himself and the fly in a poem the reader will read commemoratively. Not only does the reader "think" of the narrator as the narrator "thinks" of the fly, but the narrator and the fly are also ultimately suggested as parallel and thus similar objects of thought for the reader. Characteristic of amatory verse, such as Shakespeare's sonnets 15, 18, and 19, the convention whereby the lyric "I" immortalizes a privileged addressee is deployed here to suggest the intimacy of an identity between narrator and fly. What contradicts the predication of a total identity in the lines "Then am I / A happy fly" is the fact that narrator and fly are constituted as parallel objects of the reader's thought by an initial hierarchy that the narrator constructs and that allows no place for the fly's thought. It is the commemorative thought of the narrator alone that initiates a process of resurrection then underwritten by the reader.

The last two stanzas of "The Fly" and especially the relations between them, have been generally acknowledged as the most enigmatic portions of the poem. Another reading of these stanzas might be just as plausible as the one advanced above: the fourth stanza could be a speculation that "life" may consist only in an awareness of itself, thus precluding any awareness of its absence, while the fifth stanza could be drawing the inference that death is not to be dreaded because it is merely the absence of "thought" about both itself and everything else. If thought is what constitutes a subject in relation to itself as object, the "want" of thought will cancel both subject and object, so that oblivion will be its own consolation. The rhetorical project of these stanzas seems once again to be to urge the narrator's identification with the fly, since he is shown in the process of endorsing its apparent nonchalance about death. And yet again, this identification is highly resistible: only if the subjects "thought" and "want of thought" and their predicates "life" and "death" are read as applicable to both narrator and fly is this identification at all possible. If, on the other hand, we suppose that these subjects and predicates are not all generally applicable to narrator and fly and that it is specifically the narrator's thought or want of it that determines life and death, specifically for the fly, then the alleged identity of the two figures is denied by the unilateral characteristic of the narrator's "thought" about the fly. There is a similar denial of identity if we assume instead that it is the narrator's "thought" that assigns "life," "want of thought," and "death" to the fly. The fourth stanza will support at least three permutations of how these subjects and predicates can be correlated with the fly and the narrator.

What is perhaps most resistant in all of this to my claim of identification is not merely the power that accrues to the narrator's thought in two of the permutations above, but that it is the narrator alone who forms these propositions about "thought" and indeed about everything else in the poem. By appearing as the only discursive subject in the poem, the narrator enacts the unilateral thought that can be read in the fourth stanza. David Wagenknecht, however, suggests a provocative complication of this notion:

> But "The Fly" is unique among the *Songs* in that it is etched in two columns, the first three stanzas in one column and the two-stanza rejoinder to the right, the typographical form suggesting a dialogue with two speakers and perhaps implying "two laws." In fact we can see the last two stanzas as constituting a "reply"... to the first three, the reply of the fly addressed in the first stanza. We assume that the speaker of the final two stanzas is in fact an interlocutionary fiction of the speaker of the first, a fiction resulting from his successful identification with the fly in stanza 2.

III

... If the "thoughtless hand" is read as the hand of the writer or engraver, the complicity of the poem with the destructive act that it claims to investigate could even be registered in the first stanza. The obliteration, or dismissal, of the fly would thus be caused by and partly contemporaneous with the acts of writing and engraving, because the fly would be despatched not before but during the writing. This incriminating proximity of the writing hand to the fly's fate, however, is once again a function of how we construe the relevant lines. Our very attribution to the writing hand of an extreme power over life and death is itself figured, by the starkly alternative reading of the first stanza, as a mere attribution that originates in the more awesome power of the reader. If this reader is to be characterized by features other than the power of choice, which is the property with which the poem itself figures this persona, it is the poem's genre that must supply these elusive details. Signing itself as an instance of the chapbook and hence as a form of morally edifying literature, *Songs of Innocence and of Experience* projects a reader who must be induced by exemplary and cautionary tales to make moral discriminations between those tales. Since the chapbook was a means, in a culture with few books, of teaching literacy as well as moral judgment, the reader it supposes and consequently figures is a persona to whom considerable work is assigned.

So much labor is in fact required of this reader, who must do the work of actually becoming a reader, that the text implies the presence of another, more competent reader who might mediate, on the one hand, between the competence assumed and demanded by the text, and, on the other, the lack of such competence it also assumes of its illiterate or semi-literate addressee. "The Fly," in common with the other poems in the collection, implies an adult reader who must assist a juvenile subject to modulate from non-literacy to the condition of literacy. Explicitly invoking such an adult reader to help her or his junior counterpart is the preface to John Newbery's *A Little Pretty Pocket-Book*, published in 1767. Inscribed at the outset 'TO THE PARENTS, GUARDIANS, AND NURSES IN GREAT-BRITAIN and IRELAND,' this text features a preface that effectively instructs this adult audience how to use the succeeding text, comprising simple fables and morals.

> Would you have a Wise Son, teach him to reason early. Let him read, and make him understand what he reads. No Sentence should be passed over without a strict Examination of the Truth of it; and though this may be thought hard at first, and seem to retard the Boy in his Progress, yet a little Practice will make it familiar, and a Method of Reasoning will be acquired, which will be of use to him all his Life after. (58)

It is just such a practice of not passing over any sentence without "a strict Examination of the Truth of it" that "The Fly" is here being said to invite.

A modification of this scenario of reading, in which the juvenile reader is assisted by an adult, is proposed by Maria Edgeworth's *Harry and Lucy Concluded: Being the Last Part of Early Lessons*. Repeating a proposal featured in other examples of children's literature written by the Edgeworths and that seems thereby to be elevated into a principle, the "PREFACE; ADDRESSED TO PARENTS" makes this recommendation:

Much that would be tiresome and insufferable to young people if offered by preceptors in a didactic tone, will be eagerly accepted when suggested in conversation, especially in conversations between themselves.... The great preceptor, standing on the top of the ladder of learning, can hardly stretch his hand down to the poor urchin at the bottom looking up to him in despair; but an intermediate companion, who is only a few steps above, can assist him with a helping hand, can show him where to put his foot safely; and now urging, now encouraging, can draw him up to any height within his own attainment. (11–13)

This hierarchy of pedagogy, plotted on a vertical axis, is especially pertinent to the tableau depicted in the poem's illustrated plate where the nurse bends down towards the small child, apparently in order to elevate his arms, and the older child aims upwards in an effort to elevate the descending projectile. Whether by means of the bipolar hierarchy characterized in Newbery's preface or by means of the more mediated stratification typical of the Edgeworths' prefaces, children's chapbooks of the eighteenth century invoke a dual audience. Even if we read Blake's poem as a parody of these structural conventions of the chapbook rather than as simply instantiating them, the text still implies a bipartite audience. It is not that Blake's *Songs* in general and this poem in particular invoke these readers literally, but rather that they figure such reading positions symbolically. By identifying itself as a version of the chapbook Blake's *Songs* structurally projects these reading positions.

That these poems formally address themselves both to a juvenile persona and to an adult figure is indicated not only by their often patronizing tone and the simplicity of their vocabulary, which might in any case be purely ironic elements of the text, but also in that earlier instances of the chapbook explicitly target children as a substantial component of their audience. So many pieces of popular literature throughout the eighteenth century and earlier address themselves to children, at least rhetorically, that they seem to compose a fairly stable genre. William Sloane's *Checklist* catalogues 261 such publications, excluding primers designed specifically for use in schools, between 1557 and 1710. The most influential texts of this kind published after 1710 include William Ronksley's *The Child's Week's Work* of 1712, Isaac Watts's *Divine and Moral Songs for Children*, appearing in 1715, and Charles Wesley's *Hymns for Children* of 1763. Significant instances of this genre that appear more immediately before Blake's *Songs* and that might consequently be read as its direct antecedents include the Edgeworth's *Practical Education: The History of Harry and Lucy*, first published in 1780, Mrs. Barbauld's *Lessons for Children from Two to Three Years Old* of 1780, and her *Hymns in Prose for Children* of 1781, Thomas Day's *The History of Sandford and Merton: A Work Intended for the Use of Children*, and the prolific John Newbery's *The History of Tommy Playlove and Jacky Lovebook: wherein is shown the Superiority of Virtue over Vice*, both published initially in 1783. Since many of these works incorporate a preface evidently addressed to adult readers, along with a text that seems specifically targeted on children, the eventuality of co-reading seems to be structurally implied by this form. Even if Blake's *Songs*, and especially "Songs of Experience," is, as I have started to suggest, a parody of the children's chapbook, ironizing its pieties and certitudes by complicating the moral that it is supposed to communicate unproblematically, this parody nonetheless employs the device of team reading that is a feature of the form being satirized. The parody is, therefore, an intimate one. Moreover, such a parody may emphasize this dual readership, because it works by implying both a literal and an ironic reading of the text that might each be correlated with the innocent and more experienced readers invoked by the text's generic identity.

IV

... I suggest that to factor a reading persona into a discussion of "The Fly" is to construct a relation between reader and narrator that can in turn reconstruct the specific relation between narrator and fly that critical consensus has begun to stabilize, but has done so destructively. Insofar as the poem invokes an active and self-conscious reader, any predications made about the poem's narrator will be seen by the predicating reader to reflect on him- or herself. This version of the poem contrasts with certain other critical accounts of it by transferring to the reader any irony that the poem would otherwise be seen to direct at the narrator. Any moral judgments directed by this reader at the narrator will, in the context of a chapbook that works to teach moral discrimination, tend to return as questions about the reader's own ethics in making that moral judgment. Having merely hinted at an alternative narrator who might be constituted by a practice of reading more conscious of its own risks than either Hirsch's congratulation of the narrator or Wagenknecht's indictment, I will now supplement those hints with a fuller characterization that offers a more direct statement of the alternative than this narrator poses.

Whether we read the first stanza so that the fly dies or whether we read the fly deflecting, or at least escaping, the thoughtless hand, the remaining stanzas can provide a narrator who postulates an identification with an actual or potential victim only to question it. The second stanza comprises two questions. These often seem to be understood as merely rhetorical, and as thereby affirmative of their interrogatives, but they might also be something other than rhetorical.

> Am not I
> A fly like thee?
> Or art not thou
> A man like me?

If we assume that the fly survives, then the second-person address in these two questions has a real destination denied if we make the opposite assumption that the fly is dead. To read this stanza so that it is composed of actual questions is to invite ourselves to ask the question of whether they imply a positive answer, as a rhetorical question would, whether they beg a negative response, or whether their motivation is neutral. The relation between the two questions can also be an issue, since the word "Or" (which relates or dislocates these questions) could mean "or to put the same thing another way," but could also mean "or should I formulate this first question in another way?" The second question might be a simple repetition of the first one or it might be an interrogation of it. Depending on whether we read the word "Or" as such a reinforcement or as a questioning of the process of asking these questions, the narrator appears as either assertive or reflective.

How the narrator appears in the third stanza is determined largely by how the drama of the first stanza has been configured. If the fly is presumed to die, the narrator's notion that he resembles it by dancing, drinking, and singing is palpably spurious, since this is exactly what the fly cannot now do. If, however, the fly is allowed to survive and even win the encounter, the narrator's attempt to identify with it becomes an ennobling personification instead of an effort at self-justification by replacing the victim. Assuming a destroyed fly correlates the phrase "dance, / And drink, & sing" with the ironic "dance & sing" of the victimized child in "The Chimney-Sweeper," while assuming a victorious fly identifies the above phrase with the words "drink, & sing" as they form part of the positive proposals made by the juvenile narrator in "The Little Vagabond." Not only the internal relations of "The Fly," but also its external relations to other poems in the sequence are at stake in how the poem is construed.

The narrator of the fourth stanza can be manifested, on the one hand, as a callous, and probably empiricist, philosopher who traffics in such abstract categories as "thought" and "want of thought," or, on the other hand, as a narrator who carefully anatomizes a specific act by allocating the property of "thought" to his own role and "want of thought" to the lot of the fly. And the narrator's recognition of a difference, which is also an inequality, in the whole transaction is foregrounded if we read the condition introduced by "If" as extending only as far as "breath" but excluding "want of thought," so that the stanza comprises not two parallel conditional clauses, but two separate clauses representing "thought" as the narrator's luxurious option and "want of thought" as the fly's probable fate within that luxury. In this reading, the second clause would effectively be a parenthesis between the conditional clause and the main clause that opens the next stanza.

However we construe the fourth stanza, the narrator of the final stanza is either confident of the proposition that he deduces from the premises of that penultimate stanza, whether they be mutually universal or alleged to be applicable to narrator and fly respectively, or he is vulnerably unsure of what conclusion to draw. If we try to reconstruct a hypothetical reading experience of this stanza, we might suppose that the inversion of subject and verb in the line "Then am I" signals the introduction of a question and that the alternative condition staged by the word "or" then compounds this signal by posing a binary opposition within which the narrator is fluctuating, perhaps interrogatively. Only at the end of the sentence, which does not feature a question mark, can this hypothetical reading exclude the eventuality of a question by resolving the syntax into the equally available, but ultimately more probable, format of an indicative statement.

Resolving any momentary alternatives in the sentence into this inevitable indicative format again involves a recourse to the literary trope of anastrophe that allowed the thoughtless hand to brush away the fly and that now enables "am I / A happy fly" to mean "I am a happy fly." The difference between these inversions in the first and final stanzas is that anastrophe insists on its profile as a stylistic form conditioning the grammar far less in the first stanza than it does in the last. It seems that we have less choice about grammar at the end of the poem. What we can recognize, nonetheless, in this final stanza is a momentary manifestation of that more benign and diffident narrator that we can understand the poem as a whole to provide—or at least not to deny. Rather than immediately concluding that his happiness is as independent of his own survival as it is of the fly's, and so proving his case by appearing so insensitive as to be dead, the narrator appears instead, at least for a moment, as one who questions the oblivion of that thoughtlessness which identifies this oblivion with death itself.

Although the poem can be said to provide, at different junctures, thoroughly different narrators who can thus be fashioned into coherent alternatives, there is no necessity that these characters be so rigorously polarized throughout. While the narrator who kills the fly and the one who does not may be mutually exclusive, the destructive narrator is not incompatible with the one who then doubts his or her identification with the victim even as she or he proposes it. The opposed alternatives in the grammar that I have been suggesting need not be correlated to distill a perfect narrator on the one hand and a highly imperfect one on the other, because a narrative of moral progress, or degeneration, can be interpolated to allow less consistent narrators to emerge. While my own reading...invests in the extreme of the virtuous narrator, much of the criticism follows the more promiscuous trajectory, described above, to find a changing narrator....

What compels my reading to commit itself to the extreme of the virtuous narrator, even as it claims to be able to account grammatically for other trajectories, is that none of these readings acknowledges its implication in a grammar that will accommodate a range of options that stops, or starts, with this extreme. Also enjoining a commitment to this extreme reading is its implication that to read otherwise, once this specific choice is constituted, is, first, to participate in the fly's destruction by arranging the grammar so that the narrator kills it and, second, to repeat the crime by assassinating the narrator's character in the same grammatical arrangement. Once we acknowledge an alternative to this grammar, to read otherwise is also to abandon a narrator whom we have abetted in destruction and are now in turn destroying. But we may find at least one obvious objection to the construction of a diplomatic narrator: such diplomacy might be no more than a self-idealization performed by the reader. We behold what we would like to think we are. What answers this objection is that the alternative...produces a self-idealization of the reader that is similar, but actually more reprehensible because contingent on a denigration of the narrator.

The same gestures whereby we deny the reader's agency in the text can be seen in how criticism has treated the illustrated plate of "The Fly," and specifically in its account of the relations between text and illustration.... "The Fly is unique among the *Songs* in that it is etched in two columns" and that the second column is the fly's fictional "rejoinder,"...this typographical departure might allow us to read the poem from left to right and then downwards instead of downwards and then across the page. This is an arrangement that would yield the following sequence:

> Little Fly
> Thy summer's play,
> My thoughtless hand
> Has brush'd away.
>
> If thought is life
> And strength & breath:
> And the want
> Of thought is death;
>
> Am not I
> A fly like thee?
> Or art not thou
> A man like me?
>
> Then am I
> A happy fly,
> If I live,
> Or if I die.
>
> For I dance,
> And drink & sing:
> Till some blind hand
> Shall brush my wing.

... In a sense, this vertical reading is more sensitive to the graphic text than is the suggested horizontal reading. To read vertically may well be to confer a literary authority on the "Notebook," but it is also to accommodate that authority to the exigencies of the graphic image by supposing that the sequence of the lyric is determined, or at least indicated, by the boughs of the two trees as they separate the stanzas horizontally, but allow a space for vertical access between them. There are, however, other plates in "*Songs of Experience*" in which the branches of trees intervene between stanzas without punctuating the reading sequence so stringently. In "The Tyger," for instance, branches figure on a horizontal axis without apparently arresting the reading. Understanding "The Fly" as though its sequence is signaled arboreally presupposes a particular relation between linguistic and graphic text whereby the former is harmoniously framed by the latter; the lyric effectively doubles as the foliage of the trees. Although this graphic profile of the linguistic text is sanctioned by the conventional pun on "leaves," since the term refers to both foliage and pages, there is a signal alternative. Instead of figuring as blooms or leaves and so forming a composite with the graphics, the lyric of "The Fly" might be seen as a displaced skywriting hovering around those graphics with a spatial uncertainty matching the logical indeterminacy of its relation to them.

The significance of a horizontal reading of "The Fly" is that it stages the space between stanzas as a place for the reader-in-the-text who must arbitrate the lyric's sequence. That the stanzas themselves do not lexically resist either of these formal possibilities consolidates the power and responsibility of this reader. The main difference a horizontal configuration of the lyric produces within its plot is a more tentative identification between narrator and fly than that proposed by a vertical reading. While this usually-supposed vertical arrangement asks the questions

> Am not I
> A fly like thee?
> Or art not thou
> A man like me?

immediately after the contact between the fly and the thoughtless hand, the horizontal format prefaces these questions with hypothetical conditions that thus seem to limit the assertiveness of the questions and their implication of an identity. If one of these readings is any more plausible than the other, it seems to me that the horizontal sequence produces a lyric that avoids the problematic transition from the stanza beginning "If thought is life" to the one beginning "Then am I / A happy fly" that many critics consider the most difficult part of the poem.

What licenses the whole focus throughout this essay on matters of grammar is, as already implied, the genre of the chapbook. Like earlier instances of this genre, Blake's *Songs* seems to offer itself as an occasion for the development of reading competence at the same time as it works to inculcate morals. How the *Songs* in turn differs from, say, Isaac Watts's *Divine Songs* or Mrs. Barbauld's *Hymns in Prose for Children* is not by proposing morals more heterodox than those of these earlier works, but by providing a grammar that reflects back conventional moral judgments so that they become questions about the first person ethics of delivering such moral pronouncements. Since "The Fly," specifically, supplies a grammar that can accommodate a presumption of the narrator's innocence, as well as a presumption of his guilt, any judgment that does not recognize its grounding on a mere presumption, whichever way the judgment may ultimately incline, is more destructive than the act that it evaluates. To presume that the narrator is unequivocally innocent is more destructive than the narrator's action, not only because the narrator is, in this scenario, innocent, but also because this scenario is based on an aggressive suppression of any equivocation about this innocence. To presume that the narrator is guilty, however, is more destructive than the guilty action itself because it is a presumption that claims to be predicated on a position of knowledge even as it ignores any contraindications in the grammar. Although an inclination towards either presumption is thus potentially damaging, I have weighted my reading of the poem towards an assumption of innocence because previous critical accounts have inclined towards the opposing premise.

It is not only the poem's grammar that provides a critical perspective on efforts to read it. The format of the children's chapbook also offers a standpoint beyond the text that allows this very standpoint to be observed as it collapses into the poem. By projecting for itself two readers, a child and an adult, the chapbook allows for a reading persona able to observe itself because it is composed of two parts. In this image of a reading persona, just as an adult oversees the difficulties a child might be expected to encounter in construing the text and interpreting the moral, so any difficulties that this adult might confront in this moral grammar are monitored by the child. Each of these reading positions seems to watch the other becoming absorbed into the text. While projected by the genre of the children's chapbook, this scenario of mutual scrutiny is also depicted in the graphic in the intersecting gazes of the woman and child. Since to read the poem is also to watch oneself reading, because of the mutual monitoring implied by the chapbook's pedagogy, whereby child and adult observe one another's reading practices, the educational process can become a two-way street in which experience is not only taught to the child by the adult, but innocence is reciprocally conveyed to the adult by the child. Enabled to watch ourselves reading the poem, we need not gain our experience of the text at a cost borne by the fly and the narrator. Subject to an invigilation from the perspective of innocence, the reading experience can avoid guilt by allowing the fly to survive and by consequently exonerating the narrator.

Whether this adult reader of Blake's *Songs* is understood as an agent mediating between a real chapbook and a juvenile narrator or as the ultimate destination of a chapbook that is childless because a parody of the genre, these are questions that do not affect the *Songs*' figuring of a dual readership. Either way, this text affords a critical perspective on how it is read by implying, parodically or otherwise, this dual audience. It is, moreover, this inherent faculty of self-monitoring that prevents such a model of reading from immediately resembling those other critical readings, castigated above, that seek to empower themselves over the text. None of my argument is to imply, of course, that the poem cannot be read, as it has tended to be, so that a costly experience, rather than innocence, is what the narrator and reader exchange between themselves. My own reading is not concerned to disqualify other readings, but rather to indicate their cost.... "The Fly" could ... be a traffic in mutually destructive and self-destructive experience. Once the question "Whodunit?" is posed about events in "The Fly," however, the versatile grammar of the poem and the self-monitoring reading persona offered by the form of the chapbook answer this question with another: "Who didn't?"

Source: Michael Simpson, "Who Didn't Kill Blake's Fly: Moral Law and the Rule of Grammar in *Songs of Experience*," in *Style*, Vol. 30, Summer 1996, pp. 220–40.

SOURCES

Advertisement, in *The Complete Illuminated Books*, Thames & Hudson, 2000, back cover.

Beer, F. B., "William Blake," in *British Writers*, Vol. 3, edited by Ian Scott-Kilvert, Charles Scribner's Sons, 1979.

Blake, William, "The Fly," in *The Complete Illuminated Books*, Thames & Hudson, 2000, p. 82; originally self-published by William Blake in *Songs of Experience*, 1794.

Eliot, T. S., "Blake," in *Critics on Blake*, compiled by Judith O'Neill, University of Miami Press, 1988, pp. 24–25, originally published in *The Sacred Wood: Essays on Poetry and Criticism*, Methuen, 1920.

Frye, Northrup, "Introduction," in *Selected Poetry and Prose of Blake*, edited by Northrup Frye, Modern Library, 1953, p. xiv.

Gardner, Stanley, *The Tyger, The Lamb, and the Terrible Desart*, Cygnus Arts, 1998, p. 101.

Marsh, Nicholas, *William Blake: The Poems*, Palgrave, 2001, pp. 42–43.

Morris, G. S., "Blake's 'The Fly,'" in *Explicator*, Vol. 65, No. 1, Fall 2006, pp. 17, 18.

Richardson, Alan, "William Blake," in *British Children's Writers, 1800–1880*, edited by Meena Khorana. *Dictionary of Literary Biography*, Vol. 163, Detroit: Gale Research.

FURTHER READING

Ackroyd, Peter, *Blake*, Sinclair-Stevenson, 1995.
This biography describes the city of London as Blake knew it, his tradesman's life, and the social upheaval of his times.

Applebaum, Stanley, ed. *English Romantic Poetry: An Anthology*, Dover, 1996.
This anthology, suitable for a high school class, contains 123 poems by the six leading romantic poets: Blake, Wordsworth, Coleridge, Byron, Shelley, and Keats. Brief introductions are given for each poet's work.

Bloom, Harold, *William Blake*, Modern Critical Views, Chelsea House, 1985.
The Blake volume from the Bloom young adult series on famous authors provides a biography and the chronology of Blake's life as well as

critical essays by twentieth-century experts with various approaches to literary analysis.

Gilchrist, Alexander, *Life of William Blake*, Dover, 1998.
The book that saved Blake from obscurity is Gilchrist's exhaustive 1863 biography. This work is still essential reading for Blake scholars, although it is written in Victorian-era language. The book shaped Blake's legacy for twentieth-century readers, in part because Gilchrist was able to contact people who knew Blake.

Marsh, Nicholas, *William Blake: The Poems*, Palgrave, 2001.
This book gives direction on how to interpret Blake, with emphasis on *Songs of Innocence and Experience*. It provides an easy-to-read chapter on the poet's life and works, along with three critical essays and suggestions for further study.

O'Neill, Judith, comp., *Critics on Blake*, University of Miami Press, 1970.
This collection of criticism includes twenty-two excerpts from notables such as William Butler Yeats and T. S. Eliot in the period between 1803 and 1841, then a section of complete critical essays written up to 1969. Blake's imagery, ideas, techniques, and much more are covered, including a look at the relationship of *Songs of Experience* to the London of its times.

Porter, Roy, *English Society in the Eighteenth Century*, 2nd ed., Penguin, 1990.
Porter describes the eighteenth-century England in which Blake lived, covering various aspects of life in the villages and cities, including foods, entertainment, jobs, wages, housing, prisons, and social status.

Grandmother

VALZHYNA MORT
2008

Valzhyna Mort made her American debut with *Factory of Tears*, the first Belarusian-American publication in the United States. "Grandmother," a poem in this collection, is a tribute to the poet's own grandmother, Janina, to whom the collection is dedicated. Mort's grandmother suffered through collectivization in Belarus during the Stalinist era.

In "Grandmother," Mort presents a compelling portrait of a grandmother, noting the elderly woman's positive values and suggesting through the imagery the suffering she has experienced. The speaker simultaneously recognizes the physical vulnerability of her grandmother as she ages. Through the use of figurative language, the speaker admires the strength of her grandmother's physical resolve yet questions a world—as well as God's presence in it—where such hardships occur. As a *Blue Flower Arts* review of *Factory of Tears* states, "The music of lines and litanies of phrases mesmerize the reader, then sudden discord reminds us that Mort's world is not entirely harmonious."

Women of two generations are juxtaposed in the poem, and the speaker is unable to reconcile the differences between the two. Ultimately, "Grandmother" reinforces the power of family. However, it also hints at the effects of historical events and religion in forming cultural and personal identity.

AUTHOR BIOGRAPHY

Valzhyna Mort was born Valzhyna Martynava in 1981, in Minsk, Belarus, to Gennady Martynava, a manager in the industrial sector and former soccer player, and Tatsiana Martynava, an economist. She eventually adopted the last name Mort, an abbreviated family name and a childhood nickname, and one under which she published her early and subsequent verse. Mort was drawn to literature at a young age because of her parents' extensive library, and as a result, she early on developed a positive connection to books.

Another key influence during Mort's early years was her grandmother, Janina. Following Soviet tradition, Mort spent her childhood summers with her grandmother in the countryside. The two grew increasingly close, and Janina later moved in with the family. She eventually became a catalyst for some of Mort's poetry.

Mort's interest in poetry grew out of her early interest in the theater and music. In 1997, she aspired to being a musician and practiced for several years on the accordion. She received training at the Belarusian State Theatre of Opera and Ballet, a performing arts institution for children. During this time, she continued taking accordion lessons; however, despite her dedication to the instrument, she had difficulty composing music and turned to writing poetry at the age of eighteen. Although Russian is Mort's native tongue, she wrote her poems in Belarusian, because of its musical qualities and rhythm. She had also grown attached to speaking Belarusian during her childhood.

Mort soon became acquainted with a small circle of writers who resisted writing in Russian, creating instead works in Belarusian in an attempt to preserve the language. She objected to attempts to render the language obsolete made by Belarus's Russian president Alexander Lukashenko, but Mort claimed her decision to write in Belarusian was a personal choice rather than a political protest.

Along with her early venture into writing, Mort read extensively, especially works by Polish and Russian poets. Mort began to translate works by Rafal Wojaczek and Ewa Lipski into Belarusian. She also studied and translated works by William Butler Yeats and Ted Hughes.

During her studies at Minsk State Linguistic University, where she received her degree in English, Mort continued to write poetry in Belarusian. Between 2000 and 2004, she published several of her poems in various literary magazines and anthologies, including *Anthology of Belarusian Poetry* and *A Poem for Liberty*. Her poems caught the attention of Boom-Bum-Lit, a small group of writers specializing in poetry performances, and its members invited her to read her work at various festivals in and around Belarus. Word of her stage presence and dramatic performance spread rapidly. In 2004, reviews of her performances led to her being given the Crystal Vilenica Award, a top honor bestowed upon a writer for best poetry reading.

In 2005, Mort's first book of Belarusian poems, *I'm as Thin as Your Eyelashes*, was published in Minsk to critical acclaim. At a later performance in Galway, Ireland, she met Franz Wright, a Pulitzer Prize-winning poet, who encouraged her to translate her work into English. At Wright's suggestion, Mort submitted her manuscript to Michael Wiegers, a top American editor for Copper Canyon Press. Soon thereafter, Mort moved to the United States, married Joseph Cortese, a record label executive, and continued to work closely with Wright and his wife, Elizabeth, translating her poems into English. In 2006, she was awarded the Gaude Polonia stipendium in Poland and was later a poet-in-residence at Literarisches Colloquium in Berlin, Germany.

Mort made her much anticipated American debut in 2008 with her second collection of poems, *Factory of Tears*, published by Copper Canyon Press. With this publication, which featured stark portraits of Eastern Europe's violent past, she established her reputation as an international talent. Mort dedicated the collection to her grandmother and poems such as "Grandmother" and "Belarusian I" demonstrated Mort's emotional attachment to her. *Factory of Tears* was co-translated by Mort and Franz and Elizabeth Wright. It was the first bilingual Belarusian-English work of poetry published in the United States and was subsequently translated into Swedish and German. Praise for this collection led to Mort's receiving the Burma Poetry Prize in Germany.

In addition to writing, Mort also gave lectures that focused on the intricate relationship between language, politics, and the poetry of anti-communist revolutions in Eastern Europe that took place between 1970 and 1990. Additional poems by Mort, as well as her translations of selected Eastern European poets, were included in the anthology *New European Poets*, published by Graywolf Press in 2008.

Mort was the youngest person to be featured on the May–June 2008 cover of *Poets & Writers*. As of 2009, she resided in Alexandria, Virginia, and taught creative writing at the University of Baltimore.

POEM TEXT

```
my grandmother
doesn't know pain
she believes that
famine is nutrition
poverty is wealth                                5
thirst is water

her body like a grapevine winding around a walking
    stick
her hair bees' wings
she swallows the sun-speckles of pills
and calls the internet the telephone to america  10

her heart has turned into a rose the only thing you
    can do
is smell it
pressing yourself to her chest
there's nothing else you can do with it
only a rose                                      15

her arms like stork's legs
red sticks
and i am on my knees
howling like a wolf
at the white moon of your skull                  20
grandmother
i'm telling you it's not pain
just the embrace of a very strong god
one with an unshaven cheek that scratches when he
    kisses you                                   25
```

POEM SUMMARY

"Grandmother" opens with two short lines, offering a simple, declarative statement about the speaker's grandmother's philosophy on pain. The speaker notes the irony in her grandmother's claim that she has not experienced pain, despite the hardships endured in her past. A series of juxtaposed, conflicting images follows in lines 4 through 6, which convey the grandmother's beliefs. First, she equates a lack of food to nourishment. Then, the stanza closes

MEDIA ADAPTATIONS

- Borders presents an online poetry series, *Open-door Poetry*, at http://www.bordersmedia.com/odp/mort.asp (accessed July 20, 2009), which features Valzhyna Mort reading "Teacher" from *Factory of Tears* in English and Belarusian.
- A video of an interview with Mort, conducted while she was performing in New York, is available at http://www.pw.org/content/poet_valzhyna_mort_american_debut (accessed July 20, 2009). This interview includes the poet reading "Belarusian I" from *Factory of Tears*.

with the image of deprivation perceived as riches and thirst as water.

These images are references to the grandmother, who has lived a long life and suffered during hard times when there was not enough to eat or drink.

The grandmother's philosophy seems shaped by her faith. This influence becomes evident in the conflicting images presented in the poem's opening stanza, which suggest that the grandmother, surprisingly, has not chosen to interpret her past as painful. Without bitterness and relying on her faith, she values the life she has and does not take it for granted. The poet seems to struggle to harmonize the knowledge of this past and the pain she knows her own grandmother endured during the Stalin era

In stanza 2, lines 7 and 8, the poem shifts to the speaker's physical description of her grandmother, enriched by figurative language. First, the image of a vineyard's grape plant climbing up its trellis is likened to her grandmother's body. This image suggests the grandmother's rural upbringing. The speaker describes the trellis as a stick used for walking. This image hints that the speaker also recognizes the physical vulnerability of her grandmother. Mort then focuses her attention on the grandmother's hair, comparing it to the wings of a bee, perhaps lessening the uncomfortable image of her grandmother growing older.

In lines 9 and 10, Mort echoes the speaker's previous thoughts concerning her grandmother's mortality. First, the speaker again recognizes her grandmother's declining health, despite her fortitude. She alludes to the medication the grandmother takes, yet attaches an unexpected, life-affirming image to it. Through metaphor, she associates pills with flecks of sunlight. This incongruous imagery is consistent with that presented in stanza 1. The speaker then somewhat abruptly interjects a modern reference in line 10, giving the first concrete connection of the grandmother to modernity and to the speaker. The grandmother, still residing in Eastern Europe, views the Internet as a phone call to her granddaughter who lives in the United States. This not only emphasizes the geographical distance between the two people, but highlights their generational divide—the grandmother remains rooted in old ways, while the speaker apparently has moved on to the United States and now enjoys a cosmopolitan, Western lifestyle.

The tone shifts in stanza 3, as the speaker equates the grandmother's heart with a rose, a traditional symbol of love. Te speaker acknowledges that this is the essence of her grandmother's character, despite the cruel realities of her past. Regardless of the speaker's own difficulty in fully comprehending and possibly adopting her grandmother's philosophy on life, she concedes that her grandmother's character remains unchanged, and she offers no argument.

Lines 16 and 17 in the closing stanza return to an image of the grandmother's physical state. The speaker describes her grandmother's legs as sticklike, like those of a stork. Although a stork is often viewed as a folk symbol for childbirth, Mort uses the image here as a sign of frail health. She moves back and forth between an image of tenderness, as seen in stanza 3, and recognition that the grandmother is perhaps near death yet still harbors no ill will toward the world.

The poem then builds to a climax: The speaker throws herself at the feet of her grandmother. It is at once an image of humility and defiance as she likens herself to a howling wolf. She marvels at her grandmother's faith and her ability to use past trials as lessons for the future, yet she has trouble accepting a world in which such trials occur. She then addresses her grandmother directly, expressing her own definition of pain through a provocative, closing image of a humanized God. She boldly tells her grandmother that pain is the hug of a powerful, bearded God who leaves a scratch when he kisses a face. Subtly challenging her grandmother's religious beliefs, she offers a non-traditional vision of God as a strong, bearded man who is loving yet able to inflict pain. This acknowledgement of pain, and the deity's role in it, serves as the speaker's response to those beliefs of the grandmother offered in the opening stanza.

Overall, the poet pays homage to the strength of her grandmother, reinforcing the importance of family relationship and heritage. However, in this poem, she is dubious of a deity that can inflict pain in a gesture supposed to be of love. She also examines the power of memory and its role in shaping an old woman's identity and by extension, that of her granddaughter.

THEMES

Family Ties

"Grandmother" stresses the value and influence of cross-generational family ties, represented in the relationship between the speaker and her grandmother. The speaker, as she presses herself against her grandmother's heart and later throws herself at her feet, depicts herself as a child seeking comfort. They are bound together by blood and cultural ties, yet they face separate challenges because their experiences are different and they are different ages. Despite being in touch with modern ways (suggested in the reference to the Internet), the speaker remains firmly invested in her grandmother and her history, with which she identifies. Although she challenges her grandmother's religious beliefs because of her own doubts about God, her love and respect for her grandmother is evident.

How Experience Shapes Character

The poem suggests the effect of past experiences in shaping identity. The grandmother's philosophy that hunger is food, thirst is water, and poverty is opulence implies that she has learned to make do with what she has, to see the good side in a meager existence. She claims not to know pain that would come from starvation and poverty; instead, she denies its existence and bravely perseveres with optimism and

TOPICS FOR FURTHER STUDY

- Use the style and content of Valzhyna Mort's "Grandmother" as a model for creating an original poem of your own. Use first person point of view to describe the essence of your own grandmother and her legacy to you. Use imagery, simile, and metaphor when possible to describe your grandmother's physical traits and personality. If possible, include an important experience from her past that shaped her character.

- Read Gwendolyn Brooks's "My Grandmother Is Waiting for Me to Come Home" and "Saints" by Louis Glück. Examine how the grandmothers are portrayed in these poems and the effect they have on the each poem's speaker. Write an essay in which you compare and contrast the grandmothers (for example, by comparing the language used to describe the women) in these two poems to the grandmother in Mort's poem. Discuss what thematic connections can be made between the three poems concerning family, heritage, and personal identity.

- A central theme in "Grandmother" is the effect of past experiences on shaping personal identity. This subject is treated in the visual arts, too. Romare Bearden, a twentieth-century African American artist, who worked primarily with collage, explored similar ideas. According to Neda Ulaby, author of the National Public Radio article, "The Art of Romare Bearden: Collages Fuse Essence of Old Harlem, American South," "Shortly before he died of cancer in 1988, Bearden said working with fragments of the past brought them into the now." About these echoes of slavery and images of the South, Ulaby writes, "each piece of a Bearden collage has meaning and history all its own." Conduct further research on the work of Romare Bearden, and study a selection of his collages. Then make a collage that illustrates your past as well as your present. You can use clipart, photos, and magazine and newspaper clippings. Then write a short response paper in which you discuss the meaning and history behind each piece included in the collage and how the pieces join together to create your distinct identity.

- Read Albert Einstein's essay "The World as I See It," paying special attention to his philosophy regarding the mysteries and dangers of daily life, the greater human purpose, and the existence of a higher being. Using Einstein's perspective, consider how these ideas could be connected with those presented in "Grandmother." Consider the grandmother's philosophy regarding her memories of pain, how this shapes her present view of the world, and how this affects the speaker. Einstein's essay can be found in *Ideas and Opinions, based on Mein Wiltbild*, edited by Carl Seeling and published by Bonanza Books in 1954, pages 8–11.

---

hope. The images of the grapevine and the rose charactcrize the grandmother as being tenacious and loving, despite loss and cruelty. She continues to hold on (like a vine) and her nature is loving (like the symbolic meaning in a rose). Ultimately, the portrait of the grandmother is one of a strong woman who has been shaped by the goodness in her heart and by the hardships of the past and present.

Aging

Various images emphasize the grandmother's physical fragility despite her stalwart spirit. She takes pills to combat illness; her body, although likened to a vine, needs a stick for support; her legs are reed-thin like those of a stork; and her head is skull-like. Although these details could be viewed as harbingers of death, the poet couples them with life-affirming images that mitigate the

A Russian grandmother (Image copyright Konstantin Sutyagin, 2009. Used under license from Shutterstock.com)

darker ones. For example, her medicine is shaped like small pieces of sunlight. Her stick indicates she is mobile. She is connected to a symbol of childbirth and motherhood with the image of the stork. And, although her head is skull-like, the speaker links it to a bright moon, which is astrologically symbolic of family and home life.

Concept of Deity

The poem ends with a somewhat jarring image of God personified as a man in need of a shave, who scrapes the cheeks of those he hugs. The speaker claims that this God is her idea of a supreme being, one that paradoxically inflicts pain at the same time it embraces. The image challenges the grandmother's denial of God's responsibility for her own suffering. The oblique biblical references in the imagery, including grapevine and rose, suggest that the grandmother's present philosophy is informed by her belief in a merciful God. For example, her heart, likened to a rose, is connected with the scriptural reference of the rose of Sharon, a religious symbol that signifies unconditional love and perfection in nature.

STYLE

Paradox

In the opening stanza, the speaker presents her grandmother's philosophy on life in a series of paradoxes (explicit and unresolved contradictions). The grandmother denies the existence of pain. She believes that to starve and to need water is to be well fed. She also claims that to experience destitution is to be truly rich. This use of paradox indicates both the resilience and the resignation in the grandmother, survival skills that evolved as a result of harsh experiences. At the same time, these paradoxes express the conflict within the speaker as she at once admires and is skeptical of her grandmother's tough attitudes. This conflict is conveyed in the image of the speaker crying at her grandmother's feet like a howling wolf.

Personification

Personification is a figure of speech in which an abstraction is given human form. In this poem personification is used to characterize deity. God is depicted as an unshaven man who chafes the faces of those he embraces. By assigning human qualities to the deity, the speaker reduces God to an imperfect human being, one who hurts others in gestures of love.

Simile

To describe the grandmother's physical characteristics, Mort uses similes. Similes are explicit comparisons between unlike things, using the word *like* or *as*. The speaker likens her grandmother's body to that of a vine supported by a walking stick. The vine is supported by a trellis, as an elderly person is supported by a cane. This simile suggests that the grandmother has found enough support to move on with her life. It simultaneously hints at the grandmother's frailty and her vulnerability. She clings to the cane. The speaker marvels at grandmother's spirit but also is acutely aware of her mortality.

Another simile compares the grandmother's legs to those of a stork. Her legs are thin, straight, sinewy, and red, all of which conveys the grandmother's age. Yet storks are associated with childbirth and nurturing. They are also known to be protective guardians of their nests. The speaker, albeit briefly, becomes a vulnerable child again, with her grandmother acting as protector.

In the third simile, the speaker compares her own crying to a howling wolf in the night. She is humbled, yet kneeling down seems to be a mixture of defiance and despair. The speaker attempts to reconcile her aging grandmother's past with the present, and she questions her own worldview and the existence of God in an imperfect world.

Metaphor

Metaphors are implied comparisons between unlike things. For example, the poet compares the grandmother's medication to tiny pieces of sunlight. Her pills, evidence of an ailment, are associated with the bright sun, an invigorating image that lessens the uncomfortable picture of ill health. The pills are like bits of vitamins, strengthening her. Immediately following this comparison is one that connects the grandmother to modern technology. Here, the grandmother sees the Internet only as a telephone that can connect her to her granddaughter in the United States. The grandmother sees the modern invention only in terms of how she uses it. She does not understand the global network, World Wide Web, but she does understand how to call her granddaughter.

Finally, the grandmother's heart is said to have become a rose. The speaker tenderly describes the grandmother's essence. There are no jarring images juxtaposed with this very gentle depiction. Although the speaker still has not come to terms with her grandmother's past, she gives in, momentarily, to her. She realizes that pressing herself against her grandmother's heart, much like a child would, is all that can be done.

HISTORICAL CONTEXT

The Stalin Era (1928–1953)

Vladimir Lenin died in 1924. The next person to assume power in the Soviet Union was Joseph Stalin (1878–1953), a self-proclaimed nationalist, who endeavored to propped Russian pride by aggressively endorsing the nation's history, political and cultural heroes, and language. Later in 1924, the Soviet Union enacted a constitution that established a dictatorship and public, rather than private, rights to property. In 1928, the first Five-Year Plan was adopted, which outlined rigid regulations for industrialization. Stalin ordered forced collectivization of agriculture and overcame strong, often violent resistance, particularly in the Ukraine and Belarus. Farms were destroyed, property and possessions were confiscated, peasant farmers were abused, arrested, and millions were sent to labor camps in Siberia. Collectivization resulted in the famine of 1932 and 1933, which killed over seven million Ukrainians.

Anti-Communism, the Solidarity Movement, and the Poetry of Revolution

On August 31, 1980, a strike at the Lenin Shipyard in Gdansk, Poland, was organized and led by Lech Walesa. Over 17,000 workers protested high food prices and also advocated for a self-governed trade union. After over two weeks of meetings with the communist government of Poland, the Solidarity independent trade union was formed. The solidarity movement subsequently played a large role in bringing an end to Soviet communism.

During this volatile period, restrictions on speech prevented many poets from writing, publishing, and reading poems in public. However, some writers, including Ewa Lipska, bravely voiced anti-Communism sentiments. Lipska's often ironic poetry, including "When Our Enemies

Minsk, Belarus *(Image copyright Dontsov Evgeny Victorovich, 2009. Used under license from Shutterstock.com)*

Fall Asleep" and "If There Is a God," addresses Eastern Europe's violent past and questions the existence and role of God.

Collapse of the Soviet Union and Independence of Belarus

In 1989, when Mort was just eight years old, the Lithuanian Communist Party claimed independence from the Soviet Communist Party, spurring other Baltic states to follow suit. In 1990, after leaving the Soviet Communist Party, Boris Yeltsin (1931–2007) became president of the Russian Socialist Republic. Mikhail Gorbachev (1931–) resigned as president of the Soviet Union in 1991, when the Congress of People's Duties voted for the Soviet Union to be dismantled. Leaders of Russia, Ukraine, and Belarus drafted and signed legislation that formed the Commonwealth of Independent States.

Although Belarus attained independence in 1991, it still maintained close ties with Russia concerning governmental and economic policies. As a result, a sense of Belarus as a cultural and national identity, apart from Russia, had never been clearly established. In 1994, when Mort was a young teenager, Alexander Lukashenko (1954–) became Belarus's first president. Despite widespread hope for democratic reform in government, Lukashenko's power was considered to be largely authoritarian, with its rigid restrictions on speech and exercise of religion. Despite Belarusian being declared the state language, Lukashenko discouraged its use in public and in educational settings because it is the language of the peasant class, the poor, and the uneducated.

CRITICAL OVERVIEW

Before her first collection of poems, *I'm as Thin as Your Eyelashes*, was published in 2005, Mort was internationally recognized as a performance poet. As quoted on the back of *Factory of Tears*, the *Irish Times* reported that the young writer "dazzled all who were fortunate to hear her." After hearing Mort read at a poetry festival in Ireland, her soon-to-be co-translator Franz Wright was quoted in *Poets & Writers* as saying, "She's electrifying." In *Poetry*, Wright commented again on her reading: "I'd seldom witnessed a performance of such charismatic authenticity and power."

Mort's much heralded American debut of *Factory of Tears* in 2008, in which "Grandmother" appears, solidified her reputation as a poet to be read and heard in the United States. A review in the *New Yorker* acknowledged that Mort "strives to be an envoy for her native country, writing with almost alarming vociferousness about the struggle to establish a clear identity for Belarus and its language." As in Europe, Mort continued to impress American audiences with dramatic readings from this collection. Kevin Nance, author of "You Cannot Tell This to Anybody," a *Poets & Writers* feature story on Mort, was struck by the poet's style and delivery: "Her feet planted, her eyes fixing the audience, her voice is rich, expressive, clarion strong."

The *Belarusian Review* described Mort's voice in *Factory of Tears* as "visceral, wistful, bittersweet, and dark." Michael Wiegers, executive editor of Copper Canyon Press, is quoted by Nance as saying: "There's a voice there that you don't encounter in much contemporary American poetry." Wiegers continued: "There's something of Andrei Codrescu's early voice, I think, an attractively ironic tone." Finally, a review in *Publishers Weekly*, though not wholly positive, found the collection "decidedly exciting" and its poetry conveying "a ragged power."

CRITICISM

Wendy Perkins

Perkins is a professor of English at Prince George's Community College in Maryland and has had several articles published on American and British literature. In the following essay, she examines the biblical subtext in the imagery in "Grandmother."

In "Grandmother," Valzhyna Mort presents the unique relationship between a grandmother and her granddaughter as she focuses on the former's strength as a survivor. The complexity of this bond becomes apparent as the speaker attempts to reconcile her grandmother's difficult past with her present optimism. Mort explores this complexity in the poem through plaintive, stark, and riveting imagery. Perhaps the most striking image is one that occurs in the final stanza—God as an unshaven man who unwittingly scrapes the cheek of one whom he embraces. This jarring image is initially perplexing since prior images in the poem, such as vine, rose, stork, wolf, and moon, appear to have no religious significance, thereby making the depiction of the personified God much more isolated and resonant. However, after a closer examination of the poet's grandmother's history and its connection to Eastern Orthodoxy, a biblical subtext emerges. Mort's imagery hints at scripture from the Old and New Testament that emphasizes the grandmother's morals as well as aspects of her character.

A look at Mort's grandmother's violent past and subsequent survival under the rule of Stalin

> THE IMAGE OF THE WOLF THREATENING THE FLOCK IS HAUNTING; THE GRANDDAUGHTER AS WOLF CHALLENGES HER GRANDMOTHER'S BELIEF SYSTEM, YET IS HUMBLED BY HER, AS SHE LIES AT HER FEET."

is key to an understanding of the character of the grandmother in Mort's poem. During the Stalinist era (1928–1953), those who enforced collectivization waged a battle against peasant farmers in Belarus and the Ukraine. Stalin and Soviet forces confiscated and destroyed farms, including the one belonging to Mort's grandmother, and they campaigned to eliminate Belarusian and Ukrainian cultural institutions and Eastern Orthodox religion. Eastern Orthodox churches, which were central to community life in villages where Janina (Mort's grandmother) lived, were forced to close and priests were jailed. Church bells, a powerful voice of solidarity within the community, were removed. Despite these acts of oppression, the people of Belarus, including the poet's grandmother and her family, maintained their faith, clinging to the Old and New Testament and remaining strong and resistant.

The poem reveals that the grandmother's values are shaped by her past along with her spiritual convictions that now guide her adult life. Her claim that she does not recognize pain as part of her history is presented in a series of conflicting images, offered in the first stanza, which characterize her philosophy: to have a dearth of food and water is to have a healthy body, and to have a lack of money is considered plentiful.

This pattern of contradictory statements concerning hunger and poverty is found in various places throughout the Bible. In Isaiah 29:19, it is written that "The meek shall obtain fresh joy in the Lord, and the poor among men shall exult in the Holy One of Israel." Similarly in Luke 6:20–23, God prophecies that the poor, rather than the rich, will inherit heaven, and those who are hungry will be satisfied. Later verses in Luke also give a warning to those who are wealthy and

WHAT DO I READ NEXT?

- In "Belarusian I," another poem in *Factory of Tears*, the poet uses the point of view and voice of a person her grandmother's age. Here, the speaker confronts memories of her family's farm being destroyed and the poverty and hunger encountered during collectivization. The speaker in the poem addresses the struggle to maintain her family's identity by speaking Belarusian rather than Russian, even while the Soviet government attempts to stigmatize Belarusian as the language of uneducated peasants.

- In "You see your life as something borrowed," from *Factory of Tears*, the speaker reflects on and questions her grandmother's religious beliefs, which inform her sense that life is to be valued. The speaker boldly claims that her grandmother's life should be the model by which God lives. She then imagines God writing a letter to her grandmother, imploring her to teach him about mankind.

- "My Grandmother Is Waiting for Me to Come Home," a poem by Gwendolyn Brooks, published in 1967 in *In Montgomery and Other Poems*, addresses the strong bond between an African American grandmother and granddaughter, as the two engage in an afternoon ritual of eating apples and walnuts in an impoverished one-room apartment. The work explores how the family discovers its heritage while fostering community.

- "Saints," a poem by Louise Glück, written in 1990 and published in a collection entitled *Ararat*, compares the speaker's grandmother and her aunt. The poet uses images from the Hebrew Bible and connects them with the grandmother, while the Greek idea of fate is used to portray the aunt. Juxtaposition of spiritual and mythical imagery highlights the struggles, often violent, of the two women and demonstrates the depth of familial ties.

- *Grand Mothers: Poems, Reminiscences, and Short Stories About the Keepers of our Tradition*, published in 1996, is Nikki Giovanni's Young Adult collection of stories and poems about grandmothers, as retold to her by close friends, including Gwendolyn Brooks and Maxine Hong Kingston. Giovanni also includes recollections from writers over 90 years of age. The work attempts to honor grandmothers of all cultures who are keepers of legacies and traditions and who cultivate pride in their heritage.

- *Black Candle: Poems About Women from India, Pakistan, and Bangladesh*, published in 2000, is a collection of poetry by Chitra Banerjee Divakaruni, describing the often complicated life and experiences of South Asian women. The poetry's bicultural viewpoint, which depicts the trials and triumphs of being an immigrant woman, resonate with many readers.

---

well fed: "But woe to you that are rich, for you have received your consolation. Woe to you that are full now, for you shall hunger." Matthew 5:1–7 echoes the sentiments of Luke yet presents scripture that uses the meaning of poor, hunger, and thirst in a figurative context. Here, those who are "poor in spirit" and who "hunger and thirst for righteousness" are reassured that they will be satisfied and amply rewarded in heaven.

Mort's grandmother was heavily influenced by scripture as a child, and, as a survivor of collectivization, she later applied these tenets to her core values. It seems logical to assume the poet had her own grandmother in mind when she wrote this poem. In it, the grandmother refuses to acknowledge that the only view of her traumatic past is that she experienced pain; therefore, she denies its existence. Instead, she chooses to believe in the reward of endurance. Her hunger, thirst, and destitution ultimately equate to eternal salvation, and this belief gives her hope. She does not dwell on those who inflicted abuse, for she believes that they will have to answer to God.

In the second stanza, the poet uses the image of the grapevine, which harkens back to her own grandmother's childhood spent on her farm, where the poet's parents cultivated grapes. This image also has a biblical significance. References to grapes (and to wine that is made from them) can be found throughout the Bible. Particularly in the New Testament, which Eastern Orthodoxy predominantly uses, grapevines are symbolic of rebirth and fertility associated with Israel, God's promised land to his people. In John 15:1–2, Jesus says, "I am the true vine, and my Father is the vinedresser... every branch that does bear fruit He prunes, that it may bear more fruit." Eastern Orthodoxy urges followers to live a Christ-like life and to love unconditionally. Here, the grandmother in the poem is likened to a vine, is one with Christ. She has risen above her adversity, much like Christ did, and harbors no ill will. The notion of rebirth, of "bear[ing] more fruit," may suggest the grandmother's wish to pass down these beliefs to her granddaughter, thereby continuing her legacy.

The next stanza finds the speaker reflecting upon the essence of her grandmother's character through a description of her heart, which she believes has become a flower. The choice of a rose, often considered the perfect bloom and a traditional symbol of love, is poignant. It emphasizes the intimacy between grandmother and granddaughter and the younger woman's respect for the older one. However, beneath the surface, two sacred connections to the rose can also be discovered.

First, in Isaiah 35:1, barren locations in the wilderness and desert are described as being transformed by the glory of God as they begin to bloom like roses. Next, in Solomon 2:1, Jesus proclaims, "I am the rose of Sharon, and the lily of the valley." The allusion to scripture from Isaiah suggests that the grandmother's time of need, her ordeal of hunger and thirst (equated to the desert), is over. She has survived and now is reborn as a rose through God's word. Additionally, in the time of Solomon, it was written that a Palestinian plain, Sharon, existed as an untamed, yet lush place with fields of beautiful flowers. In the book of Solomon, Jesus is symbolically connected with the rose of Sharon. The image of the grandmother's heart becoming a rose implies that she has unconditional love (a major tenet of her religion) and has chosen forgiveness over bitterness; she continues to flourish in an imperfect world. This image also harkens back to the Orthodox teaching to live a Christ-like existence (witnessed earlier in the image of the grapevine). Jesus is the rose of Sharon and the grandmother's heart has become a rose.

Other descriptions within the poem, such as that of the stork and the moon, associated with the grandmother's legs and skull, respectively, can also be viewed through a biblical perspective. In Jeremiah 8:7–8, God is angry at those who claim to worship him, yet turn against him in sin. He praises birds, including turtledoves, cranes, and storks that know their place in the world as creatures of God, yet chastises people who do not follow his teaching. The speaker likens her grandmother's legs to the thin legs of storks, but this comparison also incorporates the significance of storks as linked in folklore with childbirth and fertility.

The poet also depicts the grandmother's head as that of a moonlike skull. In Psalms 72:5, the moon is a sign of permanence, one that endures throughout generations. Here, the poet recognizes the value of the grandmother as a permanent influence in her life, yet the image is coupled with the reality of her impending death with the reference to her skull. Also, lunar eclipses, such as those described in Joel 2:31, were taken to signify the power of God and served as a sign to his people not to be troubled by evil acts or disasters. This also correlates to the grandmother's belief in spiritual salvation, which does not waver in times of distress.

The poem's imagery—grapevine, rose, stork, and moon—is enriched by these biblical connotations. In this sense, the poem offers a complex portrait of the grandmother, demonstrating how her history and faith have shaped her character. The grandmother has been presented through the eyes of the granddaughter, yet at a slight narrative distance.

In the final stanza, however, the speaker suddenly interjects herself, throwing herself at the feet of her grandmother as a wolf, crying in the night. Ironically, John 10:12–14 depicts Jesus as a shepherd who protects his people, or flock, from the wolf, a symbol of evil. The speaker, as embodied by this image, is the antithesis of her grandmother. It is here that the work approaches its dramatic peak. Despite the homage the speaker pays to her grandmother's strong character, she struggles to fully accept her spiritual convictions that allow an acceptance of pain (and paradoxically, the denial of it) as part of a divine plan. The image of the wolf threatening the flock is haunting; the granddaughter as wolf challenges her grandmother's belief system, yet is humbled by her, as she lies at her feet.

The end of the poem comes full circle by echoing the first stanza. The speaker confronts her grandmother's philosophy about pain by offering her own perception of it. Using personification, she claims that pain is an embrace from a powerful god. The speaker's god, unlike her grandmother's, is manlike with a scruffy beard that chafes the faces of those he touches. The speaker does offer validation of the presence of a deity, yet she boldly challenges the Orthodox depiction of an omnipotent, all merciful being. Each image that illustrates the grandmother's philosophy, grapevine, rose, stork, moon, and wolf, is enriched by biblical subtext, rendering a deeper reading of the poem and a more intimate portrait of the grandmother. Mort's imagery builds to a dramatic concluding vision in which the speaker appears to counter and perhaps to balance her grandmother's beliefs, with her own vision of God. The speaker's god is loving yet hurtful, and one who must take responsibility for creating an imperfect world where pain, for both grandmother and granddaughter, exists.

Source: Wendy Perkins, Critical Essay on "Grandmother," in *Poetry for Students*, Gale, Cengage Learning, 2010.

Fiona Sampson

In the following essay, Sampson gives some basic biographical information about Valzhyna Mort and discusses her impressions of Mort's poetry.

Some facts about Valzhyna Mort: 1) Her real name is Valzhyna Martynava. 2) Belarus is a country with a GDP of something over $83 billion, a population just under ten million. 3) Mort—or, more probably, Martynava—studied at the State University of Linguistics in Minsk. 4) When she moved to the U.S. in 2005, she was twenty-four and had already published her first book, *I'm as Thin as Your Eyelashes*.

I first came across Mort in Slovenia in 2004. She seemed all energy, a striking performer with whip-crack language and the distinctive bounce of an absolutely individual poetics. The panel I was chairing (better to declare this) awarded her the Crystal Vilenica Prize. We did so for what we could glimpse, through a handful of translations, of a vivid, stripped-down, and buoyant verse, unlike anything else that was coming out of Belarus, or indeed elsewhere in the Slav world. Now that skinny kid, all nervous energy and focus, is twenty-eight, and in these fine translations by Elizabeth Oehlkers Wright and Franz Wright the Anglophone reader has for the first time an even chance at a body of her work: the thematic and structural hinterland to a rare kind of sonic brilliance.

Still, brilliance is not, perhaps, the right word. Mort is neither arbitrary nor ostentatious. She eschews the straggling surrealism, and crescendo rhetoric, still fashionable in Belarus, Ukraine, or Moldova. Instead, there's something about her writing that seems intensely personal. Perhaps that's why one is tempted to start with the biographical. But—what is this personal element? Certainly not the usual drear confession, though she can write about experiences which are typical enough for a young woman:

> men arrive like a date on a calendar they keep visiting once a month—From "Men"

Or:

> memory two fingers thrust into the mouth of life—"memory"

Or:

> it's so hard to believe that once we were even younger than now that our skin was so thin that veins blued through it like lines in school notebooks that the world was a homeless dog that played with us after class—From for "A.B."

There's a compaction of energy in Mort's line. This isn't solely a question of register, though that is never cozy. More germane, perhaps, is her habit of accelerating metaphor. Often this means a points-switch between narrative realities. "Password," by and large a bedroom poem—

> there are apples parsley and my round bare nipples like two grains of red caviar they will make a good dessert

—ends with: "where do you say you were when I / was killing you in the city square at night?" That closing couplet travels so quickly over the points it almost naturalizes its own absurdity. Meanwhile, "Men" segues into English for the last dozen lines, which use 9/11—"mama their lips fall on me / like burning planes"—in just the way Plath used the Holocaust, whatever we make of either gesture. This zigzag reality continues even within a single idea: when "Polish Immigrants" asks "is it true that their pillows / are stuffed with soil / softer than any feather," the image folds over onto, and compounds, itself.

Such density seems—I was going to write "foreign"—an inheritor of the lapidary versification of the Russian Silver Age. Yet Mort's title poem, which opens, "And once again according to the annual report / the highest productivity results were achieved / by the Factory of Tears," more suggests the mannered grotesqueries of those great Central European inventors from her grandparents' generation: Miroslav Holub and Zbigniew Herbert. But Belarus is neither Mitteleuropa nor Russia, but a somewhere-in-between (south of Lithuania, west of St. Petersburg) with an arguably more chaotic history and present. And Mort, though young, is a personal poet not least in the sense that her poetics are clearly her own. She gives the impression (always the mark of accomplishment) of having emerged entire, her writing and its strategies coterminous: certainly, there's no particular stylistic development between pieces written in Belarus and later, American work.

Another strategy common to these unrhymed poems is brilliant, glancing observation. One might be tempted to call their author a Neo-Martian, after Craig Raine's British school, if she weren't already Mort-ist. Despite that choice of pen name, though, there's nothing cloying or morbid here, even if the material such observation cuts through is often dark. (In this she resembles the Estonian Emil Tode, real name Tonu Onnepalu. An earlier chronicler of the sexual mores of transitional times, who also achieved critical success deservedly young, Tode claimed to have chosen his resonant pen name for its sound alone.) While miniatures like "Marriage" and "Alcohol" are narrative slices of incidental life, nothing in them is incidental. Every phrase is part of a masonry of both sense and rhythm, for it's Mort's diction—economic, bouncing from short line to short line, with the obvious exception of the long prose poem "White Trash"—which acts as form.

Alert to pulse, the poems in *Factory of Tears* use lineation, stepped lines, and stanza breaks—the air-sprung soles of tiny pauses—for emphasis. Sense proceeds by lines which are also phrasal units, sometimes enjambed but never uncertain or astray. To have kept the best of the Russian, this bounce and rebound, is a subtle, ballsy feat in English: our language has a lamentable tendency to explain the noble if savage original, rather than echo (i.e. sound like) it. It takes a poet to know a poet, arguably, and the Wrights have captured both diction and character with generosity, making edgy, living poems in the English. (Of course, one could argue the odd corner: those "that's" lining the left-hand margin of "for A.B.," for example, simply seem unfinished. But translation, after all, can never be the final word.)

Thus disciplined, Mort seems to eschew High Style, except for the rhetorical flights of two "Belarusian" poems:

> completely free only in public toilets
> where for a little change nobody cared what
>   we were doing
> we fought the summer heat the winter snow
> when we discovered we ourselves were the
>   language
> and our tongues were removed we started
>   talking with our eyes
> when our eyes were poked out we talked
>   with our hands
> when our hands were cut off we conversed
>   with our toes
> when we were shot in the legs we nodded our
>   heads for yes —from "Belarusian I"

When she lets herself go like this, language, body, and self turn out to be indistinguishable. After all, what's personal in Mort's poetry is the matter of voice. Her percussive, rhythmic diction, in both Belarusian and English, is impossible to read without having it fill the mouth. Beyond that, though, voice implies speaker: it's where words get embodied. In this work, we hear a persona—something like "a ball / in a lottery bubble / [who can] do somersaults / and dance / a fast fox-trot," to quote from the early poem "Lottery Wheel." It's with the concrete life of language itself—its sound—that she has constructed her textual self. When she performs in public, Mort's poems famously seem to "fit her like a skin"; she "inhabits them." On the page, too, her unique diction speaks, as if in character.

Like an aural puppet, this fictional persona performs, and is performed by, her distinctive verse.

Source: Fiona Sampson, "In Persona," in *Poetry*, Vol. 193, No. 4, January 2009, p. 353.

Svetlana Tomic

In the following essay, Tomic gives general biographical information and a basic overview of the themes present in Mort's poetry.

In a recently published anthology, *New European Poets* (2008), twenty-seven-year-old Valzhyna Mort from Belarus set herself apart from many other young poets. Recipient of the 2005 Crystal of Vilenica Award in Slovenia and of the 2008 Burda Poetry Prize in Germany, she is most characterized by an obstinate resistance and rebellion against the devaluation of life, which forces her to multiply intelligent questions, impressive thoughts, and alluring metaphors, while her rhythm surprisingly arises as a powerful tool for the most dramatic moments of her verses.

Factory of Tears is her second book of poetry and the first one to be published in the United States. (It is also the first American bilingual edition in Belarusian.) As an immigrant from a dramatically changed homeland, Mort is concerned with some of Belarus's political issues—a new national identity and a new language. As she goes about presenting these issues, a range of conflicting feelings emerge ("Belarusian I,""Belarusian II"). In the poem "The Factory of Tears," she brilliantly converts the ideological speech of a famous socialist factory reports into personal confessions that culminate in bitter irony. In other poems, Mort intensifies her connection to the past through the figure of her grandmother, who survived the Stalinist age and became the author's heroic muse.

Since her move to the States, Mort has begun dealing with another new language (one of her poems is written in English) and more new places. The poem "New York" begins with a sort of a theatrical announcement: "new york, madame, / is a monument to a city / it is / TA-DA // a gigantic pike, / whose scales / bristled up stunned," followed by verse expressing her own fascination and enchantment, and ends with wizardry—comparing skyscrapers with a rabbit pulled out by its ears from a black hat by a magician. The poem "From Florida Beaches" reads as a metaphorical postcard: "The sun is jumping among the clouds like a yellow monkey ... The beach pours like an overturned jar of honey / and waves lick the shore with their watery mouths."

Readers will enjoy the mature way in which Mort communicates the ironies and paradoxes of life and her specific bond with music, "but time will come and it will / show its tara ta ta." She has a deft ear for rhyme and a great sense of rhythm. Even in her most narrative and longest poem ("White Trash") the poetic speech is easily and smoothly transformed into different forms and structures. In her shortest poems ("Fall in Tampa,""Promised Land,""Teacher") she masters the art of saying much with a few effective details: "your body is so white / that it falls on me like snow / every night is a winter."

Factory of Tears is certainly worth reading. Moreover, readers will appreciate the talent of Valzhyna Mort, acclaimed as one of the best young poets in the world today.

Source: Svetlana Tomic, "Valzhyna Mort, *Factory of Tears*," in *World Literature Today*, Vol. 83, No. 3, May–June 2009, p. 71.

Kevin Nance

In the following essay, Nance explains how Mort bridges cultures in her life and poetry as she navigates establishing her new home in the United States while remaining in touch with her native country of Belarus.

Despite her slender frame, Valzhyna Mort can *eat*. At Veselka, a Ukrainian diner in New York City's East Village, Mort attacks a bowl of borscht, a basket of coarse crusty bread, a plate of meat-filled pierogi that she slathers individually with sour cream, and, finally, a slice of apple crumb cake à la mode, savoring it all with a deep satisfaction that suggests she is feeding more than her stomach. The twenty-six-year-old poet from Belarus, who now lives in Alexandria, Virginia, is susceptible to occasional bouts of homesickness that fortunately can be alleviated, if not quite cured, by regular infusions of beet soup and stuffed cabbage.

"As I realized after I moved to the United States, culture and agriculture are very close," says Mort, whose American debut, *Factory of Tears*, published in April by Copper Canyon Press, features her poems in the original Belarusian along with English translations by Pulitzer Prize-winning poet Franz Wright and his wife, Elizabeth Oehlkers Wright. "It's impossible to do without the food that you're used to. You miss it so much that nothing—no book, no movie, no anything—can substitute." Which is

> FOR MUCH OF MORT'S CHILDHOOD, HER GRANDMOTHER'S FAMILY HISTORY WAS NOT AN APPROVED TOPIC OF CONVERSATION."

why she's at Veselka, her favorite haunt whenever she's in New York. The day before, as part of a group event featuring Copper Canyon poets, Mort had given a reading at the Association of Writers & Writing Programs conference in midtown, but she's visibly more comfortable in the East Village, where Ukrainian restaurants are common and the sidewalks are crowded with people speaking a borscht-like stew of Slavic languages. "I've been having very hard times because of living in an English-speaking environment and lacking the Belarusian language," she admits. "The sound of it is very important for a poet—the noise, you know, the Slavic noise on the street."

Luckily for Mort, the cuisine of Ukraine is virtually identical to that of its neighbor, Belarus. But why do there seem to be no specifically Belarusian restaurants in New York? "I don't know," Mort says. "There are a lot of Belarusian people who move to the United States and are sort of Belarusians under cover, you know? They identify as Russians, or as Poles or Ukrainians, because those are the countries that are recognizable to a foreign ear, while Belarusian is something more exotic. If you say you're from Belarus, then the next question will be, 'What is it?' So you have to go into the explanation. And many people would rather not."

Mort smiles, tucking another pierogi under a blanket of sour cream. "Me," she says, "I'm still rather yes."

Valzhyna Martynava grew up in a comfortably middle-class, Russian-speaking family in the Belarusian capital of Minsk, a city of nearly two million people. Mort is at once a shortened version of her family name, a "stupid" nickname in school, and the pen name under which friends published some of her early poems. "It grew on me," she explains, "and now I don't see myself separate from it." As for the word's other association, "I certainly don't see 'death' as a negative meaning," she says. "I find it hilarious." Her parents—Gennady, a former professional soccer player who is now a manager in an industrial firm, and Tatsiana, an economist—are not especially literary, but they own a substantial collection of books, which their daughter began to read while she was in the sixth grade. "My first book happened to be the Marquis de Sade's *Philosophy in the Bedroom*," she says with an inscrutable smile. "I liked the cover, so I decided this would be the first. I liked it very much. The Marquis de Sade opened literature for me, and then I was reading more and more from my parents' library."

Another key influence in young Mort's life was her beloved grandmother, Janina, who lived with the family and took care of her while her parents worked. Born to a wealthy family in a rural area about a thirty-minute drive from Minsk, Janina suffered through the Stalinist era of collectivization, during which her family's house and farmland were seized by the Soviet authorities. "The first memory of her life is when people came to take the roof of their house," Mort says, "to make sure they wouldn't live there." Some of Janina's relatives were sent to Siberia, and by the time she was seven years old, both her parents had died. She spent World War II, including the period of Nazi occupation, in an orphanage or with aunts, in poverty and hunger.

Growing up, Mort recalls, "You could never throw away bread that you didn't eat at the table. She would say, 'I will dry it, and when we have nothing to eat, we will eat it with water.' And it was impossible to persuade her not to do it. We did not want to have this dried bread staying in the kitchen. My mom would throw it out, and my grandma would start over again. Once you live through hunger, you are afraid to go through it again, and you prepare. And so she has been preparing."

For much of Mort's childhood, her grandmother's family history was not an approved topic of conversation. "They were called Kulaks—an offensive name, it meant that you were a well-to-do farmer whose family was somewhere in Siberia," she says. "When my grandmother would tell stories about what she remembered, my mom would always come into the room and say, 'Valzhyna, you cannot tell this to anybody. We don't want people to know.'" But Mort did tell. *Factory of Tears* is dedicated to Janina, whose voice and stories appear in several of the poems, including "Grandmother":

> my grandmother
> doesn't know pain
> she believes that
> famine is nutrition
> poverty is wealth
> thirst is water....

Mort's attraction to poetry grew out of a more general interest in the arts, including music and the theater. Although she had no talent as a singer, she says, she was admitted to a studio for child performers at the Belarusian State Theatre of Opera and Ballet, where she was trained and participated in several productions as a member of the chorus. And partly because Janina enjoyed the accordion (an instrument cherished in Slavic countries) and hoped her granddaughter could learn it, Mort took lessons for eight years, playing several hours each day even though her instructor told her early on that she had no ear for music. Eventually she tried her hand at composing, only to find that she lacked a gift for it.

But the urge to create was persistent, she says, "so I started composing music using language. The first poems that I wrote were very language driven—they were all about the sound and the rhythm. And still right now, when I write a poem, I don't like having only one rhythm, the same person speaking. I like having my chorus there, changing the rhythm several times. Sometimes there are several characters in one poem. In my head, all of them have their own cues, like in the opera."

The most musical-sounding language she knew was Belarusian, though—as was the case for most people who lived in the former Byelorussian Soviet Socialist Republic—it was not her first language. (Stalin, and later Nikita Khrushchev, discouraged the use of Belarusian. "The sooner we all start speaking Russian," Khrushchev said in 1953, "the faster we shall build communism.") During Mort's childhood, Belarusian was taught in some schools as a second language but was almost never the primary language of instruction. After 1990, when Belarus declared independence from the collapsing Soviet Union, the Belarusian language surged in popularity; it was widely adopted by high schools and made significant inroads in the mass media. But with the 1994 election of pro-Russian president Alexander Lukashenko (who remains in office), the popularity of Belarusian began to wane again. Schools that had adopted it began to shut down, sometimes under pressure from the government, which for years has been in negotiations to merge with Russia.

The lack of official support for Belarusian echoes the unease with the language felt by many Belarusians. "Belarusian was the language of poor, rural people, the peasants," Mort explains. "This is the reason an ordinary person in Belarus today refuses to speak Belarusian, refuses to acknowledge that he is a native speaker of the language or that he can understand it. If you speak Belarusian, it makes you automatically someone who came from the countryside, who never went to school. People are afraid to be put into this vulnerable position in which they are constantly being made fun of."

Even so, a certain cross section of people in Belarus—including many younger intellectuals, artists, and writers—are adamant about the preservation of the Belarusian language. Mort writes in Belarusian but doesn't consider herself an activist. "It does hurt me that my language—not my mother tongue, but my blood tongue—is greeted so badly by Belarusians themselves. But it's not a political choice for me, because for me right now, I'm the last person, the *only* person speaking and writing in Belarusian. It's not so, of course, but this is how I feel to myself. It doesn't matter if somebody else speaks or writes it, because it's a personal reflection, not a political one."

In addition to her early efforts at writing poems, Mort began to translate into Belarusian the work of poets she admired, including the Poles Wislawa Szymborska, Stanislaw Baranczak, and Rafal Wojaczek, the Russian Marina Tsvetaeva, and, later, Yeats, Eliot, and Ted Hughes. "That was my manifestation of loving a poet—I wanted to own it, I wanted the poem to be mine, and the only way was to translate it," she says. "Someone said we're born as poets from this wound that is inflicted on us by other poets' poetry. And at some point I had this wound."

If the writers Mort translated were her literary parents, her delivery as a poet was at the hands of Boom-Bum-Lit, a supportive group of about ten young Belarusian poets who held readings together in Minsk. "They invited me to join, and this is how I became a poet," she says. "It was very easy, like entering a restaurant."

By the time her first book, *I'm as Thin as Your Eyelashes*, was published in Belarus in

2005, Mort was already a sensation as a performer of her work. Although she's reserved by nature, she is a commanding presence onstage, her stature seeming to grow with every line. Her feet planted, her eyes fixing the audience, her voice is rich, expressive, clarion strong. Word of her prowess at the podium spread, and soon she was in demand at literary events throughout Europe. In 2004 in Slovenia, she won a Crystal Vilenica Award for best poetry performance. Later, when Franz Wright saw her at a festival in Galway, Ireland, he turned to Alison Granucci (who later became Mort's agent in the United States) and said, "She's electrifying."

"She was very young," Wright recalls, "but it seemed to me that there was something old, something ancient about her country and her people, coming out of her and *through* her."

In a reading at New York City's Bowery Poetry Club last April, Mort shared the stage with Rives, a popular spoken-word artist who has appeared on HBO's *Russell Simmons Presents Def Poetry* series. "He had an act, basically, and it worked very well," recalls Dean Temple, the creative director of a design firm in upstate New York who attended the reading and has become a friend and fan of Mort, recording her readings for podcasts on virtualhudsonvalley.com. "But at one point they had each poet read a poem by the other poet. He read Valzhyna's poem as if he were trying to read it like she did, and it fell very flat. She read his poem as if it was her own, and it was amazing. I would say she *took* his poem from him."

What's different about Mort's reading, Temple says, is the disarming way it reveals the speaker. "A lot of really good poets who are very polished, very used to being in front of an audience—people like Robert Bly, Carolyn Forché—can't help but fall into a pedagogical state where they discuss their own work almost academically at times. Valzhyna is really an innocent who reveals so much about herself by creating an incredible intimacy with her audience. Her reading, in its own way, is titillating, in a sense; I've actually seen her embarrassed to talk to people after a reading."

Mort is not convinced by such extravagant claims, preferring to think of her performance style as directly related to her training at the Minsk opera house. "It was the drill I went through as a child—of speaking loudly, speaking slowly, of pulling myself together. No magic,

really. When you are a child on the opera stage, you have to make sure the balcony hears you, and you have to be very still. In my first opera, which was *Carmen*, you had to sit through the whole fourth act onstage. You cannot move, you are scared to breathe, you have to stay in character. And that's what reading poetry is. It's not just about the words. It's about the character. I have to take you by the collar and make you keep listening and looking. Thank you, Georges Bizet!"

Soon after her reading in Galway, Mort's life began to change quickly. She moved to the United States and married Joseph Cortese, an American she had met in Warsaw while he was looking for bands to sign for his independent record label. Wright, who with his wife had begun to convert Mort's own literal English translations of her poems into an American idiom ("we don't do much—it's not like real translation," he says), recommended her manuscript to Michael Wiegers, executive editor at Copper Canyon Press.

"There's a voice there that you don't encounter in much contemporary American poetry," Wiegers says. "There's something of Andrei Codrescu's early voice, I think, an attractively ironic tone. But mainly it was just something that was unlike anything I had been reading at the time by younger poets. There was an intimacy and a personal touch in the work, but it also didn't feel self-involved."

One sign of that lack of self-involvement is Mort's frequent use of the pronoun *we* rather than *I*. Confessional American poetry, Wiegers says, is often "centered in the *I*, centered in the autobiography. I saw her use of *we* in terms of the community from which she hails—her family, her extended family, maybe her generation—but it's still intensely personal."

Asked about the *we*, Mort says that she uses the pronoun "maybe because it takes a certain courage to say 'I' and I don't have it, and prefer to distance myself from the poem and camouflage myself in the costume of this *we*. Maybe because I feel that some poems are sort of 'generational' poems and things I'm saying in them could have been said by many people of my age. I certainly don't mean 'we—Belarusian peoples.'"

It's an important distinction for Mort to make, because several of her poems seem to speak for the nation itself, with specific references to the troubled history of Belarus, both in the

Soviet era and in contemporary times. The book's title poem, for example, is a sardonic riff on the Lukashenko government's Soviet-style annual reports about industrial and agricultural production:

> While the Department of Transportation
> was breaking heels
> while the Department of Heart
> Affairs
> was beating hysterically
> the Factory of Tears was working
> night shifts
> setting new records
> even on holidays.

And the nation's past sorrows are often conjured up by the channeled voice of Janina, as in "Belarusian I":

> even our mothers have no idea how
> we were born
> how we parted their legs and crawled
> out into the world
> the way you crawl from the ruins
> after a bombing
> we couldn't tell which of us was a girl
> or a boy
> we gorged on dirt thinking it was
> bread...

It would be understandable if readers interpreted such lines as political commentary, but Mort denies that they are. "People do assume that I'm political, but for me personally, those are not political poems," she says. "I live in a country, and I live with open eyes. I am attracted by a certain fever in the social and political situation. The fever gets to me, the high temperature, so certain poems are born. But they're not born as a protest or an exclamation from a city square. It's putting what I see through me, nothing more."

It might also be that Mort resists the "political" label because it was used to pigeonhole earlier generations of Slavic poets. "I think there's a tendency for every poet from Eastern and Central Europe to be read as political," says Matthew Zapruder, a friend of Mort's and a fellow Copper Canyon poet (his second collection, *The Pajamaist*, was released in 2006). "People think it's always about communists and Soviets and getting repressed and Stalin and all that, and they're trapped, no matter what they write about. In Valzhyna's case, I think her poems are political in the sense that they deal with circumstances in the era and age we live in, but there's an aspect of it having come out of innocence, out of childhood."

Mort's childhood inspiration—her grandmother's role in her upbringing—remains a major part of her life and art. "For a very long time I saw the world through her eyes," Mort says. "Later, we became so close that for me there is not much distinction between us. We are the same person. I'm sort of a continuation of her, a younger version of her, and I know that because she put so much into me, she is living in me. I feel that all the time, and this is why I still view the world through her eyes. This is why the book is dedicated to her. And this is why everything written in there is written by her, to some extent."

As much as her grandmother means to her, and as deep as her connection to her birthplace runs, Mort doesn't get back to Minsk as often as she'd like. Veselka and the East Village are fine as occasional substitutes, but will never replace home. Still, she keeps in touch with Janina, who doesn't read much poetry but is proud of the granddaughter who calls her regularly, playing tunes on the accordion over the phone.

Source: Kevin Nance, "You Cannot Tell This to Anybody," in *Poets & Writers*, Vol. 36, No. 3, May–June 2008, pp. 29–33.

SOURCES

Mort, Valzhyna, "Grandmother," in *Factory of Tears*, Copper Canyon Press, 2008, p. 13.

Nance, Kevin, "You Cannot Tell This to Anybody," in *Poets & Writers*, Vol. 36, No. 3, May–June 2008, pp. 31, 32, 33.

Review of *Factory of Tears*, in *Belarusian Review*, Vol. 20, No. 1, 2008.

Review of *Factory of Tears*, in *Irish Times*, http://www.coppercanyonpress.org/catalog/dsp_bookReview.cfm?Book_ID=1294 (accessed July 20, 2009).

Review of *Factory of Tears*, in the *New Yorker*, Vol. 84, No. 14, May 19, 2008, p. 81.

Review of *Factory of Tears*, in *Publishers Weekly*, Vol. 255, No. 8, February 25, 2008, pp. 54, 55.

Ulaby, Neda, "The Art of Romare Bearden: Collages Fuse Essence of Old Harlem, American South," *All Things Considered*, National Public Radio, September 14, 2003, http://www.npr.org./templates/story/story.php?storyId=1428038 (accessed July 17, 2009).

"Valzhyna Mort: Belarusian Poet," in *Blue Flower Arts*, 2009, http://www.blueflowerarts.com/valzyhna-mort (accessed July 17, 2009).

Wright, Franz, "Poem Commentary," in *Poetry Foundation*, http://www.poetryfoundation.org/archive/poemcomment.html?id=179414 (accessed July 17, 2009).

FURTHER READING

Dolot, Miron, *Execution by Hunger: The Hidden Holocaust*, Norton, 1985.

> Dolot's eyewitness account describes the violence and terror imposed by collectivization during the Stalinist era, which resulted in seven million Ukrainians starving to death during the famine of the early 1930s. Dolot describes how his relatives were victims of Soviet abuse and humiliation, yet he focuses more on their survival.

Lipska, Ewa, "When Our Enemies Fall Asleep" and "If There Is a God," in *Contemporary East European Poetry: An Anthology*, edited by Emery Edward George, Oxford University Press, 1983, pp. 148–49.

> The work of Ewa Lipska serves as a relevant compliment to Mort's poetry. Lipska's poetry describes the anti-communist revolutions in Eastern Europe and poses often controversial questions concerning the existence of God, questions that Mort explores in her own verse.

Miller, Wayne, and Kevin Prufer, eds., *New European Poets*, Graywolf Press, 2008.

> This anthology of late twentieth- and early twenty-first-century poetry includes work from every country in Europe. The collection includes poems by Mort as well as her translations of selected Eastern European poets.

Midsummer, Tobago

DEREK WALCOTT

1976

Poet Derek Walcott is one of the few writers from the West Indies to draw international attention, which peaked with his winning the 1992 Nobel Prize for Literature. The biracial Walcott has published numerous plays and collections of poetry, often addressing the subject of the region's difficult history of European rule: Tobago was controlled by France, Spain, the Duchy of Courland Latvia, and the Dutch Republic at various times before becoming a colony of the United Kingdom from 1815 until 1962, when it joined Trinidad as an independent commonwealth. While some Caribbeans write with anger and disdain about their colonial past, Walcott tends to use poetic imagery to explore daily life and regional culture.

This tendency certainly is evident in the poem "Midsummer, Tobago." In it, Walcott describes a quiet but vivid scene in a beautiful setting, with a narrator seemingly nearly drowsing in the heat until, unexpectedly, the poem mentions that days have come and then slipped away. The connection to the colonial theme is understated, but present. In few words, with just eleven lines, Walcott's poem evokes complex emotions. It gives a concise visual image, while leaving readers to intuit the broader social meaning.

"Midsummer, Tobago" was originally published in 1976, in Derek Walcott's collection *Sea Grapes*. It also appears in Walcott's *Selected Poems*, published in 2007.

Derek Walcott (AP Images)

AUTHOR BIOGRAPHY

Derek Alton Walcott was born with his twin brother Roderick on January 23, 1930, in the town of Castries, St. Lucia, which is one of the Windward Islands in the Lesser Antilles chain of the West Indies. His mother's father was Dutch and his father's father was English, while his grandmothers on both sides were black West Indians. When he and his brother were just one years old, Walcott's father died during a surgery. His mother, a teacher at the Methodist Infant School, raised her children as Protestants in the predominantly Catholic environment of Castries. Many of their father's friends helped in raising Derek and Roderick; the most notable of these was Harold Simmons, an amateur painter who taught Derek Walcott painting and encouraged him to write poetry.

Walcott attended St. Mary's College on St. Lucia, graduating in 1947. He applied for a scholarship to Oxford and to Cambridge but was denied because of his weakness in math. For a few years he taught as an assistant master at St. Joseph's Convent, and then in 1950, he won a Colonial Development and Welfare scholarship, which allowed him to attend the University of West Indies, in Mona, Jamaica. While in college, he participated in the school's literary society and founded the school's newspaper. He and his brother were among those who formed the St. Lucia Art Guild in 1950. He published his first book of poetry while he was at St. Mary's, and he had one of his plays produced in London.

After graduation in 1954, Walcott moved to Trinidad and made his living as an art critic. He moved to New York for a year and studied theater at the Jose Quintero's acting school in 1958, then returned to Trinidad. In 1961, he won the Guinness Award for Poetry, and in 1962, his first volume of poetry to appear outside the Caribbean, *In a Green Night: Poems 1948–1960*, was published in the United Kingdom.

In the following years, Walcott published poems and plays constantly. The first volume of his *Selected Poems* was published in 1964. In 1970, his play *Dream on Monkey Mountain* (1967) won an Off-Broadway, or Obie, Award. His collection of autobiographical poems, *Another Life*, was published in 1973, and in 1976, *Sea Grapes*, the volume that contains "Midsummer, Tobago," appeared.

In 1981, Wolcott was appointed professor of creative writing at Boston University, where he had been teaching on a part time basis for years. That same year he won the prestigious John D. and Catherine T. MacArthur Genius Award. There followed a brief stint at Harvard University, which the thrice-married Walcott left under a cloud of suspicion having been accused of sexually harassing a student. He returned to teaching at Boston University. In 1996, he reached a settlement with a Boston University student on charges of sexual harassment.

In 1991, Walcott was given the Order of the Caribbean Community, and in 1992, he received the Nobel Prize for Literature, the highest award a writer can win. His 1998 collaboration with pop singer Paul Simon, a musical called *The Capeman*, was much-anticipated but a critical failure.

In 2009, Walcott withdrew his candidacy as frontrunner for an appointment as professor of poetry at Oxford University, after an anonymous campaign circulated old news articles and unsubstantiated rumors accusing him of sexual impropriety with students. That year he began a three-year term at the University of Alberta, as distinguished scholar in residence, the first person to hold that position. Walcott has been married and divorced three times and has three children, a son Peter Walcott, and two daughters, Elizabeth Walcott-Hackshaw and Anna Walcott-Hardy. In 1986, he began a relationship with Sigrid Nama, who was interviewed with him for a *New Yorker* profile in 2004.

POEM SUMMARY

Line 1

The first line of "Midsummer, Tobago" ends with a period, though it is only a noun. This line describes the beaches of Tobago, not a specific beach but the beaches in general. The hyphenated word "sun-stoned" suggests two meanings. The beaches certainly have stones, and they are heated by the sun, but another interpretation is that the sun has beaten the stony beaches with its heat, making the rocks hot along the shoreline. The unusual modifier helps to establish the visual effect that the rest of the poem develops.

Line 2

In the second line, Walcott uses an unusual phrase to engage the reader's imagination. Technically, heat has no color, though flame is hot and associated with colors ranging from blue to red to white. Readers understand his reference, though. A chemical reaction like the one that releases the sun's energy is said to release white heat. The beaches of Tobago are not literally that hot, but this phrase shows, through the use of exaggeration, that they are extremely hot.

Line 3

Walcott gives an opposite image here. A river would, of course, offer relief from the tropical heat, just as its single modifier, "green," is a much cooler and more refreshing color than the blinding whiteness of the heat described above. The poem does not lay out these images in any order to indicate that they can all be seen at once, but the inference is they all exist in Tobago.

Line 4

The bridge mentioned in line 4 is not described. It comes after a line about a river, and so readers may assume that it is a bridge across that river, even though its placement in the poem contradicts that assumption. The river and bridge are separated by both a period and a stanza break,

MEDIA ADAPTATIONS

- Bill Moyers discusses language, poetry, and politics with Walcott as part of the PBS *World of Ideas* series. A video of that interview, volume 32 in the series, was produced in 1988 by PBS Video, with the title *Derek Walcott*.
- Walcott reads a selection of his poems on the 1994 Caedmon audio cassette *Derek Walcott Reads*.
- Walcott and other famous poets who were published by Farrar, Straus and Giroux read their poetry on the 1998 audio cassette collection *Poet's Night: 11 Leading Poets Celebrate 50 Years Poetry*, a tribute to the publisher's sustained record of producing books of poetry.
- Walcott is one of the authors featured on the three-compact disc collection *The Caedmon Poetry Collection*, which Caedmon made available in 2000.

creating considerable visual distance on the page between the words. Without physical details about the bridge, readers may suspect the bridge has figurative meaning, serving as an image that connects, or bridges, one idea to another.

Line 5

Intense tropical heat is rendered in the imaged of palm trees burned and yellowed. The dryness of the trees suggests they are far from fresh water.

Line 6

Walcott uses the word "from" in line 6, possibly to indicate that all of the things described above can be seen from the house he mentions in this line. The house is personified, said to be sleeping away the summer. The compound modifier "summer-sleeping" indicates that it is the heat which is making the people in the house sleep, following the tradition of siesta, or sleeping through the very hottest hours of the afternoon, that is a practice in many warm-climate countries.

Line 7

In this line, the word "drowsing" reinforces the poem's lethargic feeling. Walcott identifies the action of the poem as occurring in August, perhaps the hottest month of the year, technically late summer. August is usually a rainy month in the West Indies, though the scene described in this poem is parched from the heat.

Line 8

In the last two stanzas of the poem, the speaker reflects on his relationship to the passage of time. In these lines, the focus and tone change. Instead of describing visual images, the speaker reflects on larger concepts that have come to his mind. The speaker regrets how much time is past. What connects this line with the lines that precede it is the word "held": The first seven lines of the poem describe a static or unmoving scene, held in place by the oppressive heat. Walcott implies that on unbearably hot days like these, time seems to stand still.

Line 9

Line 9 offers a different sense with the word "lost." Another change is that this line moves the poem in a different direction: While line 8 is reflective and pensive, line 9 is explicitly remorseful. In this stanza, the poem shifts its direction, from a tropical snapshot in midsummer to a personal lament about the way time has slipped away.

Line 10

The speaker refers to days outgrowing him, showing that he realizes how the past has swollen beyond his present ability to contain the days. The line compares these days to daughters, a comparison that evokes several emotions. Included in this simile is a sense of what lies beyond the speaker's control. The simile also conveys a sense of trying to understand the right time to let go.

Line 11

In the last line of the poem, Walcott combines the nautical image of a harbor, which refers back to the beaches mentioned in line 1, with the parenting image, begun in line 10, of a parent trying to shield or protect daughters. The speaker indicates the futility of doing so. Days come and pass; one cannot contain them. Like daughters who get too big to hold on to, the days outgrow one's arms. After the description in the early lines of the island being stunned in the excessive heat, the desire to hold onto the passing days here proves to be desperate and futile.

THEMES

Lethargy Caused by Intense Heat

Walcott conveys the slowness caused by extreme heat. He describes a tranquil setting in order to make readers feel the enervation that overcomes a person in a tropical setting like Tobago. He promotes the idea of lethargy in specific images. The beaches, for instance, are not crowded or busy because they are broad and beaten in the sun and covered with stones that are red hot. The intense sun anchors objects in the scene. Walcott stresses the calm with short, declarative statements and uses three colors to paint a picture that contains no action. The two motifs, stifling heat and simple description, come together in line 6, at the center of the poem, when Walcott combines the words "sleeping" and "summer" to describe the house.

Nature, Free of Moral Complexity

The description suggests that Tobago is a place where moral complexity does not exist. The concrete images stand outside morality or philosophical meaning. The aspects of the Tobago environment that Walcott names have no moral inference—beach, river, bridge, tree and house are identified, but there is nothing in the poem to show that they are laden with any greater meaning.

In the last four lines of the poem, the speaker seems to feel that the island of Tobago is itself innocent, but it is the very innocence of the place that he uses to highlight his own sense of loss. In these last lines, the speaker confesses that the past sum of days is too large to contain; he has been lulled by the land's tranquility, and time has slipped away from him. The poem suggests that a tropical setting can lull a person into assuming incorrectly that time holds still, that what one grasps at one point will always be within one's reach.

Passage of Time

After the first seven lines present their static descriptions, the last four lines make the point that what may have seemed to be a situation immobilized in time is actually affected by time's passing. Walcott stresses a fact about the human condition: Time can only flow in one direction,

TOPICS FOR FURTHER STUDY

- Search the Internet for pictures that you think illustrate the images that Walcott renders in this poem. Then make a map that shows each item in relation to the others. Present a slide show to your class that gives them the layout of the place the poem describes.

- Interview someone who grew up in a tropical climate without air conditioning, and someone who grew up in a moderate climate without air conditioning. Chart the methods that both used to keep cool. Use your findings to imagine a new device for keeping cool, and pitch it to your class.

- Listen to recordings of calypso music, which originated in Trinidad and Tobago. Adapt the words of this poem to a song in that style.

- Research the cultural attitudes in Trinidad and Tobago toward male and female children. Write an essay that makes the case that this poem would or would not have had the same meaning if Wolcott had used the word "sons" in place of "daughters."

- Compare Wolcott's use of imagery to the images that Jamaican writer Claude McKay uses to describe his memories in his famous poem "The Tropics in New York." Rewrite "Midsummer, Tobago," from the perspective of someone who has been away from Tobago for many years, describing the elements Wolcott uses through the lens of distant memory. Be ready to explain why you chose to alter his descriptions in the ways you did.

must be a reference to the days that are gone. These other days are beyond his control, he says.

placing the things that have passed by forever out of a person's grasp. The poem's speaker becomes aware of the passage of time when he considers how many days have slipped away. His use of the word "last" in line 9 shows that he feels the days were not used as fully as they could have been.

The passage of time expands into an ever-enlarging past as a person ages. It makes sense to speak of the past as growing, and so this word

STYLE

Concrete Imagery

Concrete imagery refers to words that convey meaning through the five physical senses. Readers visualize the place that Walcott describes through visual details. A single detail conveys the whole scene. For example, readers are not told how broad the beach is. They do not know anything about the flow of the river, its width or pace. They do not know what the bridge is made of, how it is designed, or its size. They are left to fill in these details for themselves. Wolcott gives his readers a few visual cues, with which they can envision the whole scene.

Key to this approach is Wolcott's use of colors. The colors that he mentions—white, green, and yellow—are minimal, almost abstract, and yet sufficient to complete the impression.

In the poem's last line, the poet captures a psychological state of mind with a concrete image of arms that reach out in an attempt to shelter or harbor what is now past. The visual meaning of "harbouring" conveys the speaker's feelings of futility.

Free Verse

Walcott uses no traditional form in this poem. There is no recurring rhythm scheme, no rhyme pattern, and no overall format that corresponds to any previously established design. The closest feature to a regular pattern this poem has is that most of its stanzas consist of two lines, but the one-line first stanza diverts from that pattern. A poem lacking in any traditional pattern is identified as *free verse*, a term that refers to the absence of a superimposed form; the poet is free to create a new structure for the piece at hand.

HISTORICAL CONTEXT

The island of Tobago is 200 miles south of St. Lucia, where Walcott was born, and shares a similar history. Tobago, which is east of Venezuela, was first noted by European explorers when Christopher Columbus in 1498 sighted the island, which he dubbed Assumption. Having

Nariva Swamp, a protected area on the island nation of Trinidad (© *Kevin Schafer | Corbis*)

been inhabited for centuries by Arawak and Carib tribes, the island was first colonized by the British in 1626. After that first colonization, many other European governments claimed the land. The Spanish, who had colonized nearby Trinidad, invaded the island in 1636 to protect their interests. In 1639, the Duchy of Courland (a small coastal area north of modern Warsaw) took possession; in 1664, France and Holland both claimed the island, a conflict which was settled by war in 1678. Throughout the 1700s, European control shifted from one country to another, with none of the countries keeping a very close eye on the area. Daniel Defoe's 1719 novel *Robinson Crusoe*, about a sailor who is shipwrecked on an island and beset by "savages," is assumed to be set on the island of Tobago. About that time, the West Indies gained the reputation as a lawless outpost, a region dominated by pirates. In part because of the regional instability, in 1803 Tobago became a Crown Colony of the British Empire, which it remained until after World War II.

Tobago joined with Grenada, St. Vincent, and Barbados as a political unit governed through Barbados in 1833. The island was never prosperous, and the British were glad to combine it with other political entities, rather than establish a separate government for Tobago. In 1898, given its decreasing population and limited natural resources, Tobago became a ward of Trinidad. Both islands benefited from the discovery of oil off Trinidad's shores in 1910, and citizens of Trinidad and Tobago were granted voting rights in 1925, but the oil was exhausted and the sugar they provided for the British Empire diminished. After that, poverty was widespread.

During World War II, the United States, which was fighting the Japanese in the South Pacific, established military bases throughout the Caribbean with the blessing of the British. The people of Tobago briefly enjoyed prosperity during the war years, with the U.S. dollars that the troops brought with them, but after the war the economy shrunk once again, leaving the islands impoverished. The war did have one far-reaching effect, however. It weakened the British Empire. Spurred by the push for independence in India, which won its freedom from the British in 1947, British colonies around the

COMPARE & CONTRAST

- **1976:** Walcott stands out as one of the few Caribbean authors being published in the United States.

  Today: English departments have been pushing multiculturalism for school reading lists for years. Authors such as Jamaica Kincaid, V. S. Naipaul, and Aimé Césaire are familiar to students worldwide.

- **1976:** The people of Tobago have only been freed from Great Britain's colonial influence since the previous decade; many still remember the time when they did not have political self-determination.

  Today: A generation has grown up in the independent Republic of Trinidad and Tobago. Political problems are the responsibility of the country's own elected officials.

- **1976:** Walcott's racial background, coming from black grandmothers and white grandfathers on each side, makes him seem like an outsider who does not fit in with any race.

  Today: The election of President Barack Obama shows that a biracial ancestry can help one fit in with different social and racial groups.

- **1976:** The beaches described in "Midsummer, Tobago" are empty, familiar only to people of the Caribbean.

  Today: Tobago is a popular tourist destination, especially for scuba divers. The waterfront property is considered prime real estate.

- **1976:** Tobago seems like a sleepy little province, framed in the past, which is how Walcott presents it in this poem.

  Today: Technological advances such as mobile phones and Internet access have connect these remote islands to the global culture.

---

globe voted to be free and public sentiment swung against colonization. Trinidad and Tobago joined the West Indian Federation in 1958, and, when that dissolved in 1962, the Commonwealth of Trinidad and Tobago became fully independent.

Throughout the 1960s and 1970s, advances in commercial air travel helped Trinidad and Tobago build their tourism industry. The final break with Great Britain, after nearly two centuries, came in 1976, the year that Walcott published *Sea Grapes*, when the official name of the nation became the Republic of Trinidad and Tobago.

CRITICAL OVERVIEW

Derek Walcott has been a respected writer since he was twenty years old. By that time, he had published the well-received volume of poetry, *25 Poems*, and had read his poetry on BBC radio and had one of his plays produced in his native town of St. Lucia. By the time he finished college, he had a play produced in London. His constant output of poems and plays received much critical acclaim.

However, early critics faulted Walcott's poetry for not being sufficiently political, for not ruminating on the colonial history of the Antillean Windward Islands where he grew up. His early poems were criticized for being too influenced by European models. Later, after Walcott's genius was confirmed by his winning the Nobel Prize for Literature in 1992, critics looked back and wondered if these earlier critics might not have been approaching his poetry with their own predisposed assumptions, wanting him to conform to their expectations of how so-called Third World writers should introduce their native lands to readers of industrialized countries. As an example of this early reception, Julián Jiménez Heffernan stated: "Far from writing the poems of his people,

Coconuts being harvested on the island nation of Tobago (Fox Photos | Hulton Archive | Getty Images)

he rewrote the poems of a distant culture." Heffernan also asserted that "Far from imitating the rich cadences and lexical hybridism of his mongrel dialect, [Walcott] chose to suffer the accurate iambics of the imperial idiom." Even noted critic Harold Bloom, editor of the *Bloom's Modern Critical Views* series from Chelsea House Publishers, questioned Walcott's aesthetic eminence. Bloom concluded his introduction to Walcott with uncertainty: "Walcott, the leading Anglophone poet of the West Indies, is a cultural figure of real importance, and deserves his fame. If I do not find him to be a strong poet ... is that because I set too high a value upon the agonistic element in poetry? My uneasiness may reflect primarily upon myself, and not upon Derek Walcott."

One reader who expressed no questions about Walcott's maturity as a poet is Seamus Heaney, himself a poet of international repute. In his 1989 essay "The Murmur of Malvern," Heaney stated that Walcott's strength is his not being an example of West Indies culture: "Walcott's poetry has passed the stage of self-questioning, self-exposure, self-healing, to become a common resource. He is no propagandist. What he would propagate is magnanimity and courage and I am sure that he would agree with [Gerard Manley] Hopkins's affirmation that feeling, and in particular love, is the great power and spring of verse." Edward Baugh made a similar point about Walcott's maturation when discussing the poems of *Sea Grapes*, the volume that contains "Midsummer, Tobago." Baugh opened his essay "Ripening with Walcott" with this thought: "To follow Derek Walcott's progress over more than a quarter of a century, through several books of poetry, from feverish, precocious youth to mellow middle age, is to follow a process of self-discovery and self-creation." At that time, in the late 1979s, Baugh recognized Walcott as a mature poet. In the early 2000s, Walcott was still writing, a revered talent on the poetry scene.

CRITICISM

David Kelly

Kelly is a writer and an instructor of creative writing and literature. In the following essay, he explains how "Midsummer, Tobago" describes the passage of time.

An aura of melancholy surrounds Derek Walcott's poem "Midsummer, Tobago," a heavy mood that the poet establishes subtly, hinting at much more than he explains. By no means could this be considered an emotional poem. For the most part, it offers a static description—a snapshot, a picture postcard of a Caribbean setting that many people might view as a paradise. There are no actions. The only verb in the first two-thirds of Walcott's text is "drowsing," and even that intentionally passive activity does not occur until line seven. The rest of the poem's descriptions are given in nouns, modified by one or two adjectives or none at all. No people are mentioned.

The tone of the poem changes in the eighth line. A character suddenly appears: the poem's speaker, referring to himself in first person. The speaker expresses regret and a clear sense of loss. Days have slipped away from him, and time once past cannot be regained. The speaker's sense of loss is conveyed with a simile: The days have outgrown his grasp "like daughters."

By the time readers reach the eighth line of the poem, they are eager for some message, some meaning to be provided for the preceding descriptions. Wolcott provides few sensory details. Readers get an impression from these

WHAT DO I READ NEXT?

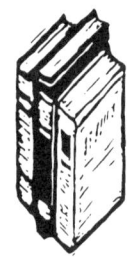

- After writing "Midsummer, Tobago," Walcott went on to publish an entire volume of poetry called *Midsummer*. Many of these poems describe life in the tropics over the course of one year. Published in 1984 by Farrar, Straus and Giroux, these poems are also included in Walcott's *Collected Poems: 1948–1984*, which Farrar, Straus and Giroux published in 1987.

- Life in contemporary Tobago is described in Amanda Smyth's debut novel *Lime Tree Can't Bear Orange*, published in 2009 by Three Rivers Press. The story concerns a young girl who runs away from her abusive uncle and moves to the city, where she works as a maid for a doctor and becomes a part of the family.

- William Shakespeare, who never left Europe, set one of his most famous plays, *The Tempest*, on a Caribbean island like Tobago. Shakespeare's play, which was written around 1610, is available in many editions.

- *The Capeman*, with book and lyrics by Walcott and music by Paul Simon, was considered a popular failure in its Broadway run, closing after just three months. Still, it won several Tony Awards and is considered an artistic, if not a commercial, success. Walcott's script, about a Puerto Rican immigrant who stabbed several bystanders during a rumble in 1959, was published by Farrar, Straus and Giroux in 1998. Out of print as of 2009, it remains available in libraries and used book stores.

- Writer V. S. Naipaul, also raised in Trinidad and Tobago, won the Nobel Prize for Literature in 2001. He gained international fame in 1961 with the publication of his novel *A House for Mr. Biswas*, which concerns a man born in rural Trinidad who is forced by a series of unlucky coincidences to travel across the island, encountering a range of social types. The novel was published by Vintage Press in 2001.

- Aimé Césaire, from Martinique, is considered among the best Caribbean writers. He is one of the founders of the Negritude literary movement, which helped bring attention to the area's post-colonial struggles. Césaire's 1939 book-length poem, *Notebook of a Return to the Native Land*, regarding his thought about his country after leaving it for the United States, is available from Wesleyan Poetry.

- Bruce King's biography, *Derek Walcott: A Caribbean Life*, was published by Oxford University Press in 2000. Written with Walcott's cooperation, the book covers both the poet's Caribbean years and his residence in the United States.

- In his interview with Derek Walcott, "This Country Is a Very Small Place," Anthony Milne records Walcott's thoughts about Tobago and his memories about growing up on an remote island. The interview is included with many like it in *Conversations with Derek Walcott*, edited by William Baer and published in 1996 by the University of Mississippi Press.

---

details and must provide the rest of the scene with their imaginations.

One part sticks out: Walcott's use of a compound modifier to describe the beach and the house. The beach is not just baked by the sun, but is assailed by it. The sun strikes the beach with its heat, stones it, in one sense, and in another makes the stones too hot to touch.

Later, Walcott describes the house as sleeping through the summer afternoon. The "sun-stoned beaches" and the "summer-sleeping house" convey in a fresh way the intense heat and lethargy of this topical place.

The first seven lines describe the scene. The last four lines take a new direction with the sudden presence of the speaker and that person's psychological state. This gives this poem its intellectual weight. There is sorrow in recognizing how many days are past, days that passed unnoticed. Walcott draws on his readers' recognition here; everyone can understand the sad realization that most of one's days are already gone. Moreover, the speaker realizes too late that inertia inevitably leads to loss.

In the last two lines, the past days are compared to daughters who have outgrown their parent's embrace. The suggestion is that when people are young and have a lot of time ahead of them, they can embrace all those days, the future, just as a parent can hold little daughters in his arms. But as time goes by, the adult realizes that time cannot be contained or shaped by the individual. Things happen, opportunities come and go, just as children get too big to be encircled in one's arms and protected. Thus, the poem takes the reader to a point of awareness. Hot summer days can seem endless in their lassitude and laziness, but they come and go, and sooner or later, one realizes more of them have gone than are yet to arrive.

Source: David Kelly, Critical Essay on "Midsummer, Tobago," in *Poetry for Students*, Gale, Cengage Learning, 2010.

Sharon McCallum

In the following essay, McCallum discusses Derek Walcott's influence in creating a Caribbean poetic tradition and how being from the Caribbean influenced Walcott.

The experience of first hearing Derek Walcott's poetry marked me such that, fifteen years later, I can conjure sitting in the wooden church pew and listening to his voice, riding the lilt of his words, a cadence at once familiar and strange. I was twenty, an undergraduate at the University of Miami. Earlier that week, my creative writing teacher had informed me that one of my countrymen, so to speak, had recently won the Nobel Prize for Literature and would be reading at an old church in Coral Gables—and that I simply could not miss it. Only in retrospect did I realize how wise she was to steer me toward the reading. As with other experiences to which she led me, hearing Walcott helped me to imagine myself as a writer. But it would be a lie to say that the reading apprenticed me to his work. Whether due to humility or ignorance, I did not immediately feel kinship with Walcott's poetry and my own incipient attempts at writing in the genre.

Three years later, Walcott was brought up again in more pointed relation to my work as an

> ONE OF WALCOTT'S MOST LASTING CONTRIBUTIONS IS TO HAVE CREATED OUT OF THE PHYSICAL ENVIRONMENT AND PSYCHOLOGICAL AND HISTORICAL CONDITIONS THAT BIRTHED HIM A CORRELATIVE IN WORLD LITERATURE."

aspiring poet in his tradition. I was completing an MFA at the University of Maryland and finishing the last hurdle: the "defense" of my thesis. One of the members of my committee was Grenadian poet and fiction writer Merle Collins. Speaking of one of my poems Merle remarked, "These lines are so Walcott. Can you say more about his influence on your poetry?" I had to admit that I couldn't. I had read one of his plays and an essay in a class I'd taken on Caribbean Literature, but knew none of his poems intimately enough to answer her question.

I realized then that I would need to correct this gap in my reading. I suspect a similar moment comes for most poets of my generation from the Caribbean, the instance when we realize that we must reckon with Walcott's poetry. Walcott, the writer, is a totemic figure and one with whom many of us, rightly or wrongly, at some point are compared or compare ourselves. He declines to place himself as the single progenitor of the Caribbean poetic tradition, but even he has had to admit that he has been instrumental in creating it and will have a notable influence on those who come after him.

In a 1977 interview with American poet Ed Hirsch, Walcott offered the following: "I think if the development of West Indian literature continues, my generation of writers will be known as people who had to go through a very anguished kind of identity crisis. And if we've set down West Indian roots, we've used the language we heard around us and described the things we saw and the experiences we went through as a people. It has been to lay the foundation for whatever masterpieces would later come out of that part of the world." Beyond the genealogical implications of his words for younger writers, what strikes me here is Walcott's emphasis on giving an account of a "people's experience." Of all the literary arts, poetry is perhaps the worst vehicle for achieving this aim, steeped as poems are in metaphor, in speaking indirectly. As compensation for this lack, I hope, what they do exceptionally well is clarify one individual's attitude toward a situation, thought, or feeling. A poem exposes and defines the moment that a particular consciousness and language meet; and Walcott's poems tilt this moment of encounter toward the light in such a way that the gesture itself and the resulting poem often reveal the prismatic nature of identity.

His poems circle a core question: is there an origin to which any of us can lay claim in order to know our self? More than my admiration for his language or the cultural relevance his work holds for me, Walcott's interest in naming the self is why I now consider his poetry an essential part of who I have become as a Caribbean poet. The lines of my own poem Merle felt were "so Walcott," not surprisingly, were these: "If we name in order to know: / say apple / it will taste red. / say bird / it will fly / from your mouth. / say home/see what stays."

In Walcott's poems, the aforementioned question regarding the self is an existential one that intersects the particulars of Walcott's ancestry. If a matrix exists at all in a Walcott poem, it is built from language, geography, history, and racial and national conceptions of identity specific to the Caribbean.

The Caribbean we come to know through Walcott's *ouevre* reflects his own lived experiences and understanding of the region while echoing a story heard across the archipelago. Walcott, like many, possesses a divided lineage: both of his grandfathers were white, his grandmothers black; he was raised speaking standard British English, English Patois, and French Creole. In 1930, when he was born on the tiny Caribbean island of St. Lucia, the country was still a colonial outpost of the declining British Empire. Like other native children living throughout the empire at that time, Walcott was given a classical education that included Latin, Greek, and the great works of Western literature and civilization.

At the same time, he was clearly outside the metropole and saw around him the landscape and experiences of a people who were not British and would never be fully admitted, as it were, into that club. Walcott's early consciousness would later be inflected by other historical incidents and pressures, notably burgeoning Independence movements throughout the 1950s and 60s, the concurrent rise of Black Nationalism, and the short-lived attempt to create a West Indian Federation. One way of reading Walcott's poems is to trace the development of a literary persona that has its analog in threads of his own life set against the backdrop of the larger history of the Caribbean in the twentieth century.

Although recent poems include American and European locales, Walcott's poetry emerges from and returns to the Caribbean as a physical setting: the sea that bears its name and the constellation of islands that run from the southern coast of North America to the northern coast of South America. Some critics suggest that the centrality of landscape in Walcott's poetry is due to the fact that he is a painter as well as poet. This is certainly one way of reading the poems; but I think Walcott's interest in visual representation of the land signals his affinity for the English poetic tradition, one with a long-standing interest in pastoral imagery.

Like Yeats's, though, Walcott's landscapes are soaked in a history that stands outside of the colonial center, so that Walcott's "wind" is not Coleridge's moving through the Aeolian Harp: "Once the sound 'cypress' used to make more sense / than the green 'casuarinas,' though, to the wind / whatever grief bent them was all the same ... but we live like our names and you would have / to be colonial to know the difference, / to know the pain of history words contain." His poems invoke the flora and fauna of this region not for decorative purpose or for easy identification with a Romantic self but, rather, to render them symbols of the Caribbean experience. One of Walcott's most lasting contributions is to have created out of the physical environment and psychological and historical conditions that birthed him a correlative in world literature.

At first glance, Walcott might appear to be a regional poet, writing a kind of poetry that evinces a longing for or simple allegiance to the concept of a homeland. Yet this would be short-sighted, as the opposite is palpable in his work: a pull toward travel and a certain restlessness of spirit. Walcott's poetry is best understood for me as a dramatization of a self filtered through many selves. These selves might be conceived discreetly as personae that include but are not limited to the poetic, autobiographical, historical, and communal. Each one of these voices brings a particular set of concerns that cleave the dramatic self at the center of the poem. I use "cleave" deliberately to evoke the conflicted definition of the word: to split and to adhere.

Walcott's work begs another question then: how does one create a singular vision and coherent persona out of fragmentation? Over the course of his early and middle poetry, the figuration of the self that gains clarity and force in order to answer this question is the Creole. By Creole, I mean an individual and collective identity Walcott and many other twentieth-century Caribbean writers helped to imagine through their poems, essays, stories, and plays. Creole identity is one these writers reveal as predicated on conflict: to exist as a Creole is to admit competing histories and cultures into a single consciousness.

Walcott's long poem, "The Schooner Flight" appears in his 1979 collection, *The Star Apple Kingdom*, and offers what is to my mind his finest articulation of Creole consciousness. At the time of its printing, Walcott was forty-nine years old and two years away from ceasing to maintain full-time residence in the Caribbean. Up to that point, he had lived in St. Lucia, Jamaica, and Trinidad. From 1981 until his recent retirement to St. Lucia, Walcott spent at least half of each year outside the Caribbean, teaching in the United States and lecturing and delivering readings around the globe.

Quasi-autobiographical, "The Schooner Flight" is a dramatic monologue in eleven parts whose back story is introduced in the poem's opening section. Shabine, the poem's persona, is leaving his home of Trinidad to "ship as a seaman on the schooner Flight." He is also, we come to discover, a poet. Shabine's story is an inversion of Odysseus's, but the shared features in the narrative are worth noting: infidelity, seafaring life, and ambivalence toward family and home. What immediately spurs Shabine's going is an affair that's gotten out of hand. His love of a woman, Maria Concepcion, has destroyed his family, leaving Shabine to feel that the best solution to the mess he's made of things in his life is desertion of the whole lot.

But this is not the whole story, as we quickly learn. The second stanza of the poem introduces other possibilities for Shabine's leave-taking: his dissatisfaction with the "corruption" of the "islands he loves." Shabine laments, "they had started to poison my soul / with their big house, big car, big-time bohlbohl, coolie, nigger, Syrian, and French creole, / so I leave it for them and their carnival." "Parades, Parades," a poem published three years earlier, offers perhaps Walcott's most bitter response to the post-Independence political climate. In the poem, the speaker suggests that Independence has led to the exchange of one self-concerned leader for another. The poem indicts the new leader, "Papa," along with his entourage, "the sleek, waddling seals of his Cabinet," as well as the poet/native Caribbean who witnessed it all and "said nothing." Interestingly, the "electorate" en masse in "Parades, Parades" is presented as duped or innocent but spared complicity in the societal failure. Three years later in "The Schooner Flight" to the contrary, everyone on the island—"bohlbohl, coolie, nigger, Syrian, and French creole"—is condemned for worshiping the petty capitalism that blossomed post-Independence, arguably partly a consequence of the United States replacing Europe as the major cultural and economic influence in the region.

In the opening section of "The Schooner Flight" Shabine defines himself first in racial terms: "I'm just a red nigger who love the sea." I'll return to the subject of race in the poem momentarily, but first wish to consider the implications of the modifier "just." A bit tongue-in-cheek as used, the word nonetheless signals Shabine's deliberate self-deprecation. As we move a bit further into the poem, though, other definitions conflict with his early humble declaration. At the end of the first section, for example, Shabine announces that he is the poet of "simple speech" with a yet quite lofty goal: "my common language go be the wind / my pages the sails of the schooner Flight." The friction created by the selves Shabine aspires to be—both the "common man" and the poet with high hopes for his work—exists throughout the poem. This tension is particularly indicative of a culture in which education, travel, and the acquisition of cosmopolitan values often separate a writer from the majority of his or her "people."

If Shabine cannot fully resolve toward an identity rooted in class, he similarly cannot fix an idea of himself in racial terms. In section three, Shabine finds himself in conflict with post-Independence ideas of Caribbean nationhood that are founded on race, as was the case with colonial society, albeit in inverse fashion. Shabine says, "I had no nation now but the imagination. / After the white man, the niggers didn't want me / when the power swing to their side … I wasn't black enough for their pride." And later: "I met History once, but he ain't recognize me, / a parchment Creole." "History" is personified in this exchange as the white colonial, the speaker as the illegitimate offspring whom History will not acknowledge. Left with untenable racial designations, Shabine forges a sense of himself as "Creole," an identity that exists outside of "History" and that belongs to "no nation but the imagination."

Over and over in "The Schooner Flight," Shabine dramatizes the question—or rather the dare, if you will—on which the poem turns: "I had a sound colonial education, / I have Dutch, nigger, and English in me, / and either I'm nobody, or I'm a nation." Given the time period in which the poem is written, his statement is pointed. Through Shabine, Walcott's alter-ego, Walcott offers his response to various black nationalistic movements that emerged from the 1950s through the 1970s in the Caribbean, ones that sought to create a new Caribbean identity, built on an affirmation rather than negation of blackness. In "What the Twilight Says," an essay published in 1970, Walcott succinctly expressed his distaste for this paradigm: "Once we have lost our wish to be white, we develop a longing to become black, and those two may be different, but are still careers." For Shabine, either the West Indian is "nobody" and does not exist because the old affiliations with Africa, Europe, or Asia are impossible—or the West Indian is a "nation" formed, however contentiously and tenuously, out of these past allegiances.

Variant levels of diction extant in this poem are the principal vehicle Walcott uses to show how the personae that constitute Shabine are in conflict but, perhaps through that conflict, are responsible for who he is. Most obviously, Shabine moves between Trinidadian English and Standard English; but the poem also uses iambic pentameter as its baseline, paying literary homage to the colonial tongue while subverting it through the use of dialect. Shabine's language is prototypically Caribbean in other ways, incorporating a kind of wit that favors puns, musicality, satire, and the speed of the "come back," as well as diction that is often highly imagistic and dense.

The speed with which Walcott moves in this poem between elevated and profane utterance, demotic and standard English, and poetic and plain diction allows us to see these "voices" as all parts of the same moment of expression and being. Most importantly, perhaps, this linguistic range is true to the way many Caribbean people speak. Walcott's wonderful ear for diction, accent, and inflection is most evident in his plays, but among his poems "The Schooner Flight" is a highlight in this regard, showing off his major gift as a composer of human speech.

Shabine embodies the Caribbean persona non grata who is also poet, historian, and social commentator. "The Schooner Flight" uses various registers of language and the sinews of personal circumstance to show how Caribbean identity comes into being but also reveals the process by which the individual comes to know him or herself. Acquiring selfhood, Walcott suggests, means navigating between the exterior world and interior life. While this negotiation is not unique to people in the Caribbean, what is heightened for many from this geo-political space is the degree to which individuation has been and continues to be historically and politically contested and constituted. These circumstances help to explain for me why Walcott has been prickly in responding to interview questions regarding identity, racial identity in particular, and yet grapples with these same questions so poignantly and paradoxically within his own poems.

I agree with Walcott when he says in an essay about V. S. Naipaul that "either every writer is an exile … or no writer is." Exile, as I think Walcott means it in this essay, is not simply the condition of being removed from one's homeland or people. This is not true of most poets' experience and is not an accurate depiction of Walcott's. The most stringent condition of exile, that it arises from political persecution in one's homeland, is not something Walcott has endured. Rather, what I think Walcott means by "exile" is a psychic condition that many writers, but especially those in the Caribbean, seem to share: a feeling of being apart from others in our community and even from ourselves, whether at home or abroad. The self-consciousness about identity that results fosters the feelings of dislocation and alienation Walcott finds resonant in the term "exile" and is one of the main reasons I think he offers Creoleness as a way out of a crisis of non-belonging. In later works, such as *Omeros* and the aptly titled *The Prodigal*, the Creole will morph into the traveler and the returning son. But in Shabine, the Creole, with all of his ambivalence, is who we meet.

As one who is a hybrid in multiple ways (in terms of race, ethnicity, nationality, and religious background), as a writer who has a foot in and out of the Caribbean in a very different fashion from Walcott and others of his "generation," I find the idea of Creoleness powerful and seductive; but it has not been a wholly satisfying way for me to achieve self-definition. If multiplicity of consciousness can be achieved, can it be sustained? Is it possible to remain adrift, without landing on this or that shore? Walcott's poems do not allay the anxiety behind my questions, but I'm not sure which poems could. More so, their lack of resolution regarding identity does not make them feel less valuable, urgent, or achieved works of art. I don't go to poems for answers. I go to them to be in the presence of the questions that matter most deeply to the poet. What Walcott's poems do, for me, is enact a struggle for selfhood in ways that make me keenly aware of the speaker's and my own fraught relationship to history.

While Walcott's work is deeply aware of the fissures of history, when I read it I find myself encountering ode as often if not more than elegy. What we frequently expect from poems that deal fervently with a place and people steeped in loss is that the voice of the poem will itself be hopelessly ruptured. The vision of a self Walcott puts forth does not shy away from confronting the entrails of history and is built on fragments, yes. But it coheres and shimmers in the moment of utterance. Walcott's poems body forth from the imagination, praising all that is possible, as well as all that is unrecoverable.

Source: Sharon McCallum, "'Either I'm Nobody or I'm a Nation': Derek Walcott's Poetry," in *Antioch Review*, Vol. 67, No. 1, Winter 2009, pp. 22–29.

T. J. Cribb

In the following essay, Cribb makes a case for ways in which Derek Walcott's poetry is seen to be influenced by the poet's other occupation as a professional painter.

I am lucky enough to have on my wall a painting by Derek Walcott, a watercolour about thirteen by fifteen inches in landscape format, dated 1988. People read the painting in interestingly different ways. Some immediately recognise the subject matter, but others at first see indeterminate shapes and colours that resolve into an identifiable subject only after an interval of time. In what follows I use these reactions to a painting as a way into what I take to be a defining characteristic of Walcott's poetry. The painting offers the pleasure of balancing between the two reactions described,

> WE ARE RETURNED TO THE FUNDAMENTAL IRRESOLUTION BETWEEN POETRY AND PAINTING; EACH INTERVENES IN OR INTERFERES WITH OUR RECEPTION AND PERCEPTION OF THE OTHER."

never settling down as one or the other. There are several levels at which this goes on. The subject is, in fact, nothing much: some bits of wood, possibly tree roots, tangled in weed, jetsam on a beach, but it affords the pleasure of recognition, the mimesis of reality traditional to Western art since the Renaissance. This carries with it the additional pleasure for cognoscenti at the painter's skill in managing the conventions of representation that enable us to accomplish the act of recognition, a pleasure, that is, in the virtuosity of performance. (In the case of this painting, the conventions are those developed by the English watercolourists and seascape artists of the eighteenth and nineteenth centuries and the optical and chromatic studies of the French Impressionists.) There is as well an abstract pleasure, akin to the pleasure of music, in which we forget the subject matter as we respond to the arrangement of planes, masses, and tones, their intervals, gradations, correspondences, and rhythms as elements in themselves. And beyond even that, just as we can lose the subject matter in its composition so we can lose the composition in the composing, in purely local effects, the run of a colour, the colour of a colour, the sweep or scribble of a brush, the myriad incidents and accidents as they occur on the paper, the marking and staining and even absence of colouring of the paper itself. This is perhaps the most rapt and wondering reception of the painting, for here we seem to share the painter's intimacy with the coming into being of the picture, to witness its process of emerging from and through the contingency of its medium in the miraculous anadyomene of art. And that returns us to the resulting image.

It is no accident that it is an image of something thrown up by the sea. As Edward Baugh, Walcott's best critic, observes in his book on *Another Life*, when the poet says "my sign was water" he alludes to being born under Aquarius. Walcott is preeminently the poet of the sea not only because he is an islander, but also because his art is like the sea. The sea carries things between continents and casts them arbitrarily into new worlds. Its tides wash beaches and make them new as if continually starting again. It suggests power even when calm, a Caribbean cool. It smoothes, shapes, and transforms anything that comes into it, even rubbish. It is the sea as medium, then, a medium like art in its capacity to transform, that supplies Walcott with an endless metaphor. Its only rival in this capacity is another medium, light. And it is Walcott's emphasis on his media that imparts the elusiveness to his poetry and affords its peculiar pleasure of balancing between the concrete image and the medium through which we perceive it.

Hence in *Another Life*, Walcott's *Portrait of the Artist as a Young Man*, it is not the artist who is the subject of the poem, but his art. From the very beginning the artist is divided between the arts he practises, with radical consequences for the reader. For if the artist presents himself not as poet but as painter, yet in a poem the reader is compelled to think of one art through the medium of another, making it impossible to settle on a simple relationship with either. Are we meant to read or simply to look?

This uncertainty is enacted in Walcott's characteristically elusive syntax. The poem opens with what sounds like a salutation: "Verandahs." So vocative an elevation of voice is unusual in English poetry after T. S. Eliot, borrowing from Laforgue, had lowered its rhetorical pitch. On the evidence of an early poem, "Origins," Walcott's reinvention of the vocative, together with a general pitching up of tone and rhetoric, is his borrowing from a very different French source, Césaire. Since verandahs have imperial associations for Walcott (see "Verandah," a poem to his English grandfather), the rhetorical elevation is appropriate enough. But it is not sustained. The line continues "where the pages of the sea," so that the ringing vocative becomes a locative, somewhat lowering the dignity of the effect. The location is now inside a verandah, looking out at the series of views its posts frame, views which are like pages, though whether written pages or the perhaps blank pages of an artist's sketchbook is left uncertain, even when the following lines seem to offer the definition that they

are a book left open by an absent master
in the middle of another life—
I begin here again,
begin until this ocean's
a shut book; and like a bulb
the white moon's filaments wane. (Book
    I, Chapter 1, Section i)

The uncertainties multiply. Who is the absent master? Could it be some Prospero who has sailed away, leaving his book behind? What other life is he leading? Is it his life that is recorded in the book that is left open in the middle, or the poet's? The latter might well be the case, since this whole poem is written over the period evoked in "Nearing Forty, " a poem brilliantly analysed by John Lennard in *The Poetry Handbook* (Oxford, 1996). And what has happened to the sentence? "Where" and "here" refer us to "verandahs," in the first case generically but in the second specifically, leaving an unresolved discord, extended into time as well as space, since "I begin" makes the poem simultaneous with the act of writing it, but "again" means it carries the consciousness of past attempts, while "until" throws the mind forward to the future completion of the current project. Meanwhile the lighting fluctuates between the natural (or literary) light of the moon and the artificial light which, we later realise, most probably illuminates the writing of the poem, for the following stanzas reveal that the poet is an apprentice painter who spends "all afternoon" labouring at a view of Castries harbour, necessarily leaving only night time for work in the other medium. We are returned to the fundamental irresolution between poetry and painting; each intervenes in or interferes with our reception and perception of the other. And in any case, who can shut the book of the sea?

These ambiguities should not be taken as a merely accidental by-product of the fact that Walcott is both painter and poet. Suspending his poem between two media is more like a strategy by which Walcott is enabled further to radicalise Joyce's innovations in *A Portrait of the Artist*. Joyce pioneered a way of writing that exploited the gap between the spoken and the written, suspending his writing between the two. Anthony Burgess's anecdote about the way the hell-fire sermons in *Portrait* oscillate between the boring and the terrifying, depending on whether they are scanned by eye or activated by voice, illustrates this perfectly. The consequence for the reader is that, as Stephen Heath has argued, a hesitation is written into our natural impulse to attribute meaning. However, one thing that is not subverted by this mode of writing in *A Portrait* is art itself (that comes with *Ulysses*). Stephen may be portrayed ironically as a particular would-be practitioner, but the practice isn't. This is where Walcott goes further. Thus, returning to the first section of the first chapter of *Another Life*, the poetry magniloquently describes a Caribbean sunset at the moment when the artist is waiting

> ... for the tidal amber glare to glaze
> the last shacks of the Morne till they
> became
> transfigured sheerly by the student's will,
> a cinquecento fragment in gilt frame.
> (I.1.i)

It is impossible to distinguish what is natural from what is artificial here, since although we move from the actual change in the light before sunset to the rendering of that light in the student's painting, the light itself is already saturated in perception conditioned by pictures of sunsets descending from the Italian Renaissance through Claude [Monet] to the English watercolourists and Turner, as we are prompted to realise by "glaze." The descent is also the descent of history and the successions of empire, in which metaphoric light the shacks take on a darker pathos, perhaps betrayed by the art that purports to represent them. The syntax refuses to order the relationships of these competing elements, letting "till" both refer to the action of the light and rhyme forward to the exertion of the student's will. And after all this, when the student presents his work at the end of the section, "Then, with slow strokes, the master changed the sketch."

The effect of suspending the writing between two different media is like a perpetual admission of failure or falling short, signalling the poem as project rather than finality. This is writ large in the structure of the poem as a whole. The first section, "A Divided Child," continues as described. The second section, "Homage to Gregorias," seems to celebrate an artist untroubled by the poet's doubts. The third section, "A Simple Flame," analyses "the noble treachery of art" in love. The poem closes with "The Estranging Sea," when the poet returns to his island to find that his erstwhile master has killed himself and Gregorias is sunk in despair. Yet this grim armature supports a radiant tissue of eloquence and what Walcott calls "elation," a continual beginning again. In the oscillation between the two, all the problematics of empire, poverty, ambition, and exile, equally with the celebrations of place, love, beauty, and home are as it were dissolved or held in a kind of limbo, or, if you prefer, *sous rature*.

It is this suspension that makes Walcott so different from that other great poet of the sea, Hart Crane. There are echoes of Crane's "The Harbor Dawn" ("gongs in white surplices") and "Voyages II" ("Samite sheeted and processioned") in the hymn to Saint Lucia that opens Chapter 6 of *Another Life*:

> Surpliced, processional, the shallows mutter in Latin, maris stella, maris stella (I.6.i)

Crane is heard again in chapter 10:

> O Paradiso! sang The pied shoal ... And it all sang, surpliced, processional, the waves clapped their hands, hallelujah! (II.10.ii)

This comes in "Homage to Gregorias," which focuses on Walcott's teenage intoxication with art, under the tutelage of Harry Simmons and his late-Romantic idols, Gauguin and Van Gogh. But that inspirational phase ends in madness and despair, as did Crane, who literalises his art in martyrdom. "Voyages II" ends:

> O minstrel galleons of Carib fire,
> Bequeath us to no earthly shore until
> Is answered in the vortex of our grave
> The seal's wide spindrift gaze toward
> paradise.

Exalting though this is, the elation is willed; it insists on an identification of art and nature, on paradise now, which neither art nor nature can supply; art is forced to become not a medium but a revelation. In contrast to this, as Harry Simmons nears his end, Walcott describes him in a line borrowed from Timon of Athens: "Harry had built his mansion / upon the beached verge of the salt flood" (IV.18.i) This sounds the note that becomes dominant in the poetry of Shakespeare's last plays, where the sea is an image of art and its strangely powerful transformations that change nothing. Walcott's relationship with his art is a Modernist one, post-tragic, post-Romantic, anti-historic.

It might be thought that Walcott's second long poem, *Omeros*, returned us to the tragedies of history. In *Another Life*, the studio of Harry Simmons occupies the former military hospital on the Vigie peninsula, facing the town of

Castries, making art the principal reference point for the poem. In *Omeros*, the former barracks on the heights of the Morne above Castries are as it were reoccupied by the retired British Sergeant Major, Plunkett, suggesting that history may now dominate the town and the poem. Such a reading might seem encouraged by the versification, since the relatively freely formed verse paragraphs of the earlier poem are replaced by Homeric hexameter and Dantean terza rima, as if taking on board the full gravitas of epic. There are no less than three visits to the underworld to receive the injunctions of dead fathers. A number of chapters are in the mode of a historical novel, following the adventures of a namesake of Plunkett's who serves in Rodney's fleet and is killed during the Battle of the Saints, a turning point in the history of the British empire. An Achilles and a Hector fight over a Helen. And so on.

But these are not the heroes of the *Iliad*, that prototype for tragedy. The deeds of history are narrated but in an oddly desubtantialized way, such that they eddy and even repeat themselves. We lose sight of the fight between Achille and Hector in a sudden gust of rain blown in from the sea; Helen returns to Achille (who is also a sort of Menelaus) after Hector's death. That death is not at the hands of another "hero," it is a road accident and results from driving made reckless by the perversion of love into frustrated desire, when Hector abandons the sea to run a transport business; it is more like a suicide caused by the psychodynamics of development economics. Hector dies of the wound from which all suffer in various ways, for Walcott has made Saint Lucia into Sophocles's magical island of Lemnos, a space from which history is certainly not absent but where its stinking wounds may be nursed. The amber light of empire that suffuses much of *Another Life* is condensed into the yellow dress Helen filches from Maud Plunkett, and the colour runs through the poem like a painterly motif. Plunkett himself, a veteran of Alamein, has retired to Saint Lucia in order to escape history and dedicate himself to Maud and her garden (a nice touch of humour), though he still hankers after a son; this last is his wound. It is desire for succession that leads him into historical research, digging in the midden of the past, where he indeed finds his namesake son, but only as an entry in a document. With the acquisition of this ghost-son the fever of nostalgia is finally appeased and he reacknowledges his wife. Achille, conversely, seeks a father, whom he finds in a dream or nightmare of Africa "where," he later explains to Helen, while she helps him don her yellow dress for the traditional Gelede carnival after Christmas, "he had been his own father and his own son" (VI.55.ii). Succession, social reproduction, history, that nightmare of the Modernist sensibility, is transmuted into the succession of the sea's waves, always different, always the same, "proving that empires vanish / while water has one tense and cannot run backwards" (IV.19.i), as Walcott muses in *Tiepolo's Hound*.

Thus the land-bound characters of the *Iliad* are reimagined in the sea-borne world of the *Odyssey*, and an Odyssey rewritten to the poetics of Ovid, for the imagery continues as metamorphic as ever. As well as a mark of ambitiousness, Walcott's combination of hexameter with terza rima, both notoriously difficult forms in English, is a stroke of genius, for by doubling the stakes he lowers the odds. It is commonly said that English lacks the number of rhymes available in Italian, but it is more that frequently recurring rhymes in a relatively uninflected language fall with such great emphasis that they impede narrative, not a problem for a language that can rhyme lightly on the inflections. Walcott solves this problem by the hexameter, which runs past the point where the English ear expects a rhyme and thus loosens the stricture of Dante's form. The length of the hexameter also accommodates Walcott's calculatedly straggling and inconclusive, indeed anti-conclusive syntax.

The presiding genius of the poem is not really Homer, not even Ovid, but Joyce, whose Bloom and Molly lie behind Walcott's Maud and Plunkett. Interestingly (given that Walcott has been accused of machismo), it is not Plunkett but old Maud who is "a bit of an artist" (LIV), reinforcing the witty and moving tribute to Joyce and the Liffey in Chapter XXXIX:

Anna Livia!
Muse of our age's Omeros, undimmed
    Master
and true tenor of the place! (V.39.iii)

Whatever a later age's final judgment on Walcott's *Omeros* as a poem, its humane values undoubtedly keep faith with those of Joyce's *Ulysses*.

In Walcott's third long poem, *Tiepolo's Hound*, he returns to the topic of painting that preoccupied him in *Another Life* but now in the life of another painter, Pissarro. He also for the first time publishes his own paintings alongside the poem. History recedes. When the Franco-Prussian war breaks out, Pissarro flees to London; when Dreyfus is exiled to Pissarro's own Caribbean, his painting continues quietly, despairingly, to render the French landscape:

> his canvases endorsed the fiction that its citizens believed, an equal France. (III.17.iii)

And the endorsement is not couched in terms of the iconography or rhetoric of a Delacroix but in the liberation of the elements of painting itself, something he has learned along with Cézanne:

> Paint had, until then,
> pretended it wasn't paint, but now an equal drama
> was made of every inch ...
> now stroke or word or note presume their intent because of what they are:
> shape, sound, and stain ... (II.9.iii)

The equality, the democracy, is in the act of painting itself. This is why Walcott's syntax has to be indeterminate, why his images refuse fixity and spin their meaning through a tissue of fleeting associations. He commits his poetry neither to the white dog of art nor the black dog of reality, instead making each reverse out the other. This is the politics of his poetics.

This is also why Walcott's paintings in *Tiepolo's Hound* are at their best when dealing with landscape and at their weakest when most directly figurative. The bands of colour running across "Preparing the Net," for example, can be read purely as paint, as can the splotches of light and shade across the sand. The figure of the fisherman emerges from and merges back into the paint, perfectly a figure in a landscape, just as the impact of Hector's death is elided in the description of its setting. But when the figures are foregrounded, as in "Baiting the Hook," "Doctrine," and even "Anna," moving though that last painting is in its resonance with the text, the plasticity of the figures resists assimilation into the ground of the painting. The pleasurable oscillation between dissolving and resolving the image jars to a halt.

The poetry never breaks down in that way. For *Tiepolo's Hound* Walcott has devised a brilliantly simple form. The poem is laid out on the page in couplets, which one inevitably perceives as visually complete; yet acoustically they are incomplete, since they do not rhyme. The reader has to wait until the next couplet for the rhymes to arrive; when they do they recompose the preceding couplet as the first part of a quatrain, though a quatrain that is never allowed to complete itself before one's eyes. Walcott plays across this gap with endless felicity of invention, as in the close to the penultimate chapter of the poem:

> There is another book that is the shadow
> of my hand on this sunlit page, the one
> I have tried hard to write, but let this do;
> let gratitude redeem what lies undone.

Perhaps this beautiful form answers one of the late John Figueroa's searching questions at the end of Stewart Brown's collection, *The Art of Derek Walcott* (Bridgend, 1991). Figueroa asked whether what he called the "whiteness is everywhere" parts of *Omeros*—Euro-American exploitation, displacement, and genocide—did not overwhelm the positive parts. It is the reader who has to find the answers to this question in the *blanc du papier* between the couplets, for it is in these gaps that Walcott, like the sea in *Omeros*, is still going on.

Source: T. J. Cribb, "Walcott, Poet and Painter," in *Kenyon Review*, Vol. 23, No. 2, Spring 2001, pp. 176–84.

SOURCES

Als, Hilton, "The Islander," in the *New Yorker*, February 9, 2004, pp. 421–51, available online at http://www.newyorker.com/archive/2004/02/09/040209fa_fact1 (accessed October 12, 2009).

Baugh, Edward, "Ripening with Walcott," in *Critical Perspectives on Derek Walcott*, edited by Robert D. Hamner, Three Continents Press, 1993, p. 278.

Bloom, Harold, "Introduction," in *Derek Walcott*, Bloom's Modern Authors Series, edited by Harold Bloom, Chelsea House, 2003, p. 3.

Breslin, Paul, "Biographical Sketch," in *Nobody's Nation: Reading Derek Walcott*, University of Chicago Press, 2001, pp. 11–45.

Cole, Olivia, "Nobel Winner Quits Oxford Poetry Race Over Sex Claims," *Evening Standard* (London), May 12, 2009, available online at http://www.thisislondon.co.uk/standard/article-23689480-nobel-winner-quits-oxford-poetry-race-over-sex-claims.do;jsessionid=415175B79A87271F69E1BC66F0714FC8 (accessed October 12, 2009).

Davies-Venn, Michael, "Nobel Laureate to Join University of Alberta Faculty," *Express News*, University of Alberta, April 21, 2009, available online at http://www.expressnews.ualberta.ca/article.cfm?id=10117 (accessed October 12, 2009).

Heaney, Seamus, "The Murmur of Malvern," in *Derek Walcott*, Bloom's Modern Authors Series, edited by Harold Bloom, Chelsea House, 2003, p. 9.

Heffernan, Julián Jiménez, "Tropical Sublime: Derek Walcott's Early Poetry," in *Approaches to the Poetics of Derek Walcott*, edited by José Luis Martínez-Dueñas Espejo and José María Pérez Fernández, Edwin Mellen Press, 2001, p. 31.

"History, 1900–1999: The History of Tobago in the 20th Century," *myTobago: The Definitive Visitor Guide to Tobago*, available online at http://www.mytobago.info/history05.php (accessed October 9, 2009).

"History of Trinidad and Tobago" *History of Nations*, 2005, available online at http://www.historyofnations.net/northamerica/trinidad.html (accessed October 9, 2009).

Thieme, John, *Derek Walcott*, Manchester University Press, 1999.

Walcott, Derek, "Midsummer, Tobago," in *Selected Poems*, edited by Edward Baugh, Farrar, Straus and Giroux, 2007, p. 119.

FURTHER READING

Als, Hilton, "The Islander," in the *New Yorker*, February 9, 2004, pp. 421–51.
  This portrait of the poet in his old age includes personal reflections and comments on his poetry.

Baugh, Edward, *Derek Walcott*, Longman Group, 1978.
  Written with student audiences in mind, this study of Walcott's life describes the important time the poet spent in the Caribbean.

Bobb, June D., *Beating a Restless Drum: The Poetics of Kamau Brathwaite and Derek Walcott*, Africa World Press, 1998.
  Bobb's survey interweaves the ideas in Walcott's work with those in the poetry of Brathwaite, a major Caribbean writer from Barbados whose works focus on the connection between Africa and the Antilles.

Burnett, Paula, *Derek Walcott: Politics and Poetics*, University of Florida Press, 2000.
  Burnett explores Walcott's drama and poetry and discusses Walcott's philosophy and technique. She covers his approach to aesthetics, myth, and identity.

Hamner, Robert D., *Derek Walcott*, Twayne, 1981.
  Another early academic survey of Walcott's career, Hamner's book is useful to readers who are focused on this early poem and the poet's career at the time he wrote it.

Ismond, Patricia, *Abandoning Dead Metaphors: The Caribbean Phase of Derek Walcott's Poetry*, University of the West Indies Press, 2001.
  This survey, written late in the poet's career, looks back at the time when "Midsummer, Tobago" was written, placing it with the perspective of hindsight regarding Walcott's growth as a poet.

Weiland, James, "Adam's Task . . . : Myth and Fictions in the Poetry of Derek Walcott," in *The Ensphering Mind: A Comparative Study of Derek Walcott, Christomper Okigbo, A. D. Hope, Allen Curnow, A. M. Klein and Nissim Ezekiel*, Three Continents, 1988, pp. 165–88.
  Weiland presents a study of Caribbean literature, placing Walcott in that genre among with others.

My Mother Combs My Hair

CHITRA BANERJEE DIVAKARUNI

1991

"My Mother Combs My Hair" is a poem by the Asian American poet and author Chitra Banerjee Divakaruni. The poem was published in 1991 in Divakaruni's first collection of verse, entitled *Black Candle: Poems about Women from India, Pakistan, and Bangladesh* (Calyx, 1991). It is also available in the revised 2000 edition, also published by Calyx.

The collection focuses on the various abuses perpetrated against women in the Indian subcontinent and in Asian American communities, particularly within the family. The main theme of "My Mother Combs My Hair" is the romantic ideal and grim reality of marriage as seen by a mother brought up in the traditional Indian ways and a daughter who is more assimilated into American culture. The poem is widely anthologized and studied in schools and colleges.

Divakaruni has gained a reputation as one of the most important South Asian writers in English. She is best known for her novels and short stories, many of which are set in the Bay Area of San Francisco, where Divakaruni lived for many years. Her stories have appeared in over fifty magazines, including the *Atlantic Monthly* and the *New Yorker*. Her writing has been included in more than thirty anthologies and has been translated into eleven languages.

AUTHOR BIOGRAPHY

Chitra Banerjee Divakaruni was born on July 29, 1956, in Calcutta, India, the daughter of Rajendra Kumar, an accountant, and Tatini Banerjee, a schoolteacher. The only girl in a family of three sons, one of her earliest memories was of her grandfather telling her stories from the ancient Indian scriptures.

Divakaruni was brought up (and remained in adulthood) a devout Hindu, but she attended a Catholic convent school run by Irish nuns, graduating in 1971. She gained a bachelor's degree in English from Calcutta University in 1976. In the same year, at the age of nineteen, she immigrated to the United States. She earned a master's degree from Wright State University in Dayton, Ohio, in 1978, and a Ph.D. from the University of California, Berkeley, in 1985, doing odd jobs to pay for her education. She began her writing career after graduating from Berkeley.

In 1989, Divakaruni was appointed professor of creative writing at Foothill College, Los Altos, California. She lived for many years in the San Francisco Bay Area of California, which forms the setting for much of her writing. In 2002, she moved to Houston, Texas, and took up a post as professor of creative writing at the University of Houston. As of 2009, she was still residing in Houston.

Divakaruni has long been active within the Asian American community. In 1991, she established Maitri, an organization for South Asian women who suffer domestic abuse. As of 2009, she served on the advisory board of Maitri in the San Francisco Bay Area and of Daya in Houston, another organization with similar aims. She was also on the board of Pratham, an organization that helps educate children in India.

While arranged marriages have formed a major theme in her work, Divakaruni herself opted for a love marriage on June 29, 1979, to S. Murthy Divakaruni. They have two sons, Abhay and Anand.

In her writing, Divakaruni draws on her own and other South Asian women's experiences as an immigrant with a foot in two cultures. The poetry collection in which "My Mother Combs My Hair" appears, *Black Candle: Poems about Women from India, Pakistan, and Bangladesh*, was published in 1991. *Arranged Marriage* (1995), a collection of short stories, followed in 1995. A collection of poetry, *Leaving Yuba City*, and a novel, *The Mistress of Spices*, appeared in 1997. In 1998, Divakaruni published a second novel, *Sister of My Heart*. *The Mistress of Spices* and *Sister of My Heart* were made into films.

Divakaruni's work has garnered many awards. In 1996, *Arranged Marriage* was awarded the PEN Oakland Josephine Miles Prize for Fiction, the Bay Area Book Reviewers Award for Fiction, and an American Book Award from the Before Columbus Foundation. *The Mistress of Spices* was named a best book of 1997 by the *Los Angeles Times* and a best paperback of 1998 by the *Seattle Times*. Poems that were later collected in *Leaving Yuba City* won a Gerbode Foundation Award (1992), a Pushcart Prize (1994), and the Allen Ginsberg Poetry Prize (1994).

POEM TEXT

```
The room is full
of the scent of crushed hibiscus,
my mother's breath.
Our positions are of childhood,
I kneeling on the floor,                          5
she crosslegged
on the chair behind.
She works the comb
through permed strands
rough as dry seaweed.                             10
I can read regret in her fingers
untangling snarls,
rubbing red jabakusum oil
into brittle ends.
When she was my age,                              15
her hair reached her knees,
fell in a thick black rush
beyond the edges
of old photographs. In one,
my father has daringly                            20
covered her hand with his
and made her smile.
At their marriage, she told me,
because of her hair
he did not ask for a dowry.                       25
This afternoon I wait
for the old comments,
how you've ruined your hair,
this plait's like a lizard's tail,
or, if you don't take better care                 30
of it, you'll never get married.
But the braiding is done,
each strand
in its neat place, shining,
the comb put away.                                35
I turn to her, to the grey
snaking in at the temples,
the cracks growing
```

        at the edges of her eyes
        since father left.   40
        We hold the silence
        tight between us
        like a live wire,
        like a strip of gold
        torn from a wedding brocade.   45

POEM SUMMARY

"My Mother Combs My Hair" opens with the speaker describing in the first person (using *I* and *my*) a sensory experience. The room in which she finds herself is filled with the scent of hibiscus, a flower with large, beautiful, and fragrant blooms that is common in tropical and subtropical regions such as India. The hibiscus flower is used in India to make an herbal tea and a hair oil called *jabakusum* oil (see line 13). The speaker identifies the scent of the crushed flower with her mother's breath, perhaps because she uses *jabakusum* oil on her own hair or because she is using it on her daughter's hair.

Lines 4 through 7 introduce the two persons of the poem: a mother and her daughter, the speaker of the poem. The speaker kneels on the floor, while her mother sits cross-legged on a chair behind her. The mother is combing her daughter's hair. The daughter has had her hair permed, a Western fashion that is alien to traditional Indian culture. Perming has the effect of drying and roughening the hair, and the mother is having difficulty working the comb through the tangled mess.

In line 10, the speaker's perm-damaged hair is likened in a simile (comparison using *like* or *as*) to dried seaweed. The speaker senses the regret that her mother feels about the state of her hair, though the mother does not say anything. The mother rubs *jabakusum* oil into the broken ends of the daughter's hair.

The second stanza marks (line 15) a flashback to a time when the mother was young and in love with her husband, the daughter's father. The mother's hair, in contrast with her daughter's, was strong and lush and so long that it reached beyond the edges of the old photographs that captured her image. In one such photograph, the husband has placed his hand over his wife's hand. Such an act is considered daring in the conservative and modest Indian culture and makes her smile.

The mother once told her daughter that when she married, her bridegroom did not ask for a

MEDIA ADAPTATIONS

- Actress, screenwriter, and producer Suhasini and her husband Mani Ratnam turned *Sister of My Heart* into an early 2000s television miniseries in Tamil, the northeast region of Sri Lanka.
- *The Mistress of Spices* is a 2006 film based on Divakaruni's novel of the same title.

dowry (a sum of money which in traditional Indian culture was given by a bride's father to the bridegroom as payment for marrying his daughter) because he felt that her hair was prize enough.

The third stanza begins (line 26) with a return to the present time. The daughter is expecting to hear the usual comments from her mother about how she has ruined her hair, how her plait resembles a lizard's tail, or how, if she does not take better care of her hair, no man will marry her. No such comment comes, however. Now that the mother has finished making the neat and shiny plait, she puts away the comb.

The fourth stanza begins (line 36) with the daughter turning to look at her mother. She sees that her mother's hair is starting to turn grey at the temples. The wrinkles around her eyes have increased since her husband, the speaker's father, left. This is the first indication that the mother's marriage is no longer intact. Mother and daughter remain silent. The silence between them has a tautness that is likened in similes to a live electrical wire (line 43) and then to a gold border torn from the rich silk brocade from which Indian wedding saris are often made.

THEMES

Attitudes toward Marriage in Traditional Indian Culture and Modern Western Culture
In Divakaruni's work, cultural conflicts often run in parallel with, and are exacerbated by,

TOPICS FOR FURTHER STUDY

- Research attitudes toward courtship and marriage in Asian American families or another immigrant group. Interview people of different generations, noting the length of time they have spent in their family's country of origin and in their adopted country, the United States. Possible topics to include in your questions are: qualities sought in a spouse; method of seeking the spouse; who has a say in the choice of spouse; expectations of marriage; experience of marriage; and experience of separation and divorce where relevant. Give a class presentation or write a report on your findings. Throughout this assignment you will need to be aware of confidentiality and anonymity issues.

- Research the topic of women's rights and roles in Asian American communities and in one other minority or majority community. Note any privileges or benefits to women in each community as well as any problems or restrictions on their rights. Find out what changes women want in those communities. Write a report or make an audio or video CD in which you compare and contrast the lot of women in the two communities.

- Write an essay in which you compare and contrast any two of the following poems about marriage: Divakaruni's "My Mother Combs My Hair," Robert Browning's "My Last Duchess," Denise Levertov's "Wedding Ring," and Wendell Berry's "The Country of Marriage." Consider such elements as authorial voice, narrative, themes, style, and imagery.

- Create a film, poem, short story, dramatic monologue, or play around the theme, portrait of a marriage.

conflicts between the generations. In the immigrant families she portrays, the parents and older people embody the traditional cultural values with which they grew up in India. Their offspring are generally more assimilated into American culture. This difference in values produces an inevitable tension between generations.

"My Mother Combs My Hair" fits into this pattern. Its main theme is the different views and experiences of marriage held by a mother and daughter. The mother exemplifies the attitudes held by the traditional culture of India and the daughter exemplifies views more typical of the Western culture of the United States, their adopted country.

The tension between mother and daughter is primarily shown through the symbolism of hair. The mother would have grown up in India, where she used traditional herbal remedies such as the hair oil she uses on her daughter. The daughter's hair has been damaged by her getting a permanent, a process which was especially common in the West in the 1980s and 1990s but unknown in Indian culture. The mother disapproves of the daughter's decision to perm her hair and tries to restore it to the same beautiful and natural state of her own hair when she was the same age as her daughter is now. Symbolically, this suggests that the mother would like to turn the clock back to when the family was united in and within the old Indian traditions.

In India, the mother's hair was seen as a glory precious enough to substitute for a dowry. Beauty was elevated above material considerations. From the point of view of a girl, marriage was a goal in itself. The daughter, by contrast, is not interested in using her hair to entice a husband. She has had her hair permed, an act that artificially changes the hair and damages it, in line with the American fashion of the time.

The drying and damaging effects of the perm symbolically parallel the decay of the ideal of marriage. The mother's marriage, which started with such romance, is no more: Her husband has left her. The beauty that temporarily made him forget financial considerations when he married her is fading, as the wrinkles around her eyes have increased since his departure. The hair that attracted him is now turning gray. The man who married her at least partly for her beautiful hair has gone, and she is unlikely to attract a replacement.

The failure of the mother's marriage explains why the comments that the daughter expects, about never getting married if she does not take better care of her hair, do not come. The mother did everything right according to the old values: She kept her hair long, lush, and beautiful—but still the husband left her. The fact that the daughter's hair already has the qualities of old age, dryness and decay, suggests that she has already acquired the skepticism about marriage that took her mother a lifetime of bitter experience to learn.

The style of hair is also significant. While the mother's hair, at the time she attracted her husband, was loose, a sign of sensuality and femininity, the daughter is having her hair plaited neatly. This containment of a major feminine attraction suggests an attitude of restraint towards sexuality and marriage. The daughter feels no need or desire to put her femininity and beauty on show or on sale to potential suitors.

Thus, while the mother has grown disillusioned about marriage, so has the daughter. This ironically subverts the tradition (strong in India) of children sitting at the feet of a respected parent or elder in order to learn their wisdom. Here, the wisdom that the daughter has learned at the mother's feet is to avoid treading the same painful path as the mother. She has learned not to place her trust in the old ideal of romance, husband, and marriage.

Women's Lot

Divakaruni is quoted in an article by Elizabeth Softky for *Black Issues in Higher Education* as saying, "Women in particular respond to my work because I'm writing about them, women in love, in difficulties, women in relationships...I want people to relate to my characters, to feel their joy and pain, because it will be harder to [be] prejudiced when they meet them in real life."

Much of Divakaruni's work has a strong feminist message, and this poem is no exception. It can be read as a warning to women against surrendering themselves to the whims of a man, who may not prove reliable. The mother followed Indian convention in trying to attract and please her husband, but his desertion shows that this was an unwise sacrifice. It is also one that the daughter is not prepared to make. She remains unmarried and has ruined her hair to the point where the mother believes she will never attract a man. The daughter does not regret this. On the contrary, she keeps her hair—and her person—out of reach.

STYLE

Irony

Situational irony is a literary device in which the actual outcome is different from the one that might be expected. This reversal of expectations often makes a strong and memorable point because it surprises the reader. In "My Mother Combs My Hair," the reversals of expectation occur on several levels. First, there is a reversal of youth and age. The mother's view of marriage has been characterized by the innocence, idealism, and romanticism typical of youth. The daughter's view is a more cynical one, tempered by the hard experience of her father's desertion of the family, such as might be expected of an older person who has seen more of the world.

This reversal of youth and age, innocence and experience, leads to a reversal in authority. While the daughter sits at the mother's feet in the traditional pose of the pupil at the feet of the respected elder, it turns out that the mother has lost some of her authority by espousing a faith in marriage that has been discredited. The mother is in no position to lecture the daughter, and she refrains from doing so, backing away from the long-term habit. The daughter, in her less trusting, less innocent, and certainly more American stance on men and marriage, has become more of an authority.

Imagery

The imagery (descriptive language evoking pictures of other sensory experiences) in "My Mother Combs My Hair" is taken from nature. It expresses the opposites of lush and sensual femininity, romance, and hope versus dried-up decay and disillusionment. The mother, though she is the older woman, is associated with the beautiful hibiscus flower and long, lush hair, whereas the daughter is associated with dried-up seaweed, lizard's tails, and a perm-damaged plait. This reversal of the expected imagery reflects the characterization of the two women. The mother has traditionally championed the romantic ideal of marriage, seeing attracting a husband as a worthy goal for her daughter. However, her marriage has failed. The daughter has learned from this failure and from the harsher, more cynical, and more realistic ways of her adopted country, the United States. She harbors no romantic ideals, but keeps her hair and her femininity strictly contained.

COMPARE & CONTRAST

- **1990s:** According to figures from the Department of Homeland Security published in the *2008 Yearbook of Immigration Statistics*, the number of people obtaining legal resident status in the United States whose previous country of residence was India was over 352,000 in the years between 1990 and 1999.

    Today: According to the same source, the number of people obtaining legal resident status in the United States whose previous country of residence was India in 2008 alone was over 59,000.

- **1990s:** In 1995, the Fourth World Conference on Women in held in Beijing, China, as part of the United Nations Commission on the Status of Women. A Platform for Action is signed, committing to gender equality and the empowerment of women.

    Today: As of 2009, the United States is the only developed country in the world that has refused to ratify the Convention on the Elimination of All Forms of Discrimination Against Women (CEDAW), a United Nations (UN) bill of rights for women adopted in 1979 by the UN General Assembly.

- **1990s:** Maitri, an organization that helps women of the South Asian community who are suffering domestic abuse, is founded in California in 1991 by a group of Indian women, Divakaruni among them.

    Today: A 2007 report by the Family Violence Prevention Fund, "(Un)heard Voices: Domestic Violence in the Asian American Community," concludes that there is "clear consensus that domestic violence is a serious issue in all the Asian American communities."

- **1990s:** Arranged marriages in the Asian community are organized by relatives or professional marriage brokers, though classified advertising is also used.

    Today: As Asian American immigrants increasingly lose contact with their country of origin, the role of newspaper classified advertisements and Internet agencies in facilitating arranged marriages grows.

HISTORICAL CONTEXT

Indian Immigration to the United States

Few people immigrated to the United States from India before 1900. Hindu beliefs discouraged it and so did the British colonizers of the Indian subcontinent, who restricted the movements of the Indian people. The situation changed in 1946 when the Luce-Celler Act allowed 100 Indians per year to immigrate to the United States and allowed them to become citizens. In 1947, India gained independence from Great Britain, marking a second wave of Indian immigration, which saw over six thousand Indians come to the United States to live between 1948 and 1965.

The passage of the Immigration and Nationality Act Amendments of 1965 ended discrimination in immigration quotas based on race or nationality.

According to a 2008 Census Bureau population estimate cited on the U.S. Department of Health and Human Services Website, there are 15.5 million Asian Americans living in the United States. Asian Americans comprise people originating from the Far East, Southeast Asia, or the Indian subcontinent. Asian Americans make up 5 percent of the nation's population. In 2008, the states with the largest Asian American populations are California, New York, Hawaii, Texas, New Jersey, and Illinois.

Marriage in Indian and American Asian Culture

Arranged marriages are common in Asian culture and have been carried over into American

Asian culture. The marriages may be arranged by the bride and bridegroom's family, through marriage bureaus, or through paid matchmakers. In the 1990s, it became common for parents of prospective brides and grooms to place advertisements for spouses in the classified sections of publications targeted at the Asian American community. In the late 1990s, the growing popularity of the Internet made it easy to conduct searches online.

While the tradition of arranged marriage has its critics, it also has its defenders, who point out that the separation and divorce rates of such marriages are lower than those of modern Western-style love marriages. They point out further that a couple is matched by rational considerations that are more likely to provide a solid foundation to a partnership than the passions or infatuations that can prompt Western-style love marriages, which may not last. These rational considerations include education, financial status, and caste (the social stratification of India). When the foundation is in place, it is argued, love grows later. Finally, supporters of arranged marriage argue that the institution now operates much like a dating agency, which simply introduces the prospective couple and leaves the choice up to them of whether to take the relationship further.

The mother's marriage in "My Mother Combs My Hair" may or may not have been an arranged one. This point is not made explicit. Undoubtedly, it is at the same time a love marriage, but it does not last.

Bride Burning

Some commentators link the tradition of arranged marriages to spousal abuse and so-called bride burning or dowry death incidents in Asian communities. In such incidents, the bridegroom marries a young woman to collect her dowry (money settled on a bridegroom by a bride's parents in return for his marrying her) and then arranges an apparent accident in which the woman burns to death in a kitchen fire. Alternatively, the bridegroom may feel that the dowry was inadequate and demand a further dowry from the bride's parents. When it is refused, the bridegroom arranges the bride burning.

It is significant that the husband of "My Mother Combs My Hair" does not ask for a dowry, out of appreciation for his bride's beautiful

Portrait of an Indian bridal couple in their finery
(Image copyright Thefinalmiracle, 2009. Used under license from Shutterstock.com)

hair. While this may seem romantic, the dream ends in bitterness and disappointment when the husband leaves the marriage.

CRITICAL OVERVIEW

Divakaruni is better known for her fiction than her poetry, and she did not begin to write prose until after the 1991 publication of *Black Candle*. Thus Nina Mehta's 1992 review for the *Bloomsbury Review* is one among few. In comments that could apply to "My Mother Combs My Hair," Mehta called the collection "unsettling" on the grounds that the poems catalogue "an assortment of sins" perpetrated against "desolate, soul-sick women," from *sati* (the immolation of women on their husbands' funeral pyres) to dowry death, domestic abuse, and female infanticide. She considered the collection's title an apt metaphor for the "scorched lives" of the women portrayed.

Mehta wrote that the poems' straightforward and descriptive style helps give them their "emotional heft." The focus of the poems, she pointed out, is "connubial despair and the ritualistic sacrifices expected and demanded of women." In a comment that raises a question about the fate of the daughter in "My Mother Combs My Hair," Mehta pointed out that even poems about adolescent girls are "full of tension and foreboding," in that "Young girls are bound to become hopeless and helpless women." Mehta drew attention to a common theme in the collection of the failed "promise of marriage."

Mehta concluded that while the poems in the collection are not of a consistent quality, "at their best, they constitute a series of verse dispatches from an all-too-quiet home front that makes one wish India's sentimental films were the worst of women's problems."

Sudeep Sen, in his essay for *World Literature Today*, "Recent Indian English Poetry," mentioned *Black Candle* and other volumes of Divakaruni's poetry as having similar subject matter to her later novels: "womanhood, family life, American exile, alienation, exoticism, ethnicity, domesticity, love and romance."

Divakaruni's 1997 poetry collection, *Leaving Yuba City* contains poems from *Black Candle*. Amy van Buren's comments on *Leaving Yuba City* could apply to "My Mother Combs My Hair." Van Buren noted the "beauty and sensitivity" with which Divakaruni "guides the reader through stories of immigration, changing traditions, and family violence." Van Buren added, "It is emblematic of Divakaruni's work that she connects personal experience with cultural history in a soft but powerful voice."

Donna Seaman's review for *Booklist* of *Leaving Yuba City* is also relevant to "My Mother Combs My Hair". Seaman noted the "bittersweet" quality of Divakaruni's poetry and commented, "Everything Divakaruni touches with her exquisitely sensitive writer's mind—whether it's a memory, or a scene between wife and husband—turns to gold." Seaman noted that each of Divakaruni's "lyrical and haunting poems opens slowly, like a flower," but then "rapidly picks up speed and intensity until it glows like a meteor as it plunges into the deepest recesses of the heart."

Seaman called Divakaruni's poetry "Strongly narrative, shimmeringly detailed, and emotionally acute," adding that it "embraces pain and beauty in its affirmation of grace."

In a review of *Black Candle* printed on the back cover of the revised Calyx edition of 2000, the poet Jane Hirshfield is quoted as having written that the book "bears witness to the condition of women and to the condition of the world." Hirshfield testified to the poems' sensory power, calling them "Rich with colors, sounds, scents, with flowers and spices and fabrics and waters and sorrows and smoke." The quotation from Hirshfield concluded that the poems demonstrate the "compassion" of the poet's "fiercely seeing heart."

CRITICISM

Claire Robinson

Robinson has an M.A. in English. She is a former teacher of English literature and creative writing and a freelance writer and editor. In the following essay, she examines how "My Mother Combs My Hair" uses imagery to trace two women's attitudes toward marriage across generations and cultures.

Typical of poetry by Divakaruni, "My Mother Combs My Hair" has a narrative on the surface level that is straightforward. On a deeper symbolic level, the poem describes through the use of imagery a journey to bitter self-realization. In the first stanza, the mother is associated with the hibiscus flower. The hibiscus is a tropical or subtropical plant with beautiful, showy, and fragrant blooms, often of a deep pink or red color. It is common in India and is used to make *jabakusum* hair oil. The blooms are also used to decorate the hair. The seeds of some members of the hibiscus family are chewed in order to sweeten the breath. This may explain the reference to the mother's hibiscus-scented breath in line 3 of the poem.

The fact that the hibiscus is described as crushed has two meanings. On the literal level, hibiscus blooms are crushed in order to make *jabakusum* hair oil or hibiscus tea, so the fragrance in the room would be of crushed hibiscus. On the symbolic level, the hibiscus is identified with the mother (line 3) at that point in her life when she was in full glorious bloom as a desirable woman. In this context the crushing refers to the destruction of her marriage and her romantic ideals.

WHAT DO I READ NEXT?

- Chitra Banerjee Divakaruni's poem "The Woman Addresses Her Sleeping Lover" (also in *Black Candle*, 1991), like "My Mother Combs My Hair," explores the theme of marital abuse. Divakaruni has dedicated the poem to a woman at the Women's Shelter in Oakland, California. Readers should be warned that the poem contains images of domestic violence.

- Chitra Banerjee Divakaruni's collection of short stories *Arranged Marriage* (Anchor, 1996) explores Indian women's experiences of arranged marriages and their attempts to find a way through cultural and generational conflicts, both in India and in their adopted country of the United States.

- Arundhati Roy's debut novel, *The God of Small Things* (Random House, 1997), won the prestigious Booker Prize in the UK and has been translated into forty languages. The novel examines relationships in a family based in Kerala, India, which loses members to the United States and Great Britain. Events are seen from the viewpoint of twin siblings.

- Amy Tan's novel *The Joy Luck Club* (Putnam, 1989) explores the relationships between four immigrant women from China and their American-born daughters. The mothers want their daughters to make the most of the opportunities available in their adopted country, but at the same time, they want them to uphold Chinese tradition.

- *Asian American Studies: A Reader*, by Jean Yu-wen Shen Wu (Rutgers University Press, 2000), is an anthology of writing by and about Americans of South Asian, East Asian, Southeast Asian, and Filipino ancestry. Subjects covered include cross-racial marriage, success stories of minority groups, Asian American activism, and attitudes toward feminism. Readers should be warned that the book contains a chapter on pornography.

- *Growing Up Filipino: Stories for Young Adults*, by Cecilia Manguerra Brainard (PALH, 2003), is a collection of short stories for young adults by Filipino American writers, which explores the challenges of adolescence from the viewpoints of teens in the Philippines or the United States.

At the opposite pole to the hibiscus imagery is the reptilian imagery. Two similes are used to describe the daughter's perm-ruined hair. Her hair is rough like dried seaweed, an unattractive image that connotes an absence of life and luster. The roughness means that unlike the mother's hair when she was younger, the daughter's hair does not invite touch. In an old photograph, the mother's hand is covered protectively by her husband's hand, but no man, it seems, would want to touch dried seaweed. The contrast is reinforced by the imagery of color. Unlike the rich pinks and reds of hibiscus flowers, dried seaweed is black or brown.

The other simile used to describe the daughter's hair is that of the lizard's tail. A lizard is a cold-blooded reptile that must bask in the sun in order to warm itself sufficiently to become active. *Hot-blooded* is a synonym for *passionate*. When applied to the daughter in the poem, the lizard imagery suggests that she is not interested in passionate relationships with men or that it would take much effort to warm her up to the idea.

It may or may not be significant that many types of lizard can shed their tail if a predator catches them by the tail. It is a defense mechanism that can save the lizard's life, as the predator is left holding the tail while the lizard escapes. Again, this imagery applied to the daughter suggests that she is more likely to try to escape from any man who tried to capture her than to offer herself up for plucking like some beautiful flower.

> "THE DAUGHTER OF THE POEM IS UNMARRIED YET KEEPS HER HAIR TIGHTLY BOUND, MARKING HER UNWILLINGNESS TO GIVE HERSELF TO A MAN IN THE WAY THAT HER MOTHER DID."

The ironic twist of this poem (irony in this context means that the actual outcome is the opposite from the one that might be expected) lies in the fact that although the mother conformed to the conventional Indian expectation of attracting a husband, the husband left her. This casts doubt on the value of the conventional behavior that the mother would once have wanted her daughter to follow.

This twist is reflected in the change in imagery that the poet uses to describe the mother. Thus in the final stanza, the mother acquires some of the reptilian imagery that in the previous stanza (stanza 3) was the province of the daughter. The appearance of the graying hair that helps mark the end of her role as a woman who is attractive to men is described in a reptilian image connoting snakes. The image is reinforced by the description of the cracks that have been growing around her eyes since her husband left. The reference to cracks suggests a parched surface and reflects the fact that the family has been broken.

The reptilian imagery, especially when applied to women, may connote for some readers the biblical serpent who successfully tempted Eve, the first woman, to disobey God and eat the forbidden fruit of the tree of the knowledge of good and evil in the Garden of Eden (Genesis 3:1–6). Eve ate the fruit and tempted her husband, Adam, to eat it too. This marked the Fall of Man, in that humans were forever condemned to live life in suffering because they had rebelled against God. The serpent is identified by some Christian authorities as Satan (the devil) in disguise, though the Bible does not itself identify the serpent of the Garden of Eden with Satan. The forked tongue of the snake is associated with deceit, and Satan is seen as the deceiver of mankind.

Some feminist commentators object to the implication that Eve is portrayed in the Bible as the weaker half of the partnership and as the devil's ally and agent: in other words, the person who is responsible for bringing evil into the world. Certainly some strands of Christian thought have portrayed women as the evil tempters of men, using their female beauty to lure men into the sin of lust.

Any reader of Divakaruni's poem for whom such Biblical associations are lively may see some complex variations and twists on the serpentine symbolism. In this case, the one who spoke with a forked tongue (deceitfully) was not a woman but a man. The women who partake of reptilian imagery are emphatically not trying to attract or tempt men. On the contrary, the mother has good reason to regret ever having done so. Both women seem more likely to repel men, in the daughter's case consciously and in the mother's case because she is growing old and gray. The mother's feminine allure is decayed and the daughter's is damaged and contained, just as her hair is bound in a thin reptilian tail, with every hair in place and kept within the bounds of her own self.

The strict containment of the daughter's hair is contrasted with the mother's hair at the height of her beauty, which is so long and full that it cannot be enclosed within the photograph, but flows beyond the edges. Symbolically, this connotes the mother's lack of control over her feminine charm and beauty, which is freely and trustingly offered up to the claimant, the husband. His hand covering hers implies that her identity is eclipsed and suppressed by his ownership.

Relevant to the question of hairstyles in the poem is the fact that in more conservative cultures, and in Western cultures until the early decades of the twentieth century, a woman's wearing her hair loose and uncovered is a sign that she is not yet married and is therefore available. Married women were and are expected to bind, put up, or cover their hair, so that only their husbands see it loose. The daughter of the poem is unmarried yet keeps her hair tightly bound, marking her unwillingness to give herself to a man in the way that her mother did.

In the light of the significance in the hair, it is useful to return to the serpentine symbolism. Divakaruni's women are not the fallen tempters of certain strands of Christian thought but share in a much wider serpent symbolism. The serpent or snake is a symbol in many cultures and religions. In Hinduism, the god Vishnu, who maintains creation, is said to sleep on a serpent that floats on the waters of the cosmos. In the Indian yogic tradition, *kundalini* (a Sanskrit word meaning *coiled*) is the primal force associated with life, power, and sexual energy. It is portrayed either as a goddess or as a serpent coiled at the base of the spine.

In ancient Roman mythology, two serpents coil up the caduceus or wand carried by Mercury, the messenger god, in a double helix shape. The symbol strangely prefigured the discovery of the double helix structure of DNA, an organism's genetic blueprint, which can be said to carry the *message* of how the organism develops. Modern medicine has taken from ancient Greek mythology the symbol of the rod of Asclepius, which has one serpent coiling up it. Asclepius was a god associated with healing and astrology.

Many cultures, including the ancient Greeks and the Aztec peoples of ancient Mexico, had a version of the *ouroboros*, the serpent that is depicted swallowing its own tail. The *ouroboros* is variously interpreted as symbolizing life energy; eternal life; and the cycle of birth, death, and rebirth.

While it would be simplistic to say that the women of "My Mother Combs My Hair" perfectly embody any one of these symbolic elements, it would be true to say that they evoke many qualities suggested by symbolic serpents. Wisdom and female sexual power are two that come to mind. Interestingly, the concept of the serpent as an embodiment of wisdom links to the Biblical serpent of the Garden of Eden that tempted Eve to eat the fruit of the tree of knowledge of good and evil, which he promised would elevate her and Adam to the level of gods. The women of the poem have come to know good and evil through the painful experience of the family breakup.

Half-way through the final stanza is a caesura (pause) created by the period at the end of the fifth line, which forms the turning point of the poem. Up to this point, the mother has been in the apparent position of authority in the mother/daughter relationship. The mother sits above her daughter while the daughter kneels before and below her. The mother is pictured lecturing her daughter on hair care. But this time the accustomed lecture does not come. In a poem or a speech, information that comes just before or just after a pause has most power. Here, that information is the fact that the husband has left. This totally undermines the mother's lifelong position as the champion of marriage and her commitment to a woman's surrender to a man's dominance. In the line that follows the caesura, the poet reinforces the effect created by the caesura by explicitly describing the silence that falls between the two women.

The silence, weighty with the knowledge and wisdom gained by both women, is characterized in two similes. In the first, the silence is likened to a live electric wire, suggesting that it is full of meaning and communication and also that it is threatening, perhaps because it reflects discord between the women. In the second simile, the silence is likened to a strip of gold torn from a wedding brocade. The torn brocade symbolizes the destruction of the romantic ideal of marriage. The two women are holding opposite ends of the strip of gold like adversaries preparing for a tug-of-war. This may suggest that the mother still clings to her ideal of marriage on some level, in spite of the fact that the brocade is torn.

Something of value has been salvaged from the wedding brocade: the strip of gold. Gold famously does not rust or corrode and is, therefore, a universal symbol of value and incorruptibility. The simile of gold can be taken to suggest the preciousness of the connection that endures between the two women and the unity created from their common experience of suffering the breakup of the family.

The poem ends not in resolution, but in the recognition of a tension consisting equally, it seems, of love and exasperation. It is a tension that will be familiar to anyone who has lived with cultural or generational conflicts among their loved ones.

Source: Claire Robinson, Critical Essay on "My Mother Combs My Hair," in *Poetry for Students*, Gale, Cengage Learning, 2010.

Melodie Monahan

Monahan has a Ph.D. in English and operates an editing service, The Inkwell Works. In the following essay, she discusses the cultural significance of women's hair in the West and how hair is handled specifically in two poems by Robert Browning, a discussion that is relevant to "My Mother Combs My Hair."

Hair that grows on a person's head has been assigned cultural significance in societies around the world and across the centuries. In regard to

> EVERY PERSON INHERITS FROM THE CULTURE IN WHICH THAT PERSON LIVES; CHANGE THE CULTURE, AND THERE IS STILL AN INHERITANCE."

women particularly, hair has been and continues to be seen as an indicator of beauty, sexual maturity, vitality, status, and financial worth. From the hip-long hair of women in India to the practice among some Jewish wives of shaving their heads and wearing wigs to magazine and online ads on how to have younger hair and compensate for thinning hair, in these and countless other ways the hair on a woman's head is evaluated and assigned cultural significance, and that significance is ever changing through time with shifting local beliefs and fashion. Given the way hair signals so many social values, it makes sense that writers would use it to signify more than what it literally is, describing the physical nature of a woman's hair in such a way as to reveal the character of the woman and the character of those who view her and use hair as a means of explaining how these characters interact.

In Europe and in the United States, particularly in light of Sigmund Freud's nineteenth- and early-twentieth-century theories of sexuality, female Caucasian hair styles were often aligned with sexual development. Before puberty a middle- or upper-class female could wear her hair loose or loosely tied back with a ribbon or braided down her back, but after puberty, a female wore her hair pinned up in a bun or rolled tightly across the nape of her neck, and particularly after marriage, she covered her hair with a simple cap worn in the house and covered that cap with a more structured bonnet when going outdoors. By contrast, low-class women and women who marketed their sexual appeal either as stage performers or as prostitutes tended to wear their hair loose or down, such that females seen with their hair uncovered and loose were perceived to be sending the message of sexual availability. Depictions in literature and the visual arts often capitalized on this pattern in order to use hair to convey certain messages.

Diverse disciplines, such as sociology, anthropology, psychology, and literary criticism, and notably in feminist approaches in them, have explored the image of the female as a signifier of social value. In art, the depicted female is transformed into an object, is objectified by the artist. The viewer/reader of the art *reads* or *interprets* the female image. In this sense, then, art comments on real life, and real-life individuals may adopt the fashion and behavior depicted in art. This intersection of art and life is illustrated in the geisha, who in her formal dress with her hair sculptured into complicated arrangement complete with decorations and her cosmetic-covered porcelain-looking face and her figure disguised in structured silk panels presents a real-life woman as an artificial construction, replete with social significance and value and with a predetermined role to play. Westerners may see this as obvious in a geisha, a product of a distant culture, and yet less quickly recognize women on Hollywood red carpets as American equivalents, at least from a sociological perspective. In the role of geisha or in the role of actress posing on a red carpet, these women present manufactured images of themselves; they have become identified with the masks they wear.

The pervasive and varied correlation between hair and female character and role is an obvious resource for writers. In literature, how a female character's hair is described and handled often has thematic or psychological significance. As with other aspects of any given literary work, this element reflects the cultural context, its assumptions and mores, within which the work of literature is composed and by which it is framed. For example, in two dramatic monologues by the Victorian poet Robert Browning (1812–1889), "Soliloquy in a Spanish Cloister" and "Porphyria's Lover" (both published in 1842), references to a woman's hair reveal something essential about the poems' meaning. In the first, the speaker's description of a woman's hair betrays his lascivious nature, and in the second, the speaker's reaction to the way a woman loosens her hair is used to propel the action, the hair itself functioning as a key element of both characterization and plot. Both handlings suggest a correlation between a woman's hair and her sexuality, and they capitalize on the nineteenth-century values of Browning's English middle-class upbringing.

The speaker in "Soliloquy in a Spanish Cloister" is an envious, mean-spirited monk, a man who specializes in living his cloistered life according to the letter of his Catholicism rather than to its spirit. The speaker hates the placid, mild-mannered gardener Brother Lawrence, who goes along tending his flowerpots and herbs and talking at mealtime about the weather. The speaker secretly trims the flowers off Brother Lawrence's melon plants, taking pleasure in frustrating the other monk's efforts and resenting the fact that when melon is served, a whole one goes to the abbot's table while the brothers share a melon, each receiving only a thin slice. The speaker prides himself on laying his silverware in the sign of the cross and in drinking his orange juice in three swallows in memory of the trinity, but his heart is actually full of hatred and unsatisfied longing. His mechanical gestures at piety, in his mind, set him above Lawrence, who peacefully works with a sweet temperament and by his selfless efforts enacts a life of loving kindness.

In this dramatic monologue, Browning poses the speaker off to one side of the cloister courtyard, secretly observing Brother Lawrence at work in his garden. The speaker is also observing two females visiting outside the cloister gates. The speaker's lusty nature is revealed in the way he describes one of these girls: "brown Dolores/ Squats...telling stories, / Steeping tresses.../ Blue-black, lustrous, thick like horsehairs." The speaker imagines Lawrence see her, too, but Lawrence busy with his roses does not look up, much less beyond the gate. The inference in the word, "Squats," and the description of her hair as being like that of a horse is the speaker's way of *reading* Dolores as a sexual object. Though a cloistered monk, he has fixated on Dolores, dwelling on the titillation he feels in observing her position and her hair. He may pride himself on his attention to details when it comes to cutlery and swallowing juice, but in secret he lusts after Dolores. Browning underscores the monk's own earthy and worldly nature through the way he interprets others' activities and secretly acts out his vindictiveness.

The sexual significance conveyed by hair is used by Browning in a different, far more overtly dangerous way in "Porphyria's Lover." The speaker of this monologue is a man who waits alone in a poor cottage and is visited during a stormy night by Porphyria, a woman of some refinement, who leaves a dinner party to be with him. While the poem is ostensibly about the speaker's fixation on Porphyria and his obsession with taking control of her, Browning also implicates Porphyria, a kind of blaming-the-victim scenario. The speaker describes how Porphyria arrives alone, builds up the fire, and takes off her cloak, shawl, and gloves. She removes her hat and loosens her wet hair letting it fall. She seats herself next to the speaker, pulling her hair aside to expose her bare shoulder and arranging herself so the speaker can rest his head directly on her skin:

> She put my arm about her waist,
> And made her smooth white shoulder bare,
> And all her yellow hair displaced,
> And, stooping, made my cheek lie there,
> And spread, o'er all, her yellow hair.

Victorian readers would have immediately noted (and perhaps secretly enjoyed) all the titillating improprieties here. Porphyria leaves a feast alone, goes out into the night alone, and visits a man alone. All of this is most inappropriate for a woman of her class. Once in the cottage, she takes off her outer garments and lets down her hair, a gesture signaling sexual availability, and finally she positions herself so that the man's face can touch her bare shoulder. Why Porphyria acts in this unbecoming and indeed dangerous manner is left unexplained. Readers see the action only through the speaker's words, and the reliability of the speaker is soon called into question.

Having taken control of the cottage setting and the speaker, Porphyria has placed herself in a vulnerable position. The speaker in his twisted way fixes on the idea that Porphyria worships him. He is triggered by sexual arousal and charged with the sudden plan to capture this moment and take possession of Porphyria, once and for all:

> ...I found
> A thing to do, and all her hair
> In one long yellow string I wound
> Three times her little throat around,
> And strangled her. No pain felt she;
> I am quite sure she felt no pain.

With his repeated assertion that strangling Porphyria caused her no pain, readers realize the speaker is out of touch with reality. Once she is dead, he opens her eyes and releases her hair. The blood moving back into her face makes her appear to blush, and he cradles her corpse now in his arms. Readers discover with a shock that he has narrated this monologue while holding the dead body of Porphyria in his arms, her head now resting appropriately on his manly shoulder. He waits in silence and is convinced that all is right because "God has not said a word!"

In a court of law, the speaker would likely be found criminally insane. But the poem ends with this line, weirdly suggesting God's approbation. Readers are left to consider what the dramatic monologue, delivered by a clearly unreliable narrator, means. In part, the poem enacts the lethal danger of female enticement, communicated in the speaker's view by Porphyria's actions, her handling of her clothes and her hair, and in her willingness to make herself physically available by embracing the speaker, almost as though he were a nursing child. It also enacts the danger that may befall an autonomous, powerful woman. Porphyria takes charge of the scene and the speaker and leaves herself open for attack. In these ways, the poem becomes a cautionary tale for Victorian readers, one that insists if females act independently and in promiscuous ways they may pay with their lives. Porphyria asks for it, Browning seems to be suggesting, and any man would have taken advantage of her. What distinguishes this man from any other, however, is how he does it. In Browning's use of hair, the suggestion seems to be that a woman's hair can excite a man to the extent that he may destroy her. The same feature women are taught to cultivate in order to attract men can become a weapon used against them. That is ironic, as ironic as identifying the speaker as Porphyria's *lover*.

Browning's two poems are just small instances in the vast literary tradition that Chitra Divakaruni draws upon in writing her poem, "My Mother Combs My Hair." This poem published in 1991 bespeaks the cross-cultural intersection of two generations of Indian women, the mother who was born and raised in India and the daughter who grows into her sexual adulthood in the United States. The history of hair and its sexual connotations creates the background context. Another framing element is the complexity in the collision of cultural beliefs across two generations of immigrants who are shaped by them. Culture is temporally and spatially determined: Place and time define culture. But culture is dynamic, and people who emigrate get exposed to and changed by the subsequent environment. The Americanized daughter/speaker in Divakaruni's poem can anticipate her mother's unspoken yet changing beliefs given her marital experiences, and the

> ALTHOUGH TODAY HER OUTLOOK HAS SOFTENED, AND HER INTEREST HAS SHIFTED TO MORE GENERAL HUMAN THEMES OF MEMORY AND DESIRE, AT THE TIME, SHE SAYS, SHE FELT MILITANT."

daughter also interacts with her American context by cutting her hair and getting a permanent wave. Without explaining in detail, the women recognize hair for its sexual energy, and in the light of the father's departure, they see the risk that sexual relationships can present. That risk is communicated in the description of their hair. Every person inherits from the culture in which that person lives; change the culture, and there is still an inheritance. The same is true for the poet and the poem the poet writes.

Source: Melodie Monahan, Critical Essay on "My Mother Combs My Hair," in *Poetry for Students*, Gale, Cengage Learning, 2010.

Roxane Farmanfarmaian

In the following essay, Farmanfarmaian describes Divakaruni's creative process and gives an overview of her works.

Above the door to Chitra Divakaruni's house in a development off a main highway of San Francisco's East Bay, a little sign in Bengali proclaims, "Hail to the Lord of the Universe." The house is an ordinary dwelling, and the sign a simple Hindu invocation. But in Divakaruni's world, nothing is really simple. The sign is as much a pledge to the world outside the house as it is to the writing muse that Divakaruni calls on from within. "Each time we enter the house, it reminds us," she explains, "that we live in a spiritual place, and we must make it so." As the title of her most recent collection of short stories, *The Unknown Errors of Our Lives* (Doubleday; Forecasts, Mar. 12 [2001]) hints, life to her is forever mysterious—always complicated by the conflict between destiny and desire.

"When I write a book, I try to make it the very best it can be," she says. "But once a book is done, I put it aside. I do my part of the job, and then let the universe do the rest because, when I look back, the best things, in terms of my career, have been serendipitous." By any measure, the prolific Divakaruni has been touched by a lucky star in her publishing life. Since her first book of poetry came out in 1991, she has written three more books of poetry, two collections of short stories (her first, *Arranged Marriage*, won the American Book Award in 1995) and two novels (including the bestselling *Mistress of Spices*); she's also edited two anthologies on multiculturalism. In addition, she has taught creative writing full time, first at Foothill College in the Bay Area and then at the University of Houston until last year; she is the mother of two boys; and she cofounded Maitri, a Bay Area hotline for South Asian abused women.

Born in Calcutta, the only girl in a family of four children, Divakaruni, now 44, came to the U.S. to study for a master's degree at Wright State University in Ohio, and from there went on to Berkeley for a Ph.D. in Renaissance literature. At the time, her focus was on teaching. But then her grandfather died back in her ancestral village in India, and she began to write poetry. "I was going through Berkeley on a scholarship," she recalls. "I didn't have any money, and I couldn't go back for his funeral. It was very difficult." One day, she woke up and couldn't picture his face. Shocked, she realized she needed to write her memories down so as not to forget them. "It was very personal," she says, "and poetry was closest to my psyche. Poetry focuses on the moment, on the image, and relies on image to express meaning. That was very important to me, that kind of crystallization, that kind of intensity in a small space."

Divakaruni is dressed in sweatpants and a T-shirt, her long dark hair tied in a knot at the back of her head; her voice is melodious, and she interrupts herself frequently with sudden laughter. "I started by writing some very bad, very sentimental poetry. And anything I wrote, I went, 'Wow! Straight from the brain of God through my pen into the world!'"

It was not long, however, before she joined the Berkeley Poet's Workshop and began sending poems to *Calyx,* a women's magazine in Oregon. *Calyx* liked them so much that its publishing arm offered to bring out a collection of her poetry once she had completed enough work. *Black Candle* was published in 1991. "*Calyx* has always kept it in print, and just reissued it, which is the wonderful thing about our small presses," says Divakaruni, who is keenly cognizant of how easily, as a poet, she found a place with a publisher.

Good fortune would accompany her into the realm of fiction. "My poetry was becoming more and more narrative," she says, "and I was becoming more interested in the story element, and the nuances of character change." But the format of short story writing was foreign to her, and so in 1992, she joined an evening fiction class at Foothill, where she had started teaching 20th-century multicultural literature the year before.

"I was still writing very much for myself," she says, "but my teacher, Tom Parker, said I should send my stories to an agent." Not knowing any agents, and having just had her first baby, as well as having just founded Maitri, Divakaruni didn't take his advice. Instead, it was Parker who sent her stories to Sandy Dijkstra. She laughs. "A few months later, Sandy called and said, 'I sold your book to Anchor,' and I said, 'What book?' because I only had three stories."

It was then that Divakaruni began keeping to the rigorous writing schedule that has governed her life ever since. "My writing time is my writing time, though my children may eat microwaved burritos and I may not clean the house," she says. At Foothill, she taught every morning, and then wrote in the afternoon, dropping a curtain over her office door so her students would know they were not to disturb her.

Her approach to composition is intuitive. She begins with half an hour of meditation and sometimes even comes up with good ideas in the process. "I realize that means it's a failed meditation," she says cheerfully, "but boy, I got this great idea! so I ask forgiveness." When she starts to write, she begins with a scene. "I believe in scenes. I know the characters, but I don't know a lot about them," she says. "The advantage is that the book unfolds organically; the disadvantage is that I have to go back for a lot of rewriting."

Divakaruni's revision process, by contrast, is highly structured. "I'll write a story over the period of a month, and then put it aside for eight or nine months," she explains. Then she does a "prerevision" in which she writes "This scene needs to be changed" or "This sentence isn't right" in the margins. Next, she lays the story aside. When she goes back to it again, she does a "How-to-fix-it" revision, making a second set of notes in a different color. "I'll say, 'I need to have this person come in and give this kind of information here, or I need this to happen here.' But I still haven't done it." Only later, when she feels she's digested what she's written down, does she go back to make the final changes.

"You can't hurry writing if you're going to do it well," she says. "Otherwise, what is the point of being a writer? If you're going to create art, the least you can do is give it your best attention and as much time as it takes."

The stories that eventually composed *Arranged Marriage* focused on the immigrant experience, particularly from the female point of view, a theme that has continued to inform Divakaruni's work. "It was while I was at Berkeley that I became aware of women's issues and the need for me to do something about them," she says. Although today her outlook has softened, and her interest has shifted to more general human themes of memory and desire, at the time, she says, she felt militant. "I really wanted to focus on women battling and coming out triumphant."

As a student in India, she loved Bengali women writers like Mahasveta Devi, who has now been translated into English. In Ohio, she came across Maxine Hong Kingston's *The Woman Warrior*, which had a profound effect on her thinking. Today, the roster of writers she considers most influential includes Toni Morrison, Christina Garcia, Sandra Cisneros and Louise Erdrich (particularly her book *Tracks*, told from Native American perspectives). "The South Asian writers I read very carefully," she says, are writers like Bharati Mukherjee, whom Divakaruni admires for her focus on the immigrant experience, and Anita Desai.

"But," she cautions, "I don't believe you can be a writer saying I will now bring attention to some of these issues. You have to start with the story, the character, and then hopefully..."

Arranged Marriage, published in 1995, won the PEN Oakland Josephine Miles Prize, the Bay Area Book Reviewers Award and the American Book Award. But Divakaruni's own life took a sudden turn for the worse. When her second son was born, serious complications led to her close brush with death. "I gave up. And I really felt I left the body, and was up there somewhere looking down." When she recovered, she felt strongly that she had returned for a purpose. "It was very positive, actually," she says of the experience. "And it gave me the sense that we're here in this body only for a little while, and then we go on, we go on to other existences and maybe other worlds that we don't know, and I wanted to write about this, fictionalize it in some way."

So her next book, *Mistress of Spices*, was born. She'd never tried writing a novel before and had never experimented with magical realism, but when one day she heard a voice—"you know how writers sometimes hear their characters?"—saying, "I am the Mistress of Spices," she knew she had the first line of what was going to be a much larger work than anything she'd previously written, and that it was going to be a magical tale.

The setting of the *Mistress of Spices*, a little Indian grocery in Oakland, became a metaphor for the world within a world so typical of the immigrant experience. "You know those little ethnic groceries, where you go through the door and you step into a different country?" she says. In order to put it all together, Divakaruni conducted research on the Internet and in the library, watched Indian movies, read Indian magazines, talked with people informally in Indian groceries and drew from her work helping women through Maitri.

Her own immigrant experience in Ohio also helped her express the feelings of loneliness and cultural separation that suffuse *Mistress of Spices*. Sent to Ohio to be under the watchful eye of her older brother, she often found herself isolated and neglected as he struggled to establish a life of his own as a doctor and father—a situation she describes more closely in "The Intelligence of Wild Things" in *The Unknown Errors of Our Lives*. Many immigrant experiences that she describes, however—those of the bullied teenager, or the Muslim taxi driver, or the Hindu grandfather—she did not know firsthand, and yet she speaks of them as though she had.

"These are my people no matter what their economic or religious background," says Divakaruni by way of explanation. "I think the way I do it is to listen while they are talking and really think about their lives. And then it has to come into you, be transformed deep down inside you, in your gut. You have to live that person's life, in a way."

To promote *The Unknown Errors of Our Lives*, Divakaruni is going on a four-week, 17-city tour. As she always does when she is in what she calls her "formal persona"—out at someone's house, doing readings, teaching—she will wear a sari. "The Indian part of my culture is very important to me," she explains, "and when I wear my Indian clothes, I feel a certain way, so it's as much for me as for anyone." Her readings are often well attended by the Indian community. "But," she says, "the response at times can get very heated if they feel I'm betraying the community by pointing out problems." Still, she considers it a worthwhile price to pay. The strong response means the book has touched them, made them think about their lives more deeply, and that means, she says, "the book has done what I hoped."

Going on tour and seeing all her backlist at the bookstores is one of the many reasons she's pleased she's stayed with Doubleday. "They think of me as one of their authors, someone they discovered and whose career they have helped grow," she says. Though she has had three different editors—all of whom she's liked—because the first two left for other houses, she and her agent, Sandy Dijkstra, decided it would be best for her to stay with Doubleday. "And that's where Sandy was very helpful, because she knows the editors really well, and she helped decide who would understand my work, and she was right."

Today, Divakaruni works with Deb Futter, who edited *The Unknown Errors of Our Lives* and who will be reading her next novel, a sequel of sorts to her second book, *Sister of My Heart*. But she cautions, "With each book, I try something different. If I didn't, what would be the point of being a writer any more?" In a recent piece for the *New York Times* series Writers on Writing, Divakaruni admits she threw out 200 pages of this newest novel after having served as a judge for the 2000 National Book Awards. "The whole experience taught me a great deal as a writer," she says, almost shyly. "And the writing comes from a different place, which is not a conscious part of myself—that's why I'm not egoistic about it." This perspective, which she comes to through the spiritual teachings of Gurumayi Chidvilasananda and Baba Muktananda (whose pictures she has on her writing table and whom she includes in the acknowledgments of each of her books), is what enables her to pour everything she has into the book she's working on, and then, feeling that she's done her best, let it go. "I think of writing as a very sacred activity," she says. "I'm only the instrument."

Source: Roxane Farmanfarmaian, "Chitra Banerjee Divakaruni: Writing from a Different Place," in *Publishers Weekly*, Vol. 248, No. 20, May 14, 2001, pp. 46–47.

SOURCES

2008 Yearbook of Immigration Statistics, Office of Immigration Statistics of the U.S. Department of Homeland Security, August 2009, pp. 8, 10, available online at http://www.dhs.gov/xlibrary/assets/statistics/yearbook/2008/ois_yb_2008.pdf (accessed September 8, 2009).

"Asian American Profile," Website of the Office of Minority Health, U.S. Department of Human Health and Services, available online at http://www.omhrc.gov/templates/content.aspx?ID=3005 (accessed September 10, 2009).

"Beijing Declaration and Platform for Action," Fourth World Conference on Women, United Nations, September 1995, available online at http://www.un.org/womenwatch/daw/beijing/pdf/BDPfA%20E.pdf (accessed September 10, 2009).

Browning, Robert, "Porphyria's Lover," in *The Norton Anthology of English Literature*, Vol. 2, 7th ed., edited by M. H. Abrams, Norton, 2000, pp. 1349–50.

———, "Soliloquy in a Spanish Cloister," in *The Norton Anthology of English Literature*, Vol. 2, 7th ed., edited by M. H. Abrams, Norton, 2000, pp. 1350–52.

"Convention on the Elimination of All Forms of Discrimination Against Women," United Nations, available online at http://www.un.org/womenwatch/daw/cedaw/states.htm (accessed September 12, 2009).

Divakaruni, Chitra Banerjee, "My Mother Combs My Hair," in *Black Candle: Poems About Women from India, Pakistan, and Bangladesh*, rev. ed., Calyx, 2000, pp. 75–76.

Hirshfield, Jane, Review of *Black Candle*, in *Black Candle: Poems About Women from India, Pakistan, and Bangladesh*, Calyx, 1991, rev. ed., 2000, back cover.

Mandal, Somdatta, "Chitra Banerjee Divakaruni," in *Dictionary of Literary Biography, Vol. 323: South Asian Writers in English*, edited by Fakrul Alam, Thomson Gale, 2006, pp. 112–22.

Mehta, Nina, Review of *Black Candle: Poems About Women from India, Pakistan, and Bangladesh*, in *Bloomsbury Review*, September 1992, p. 19.

Seaman, Donna, Review of *Leaving Yuba City*, in *Booklist*, Vol. 93, No. 22, August 1997, p. 1871.

Sen, Sudeep, "Recent Indian English Poetry," in *World Literature Today*, Vol. 74, No. 4, Fall 2000, p. 783.

Simpson, Peggy, "Chances Improve for Ratification of CEDAW," Women's Media Center, March 30, 2009, available online at http://www.womensmediacenter.com/ex/033009.html (accessed September 12, 2009).

Softky, Elizabeth, "Cross-cultural Understanding Spiced with the Indian Diaspora," in *Black Issues in Higher Education*, Vol. 14, No. 15, September 18, 1997, p. 26.

Van Buren, Amy, Review of *Leaving Yuba City: New and Selected Poems*, in *Library Journal*, Vol. 122, No. 16, October 1, 1997, p. 86.

Warrier, Sunjata, "(Un)heard Voices: Domestic Violence in the Asian American Community," Family Violence Prevention Fund, 2007, p. 16, available online at http://endabuse.org/userfiles/file/ImmigrantWomen/UnheardVoices.pdf (accessed September 11, 2009)

FURTHER READING

Cherian, Anne, *A Good Indian Wife*, Kindle, 2008.
 This novel tells the story of a Americanized and successful Indian man who finds himself in an arranged marriage to an Indian woman. At first, he ignores his new wife and lets her fend for herself in her new environment, but eventually he has to face her and decide on their future.

Lee, Jennifer, ed., *Asian American Youth: Culture, Identity, and Ethnicity*, Routledge, 2004.
 This book is a collection of essays that consider how young people from Asian American communities forge an identity for themselves in the United States. It covers such topics as immigration, assimilation, intermarriage, and sexuality.

Ling, Huping, *Voices of the Heart: Asian American Women on Immigration, Work, and Family*, Truman State University Press, 2007.
 This book is a compilation of oral histories in which American women of Chinese, Japanese, Filipina, Korean, Indian, Vietnamese, Laotian, Thai, and Pakistani origin tell their stories. The book covers their aspirations, education, employment, attitudes to their culture of origin, and family relationships.

Seth, Reva, *First Comes Marriage: Modern Relationship Advice from the Wisdom of Arranged Marriages*, Kindle, 2008.
 This is a self-help book for people of all cultures. The author is a Toronto-based journalist who has written at length about arranged marriage and who married her husband after only meeting him seven times. It contains advice on how to find a spouse who will make you happy and how to keep the relationship alive.

Possibilities

WISŁAWA SZYMBORSKA

1986

In her 1996 Nobel Prize for Literature acceptance speech, Wisława Szymborska declared her appreciation for the phrase "I don't know," which she claims is "small, but it flies on mighty wings. It expands our lives to include spaces within us as well as the outer expanses in which our tiny Earth hangs suspended." Szymborska explained that this confession defines "restless, questing spirits" who continually ask questions about their world. This questioning and searching spirit is at the center of much of her poetry, including her poem "Possibilities." Szymborska's questioning of dogmatic platitudes in this poem suggests possibilities for the reader's own determination of personal freedom. The poem can be read as a statement regarding the oppression Poland suffered under Germany and the Union of Soviet Socialist Republics (USSR) when these foreign powers took control of the country during the twentieth century, or it can be seen as functioning beyond a political context, expressly dismissing in more general terms a devotion to any type of restrictive ideology. The poem presents a list of preferences made by the speaker that set up contrasts between her own choices and those proscribed by conventional beliefs. The contrasts challenge these conventions and illuminate the absurdity of blindly following them. "Possibilities" is one of the selections in Szymborska's *Poems New and Collected: 1957–1997*, published in 1998.

Wisława Szymborska (AP Images)

AUTHOR BIOGRAPHY

Wisława Szymborska was born on July 2, 1923, in Prowent-Bnin, Poland, one of two daughters of Wincenty and Anna Szymborski. When she was eight, her family moved to Krakow where she went to school illegally after Germany occupied Poland during World War II and banned Poles from advancing their education. Her father encouraged her literary skills by offering to give her money every time she wrote a poem. She published her first poem, "Szukam slowa" (I am Looking for a Word) in 1945, the same year she began taking classes at Jagiellonian University in Krakow, where she studied Polish literature and sociology but without completing a degree. By 1948, she had written enough poems to fill a collection but could not find a publisher since the Communist Party judged her work to be unsuitably pessimistic. When she rewrote the poems, giving them political themes that she later regretted, she was able to publish them as *Dlatego zyjemy* (That's What We Live For) in 1952.

In 1953, Szymborska was hired as a poetry editor and critic for the Krakow literary magazine *Życie literackie*, a position she held until 1981. She later collected several of the pieces she had written for them and had them published as *Lektury nadobowiazkowe* (Optional Readings). During this period, she continued to publish poetry that was well received.

In her second collection of poetry, *Pytania zadawane sobie* (Questions Put to Myself), published in 1954, she abandoned the propaganda of her first collection and began to find her own voice. Her third collection, *Wolanie do Yeti* (Calling Out to Yeti), published in 1957, established her reputation as an important new Polish writer. That reputation grew with her subsequent collections, including *People on a Bridge: Poems*, published in 1986, which contains her poem "Possibilities."

Several of her works have been translated into English, including *People on a Bridge: Poems, View with a Grain of Sand: Selected Poems, Poems New and Collected: 1957–1997*, and *Nonrequired Reading: Prose Pieces*. Her works have also been published in other languages, such as Arabic, Hebrew, Japanese, and Chinese, which has generated for her a worldwide readership. Her poetry has been reprinted in several anthologies, such as *Polish Writing Today*, published by Penguin in 1967; *The New Polish Poetry*, published by the University of Pittsburgh Press in 1978; and in more general collections such as *Legacies: Fiction, Poetry, Drama, Nonfiction*, published by Wadsworth in 2008. Her awards include the Krakow Literary Prize in 1954, the Ministry of Culture Prize in 1963, the Knight's Cross, Order of Polonia Restituta in 1974, the Goethe Prize in 1991, the Polish PEN Club Prize in 1996, and the Nobel Prize for Literature in 1996.

Szymborska gained much attention after winning the Nobel Prize, which sometimes challenged her shy nature. As of 2009, she continued writing poetry, living in Krakow, and publishing a new collection every six or seven years.

POEM SUMMARY

Szymborska constructs "Possibilities" as a list of her speaker's personal preferences. The title highlights the tentative nature of the preferences that make up the poem. The speaker lists only what she prefers, not necessarily firm choices that she has made or will make. So the preferences become possibilities, not definitive statements of what she values. Each line of the poem contains a choice

MEDIA ADAPTATIONS

- Audio recordings of some poems by Szymborska as read by Charlotte Maier and an interview with the poet's translator Clare Cavanagh can be heard at the Poetry Foundation Website, available online at http://www.poetryfoundation.org/archive/poet.html?id=6744 (accessed October 16, 2009).

made by the speaker concerning a wide range of subjects, which includes every day items as well as more general, philosophical ideas or values. By characterizing her taste in terms of preferences, the speaker suggests that she is choosing one thing over another, which gives readers some clues into her personality.

The speaker begins her list with preferences concerning ordinary objects. Her choice of movies in the first line suggests that that form of entertainment is more pleasing to her than others such as television or radio programs. She may have made this choice because films are more highly regarded than television and more visual than radio.

The speaker then notes her preference for cats over dogs or other pets. The speaker's personality is implied by this choice since distinctions can be made between cats and dogs. Dogs are more dependent and social in general than cats, but dogs require more care since they need to be walked every day and cannot be left alone for long periods. These differences suggest that the speaker enjoys the self-sufficiency and aloofness of cats but still enjoys the affection and comfort a pet provides.

The third line identifies her preference for specific trees along the Warta, a river in central Poland. She singles out oaks, which often are used as a symbol of strength and consistency. She apparently enjoys either spending time walking or boating along the river observing these trees.

The fourth line identifies her reading tastes; she prefers Dickens to Dostoyevsky. Charles Dickens (1812–1870), an English novelist, described the plight of the poor in Victorian England and the institutions such as schools, debtors' prisons, and government agency that often contributed to their suffering. The Russian Fyodor Dostoyevsky (1821–1880) explored such complex subjects as religion, psychology, and philosophy. The inference is the speaker would rather focus on the individual than on concepts; she remarks that she likes individuals but is not as inclined to love mankind in general.

Next she returns to ordinary objects, in this case a needle and thread, but places them in a specific context, which she has not done previously. She notes that she likes to have these nearby in case they are needed. She does not, however, name a situation that would require them. They could be used to repair a tear in clothing or in skin. The eighth line states that she prefers the color green.

The next line becomes more abstract when the speaker states that she blames reason for everything. Here for the first time she uses a negative to show her rejection of an established belief, that relying on reason causes problems. The speaker's other preferences imply rather than name a particular belief.

In lines 11 and 12, the speaker reveals her aversion to established rules when she notes her preference for exceptions and for leaving early. Readers can assume that she would rather leave early than fulfill a social obligation by staying for the expected length of time. The next line shows her affinity for hope when she writes that she would rather talk to doctors about something other than medical problems, which could be concerning herself or someone close to her.

In lines 14 through 16, the speaker addresses the subject of art, noting her preference for old-fashioned lined illustrations and for writing poems. She finds writing poetry just a bit less absurd than not writing it.

In the next five lines, the speaker makes general choices that again reveal her aversion to rules. She prefers expressing love every day rather than on proscribed dates, moralists who cannot make definite promises to her, and kindness that is more cunning than trustful.

Lines 22 through 26 focus on historical conflict. First, the speaker addresses the issue of war, noting her preference for civilian clothes and for countries that are conquered rather than those that do that conquering. Her choices become more abstract in the next few lines but can still be seen as relating to her position on war. She prefers using restraint, and while she finds suffering a part of both order and chaos, she determines that order is worse, which links to her previous condemnation of conquering countries. The last line in this sequence conveys her reluctance to read the front pages of newspaper, which present images of war.

In the next two lines, the speaker returns to ordinary objects but maintains her attraction to what is natural over what is reshaped by humans. She prefers leaves by themselves to flowers that have been stripped of their leaves and dogs that have not had their tails cropped.

Lines 29 and 30 appear to be random preferences, but they could also suggest a historical context. The speaker's eyes are dark, perhaps meaning that they have seen much suffering. She prefers light eyes, perhaps because they do not remind her of a dark past. The preference for desk drawers in the next line could be a reference to a safe place for things that must be hidden away when living in an oppressive society.

The speaker then explains in lines 31 and 32 that she has left some of her preferences unlisted, perhaps because she does not want to reveal too much about herself. She continues in these lines to identify what she likes but in an abstract sense. Referring again to her distaste for order, she admits she prefers random numbers to those used in a cipher, a method employed when transforming messages so they cannot be read. Here, then, she seems to suggest that those unspoken thoughts should not be hidden.

In line 35 she notes that she would rather look at the tiny bits of time than consider time in terms of light years. She prefers in the next two lines to be superstitious but will not worry about time limits.

In the closing line, the speaker comments on the nature of existence, believing in the possibility that it has its own reason for being and does not necessarily follow any specific laws.

THEMES

The Preference for the Ordinary and Specific

Many of the speaker's preferences in the poem are for the ordinary rather than the abstract. She begins her list with an outline of her own tastes in entertainment (movies), pets (cats), nature (oak

TOPICS FOR FURTHER STUDY

- Write a story about the speaker based on what you learn of her in the poem "Possibilities." Imagine a scene in her past when she had to suffer under a totalitarian government. You can set this scene in any time and place in history. Make sure you provide enough historical details to make the story come to life. End the scene in the present time with the speaker reflecting back on this event and how it has affected her life.

- Research the period when Poland was a part of the communist bloc, including all of the restrictions that the communist government imposed on Polish citizens. Prepare a PowerPoint presentation that highlights the details of the communist takeover of Poland, the totalitarian society it created there, and how some individuals resisted and fought the system.

- Write a poem that lists your own preferences. Try to choose details that express your personality, much like Szymborska does in "Possibilities."

- Read other poems by Szymborska from *Poems New and Collected*. Find at least two that focus on the rejection of traditional ideals and beliefs. Write an essay that incorporates scholarly research, comparing and contrasting the poems' treatment of this subject.

- The 1993 film *Swing Kids*, starring Christian Bale and Robert Sean Leonard, chronicles the lives of a group of teenage friends in Nazi Germany who get caught up in the underground world of American swing music during the war. Watch the DVD version of this film and prepare a presentation, incorporating film clips, that depicts the teens' rebellion against Nazi rule and the results of that rebellion. Lead a discussion on the options these teens had and how their actions helped shape their character.

trees), and literature (Dickens). Often her everyday preferences illustrate the poem's main focus on the rejection of dogma, as in her choice of novelists. Dickens is known for his sympathetic depictions of the poor, whereas Dostoyevsky is known for his complex philosophical discussion. At other times, though, the speaker's choices betray personal experience.

Szymborska celebrates ordinary pleasures in the poem, such as oak trees along a river and fine-lined drawings. The speaker prefers the tiny progress of insects rather than the lifespan of stars. The accessible object can be experienced in the present, like the color green, rather than an abstraction promoted by philosophers.

Surface versus Depth

Another contrast that plays out in the poem is between surface and depth. While Szymborska's direct, simple language describes ordinary pleasures that appear to be merely statements of the speaker's preferences, the poet hints at an underlying significance that becomes a condemnation of dogmatic generalizations that require strict compliance. The speaker's deceptively straightforward announcements declare her preference for exceptions and for leaving early, both of which reveal her penchant for breaking the rules. She also notes that she likes dogs with their tails left natural, promoting humane treatment of animals over devotion to fashion. She prefers messiness over enforced order, including desk drawers that can contain a jumble of one's possessions and random arrangements of zeros rather than those neatly ordered behind a cipher.

STYLE

Listing and Repetition

The lines in "Possibilities" create of list of things that the speaker says she prefers. Szymborska uses the list to common on the relationship between dogma and order. Those who make lists are trying to organize their thoughts. Lists are also used when one is setting out all of the beliefs that make up a specific type of dogma or ideology. In this poem, however, Szymborska constructs a list to subvert the sense of order usually achieved by this process. Her list contains seemingly unrelated items such as trees and kindness that do not appear to reveal any sense of order. This lack of organization, however, makes a clear point in the poem, that trying

Illustration for "The Goose-Girl" from Brothers Grimm Children's and Household Tales *(© Lebrecht Music and Arts Photo Library / Alamy)*

to establish order, especially when enumerating one's preferences, is pointless, even absurd.

The list in the poem reveals what the speaker prefers. Thirty-one out of thirty-nine lines begin with the same two-word phrase. Here the speaker emphasizes over and over again that her choices are preferences, not parts of any specific set of beliefs that govern her life, and they are hers and not someone else's. She is reluctant to give definite answers concerning her tastes, either because she is uncertain about them or because she wants the option of changing her mind. Either motive would contradict a fixed and superimposed doctrine. The repetition, like the list, is also used ironically. Often, followers of a specific ideology are taught to repeat its platitudes, designed to be a kind of mantra that can help them maintain obedience to that ideology. However, in "Possibilities," the repetition serves to reinforce the speaker's individuality.

HISTORICAL CONTEXT

Socrealizm

Socrealizm is the term used in Poland to describe socialist realism, a movement sponsored by the

COMPARE & CONTRAST

- **1980s:** Marshal law imposed in Poland in 1981 calls for the censorship of speech and publications. An underground press emerges, however, that publishes works that protest against the country's communist government.

  Today: Americans have few limits on their right to express themselves verbally and in print. However, some states such as Texas and Kansas try to ban certain books, including *Huckleberry Finn*, from school libraries due to content that is considered inappropriate.

- **1980s:** Poor economic conditions and lack of government aid prompt Polish workers to strike.

  Today: Debates continue in Congress about how to get the United States out of the deep recession that has caused thousands of Americans to lose their jobs and in many cases their homes.

- **1980s:** The collapse of the Soviet Union and that country's control of the communist bloc begins in 1985.

  Today: Under Vladimir Putin's leadership, Russia tries to regain some of the political power it lost during the 1980s when the Soviet Union dissolved into independent states.

---

communist government in Poland in 1949. Socrealizm was introduced by decree at the Fourth Writers' Union Congress in Szczecin in January 1949. For the next six years, Polish writers and artists were forced to conform to strict guidelines in the construction of their works. In Poland and in other European countries, the period between World War I and World War II was a time of avant-garde experimentation. That period came to an end under the new decree of socrealizm, which forced artists to produce works that asserted the supremacy and superiority of Marxist ideals. Any literary work that did not conform to the decree would not be published.

Ruth Franklin, in her review of *Miracle Fair: Selected Poems of Wisława Szymborska* for the *New Republic*, notes: "Some writers, including the critic Jan Kott and the poet Adam Ważky, embraced early on the idea of basing literature on Marxist criteria." This group also included Szymborska, who revised a group of her poems when the communist officials would not allow them to be published. The revised collection, *Dlatego zyjemy* (That's What We Live For), was eventually published in 1952. Franklin finds "propagandistic tendencies" in the poetry in this volume that "reflect the anti-Western and anti-capitalist tendencies of the time."

After the death in 1953 of Joseph Stalin, the Soviet Union's brutal, tyrannical leader from 1924 to 1953, literary restrictions eased in Poland and writers began publishing works that spoke out against communist doctrines.

The Solidarity Movement

The solidarity movement helped end Soviet control of Poland and led the country's transformation into a European democracy. It also encouraged anti-communist protests and political action throughout Europe, particularly in the communist bloc countries still under Soviet control, including Albania, Bulgaria, Romania, Mongolia, Eastern Germany, and Hungary. Eventually, these activities helped to enable the people of the communist bloc countries to free themselves from Soviet domination.

The movement began at the Gdańsk shipyards in August 1980, when Solidarity, an independent Polish labor union, protested the firing of one of their members. The workers, led by Lech Walesa, who had been fired four years earlier, decided to strike. Their action inspired other strikes across the country, also spurred by increasing economic problems in Poland. Demands by striking workers included the legalization of independent labor unions, permission for a monument

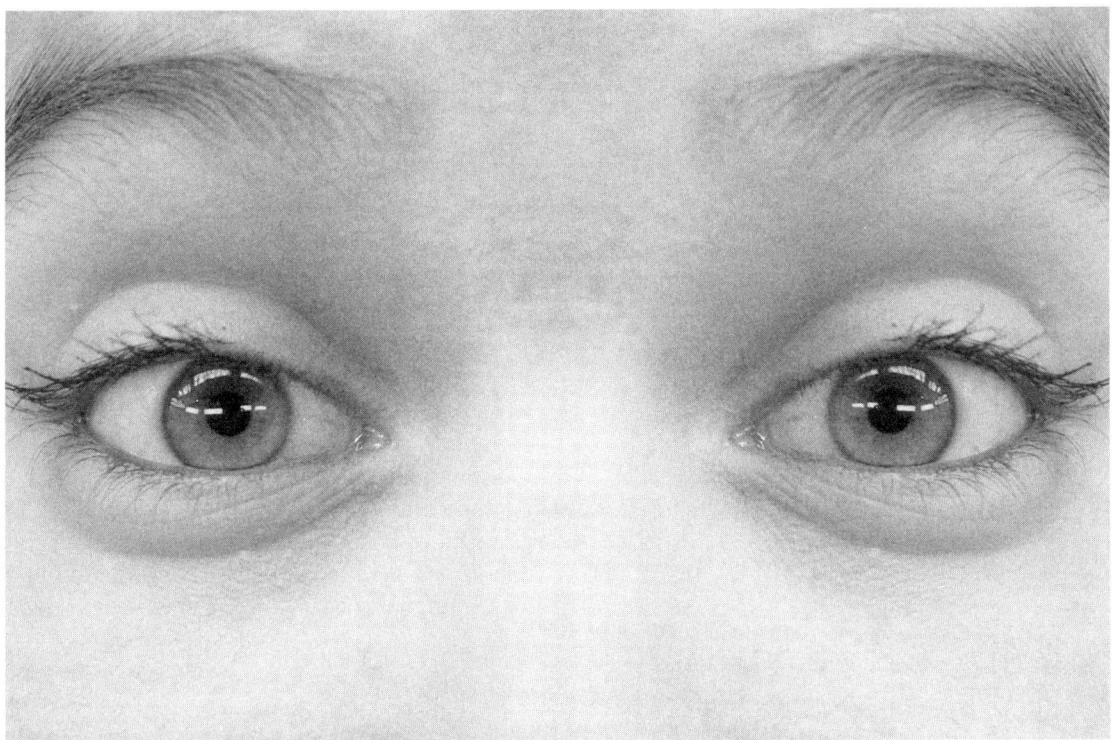

Close up of light-colored eyes *(Image copyright Andresr, 2009. Used under license from Shutterstock.com)*

to be built honoring 80 workers who had been murdered during a labor dispute in Gdańsk, the elimination of media censorship, freeing of political prisoners, lifting of restrictions on religious expression, and better health care. Underground publications spread news of the strikes, which helped the movement grow.

The strikes forced the government to begin negotiations with Walesa, who had become the leader of the movement, and on August 31, 1980, the Gdańsk Agreement was signed, allowing workers to form independent unions. In 1981, however, the government, fearing a harsh Soviet backlash, imposed martial law and arrested several Solidarity leaders, including Walesa. During the next few years, economic conditions worsened, and workers continued their protests against government control. By 1990, fears about Soviet intervention had lessened, and the government began talks with the workers, which ultimately resulted in the establishment of a democratic state government led by Walesa.

During the period of martial law in Poland, Szymborska supported the protest movement and initiatives proposed by human rights groups such as Workers' Defense Committee (KOR). She also helped establish the Association of Polish Writers, a group that sought to overturn literary censorship. Szymborska continued to publish during the 1980s in Parisian periodicals and in the underground press in Poland under the penname, Stanszykówna. Stańczyk was a famous court jester in Poland who was heralded for his political wisdom.

CRITICAL OVERVIEW

Szymborska's first two volumes of poetry were generally regarded as little more than communist propaganda. By the 1950s, she had recognized the abuses imposed by communist control in Poland and broke with the party in a personal and political sense. After the 1957 publication of her third volume of poetry, *Wolanie do Yeti* (Calling Out to Yeti), which was free of the political dogma of her earlier collections, she was heralded as a new fresh poetic voice in Poland. She received similar attention after her collection *Sounds, Feelings, Thoughts: Seventy*

Poems (1981) was published in English, the first of her works to be translated. Her reputation as one of the best poets of her generation was established when she won the Nobel Prize for Literature in 1996.

In a review of *Sounds, Feelings, Thoughts: Seventy Poems* for the *Slavic Review*, Madeline G. Levine concluded that Szymborska's "poems are tightly crafted, intelligent commentaries on the human condition." She determined that they "encompass potentially ponderous themes" and concluded that "despite the serious philosophical underpinnings, the poems are written...with a light hand." Levine found that the poems in this volume are "marked by a wry wit which is reinforced by [Szymborska's] characteristic combination of sophisticated literary Polish with colloquial turns of phrase and bursts of linguistic inventiveness."

Szymborska's *Poems New and Collected: 1957–1997*, which includes "Possibilities," was met with similar glowing responses. E. J. Czerwinski wrote in a review for *World Literature Today* that Szymborska is "a superb master of metaphor": "Metaphor not only defines her verse but is the driving force of her genius." Czerwinski explained, "The moment of truth in each poem contains a philosophic twist of irony that is arrived at after great mental anguish.... Her closing words in each poem illustrate the soul-searching thought behind even the simplest of metaphors." The review concludes with the argument that Szymborska's work "pays homage to man's weakness and fragility. Perhaps... it is this quality that endows her voice with such resonance and conviction—and makes it totally her own." While as of 2009, a full-length study of "Possibilities" had not been written, the poem has been singled out in several reviews as a successful example of Szymborska's poetic talents.

Another review of this collection, appearing in *Publishers Weekly*, claimed, "Szymborska's tough naturalism does allow rays of light to penetrate its bleak landscapes, leaving lasting, sustaining impressions."

The praise continued for her work in reviews of *Miracle Fair: Selected Poems of Wisława Szymborska*, published in 2001. Ruth Franklin, in a review of the collection for the *New Republic*, claimed that Szymborska writes "in carefully apportioned and gently administered measures" and that "the neatly assembled sentences of which her poems are constructed are miniature marvels of precision in a Polish literary tradition famous for lines and constructs of Latinate complexity." Franklin determined that the poet is one of "the plainest and most lucid writers of [her] generation" and praised her ability to "play with traditional forms to create a poetry that manages to feel modern within the very constraints of its formalism." Szymborska is, she concluded, "one of the great humanists of our time" but also should be recognized for her "mischievous, whimsical sense of humor."

In another review of the collection, Maya Peretz, in *The Slavic and East European Journal*, wrote that Szymborska "manages to grapple with the gravest and most brutal problems of our age with unusual sensitivity and subtlety." Peretz found the poet to be "discriminating and graceful, while at the same time penetrating and analytical" as she "combines a razor-sharp mind with humor and wit."

CRITICISM

Wendy Perkins

Perkins is a professor of English at Prince George's Community College in Maryland and has had several articles published on American and British literature. In this essay, she explores the rejection of political dogma and conventional beliefs in "Possibilities."

Polish-born Wisława Szymborska experienced firsthand the oppressive effects of foreign occupation in her country. Poland suffered first under the rule of Nazi Germany during World War II and later, as part of the communist bloc, under the control of the USSR. During the war, over six million Poles lost their lives in military service and in concentration camps and ghettos. Szymborska survived but was forced to go to school in secret since the Nazis declared education illegal for Poles. When the USSR under Stalin took control of Poland after the war, severe restrictions on personal and professional activities were imposed, including the censorship of literary works if they did not promote Marxist rhetoric. Questioning the imposed ideology emerges as a dominant theme in many of Szymborska's works. A successful handling of this theme occurs in "Possibilities," a poem that quietly subverts dogmatic principles in any form.

As "Possibilities" questions and subverts the validity of dogma, it also rejects the devotion to

WHAT DO I READ NEXT?

- Szymborska's "Thank-You Note," from her collection *A Large Number* (1976), is also written in first person, here expressing the speaker's feelings about the responsibilities of love. The speaker lists how she would respond, or not respond, to people she does not love.

- In "Funeral (II)," from *The People on the Bridge: Poems* (1986), Szymborska lists comments gathered from people attending a funeral. Their comments, mostly disjointed fragments, express their lack of caring or respect for the one who has died.

- Szymborska's Nobel Prize acceptance speech, published in *Poems New and Collected: 1957–1997* (1998), outlines her philosophy on writing, which includes the importance of questioning.

- Pablo Neruda's *The Book of Questions*, translated by William O'Daly (1991), collects 316 brief poems that are written in the form of philosophical questions that are not answered, a form that Szymborska often uses in her poetry.

- *New and Collected Poems: 1931–2001* (2001) is a collection by the Polish poet Czeslaw Milosz, who won the Nobel Prize for Literature in 1980. His poetry, like that of Szymborska, often describes Poland's troubled history in the twentieth century.

- Margarita Engle's *The Surrender Tree: Poems of Cuba's Struggle for Freedom* (2008) focuses on a young girl's struggle to help others survive Cuba's three wars of independence (1850–1899).

speaker describes the items on the list as preferences rather than absolute choices, she refuses to align herself with any set philosophy or ideology. Her list is open to change since she may at some point decide that she prefers something else, and so it is not rigid in any sense. The list appears random with no set pattern, moving back and forth from the concrete to the abstract, from reference to a needle and thread to the nature of reason, suggesting that objects and ideas and what attracts and repels cannot be so neatly packaged. Yet the list expresses her individual preferences, no one else's.

As she constructs the list, Szymborska sets up a pattern of opposites, subtly pitting the doctrine against a preference for something that contradicts it. The doctrine is implied rather than explicit. This technique also causes the statement of preferences to seem less combative and assertive, which reflects the poem's rejection of ideological pronouncements. The preferences suggest an alternate point of view that prompts readers to see the fallacy of the implied, apparently widely accepted rule. As the speaker notes in line 11, she prefers exceptions to rules.

Some of the items on the list are overtly political in a general if not specific sense. They hint at the oppression that she and her countrymen and women suffered under Germany and the USSR but expressly dismiss the ideology of occupation. In line 22, the speaker rejects the state of war when she decides that she prefers people dressed in civilian clothes, which automatically implies the less preferred opposite: military uniforms. She then subtly attacks commonly shared views, which she does repeatedly in the poem, when she notes her preference for occupied countries rather than for invading countries. Here Szymborska identifies the contrast she has in mind, which she does not often do in the poem, in order to make clear what common view she is challenging. She pits the occupied people against the occupiers to stir the readers' sympathy for the former rather than to generate praise for the strength of the latter.

The next three lines are more general statements on war and occupation but make the same point. Line 24 appears to link to the speaker's position in the previous line when she announces that she prefers having some reservations. Occupying countries, she suggests here, do not have any reservations. If they did, they would see the

order that that dogma requires. This rejection first is apparent in the title and in the form of the poem. The list the speaker constructs presents possibilities, not prescriptions for her or anyone else. The list itself creates an ironic counter to the imposition of doctrine and order. When the more humane value in not trying to take over other countries.

The next line presents a different point of view on the same subject. Occupiers often justify occupation by insisting that their takeover will help restore order and peace. The speaker contradicts this commonly held belief, noting that states of both chaos and order can be miserable, but she prefers chaos, suggesting that imposed order can cause more suffering than chaotic but free disorder. The last line in the sequence compares Grimms' fairy tales, noted for their often gruesome story lines, to the front pages of newspapers that often report scenes of war. She would rather read about fairy tale violence than about the violent real events.

The poem's remaining lines function beyond the political context of the sequence just quoted. They do, however, accomplish the same goal: rejection of an adherence to platitudes that when examined closely, often appear absurd. The other items on the list are a combination of the every day and the philosophical. Szymborska continues the pattern of contrasts between her speakerapos;s point of view and that of convention, but often adds her witty, ironic take on the absurdity of blind obedience to what is accepted as common wisdom.

In line 13, when the speaker refers to a doctor visit, she notes that she does not want to talk about her medical problems, which of course is why one goes to see a doctor. She would rather discuss another subject, which actually makes perfect sense, however, if the doctor is about to tell the patient any bad news.

The belief that people should love all mankind appears absurd in lines 5 and 6 when the speaker suggests people should focus on individuals rather than the unknown entire population of the world. Showing love for individuals is more time-consuming but more beneficial and rewarding than believing in a love that is generic and abstract.

The speaker then focuses on moralists in lines 19 and 20 who insist that if one acts properly, he or she will be rewarded, which of course, sometimes does not happen. She prefers those who do not make such promises. When it comes to writing poetry, the speaker finds absurdity in both writing and not writing. Accepted wisdom is that writing poems helps a poet express him or herself, but the speaker realizes that words can never express absolute truths, only hint at possibilities, as the title suggests.

Accepted wisdom also insists that true acts of kindness are selfless and so should be trusted. The speaker, however, decides that she prefers kindness that is cunning rather than too trustworthy, suggesting that she does not believe the later really exists.

The last lines of the poem sum up Szymborska's main point. The speaker's final preference is for thinking that existence may have its own reason for being instead of expressing some dogmatic government, religion, or given institution. Throughout the poem, Szymborska insists that there are no concrete answers to puzzling aspects of life, to people's visions of their identity, or to the purpose of their lives. Yet when the speaker expresses her preference for thinking about possibilities rather than any absolutes, she suggests that the search for those possibilities can be a fruitful one.

Source: Wendy Perkins, Critical Essay on "Possibilities," in *Poetry for Students*, Gale, Cengage Learning, 2010.

Eva Badowska

In the following essay, Badowska discusses the themes that are present in Szymborska and relates these to events in the poet's life. She suggests that Szymborska's poetry exhibits philosophical precision, intellectual playfulness, and wit.

For all their philosophical precision, intellectual playfulness, and emotional detachment, the poems of Wisława Szymborska, who was awarded the Nobel Prize in 1996, are much more than thought experiments in verse. That "the unthinkable / can be thought" is for her the "miracle" of poetry. A wit rather than a sage, she proclaims nothing and dictates less, teasing the reader with unsettling queries and suggestive contrariness. Having become disenchanted with dogmatism in her Communist youth, Szymborska has no patience for formal philosophical systems. She appreciates, rather, the natural perversity of all thought worthy of the name. If she thinks against the grain, her defiance isn't programmatic. She genuinely delights in asking questions and gently poking holes in established wisdoms and unexamined assumptions. With her, even metaphysical questions about Plato's Ideal Being turn into teases: "Why on earth did it start seeking thrills / in the bad company of matter? Citing the conclusion of "Century's Decline"—where she observes that "the most pressing questions / are naïve ones"— Stanisław Barańczak, Szymborska's award-winning translator (together with Clare Cavanagh), comments: "Many of her poems start provocatively, with a question, observation or statement

Tree-lined bank of the Warta River in Poland (Image copyright Pawel Kielpinski, 2009. Used under license from Shutterstock.com)

that seems downright trite, only to surprise us with its unexpected yet logical continuation." Despite her "metaphysical imagination," Szymborska is no armchair philosopher. She revels in poetry's intellectual potential because, as she once remarked, "the word 'why' is the most important word in any language on earth, and probably also in the languages of other galaxies; the poet must know it and use it adroitly." This lively curiosity has led her to a humble but profound respect for the quiddity, the otherness, of all persons, animals, plants, and things. Her emotional reserve, which has nothing to do with reasoned dispassion, has an ethical dimension. She likes to get up close to the object but refuses to merge with it.

A good starting point for a consideration of her poetry is "An Opinion on the Question of Pornography," from *The People on the Bridge,* a volume widely regarded as Szymborska's masterpiece. The poem entertains, inflames, even disturbs. It plays with the notion that thinking is like pornography, that paradoxical equalizer, abhorred by the Communist authorities, but furtively imported, in Soviet-style cardboard suitcases, by party officials and dissident activists alike. Opening with an incendiary proposition—"There is nothing more debauched than thinking"—it goads the reader with further provocations:

> Nothing's sacred for those who think.
> Calling things brazenly by name,
> risqué analyses, salacious syntheses,
> frenzied, rakish chases after the bare
>   facts,
> the filthy fingering of touchy subjects,
> discussion in heat—it's music to their
>   ears...

We are barraged with ever more intense images of the debauchery of thought, only to be left disoriented at the end of the stanza with the sudden calm of "music to their ears." When it

> **SYMBORSKA, UNLIKE MOST POLISH POETS OF THE LAST TWO CENTURIES, FLATLY REFUSES TO DON THE "PROPHET'S STAFF AND RIBBONS." WITH HER, THEY BECOME ONLY A THEATRICAL COSTUME, "PROPHET'S JUNK."**

comes to wordplay, Szymborska has the Midas touch. Every line couples conceptual nouns with spicy modifiers, suggesting that thinking, if done right, will bring out your inner libertine, for it respects no restrictions, be they puritanical or political. The poem's raciness also reflects a particularly effervescent quality of Szymborska's intellect. She positively gets off on unearthing the forgotten thought still living in dead metaphors. "Bare facts" exude nudity and make the "heat" of a discussion take on a fresh sense. The undoing of dead metaphors generates new ones.

"An Opinion on the Question of Pornography" was probably written during or shortly after the martial law in Poland. Szymborska first read the poem in December 1984 at the first meeting of NaGłos (Out Loud), a gathering of the kind that her generation remembered from the time of the German occupation, and which was now revived in defiance of censorship.

The event took place in Cracow's Catholic Intelligentsia Club (KIK), an elite association of Catholic intellectuals, whose activities had been suspended by the government. Though programmatically KIK was an apolitical organization, for years it had provided refuge for writers and intellectuals, not necessarily Catholic and often agnostic or even atheist. The occasion of the poem's performance certainly influenced its reception. It is often read less as a critique of false morality than as a defense of underground intellectual gatherings. Indeed, the last stanza gives a realistic sketch of just such forbidden "trysts":

> During these trysts of theirs, the only
> thing steamy is the tea.
> People sit on their chairs and move their
> lips.
> Everyone crosses only his own legs
> so that one foot is resting on the floor
> while the other dangles freely in midair.
> Only now and then does somebody get
> up,
> go to the window,
> and through a crack in the curtains
> take a peep out at the street.

For Szymborska, the dissident underground was a new and unfamiliar environment, but her relationship to it, as the poem makes clear, was typically "aslant" ([Emily] Dickinson and Szymborska share a strain of contrariness). Though the poem contemplates the problem of pornography in order to defend free speech, Szymborska refuses to become an apologist for any political movement and lavishes not praise but ambivalence on her subjects, the somewhat bloodless intellectuals who "prefer the fruits / from the forbidden tree of knowledge / to the pink buttocks found in glossy magazines." If the poem strikes at the heart of censorship, it also doesn't spare a typical member of the KIK, or for that matter any academic the world over, turned on by "the filthy fingerings of touchy subjects." Its last lines can of course be read politically—that "someone" furtively lifting the curtain is on the lookout for the police—but they also suggest the stifling claustrophobia of intellectual stimulations. Those sequestered in the hothouse of the mind secretly long to flee the pathetic "tryst" for a single "peep out at the street." Though English "peep" is used in such prurient phrases as "peep show" and "peeping Tom," it has a perfectly innocent meaning as well. But Polish "*podglądać*," which is less nuanced, has the effect of infantilizing the freethinkers. The image that comes to mind is that of precautious boys who "*podglądają*" girls in school bathrooms, not of adult deviants. The corporeal diction of the stanza and the many verbs of physical movement further amplify the mood of restlessness. Thinking is wicked: it makes us yearn for what is hidden just out of reach, behind curtains. Those who truly prefer forbidden fruit are not satisfied to be part of any club, however dissident, that would have them as a member. Yet freethinking has its risks. It can become its own prison house, complete with a longing for the lost paradise of the "street."

Szymborska had good reasons to feel ambivalent about joining the underground. As soon as martial law was imposed on the country, she began writing for dissident publications, but her poetic career before 1981 had a very different coloration. Born in 1923, Szymborska became a poet under the German occupation. During the war she got involved with a Communist youth group; her first poem appeared in a Communist daily in 1945. The trajectory of her political life was typical of the vast majority of Eastern European intellectuals of the period. In 1952 she joined the Communist Party (PZPR), out of genuine, it seems, ideological commitment. She remained a member until 1966, when, following the reprisals against Leszek Kołakowski, a respected philosopher, she turned in her party membership card as a gesture of protest. If anything should surprise us about Szymborska's Communist past, it's not the fact of her having been a member of the PZPR. Czesław Miłosz, for one, was an employee of the Communist government (the Ministry of Foreign Affairs) until his defection in 1951. What might take us aback, rather, is how long Szymborska remained in the party's ranks, while many fellow writers left during the thaw of 1956.

By the late 1940s she had a volume of poems but found no publisher, not having fulfilled the political mandates formulated at a writers' congress in 1949—her poems were deemed too "bourgeois" and "pessimistic," the decade's favorite critical epithets. Changing tack got her a job at *Życie Literackie,* the official weekly of the literary arts, a post in which she stayed for thirty years, until the events of 1981. At the height of the Stalinist period, she published two volumes of poems in the vein of Soviet social realism, including poems extolling the virtues of Lenin and mourning the death of Stalin. In a post-Nobel interview with the *Los Angeles Times,* she explained that

> I really wanted to save humanity, but I chose the worst possible way. I did it out of love for mankind. Then I came to understand that you should not love mankind, but rather like people. Like, but not love. I don't love humanity; I like individuals. I try to understand people, but I cannot offer salvation to them. That was a very hard lesson for me. It was a mistake of my youth. It was made in good faith, and, unfortunately, a lot of poets have done the same. Later they would sit in prison for changing their ideology. I was fortunately spared that fate, because I never had the nature of a real political activist.

This was an important moment. Szymborska, unlike many of her contemporaries, had not made a show of repentance and had barely spoken about her Communist past, leading some extreme commentators to draw comparisons between her and Martin Heidegger, who never publicly acknowledged his membership in the Nazi party. Though in "Writing a Résumé" she criticized official biographies for talking about "Memberships in what but without why," reticence was a perilous stance to take in a country whose hunger for public disclosure remains well-nigh insatiable. (Writers and intellectuals make a habit of confessing that they "prostituted themselves" under communism, adding a further sardonic twist to Szymborska's central metaphor in "An Opinion on the Question of Pornography.") Critic Tadeusz Nyczek provides a more measured perspective: "Szymborska remains silent. She doesn't explain herself, she doesn't talk back, she doesn't prostrate herself, she doesn't apologize... Perhaps she came to the conclusion that evil or stupid words can't be erased with other words, other gestures. What would she have to think about literature, its fragile sense, if she thought that words were so easily altered?"

Her *Los Angeles Times* interview included words she used on previous occasions and that held for her a special significance. In one of her weekly feuilletons for *Życie Literackie,* later collected as *Nonrequired Reading,* she praised Charles Dickens, whose *Pickwick Papers* remains a personal favorite. Dickens, she wrote, "not only loves humanity, but what is much more rare—likes human beings," and the same words reverberate in "Possibilities," from *The People on the Bridge:*

> I prefer movies.
> I prefer cats.
> I prefer the oaks along the Warta.
> I prefer Dickens to Dostoevsky.
> I prefer myself liking people
> to myself loving mankind...

This is as much as Szymborska is ever likely to dabble in confessional poetry. The poem tempers its sundry disclosures with a polite anaphoric emphasis on "preference" (thirty-one of thirty-nine lines begin with the same simple phrase). If the juxtaposition of "I prefer cats" with "I prefer myself liking people" isn't merely incongruous, it's because the incantatory form transmutes these statements of predilection into charms and spells. The lethal tendency to "love humanity" is also exorcised by irony: "I prefer talking to doctors about something else." But the reiteration also hints that preference offers no guarantees (while I *prefer* myself snacking on carrot sticks to myself inhaling chocolate squares, I more often wind up doing the latter) and thus discourages us from seeing the poem as a poetic manifesto.

Szymborska may refuse to prostrate herself, but the Communist experience changed her. With her biographers, Bikont and Szczęsna, she was clear: "I have no collective feelings," she said, "No one will ever catch sight of me in a crowd. Perhaps the lesson, which I once received, caused me to be no longer capable of belonging to anything at all? I can only sympathize. Belonging is for a writer an obstacle..." The Polish title of "An Opinion on the Question of Pornography" confirms this. "*Głi*" (rendered as "opinion" by Barańczak and Cavanagh, and "contribution" by Adam Czerniawski) literally means "voice" and echoes the name of the event, *NaGł*, where it was first read. The word is often used in the collocation "*zabierać głos,*" to voice an opinion, which positions Szymborska as part of a larger debate (as in "*głosy w dyskusji*": voices in a debate). "*Głos*" is also used in the expression "*oddać głos,*" which means "to vote," making the poet's contribution a kind of individual vote on the issues raised in the poem. A "*głos*" is always one of many and never represents a collectivity; Szymborska claims no special status for her "opinion." Even in this most political of her poems, then, she casts doubt on her own propositions, showing that they are impossible to mobilize in the service of any cause.

One of her most frequently anthologized poems is "Soliloquy for Cassandra," from the 1967 volume *No End of Fun*, published a year after Szymborska left the party. The poem, by entering into the plight of Cassandra, a failed prophet, reflects on the role of poetry after the great catastrophes of history. Szymborska identifies with Cassandra, but *at a distance*, marking her separateness and distinct voice with the humble proposition "for" ("*dla*") in the poem's title. Here and elsewhere, her empathy shuns complete identification and preserves a tension between the self and another being, however mythical.

Not quite a dramatic monologue, the poem helps the Trojan princess descend from the "heights beyond life" and makes her appear warm and approachable, full of regrets and irony. Having learned from past mistakes— as did Szymborska, who no longer "loved humanity"—Cassandra apologizes for her aloof and presumptuous manner towards the Trojans:

> I loved them.
> But I loved them haughtily.
> From heights beyond life.
> From the future. Where it's always empty
> and nothing is easier than seeing death.
> I'm sorry that my voice was hard.

The prophetess failed to save her people because she was alienated from their mortal fates. The very transcendence that gave her foresight also made her words hollow and her prophecy ineffective.

But when Szymborska's Cassandra later soliloquizes over the ruins of Troy, reflecting on her prophetic fiasco, her speech is informal and her easy demeanor compels listeners in a way that her prophesy could not. She introduces herself not, as Barańczak and Cavanagh would have it, with "Here I am, Cassandra," but even more colloquially, in a phrase that could be rendered as "Hi, it's me, Cassandra." She atones by becoming one of those who "knew what a moment means." The poem is framed by two stanzas that echo each other:

> Here I am, Cassandra.
> And this is my city under ashes.
> And these are my prophet's staff and ribbons.
> And this is my head full of doubts
>
> It turns out I was right.
> But nothing has come of it.
> And this is my robe, slightly singed.
> And this is my prophet's junk.
> And this is my twisted face.
> A face that didn't know it could be beautiful.

"Soliloquy for Cassandra" unfolds, then, in the shadow of the question posed by Miłosz in *Rescue* (1947): "What is poetry which does not save / Nations and peoples?" Though Miłosz challenges the Polish Romantic tradition of the Poet-Prophet, his question is rhetorical: it is essential that poetry retain its "salutary aim." But, for Szymborska, "uncertainty is more beautiful still," as she puts it in "Love at First Sight." The poet, like the doomed Trojans, should embody the Socratic disclaimer, "I don't know." Not to know is, actually, according to Szymborska's Nobel lecture, "The Poet and the World," the poet's ethical obligation: "Poets, if they're genuine, must also keep repeating, 'I don't know.' Each poem makes an effort to answer this statement, but as soon as the final period hits the page, the poet begins to hesitate, starts to realize, that his particular answer was pure makeshift, absolutely inadequate." Unlike "torturers, dictators, fanatics, and demagogues," that is, those who zealously profess to know, poets must concede that their authority is nothing but a fiction. They might even find joy and succor in the humbling fact:

> Is there then a world
> where I rule absolutely on fate?
> A time I bind with chains of signs?
> An existence become endless at my bidding?
>
> (from "The Joy Writing")
>
> Poetry—
> but what is poetry anyway?
> More than one rickety answer
> has tumbled since that question first was raised.
> But I just keep on not knowing, and I cling to that
> like [sic] to a redemptive handrail.
>
> (from "Some People Like Poetry")

What sort of "redemptive handrail" is poetry to Szymborska, for whom Troy was a figure for the devastations of history in her own life? Though she was born elsewhere, her literary life is associated with Cracow, a city she is notorious for hardly ever leaving. In the 1960s, she faced the "moral pressure to remember" the Holocaust. The crematoria of Auschwitz, not thirty miles from Cracow, cast a long shadow. Shortly after the war, Szymborska and fellow writers cooped up in a Soviet-style writers' colony in the Old Town knew little about the genocide that took place so close to home. Her biographers go to the extreme of suggesting that "in her memory about the war there are no Jews." Critic Artur Sandauer explains that even poems about the death camps contemplate "not the event itself but her ignorance of it." The knowledge came gradually, and became more demanding with time. According to Miłosz, Szymborska belongs to a generation that wrote "in the place of the generation of poets who made their debut during the war and did not survive." Such a survival in the place of another resembles Cassandra's and like hers, poses an ethical problem. In this way, "Soliloquy" questions, as did [Theodor W.] Adorno, the viability of poetry after Auschwitz.

The poem carries, in fact, the echoes of an earlier poem about the death camps, "Still" (from her 1957 volume *Calling Out to Yeti*). The "short-lived names" of the Trojans, doomed by history, recall the "names" of Jews transported to the death camps in "Still":

> Across the country's plains
> sealed boxcars are carrying names:
> how long will they travel, how far,
> will they ever leave the boxcar—
> don't ask, I can't say, I don't know.
>
> The name Nathan beats the wall with his fist,
> the name Isaac sings a mad hymn,
> the name Aaron is dying of thirst,
> the name Sarah begs water for him...

Imitating the rhythmic sound of the rail and the wheels, the poem paints a disturbing picture of the fate that carries "the names" towards perdition. The absence of whole human beings on either side—if the victims have been reduced to metonymic names, the perpetrators have been replaced by runaway trains—makes the journey seem mechanical and unstoppable. Their fate is so inexorable that it resembles the Greek *moira*, which determined the Trojans' destiny.

Szymborska nonetheless offers a more hopeful, almost commonsensical ethics of survival:

> After every war
> someone has to tidy up.
> Things won't pick
> themselves up, after all.
>
> Someone has to shove
> the rubble to the roadsides
> so the carts loaded with corpses
> can get by...
>
> (from "The End and the Beginning")

That the "someone" Szymborska has in mind is the poet becomes clear in an essay from *Nonrequired Reading*, where she writes. "The poet can't keep up, he lags behind. In his defense I can only say that someone's got to struggle in the rear. If only to pick up what's been trampled and lost in the triumphant procession of objective laws." The poet's role is to "trudge / through sludge and ashes," to be a sort of janitor to the bedlams of history, or else a stage manager tidying up after a dramatic performance:

> ...the tragedy's most important act is the sixth;
> the raising of the dead from the stage's battlegrounds,

> the straightening of wings and fancy
>   gowns,
> removing knives from stricken breasts,
> taking nooses from lifeless necks,
> lining up among the living
> to face the audience...
>
> (from "Theater Impressions")

Symborska, unlike most Polish poets of the last two centuries, flatly refuses to don the "prophet's staff and ribbons." With her, they become only a theatrical costume, "prophet's junk,"... which can be worn as a gag or not at all. Patently uninterested in saving nations, or for that matter belonging to them ("Oh, the leaky boundaries of man-made states!" she intones in "Psalm"), she can proffer only a "head full of doubts." Szymborska shows no interest in prophetic "heights beyond life," and so the destruction of transcendence, described by Adorno in *Prisms*, if itself an ethical catastrophe, has little impact on her conception of poetry.

But Szymborska's poetry is by no means all about anguish. "My identifying features / are rapture and despair," she writes in "Sky," and the former feeling is expressed as insistently as the latter. When operating in this mode, a favorite word of hers is "*zdumienie*" translated as "astonishment" by Barańczak and Cavanagh). In her Nobel lecture, she remarks that whatever "we might think of this world—it is astonishing":

> But "astonishing" is an epithet concealing a logical trap. We're astonished, after all, by things that deviate from some well-known and universally acknowledged norm, from an obviousness to which we've grown accustomed. But the point is, there is no such obvious world. Our astonishment exists per se, and it isn't based on comparison with something else.

"Astonishment" is also the title of a poem included in the 1972 volume *Could Have*. It consists of seventeen questions permitting no apparent answers.

> Why after all this one and not the rest?
> Why this specific self, not in a nest,
>   but a house? Sewn up not in scales, but
>   skin?
> Not topped off by a leaf, but by a face?
> What made me fill myself with me so
>   squarely?
> Why am I staring now into the dark
> and muttering this unending monologue
>   just like the growling thing we call a
>   dog?

Szymborska's astonishment, obviously philosophical, is also embodied—and that's something she cares deeply about. If she puzzles at the nature and contingency of consciousness, she never does so abstractly. The poem depicts living beings by means of synecdoche, in a series of startlingly concrete images: a tree is represented by a "leaf," fish by "scales," birds by "a nest," and a human person by "skin" and "face." Without these material markers of identity, no one can claim to be "this one and not the rest." The poem bewitches with its offbeat analogies and throwaway charm. It implies that our very capacity to pose such questions in just such a way is all that really matters.

Szymborska's "continuous 'I don't know'" harmonizes with her delighted curiosity, her philosophical interest in the "why." She often writes about the limitations of human knowledge, especially in regard to the natural world. Though she has a keen interest in biology and has reviewed many books on evolution and related topics, she believes that our often professed love of nature is "warped by perversity and double-dealing." All that we can really do is gape in amazement at the world's rich variety:

> So much world all at once—how it rus-
>   tles and bustles!
> Moraines and morays and morasses
>   and mussels,
> the flame, the flamingo, the flounder,
>   the feather—
> how to line them all up, how to put them
>   together?...
>
> (from "Birthday")

Here is the same passage in Polish:

> Tyle naraz świata ze wszystkich stron
>   świata:
> moreny, mureny i morza i zorze,
> i ogień i ogon i orzeł i orzech—
> jak ja to ustawię, gdzie ja to położę?...

The poem transforms "world" into a quantifiable noun, bursting the seams with its medleys. The translation does a superb job of reproducing the mimetic effect of the original, in which ecological interconnectedness is stressed by means of alliteration (in Polish, the third line lists fire, tail, eagle, and walnut), and the rhyme of "bustles" with "mussels" is delightful. The only striking difference in the translation is that the "I" has been removed from the last line—in Polish it runs, "how shall I line them up, how shall I put it all together?" It matters to Szymborska that a particular person is perplexed by the lushness of the world. She treasures our individual capacity to be astonished.

She also likes to muse on the human desire to experience—to empathize with—other forms of being despite our better knowledge that it is futile. In "Conversation with a Stone, " she wants "out of pure curiosity," "to enter... [the] insides" of the stone and insists on being "let... in." The stone patiently explains that the speaker "lack[s] the sense of taking part"; she may come to "know" the stone, but she will never "know [it] through." The Polish word Barańczak and Cavanagh translate as "know through" is zaznać, or experience something for oneself, in one's own body. The poem distinguishes between intellectual and sensory knowledge, clearly favoring the latter, which remains outside the human supplicant's reach (after all, the stone is "made of stone"). In Szymborska's Leibnizian view, each being is "shut tight" to all others. By the poem's end, the stone, "bursting with laughter," discloses that it doesn't "have a door" for her to pass through. Tropes are but "poor senses" with which to "zaznać" the world.

While Szymborska's dismay at our alienation from the natural world doesn't make her succumb to doubts about representation, she isn't averse to pondering its consequences. In "View with a Grain of Sand, " she writes:

> We call it a grain of sand,
> but it calls itself neither grain nor sand.
> It does just fine without a name...
> Our glance, our touch, mean nothing to it.
> It doesn't feel itself seen or touched.

Plants and animals and grains of sand do not reciprocate our curiosity and remain placidly unperturbed by our desire to name them. "Our one-sided acquaintance / grows quite nicely," Szymborska remarks with biting irony in a recent poem. The "silence of plants" perplexes her, but doesn't detract from the "joy of writing." The alienation of human consciousness causes her no existential angst. On the contrary, it rather charms her.

Szymborska's recent poems are more darkly inquisitive. Her only volume published after the Nobel Prize, Moment has all the usual quiet wonder at the world's stunning contrasts of animal and human, peace and war, philosophy and history, but there are also flashes of something tenebrous, all the more disquieting for the calm that continues to underpin it. Though she still assures us that "this is / misery and happiness enough," she also begins to question such stoicism.

As with all her books, Moment is a tightly woven collection, unified by a set of recurrent themes. Philosophically, it revisits the problem of time and transcendence raised in "Soliloquy for Cassandra," where Cassandra was tragically estranged from those who "knew what a moment means." The volume opens with the title poem:

> I walk on the slope of a hill gone green.
> Grass, little flowers in the grass,
> as in a children's illustration.
> The misty sky's already turning blue.
> A view of other hills unfolds in silence.
>
> As if there'd never been any Cambrians, Silurians,
> rocks snarling at crags,
> upturned abysses,
> no nights in flames
> and days in clouds of darkness...

An interval of time, like Zeno's arrow seeming to stand still in mid-flight, projects a bucolic calm, "as in a children's illustration." But behind the placidity of "nine-thirty local time" lie the massive and violent confluences of geology and history, "upturned abysses" and "malignant fevers," which the poem illustrates in its form: the second stanza's brief staccato lines contrast with the legato rhythm of the first. In her conversations with Bikont and Szczęsna, Szymborska admits that she "experiences moments of genuine despair because of what is happening in the world; she fears that the twenty-first century will be an age of great fundamentalisms, of a massive settling of accounts, of great wars." The calm of a moment depends on a vital illusion: it is "as if seas had seethed only elsewhere / shredding the shores of the horizons."

Towards the end of Moment comes "Photograph from September 11":

> They jumped from the burning floors—
> one, two, a few more,
> higher, lower.
>
> The photograph halted them in life,
> and now keeps them
> above the earth toward the earth.
>
> Each is still complete,
> with a particular face
> and blood well-hidden.
>
> There's enough time
> for hair to come loose,

for keys and coins
to fall from pockets.

They're still within the air's reach,
within the compass of places
that have just now opened.

I can do only two things for them—
describe this flight
and not add a last line.

The terse stanzas enact a quiet drama in what is otherwise a tragically static picture, its tercet pattern interrupted by a single four-line stanza, incongruously claiming that "there's enough time." Clearly not, and for what? For life literally to fall apart, in a metonymic shower of keys, coins, and hair. Unlike the idyllic interval in *Moment*, which obscures the forces behind it, this photographic still only intensifies our knowledge that the bodies' movement is "toward the earth." Traveling from life to death, the arrow can't stand still. Caught in flight—for they are, for Szymborska, in "flight," not in free-fall—the jumpers are, for the moment, "complete." Though the instant itself could be "invited to linger" only in vain, the photograph demands a closer look at that which, in a matter of seconds, is obliterated. The victims of September 11 are, for Szymborska, suspended by history in the midst of forces which tend, as do all historical forces, toward the undoing of their human particularity. By her own account, her imagination is "still particularity ... / illuminating only random faces," holding fast to "singular faces, / each the first and last for all time, in each a pair of inimitable eyes." The Polish word here rendered as "particular" is "*poszczególny*," which emphasizes singularity within a group: it considers "each part from the others." Uniqueness is an attribute of human faces, which, arresting and elusive, remain on the verge of becoming nameless and unrecognizable.

The Swedish Academy, in awarding Szymborska the Nobel Prize, praised the way her poetry "with ironic precision allows the historical and biological context to come to light in fragments of human reality." Malgorzata Baranowska, a poet and critic, writes that Szymborska "always brings out a certain fragment as in a photographic close-up, as though she had a suspicion that the whole is by nature unknowable." But for Szymborska the world isn't itself fragmented, though it can be apprehended only in poetic stills. She highlights moments and fragments from the earliest volumes, underlining the distance between "us" and those who "jumped from the burning floors," for such barriers can only be "describe[d]"—they cannot be traversed by any effort of the imagination or bridged by any act of empathy. Paradoxically, what poetry can do is only protect "them" against facile and spendthrift sympathies, mindless of differences.

If Szymborska makes only a reticent witness to history, it's partly because she despises sentimentality. "No one in this family has ever died of love," she asserts, mocking "death-defying vigils, love-struck poses," and "Bosch-like hell within." A staunch anti-Romantic, she rejects the view that "the artist must be dutifully unhappy. Nothing comes to him without hellish sufferings, which his own personality, fate, and society try hard to make a reality." She opens vistas that are truly worldly, for she sees poetry as a cosmopolitan art. Her realism moves, frightens, saddens, and astonishes us. Her love of detail, which springs from her belief that truth resides in the particular and the contingent, flies in the face of fundamentalism, while her dazzling wit wreaks havoc with universal truths. In all her poems, Szymborska reminds us that "Everything" is "a bumptious stuck-up word," nothing but "a shred of gale," and "should be written in quotes."

Source: Eva Badowska, "'My Poet's Junk': Wislawa Szymborska in Retrospect," in *Parnassus: Poetry in Review*, Vol. 28, Nos. 1–2, 2005, pp. 151–68.

Jacqueline Osherow

In the following essay, Osherow discusses how she enjoys reading translations of the poetry of Wislawa Szymborska.

Let me begin by making a peculiar confession: I love reading poetry in translation. I suppose this has to do with the way you experience what you're reading as inaccessible, so that the poem, elusive as it necessarily is, becomes, itself, almost an object of poetic longing. But there are also less heady reasons for reading poems in languages we don't know. One can go on and on about what is not translatable in poetry—and certainly no dearth of eloquence has been expended on this subject—but I want to focus here (as indeed I must, since I don't know Polish) on what isn't lost in translation. It seems to me that we in America—especially as we scramble to find places for ourselves in the line-up from, say, language poetry to new formalism—put far too much weight on a poem's surface. What the pleasures of poems in translation prove—and Wislawa Szymborska's do this exquisitely—is

WHAT WOULD BE ANOTHER POET'S TRIUMPH IS, FOR SZYMBORSKA, A SOURCE OF SHAME."

that there is something essentially poetic that does not inhere merely in a poem's surface. Call it substance. Call it thought. Call it wild association. What poetry does with these—and so many other—imaginative possibilities is at least as interesting as what it does with language. That said, let me also make clear that I wish I knew Polish, and remind myself, even as I make this case for poems in translation, how I came to love Eugenio Montale from a single translation of Robert Lowell's that I loathed when I finally learned Italian. The surface of a great poem is always miraculous; it's no wonder we are often too bewitched to look beyond it. And even as I admire—and I do, wildly—these poems of Szymborska's, I know I am being extravagantly short-changed.

Stanislaw Baranczak and Clare Cavanagh make her poems read like excellent English poems, and I am certainly grateful for that (*View with a Grain of Sand: Selected Poems*, Harcourt, Brace, 1995). These translations are far smoother and more colloquial and, frankly, more poetic than those I've seen before. Nonetheless, earlier translations never got in the way of my immense enthusiasm. I do suspect, however, from trying to piece together the Polish in an earlier bilingual edition (*Sounds, Feelings, Thoughts*, translated by Magnus J. Krynski and Robert A. Maguire, Princeton University Press, 1991), and from my sense that its translators have stayed very close to the literal meaning of the text, that Baranczak and Cavanagh make free, at times, with the poet's meaning. Occasionally, I prefer other translations to theirs: John and Bogdana Carpenter's version of "The Joy of Writing," for example, begins "Where is the written doe running, through the written forest?" (from *Contemporary Eastern European Poetry*, edited by Emery George, Oxford, 1993). Baranczak and Cavanagh's reads, "Why does this written doe bound through these written woods?" (Krynski and Maguire opt for "Where through the written forest runs that written doe?"—

which is why I suspect this team of accuracy. What else could explain that sort of awkwardness?) What's the point of changing "Where" to "Why"? And where else have I been duped?

I also find no reference to the game "solitaire" in Maguire and Krynski's version of the "Notes from a Nonexistent Expedition to the Himalayas" (see below), nor can I find room for it in the Polish; but there it is, in Baranczak and Cavanagh. It's worrying, but then, I do love these versions of the poems (indeed, I have to admit, I even like the "solitaire") and most of the time they appear to offer, with real grace, the same meanings given far less effectively by other translators.

Whether they're perfectly accurate or not, the rewards of reading Baranczak and Cavanagh's renderings are real. But I doubt that even the clumsiest language could entirely mask Szymborska's endearing sense of humor, her finely tuned but matter-of-fact self-consciousness, her genius for the unexpectedly resonant detail. What most distinguishes her poems is the quality and complexity of her thought, the pressure she puts on what already seem like revelations, the way she moves not only in unexpected but unimagined directions, or, as she herself puts it, in the poem "Into the ark," that "eagerness to see things from all six sides."

Szymborska's poems are demanding ones—less on her readers than on herself. Even in her earliest poems we benefit from these demands. She begins "Notes from a Nonexistent Himalayan Expedition" with an observation many poets would be pleased to arrive at in conclusion: "So these are the Himalayas. / Mountains racing to the moon." We see her characteristic combination of seriousness and whimsy, her cataloging of incongruous and telling details:

Yeti, down there we've got Wednesday,
bread and alphabets.
Two times two is four.
Roses are red there,
Violets are blue.

Szymborska doesn't belabor a proposition to which a lesser poet would devote at least an entire poem, namely, that "two and two" aren't necessarily "four" elsewhere. And that lesser poet would not have trusted the specificity of "Wednesday," the generality of "bread." (We might have been stuck with, say, "daylight" and "croissants.")

And the characteristic coexistence of bleakness and optimism that gives such breadth to

Szymborska's work is also apparent in this early poem: "We've inherited hope— / The gift of forgetting." But it is her simultaneous fusion and inversion of the ordinary and the extraordinary, her way of revelling in that fusion, and, above all, that inversion, that is, finally, her trademark:

> Yeti, we've got Shakespeare there.
> Yeti, we play solitaire
> and violin. At nightfall,
> we turn lights on, Yeti.

"Solitaire" aside, not only are "Shakespeare," the "violin" and "turn[ing] lights on" placed on the same level, but we arrive at the turning on of lights—needless to say, a well-chosen representative of the miracle of the ordinary—as if it were the greatest of the treasures "down there" has to offer. Of course, the effect is double edged. Is this an exaltation or a trivialization of earthly experience? Both, of course. And then there is the pure wonder of the conceit of the poem, that we readers should have the experience, once in our lives, of being addressed, even for a moment, as "Yeti."

Szymborska perpetually insists on and delivers a wide scope of vision, despite her indebtedness to tiny details; at the same time, she begs our pardon for those expectations. In another fairly early poem, "Museum," I suppose she's talking about her own enterprise when she says: "Since eternity was out of stock / ten thousand aging things have been amassed instead." In that poem too she begins with what some would have found an opportune conclusion:

> Here are plates but no appetite.
> And wedding rings, but the requited love
> has been gone now for some three hundred years.

and ends by making the thing surprisingly personal:

> The battle with my dress still rages on.
> It struggles, foolish thing, so stubbornly!
> Determined to keep living when I'm gone!

That turn—calling the "dress" the "foolish thing" instead of herself—and revising the notion of who's a patsy in the "struggle . . . to keep living" strikes me as the only way to bring off a poem in which a museum's leftover things call to mind one's own mortality. The charm and humor and surprise leave potential self-pity behind.

But the only proper way to appreciate Szymborska—and this is clearly turning into an appreciation—is to look at a poem in its entirety. I choose "Under One Small Star":

> My apologies to chance for calling it necessity.
> My apologies to necessity if I'm mistaken, after all.
> Please, don't be angry, happiness, that I take you as my due.
> May my dead be patient with the way my memories fade.
> My apologies to time for all the world I overlook each second.
> My apologies to past loves for thinking that the latest is the first.
> Forgive me, distant wars, for bringing flowers home.
> Forgive me, open wounds, for pricking my finger.
> I apologize for my record of minuets to those who cry from the depths.
> I apologize to those who wait in railway stations for being asleep today at five a.m.
> Pardon me, hounded hope, for laughing from time to time.
> Pardon me, deserts, that I don't rush to you bearing a spoonful of water.
> And you, falcon, unchanging year after year, always in the same cage,
> your gaze always fixed on the same point in space,
> forgive me, even if it turns out you were stuffed.
> My apology to the felled tree for the table's four legs.
> My apologies to great questions for small answers.
> Truth, please don't pay me much attention.
> Dignity, please be magnanimous.
> Bear with me, O mystery of existence, as I pluck the occasional thread from your train.
> Soul, don't take offense that I've only got you now and then.
> My apologies to everything that I can't be everywhere at once.
> My apologies to everyone that I can't be each woman and each man.
> I know I won't be justified as long as I live,
> since I myself stand in my own way.
> Don't bear me ill will, speech, that I borrow weighty words,

then labor heavily so that they may
   seem light.

There are many ways to read this poem, it seems to me, all of them correct. The speaker could, I suppose, be apologizing for her poetry not being "everywhere at once," not representing "each woman and each man." At the same time, the poem delights so much in its own specificity—in its own "small answers" to "large questions"—apologizing not for the "table," for example, but for "its four legs," that it resists such a reading.

Even the endearing gesture of the first two lines, of covering all bets in the face of her own confusion, is only, as it turns out, an opening gambit. After all, the speaker does make extraordinary claims for herself, even if she does so (in what strikes me as a very Dickinsonian gesture) with immense humility. It may be a mere "thread"; it may be only "occasional," but she is telling us that she has managed to "pluck it" from no less a garment than the "mystery of existence."

Her apologies are sincere, but this is a woman aware of her achievements. For those who are not convinced, we have the authority of the last two lines, which soar, even as they deflate themselves. What would be another poet's triumph is, for Szymborska, a source of shame. As she masterfully puts one last thing over on us, she apologizes with such genuine pathos that the newly completed poem seems like the ultimate act of treachery. She places before our eyes the possibility of another poem: one that speaks head on, that doesn't "make light," that doesn't "labor," that doesn't shy away from "weighty words." So, even as we admire her, we are left dreaming of that other poem until that poem, finally, is this poem's great achievement, despite the fact that it appears only as shadow.

But Szymborska is not only talking about her poetry. The poem moves easily between the world at large and poetry: those "flowers" the speaker's been "bringing home" despite the "distant wars" could be poems, but, then again, they could be flowers. And the person in the railway station at 5 a.m. who is more real to us than the "distant wars" is meant to be more real. We've been in that damned railway station; we haven't, thank God, been in those particular wars.

Szymborska doesn't shy away from addressing enormous subjects head on. In the relatively recent poem, "The Century's Decline," an impossible subject she knows first hand, her capacity for epigram is suddenly given wings:

God was finally going to believe
in a man both good and strong,
but good and strong are still
two different men

It is, of course, the mitigating and insistent "still" that gives the stanza its power, simultaneously undercutting the otherwise pompous epigram and rendering it eternal. In her provocative, imaginative, and nervy use of God, one is reminded of the dress in "Museum." Here, the inversion is of God and man; surely it's God's apparent inability to be both "good" and "strong" that Szymborska is also surreptitiously lamenting.

Effectively, she is being indirect even when she appears to be direct, and it is, after all, the power—and ultimate marksmanship—of her indirection that is Szymborska's crowning achievement. Take "In Broad Daylight," a poem that begins in this deadpan fashion:

He would
vacation in a mountain boarding house,
   he would
come down for lunch, from his
table by the window he would
scan the four spruces, branch to branch,
without shaking off the freshly fallen
   snow

One is a trifle bored, but this is Szymborska, so one goes on reading.

One should, I suppose, begin suspecting something with:

About his ear, just grazed by the bullet
when he ducked at the last minute, he
   would
say: "I was damned lucky."

but I admit that it was only when I read:

Sometimes someone would
yell from the doorway: "Mr. Baczynski,
   phone call for you"—
and there'd be nothing strange about
   that
being him, about him standing up,
   straightening his sweater,
and slowly moving toward the door

along with the accompanying translators' note—"Krysztof Kamil Baczynski, an enormously gifted poet of the 'war generation,' was killed as a Home Army fighter in the Warsaw Uprising of 1944 at the age of twenty-three"—that I recognized the gift I was being given. My first reaction was fury at myself for never having thought of writing a poem in which antibiotics were invented 175 years earlier and Keats is an old man on a trip to Rome; but I'd stupidly have imagined Keats writing poems, instead of "moving toward the door." And even if I had managed to come up with that "door," never, in a million years, would I have pushed it further:

> At this sight no one would
> stop talking, no one would
> freeze in mid-gesture, mid-breath
> because this commonplace event would
> be treated—such a pity—
> as a commonplace event

And so of course, we arrive, through the war, through poetry, through what might have been, through all kinds of weighty and important subjects, back at that one "mystery of existence" that Szymborska has "plucked out" so magisterially: the impenetrable mystery of the "commonplace."

And each time Szymborska makes the "commonplace" miraculous, the miracle is newly astonishing. The poem "In Praise of Dreams" begins, "In my dreams / I paint like Vermeer van Delft", and I am forced, once again, to recognize the futility of my own jealousy (as in, why the hell didn't I write those lines? haven't I always wanted to paint like Vermeer van Delft?). Good as those lines are, they would never have led me through her particularly graceful and amusing list of examples—(my favorite: "I can't complain: / I've been able to locate Atlantis"). And certainly never, in my wildest dreams, would I have thought to end:

> A few years ago
> I saw two suns
> And the night before last a penguin,
> clear as day

Source: Jacqueline Osherow, "'So These Are the Himalayas': The Poetry of Wislawa Szymborska," in *Antioch Review*, Vol. 55, Spring 1997, pp. 222–28.

SOURCES

Czerwinski, E. J., Review of *Poems New and Collected: 1957–1997*, in *World Literature Today*, Vol. 74, No. 2, Spring 2000, pp. 440, 441.

Franklin, Ruth, "The Storm Before the Calm," in *New Republic*, June 4, 2001, pp. 58, 59, 61.

Levine, Madeline G., Review of *Sounds, Feelings, Thoughts: Seventy Poems by Wisława Szymborska*, in *Slavic Review*, Vol. 41, No. 3, Fall 1982, p. 586.

Peretz, Maya, Review of *Miracle Fair: Selected Poems of Wisława Szymborska*, in *Slavic and East European Journal*, Vol. 46, No. 1, Spring 2002, pp. 187, 188.

Review of *Poems New and Collected: 1957–1997*, in *Publishers Weekly*, March 30, 1998, p. 77.

Szymborska, Wisława, "The Poet and the World: Nobel Lecture, 1996," in *Poems New and Collected: 1957–1997*, translated by Stanislaw Baranczak and Clare Cavanagh, Harcourt, 1998, p. xvi.

———, "Possibilities," in *Poems New and Collected: 1957–1997*, translated by Stanislaw Baranczak and Clare Cavanagh, Harcourt, 1998, pp. 214–15; originally published in *Ludzie na moscie* (The People on the Bridge: Poems) Czytelnik, 1986.

FURTHER READING

Ash, Timothy Garton, *The Polish Revolution: Solidarity*, 3rd ed., Yale University Press, 2002.
> Ash tells the exciting story of the Polish shipyard workers whose defiance of Soviet control sparked the Solidarity movement and helped propel Lech Walesa into the national spotlight.

Baranczak, Stanislaw, "The Szymborska Phenomenon," in *Salmagundi*, Vol. 103, Summer 1994, pp. 252–65.
> In this essay, Baranczak explores Szymborska's use of language and her focus on questioning.

Gajer, Ewa, "Polish Poet Wisława Szymborska," in *Hecate*, Vol. 23, No. 1, May 1997, pp. 140–42.
> In this essay, Gajer provides an overview of Szymborska's career and offers insight into how her work was shaped by her life in Poland.

Michener, James A., *Poland*, Fawcett, 1984.
> In this bestselling novel, Michener mixes fact and fiction as he traces the lives of three Polish families over eight centuries.

Zamoyski, Adam, *The Polish Way: A Thousand-Year History of the Poles and Their Culture*, John Murray, 1989.
> This work serves as an impressive introductory history of the art, politics, and customs of Poland from its founding during the dark ages into the early 1990s.

since feeling is first

E. E. CUMMINGS

1926

The American poet Randall Jarrell stated in an article published in 1950 in *Partisan Review* that e.e. cummings "will remain popular for a long time" because "he is one of the most individual poets who ever lived." Jarrell's assessment has been echoed throughout the twentieth century and into the twenty-first by readers and scholars alike. One of cummings' most popular pieces is the love poem "since feeling is first," which first appeared in *Is 5*, a collection of his poetry that was published in 1926. The collection was highly praised, and the poem has been widely anthologized. One such anthology is the fourth edition of *The Heath Anthology of American Literature*.

In "since feeling is first," cummings presents a young man who is trying to convince his lady to indulge in her passions for him. In order to accomplish this, the speaker carefully constructs an argument that he hopes will prompt her to accept him as her lover. Cummings presents two themes in this argument: to privilege emotional responses to experience over intellectual ones and to live fully in the moment. Readers delight in the poem's playful, innovative call for individual expression and the rightness of sexual passion.

AUTHOR BIOGRAPHY

Edward Estlin Cummings was born in Cambridge, Massachusetts, on October 14, 1894, to

e.e. cummings (The Library of Congress)

Edward Cummings, a Unitarian clergyman and sociology professor at Harvard, and Rebecca Haswell Clarke Cummings, who encouraged her son's early interest in art and poetry. Cummings was called by his middle name by his family, but when he began publishing his poetry, he shortened Edward Estlin to E. E. and would often use all lower case letters when he signed his name.

Cummings grew up in Cambridge, and in 1911 he began his studies at Harvard. During his college years, he worked as an editor for the literary magazine and became interested in the modernist movement, which would later influence his own paintings and poetry. He left Harvard in 1916 with a master's degree, and his first poems were published the following year in the anthology, *Eight Harvard Poets*. The poems included in this volume illustrate his early experiments in style and language for which he later became famous.

During World War I, cummings volunteered to be an ambulance driver in France where he was later held for a few months in an interment camp on suspicion of treason, charges that were soon dropped. This experience was fictionalized in his first book, *The Enormous Room*, which was hailed by the critics.

After the war, he, like many other disillusioned writers and artists, traveled and worked for a time in Europe before settling in New York's Greenwich Village. His first poetry collection *Tulips and Chimneys*, published in 1923, established him as an important new American poet, a title that was confirmed by his subsequent collections, including *Is 5* in 1926. One of the poems in the latter collection is "since feeling is first," considered to be one of his finest.

Cummings' steady work from the 1930s through the 1950s was well received by the critics and the public. He earned a number of poetry awards during his lifetime, including the *Dial* (magazine) Award in 1925, a Guggenheim fellowship in 1933 and 1951, the Shelley Memorial Award in 1944, the Charles Eliot Norton Professorship at Harvard for the academic year 1952–1953, the Bollingen Prize for Poetry in 1958 and three *Poetry* (magazine) awards (1939, 1952, and 1962). In 1955, he received a special citation from the National Book Award for *Poems, 1923–1954*. Cummings stayed active until his death in New Hampshire on September 3, 1962, writing, painting, and reading his poetry on college campuses.

POEM TEXT

```
since feeling is first
who pays any attention
to the syntax of things
will never wholly kiss you;

wholly to be a fool                              5
while Spring is in the world

my blood approves,
and kisses are a better fate
than wisdom
lady i swear by all flowers. Don't cry           10
—the best gesture of my brain is less than
your eyelids' flutter which says

we are for each other: then
laugh, leaning back in my arms
for life's not a paragraph                       15

And death i think is no parenthesis
```

POEM SUMMARY

The first line of "since feeling is first" conveys the main statement that the speaker makes in the

MEDIA ADAPTATIONS

- On the CD *The Voice of the Poet: e.e. cummings*, published by Random House Audio Voices from *The Voice of the Poet* series, cummings reads selections of his poetry. A book containing the texts of the poems on the CD accompanies the CD.
- The CD *Essential Cummings*, published by Caedmon Essentials, presents another collection of poems read by the poet.

poem. He asserts that one's emotional response occurs first. The speaker does not qualify his statement that feeling should be first; he asserts by using the word "is": Feeling is immediate, occurs before other responses, and it also takes precedence over any other response.

In the next line, he notes, that people who pay attention to the order of things cannot engage fully in a kiss, cannot kiss fully the person whom the speaker addresses in the second person as "you" and later calls "lady." Anyone who is more concerned with the proper sequence of things, with the proper relationship between parts, which the poet calls "syntax," cannot engage fully in a passionate way with another person.

In the second stanza, the speaker accuses this type of person of being a complete fool, especially during spring when there is so much stimulation for the senses and emotions. Implicitly, he distinguishes himself from such a fool and suggests his lady is above one, too. In the first line in stanza three he admits that he, of course, would respond emotionally not only to the beauty of spring, but also to the loveliness of his lady, whom he now speaks to directly.

In stanza three, he declares his physical attraction to his lady who has stirred his blood. He argues that a physical relationship, symbolized by kisses, is more important than gaining wisdom. He tries to convince her that spring approves of his declarations as he swears the truth of them "by all flowers."

In the middle of this stanza, his lady cries, perhaps because she is afraid to indulge with such abandonment or because she is touched by his affection. The speaker insists that true emotions must take precedence over any other response, claiming that his best thoughts account for less than the movement of her eyelids.

The speaker links the third stanza with the fourth, declaring to his lady that the fluttering of her eyelids tells him she recognizes that the two of them belong to each other. In this sense, he is suggesting that she wants a physical relationship with him as much as he does with her, which would then mean that the two of them are in complete agreement.

As a result of this agreement, the speaker is ready to engage physically with his lady, and so he tells her that she should laugh rather than cry and lean back in his arms. He then reinforces his initial claim of the supremacy of feeling when he insists that life is more than a paragraph, that it should be experienced fully through the emotions.

The speaker continues this line of reasoning in the final stanza, which consists of only one line. He comes full circle in the last two lines, citing the life is not a single experience but a sequence of them and death cannot be placed into a parenthesis, meaning there is nothing beyond dying. In that case, then, life must be lived fully in the moment.

THEMES

Cycle of Life

In many poems that have a *carpe diem* (seize the day) theme, the poet includes a secondary, related theme: the cycle of life. In "To the Virgins, to Make Much of Time," Robert Herrick refers to the sun's rising and setting as a sign of this cycle: Life is short, and so the young must seize the day. Blooming and fading roses also suggest the passage of time. Flowers are often used in *carpe diem* poetry as symbols of the brief blooming time, of spring as the time of ripening, youthful energy. In "since feeling is first," cummings refers to the spring and flowers in both traditional and innovative ways, all related to the cycle of life and all an integral part of the speaker's argument that the lady should live in the moment.

TOPICS FOR FURTHER STUDY

- Draw an illustration of the central scene of the poem, depicting the speaker comforting his crying lady. As you construct your illustration, think about how you would stage this scene if it were part of a play. Draw another picture of the lady after she has listened to her lover, showing her response to his words.
- Decide whether the lady rejects or accepts the speaker's argument and write a poem from her point of view. Try to mimic cummings' style in your poem.
- Research the cubist movement, which had a great influence on cummings' poetry. Also look at Rushworth Kidder's article, "Cummings and Cubism: The Influence of the Visual Arts on Cummings' Early Poetry" in *Journal of Modern Literature* and prints of cummings' own paintings. Then read the poem again and see if you can determine how this movement influenced the poem. Write up your analysis in a research paper that includes background information on cubism and any relevant points from Kidder's article.
- Read some of the poems in *The Collected Poems of Langston Hughes*, edited by Arnold Rampersad, especially those such as "Weary Blues" and "Song for a Dark Girl" that show Hughes's innovative style and form. Make a list of Hughes's innovations and those of cummings. Present your findings in a PowerPoint presentation that includes illustrations from each poet's work.
- Think about situations in which people must decide whether to listen to their head or their heart. This struggle can occur over important matters or insignificant ones, over career choices or over whether to order dessert or keep to one's diet. Write about an incident, either fictional or autobiographical, which dramatizes this type of struggle.
- In the early twentieth century, feminist thinkers began to engage in a rigorous investigation of female identity as it related to all aspects of a woman's life. The New Woman was a label applied to women who rejected traditional roles and set off to enjoy male prerogatives in social settings and in the workplace. Many of these women demanded the right to the same kind of sexual freedom that men typically enjoyed. Research the topic of women and sexuality in the United States in the 1920s. How much sexual freedom were women able to gain during this decade? Did urban women have fewer restrictions than those who lived in rural communities? What might be the social consequences for the woman in cummings' poem if she gave in to the sexual urgings the speaker recommends? Write a paper that places the woman in the poem in her historical context and explore possible answers to these questions.

Cummings introduces spring, which he capitalizes, in the second stanza, indicating this season's importance. Spring is one of only two words he capitalizes in the poem. He uses spring to indicate the season in which the poem is set, which coincides nicely with his argument. Clever word play here points to the imagined rival's failure as a lover as well as the speaker's own appropriateness. The rival is a fool in this season since he thinks rather than feels, while the speaker's superiority is proven by his racing pulse. His heart beats strong, he is full of youthful energy, and he can be an excellent lover.

Cummings employs the image of flowers in the third stanza in three traditional ways: as the symbol of spring, of beauty, and of the transitory nature of life. As Herrick notes in "To the Virgins, to Make Much of Time," flowers follow the cycle of life, beginning as buds and blossoming into lovely flowers that "tomorrow will be dying." Like Herrick, cummings uses them to create a sense of urgency; the speaker insists that his lady use her time wisely by enjoying sexual love. Her fluttering eyelids suggest to the speaker that she has blossomed like a flower and may be ready to indulge her passions.

Celebration of the Individual

One of cummings' favorite themes is the rejection of the conventional in favor of the celebration of the individual. In his satiric poems like "the Cambridge ladies who live in furnished souls," and "next to of course god America i," he gives full voice to this theme when he attacks traditional beliefs and social restrictions on self expression. In "since feeling is first," cummings rejects restrictions on physical love and celebrates the individual's desire for sexual fulfillment.

Conventional thinking inhibits those who focus on the rules of courtship, who are so preoccupied with syntax that they cannot fully express their feelings. The speaker warns his lady against allowing the same kind of emotional repression in her response to him, insisting that the fluttering of her eyelids proves that she desires physical fulfillment with him.

The speaker presents himself as a free individual who refuses convention and encourages unaffected delight in spontaneous expression. He is convinced he is right and is completely free of guilt in his call to celebrate love and to indulge in sexual pleasure.

The primacy of the individual is also evident in cummings' experimentations in poetic style and in his construction of the poem. He refuses to follow conventional patterns of rhyme and meter and to capitalize the beginning or to provide punctuation at the end of sentences. He arranges his words on the page not according to poetic or grammatical rule, but to the free expression of his themes. Thus, no two stanzas have the same number of lines. He breaks the lines according to the images he presents, saving the shorter stanzas for his most important pronouncements. He makes these in the second, fourth, and fifth stanzas: that anyone would be foolish to restrict feeling, that he and his lady were meant for each other, and that they must live life to the fullest since death marks the absolute end of possibility.

STYLE

Imagism

In his analysis of cummings' poetry in his *A History of Modern Poetry* David Perkins writes: "To most American poets Imagism meant a short, free-verse impression of some object, scene, or happening. The impression would be conveyed in a few, carefully selected and vividly rendered details and metaphors." The poems would also be characterized by "understated emotion, and maybe a mute, musing implication of further meaning." cummings was drawn to this literary movement because its poetry was liberated from traditional forms. The influence that imagist style had on cummings is evident in "since feeling is first."

This short poem shows the imagists' rejection of formal structure and complicated subject. Cummings writes the brief scene in free verse, a poetic form that does not have any set rhyme or meter, and employs contemporary language. Rejection of poetic conventions is matched by the speaker's argument for his lady to ignore social dictates and give in to her emotions and physical yearnings.

Cummings employs an extended metaphor to show his lady how not to act. His references to syntax, paragraph, and parentheses, to the rules of language, are used to suggest a life of the mind that takes precedence over a life of sensation and romance. His word play, which invites more than one meaning, also steps outside the boundaries of imagism, as in his use of the word "wholly," first to describe a kiss and immediately after to describe a fool. In this sense, cummings used imagist style in his own playful way.

HISTORICAL CONTEXT

Modernism

The term *modernism* refers to an artistic movement in Europe and the United States during the first few decades of the twentieth century, which shaped the literature, painting, music, and architecture of the period. Modernism in the United States reached its height in the second decade and extended until the early 1930s. Modernist American literature expressed a growing sense of disillusionment with traditional social, political, and religious doctrines experienced by Americans at

COMPARE & CONTRAST

- **1920s:** The modernist writers during this period express a growing sense of disillusionment with Christian beliefs. Many begin to doubt that people are protected by a benevolent God, especially given the carnage and casualties caused by World War I.

    Today: Many Americans return to their faith and to traditional values in the first years of the twenty-first century. Several conservative Christian groups, usually referred to as the religious right, lobby for a return of Christian values in schools, including a return to prayers in the classroom and the promotion of sexual abstinence in sex education classes.

- **1920s:** American poetry often presents a pessimistic view of contemporary society as a reaction to perceived notions of complacency and conformity. T. S. Eliot's *The Waste Land*, published in 1922, is an important poetic expression of this perspective. e.e. cummings criticizes the age in his poetic satires.

    Today: Contemporary poets tend to use more concrete images and fewer literary allusions than modernist poets. But contemporary poets often continue the pessimistic zeitgeist of the twentieth century, which spills into the early years of the twenty-first. Their poetry frequently presents social critiques in a stripped down form, reflecting the rhythms and diction of spoken language.

- **1920s:** The flapper, who presents a new, freer female image, becomes the model for young American women as they begin to express a sense of individuality in terms of dress and behavior. However, women mostly follow traditional gender roles, especially after they marry.

    Today: American women enjoy major gains in their fight for equality, and in the twenty-first century they make their own life and career choices without bowing to the pressure of former social conventions. In 2008, Hillary Clinton is the first woman to be nominated by a major political party for president of the United States. When Barack Obama is elected president, she is appointed secretary of state, the third female secretary of state in the past two decades.

---

the beginning of the twentieth century but especially after World War I.

This time of confusion, redefinition, and experimentation produced one of the most fruitful periods in American letters. Modernist writers such as Ernst Hemingway, F. Scott Fitzgerald, and cummings helped create a new form of literature that repudiated traditional literary conventions. Late nineteenth-century works often expressed their authors' belief in the stability of character and the intelligibility of experience. Typically, nineteenth-century novels, stories, and poetry ended with a clear sense of closure as conflicts were resolved and characters gained knowledge about themselves and their world. Modernist authors challenged these assumptions as they expanded traditional form to accommodate their questions about the individual's place in the world.

The Lost Generation

Gertrude Stein, an important author and patron of the arts during this period, dubbed the group of authors that expressed its zeitgeist, the "lost generation," a label Ernest Hemingway used as an epigraph in his first novel, *The Sun Also Rises*. This novel portrays a band of expatriate American and English writers, who gather in Paris during the 1920s in search of a venue that allows them the artistic and intellectual freedom they do not experience at home. T. S. Eliot and Ezra Pound initially relocated to London, while Fitzgerald, Hemingway, and cummings traveled to Paris, which became a mecca for notable artists, critics, and writers who congregated in literary salons, restaurants, and bars to discuss their work. One such salon was provided by Gertrude Stein who

A spring landscape (Image copyright Jerry Whaley, 2009. Used under license from Shutterstock.com)

supported and publicized contemporary artists and writers.

The characters in works by these authors express a loss of faith in traditions and an interest in new ideas in psychology, anthropology, and philosophy. The theories of psychologist Sigmund Freud, for example, which contributed to a loosening of sexual behavior during the 1920s, began to be studied by these writers and used in their handling of characterization in their fiction. Hemingway's men and women face a meaningless world with courage and dignity, and Fitzgerald's seek the redemptive power of love and the insulation of alcohol among the wealthy, materialistic class. In his poetry, cummings' speakers satirize social hypocrisies and celebrate the physical and emotional pleasures of love.

Imagists

The Imagists were a group of poets that gained prominence in the second decade of the twentieth century and had an important effect on modernist poetry. These poets rejected traditional poetic diction and regulated meter in favor of more natural expressions of language written in free verse. One of the leading proponents of this movement, Ezra Pound, published his anthology *Des Imagistes* in 1913, with examples of what he considered to be imagist poetry by James Joyce, H. D. (Hilda Doolittle), William Carlos Williams, F. S. Flint, Ford Madox Hueffer (later Ford Madox Ford), and Amy Lowell, among others. Pound included in the collection his imagist doctrine, which insisted on direct treatment of the poetic subject, discarding any language that did not contribute to the presentation of this subject, and the emphasis on a sequence of musical phrases rather than on rhythm.

The imagists were greatly influenced by abstract painting, especially cubism. Imagism and cubism influenced cummings' poetry and his own paintings, for example some of his early poetic sequences, "Impressions," "Post Impressions," and "Portraits." His experimental juxtapositions of words, use of fragments, and variation of line length and space reflect this impact.

Sexuality in the 1920s

Feminist Victoria Woodhull (1838–1927) embarked on a lecture tour in 1871, in which she recommended a free-love philosophy, advocated for the women's movement, and approved the growing willingness to discuss sexual issues. Social attitudes toward sexuality did not begin to change, however, until the 1920s. Prior to that decade, many young women lived at home with their parents and were chaperoned when they went out in mixed company. Sexual relations outside marriage were taboo, especially for women who feared being branded as loose and unmarriageable.

In the aftermath of World War I, dramatic changes occurred in American society. In the 1920s, Americans recognized that the pre-war Edwardian formality had been replaced by a new, freer society, one that adopted innovative fashions in clothing, behavior, and the arts. Fitzgerald called this decade the Jazz Age, a label that along with the Roaring Twenties came to express the cultural revolution then taking place. Americans experimented with personal and social choices in the way they looked and the way they acted, especially concerning premarital sex, alcohol use, and exorbitant spending. In this decade, sex outside marriage began to lose its stigma as more women became sexually active.

CRITICAL OVERVIEW

At the time of his death in 1962, e.e. cummings was one of the most popular American poets of the twentieth century. He has retained that title into the beginning of the twenty-first century as his poems, including "since feeling is first," are widely anthologized. Cummings has been celebrated for his innovations in style and poetic form, for his love poetry, and for his sometimes scathing social critiques. In the 1920s, he was recognized as a modernist poet, but some scholars also found elements of American transcendentalism in his work. Transcendentalism is a nineteenth-century philosophical movement, and its ideas were expressed by Americans Ralph Waldo Emerson and Henry David Thoreau and by English romantic poets such as William Wordsworth and John Keats. Cummings' attention to the individual's thoughts and emotions harkened back to these earlier writers.

Laura Riding and Robert Graves, in *A Survey of Modernist Poetry*, praised cummings' experimentations in style and form: "Poems like cummings' and the attention they demand should make it harder for the standardized article to pass itself off as poetry." In agreement, Randall Jarrell applauded "how wonderfully individual, characteristic, [and] original" cummings' poetry is.

While Jarrell wrote that "cummings' poems are full of perceptions pure as those in dreams, effects of wonderful delicacy and exactness," he also pointed out that the poet avoids darker, more complex themes that involve suffering and heartache. Other scholars agreed with Jarrell's criticism, complaining that cummings did not develop his poetic talents after he established his unique style during the 1920s.

Some critics found cummings' love poetry too traditional, but Jarrell insisted that "love, in [cummings'] poems, is so disastrously neoprimitive, has been swept so fantastically clean of complication or pain or moral significance, that it seems a kind of ecstatic chocolate soda which is at once a sin—to the world—and a final good—to us happy few." Literary scholar R. P. Blackmur, describing *Is 5* in *The Hound and Horn*, praised some of the poems but found many others in the collection "more sentimental and less successful, where the realism is of a more obvious sort; not having reference to an ideal so much as to a kind of scientific reality."

"since feeling is first," however, is regarded as one of the best of the collection. William Heyen, in *Southern Humanities Review*, wrote: "I am more than fond of this poem. I think it is imaginative and compelling, convincing and even deep." In his explication of the poem published in *Spring: The Journal of the E.E. Cummings Society*, John M. Gill determined that it "remains a quintessential 'heart' poem in the cummings canon." Gill argued that its feeling-first theme "is a major and constant electrifying current in cummings' work." He also found a satisfactory complexity, claiming that "the movement of the poem is from the intensity and immediacy of the love scene to the abstractions of philosophic contemplations."

CRITICISM

Wendy Perkins

Perkins is a professor of English at Prince George's Community College in Maryland and

WHAT DO I READ NEXT?

- In cummings' "O sweet spontaneous," published in *Tulips and Chimneys* in 1923, the speaker insists that nature should not be analyzed from a religious, philosophical, or scientific point of view. It must be experienced emotionally rather than intellectually.

- In cummings' "the Cambridge ladies who live in furnished souls," published in *Tulips and Chimneys* in 1923, the speaker criticizes the superficial concerns of university wives who should instead be appreciating the beauty of nature.

- T. S. Eliot's *The Waste Land*, published in 1925, presents more examples of innovations in style and form. Many consider the poem one of the finest examples of modernism.

- *The Sun Also Rises* (1926) by Ernest Hemingway, one of cummings' lost generation compatriots, focuses on a group of disillusioned Americans living in Paris after World War I. Critics consider this novel to be the voice of its generation.

- Kate Chopin's short stories and her 1899 novel *The Awakening* center on women who act out against various social restrictions. Two of her best known stories are "Story of an Hour" (1894), which focuses on a woman's vision of a future life without her husband, and "The Storm," written in 1898 but not published until 1969, which explores the attraction of adultery from a woman's perspective.

- *Discontented America: The United States in the 1920s (The American Moment)* (1989), by David J. Goldberg, presents an overview of this decade and focuses specifically on how World War I affected American society.

- Kidder's 1979 *E.E. Cummings: An Introduction to the Poetry* is an excellent source for students who are just beginning a study of cummings.

- Arnold Adoff's *Love Letters*, published in 1997, is a collection of love poetry for young adults and is beautifully illustrated by Lisa Desimini. Included in this collection is "Dear Playground Snow Girl," a humorous look at unrequited love, and "Dear Tall Girl at Front Table," a poem that focuses on teenage body image.

- *The Collected Poems of Langston Hughes*, published in 1979 and edited by Arnold Rampersad, presents the work of this famous Harlem Renaissance poet, who, like e.e. cummings, was celebrated for his experimentation in poetic style and form. Two of his most famous poems are "Weary Blues," published in 1925, and "Song for a Dark Girl," published in 1927. The first has the same rhythm and tempo as a blues song and the second as a minstrel, both popular musical forms during the Harlem Renaissance.

---

has published several articles on American and British literature. In the following essay, she examines how cummings pairs the ideas of carpe diem *and head-versus-heart in "since feeling is first."*

Carpe diem, a Latin phrase from Horace's *Odes*, translates as "seize the day." The importance of living fully in the moment, which this phrase recommends, is a common literary idea, especially in lyric poetry. Love poems from the sixteenth- and seventeenth-century that incorporate this idea include Edmund Spenser's *Faerie Queen*, Robert Herrick's "To the Virgins, to Make Much of Time," and Andrew Marvell's "To his Coy Mistress," and from the nineteenth-century Edward Fitzgerald's "The Rubaiyat of Omar Khayyam". Twentieth-century writers have also employed the theme, for example, Henry James in his novel *The Ambassadors* and his short story "The Beast in the Jungle," Saul

> CUMMINGS JUGGLES DICTION IN THESE LINES, INFUSING THEM WITH NEW ENERGY IN ORDER TO MAKE READERS SEE CONVENTIONAL LANGUAGE IN FRESH WAYS."

Bellow in *Seize the Day*, and e.e. cummings in "since feeling is first." Typically, the speaker in a poem that expresses a call to seize the day proposes that since death is unavoidable and life is brief, the listener, often a reluctant virgin, should take advantage of the sensual pleasures the speaker is offering to her. What makes cummings' "since feeling is first" unique is its combination of two traditional themes, seize the day and head versus heart.

Many poems recommend the *carpe diem* approach to experience, promoting indulgence in natural physical impulse over abiding by the constraints of social decorum; young ladies are urged to give themselves up to sensual pleasure for its own sake. For example, in Marvell's "To his Coy Mistress," the speaker's goal is to convince his hesitant mistress to join him in becoming like "amorous birds of prey" so they can "tear [their] pleasures with rough strife / Through the iron gates of life."

In "since feeling is first," the speaker cleverly delays the suggestion that his lady give herself over to sensual pleasures until after he has offered a second approach, that of head versus heart, which recommends controlling impulse with thoughtful deliberation. Such an approach the speaker assigns to those who consider orderliness, signified by their interest in syntax, and cannot kiss with full passion. Laura Riding and Robert Graves, in their essay on innovations in modernist poetry, state: "To write a new poem on an old subject... and avoid all the obvious poetical formulas, the poet must write in a new way if he is to evoke any fresh response in his readers at all." Cummings' unconventional combination of these themes evokes this type of response.

The speaker begins with the value he promotes, that feeling should be the primary response to experience. He suggests that the intellect can suppress and inhibit the emotions, much like the rules of punctuation, syntax, or paragraph delineation can restrict creative writing. Cummings refuses to capitalize the first word in the first line of the poem, or in any line except for the last. He also refuses to punctuate the lines in the stanza except for the last line, which ends with a semi-colon. This lack of capitalization and punctuation conveys his insistence that people should not be governed by the intellect or by superimposed rules, not by rules for writing or for human relationships. Feeling, then, must come first, breaking through the restrictions of the objectivity and dispassionate analysis.

Cummings' lack of punctuation, coupled with his syntactical agility, allows a free play of lines and fragments of thoughts that come together to create an organic whole. In this poem, he uses the poetic technique of enjambment, allowing one thought to run over one line and into the next, which can create different meanings depending on how people read the lines.

At first reading, the first three lines seem to flow together to suggest that no one would ever pay attention to the rules of syntax since free thought and expression would always take precedence. However, when the fourth line is put together with the second and third, the meaning shifts to the speaker's perceived rival for the lady's affections, someone who *would* grant the intellect supremacy over emotions. That person, whom the speaker calls a "fool" in the second stanza, could never wholly kiss the lady and, thus, could never be a true lover to her.

Cummings then plays with the word "wholly" when he shifts its meaning at the beginning of the second stanza from a description of the act of kissing to a description of the fool. This hapless lover becomes wholly a fool when he cannot give himself completely to the kiss. Cummings juggles diction in these lines, infusing them with new energy in order to make readers see conventional language in fresh ways, to force readers out of commonplace associations, much like he later attempts to persuade his lady to reorder her priorities.

The introduction of the false lover provides the perfect link to his primary theme: *carpe diem*. The third stanza makes a formal call to seize the day, a call that is linked to the previous stanza. In this third stanza, cummings again constructs a line devoid of punctuation that can be linked either to the line that comes before or after it. If the line is linked to the previous one, the lover the speaker insists the lady should reject is characterized as a fool who will not give himself completely to feeling, especially during spring, a season that symbolizes budding life and new possibilities. Spring is one of only three words that cummings capitalizes in the poem, highlighting its symbolic power. If readers link the line to the one that follows it, however, which opens the third stanza, the speaker is able to reinforce his declaration that he is the more appropriate lover. Spring stirs not the fool's blood but his own, which approves of and so heightens his desire for his lady. Cummings unites his two themes in this stanza and so strengthens each by bringing the speaker and his lady together. He declares that kisses are more enjoyable than gaining wisdom, swearing the truth of his statement on "all flowers," again evoking the image of spring.

The lady's response to the speaker's words is mixed. The first indication of her reaction is in stanza three when the speaker begs her not to cry. Her distress suggests that the lady has come to understand what the speaker is proposing—to abandon any traditional social convention that would insist that she suppress her physical response to him. In an effort to comfort her, the speaker immediately reasserts his position that the physical should take supremacy over the intellectual. He states that his brain could not produce anything more compelling or more real than her emotional response to him, which, he suggests, she expresses by the flutter of her eyelids. This flutter, he assumes, proves her desire for him and confirms that the two were meant to be united.

He hopes that her acknowledgement of this truth will prompt her to accept his proposal, to laugh and lie back in his arms. In case he has not convinced her, the speaker reinforces his position by calling her attention to life's brief cycle, a common symbol used in support the *carpe diem* idea. His references to both life and death in the last two stanzas suggest that if they do not grab this opportunity now, they may lose it forever. Marvell offers a similar message in "To his Coy Mistress" when his speaker slyly notes, "The grave's a fine and private place, / But none, I think, do there embrace."

Cummings closes the poem by bringing the two themes together, arguing that life is not a paragraph nor is death a parenthesis. Here he continues his head-versus-heart theme by

> SILENCE IS, AFTER ALL, HARDLY LESS AUDIBLE THAN A SNOWFLAKE, A RAINDROP, OR A FALLING LEAF THAT IS SCATTERED ON THE PAGE."

recalling the poem's controlling metaphor of a grammatical and correctly punctuated piece of writing. By insisting that life cannot be placed into the same restrictive format, he reasserts his call to his lady to seize the day by putting feeling first. His mention of death in the final line asserts the urgency of his call. Parentheses are traditionally used to enclose additional information that is not essential to an understanding of the sentence. When cummings declares that death is not a parenthesis, he asserts its finality and its importance. Death marks the end of life; it is not an additional bit of information. The inevitability of death reinforces the need to pursue sensual pleasure now.

Source: Wendy Perkins, Critical Essay on "since feeling is first," in *Poetry for Students*, Gale, Cengage Learning, 2010.

Isabelle Alfandary
In the following essay, Alfandary makes a case for silence alternating with voice as a thematic unity running through the poetry of e.e. cummings.

"Japanese poetry is different from Western poetry in the same way as silence is different from a voice" (Houghton bMS Am 1892[94]). Such an aphorism is not to be found in a critical essay but in a college paper entitled "The Poetry of Silence" in which a student discusses the comparative forms and techniques of traditional Far-East and twentieth-century modernist poetries. The author of the paper was e.e. cummings when he was a college student at Harvard University in the years immediately before World War I. Even as a young man and poet, e.e. cummings had already connected voice and silence. Indeed, the relationship between silence and voice became fundamental in his poetry. How different is silence from voice is the question I would like to ask of cummings' poetry.

e.e. cummings' poems are filled with references to silence and voice. In *Is 5*, section Four

(1926), the poet, interestingly enough, gives an account of his poetic activity in these words:

> some ask praise of their fellows
> but i being otherwise
> made compose curves
> and yellows, angles or silences
> to a less erring end)
>
> myself is sculptor of
> your body's idiom:
> the musician of your wrists;
> the poet who is afraid
> only to mistranslate
>
> a rhythm in your hair,
> (your fingertips
> the way you move)
> the
>
> painter of your voice—
> beyond these elements
>
> remarkably nothing is....
>
> (*CP* 292)

The poem, as cummings suggests, is a composition of silences among such other different things as "yellows," "curves," and "angles." e.e. cummings was at least partly a modernist poet, as Norman Friedman argues in his essay "Cummings and the Modernist Tradition" (16). Just as he was a modernist painter in Kandinsky's and Picasso's wake, silence is poetic matter in his poetry as colors or shapes in his painting. More than just a poetic means, silence is a poetic end, may be even "a less erring end" as the poet ironically remarks. Of course, cummings did not devise the notion but to some extent discovered or rediscovered it. Christopher Columbus did not invent America either. And indeed silence is this long-ignored and new-found land, the impossible and engulfed continent the poet reaches. It is just as if cummings' poetry took up a lost and forlorn object in Western poetry. Now why had silence been silenced? If the poet-to-be did not give the answer, at least he raised the question and came to the conclusion that Western poetry—especially the romantic poets whom cummings admired and to whom he owed his early inspiration and more—had overinvested the voice to the detriment of silence.

But of course, it would be impossible to think of a voice without thinking of silence, for the two are undoubtedly inseparable. Only the connection between the two is problematic— what our college student referred to as their "difference." The reference to silence hardly ever comes without that of voice because silence implies voice just as voice does silence. Yet silence does not logically contradict voice in cummings' mind. We could even say (taking up one of cummings' well-known phrases devised on the occasion of a fictitious interview he gave to himself and in which he related his painting to his poetry [*Miscellany* 316]) that the two even "love each other dearly." Silence is a prerequisite for the voice, a space for it to invest, a resonance chamber in which to reverberate. In silence resounds voice, in voice silence is present. Poetry consists in turning the invisible—silence or a voice—into perception and presence.

Silence is experience. And that may be the reason why it usually comes up equally as an adjective, an adverb, or a noun in e.e. cummings' poems. Silence is a quality, or even more, emotion itself. It may either qualify a noun ("silent shoulders"), be a qualified substantive ("nervous and accurate silence" [*CP* 114]), or be presented as a quality in itself ("she smelled of silence" [*CP* 208]). Of course, silence is a quality the senses perceive even if we cannot properly name it. And indeed, the poet hardly ever uses the word "silence" alone. But silence is not completely unknown to us even though it remains almost unnamed. How would we be able otherwise to understand the phrase "she smelled of silence" without having at least once felt it? Unspeakable, silence is not imperceptible but can only be attained by indirect means. One of them is synesthesia. Silence is more than just an idea or a thing, it is a phenomenon, a form for emotion to occur. Being an abstraction, as is always the case with abstraction in cummings' poetry, does not prevent it from being essentially tactile. The abstraction of silence is more than perceptible—it is purely sensuous.

If the very words of "silence" and "voice" are repeated throughout the poems and tend to compose a recurrent motive, a literal *ritornello*, silence and voice are not only evoked as words or values but performed as poetic events. But what do voice and silence have in common after all? Silence as well as the voice are unspeakable. Both are located on the margins of language, on the two ends of the linguistic field. And cummings as we know was highly interested in limits and frontiers, being fond both of exploration and transgression. Silence is in fact beneath linguistic expression, while the voice is beyond it. Although the voice can be heard even in the silence of a speechless reading, it can by no means be uttered. If the poet can "utter a tree" (*CP* 114) and effectively does in one of his poems, all he can do is utter words but never the voice itself. For the voice exceeds sound and phonetics.

Paradoxically, reading gives access to the voice, the poetic voice, even though the reading is silent, or maybe precisely because it is silent. In most cases, at least as far as visual poems are concerned, the reader does not have the choice but to read in silence, to utter the syllables and eccentric letters in order to recompose the dismembered words and syntagms, to literally chew them to rearticulate what has intentionally been dislocated. Only mute speech makes it possible for the reader to recover meaning and sound at the same time. If the voice does not exclude the sound, it cannot be reduced to it. The voice is in fact sound but also contrast. If Chinese characters inspired the young author of "The Poetry of Silence," it is precisely because as a monosyllabic word, each character "differs from its neighbor not only in phonetic sound but also in pitch and 'tone'" (Houghton 1892.6[94]). The poem is thus to be read as a score, as an alternation of differences. The written sign eventually releases its intensity in the surrounding blankness of the page. As paradoxical as it may sound, the voice is beyond the reach of language, just as silence is said to be "beyond the mystery of rhyme" (*CP* 143) in one of the "Sonnets—Unrealities."

The pictorial equivalent to silence and voice that keeps coming up in cummings' texts on his painting as well as in his poetry is color. In a love poem, the poetic voice invites the beloved to come closer and enjoins her: "live with me in the fewness of / these colors; / alone who slightly / always are beyond the reach of death // and the English" (*CP* 358). Color as well as silence is unspeakable, sheer difference that can only be imperfectly qualified and impossibly uttered, pure emotion that can only be experienced without being named. The comparison between silence and colors is not gratuitous at all, for the poet constantly associates disparities of what he acknowledges as the fundamental mysteries as well as basic resources of his art.

The unspeakable is precisely the region the poet&painter is to explore, the territory he tries by all means to capture. The more unspeakable a concept is, the more cummings works at defining it. Definition is the alternative to the most problematic utterance of silence. As metaphysical poets were before him, cummings is very fond of definitions. Silence is, moreover, one of cummings' favorite conceits, together with love, life and death.

silence

.is

a

looking

bird:the

turn

ing;edge, of

life

(inquiry before snow

(*CP* 712)

In this brief and intense poem from *95 Poems* (1958), silence is defined through two remarkable images I would like to dwell upon. First of all, "the looking bird" symbolises the potentiality of the voice unactualized. The underlying metaphor that has been displaced is that of the singing bird: the looking bird is the bird literally "unsinging." The poet actually forged the adjective that comes up from time to time in the poems, especially in a poem on silence (*CP* 839): "enter no(silence is the blood whose flesh / is singing)silence:but unsinging." Now "the looking bird" makes it possible to understand the adjective "unsinging," which the poet did not devise thoughtlessly. The negation is here the only linguistic possibility for expressing silence. If we know what singing means, then we may have a chance to understand its transgressive negation, "unsinging." Neither figures of speech nor linguistic games, even though witty or powerful, will ever convey the universal meaning of a voice or silence. For they are a matter of private experience and of singular comprehension.

As for the second image, "the turning edge of life," it refers to the unlikely point where speech ceases, the unimaginable passage where speech turns into speechlessness, that no one can experience unless it is already too late to testify. These two images are literally beyond representation. The looking bird and the turning edge of life can hardly be met. They challenge not only conventional representations but the faculty of imagination itself. Is a looking bird still a bird? Can the turning edge of life still be called life? To express silence, the poet has to work on the limit of representation to adjust to the nature of its escaping object. The image is here more than just an artifact. Displacement is the only way to express silence, if such thing be possible at all. Since silence is what cannot be articulated, it has to be experienced otherwise.

Still, silence partly resists definition. For silence is self-sufficient as the full stop at the beginning of the second line clearly demonstrates. Silence is in itself a sentence that hardly needs any verb. The punctuation mark, however, draws an invisible line between silence and "is." The "is" is, by the way, a major concept in e.e. cummings' poetry and really what his poetry is about. The "is" is what happens.

What the speaker cannot pronounce may be heard, what the mouth cannot utter can be seen. Even imperceptible sounds can be perceived on the flat surface of the poem just as a "dead leaf stirring makes a crash" the poet mentions in a late poem devoted to silence (*CP* 839). So why not silence itself? Where the voice stops at the end of a line or even within a line, silence can be encountered, almost heard as an echo of it. Silence is, after all, hardly less audible than a snowflake, a raindrop, or a falling leaf that is scattered on the page. The poet himself points out the analogy between silence and snow, which constitute the first and last words of the poem. This poem may to some extent be considered a visual one, for its last line is followed by a huge blank: "inquiry before snow" announces a white downpour, a visual snow that effectively occurs and covers the rest of the page. In spite of its performative and prophetic power, the voice eventually ends in silence that it can foretell but is unable to rival.

To express silence as well as voice, cummings resorts to the eye. The most efficient way to render the unspeakable is to make it visible. Exchanging senses through synesthesia or crossing domains makes it possible for the poet to express what cannot be represented. Vision is the most appropriate sense available for fulfilling this complicated requirement. Why? Because the eye sees even what the mouth cannot articulate, and to some extent it can touch what language cannot reach. And in fact, the reference to silence is not only to be encountered in cummings' poetry but also in his painting. Silence apparently plays a decisive role in cummings' æsthetics. In a personal note, the poet&painter (as he liked to call himself and to be called by others), surprisingly enough, referred to silence as the core of the pictorial emotion as well as the cause of his urge to paint and linked it explicitly with color: "To start with I have a strong desire to paint, by 'a desire to paint' I mean an impulse to feel before me a good deal of color.... Eventually, soon or late, color begins, a particular chromatic instant roots gradually upon a certain moment of silence. I turn to my paints, catch with every possible speed the visitor, and place him where he most desires to be, place him wheremost he will devour the silence." And cummings insistently gave a clue to the interpretation of his painting, which is quite surprising if we consider his well-known reluctance to explain his technique: "When I say wheremost he will devour the silence I am indicating the fundamental significance of my painting." Silence stands thus on both sides of the pictorial scope and process.

Now why does color involve silence? Because colors are unspeakable. Language is unable to convey the chromatic emotion. Color is beyond the realm of articulation and words. For colors are neither signs nor symbols; they do not represent, do not mean anything. And yet colors speak to the senses, the mind, and the body altogether. But this language cannot be formalised, for its syntax is not systematic. And because you do not recognize a color, you cannot name it. Silence is consequently derived from the impossibility of color to be properly voiced. Color is sheer emotion. And as cummings' poetry and painting constantly demonstrate, emotion lasts only as long as recognition can be postponed. Color is, according to cummings, what is edgeless: "Colors...are exempt from the taxation of recognition" (Houghton 1892.7 [68]). An edge is indeed what makes a sign or a shape distinct and likely to be recognized. It is with painting just the way it is with language. As soon as words or forms are perceived, then emotion originating in the unknown, what cummings calls "the invisible", has lapsed. That is why cummings' painting and poetry attempt to delay as much as they can the conditions and the time of recognition.

Silence and color are to be devoured, for they cannot be articulated. Sigmund Freud, whom cummings had read extensively, remarks that the same organ is meant for two antagonistic activities: eating and speaking. Oral satisfaction is the end of painting and may be the end of poetry too. Whenever words cannot be spoken or read, they are likely to be visually devoured.

If silence cannot be outspokenly uttered, it has to be expressed using inarticulate means. The realm of inarticulateness is the eye. Silence is materially made visible on the page by being metonymically identified with the surrounding blank space, as is the case here. On the canvas, or on a page, silence is a matter of space and surface, of infinite space and of unrecognizable surface. The written text plays here a decisive role. Without the physicality of writing, silence could not be properly conveyed. Then, reciprocally, the vocal part should not be underestimated either, for the voice enables the reader to decipher the mute hieroglyphs of the page and to turn them into speech. However, muteness essentially differs from silence, for muteness implies a dead letter while silence does not imply a letter at all. Silence is neither want of language, nor inability to speak, but the unspoken.

Cummings' poems are filled with silences made visible: blanks between words, between syllables or even letters, are encountered more than just occasionally. Language is thus pierced with silence which does not remain confined to the limits of the written text. If silence is unspeakable by definition, the experience of silence, and the expression of silence, will take place on the page visually within the poem as well as on the margins. The poet was used to checking and double-checking the visual and material aspect of the poems for that purpose: his correspondence with his publisher as well as with his personal typesetter Samuel A. Jacobs is full of what may be considered minor typographical details, or even worse, the symptoms of some unknown form of obsession: the typographical obsession. But there is nothing pathological about it. Silence is performed so; the poet needs to make sure that the conditions of the performance are under control. Punctuation marks especially matter since they interrupt the voice but also prefigure the unspeakable. A comma, a colon, or a semicolon, as in "silence / .is", can be seen but hardly spoken. Of course, cummings could not help playing from time to time with them and replacing the punctuation marks by their names in black and white on the page. Part of the obsession of what he calls "that precision which creates movement" (*CP* 221) can be related to the urge to attain the unspeakable, to express silence and voice, to render rhythm. For rhythm is the alternation of voice and silences, a fabric of differences called a poem.

But let's come back for a minute to the "is" of the definition poem. What happens really is either voice or silence, for what happens is rhythm. Thin, forlorn and lyrical, the voice resounds in the immensity of the silent page. The voice cannot be reduced to the first person singular, nor to the poetic instance, not even the lower case "i." In fact, it transcends the division between subject and object, and all forms of categories. A singular voice is what brings the poem together and generates the poetic emotion and eventually what is idiosyncratic in e.e. cummings' poetry. It unifies the poem beyond syntactical disruptions and visual games of all sorts. In fact, the voice is what goes on whatever the discontinuities of syntax or typography might be, whatever the threat of silence, solitude and loss may be, and even though it seems to be on the verge of fading.

The lyricism of cummings' poetry, which is almost everywhere acknowledged, has its roots deeply in the echo, visual and oral, of the voice reverberating in the silence of the page. I would like to conclude with the second stanza of one of the more moving love sonnets e.e. cummings ever wrote, "it may not always be so," for it exemplifies to perfection the attitude of the voice towards silence:

> if this should be,i say if this should be—
> you of my heart,send me a little word;
> that i may go unto him,and take his
>   hands,
> saying,Accept all happiness from me.
> Then shall i turn my face,and hear one
>   bird
> sing terribly afar in the lost lands. (*CP*
>   146)

Source: Isabelle Alfandary, "Voice and Silence in E.E. Cummings Poetry," in *Spring: The Journal of the E.E. Cummings Society*, No. 9, October 2000, pp. 36–43.

Michael Webster

In the following essay, Webster discusses the nature poetry of e.e. cummings.

This essay takes its title from a 1959 essay by Robert Langbaum called "The New Nature Poetry." Langbaum's essay was a pioneering foray into the vast and complex topic of modernist nature poetry: as such, it provides us with a convenient and logical starting point for an investigation into cummings' nature poetry. Langbaum's essay makes two large claims: first, that in contrast to the Romantics' religious veneration of nature as teacher, guide, and nurse, the nature poetry of

> "AS IN MANY OF CUMMINGS' NATURE POEMS, THIS ONE INVOKES A DISAPPEARANCE INTO A SILENCE THAT IS SEEN AS THE ESSENCE OF IMAGINATION."

modernists like Wallace Stevens, Marianne Moore, Robert Frost, and D. H. Lawrence stressed "the mindlessness of nature, its nonhuman otherness" (102). To that end, modernist poets avoided projecting "human feelings into natural objects" (104). In other words, they avoided what critics call the pathetic fallacy.

The term was coined by 19th century art critic John Ruskin as a way of describing what he viewed as a typically modern relation to nature. Ruskin claimed that the 19th-century writer could not look at nature in and of itself, but must attribute some human emotion to it, as when Charles Kingsley wrote:

> They rowed her across the rolling foam,
> The cruel, crawling foam. (quoted in Ruskin, 12.11)

Langbaum shows how modernist poems like Wallace Stevens' "The Snow Man" avoid this animated, humanized, "pathetic" nature. The speaker of Stevens' poem asserts that "one must have a mind of winter" not to think of "any misery in the sound of the wind." As we read, we realize that the speaker of the poem and the snow man of the title gradually merge together to become a symbol for the dispassionate poetic observer of nature: "the listener, who listens in the snow, / And, nothing himself, beholds / Nothing that is not there, and the nothing that is" (Stevens 9–10).

Langbaum's second claim is more difficult to summarize. For he says that "to feel in nature an unalterably alien, even an unfeeling, existence is to carry empathy several steps farther than did the nineteenth century poets" (104). By this he means, I think, that one has to work that much harder to feel into the life of the "nonhuman other" if the gap between poet and natural object is greater. The gap requires poet and reader to work harder to empathize with creatures as seemingly alien to us as Moore's pangolins and basilisks or Lawrence's tortoises and snakes. That's one reason why, Langbaum says, the new nature poetry "is so often about animals rather than landscapes. The poet is less likely to commit the pathetic fallacy with animals, for they have a consciousness of their own" (112). I would go further: animals have feelings of their own, which may or may not have a relation to ours. And yet, the modern poet empathizes with the "living unconsciousness" of nature, perhaps because it represents a deeper truth about human nature. For example, in D. H. Lawrence's much-anthologized poem "Snake," Langbaum says that the snake represents "the alien god of our submerged unconscious and libidinal life" (115).

If Langbaum is saying that poets avoid the pathetic fallacy only to create a deeper, less ego-driven bond between humans and nature, then he ironically recapitulates the argument of the fellow who invented the term in the first place, John Ruskin. For Ruskin, the pathetic fallacy was symptomatic of a characteristically modern and muddled attitude towards nature. The pathetic fallacy, "a dim, slightly credited animation in the natural object" (16.37), is only a remnant of classical and medieval beliefs that saw gods in every hill and stream and angels in the clouds (16.7). Paradoxically, the ancients had no need of the pathetic fallacy since they already had a more deeply felt vision of nature as divinity. Equally paradoxical was Ruskin's insistence that the modern way of finding god in nature was to see clearly the plain fact of nature: such seeing led to a deeper understanding of its spiritual animation. "To see clearly is poetry, prophecy, and religion,—all in one" (16.28). Josephine Miles has shown how, as use of the pathetic fallacy declined throughout the 19th century, poets began to attribute less feeling to objects and to concentrate more on the object's connections "with color, shape, and quality" (83). There occurred a subtle shift "from object and emotion to quality and sense perception." People began to *see* things more closely and clearly, "working inward from outline to detail, as men discerned more and more" (103). This new concentration on the details of objects is emblematized by the difference between Wordsworth the meditative walker and Ruskin the sharp-eyed painter and critic. As a perceptive art historian, Ruskin knew that the 19th century passion for painting landscape alone, as itself and not as some backdrop for a heroical, historical, religious, or aristocratic genre painting, was something new in the world. To this new concentration on the details of object and image, cummings would add movement—activated in the reader by syntactic dislocation and the visual arrangement of words and letters on the page.

As is true of many sweeping theories of modernist poetry, Langbaum's interesting thesis fails even to mention cummings, much less place him within his new paradigm of the modernist nature poet. Usually cummings is slighted because he is perceived as too idiosyncratic or too romantic or too lyrical, or perhaps too a-political to fit into the grand scheme. In this case, however, cummings fits certain aspects of the paradigm quite well. For example, he wrote many more poems about animals than Marianne Moore or possibly even D. H. Lawrence. (By a quick count, cummings wrote at least 46 poems about animals, in addition to 43 other kinds of nature poems.) One of Langbaum's chief examples of anti-pathetic modernist nature poetry, Marianne Moore's "A Grave," was in fact declared by cummings in 1933 to be his favorite poem. There are some differences: cummings' subjects are more conventional and less exotic than those of his contemporaries: his animal poems are mostly about birds of all sorts (including two poems about hummingbirds), along with other subjects like mice (3 poems), bats, porcupines, a bee, a chipmunk, a very famous grasshopper, and a baby elephant (one poem each). With the exception of the elephant (and even that is a baby), the animal poems focus on smaller, less powerful creatures who often function as stand-ins for the poet's own persona of "small eye poet" (*Letters* 109). Cummings' nature poems seldom if ever treat whole landscapes, but instead focus on somewhat generalized and also rather conventional natural elements (often in the sky-scape of the city) like the moon, stars, snow, rain, mist, and trees. If cummings' subjects are more conventionally "Romantic" than those of his contemporaries, his manner of creating syntactic and visual movement of those subjects was "modernist," if not avant-garde. Instead of Lawrence's sometimes pedestrian and rhetorical free-verse or Moore's finely-wrought and formal montages, the reader of cummings is greeted by his characteristic syntactic deformations and visual puzzle-making. In many of his poems, cummings, too, avoids the pathetic fallacy in order to present a natural fact, but never with the carefully researched details we find in Moore or with the overt psychologizing we see in Lawrence.

Cummings has two basic modes of nature poetry: 1) presentation of an image, often of an animal and often in a visual format, and 2) more rhetorical poems, often sonnets, using cummings' characteristic syntactic deformations and abstract nominalized vocabulary. While these modes intertwine to some degree, many of the poems in the first mode comprise a sort of imagist haiku with a high degree of word-splitting, radical spacing, and visual use of punctuation marks. Rather curiously, Langbaum never mentions imagism, which surely must have been an influence on many poets' "direct treatment of the 'thing'" and the effort to present "an intellectual and emotional complex in an instant of time" rather than simply describe a scene or object (Pound 3–6). Cummings' animal poems are certainly more sparing of verbiage than those of his contemporaries, and more radically imagist in their use of visual effects and in the elliptical ways they present "an intellectual and emotional complex." Let's look at two examples of nature poems with imagist leanings, companion pieces about a grasshopper and a mouse, poems 13 and 14 from the 1935 volume *No Thanks* (*CP* 396–397).

The first, the famous grasshopper poem, visually and verbally scrambles the letters of the grasshopper's name in three different ways, turning a common insect into three exotic beasts.

```
r-p-o-p-h-e-s-s-a-g-r
who
a)s w(e loo)k
upnowgath
PPEGORHRASS
eringint(o-
aThe):l
eA
!p:
S a
(r
rIvInG .gRrEaPsPhOs)
to
rea(be)rran(com)gi(e)ngly
,grasshopper;
```

The first scrambled beast, the "rpophessagr," is in lower case with each letter separated by a hyphen. The second, a "PPEGORHRASS," is all in caps with no intervening punctuation. The third specimen, a ".gRrEaPsPhOs)" (grreaps-phos), begins with a period and thereafter alternates lower case with capital letters. In this third version, a mostly reversed, mostly uppercase "hOPPER" sticks out of the lower-case "grashs." The most obvious function of these rearrangements is signaled by the (not rearranged but estranged) text of the poem, which minus the three exotic beasts, reads, "who as we look up now gathering into a The leA!p:S arrIvIng to rearrangingly become, grasshopper;". (Just like a grasshopper to split an infinitive.) The seemingly arbitrary use of spacing, capitalization, and punctuation shows, or better, re-enacts the seemingly arbitrary leap(s) of grasshopper. Far from using the pathetic fallacy, cummings instead attempts to present the life-essence of "grasshopper" though a formal visual and verbal patterning of words and letters. Or perhaps he takes the pathetic fallacy to an extreme: instead of humanizing the grasshopper by writing something like "the grasshopper's erratic, willful, athletic leap," cummings presents the otherness of the insect by deforming that most distinctive human invention, language.

We can see how arbitrary and yet how constructed and patterned this poem is if we look at the corrected proof sheets of the poem that cummings sent to his Brazilian translator, Augusto de Campos (figure 1). At the top of the proof sheet cummings notes that "this poem has a righthand margin as well as a left," but the system of elaborate spatial alignments exists only to be broken: the "S" of "leA!p:S" and the "a" of "arrIvIng" lie outside the left and right margins, respectively. The end of the grasshopper's leap and the beginning of its arrival cannot be contained within the formal boundaries of the poem. All the orthographic, syntactic, and visual rearrangements of the poem show the inability of arbitrary language to capture the essence and presence of a being.

At the same time, however, cummings' deformations of language symbolize the arbitrary, ordered otherness of a grasshopper's seemingly random leap(s). Perhaps the grasshopper's leap(s) conform to a hidden but arbitrary set of rules, analogous to the ones cummings invented to create this poem.

It is not often noticed that the poem is paired with its opposite: the grasshopper poem is about unaccountable life and uncontainable movement, while its partner is about a motionless, dead mouse who is wholly contained, wrapped in a leaf and placed in the earth:

mouse)Won
derfully is
anyone else entirely who doesn't
move(Moved more suddenly than)whose

tiniest smile?may Be
bigger than the fear of all
hearts never which have
(Per

haps)loved(or than
everyone that will Ever love)we
've
hidden him in A leaf

and,
Opening
beautiful earth
put(only)a Leaf among dark

ness.sunlight's
thenlike?now
Disappears
some

thing(silent:
madeofimagination
;the incredible soft)ness
(his ears(eyes

The containers of leaf and earth are perhaps symbolized by the rather arbitrary four-line stanzas. In contrast to the assertive grasshopper, the dead mouse's "tiniest smile?" is somehow (perhaps) bigger than the fears of lovers and nonlovers alike. This tiny smile has a question mark after it to indicate uncertainty (or mystery?) about the blatant anthropomorphism or pathetic fallacy. Though the narrator is also unsure what sunlight looks like to a dead and buried mouse ("sunlight's / thenlike?"), he is "Won / derfully" sure that the mouse represents all the dead and disappeared (line 3—"anyone else entirely who doesn't / move"). Yet this silent, non-present, non-moving, non-corporeal ("madeofimagination") thing is nevertheless present in the poem in several ways.

Though dead, the mouse has somehow "Won"; and through the common magic of a pun, it is also "one." The mouse's continued Being is indicated by the capital letter in line five. If we read only the capitalized words in the poem, we get: "Won / derfully Moved Be (Per / haps) Ever A Opening Leaf Disappears." This second telegraphic poem hidden within the first recapitulates the cycle of nature, stating how wonderfully moved the speaker is by this dead mouse, which perhaps will have an everlasting being by fertilizing an opening leaf, destined to disappear as the mouse did. Like Wordsworth's Lucy, "Rolled round in earth's diurnal course, / With rocks, and stones, and trees," the mouse becomes one with earth. As in many of cummings' nature poems, this one invokes a disappearance into a silence that is seen as the essence of imagination. This silence has profound, transcendent meaning for the poet, as his many poems on silent singing testify. In his notes at the Houghton Library, cummings wrote, "it is this silence which P[oetry] translates into sound" [quoted in Heusser 227; bMs Am 1892.7 (90, #432)].

This vision of nature as transcendent, and at the same time as sparking creativity obviously owes a great debt to the entire Romantic tradition, from Wordsworth to Emerson. Rather than an easy projection of human feelings onto nature (the pathetic fallacy), cummings creates in the mouse a complex symbol of death and imagination, of a tiny, silent being that transcends (perhaps) the fears and hopes of human lovers. In contrast to the grasshopper poem, this one emphasizes rhetoric more than image. Certainly, cummings was capable of seeing the dead mouse as fact: consult his drawing of a (the same?) dead mouse above (reproduced from Kennedy's biography, page 369). Another much later mouse poem (*CP* 784) illustrates how cummings' version of the pathetic fallacy carries "empathy several steps farther" (Langbaum 104) into the life of the other.

> Me up at does
>
> out of the floor
> quietly Stare
>
> a poisoned mouse
>
> still who alive
>
> is asking What
> have i done that
>
> You wouldn't have

Here, the mouse is seen as other, even while the poet translates the mouse's "still" silent stare into a very human question. While maintaining a distance between himself and the poisoned creature staring up out of the floorboards (referring to himself as upper-case Me and You, while the mouse is lower-case "i."), the poet nevertheless asserts a radical identity between humans and animals. Even the mouse's lower-case "i" links it (him/her?) with the poet's familiar lower-case persona of child-like seer, adrift in a world that has forgotten how to wonder and that destroys the other without thinking. In addition, as J. E. Terblanche has pointed out to me, if we read only the capital letters of this poem, we get "Me Stare What You"—the mouse becomes "Me," asking in effect, "what are you looking at?" This ecological sense of an animal's right to be in the world and of the profound connections between animal and human consciousness that should exist, but often do not, lie at the heart of many of cummings' animal poems.

Like cummings' lower-case persona, these poems function as a kind of counter-sublime, magnifying the importance of their small protagonists while reducing the pretensions of the human ego. The sublime, by the way, is a topic never mentioned by Langbaum. It seems to me that the origin of the modernist stress on "the mindlessness of nature, its nonhuman otherness" (102) can be found in the Romantic sublime, which stresses the awesome, terrifying (sublime) in nature over its loving, nurturing, inspiring (beautiful) aspect. For example, in "Mont Blanc" Shelley sees the glacier on the mountain as a "city of death" from which "[t]he race / Of man flies far in dread," and he ends the poem by wondering how we would view the mountain "If to the human mind's imaginings / Silence and solitude were vacancy?" In his counter-sublime mood, cummings stresses the transformative aspects of nature's small, silent creatures. When cummings does write in the sublime mode, he often opposes the frailty of the self to the immense power of nature. In some ways atypical of his more rhetorical nature poems, "whose are these(wraith a clinging with a wraith)" (*CP* 639) is one of cummings' few works in a sublime mode. The poem also shows that like many of his contemporaries, cummings does see nature as radically other; however, unlike them, he seeks "miracle" and imaginative transcendence against or within the other.

> whose are these(wraith a clinging with a
>   wraith)
>
> ghosts drowning in supreme thunder?ours
> (over you reels and me a moon;beneath,
>
> bombed the by ocean earth bigly shudders)
>
> never was death so alive:chaos so(hark
> —that screech of space)absolute(my soul
> tastes If as some world of spark
> 's gulped by illimitable hell)
>
> and never have breathed such miracle
>   murdered we

whom cannot kill more mostful to arrive
each(futuring snowily which sprints for
    the
crumb of our Now)twiceuponatime wave—

put out your eyes, and touch the black skin
of an angel named imagination

The octet of this sonnet depicts two lovers (the "ghosts" of line two—the manuscript has "selves") standing above a coast at night being "bombed" by and "drowning in" the ocean's surf—"supreme thunder." This experience creates a terror ("never was death so alive:chaos so...absolute") typical of the Romantic sublime. The third quatrain's syntax falls over itself, possibly like the "twiceuponatime wave." I unscramble the syntax like this: "And, [though] murdered, we have never breathed such [a] miracle [as] each more-mostful-to-arrive wave [which] cannot kill [us]." Even though the wave gulps down stars ("some world of a spark") and even though the lovers are annihilated (they are murdered ghosts), they cannot be killed because "the / crumb of [their] Now"—the angel of imagination which they can access merely by shutting their eyes and touching—is more than the "more mostful" wave. The crumb of self within is both inspired by and resistant to "drowning" in the Romantic sublime. Put another way, the lover's alive touch sparks more imagination than the deadly terrors of the sublime. Or to put it most simply: small and beautiful counters big and sublime.

It is instructive to compare this poem (first published in 1947) with cummings' favorite poem of 1933, Marianne Moore's "A Grave." Moore's poem also depicts two people standing before the sea, though in Moore's case the two people in question were Moore and her mother, and their view was obstructed by the "Man looking into the sea" of the first line. Though not as bombastic as cummings' wave, Moore's sea is even more menacing: "you cannot stand in the middle of this; / the sea has nothing to give but a well excavated grave." Moore's poem goes on to describe how the bones of the dead "have not lasted" in the sea and how fishermen "lower nets, unconscious of the fact that they are desecrating a grave" (49). The poem ends with an image of how "dropped things...turn and twist" when they sink, and that turning and twisting is "neither with volition nor consciousness" (50). This chilling finale contrasts sharply with the ending of cummings' sonnet, which explicitly states that the sea "cannot kill" the lovers and that their inner consciousness or imagination eclipses the booming sea with the touch of a hand and a blink of the eyes. In imagination at least, the crumb of the lovers' Now cannot be engulfed by the "twiceuponatime wave." Guy Rotella summarizes the more stringent atmosphere of Moore's poem quite well:

> [In "A Grave"] Nature neither signifies nor speaks: it is. Moore once said, "Any pastoral seems to pall," and one of the things she erases in "A Grave" is pastoral elegy, that classic mode in which fears of death find comfort in a healing nature that reflects our moods. (*Reading and Writing* 173)

Cummings' poem certainly does not minimize the destructive potential of the sea, nor does it find the traditional comfort of the pastoral elegy; it replaces that comfort with an assertion of the power of the self and the imagination.

In his later nature poetry, cummings more and more writes of a self that merges with nature, often at the liminal moment of twilight. For example, the poem "birds" (*CP* 448) presents an image of birds and their songs fading into the vastness of a twilight sky. The parentheses in the poem represent swallows flying at dusk, while the diminishing stepped letters at the end depict the birds' vanishing, soon silent, singing "voices." The birds' voices fade into "Be" and "now" and "soul" until they "are" "a" part of the silence:

birds(
here,inven
ting air
U
)sing
tw
iligH(
t's
v
va
vas(
vast
ness.Be)look
now
(come
soul;
&:and
who
s)e
voi
c
es

(
are
ar
a

There is much to be said about this poem, but I'd like to concentrate on its ending. The hardly-pronounceable dying fall of the ending refers not only to the fading cries of the birds, but also to the dissolution of the self [addressed in the third stanza: "Be)look / now / (come / soul;"] into twilight, and to the paradoxical oneness of song and silence, of bird-voices and man-soul. The question "who / s)e voi / c / es / are" is deliberately left incomplete: who sings here? Part of the answer is in the first stanza: not only the birds, but "U" sing with their silent song of flight. And further down the page, the Italian plural "you" ["voi"] is integral with the "voi / c / es" that "are" on the page even as the poet questions "who / s)e" they are. The polyglot sequence continues in Franglais with "c / es (/ are", meaning "these (birds, voices, humans) are being, are one." And the "voices" represented by "are / ar / a" mirror the shape of the "v / va / vas / vast// ness" of the sky. Both poet and birds invent with air, one with the column of air that forms the sounds of words, the others with the air that fades in the twilight. Both the poet's air and the birds' voices fade in the dying fall at the end of the poem. Mysteriously, each succeeding "stanza" of the poem is stepped one space further to the left than its predecessor, initiating a subtle counter-descent to the rightward sweep of "twilight's vastness" and the birds' disappearing song at the end of the poem. Through the silently singing visual sign, cummings represents a mysterious oneness of poet and birds that cannot be put into words.

With the exception of the waves in "whose are these," each of the poems we have looked at has called the natural object a "who." These are not isolated instances: in one poem, cummings calls the starry night sky a "millionminded Who" (*CP* 633); another calls a "brIght" star a "Who" (*CP* 455); another asks "who is the) [moon?]" (*CP* 571); and an early poem asserts that "only Nobody knows / where truth grows why / birds fly and / especially who the moon is" (*CP* 368). One poem even addresses a phoebe as "you darling / diminutive person" (*CP* 678), but this anthropomorphism is something of an extreme. In general, cummings stresses both the personality (the "who") of natural objects and their mysterious otherness. (See the appendix.) Natural objects are selves, "whos," and yet radically other: in one poem cummings calls a star a "morsel miraculous and meaningless," an "isful beckoningly fabulous crumb" (*CP* 456). Thus the star is both big and small, sublime and beautiful, a "fabulous" miracle full of life ("isful") and a morsel, a crumb. In these more rhetorical poems, natural objects are often invoked or addressed directly (the trope known as apostrophe) as Shelley does the West Wind. Jonathan Culler has noted that "the apostrophizing poet identifies his universe as a world of sentient forces" (139). To address natural objects as sentient will also reflect back on the self of the poet:

> ...apostrophe is a device which the poetic voice uses to establish with an object a relationship which helps to constitute [the poet]. The object is treated as a subject, an *I* which implies a certain type of *you* in its turn. One who successfully invokes nature is one to whom nature might, in its turn, speak. He makes himself a poet, a visionary. (Culler 142)

To apostrophize, to summon forth or to lecture or to ask favors of nature, is a rhetorical speech-act form of the pathetic fallacy. The natural object in cummings' poems is seen both as object and subject, as profoundly other and as a sentient being, a "who." For example, in the poem just quoted, even though the poet describes the star as being hurled "out of serene perfectly Nothing," at the end of the poem (like Keats addressing his "Bright star") cummings speaks directly to the star, asking it (him/her?) to "nourish my failure with thy freedom."

Cummings' view of nature may not be as contradictory as it seems. Guy Rotella quotes Wallace Stevens: "It is not the individual alone that indulges himself in the pathetic fallacy. It is the race." Rotella comments: "From that definition of the fallacy as no fallacy at all but the expression of a natural human need, he would construct his belief that the urge to meaning must constantly be exercised as well as restrained" (Rotella 112). In a different way, cummings acknowledges his own need to construct meaning out of a possibly empty nature. His use of the words "nothing" and "nowhere" illustrates his awareness of these contradictions. For example, "this man's heart" (*CP* 676) ends like this:

a snowflake
twi-
sts
,on
its way to now
-here

"Nowhere" is here and now, yet the snowflake will melt into some "nowhere." The poet is like this snowflake, both part of the world and transcending it. Another example: in "but also dying" the poet reminds his lover that they exist "wherever the sun and the stars and // the // moon // are... but/ also // nowhere" (*CP* 676). I do not have space in this paper to discuss properly what Guy Rotella calls "the transcendentalist paradox of using nature as a model for getting beyond nature and its built-in limits" ("Nature, Time" 290), but perhaps a riddling conclusion will point the way.

In both visual and rhetorical modes, cummings' nature poetry presents us with contradictions: nature is seen as radically other, yet addressed as a fellow being; the small and beautiful become transcendent and sublime; the fractured syntax of culture represents the beasts of nature. Both nature and language mean and "unmean"; nature is seen as other and yet completely transcendent, while language must bear sublime truth and beauty and yet be split into "unmeaning" syllables and letters:

Beautiful

is the

unmea

ning

of(sil

ently)fal

ling(e

ver

yw

here)s

Now

(*CP* 713)

The snow is everywhere, yet it is also here, now. Many of the words have been sliced into "unmea / ning" fragments, yet the last two mean "snow and "now" and "here's now." The snow is silent, yet voiced in the poem. In fact, it is quite similar to the "nothing that is" in the Wallace Stevens poem quoted at the beginning of this paper. Cummings was enough of modernist to avoid a too-easy use of the pathetic fallacy, but he was also enough of a Romantic to believe that nature and animals possessed a personality which he could address directly. He was enough of a painter and poet to note specific qualities and movements in animals, yet enough of a Buddhist to see that nature was both nothing (an illusion) and everything (the all of the here and now). Finally, he was enough of an ecologist (quite ahead of his time) to see the interconnectedness that should exist among all living things.

Source: Michael Webster, "E.E. Cummings: The New Nature Poetry and the Old," in *Spring: The Journal of the E.E. Cummings Society*, No. 9, October 2000, pp. 109–24.

SOURCES

Blackmur, R. P., "Notes on E.E. Cummings' Language," in *The Hound and Horn*, Vol. 4, No. 2, January–March 1931, pp. 163–92.

Cummings, e. e., "since feeling is first," in *The Heath Anthology of American Literature*, 4th ed., edited by Paul Lauter, Houghton Mifflin, 2002, p. 1355; originally published in *Is 5*, Horace Liveright, 1926, p. 93.

Gill, John M., "A Study of Two Poems," in *Spring: The Journal of the E.E. Cummings Society*, Vol. 5, October 1996, pp. 105, 109.

Herrick, Robert, "To the Virgins, to Make Much of Time," in *The Longman Anthology of British Literature*, Vol. 1B, edited by David Damrosch and Kevin J. H. Dettmar, Pearson Longman, 2006, p. 1709.

Heyen, William, "In Consideration of Cummings," in *Poetry Criticism*, Vol. 5, 1992, p. 86; originally published in *Southern Humanities Review*, Vol. 7, No. 2, Spring 1973, pp. 131–42.

Jarrell, Randall, "The Profession of Poetry," in *Poetry Criticism*, Vol. 5, 1992, pp. 80, 81; originally published in *Partisan Review*, Vol. 17, No. 7, Fall 1950, pp. 124–31.

Marvell, Andrew, "To His Coy Mistress," in *The Longman Anthology of British Literature*, Vol. 1B, edited by David Damrosch and Kevin J. H. Dettmar, Pearson Longman, 2006, pp. 1749–50.

Perkins, David, *A History of Modern Poetry: Modernism and After*, Harvard University Press, 1987, p. 41.

Riding, Laura, and Robert Graves, "Modernist Poetry and the Plain Reader's Rights," in *Poetry Criticism*, Vol. 5, 1992, pp. 71, 72; originally published in Laura Riding and Robert Graves, *A Survey of Modernist Poetry*, William Heinemann, 1927, pp. 9–34.

FURTHER READING

Fairley, Irene R., *E.E. Cummings and Ungrammar: A Study of Syntactic Deviances in his Poems*, Watermill, 1975.
> Fairley examines Cummings' unusual placement of words and his creation of new ones and their impact on his poetic themes.

Friedman, Norman, *E.E. Cummings: The Art of His Poetry*, Johns Hopkins Press, 1960.
> Friedman presents a comprehensive study of themes and style in cummings' poetry, exploring how the poet uses innovations such as lack

of punctuation, wordplay, line breaks to illustrate his main points.

Kennedy, Richard S., *Dreams in the Mirror: A Biography of E.E. Cummings*, Liveright, 1980.

> Kennedy provides insights into the relationship between cummings' life and his works and includes several previously unpublished poems and drawings, along with photographs.

Kidder, Rushworth, "Cummings and Cubism: The Influence of the Visual Arts on Cummings' Early Poetry," *Journal of Modern Literature*, No. 7, April 1979, pp. 255–91.

> Kidder examines the important relationship between cummings' poetry and modernist painting, including cummings' own works, which are illustrated in the article.

The Snow-Storm

RALPH WALDO EMERSON

1847

Ralph Waldo Emerson's often anthologized poem "The Snow-Storm" was one of the most popular pieces in his well-received first collection of poetry, *Poems*, published in 1847. "The Snow-Storm" has also been recognized as one of the most important statements of American transcendentalism, an influential nineteenth-century philosophical and literary movement that celebrated the beauty and power of nature and how the establishment of a communion with nature can benefit humans. The poem can be found in several anthologies, including volume one of *Anthology of American Literature*, published by Pearson Education in 2004.

"The Snow-Storm" describes a farmhouse and the surrounding area, which snow covered one night by a severe storm. The wind and snow work together during this night, first to cover and then transform the ordinary farm buildings into works of art. Those inhabiting the farmhouse are unable to appreciate the majesty of the storm and so refuse the communion with nature that the speaker offers them. Emerson also makes a clear statement in the poem concerning the power of the poet. He uses the actions of the wind and snow as illustrations of the creative genius of the poet, for, as Emerson explains in his essay, "The Poet," "the beauty of things...becomes a new, and higher beauty, when expressed."

Ralph Waldo Emerson (The Library of Congress)

AUTHOR BIOGRAPHY

Ralph Waldo Emerson was born in Boston on May 25, 1803, to Ruth Haskins Emerson and Reverend William Emerson, a Unitarian minister. After his father died in 1811, his mother ran a succession of boarding houses in the city, in order to support him and his four brothers. The following year, she enrolled him in Boston Latin School. During his childhood, he was greatly influenced by his aunt, Mary Moody Emerson, a brilliant, eccentric woman who encouraged him to write poetry. His early writings, however, showed little promise.

Emerson entered Harvard in 1817 where he studied divinity. After graduating in 1821, he taught school for a time but soon realized that he was not well suited for a position that required him to enforce his authority upon others. Emerson turned to preaching in 1826 and three years later became a junior pastor at the Second Church in Boston where the famous orators Increase Mather (1639–1723) and Cotton Mather (1663–1723) had preached in the early 1700s. His interest in preaching stemmed more from his love of oratory than from a devotion to theology. Also in 1829, Emerson married Ellen Tucker. Her death in 1831 of tuberculosis devastated him. Soon after her death, Emerson resigned his position at the church, insisting that he could no longer participate in rituals that he doubted were valid. In 1832, he began traveling in England and Europe. He studied art and natural science and enjoyed the company of such literary figures as Samuel Taylor Coleridge and Thomas Carlyle.

Emerson returned in 1834 to a new life in Concord, Massachusetts, just outside Boston, where he preached occasionally and began his literary career. In 1835, he married Lydia Jackson and later began associations with authors such as Margaret Fuller, Henry James, Nathaniel Hawthorne, and Henry David Thoreau. He soon turned to the lecture halls, reciting speeches that later evolved into his celebrated essays, including "Nature," published in 1836, and "The American Scholar," published in 1849. He also gave speeches on such diverse topics as literary criticism, slavery, and American leadership. During his lifetime, he would give over 1,500 lectures.

While he was composing his essays, Emerson began to pay more attention to his poetry. His first publication was his essay "Nature" (1836), which was well received as was his first collection of poetry, *Poems*, published in 1847. This collection included "The Snow-Storm," a poem he composed in 1841. While some of his lectures, especially the 1838 address he gave at Harvard that resulted in his being barred from speaking there for three decades, were criticized for heretical ideas, his reputation as an essayist and poet grew steadily until he earned the reputation as one of the leading philosophers, essayists, and poets of his age. Although his failing memory prevented him from writing any more significant essays or poetry in the last decade of his life, collections of his lectures, journals, letters, and poetry were published up until his death from pneumonia on April 27, 1882, at Concord.

POEM TEXT

Announced by all the trumpets of the sky,
Arrives the snow, and, driving o'er the fields
Seems nowhere to alight; the whited air
Hides hill and woods, the river, and the heaven,
And veils the farm-house at the garden's end.   5

The sled and traveller stopped, the courier's
    feet
Delayed, all friends shut out, the housemates
    sit
Around the radiant fireplace, enclosed
In a tumultuous privacy of storm.
Come see the north wind's masonry.   10
Out of an unseen quarry evermore
Furnished with tile, the fierce artificer
Curves his white bastions with projected roof
Round every windward stake, or tree, or door.
Speeding, the myriad-handed, his wild work   15
So fanciful, so savage, nought cares he
For number or proportion. Mockingly,
On coop or kennel he hangs Parian wreaths;
A swan-like form invests the hiddden thorn;
Fills up the farmer's lane from wall to wall,   20
Maugre the farmer's sighs; and at the gate;
A tapering turret overtops the work.
And when his hours are numbered, and the
    world
Is all his own, retiring, as he were not,
Leaves, when the sun appears, astonished Art   25
To mimic in slow structures, stone by stone,
Built in an age, the mad wind's night-work,
The frolic architecture of the snow.

MEDIA ADAPTATIONS

- On the audio cassettes *Great American Poetry: 3 Centuries of Classics*, published by Audio Partners in 1993, actors such as Julie Harris and Vincent Price read selections from American poets, including Emerson, Emily Dickinson, and Walt Whitman.

- *Essential Emerson*, a CD published in 2008 by Caedmon Essentials, is a collection of Emerson's poems read by poet Archibald MacLeish.

POEM SUMMARY

Stanza 1

In the first two lines of "The Snow-Storm," "trumpets of the sky" announce the snow's arrival. These trumpets are most likely the sounds of the wind. An indication of the speed and severity of the storm appears in the second line when the speaker describes the snow "driving o'er the fields" and in the third line creating "whited" air that "Seems nowhere to alight." The wind is blowing the snow around so quickly and to such a degree that the landscape becomes hidden. The hills, woods, river, sky, and farmhouse disappear in the air made white by the blowing snow. The trumpets that greet the snow's arrival suggest the welcome of fanfare for an important person, someone who is anticipated and demands appropriate attention.

Toward the end of the first stanza, the focus shifts to those inside the farmhouse who have been cut off from others by the blizzard. The traveler on the sled, the courier, and all friends cannot get to the farmhouse. Isolated by the storm, those in the house sit around a fire. They have the opportunity to view nature's handiwork during the night and appreciate its beauty.

Stanza 2

At the beginning of the second stanza, the speaker invites someone to "see the north wind's masonry." The speaker never identifies the person to whom he is speaking. He could be offering this invitation to those shut in the farmhouse or to the reader. The word "masonry" refers to the ancient art of building a structure in stone. The speaker's use of this word anticipates the architectural metaphors used to describe what the wind does with the snow. This is the only time that the speaker calls out directly to a listener; it suggests that he believes the snowstorm will be an important event to watch during the night.

In this stanza, the wind becomes an "artificer," a skilled craftsperson who recreates the landscape, using the snow as "tile" from "an unseen quarry evermore." The word "evermore" indicates that the storm will continue and there will be lots of snow to serve as tile. The adjective "fierce" denotes the aggressive, perhaps violent nature of the wind as it crafts the snow into new art forms. The wind puts its creative stamp on every detail of the landscape, both natural and man-made, constructing "white bastions with projected roof / Round every windward stake, or tree, or door." A bastion is a type of stronghold or fortified area, suggesting in this poem that the wind is strengthening the windward side (that which is facing the wind) of every object it encounters.

The wind is "speeding" through its tasks with a great number ("myriad") of hands. As a result, the work becomes "wild" and "savage," yet also "fanciful." This artificer rejects traditional methods of construction as it ignores the "number or proportion" of its creations. The wind also rejects the traditional placement of artistic works. On such common things as a chicken coop or a dog kennel, it hangs wreaths that appear made of "Parian" marble (white marble found on the Greek island of Paros). This placement mocks nineteenth-century architectural tastes that often added Greek flourishes to buildings.

The farmer does finally leave the fire to observe the storm, but he does not respond the way the speaker has apparently hoped. As he watches the snow and wind fill up his "lane from wall to wall," he can only sigh, most likely because it will impede his work the next day. In spite of the farmer's displeasure, the wind continues its artistic activities, covering thorns with "swan-like forms" and constructing a "tapering turret" (tower) over them.

As the storm comes to an end, the speaker notes that the wind has redesigned the entire landscape, which is now "his own," and so departs. When the sun appears, the speaker compares the art of the wind to that of the traditional artist, who creates "slow structures, stone by stone," which are referred to as "Art." The "mad wind's night-work" has constructed a "frolic architecture of the snow."

THEMES

Human Responses to Nature

In "The Snow-Storm," Emerson celebrates the beauty and artistry of snow. He illustrates how in one evening the wind and snow can work together to create new and beautiful forms. The poem's setting provides a perfect opportunity for humans to recognize the power of nature and to forge a closer relationship with it. Emerson sets the stage for this communion when the wind and snow create a "tumultuous privacy of storm," effectively cutting off the farmhouse inhabitants from the outside world and thus removing any distractions. However, the housemates refuse to recognize the importance of this opportunity and see the storm only as an encumbrance in their lives.

The family will not watch the storm at its onset and, instead, sit around the fireplace, turning their backs to the storm and refusing to watch it recreate the landscape. The speaker understands that they are missing an opportunity to commune with nature when he calls out to them to "come see the north wind's masonry." He explains the process of creation in the second stanza, pointing out how nature can transform ordinary objects into true works of art. Yet, the inhabitants again reject the opportunity to recognize the beauty of the "mad wind's nightwork." The farmer does eventually leave the fireside and watch the storm's activities, but he does not appreciate them. Instead, he "sighs," thinking about only practical concerns when he sees the snow fill up his lane "from wall to wall."

Man-made versus Natural Art

Emerson compares man-made structures and art to that created by nature and finds the former lacking in beauty, grace, and a sense of playfulness. The man-made structures in the poem are functional. Emerson does not adorn them with adjectives that would provide distinctive qualities. They are merely doors, walls, gates, coops, and kennels. When the storm arrives and transforms the landscape, these objects are made even more plain and ordinary through a comparison to the wind and snow's dynamic and fanciful creations.

Each stage of the transformation of the man-made landscape illustrates the superiority of nature's artistry. During the first stage, Emerson suggests the inferior quality of the farmhouse objects when the snow hides them from view. The wind then creates "white bastions with projected roof" on each structure, imbuing them with strength and beauty. Unlike the objects they have covered, these new creations are "so fanciful, so savage," so unconventional. Nature provides a final unifying element to the landscape when the wind creates "a tapering turret" to crown his work.

Emerson suggests that nature understands its superiority to traditional, made-made forms when the wind mocks and mimics those forms. Conventional nineteenth-century American tastes demanded that architecture be adorned with imitations of the Greek style. The wind highlights the inferiority of these imitations by hanging "Parian wreaths" on chicken coops and dog kennels.

The wind and snow also mock the traditional processes of creation, which appear in the poem as plodding and conforming. The wind mimics (a

TOPICS FOR FURTHER STUDY

- Draw two illustrations that depict the two settings described in "The Snow-Storm." First draw the farmhouse and its surroundings without the snow, paying special attention to the plainness of the structures. Then draw the poem's central scene, depicting the artistry of the wind and snow after they have blanketed and transformed the farm buildings and landscape.

- Write a scene that could be incorporated into a short story depicting the thoughts, actions, and dialogue among the farmhouse inhabitants, offering their points of view concerning the storm. Develop the individual characters so each has a distinct personality and voice.

- Research the transcendentalist movement in the nineteenth-century United States, which had a great influence on many important writers of this period, including Nathaniel Hawthorne, Edgar Allan Poe, and Henry David Thoreau. Prepare a PowerPoint presentation that highlights the main philosophy of this movement, how it originated and how it influenced a generation of writers.

- Read Thoreau's *Walden; or Life in the Woods* (1854) and think about how you would be able to survive in nature on your own. Write journal entries that chronicle a fictional account of a year in your life spent living alone in the woods. Include details about day-to-day activities and also your appreciation of nature.

- Read other poems by Emerson from a collection of his works such as *Ralph Waldo Emerson: Collected Poems and Translations*, published by the Library of America in 1994. Choose at least two that focus on the subject of nature. You could, for example, consider "Each and All," "Hamatreya," "The Rhodora," "Threnody," and "Merlin." Write an essay that incorporates scholarly research comparing and contrasting the poems regarding how they depict nature.

- The film *Lord of the Flies*, directed by Peter Brook and released in theaters in 1963, is based on William Golding's novel (1954) of the same name. The film and book chronicle the lives of a group of British teenagers who have crash landed on a tropical island and who have to survive on their own without adult supervision. Watch the DVD version of this film and prepare a presentation, incorporating film clips, that depicts the boys' experiences in their natural environment and what those experiences reveal about human nature.

---

form of mockery) the man-made "slow structures" that took "an age" to build, "stone by stone." Nature's "myriad" hands have taken only one night to construct a masterpiece. Its "frolic architecture" rejects traditional "number or proportion" that is reflected in conventional art.

STYLE

Personification

Personification is giving human qualities to nonhuman objects. Emerson personifies the snow and the wind in the poem. The trumpets' announcement of the arrival of the snow immediately transforms this act of nature into an important personage. The snow, in conjunction with the wind, becomes both builder and building material as it playfully participates in "the frolic architecture" that is created around the farmhouse. In the initial construction stage, the snow "drive[es] o'er the fields" and actively "hides hills and woods, the river, and the heaven, / And veils the farm-house."

Then the wind takes the lead role in the transformation of the landscape when it adopts the

Farmhouse in a snow-covered landscape (Image copyright SF photo, 2009. Used under license from Shutterstock.com)

characteristics of a builder and an artist. The wind directs the snow to transform the landscape, first by covering it and then by creating new forms on top of existing objects. Identified in the poem as "he," the wind applies his "masonry" to "every windward stake, or tree, or door," constructing "white bastions with projected roof," using the snow as tiles "out of an unseen quarry." The builder transforms into "the fierce artificer" when his "wild work" rejects traditional proportions and instead creates wreaths on chicken coops and dog kennels and swans on thorns.

The wind also adopts human qualities in its role as "myriad-handed" artist, becoming at times "mad," "fierce," "fanciful," and "savage." He also mocks and mimics traditional art as he "frolic[s]" with the snow as they create their architectural masterpiece. The final image of the wind is of a conqueror who has made "the world...all his own." After the wind and the snow have created fanciful, unconventional designs through the night, the sun rises and reveals their work as "Art."

HISTORICAL CONTEXT

Transcendentalism

Transcendentalism is an idealist philosophy developed and promoted by a group of writers and thinkers centered in the Boston area during the mid-nineteenth century. The movement was influenced by the works of German philosopher Immanuel Kant (1724–1804) and novelist Johann von Goethe (1749–1832) and by the English romantic poet, William Wordsworth (1770–1850). Emerson was a leading figure in the transcendental movement. His long essay "Nature," published in 1836, explains his belief that the natural world is the physical expression of the spiritual world and when people realize this connection they can find spiritual wellbeing by being in a natural setting. Thoreau's back-to-nature description of the time he spent in a cabin on Walden Pond described both the importance of nature and the ways in which city dwellers lost track of their spiritual selves in their work-a-day lives. Amos Bronson Alcott,

COMPARE & CONTRAST

- **Mid-nineteenth century:** Settlers are encouraged to strike out for the western territories and begin new lives there. On May 1, 1841, the first wagon train, with forty-seven travelers, departs for California from Independence, Missouri, and on May 22, 1843, one thousand Americans join a wagon train that travels to the Northwest via the Oregon Trail. By December 2, 1845, President James Polk urges Congress to support the concept of Manifest Destiny, the belief that Anglo Americans are destined and/or ordained to settle lands from the Atlantic to the Pacific Ocean. He also urges acceptance of the Monroe Doctrine, which asserts that the United States should block any European government that tries to interfere with the settlement of the West.

  Today: The largest group of immigrants, legal and illegal, in the United States comes from Mexico. Most settle in the Southwest. Illegal immigration is a contentious topic for many Americans who are concerned about crime and the economy, and for politicians, especially in the Southwest.

- **Mid-nineteenth century:** Unitarianism, a movement that promotes a belief in one individual God rather than a trinity, replaces the doctrine of original sin with a more optimistic vision of human nature. After the publication of Emerson's "Nature," the transcendentalist movement becomes a splinter group and later separates from organized religion. By 1838, Emerson denounces mainstream Unitarianism in his Divinity School address at Harvard, which causes him to be barred from speaking at the school for three decades.

  Today: The Unitarian Church is less popular than it was in the nineteenth century. Only about 1,000 congregations remain in the United States. After several decades of humanism, the American Unitarian Church focuses more on the scriptures. Unitarianism, however, retains some of its liberal precepts and welcomes like-minded Christians, Jews, and Buddhists into its congregations.

- **Mid-nineteenth century:** The environmental movement, started by Benjamin Franklin and like-minded Philadelphians in the mid-1700s, begins in earnest as Americans consider protecting natural resources during the westward expansion. Thoreau's *Walden; or Life in the Woods*, which depicts his experiment in living close to nature and minimizing personal consumption, is published in 1854.

  Today: The environmental movement gains increased public support in the 1990s and early 2000s as more Americans become concerned about global climate change, which results from various human activities that create pollution, ecosystem deterioration, and the short-sighted treatment of nonrenewable and other natural resources.

Margaret Fuller, and William Ellery Channing were also proponents of transcendentalism. This most democratic of philosophies affirmed that the sacred can be experienced within the individual and in direct communion with the divine as it is expressed in nature. People did not need theology and ministers to structure and define their spiritual experience. Popular ideas about the connection between humans and nature influenced other writers of the age, including Nathaniel Hawthorne, Herman Melville, and Walt Whitman. Emerson helped found the Transcendentalist Club and became editor of the transcendentalist magazine, *The Dial*.

Transcendentalists believed that the human mind engages creatively with nature. They also believed that humans should experience intuitively their spiritual connection to the environment. Transcendentalist views of nature follow those of pantheism, a religious philosophy that promotes

A horse-drawn sleigh ride (Image copyright UncleGenePhoto, 2009. Used under license from Shutterstock.com)

the idea that the divine is expressed directly through the material universe.

Barbara Packer, in her essay on Emerson in the *Columbia Literary History of the United States*, comments on Emerson's reliance on direct intuition of spiritual truth. She writes that Emerson "never lost faith in the existence or accessibility of the divine mind," but he refused to believe in "external 'proofs'" such as "miracles, testimony, even Scripture itself." He insisted, she states, that these types of proofs "were doomed to fall before the corrosive effects of nineteenth-century philosophy, natural science, historical criticism, and comparative anthropology." Emerson instead argued "that the only proof of faith is the experience of faith in the individual's own soul, which can *confirm* the truths of doctrine but never be convinced by them." In this way, Emerson located spiritual understanding and experience in the privacy of the individual and not in the social structure of established religion.

American Lyceum Movement

The American lyceum movement, named for the place where the ancient Greek philosopher Aristotle lectured the youth of Athens, was founded in 1826 in Millbury, Massachusetts, by teacher and lecturer Josiah Holbrook. But the movement originated in Scotland during the early 1800s when George Birbeck, an early pioneer in adult education, gave lectures on science to audiences in Glasgow. The movement then spread to France and later to the United States.

The goal of the American lyceum movement was to encourage learning in the United States through the establishment and support of an organized form of adult education. This purpose was served by public forums, led by local associations that presented lectures and debates on current issues, such as the establishment of a public school system. American lyceums became popular as the middle class increased in the northeast after the opening of the Erie Canal in 1825. As a result of economic growth in this region, Americans had more money to spend on education and culture. Many also wanted to have a voice in local and national politics. Within five years, some 3,000 lyceums had been established in the Northeast and Midwest.

Initially, local groups met weekly and asked community residents to sign up as speakers. By 1840, however, the movement had expanded and created more formal institutions that hired professional lecturers who pulled in huge audiences. Emerson, who turned to this venue in order to help support himself after he returned from Europe, became a popular speaker and later converted many of his lectures into essays. Other famous lecturers were Frederick Douglass, Henry David Thoreau, Nathaniel Hawthorne, and Susan B. Anthony. The movement also influenced school curricula in the United States and encouraged and sponsored local museums and libraries.

After the Civil War, the lyceums transformed into events aimed more for entertainment than education. The movement expanded west after the first continental railway was completed in 1869. By the early part of the twentieth century, the movement had died out but not before its effects were felt through the formation of literacy programs and higher standards in public schools.

CRITICAL OVERVIEW

Packer, in her essay in *Columbia Literary History of the United States*, wrote that Emerson held a "commanding position... in the cultural landscape of mid-nineteenth-century America." He was also highly regarded in Europe. During his lifetime few American authors were recognized outside the United States. However, Emerson's essays were translated into French and German, and his work was reviewed in newspapers and journals in England and France.

Emerson's first collection of poetry, *Poems*, published in 1847, initially received mixed reviews. Critics found his essays to be much more fluid than his poems, which some thought were awkwardly constructed. Yet within a year of publication, enough reviewers found original passages to praise in the collection for Emerson to gain a small profit from the book. Edwin P. Whipple acknowledged scholars' contradictory responses to Emerson's poetry in an 1882 article on him for the *North American Review*. Whipple noted that Emerson "often takes strange liberties with the established laws of rhyme and rhythm; even his images are occasionally enigmas." However, Whipple insisted that Emerson "still contrives to pour through his verse a flood and rush of inspiration not often perceptible in the axiomatic sentences of his most splendid prose. In his verse he gives free, joyous exulting expression to all the audacities of his thinking and feeling." W. Robertson Nicoll, in a 1903 article on Emerson for the same journal, stated, "there is little doubt that Emerson is a great and admirable poet, and that this will be increasingly recognized."

However, opinions of Emerson's poetry and prose would continue to be mixed. Before World War I (1914–1918), Emerson retained the popularity he held during the last half of the nineteenth century. His combination of optimism and individualism continued to have an impact on philosophers such as William James (1842–1910) and John Dewey (1859–1952) and poets such as Walt Whitman (1819–1892) and Robert Frost (1874–1963). However, his reputation suffered between the two world wars as many scholars considered him too sentimental for the age. Packer noted "the precipitous decline his reputation took in the middle decades of the twentieth century, when it became fashionable to belittle Emerson as a bloodless optimist who lacked a Vision of Evil." In the closing decades of the twentieth century, he regained something of his early stature as an American sage as critics rediscovered the innovative thinking in his essays and the romantic aesthetics in his poetry. The multivolume edition *The Journals and Miscellaneous Notebooks of Ralph Waldo Emerson*, which began appearing in 1960 and continued through the next two decades proved renewed and sustained interest in Emerson's thought and writings.

Opinions on Emerson's "The Snow-Storm" have been consistently positive. Joseph M. Thomas, in his review of *Poems* in *New England Quarterly*, argued, "In the 1830s, a watershed period for his growth as a poet, Emerson forsook the often sonorous and grandiloquent eighteenth-century style of his dead-end apprentice verse for a freer prosody of self-discovery." Thomas insisted that Emerson's "*Poems* reflects this new maturity and contains a large portion of the poetry for which he is known, including... 'The Snow-Storm.'" Packer singles out this poem for its "descriptive exuberance." Mario L. D'Avanzo, in an essay on Emily Dickinson and Emerson for *New England Quarterly*, noted that "The Snow-Storm" was one of Dickinson's favorite poems. In the fourth chapter of his piece on Emerson for Twayne's United States Author Series, Donald Yannella stated, "The nineteen lines which comprise the second stanza are among the most vivid and artistically wrought performances in poetic imagery in Emerson's canon." He stated that "with dazzling simplicity Emerson conjures up the classic and gleaming white statuary of ancient Greece" in his reference to the marble used in Greek sculpture. In an assessment of Emerson as a poet, Yannella wrote, "the number of Emerson's poems which have endured, and those which might continue to, may be modest," yet "among American poets Emerson does deserve, by virtue of those remarkably intense and technically accomplished works...to hold a place equal to that of our dozen most important poets." He concluded that "Emerson at his best gave us some of our finest poems."

CRITICISM

Wendy Perkins

Perkins is a professor of English at Prince George's Community College in Maryland and has published several articles on American and British literature. In the following essay, she interprets "The Snow-Storm" as an example of Emerson's beliefs about nature and the role of the poet.

Emerson's "The Snow-Storm" is typically read as an illustration of the beauty and creative power of nature. In this poem, Emerson presents a traditional setting and event in New England, a snowstorm in the country and depicts how in one evening it transforms the landscape. Yet, a look at Emerson's statements on the interaction between nature and the artist, specifically in his essays "Nature" and "The Poet," provides another view of the poem. When these two essays are read in conjunction with the poem, "The Snow-Storm" becomes an illustration of the poet's ability not only to express the beauty and power of nature through art, but also to enhance those attributes for the reader.

The first two lines of the poem, declaring that "all the trumpets of the sky" herald the arrival of the snowstorm, identify the reverence paid to this act of nature and create a sense of anticipation. Here, Emerson uses hyperbaton, an inversion of conventional word order, so that the snowstorm is announced before it arrives. This technique highlights the magisterial fanfare afforded the storm, suggesting its power and prestige. The speaker then denotes its sense of purpose and energy in his description of it "driving" over the landscape as it "white[s]" the air.

WHAT DO I READ NEXT?

- "Nature" (1836), Emerson's first published essay, presents his philosophy on how humans can discover their spiritual connection to the divine by connecting with the natural world. He argues in this essay that nature can enrich one's soul in four ways: by serving the body's needs, through the aesthetic experience of viewing it, by providing metaphors for communication, and by teaching a moral sensibility.

- Emerson's "The Poet," published in his second collection of essays in 1844, expresses his philosophy of the role of the poet and the process of poetic inspiration and creation.

- Emerson's poem "Each and All," published in 1844, is one of his well-known nature poems. It expresses Emerson's view that everything in nature makes up part of an organic whole, that the components of nature work together to create beauty and enrich the soul.

- *Rising Voices: Writings of Young Native Americans* (1993), edited by Arlene Hirschfelder and Beverly Singer, is a collection of poetry, stories, songs, and essays written by Native Americans from 1887 to 1990. Several of these works, including "Homelands," "Identity," and "Ritual Ceremony," express their young authors' spiritual connection to the land.

- *Walden; or Life in the Woods* (1854) is by Henry David Thoreau, Emerson's friend and fellow transcendentalist. The book chronicles two years Thoreau spent living on the edge of Walden Pond on the outskirts of Concord, Massachusetts. During this period, Thoreau adopted a simple lifestyle and observed nature.

- In *American Transcendentalism: A History* (2008), Philip F. Gura focuses on the main figures of this important nineteenth-century literary movement, including Emerson, Thoreau, and Margaret Fuller. Gura presents biographies and analyses of their writings and their influence in the early 2000s on American thought in such areas as religion, politics, and human rights.

> EMERSON'S NORTH WIND TRANSFORMS THE LANDSCAPE AND AT THE SAME TIME SERVES AS A SYMBOL OF THE POET'S CREATIVE POWERS."

Emerson's reverence for nature infuses many of his writings, especially his first published essay, "Nature." In this work, Emerson insists that humans should turn to nature to discover how to live a fuller and more complete life. Emerson believed that nature can inspire a "wild delight" in those who establish a connection with it. "In the woods, we return to reason and faith," he writes, and this experience nourishes the soul. Nature, then, becomes an appropriate subject for poetry.

In "Nature," Emerson complains that many people have not turned to nature for inspiration and solace and so are alienated from it. "Few adult persons can see nature," he argues, or "At least they have a very superficial seeing." Emerson believed that humans must engage with nature through an active mind in order to appreciate it, and this engagement comes naturally to children but is often lost on world-weary adults.

The farmhouse inhabitants illustrate these assertions in their apparent sense of being cut off from the outside world by the storm. Huddled near the fire, these inside people refuse even to watch the snow. They turn their backs on the storm and try to protect themselves from the winter weather.

Realizing that they will likely miss the opportunity to appreciate with the majesty of the storm, the speaker urges them to "come see the north wind's masonry." By necessity made idle from their work and visitors or travel, the people have this chance to focus on nature and what it does.

Emerson recognized nature as engaged endlessly in a fluid process that continually changes all that it contains. Packer, in her article on Emerson in the *Columbia Literary History of the United States*, notes Emerson's view that the fluidity of nature, what he calls "'the metamorphosis'—that all things are in flux, that all created things are only the temporary incarnation of a divine energy always on the brink of transformation into something else." This idea of cosmic flux, endless creativity, and metamorphosis was evidence for Emerson of the divine conveyed through nature.

In "Nature," Emerson argues that only the poet's eye can "integrate all the parts" of nature. It is the poet's role then to help others observe and appreciate it. Emerson explains in "The Poet": "We are like persons who come out of a cave or cellar into the open air. This is the effect on us of tropes, fables, oracles, and all poetic forms. Poets are thus liberating gods." The poet, whom he addresses throughout the essay with a masculine pronoun, "unlocks our chains, and admits us to a new scene."

In "The Snow-Storm," Emerson creates a symbolic representation of these two main arguments: the poet has the power to enhance nature as well as to encourage others to appreciate and embrace it. Emerson's north wind transforms the landscape and at the same time serves as a symbol of the poet's creative powers. The speaker's invitation to the farmhouse inhabitants to come out into the open air and see the results of the north wind's artistry illustrates Emerson's own call to readers to recognize the poet as a liberating agent who can help them understand and appreciate nature by showing them its coherence and value.

The main purpose in the second stanza of "The Snow-Storm" is the poet's literary transformation of the landscape through his poetic expression of it. Emerson insists in "The Poet" that what makes a poem is "a thought so passionate and alive, that, like the spirit of a plant or an animal, it has an architecture of its own, and adorns nature with a new thing." The farmhouse scene, then, is not transformed through random swirling of the snow, but by the effort of the artificer-poet, whose playful, artistic genius emerges as he constructs his poem.

The second stanza explores this creative interaction between poet and nature. Here, the poet becomes the "fierce artificer" who gathers materials from "an unseen quarry" to decorate and thus to transform natural and man-made objects in the landscape. Using snow like tile, he designs and builds "white bastions.../ Round every windward stake, or tree, or door." The word "bastions" suggests the strength of the poet's creations.

The poet rejects the traditional in order to create and illustrate a new vision of nature. In "The Poet," Emerson writes, "The poet, by an ulterior intellectual perception, gives [things] a power which makes their old use forgotten, and puts eyes, and a tongue, into every dumb and inanimate object." In "The Snow-Storm," the poet is "myriad-handed" as he creates on top of old ones "fanciful" yet "savage" images that ignore standards of "number or proportion."

The poet first hides conventional man-made objects such as chicken coops and dog kennels in the beginning of the evening in "the whited air." He then builds his new creations on top of the old. He transforms thorns into "swan-like forms" and, in an organizing and finishing touch, he creates "a tapering turret" over the transformed landscape.

The speaker adds a note of humor when he describes the poet "mockingly" hanging "Parian wreaths" on the objects. The addition of the wreaths made from Greek marble suggests the nineteenth-century American habit of adorning homes with Greek architecture. Here then, the poet makes fun of this conventional decoration as he creates his own untraditional vision.

When the evening ends and the morning sun appears, the poet sees that "the world / is all his own" and so he retires. Emerson frames the poem with the image of the conqueror. In the opening lines, trumpets herald the snow's power to reshape the landscape, and at the close, the speaker declares the poet's similar ability. This framing device, coupled with the last few lines, reinforces the poem's first point: A creative interaction exists between the poet ("the mad wind's night-work") and nature ("the frolic architecture of the snow").

The speaker has given those in the farmhouse, who have been "enclosed / in a tumultuous privacy of storm," the opportunity to view this interaction and so experience a communion with nature. He has pointed out to them how the wind/poet has created his works of art, but he has not been able to encourage them to engage with the altered landscape. During the course of the evening, the farmer does eventually leave the comfort of the fire to view this transformation, but he refuses to see past the fact that the snow is filling up his "lane from wall to wall" and so only "sighs." He becomes the embodiment of those who see nature only as an impediment to the daily tasks people have to accomplish.

The act of reading Emerson's essays "Nature" and "The Poet" deepens one's understanding of "The Snow-Storm," because the essays explain the philosophy behind the poetry. Thus informed, readers see how, according to Emerson, the poet can shape, order, and ultimately enhance nature for those who are willing to look at its constant flux with an integrative eye.

Source: Wendy Perkins, Critical Essay on "The Snow-Storm," in *Poetry for Students*, Gale, Cengage Learning, 2010.

Jean Gorely

In the following excerpt, Gorely discusses Emerson's ideas about the composition of poetry.

In the first essay of the series of 1844 [*The Poet,*] Emerson considers the nature and function of the true poet. He begins his discussion with these words: "The breadth of the problem is great, for the poet is representative. He stands among partial men for the complete man, and apprises us not of his wealth, but of the common wealth." The significance of this thought can only be understood after a study of Emerson's theory of man. That is fundamental. Therefore, very briefly, the main lines of the doctrine must be indicated, especially man's relation to the rest of the world, his nature, and his problem.

Emerson believes in the oneness of the world. God, or the Oversoul, is the life or essence in all things "swallowing up all relations, parts, and times within itself." This life is transcendent. It is the source of thought, the starting point of action. Emerson writes that "the sovereignty of this nature whereof we speak, is made known by its independency of those limitations which circumscribe us on every hand." Moreover, it is immanent, pervasive. "God is, and all things are but shadows of him." The closing lines of "Woodnotes" say:

> Thou metest him by centuries,
> And lo! he passes like the breeze;
> Thou seek'st in globe and galaxy,
> He hides in pure transparency;
> Thou askest in fountains and in fires,
> He is the essence that inquires.
> He is the axis of the star;
> He is the sparkle of the spar;
> He is the heart of every creature;
> He is the meaning of each feature;

> "BESIDES STIMULATING TO THOUGHT ABOUT POETRY AND THE LIFE OF THE SPIRIT, EMERSON'S THEORY GIVES A STANDARD FOR CRITICISM OR COMPARISON."

And his mind is the sky,
Than all it holds more deep, more high.

Thus man, with nature, is a part of this great whole. Both are revelations or manifestations of the Oversoul with the distinction that nature is its expression in the unconscious and man in the conscious.

There is a certain infinitude in man. Over and above his own life or spirit he has this greater life, within which he is contained, to draw upon.

> It is a secret which every intellectual man quickly learns, that beyond the energy of his possessed and conscious intellect he is capable of a new energy,... by abandonment to the nature of things; that beside his privacy of power as an individual man, there is a great public power on which he can draw, by unlocking, at all risks, his human doors, and suffering the ethereal tides to roll and circulate through him; then he is caught up into the life of the Universe, his speech is thunder, his thought is law, and his words are universally intelligible.

Man is also unique. Each is different from every other. Each is given a particular work to do in the world and each must carry it out alone. Upon its realization, the success of the world depends.

Man has a means of communication with the Oversoul. He is aware of his relation by intuition or inspiration. What this experience is is not explained. All we know is that "this sense of being which in calm hours rises, we know not how, in the soul, is not diverse from space, from light, from time, from man, but one with them, and proceedeth obviously from the same source whence their life and being also proceedeth." It is miraculous only in so far as all life is miraculous. It is a positive universal fact. All tools, inventions, books, and laws came out of the invisible world through the brains of men. When this state, Emerson says, is attributed to one or two persons and denied to all the rest, the doctrine of inspiration is lost.

"God is the all-fair." "Truth, goodness and beauty are but different faces of the same all." Man, then, by virtue of intuition has access to truth, goodness, and beauty. But it is not sufficient to know these. Man must give them expression. This is the problem of man, namely, to listen, to hear and to report. Truth comes

> to the end that it may be uttered and acted. The more profound the thought, the more burdensome. Always in proportion to the depth of its sense does it knock importunely at the gates of the soul, to be spoken, to be done.

These powers, however, are seldom found in perfect equipoise. Rarely is the expression adequate to the thought. "I know not how it is," Emerson says, "that we need an interpreter, but the great majority of men seem to be minors, who have not yet come into possession of their own, or mutes, who cannot report the conversation they have had with nature."

It is the poet who solves the problem. For this reason, he is the representative man. Because of deep insight and a corresponding power of expression "he stands among partial men for the complete man." He is nearest to the centre of the Universe and sees all things in their relation to the Infinite and to each other. "The factory-village and railway fall within the great Order not less than the beehive, or the spider's geometrical web." He

> perceives that thought is multiform; that within the form of every creature is a force impelling it to ascend into a higher form; and, following with his eyes the life, uses the forms which express that life, and so his speech flows with the flowing of nature.

The life may be likened to a light with its rays shining in all men. Ordinarily, it is not tended and burns but dimly. Then men must resort to reason. But the poet frees it from all obstruction. It has a brighter flame and things appear in their true relations. His report or expression is poetry. According to Emerson, it is oracular, the report of one who retires into himself to listen, one who is passive, who trusts to instinct and demands no authority but instinct.

> For poetry was all written before time was, and whenever we are so finely organized that we can penetrate into that region where the air is music, we hear those primal warblings and attempt to write them down, but we lose ever and anon a word or a verse and substitute

something of our own, and thus miswrite the poem. The men of more delicate ear write down these cadences more faithfully, and these transcripts, though imperfect, become the songs of the nations.

Fundamentally, Emerson's theory of poetry can be divided into two parts. The first of these is concerned with genesis; the second, with the finished work. In the order of genesis, thought precedes form. Therefore, we shall consider first, the getting of the idea, and, second, the execution or elaboration.

The asthetic critic, like Pater, analyzes a poem, finding and noting the virtue or virtues by which it produces its effect. But, given all these virtues, he could not create or recreate the poem any more than the scientist can put together the parts of a flower and have a flower. The power comes from without oneself.

It was Emerson's belief that thought comes from the "inner mind," the "mind of the mind," and brings with it the power of expression. At the time of its reception the poet is inspired. In this, as we have seen, he is not different from ordinary men. It is a universal experience and has certain more or less definite characteristics. Inspiration is inconsecutive. There is a flash, a "point of view," a "glimpse," a "mood" and no more. Nor can it be controlled in any way. It comes spontaneously. "When we discern truth, we do nothing of ourselves, but allow a passage to its beams." The poet can neither incite nor prolong it, but he can clear away obstruction.

Moreover, it is unconscious. The worker is often as much surprised at his work as we. Emerson, for example, could never recall having written the poem "Days". He says in the *Journal* of 1852:

> I find one state of mind does not remember or conceive of another state. Thus I have written within a twelvemonth verses ("Days") which I do not remember the composition or correction of, and could not write the like to-day, and have only, for proof of their being mine, various external evidences, as the MS. in which I find them, and the circumstance that I have sent copies of them to friends, etc., etc.

But the unconsciousness is merely in relation to us.

> We speak, we act, from we know not what higher principle, and we describe its circumambient quality by confessing the subjection of our perception to it, we cannot overtop it, . . . nor see at all its channel into us. But in saying this we predicate nothing of its consciousness or unconsciousness in relation to itself. We see at once we have no language subtle enough for distinctions in that inaccessible region.

Finally, inspiration is advancing in its nature. The inspired man sees something new, something that nobody else has seen. He does not revert to the past or look to the future, but "lives now and absorbs past and future into the present hour." "Inspiration will have advance," Emerson writes, "affirmation, the forward foot, the ascending state; it will be an opener of doors; it will invent its own methods."

Enthusiasm usually accompanies the state in varying degrees. It may exhibit itself in frenzy or ecstasy, but more often in a warm glow, a thrill of awe and delight.

Although inspiration cannot be brought about at will, there are certain favouring conditions. We all have heard of the ways in which great composers and artists have worked. How Haydn had to be very carefully dressed. How Mozart did best while riding in a comfortable carriage, or lying awake in the silence of the night. In Emerson's *Journal* of 1852 there are these lines:

> Poppy leaves are strewn when a generalization is made, for I can never remember the circumstances to which I owe it, so as to repeat the experiment, or put myself in the conditions.

Emerson does, however, give a list of conditions drawn partly from literary biography and partly from his own experience.

Health, first of all, is indispensable for good work and it can only be maintained by sleep and exercise and a simple life. Wine, narcotics, opium, and sandlewood fumes are not for the poet. They are procurers of animal exhilaration. "The poet's habit of living should be set on a key so low that the common influences should delight him. His cheerfulness should be the gift of the sunlight; the air should suffice for his inspiration." Besides daily rest, rest after years of service renews the faculties.

Human intercourse with its letter-writing, its travel, its conversation, and its reading is of value. Emerson found letter-writing a good companion, or a book very helpful.

A third condition, in contrast to the last named, is retirement into self or "solitude of habit." The poet should go to some place remote from the sounds and work of the house, where he can sit alone and think. Emerson put up at a country inn in summer, or a city hotel in winter when he had a difficult piece of work to do. There, no cares of the farm could disturb him. This need of solitude is organic.

> To the culture of the world an Archimedes, a Newton, is indispensable. If these had been good fellows fond of dancing, port and clubs, we should have had no 'Theory of the Spheres' and no 'Principia.' They had that necessity of isolation which genius feels.

Allied to this solitude of habit, is solitary converse with nature. As nature is the "projection of God in the unconscious," it is a revelation to the poet of the life of which he is a part. In it there is perfect order, for all things are regulated by the laws of the Infinite. Thus, if the poet comes close to nature, he can see truth everywhere. This thought is crystallized in "The Poet":

> The gods talk in the breath of the woods,
> They talk in the shaken pine,
> And fill the long reach of the old seashore
> With dialogue divine;
> And the poet who overhears
> Some random word they say
> Is the fated man of men
> Whom the ages must obey.

The idea of the work, then, comes in inspiration. The poet submits himself to the Universal Mind and is shown things in their right relations. The cares and fears of the day, income tax returns and wireless, sunshine and shadow, have each their place in the order of the world. To us they appear as parts out of place, detached from the whole.

The carrying out of the final work does not receive a very full treatment in Emerson. The poet does not so much create as report. The words he seems to speak are but spoken through him. So the idea takes its own form. The words come naturally and the intensity of the thought makes the language rhythmical. This is the difference between true poetry and the work of a versifier. In the one, sense dictates the rhythm; in the other, sense is adapted to the rhythm. As we have seen, there was no memory of the execution of the poem called "Days". In most cases, however, Emerson revised his work. Here is the record of the effect of the sea as it is found in the *Journal* of 1856:

> 'Tis a noble, friendly power, and seemed to say to me, why so late and slow to come to me? Am I not here always, thy proper summer home? Is not my voice thy needful music; my breath thy healthful climate in the heats; my touch thy cure?
>
> Was ever building like my terraces? Was ever couch so magnificent as mine? Lie down on my warm ledges and learn that a very little hut is all you need. I have made this architecture superfluous, and it is paltry beside mine. Here are twenty Romes and Ninevehs and Karnacs in ruins together, obelisk and pyramid and Giant's Causeway; here they all are prostrate or half-piled.
>
> And behold the sea, the opaline, the plentiful and strong, yet beautiful as the rose or the rainbow, full of food, nourisher of men, purger of the world, creating a sweet climate and in its unchangeable ebb and flow, and in its beauty at a few furlongs, giving a hint of that which changes not and is perfect.

It reads like blank verse. With very few changes it forms the first twenty-seven lines of the "Seashore". How closely they compare:

> I heard or seemed to hear the chiding sea
> Say, Pilgrim, why so late and slow to come?
> Am I not always here, thy summer home?
> Is not my voice thy music, morn and eve?
> My breath thy healthful climate in the heats,
> My touch thy antidote, my bay thy bath?

The history of "Two Rivers" was very similar. I give it as he wrote it sitting by the river one April day in 1856 and as it appeared when published:

> Thy voice is sweet Musketaquid, and repeats the music of the rain, but sweeter is the silent stream which flows even through thee, as thou through the land.
>
> Thou art pent in thy banks, but the stream I love flows in thy water, and flows through rocks and through the air and through rays of light as well, and through darkness, and through men and women.
>
> I hear and see the inundation and the eternal spending of the stream in winter and in summer, and in men and animals, in passions and thought. Happy are they who hear it.

Here are the first three stanzas of the poem:

> Thy summer voice, Musketaquit,
> Repeats the music of the rain;
> But sweeter rivers pulsing flit

Through thee, as thou through Concord
   plain.
Thou in thy narrow banks are pent:
The stream I love unbounded goes
Through flood and sea and firmament,
Through light, through life, it forward
   flows.

I see the inundation sweet,
I hear the spending of the stream
Through years, through man, through
   nature fleet,
Through love and thought, through
   power and dream.

These examples suffice to show how the thought finds its proper wording, rhythm, and melody. There was careful revision. An adjective or a superlative was omitted. Words were changed. Yet there is no loss in the spontaneity. These first expressions, like the blocked-out sketches of an artist, are in complete analogy with the finished work.

And the finished work is organically beautiful. The materials that went into its making—the thought, the melody, the phrasing, the imagery—were all only means to an end. This end in Emerson's doctrine is called Beauty. Although there is no definition of beauty, its conception is deep. It involves not only qualities of sound and colour and excellence of structure, but something deeper. Only through knowledge of the true, can one attain the beautiful.

> Wherever snow falls, or water flows, or birds fly, wherever day and night meet in twilight, wherever the blue heaven is hung by clouds, or sown with stars, wherever are forms with transparent boundaries, wherever are outlets into celestial space, wherever is danger and awe and love, there is Beauty, plenteous as rain, shed for thee, and though thou should'st walk the world over, thou shalt not be able to find a condition inopportune or ignoble.

Poetry shows nature and humanity not fancifully, not fictitiously, but more truly as they are by reason of the poet's central position. Truth to the true requires that it have its proper melody and phrasing though often the odds are immense against finding it. Then, each word, and image, and rhyme answer their ends exactly, just as in Amiens Cathedral the covering of enclosed spaces, the forms of the supports, the arches, the tracery and decorative detail have each a constructive reason. Intangible, evanescent, beauty is something to which the whole of man's nature responds. It brings about harmony between all his powers. Reason acting upon the work finds it true in the proportions and the relations of its parts. The melodious language, the imagery appeal to the senses and the feelings, while the spirit finds radiating from it something "immeasurable and divine."

"Threnody," "Musketaquid," "The Seashore"—any of these might illustrate this. "Days" is short and more suited to quotation:

> Daughters of Time, the hypocritic Days,
> Muffled and dumb like barefoot dervishes,
> And marching single in an endless file,
> Bring diadems and fagots in their hands.
> To each they offer gifts after his will,
> Bread, kingdom, stars, and sky that
>   holds them all.
> I in my pleached garden, watched the
>   pomp,
> Forgot my morning wishes, hastily
> Took a few herbs and apples, and the Day
> Turned and departed silent. I, too late,
> Under her solemn fillet saw the scorn.

Finally, the measure of greatness in poetry is the "cosmical quality, or power to suggest relation to the whole world."

One unfamiliar with Emerson, who reads his work only cursorily says that he lacks method; that his idea of poetry is too vague, too much of a theory. Emerson, himself, acknowledged that he lacked method. "I need hardly say to anyone acquainted with my thoughts that I have no system," and again, "my method is purely expectant.... I confine my ambition to true reporting, though I only get one new fact in a year." The theory, however, is a noble one, one that could only be conceived by a man of great intuitive and speculative power. It deals with poetry at its highest. Theorists in this field generally belong to one of two schools. Either they believe that poetry should have no contact with ethics or science but be the expression of emotion in beautiful phrase, image, and melody; or that it should be concerned with truth and human values in life alone. Emerson's theory includes both of these views. Poetry is not poetry if it cloys with the lusciousness of its melody and imagery. Poetry is based on truth and truth requires a consideration of the meanings of things. Moreover, the true is beautiful and its expression will be beautiful in its symbols, its rhythm, and its form. The stress on inspiration and the intimate relation with the life of the spirit makes the theory something almost religious.

Besides stimulating to thought about poetry and the life of the spirit, Emerson's theory gives a standard for criticism or comparison. It is an aid in distinguishing the good from the bad in what we read. Our personal standards are changeable. Now one type of poetry seems to satisfy them, now another. If we measure by such a standard as this of Emerson's, however, we can have results which are more lasting than our own hastily formed impressions. How this works out in English poetry can be shown almost diagramatically by a series of circles concentric with the ideal of the theory. Very near the centre would be Shakespeare. On the next circle, might come Chaucer and Spenser; farther out, Marlowe, Ben Jonson, Keats, Byron, and Wordsworth. With these the expression is usually outweighed by some deficiency in the thought. Wordsworth is peculiarly a poet of nature. There is too much of the personal element in Byron. "What has Lord Byron at the bottom of his poetry," says Emerson in his *Journal* of 1839, "but 'I am Byron, the noble poet, who am very clever, but not popular in London?'" Next to these would be writers who, in rare moments of greatness, are able to seize the inner meaning of a scene or a life and body it forth. Then would come most of us. "Deep in the heart of man a poet sings." We are capable of poetic thought, but we lack the power of expression. Last of all, on the outer circles, would be the versifiers who care only for form and effect.

Emerson, then, believed that poetry is mystical; that it comes into being as the result of inspiration. In that moment the poet sees the very essence of things. But vision is beyond his will. It comes to him unawares. Moreover, it is sudden and inconsecutive. It is advancing. Health, rest, human intercourse, solitude of habit, and a life in the open are all favouring circumstances. The poet makes the unseen visible by means of language. But he is not here the conscious creator. Vision, also, shows him the symbols and the thought takes its own form in language that is rhythmical. Because of this, there is a certain indwelling beauty in poetry and we measure its greatness by its cosmical quality. In such a theory, *poetry is spiritual and forms a link between the visible and invisible worlds.*

Source: Jean Gorely, "Emerson's Theory of Poetry," in *Poetry*, Vol. 22, July–August 1931, pp. 263–73.

ABOVE ALL ITS OTHER MERITS HIS POETRY IS *SUI GENERIC*, ORIGINAL AND HIS OWN."

Anonymous

In the following excerpt, the author gives an early positive review of Emerson's poetry.

The venerable and historic town of Concord (not Concord, New Hampshire, famous for its small-beer school of politicians) is likely, in addition to its Revolutionary renown as the spot where

once the embattled farmers stood,
And fired the shot heard round the world,

to be famous hereafter as the residence of the essayist, poet, popular lecturer, and transcendental philosopher, Emerson, who, whatever may be thought of him by his contemporaries hereabouts, is certainly destined to a permanent and world-wide reputation,—to become a fixed star in that luminous cluster of original thinkers who from their high places exercise a steady and never-waning influence on the intellectual growth of mankind. Concord, Massachusetts, therefore, as the scene of one of the events which inaugurated the American Revolution, and as the home of one of the first intellectual men of the age, is in no particular danger, in the long run, of being eclipsed by its namesake in New Hampshire, though that be the capital of a small State and the home of a small President. However this may be, one thing is certain, that there are few places better adapted to study and the cultivation of letters. Through its meadows and shady intervale lands winds a slow stream, synonymous with the town itself, a stream like the English Ouse or Avon, or the smooth gliding Mincius of classic song, not rapid or turbulent, but with just such a clear and languid current as poets have loved to prose upon from time immemorial....

As a lecturer and prose essayist, Mr. Emerson is even *popularly* known, that is, to the mass of his countrymen; but as a poet he has found a smaller audience, though a fit one. His verses can never become popular. He cannot therefore cry out with Horace, "*profanum vulgus et arceo*," for the mob of people that read with ease (to alter slightly Pope's lines for the sake of adapting it to the times) will never defile his poetry with their vulgar admiration. It will never fly through the mouths of men like Pope's pithy couplets, or Gray's "Elegy," or Longfellow's "Psalm of Life," but it has already secured for itself a select circle of admirers among the highly cultivated and intellectual, and such a circle it will always retain. It is even now frequently quoted by the ablest writers in the leading reviews and periodicals of England and this country. Indeed, we venture to assert that there are few writers of eminence, either in America or Great Britain, who are not perfectly familiar with the products of the Emersonian Muse, with the strange, weird, abstruse notes of the Emersonian lyre. Like the Theban poet Pindar, Emerson, when he wraps his singing robes about him, addresses himself only to the wise. He has many musical shafts in his quiver, but their music is only audible and intelligible "ὀοῖ ὀοöοῖ." His poems are as utterly devoid of anything like sentiment or passion as the versified apothegms of the old Greek philosophers and didactic bards. In fact, sentiment and passion, which are ordinarily supposed to be the very soul and essential principle of poetry, he utterly ignores. His best passages have "the sparkle of the spar," but none of the warmth of flesh and blood. They appeal not to the heart, but to pure intellect. He is not of the romantic school of poets. He is entirely free from "dark imaginings" of the Byronic stamp, and from maudlin, lovesick, moon-nursed fantasies. His Muse traffics not in these woes. She haunts "an intellectual bower." Some of his poetical pieces are pearl-like strings of glittering *sententio*, of brilliant and grand thoughts set in a most transparent and crystalline diction. Emerson's poetry, like his prose, is all permeated with emanations from one great central ideal. His peculiar philosophical system, call it by what name you choose, Spinozism, Pantheism, or Transcendentalism, is the master chord of his lyre, as it is the keynote of all his writings, whether in verse or prose. Around this central idea his poetry winds in luxuriant wreaths and festoons, like the leaves and flowers of some gorgeous parasite about a massy trunk. What Emerson's system of philosophy is exactly, it is no easy task to determine...Whatever it is, Mr. Emerson seems to entertain the most sublime confidence in its entire correctness. He evidently looks upon it as the master-key which unlocks the secrets of the universe and the most hidden recesses and profoundest Domdaniel caverns of Nature. Beyond a doubt, Mr. Emerson has the highest qualifications for a poet. Even his prose itself has in passages the golden *rythmus* of the most exquisitely modulated versification. He is profoundly learned, not only in printed books, but also in the book of Nature. All the lore of the East and the West is his. He is as familiar with Hafiz and Firdusi, as he is with Homer and Shakespeare; with the sages and philosophers of India, China, Persia, and Arabia, as he is with those of Greece, Rome, Germany, England, and France. He is deeply versed in the lore of plants, stones, and stars. He has looked on Nature with a lover's eye, and pursued her through all her most intricate windings, and learned to interpret her most mysterious symbols. Mr. Emerson is happy in his choice of language, which in his hands is perfectly plastic and flexible. His words are culled and marshalled with the most exquisite taste. Many of his periods are rounded and enamelled to absolute perfection. It used to be fashionable to speak of Emerson as an imitator of the rough, craggy Carlyle. This idea was without doubt engendered by the fact that several of Carlyle's works were published in this country under the supervision of Emerson, and the editor was naturally confounded with his author. Emerson, in fact, is the very opposite of Carlyle both in style of thought and composition. They no more resemble each other as writers than would an Ithuriel and a Caliban in form and feature if matched together.

But there are great inequalities in Emerson's poetry. While he has passages, indeed whole pieces, which are as faultless, flawless, and beautiful as some costly gem, he has others which, to the understanding of the uninitiated reader at least, appear to be mere unmeaning strings of words, vague, hyper-metaphysical formulas, and pure balderdash. They are hard sayings, too hard indeed for the comprehension of any human being except a *Dialist*. In nearly all Mr. Emerson's poems, it is evident that more is meant than meets the ear and eye. He has an Oriental love of the allegoric and mystical. But above all its other merits his poetry is *sui generis*, original and his own. It is not the product of any second-hand inspiration, awakened by the works of this or that great poet beyond the water, as is the case with the bulk of American poetry. It is not this or that English or German bard diluted and sophisticated, but genuine, unadulterated Emerson, with an unmistakable smack of the soil of his fatherland about it; for if he has occasion to apostrophize a mountain or river in his verse, he gives a decided preference to Monadnock or the Alleghanies over Olympus and the Alps,—to the beautiful rivers of his native New England, with their wild Indian names, hitherto "unmarried to immortal verse," over the most vaunted streams of the Old World. This is as it should be. But for the most part it is with our poetry as with the wines which we use; both are mere imitations and not natural products, the latter generally consisting of ingenious chemical mixtures, whose rich vinous *hue* and *bouquet* and flavor were not imparted by the glowing sun and genial soil of Burgundy, Champagne, and the African Islands, but by artificial perfumes and dye-stuffs. But we have one American vintage, at least, which does not smell of the apothecary-shop, but of the American soil, of the banks of the Ohio. In like manner we have a few poets who do not derive their inspiration from Tennyson or Wordsworth or Browning, or any other European bard, living or dead, but directly from Nature herself. Mr. Emerson's published poems are all included within the limits of a single small volume; but that volume is infinitely suggestive, and contains matter enough, if wire-drawn and reduced, to fill many tomes. In it all the Emersonian prose essays are presented in brief, fused, intensified, and hardened, as it were, into crystals. Virgil himself could not originate a system of philosophy in more honeyed verse. With three or four exceptions, each poem is a chip from a different side of the same block, a variation of the same key-note, a new illustration of one master idea, for there is but one string to Emerson's lyre; but he draws from that solitary chord as many variations as ever did a Paganini. Four, at least, of his poems have become popular, and have been reprinted a thousand times in newspapers, reviews, and specimens of American verse. We allude to the pieces entitled "Good-Bye," "Rhodora," "The Humble-Bee," and "The Problem." These are pure ambrosia. The Good-Bye to the world is worthy of the age of Elizabeth, and might have been penned by a Wotton or Raleigh after they had "sounded all the depths and shoals of honor"; indeed, it reminds one of verses which those great statesmen and scholars actually did write after they had become satiated with the world. The lines to the "Humble-Bee," have been compared to the Allegro and Penseroso of Milton. It seems to breathe the very spirit of the delicious months of May and June. It might have been written upon a bank of violets, fanned by the sweet South, such as the impassioned Duke Orsino speaks of. It is enough in itself to give its author a permanent place in English literature. Anacreon has an ode, and Mr. Leigh Hunt has a sonnet, addressed to the grasshopper, both exquisite in their way, but neither comparable to Emerson's lines on the "yellow-breeched" American insect, the tiny and erratic

> Sailor of the atmosphere;
> Swimmer through the waves of air;
> Voyager of light and noon;
> Epicurean of June.
>
> When the south wind, in May days,
> With a net of shining haze
> Silvers the horizon wall,
> And, with softness touching all,
> Tints the human countenance
> With a color of romance,
> And, infusing subtle heats,
> Turns the sod to violets,
> Thou in sunny solitudes,
> Rover of the underwoods,
> The green silence dost displace,
> With thy mellow, breezy bass.
> Hot midsummer's petted crone,
> Sweet to me thy drowsy tone
> Tells of countless sunny hours,
> Long days, and solid banks of flowers;
> Of gulfs of sweetness without bound
> In Indian wildernesses found;
> Of Syrian peace, immortal leisure,
> Firmest cheer, and bird-like pleasure.

The very genius of dreamy May and voluptuous June seems to brood over the above lines. A few such passages would be enough to redeem the character of the American Muse from the charge of barrenness and want of originality. Mr. Emerson looks on nature and the visible universe with the eye of a poet and a man of science both. He is a Wordsworth and Linnaus combined. New-England scenery is almost as much indebted to him as the lakes and mountain regions of Northern England are to Wordsworth, Coleridge, and De Quincey. Mount Monadnock, since it has been embalmed in Emerson's verse, need not fear to lift its head beside the most vaunted hill visible from Rydal Mount, where not long since lived the great English high-priest of nature. Emerson's "Monadnock" is one of the richest, most suggestive, and picturesque pieces in the language. What Wordsworth called "the power of hills" must have been on him when he wrote it. The tall form of Monadnock towers in his verse with as much majesty as it does in its native heavens, and henceforth is entitled to be ranked with those immemorial mountains of the Old World, renowned in song.

> Cheshire's haughty hill

has its poet, too, as well as the giant Swiss mountain, whose shadow glides over the valley of Chamouni. A voice, perhaps of the Genius of Monadnock, summons the poet:

> Up!—If thou know'st who calls
> To twilight parks of beech and pine,
> High over the river intervals,
> Above the ploughman's highest line,
> Over the owner's farthest walls!

Mr. Emerson's poetry concerns itself but little with human joys or sorrows. His Muse oftenest affects the "heights of abstract contemplation." His religion (for it is on this subject that his Muse chiefly delights to dwell) appears to be borrowed from Plato and the dreamy mystics of the Ganges. The visible universe, with its myriad forms of animal, vegetable, mineral, and impalpable aerial existences, is in his view simply a masquerade of the World-Soul or Godhead, an infinite variation of the eternal unit, a *monad* which underlies and constitutes everything. God is a vast impersonal, unimpassioned energy merely, a "*vivida vis*," or creative potency. Man himself, though the highest manifestation of Deity, is, so far as his identity and individual being are concerned, a mere foambell, which arises for a moment on the rushing tides of existence, and is quickly reabsorbed into the oceanic essence of Deity...

It seems to us, in our ignorance, not a little singular that Emerson, with his keen intellect, piercing as a Damascus blade, and his upright moral character, could deliberately turn away from what he himself calls

> The riches of sweet Mary's son,
> Boy-Rabbi, Israel's paragon,

to the altars of a vague, defied abstraction, like the Platonic *Zeus* or the Oriental *Brahma*, for such, as near as we can gather, is the God of his idolatry.

But to attempt anything like a careful examination of Emerson's poems within the compass of a short essay would be impossible, for each would furnish matter sufficient for an article. Suffice it to say, that these poems are among the most remarkable contributions to the literature of the present age, and as such they will undoubtedly be regarded by posterity.

Source: Anonymous, "Emerson as a Poet," in *Harvard Magazine*, Vol. 1, October 1855, pp. 422–33.

SOURCES

D'Avanzo, Mario L., "'Unto the White Creator': The Snow of Dickinson and Emerson," in *New England Quarterly*, Vol. 45, No. 2, June 1972, p. 278.

Emerson, Ralph Waldo, "Nature," in *The Norton Anthology of American Literature*, edited by Nina Baym, Vol. 1, 5th ed., Norton, 1998, pp. 1074, 1075, originally published separately as *Nature*, James Munroe, 1836.

———, "The Poet," in *The Norton Anthology of American Literature*, edited by Nina Baym, Vol. 1, 5th ed., Norton, 1998, pp. 1146, 1148, 1150, 1154, 1155, originally published in *Essays: Second Series*, James Munroe, 1844.

———, "The Snow-Storm," in *Anthology of American Literature*, edited by George McMichael, James S. Leonard, Bill Lyne, et al., Vol. 1, 8th ed., Pearson Education, 2004, pp. 908–909, originally published in *Poems*, James Munroe, 1847.

Nicoll, W. Robertson, "Ralph Waldo Emerson," in *North American Review*, Vol. 176, No. 5, May 1903, p. 683.

Packer, Barbara, "Ralph Waldo Emerson," in *Columbia Literary History of the United States*, edited by Emory Elliott, et al., Columbia University Press, 1988, pp. 381, 384, 388, 390, 395.

Thomas, Joseph M., "'The Property of My Own Book': Emerson's *Poems* and the Literary Marketplace," in *New England Quarterly*, Vol. 69, No. 3, September 1996, p. 408.

Whipple, Edwin P., "Emerson as a Poet," in *North American Review*, Vol. 135, No. 308, July 1882, pp. 25–26.

Yannella, Donald, "Chapter 4: Artful Thunder," in *Ralph Waldo Emerson*, Twayne's United States Author Series 414, Twayne, 1982, pp. 4, 12.

FURTHER READING

Matthiessen, F. O., *American Renaissance: Art and Expression in the Age of Emerson and Whitman*, Oxford University Press, 1941.

> Matthiessen's seminal study of the major authors of this period, such as Emerson, Nathaniel Hawthorne, and Walt Whitman, explores the integral connection between the man and his work and situates each in his historical moment. This study is also available in several paperback editions, including one by Kessinger (2007).

Porte, Joel, and Saundra Morris, eds., *The Cambridge Companion to Ralph Waldo Emerson*, Cambridge University Press, 2008.

> The editors of this collection present new interpretations of Emerson's writings, the cultural and philosophical influences on his work, and his influence on other writers.

Richardson, Robert D., Jr., *Emerson: The Mind on Fire*, University of California Press, 1996.

> In his study of Emerson's life, Richardson cites Emerson's journals, letters, and lectures. He also examines cultural and literary influences in analyses of his major works.

Waggoner, Hyatt H., *Emerson as Poet*, Princeton University Press, 1974.

> Waggoner conducts a comprehensive study of Emerson's poetry, his philosophy of poetics, and the poetic tradition that influenced him.

Yoder, R. A., "Toward the 'Titmouse Dimension': The Development of Emerson's Poetic Style," in *PMLA*, Vol. 87, No. 2, March 1972, pp. 255–70.

> Yoder explains how Emerson's poetry evolved.

The Stolen Child

WILLIAM BUTLER YEATS

1886

"The Stolen Child," by William Butler Yeats, tells about a child being enticed by fairies to go away with them. Based on Irish legend, the poem was written in 1886, at the beginning of Yeats's career, and is one of the best and most popular of his early poems. It was first published in *Irish Monthly* in December 1886. In 1888, it appeared in *Poems and Ballads of Young Ireland*, a collection of several poets' work, and in Yeats's book of folklore *Fairy and Folk Tales of the Irish Peasantry*. In 1889, it appeared in Yeats's first book of poetry *The Wanderings of Oisin and Other Poems*. "The Stolen Child" shows both the influence of romantic literature and Pre-Raphaelite verse and Yeats's desire to preserve and promote Irish literature. What Yeats did not realize until he got a few years deeper into his folklore work was that the romantic atmosphere of this poem was not typical of the robust and homely nature of Irish legends. Yeats originally thought that all Irish folk tales were melancholy, so he made his version of this tale dreamy and unearthly. Ironically, it was this tone that made the poem so popular because the Victorians liked stories about sensitive children who escape from this harsh world to a fairyland or magical place. In addition, the story was made to seem quite realistic by Yeats's use of local place names and precise imagery typical of County Sligo, his family home. The poem can be found in any number of collections of Yeats's poetry or in anthologies that include Yeats. One source is *Collected Poems: Yeats*, a 2003 Picador paperback that is also available in a 2009 Kindle edition.

William Butler Yeats (The Library of Congress)

AUTHOR BIOGRAPHY

Yeats was born on June 13, 1865, in Sandymount, County Dublin, Ireland. His father, John Butler Yeats, was studying law when he married Susan Mary Pollexfen from a wealthy County Sligo family. Soon, however, he abandoned law to become a portrait painter. After Yeats was born, the family moved to Sligo, but when the boy was two they moved to London so that his father could study art. Eventually John Yeats became well-known and successful, but during some lean times the family again lived in Sligo while the father remained in London. Yeats was home schooled until 1876 when he entered Godolphin Primary School in London, and he attended Erasmus Smith High School when the family moved back to Dublin in 1880. Not a good student, he did not go to a university but spent from 1884 through 1886 at the Metropolitan School of Art. Eventually, he realized that his talent and passion lay more in writing than in painting. He returned to London for a time and had opportunities to meet some of the leading literary figures of his time.

Yeats's first poems were published in the *Dublin University Review* in 1885 and a volume of poetry was released two years later. In 1887, he joined Golden Dawn, an organization dedicated to the study of the supernatural, and remained a member for thirty-two years. In 1888, he joined the Theosophical Society, and in 1890, he co-founded the Rhymers Club, a poets' group that met regularly to recite their own work. During these years, he published another volume of poetry and began his extensive research and publications in folklore.

In 1894, Yeats met Lady Augusta Gregory whose financial support and long friendship included establishing the Irish Literary Theatre in 1899 (later known as the Abbey Theatre or the National Theatre of Ireland). As its resident manager, Yeats wrote and produced many works, including *The King's Threshold* (1904) and *Deirdre of the Sorrows* (1907). He also developed an appreciation for Japanese Noh theater after meeting Ezra Pound in 1913. In addition, Yeats co-founded the Cuala Press with his sisters, which would publish over seventy titles during its forty-two years in existence.

In 1889, Yeats met Maud Gonne, an actress and political activist who had a big influence on him. He repeatedly and unsuccessfully proposed to her until 1917 when, determined to get married and have children, he wed Georgie Hyde Lees, who was twenty-seven years his junior and who shared his interest in the occult. They had two children: Anne in 1919 and Michael in 1921. In 1922, Trinity College, Dublin, awarded Yeats an honorary degree, and he was appointed to the Irish Senate where he served for six years. In 1923, he was awarded the Nobel Prize for Literature. His finest works, however, were written after that time. In poor health for the last decade of his life, Yeats often went to France to convalesce, and he died there on January 28, 1939. Because of World War II, his body was not returned to Ireland until 1948.

POEM TEXT

```
Where dips the rocky highland
Of Sleuth Wood in the lake,
There lies a leafy island
Where flapping herons wake
The drowsy water-rats;                                5
There we've hid our faery vats,
Full of berries
And of reddest stolen cherries.
Come away, O human child!
```

To the waters and the wild 10
With a faery, hand in hand,
For the world's more full of weeping than you
    can understand.

Where the wave of moonlight glosses
The dim grey sands with light,
Far off by furthest Rosses 15
We foot it all the night,
Weaving olden dances,
Mingling hands and mingling glances
Till the moon has taken flight;
To and fro we leap 20
And chase the frothy bubbles,
While the world is full of troubles
And anxious in its sleep.
Come away, O human child!
To the waters and the wild 25
With a faery, hand in hand,
For the world's more full of weeping than you
    can understand.

Where the wandering water gushes
From the hills above Glen-Car,
In pools among the rushes 30
That scarce could bathe a star,
We seek for slumbering trout
And whispering in their ears
Give them unquiet dreams;
Leaning softly out 35
From ferns that drop their tears
Over the young streams.
Come away, O human child!
To the waters and the wild
With a faery, hand in hand, 40
For the world's more full of weeping than you
    can understand.

Away with us he's going,
The solemn-eyed:
He'll hear no more the lowing
Of the calves on the warm hillside 45
Or the kettle on the hob
Sing peace into his breast,
Or see the brown mice bob
Round and round the oatmeal-chest.
For he comes, the human child, 50
To the waters and the wild
With a faery, hand in hand,
For the world's more full of weeping than he
    can understand.

POEM SUMMARY

The narrative of the poem follows a child who is taken by fairies on a tour of what is presented as a wonderful exotic place. The different geographical points that are named are actual places that can be found on a map, thereby giving a sense of reality to the legend about how fairies

MEDIA ADAPTATIONS

- Considered one of his finest achievements, English composer Cyril Rootham, a master of choral setting, set "The Stolen Child" to music in 1911.

- Composer Gloria Edith Manson created a version of "The Stolen Child" for voice, chorus, and piano in 1956.

- Loreena McKennitt set to music and recorded some adaptations of tradition Celtic songs and poems, including "The Stolen Child," as part of her 1985 debut album *Elemental*.

- With music written by the band's leader, Mike Scott, and parts spoken by Tomás Mac Eoin, "The Stolen Child" was recorded by the folk rock group The Waterboys for their 1988 album *Fisherman's Blues*.

- Heather Alexander's 1994 debut CD of original and Celtic songs, *Wanderlust*, includes "The Stolen Child" in a rendition set to music and played on violin by Alexander.

- A musical version of "The Stolen Child" was written by composer Gary Bachlund for baritone and piano in 2005 for his song cycle *Three Magical Songs*.

- Hamilton Camp, on his 2005 and final album *Sweet Joy*, includes a song called "Celts," which combines "The Stolen Child," as set to his original music, with "Go No More a-Rovin'."

- Parts of the poem "The Stolen Child" are recited in Steven Spielberg's 2001 film *Artificial Intelligence: A.I.*, a futuristic movie about a child-like android capable of feeling love.

- The poem "The Stolen Child" is spoken by a fairy who steals a young girl in the "Small Worlds" episode, first broadcast on November 12, 2006, of the BBC science fiction television series *Torchwood*.

- In 2008, Eric Whitacre set "The Stolen Child" in a piece for The King's Singers and the National Youth Choir of Great Britain.

steal children. The tight metric stanzas are of different lengths: stanzas one and four are twelve lines long, while stanza two is fifteen lines long and stanza three is fourteen lines long. The rhyme scheme therefore varies somewhat to accommodate the different number of lines. Each of the first three stanzas begins with the word "where," describes a scene, then ends with the same four line refrain in which the fairies invite the child to come away with them, hand in hand, to their mystical wilderness.

Stanza 1

This twelve-line stanza has a rhyme scheme of *ab, ab, cc, dd* for the first eight lines and then *aabb* for the four-line refrain. The child's journey with the fairies starts at Sleuth Wood, also known as Slish or Sloped Wood because it is a forested area on high ground that seems to slide down, or dip, into the south side of the lake called Lough Gill. The leafy island is probably the Isle of Innisfree, although there are about twenty small islands in the lake. There, where the noise of the herons (large wading birds) on the lake wakes up the water rats, the fairies have hidden vats full of berries and cherries. The entire stanza is designed to present a calming, yet enticing picture of this other world.

Yeats uses alliteration in lines 2 and 3 to add to the sense of calm with the soft sound of *l* in the words "lake," "lies," and "leafy." The rats are described as drowsy for three possible reasons. For one, drowsy is an indication that night is coming on, and for another, drowsy implies a dreamlike state, and the fairies want to fill the child with dreams of their wondrous home. Finally, drowsy is an appropriate term for a lullaby. Since these tales of stolen children were intended to urge children to go to sleep quickly at night because the fairies stole naughty children who were awake too far past their bedtime, the lullaby connection is appropriate. The use of "we've" in line 6 with "faery" lets the reader know that the speakers in the poem are fairies. The cherries are described as the reddest because the fairies are trying to convince the child that they have the best of everything, but they are also described as stolen, which is a hint about the intent of the fairies toward the child.

Refrain

The refrain speaks directly to the child and is an invitation to go away with the fairies. It is significant that the fairies don't say "Come away, O child!" but specify that the child is human. The invitation is to go to the magical land and waters that nature provides in the wild. Again there is a hint of abduction because the child does not go on its own but a fairy holds its hand and leads it away. The motivation given is that the child's home world is a worse place than the childish mind can comprehend. Yeats uses alliteration with the letter *w* in "away," "waters," "wild," "world's," and "weeping." The first three lines of the refrain have a sing-song rhythm. The fourth line is conversational in rhythm and is surprisingly twice as long as any other line in the poem; it could easily be two lines, but Yeats is making a point by keeping the one thought in one line. This choice is more dramatic and makes more impression with the message that the human world is a hard, sad place. The tone of the refrain seems to change with each stanza, starting out like a lullaby, then a mischievous invitation for fun, then more sinister like the siren's song in mythology luring sailors to their doom, and finally as a fait accompli. It is a subtle move from the guise of a rescue to a kidnapping.

The final refrain is slightly changed from the others in that the invitation "Come away, O human child!" becomes "For he comes, the human child," letting the reader know that the child is going away with the fairies. There is no exclamation mark to punctuate the first line, but a comma that connects the child to the new world it is entering. In the last line, the direct address to the child designated by "you" in the previous stanzas becomes a statement to the reader about the boy with the use of "he." This last line also perhaps is an admission by the fairies that there will be more weeping in the world because of his loss than the child has considered.

Stanza 2

This fifteen-line stanza has a rhyme scheme of *ab ab, cc, b, de, ed* for the first nine lines, then repeats the refrain. Yeats uses assonance in the words "wave," "gray," "dances," "hands," and "glances" and alliteration with the *f* sound in "far," "furthest," "foot," "flight," "fro," "frothy," and "full." These sound devices connect the sentences and produce a trance-life effect. Yeats also uses the figure of speech of personification in describing the moon as taking flight and in describing the world as anxious in its sleep.

The fairies paint a magical picture of moonlight glossing or illuminating the sands like a soft spotlight. The "Rosses" refers to Rosses Point, a small seaside village near Sligo, so the "furthest Rosses" is far outside the village in the area of the woods and streams. According to local legend, if anyone falls asleep at this point in the rocks, the person is likely to wake up crazy because the fairies have stolen the person's soul. This legend provided the poet with an obvious setting in which to locate fairy activity.

The fairies say they dance with mingled hands until daylight. Irish folklore has it that the fairies dance in circles, thus leaving rings in the grass or sand to let humans know the fairies had been there. Perhaps Yeats uses the term "olden" to indicate that he is copying from known tales. The fairies "chase the frothy bubbles," that is, the waves going in and out on the shore. The scene is intended to impress upon the child that fairies can play and jump and dance all night, whereas adults in the child's world have worries that disturb their sleep.

Stanza 3
This fourteen-line stanza has a rhyme scheme of *abab, cde, cde* for the first ten lines, then repeats the refrain. The first line is full of alliteration with the use of *w* in "Where the wandering water."

The third stop on the journey is Glen-Car, which means Valley of the Monumental Stone, or Glen of the Standing Stone, at a fifty-foot waterfall that comes into a lake where the waters are narrow and shallow. Here the fairies lie on the ferns that bend over the waters so that they can be close enough to the trout to tease them as they sleep. This behavior is a contrast to the herons that unintentionally disturb the drowsy water rats, but the fairies purposely and maliciously disturb the dreams of the trout. This is another clue from Yeats about their false friendliness to which he adds that the ferns weep, perhaps because they know the fairies are being mean. Once again, Yeats emphasizes the enticing power of the call of the fairies by using alluring terms such as "wandering water," "star," and "young streams" and soft terms such as "rushes" (tall grasses that grow in marshes and pools), "whispering," "softly," and "ferns."

Stanza 4
Like the first stanza, this fourth stanza is twelve lines long, but the rhyme scheme is different: *abab* then *cdcd* instead of *ccdd* as in the first stanza. The refrain is slightly different, too. While the other three refrains start with "Come away, O human child!" the fourth refrain has as its first line: "For he comes, the human child," the invitation changed here to an announcement.

The opening line of the last stanza lets the reader know that the child has succumbed to the lure of the fairies and is going away with them. The child is referred to as "The solemn-eyed." (Using a part (eye) to stand for the whole (child) is a figure of speech called synecdoche.) The trance-like state may suggest that the child realizes the detrimental life-changing decision that has been made. As he is going away, the fairies admit, perhaps with sinister glee, that he is leaving behind the comforting features of his home: the lowing or mooing cattle on the hillside, the singing teakettle on the hob (a nail on which the kettle hangs within the fireplace), and even the little mice that run around his house. The last stanza, then, is a reminder that the human world has its comforting domestic features. Thus, Yeats counters the popular demand for tales of escapism with a warning that charming fairies actually come from a frightening world of shadows.

THEMES

Worldly versus Other-Worldly
Yeats had a lifelong curiosity about what might lie beyond known material reality. He studied the supernatural and occult, looking for other worlds that might co-exist with the material one. He was fascinated by Irish tales of fairies, leprechauns, banshees, and similar creatures. He heard stories about changelings, that is, human children replaced by sickly fairies or enchanted objects that look like the actual child. The poem "The Stolen Child" resulted from this interest. In it, Yeats develops the Irish theme that runs through much of his poetry and promotes Irish identity and nationalism; he also contrasts the real world with that of the fairies.

County Sligo is a real place one can visit. But the world of legend, which some people say is also real, is visited by an act of imagination. Yet some believe it can be reached by extrasensory, magical, or imaginary means. If these believers are correct, then this magical world provides hope for those who seek to escape the difficulties of real life. Since Yeats believed in other realms, he sought a way to combine realism and transcendence in his poetry, thus helping his readers

TOPICS FOR FURTHER STUDY

- Yeats drew the story of "The Stolen Child" from folklore, that is, traditional stories and social practices that have been passed down mostly by word of mouth rather than being written down. Folklore includes tales; superstitions; proverbs; weather predicators; customs for births, deaths, and weddings; cultural dances; and much more. Do some library research to find a definition or description of folklore then interview a family elder or older neighbor to find out what folklore that person knows from his/her childhood. Make a classroom presentation of your findings.

- Conduct a geographical study of the area of Ireland described in "The Stolen Child." Use Google Earth, if available, to study the area. Otherwise, find Sleth Wood, Sligo, Innisfree, Rosses Point, and Glen-Car on a map. In what part of Ireland are they situated? Divide the class into five groups, each taking a different site to locate, learn about, and describe.

- Yeats chose to emphasize Irish themes in his writings as part of an effort to perpetuate an Irish identity. As a class project, dividing the task by eras, trace the history of the relationship of Ireland to England though the nineteenth century, creating an outline of events and major persons. For the twentieth century, continue the outline, but provide more in-depth reports on major events and conflict and on the Irish Republican Army. What do you think could have been done to prevent the twentieth-century violence? What is the situation in Northern Ireland and Ireland now?

- As part of perpetuating an Irish identity, efforts have been made to preserve Gaelic, the old Irish language. Perhaps as an extra credit project, find some recordings of spoken Gaelic and examples of Gaelic in print on the Internet and share them with the class.

- *Angela's Ashes* (1996), the bestselling memoir by Frank McCourt, has been popular among high school and college readers. The Irish characters in the story often express superstitions and perform traditional rituals. Find three examples of these superstitions or customs in the novel and write a report describing them or, perhaps in conjunction with a class reading of the book, have a classroom discussion about them. These superstitions and customs may provide topics for a term research paper on the novel.

---

visit in their own way the supernatural world described in Irish folklore.

Ominous Threat

Yeats suggests in "The Stolen Child" that the supernatural poses an ominous threat. The fairies pretend to have a life of irresistible delight, but behind the facade of dancing and gaiety is the wickedness expressed through knowing glances, teasing trout, and stealing cherries and children.

Ominous threat is also expressed in the child's willingness to enter a magical place, despite a natural reluctance to enter the unknown. The reader experiences this same ominous sense of wanting a peek at fairyland but leery of the dangers there. After all, the title describes the child is "stolen," and Yeats hints that the fairies are both deceptive and mean.

The last stanza counters the attraction of the imagined paradise with a reminder that the child's home is comfortable and reliable. The mortal world may be full of anxiety and weeping, but it has its peaceful and comforting aspects. Will the child really come out ahead in the exchange, or is he making a terrible mistake? Yeats was fascinated with the possibilities of other worlds, but apparently he suspected that the yearning for supernatural otherness might be a futile treasure hunt taken to avoid coming to terms with reality.

Fairy illustration by Arthur Rackham from the book Peter Pan in Kensington Gardens *by J. M. Barrie, published 1910* (© Classic Image | Alamy)

Loneliness and Loss

The theme of loneliness and loss is represented in three different ways in "The Stolen Child." For one, if the child goes away with the fairies, his parents will experience a terrible loss. For another, the term "solemn-eyed" suggests the child's loss of the familiar and beloved comforts of his home. He will be lonely without his family no matter how nice life is among the fairies. Further, he forfeits his liberty in going with the fairies, who are known to use children as slaves, according to some legends. A third kind of loneliness is that of the human condition that yearns to know if anyone else is out there. Are there beings on other planets? Are there unseen beings such as fairies on earth? Just as a lonely child will create an imaginary friend, humans throughout the ages have imagined, suspected, or felt "others," and legends to explain the loss of a child have resulted.

STYLE

Visual Imagery

"The Stolen Child" is like a painting in words that describe places intimately familiar to Yeats. In the first stanza, readers imagine the rocky ground of Sleuth Wood sliding down into a lake and envision an island covered with greenery. The herons come alive with the use of the word "flapping," which draws attention to the drowsy water rats who have been disturbed. In line 8, Yeats uses two adjectives for one noun, describing the cherries as the reddest and, therefore, the best, which tells readers that the fairies have desirable things. Then Yeats inserts the word "stolen" to hint at the negative side of the fairy world.

In the succeeding stanzas, readers imagine moonlight upon "dim grey sands," dancing fairies amidst the frothing waters, a waterfall, scant pools of water, trout, ferns, streams, calves on a hillside, a kettle on the hearth, mice, and an oatmeal chest. The poem presents the details of County Sligo, the home of Yeats and of magical enticement to any child.

Poetic Sounds

Yeats believed that a poem is a song, so he wrote his verses as lyrics. In fact, Yeats often had a tune in mind as he wrote a poem, and he sang his poems. His intention in "The Stolen Child" is to make the poem as attractive in its sound as it is in its images. He wanted it to be read aloud in the sensuous way that the country folk would tell a story. The poem's sound is reminiscent of a bedtime story or a lullaby, especially in the refrain, but the voice is haunting and passionate. Yeats used conventional poetic devices to achieve his effects in sound: "The Stolen Child" has alliteration, assonance, and rhyme, with the alliteration and assonance drawing attention to important words. Although visual imagery dominates the poem, certain words describe sounds such as "gushes," "unquiet," and "softly." Then, in the last stanza, Yeats specifically calls attention to the sounds that the child will no longer hear after he leaves his mortal home: the lowing calves and the singing kettle.

HISTORICAL CONTEXT

Irish Nationalism

Twenty years before Yeats was born, the potato blight reached Ireland and three periods of famine occurred as a result. The loss of two million of Ireland's 8.5 million people between 1845 and 1851, about half to starvation and half to emigration to North America and other places, made a huge impact on Irish society. In the face of slow and ineffectual aid from the British government in London, coupled with the continued export from Ireland to England of wheat and corn despite local starvation, a resurgence in Irish efforts for independence intensified. Various organizations promoting Irish nationalism arose, some militant and secretive, but by the end of the 1860s, people were rejecting violence for mainstream political activity.

From 1870 to 1886, two leaders from the Protestant ruling class guided this activity: first, the Irish lawyer and member of the House of Commons Isaac Butt (1813–1879), and then Charles Stewart Parnell (1846–1891), under whom the movement became the Irish Parliamentary Party. In 1880, this party won 63 seats out of the 103 Irish seats, and in 1885, it won 85 seats. At this point, Prime Minister William Gladstone argued for the Irish Home Rule cause. A bill was introduced in 1886 but was defeated by the House of Commons and then again in 1893, but it was defeated by the House of Lords. A third Irish Home Rule bill passed in 1914 but never went into effect because of World War I (1914–1918). Finally, in 1920, Home Rule was passed, but it divided Ireland with the creation of mostly Protestant Northern Ireland, a decision that caused violent conflict for decades thereafter.

In the midst of the political efforts for a separate national identity, other efforts were fostered. For example, in 1884, the Gaelic Athletic Association was established to foster traditional Irish games such as hurling over British games such as cricket. Also, the Gaelic League was formed in 1893 to promote and preserve the use of the indigenous Celtic language. Yeats, early in his career, seized upon Irish subjects as appropriate and necessary to the preservation of the culture. "The Stolen Child" is an example of his use of Irish lore in his poetry. Between 1888 and 1893, he published five books of Irish folklore. In 1892, the Irish Literary Society was founded with Yeats as its first president. Further, in 1897, Yeats helped to found a national theater for Ireland that still functions in the early 2000s.

Pre-Raphaelites

In his earliest poetry, Yeats was influenced by the Pre-Raphaelite movement. The name comes from a group of painters who began around 1848 to try to move art from a conventional, mechanistic approach to the complex detail and color of painters prior to the Italian master Raphael (1483–1520), whose style was considered the ideal in the mid-nineteenth century. The Pre-Raphaelites sought freshness, closer fidelity to nature, and new moral seriousness and sincerity in their works. Influenced by the romantics, they emphasized the connection between freedom and responsibility and the belief that art was essentially spiritual in its origins. Before long, however, the Pre-Raphaelites split into two groups, and the later development of the Aesthetic Pre-Raphaelites had more effect on poetry by emphasizing themes of sensual medievalism and moody atmospheres. Pre-Raphaelite poets drew upon the poetic tradition established by Spenser (often mentioned as an influence on

COMPARE & CONTRAST

- **1890s:** Yeats studies the Kabbalah, a system of thought in Jewish mysticism that explores the paradoxical relationship between an eternal and indecipherable creator with the finite created universe. Kabbalah seeks to reveal the nature and purpose of God, and provide a way for people to increase their spiritual understanding.

   Today: Kabbalah is an interest of certain American celebrities such as Madonna, Ashton Kutcher, Demi Moore, Brittany Spears, Elizabeth Taylor, and David and Victoria Beckham. At centers in the United States, 15,000 to 20,000 people attend prayer and meditation sessions and participate in workshops. Each month, about 30,000 people take Kabbalah Centre distance learning courses, and about 120,000 visit its Website.

- **1897:** Yeats and Lady Gregory establish the Irish Literary Theatre. In 1903, it becomes known as the Irish National Theatre Society and, in 1904, establishes its home in Dublin's Abbey Theatre. In 1925, the Abbey becomes the first state-subsidized theater in the English-speaking world.

   Today: The Abbey Theatre, also known as the National Theatre of Ireland, is home to many notable Irish dramatists. In 2007, plans are announced for a new building containing three auditoriums.

- **1886:** In Ireland, if a stolen child in a city is reported, the police have few resources for tracking the kidnapper and finding the child. In rural villages, neighbors are called upon to hunt for the child, but if the search fails, people who live in such superstitious areas as Sligo may assume that the fairies have stolen the child.

   Today: In the United States, when a stolen child is reported to the police, an Amber Alert (named after a particular stolen child) is issued over news media so that everyone in the community, even across the country, immediately learns of the kidnapping and may note and report relevant information. Various sophisticated crime scene investigation tools are available as well as electronic media for rapid communication about the case.

Yeats) and continued through Keats and Tennyson, which was marked by vibrant vowel sounds and subjectivity.

Symbolism Movement

Symbolists, whether visual artists or poets, longed for an out-of-world transfiguration, a subject that intrigued Yeats throughout his life and is manifested in poems such as "The Stolen Child." The symbolism movement started in France and Belgium in the late nineteenth century out of admiration for the poetry of Edgar Allan Poe. It was a reaction against the realism and naturalism, which focused on the ordinary in graphic detail. Rather than be obvious with plain meaning, symbolic writing evoked a certain kind of reader response, thus the name symbolism. In fact, anything in a poem could be symbolic as opposed to the selected symbols of the romantics, and they were intended to suggest a state of mind rather than to represent or be an allegory for a specific thing. The symbolists enjoyed word play, and the fluidity of their compositions eventually led to free verse. They admired the ideal of art for art's sake and ironic detachment. A influential explanation of symbolism was written in 1884 by Paul Verlaine, just two years before the publication of "The Stolen Child". Since symbolists saw art as a means of escaping worldly concerns, they explored themes about mysticism and mortality, which had fascinated Yeats since childhood and which combined perfectly into his study of folklore and fairies.

Rushy pond among the hills (Image copyright Eugene Barzakovsky, 2009. Used under license from Shutterstock.com)

CRITICAL OVERVIEW

Although a favorite from among his early poems and considered of very good quality, "The Stolen Child" is not often given much consideration by critics because it pales beside Yeats's later works. "The Stolen Child" was one of the first notable poems from a literary career of over fifty years, so it is understandable that critics have given more attention to his mature and complex works. "The Stolen Child" is often mentioned, though, in general discussions of his early themes and interests as that poem in which Yeats borrows from Irish folklore to describe a child lured away by fairies.

Among those who provide specific commentary on "The Stolen Child" is Robert Lynd who, in his book *Old and New Masters*, commented on the simplicity of the language in the last stanza: "There is no painting here, no adjective-work. But no painting or adjectives could better suggest all that the world and the loss of the world mean to an imaginative child." Lynd addressed the fact that "The Stolen Child" is an early work by complimenting Yeats on a genius that "had its birth in a sense of the beauty of common things" and that "brought a new and delicate music into literature."

M. L. Rosenthal, author of *Running to Paradise: Yeats's Poetic Art* stated that "The Stolen Child" is a "lovely early poem," a simpler example of his life-long obsession with a pursuit of ideals mixed with the "dangerous seductiveness of unholy spirits or of death." In addition, B. L. Reid, writing in the *Dictionary of Literary Biography*, volume 19, for *British Poets, 1880–1914*, described "The Stolen Child" with a phrase that is echoed in many critical reviews: "a haunted and haunting lyric."

CRITICISM

Lois Kerschen

Kerschen is an English instructor and freelance writer. In this essay, she explores the Irish background that led Yeats to write "The Stolen Child."

Through his poetry, Yeats wanted to promote an Irish identity and create an imaginative contrast to the rationalism of his time. Since the Irish are storytellers, he knew that his native folklore, filled with fairies and other supernatural creatures, could inspire readers' imaginations. These stories represented a heritage that needed to be preserved and celebrated in new works. Therefore, he drew on what is typically Irish in fairy legends in writing his poem "The Stolen Child."

Yeats started composing poetry in 1882 when he was about seventeen years old. He embraced the work of the romantics in a rejection of the new urbanization, the scientific rationalism prevalent during the Industrial Revolution, and the orthodoxies of Victorians. He felt that romanticism would allow him more freedom of imagination and self-discovery. Showing his admiration of Shelley and Keats, his teenage poems were escapes into ancient times and dreams. They followed classical themes and imitated Wordsworth's observations of nature. At first, he wrote about India because of his fascination with the exotic.

However, in 1885, upon the return of John O'Leary, the militant Irish independence leader,

WHAT DO I READ NEXT?

- *The Major Works: including poems, plays and critical prose* is the Oxford World's Classic 2008 publication edited by Edward Larrissy that gives readers access to Yeats's diverse work and his artistic, political, and spiritual development across his career.
- *The Concise Oxford Companion to Irish Literature*, edited by Robert Welch and published in 2000, contains sixteen centuries of Irish poetry, drama, and fiction with commentary by a team of experts. This comprehensive and understandable guide is excellent for both pleasure reading and research.
- *Favorite Celtic Fairy Tales* (1995), by Joseph Jacobs, is a small Dover collection of eight traditional Irish fairy tales that illustrate the magical, humorous, and charming folk legends that influenced Yeats.
- The backdrop of the young adult novel *Bog Child* (2008), by Siobhan Dowd, is the 1981 Irish conflicts. This book is about a stolen child, one who has been murdered and buried in a bog. Eighteen-year-old Fergus follows a voice in his dreams to solve the mystery.
- *Favorite Folktales from Around the World* (1988), by Jane Yolen, is a young adult edition from the Pantheon Library that contains 160 stories from the oral tradition of various cultures, grouped thematically and with introductions.
- *The Pre-Raphaelites* (2001), by Christopher Wood, charts the history of this British movement in art, which also influenced Irish authors such as Yeats. Dozens of reproductions by over forty artists are included.
- W. H. Auden and Norman Holmes Pearson edited *Romantic Poets: Blake to Poe* (1978), a Penguin Books Portable Library edition containing an extensive selection of works from both British and American romantic writers. This edition includes historical context and a chronology of the period.

> ONCE YEATS PUT TOGETHER HIS TWO PASSIONS, FOR AN IRISH IDENTITY AND THE POWERS OF IMAGINATION, HE FOUND IN IRISH FOLKLORE ALL THE MATERIALS HE NEEDED TO ESTABLISH A NATIONAL LITERATURE."

from twenty years of exile, Yeats became a fervent Irish nationalist and joined the Dublin Young Ireland Society. Through conversations with O'Leary and an intense study of Irish literature and history, Yeats became convinced that there needed to be a distinct Irish identity. When he began his studies, there were only a few books of legendary history then in print, and some resources were not translated or published. The lack of published material caused him to embark on a crusade to create and preserve Irish literature with its distinctive themes and styles. Not only did he research and publish his own books on the Irish literary heritage, but by 1886, he was publishing "The Stolen Child" and other poems that illustrate and contribute to this heritage.

According to James Hall and Martin Steinmann in *The Permanence of Yeats*, the maturing Yeats found in Irish folklore a "much less hackneyed" and more purposeful and effective subject than what he had achieved in copying the romantics. In the imagination and peasant speech of the Irish country people he found a "new precision of imagery and a greater vitality of diction" as well as "a rhythm which, while poetic, was fresh and vigorous." Hall and Steinmann add that by substituting specific Irish scenes from Rosses, Sleuth Wood, and Sligo for "vague romantic landscapes," Yeats was able to draw upon the "wild imagination" and "homely realism" of the folklore he knew, thereby taking "the first important step in the development of Yeats's individuality as a poet." As Neil Philip writes in his introduction to a 1990 publication of Yeats's *Fairy Tales of Ireland*, "Yeats...recognized in the melancholy, extravagant, spellbinding narratives of unlettered Irish storytellers a poetry and a passion akin to his own." So it was to the Irish stories he had heard in his youth that Yeats turned for his themes and imagery.

Between the ages of seven and nine, Yeats lived in the home of his wealthy maternal grandparents in Merville, Ireland, and later he spent summers there. He delighted in the frequent exchange of stories among the servants about supernatural events, although the fairies they knew were not the cute ones found in children's stories but treacherously clever and mischievous. Also, Yeats often visited his cousin George Middleton at Rosses and enjoyed the storytelling of his aunt and one of her servants. He later published a group of their fairy stories in his book *The Celtic Twilight*. One of his cousins was reputed to have almost been captured once herself by fairies.

An avid naturalist as a youth, Yeats would go fishing with his uncle in the waters near Rosses Point, take long walks, and sometimes spend the night in woodland caves. His familiarity with fairy lore and the countryside of Sligo are woven throughout "The Stolen Child." No doubt Yeats was always hoping to see fairies on these outings. Finally, on October 14, 1872, on one of these excursions with his uncle and a cousin, Yeats claimed he saw a fairy. According to a letter that Yeats wrote the next day, they were near a cave close to Rosses sands, which he describes in "The Stolen Child," a place known to be populated by fairies. He invoked the fairies, and soon his uncle thought he heard voice and music, but did not see anything. The cousin also heard the voices and music then saw a bright light and small figures dressed in crimson. Yeats heard cheering and a stamping of feet from among the rocks. Then he saw the queen of the fairies. She talked with the three mortals at length but warned them with a message written in the sand not to try to learn too much about the fairies.

Considering that he was imbued as a child with stories of phantasmagoria, it is no wonder that Yeats became fascinated with "the mystical, the paranormal, and the occult," as Jonathan Allison explains in his introduction to "The Stolen Child" in *Poetry for Young People*. Allison further reports that at age twenty, Yeats helped to found a club for a "group of students devoted to studying Indian philosophy and mysticism." The next year, the same year that he wrote "The Stolen Child," Yeats attended a séance and "later joined the Order of the Golden Dawn, a secret society that promoted the study and practice of ritual magic." He was also interested in "telepathy and astral projection, and he spent a great deal of time having visions or trying to have visions of the supernatural."

Among these supernatural interests, Yeats had a youthful obsession with the motif of the abduction of the changeling, which was popular not only among Irish storytellers but also among English Victorians as a whole. In his 1888 book *Irish Fairy and Folk Tales*, Yeats describes the legend of the changelings:

> Sometimes the fairies fancy mortals, and carry them away into their own country, leaving instead some sickly fairy child, or a log of wood so bewitched that it seems to be a mortal pining away, and dying, and being buried. Most commonly they steal children.... Those who are carried away are happy, according to some accounts, having plenty of good living and music and mirth. Others say, however, that they are continually longing for their earthly friends. Lady Wilde gives a gloomy tradition that there are two kinds of fairies— one kind merry and gentle, the other evil and sacrificing every year a life to Satan, for which purpose they steal mortals.

In popular lore, the story usually focuses on the mother's sorrow at losing her child and being forced to raise the sickly substitute. Yeats, by contrast, in "The Stolen Child" focuses on the seduction and has the fairies speaking directly to the child.

In his early twenties, Yeats got a commission to compile a representative assortment of Irish fairy stories. He enthusiastically researched all the books and journals he could find and began searching for people to tell him fairy stories. Yeats preferred oral to published tales because they were more likely to have been passed down directly from those who truly believed in fairies and other supernatural creatures. In fact, some storytellers would gather periodically to compare their stories for accuracy and prevent distortions from accidentally slipping in after multiple retellings. Soon he realized that most of what he was recording in his field work had not been written down before. Often what had been written failed to convey the storytellers's enchanting speech rhythms. Therefore, as he wrote "The Stolen Child," he tried faithfully to incorporate this unique sound.

In 1888, two years after the first publication of "The Stolen Child," Yeats included the poem in *Irish Fairy and Folk Tales*, the first book resulting from his folklore research. Academic folklorists were dismayed that Yeats's book was not scientific. James Pethica, in his chapter for the *Cambridge Companion to W. B. Yeats*, reports that Yeats responded to the criticism by saying that "the folklorist who is 'merely scientific'

A great blue heron flies into the early morning sunlight (Image copyright Jerry Segraves, 2009. Used under license from Shutterstock.com)

inevitably 'lacks the needful subtle imaginative sympathy to tell his stories well.'" However, Yeats realized that to be literary likewise raised the risk of merely indulging one's imagination, that the folklorist might hear only what fit his personal agenda "rather than capturing 'the innermost heart of the Celt.'"

Yeats's early literary achievement rested on his folklore work. Besides the aforementioned *Irish Fairy and Folk Tales* in 1888, he published *Representative Irish Tales* in 1891, *Fairy Tales of Ireland* and *The Countess Kathleen [a play] and Various Legends and Lyrics* both in 1892, *Stories from Carleton* in 1889, and *The Celtic Twilight* in 1893. To further alleviate the gaps of knowledge about Irish literature, he also put more and more explanatory material in his books of poetry in the 1890s.

A problem for Yeats in publishing these books was that while Yeats believed in the supernatural, he realized that his audience most likely did not and would read the tales as merely a preservation effort or as an attempt to bring back a sense of the old romantic to the new industrial age. Consequently, Yeats worded his prefaces carefully to describe the stories as coming from those who still believed in fairies, not from his imagination. He also allowed a touch of skepticism about the reality of the tale to be expressed with some of the stories. Nonetheless, by 1893, Pethica reports, Yeats had an "increasingly forceful conviction that imaginative inspiration, and not scientific authenticity, should be the true concern of the folklorist."

Once Yeats put together his two passions, for an Irish identity and the powers of imagination, he found in Irish folklore all the materials he needed to establish a national literature. Just as he felt that Irish poetry and magic had always been somehow connected, Yeats also felt, like the romantics who first influenced him, that the past provided an emotional energy and visionary awareness that could not be found in contemporary urban settings. Therefore, he believed that Irish legends could help to heal a nation trying to recover from the Great Famine and contending with English occupation. Just as Ireland had molded Yeats into its greatest poet, so he molded an Irish identity through its rich literature and strengthened Irish pride in its own past.

Source: Lois Kerschen, Critical Essay on "The Stolen Child," in *Poetry for Students*, 2010.

Harriet Devine

Devine has a Ph.D. in English literature and is emeritus professor in English literature at Edge Hill College, Lancashire, United Kingdom. In the following essay, she explains how "The Stolen Child" reflects the cultural and political views of William Butler Yeats.

An interpretation of "The Stolen Child" by William Butler Yeats is enhanced by knowledge of the poem's historical background and of Yeats's views of Irish mythology and Irish politics. The poet's own family history and early upbringing are also relevant. Although Yeats was born in Dublin and lived for most of the first ten years of his life in Ireland, he was not, strictly speaking, what was known as native Irish. His family on both his father's and his mother's side were what was called Anglo-Irish. In other words, they were members of the Protestant Ascendancy, members of the English ruling class who had established themselves in Ireland in the late seventeenth century.

Relations between England and Ireland had been strained for centuries, with numerous attempts being made by England to conquer and control its smaller neighbor, which met with varying amounts of success. Henry VIII of England (reigned 1509–1547) was the first English king to proclaim himself to be King of Ireland in the year 1541, and over the next century, despite several brutal conflicts between the native Irish and the English authorities, the English gained an increasingly secure foothold. This dominion was partly achieved by sending English and Scottish Protestant settlers (the Protestant Ascendancy) to colonize the country, annexing lands formerly owned by the native Roman Catholic Irish. In 1691, the Irish parliament passed a series of Penal Laws banning all Irish Catholics from voting or becoming members of the Irish Parliament. As nearly 90 percent of the

> THE ONLY VALID MEANS OF ESCAPE FROM THIS CONTINUING UNREST, THE POEM SUGGESTS, IS TO ESTABLISH A LINK WITH THE REALM OF THE SUPERNATURAL."

population of the country at that time was native Irish Catholics, this law caused great unhappiness and unrest, and more bloody rebellions followed. The Irish became increasingly antagonistic to the English in the eighteenth century. Many English landlords in this period either neglected their Irish properties or exported the food grown there, a practice which led to the first great Irish famine, in which an estimated 400,000 people died of starvation. A second famine, in the mid-nineteenth century, effectively halved the population of Ireland, either through death or emigration. During this period, too, the spoken language of Ireland, Gaelic, was all but totally eradicated through the establishment of English schools and the banning or suppressing of literature written in the native Gaelic.

In 1800, the British parliament passed the Act of Union, which made Ireland, along with Scotland and Wales, a member of the United Kingdom and thus subject to its laws. The Irish were deeply unhappy with this state of affairs, and from the middle of the nineteenth century several attempts were made to establish Irish Home Rule. One of the most important of these, though it was ultimately unsuccessful, was the pro-Irish Home Rule speech made in the House of Commons in June 1886 by William Gladstone, the British prime minister. Although these efforts failed, the issue of Home Rule was very much alive in the minds of both the British and the Irish at this period. Yeats, just twenty-one years old and living in Dublin, now began to take a lively interest in the turbulent politics of his country. He met and was greatly drawn to the charismatic Republican leader and avid supporter of Irish independence John O'Leary (1830–1907), who had recently returned to Dublin after nine years in an English prison on charges of high treason followed by ten years exile in France to become president of the radical

Irish Republican Brotherhood. A poet himself and recognizing Yeats's genius, O'Leary made available his own very considerable library for Yeats to use. The voracious and intensive reading Yeats began at this time undoubtedly led directly to the political and patriotic views he would hold for the rest of his life.

Most important, his reading at this period led him to recognize the value and importance of the literature and beliefs of the ancient Gaelic culture of Ireland. Suppressed, undervalued, and misunderstood by generations of English commentators, this romantic world of heroic myth and fairy legend needed to be appreciated and preserved. The authentic Irish people, Yeats came to believe, knew the true value of the world of the imagination and were thus superior to the English. Yet, in Yeats's day, the great ancient Celtic mythological literature of Ireland, which predated both Christianity and the English conquest, was mostly unread and forgotten by all but a small number of antiquarian scholars. But, as the poet came to recognize, elements of its fundamental beliefs in magic and the supernatural could still be found in the fairy tales and legends with which he himself was familiar from his childhood in the Sligo countryside. The two years between the ages of seven and nine that he had spent with relatives in this remote rural area had brought him into contact with local native Irish people, whose belief in fairies and supernatural happenings remained vivid and certain, untouched by colonization and the developments of English culture and education. The stories they told to this receptive and sensitive little boy took a firm hold on his imagination and would resurface in his poetry and prose throughout most of his adult life. Although these fairy tales and old legends may seem a far cry from Irish politics and the need for Irish Home Rule, both O'Leary and Yeats saw this ancient culture as the essential foundation of Irish national identity. The passionate, heroic, imaginative world of Celtic mythology was one with which, they believed, all Irish people needed to reconnect. Only by recognizing its profound connection with their country's once great past could this long repressed nation achieve a true sense of solidarity. On that basis could be built a newly regenerated and free Ireland with the strength and confidence to govern itself successfully.

O'Leary had returned to Ireland at the beginning of 1885, and Yeats probably met him for the first time shortly afterwards. Their relationship developed over the following year, leading to Yeats's intensive period of reading and the development of his ideas about cultural nationalism, myth, and legend. It seems likely, then, that these ideas fed directly into his poem "The Stolen Child," which was, presumably, written some time in the second half of 1886, as the poem was first published in the *Irish Monthly* in December of that year. The poem appeared again two years later in the anthology he compiled and published, *Fairy and Folk Tales of the Irish Peasantry*. In his introduction to this collection of stories (mostly tales recalled from his own childhood), he wrote that in the best of them could be found what he called "the innermost heart of the Celt."

With this background in mind, interpretation of "The Stolen Child" acquires an extra dimension. The poet's use of real Irish place names, which might seem slightly incongruous in a fairy story, can be seen to serve a purpose. By firmly rooting the realm of magic, myth, and legend in the tangible, recognizable everyday world, Yeats is reminding his readers of what he saw as the fundamental truth of Irish identity: the possession of a vivid and imaginative grasp of a deeper and more significant knowledge lying beyond the world of surface appearances. The phrase "*world's more full of weeping*" gains an added significance, too. Although the child is still too young to understand it, as he grows into adulthood he will become aware of the troubled state of the country where he has been born, the legacy of its centuries of unrest still affecting the minds and actions of his contemporaries. The only valid means of escape from this continuing unrest, the poem suggests, is to establish a link with the realm of the supernatural. Even the rather disturbing elements of the poem, both in structure (line lengths, rhythm, and rhyme) and meaning (the doubts set up at the end about how happy the child will be to have left his home) can be seen as Yeats's attempt to shake his readers out of their complacency. Yeats's fairyland is not a comfortable place, but it is, he seems to be suggesting, a world whose existence his readers need to acknowledge. By confronting all its contradictions and uncertainties, they may reawaken that vital faculty of imagination that he saw as essential to Irish national identity.

Source: Harriet Devine, Critical Essay on "The Stolen Child," in *Poetry for Students*, Gale, Cengage Learning, 2010.

"IRONY, REALISM, AND HUMOUR ALMOST ALWAYS ARE INVOKED, SINGLY OR IN COMBINATION, TO STOP THE POEM SHORT OF THE WORST EXCESSES OF IDEALIZING OR SENTIMENTALIZING OF CHILDHOOD."

Desmond Pacey

In the following excerpt, Pacey discusses the progression of Yeats's ideas on children from the romantic to the realistic.

Yeats' multiplicity of powerful poems about sexual love, old age, and Irish society has distracted attention from his poetic treatment of children. Apart from a number of articles and essays on "Among Schoolchildren", the subject remains literally unexplored. And yet four of Yeats' finest poems—"A Prayer for My Son", "A Prayer for My Daughter", and "The Dolls", and especially "Among Schoolchildren" (which many readers consider his greatest single poem)—are specifically about children, and there are many references to children and childhood scattered throughout his *Collected Poems*.

The strongest single impression with which one comes away from reading Yeats' poems on children, and his references to them, is of the consistency, clearsightedness, and realism of his attitudes. Although he may have been, as he has said, a Romantic writing when Romanticism had reached its most extravagant phase, he is seldom if ever prone to Romantic exaggeration in his treatment of childhood—nor, for that matter, to any other exaggerations. Attitudes to children in literature—as they are intelligently discussed, for example in Peter Coveney's *Poor Monkey* or in Leslie Fiedler's essay "The Eye of Innocence" in his *No! in Thunder*—have generally fallen into three groups: the eighteenth-century rationalist view, which saw the child as a small adult to be regulated as quickly as possible into rational and moral perfection; the Puritan Christian view, which saw the child as a miserable sinner in desperate need of salvation; and the Romantic view, expressed most clearly by Blake and Wordsworth but given premonitory utterance by Vaughan and Traherne in the seventeenth century, which saw the child as innocent, intuitively wise, spontaneous, happy, perceptive, sensitive, or "trailing clouds of glory." Of these three attitudes, it need scarcely be said, Yeats' comes closest to the Romantic, but he is singularly free from its more extreme manifestations.

This is the more remarkable when we recall that Yeats came to maturity when the Romantic cult of the child was at its apogee of decadence, the last decades of the nineteenth century. Of those decades, Coveney writes: "Writers began to draw on the general sympathy for childhood that had been diffused; but for patently subjective reasons, their interest in childhood serves not as a means for integration of experience, but creates a barrier of nostalgia and regret between childhood and the potential responses of adult life. The child becomes a means of escape from the pressures of adult adjustment..." (*Poor Monkey*). Marie Corelli, J. M. Barrie, A. E. Housman, and Hugh Walpole all provide examples of this escapist tendency; in Yeats—at least in the mature Yeats—it is found not at all. Where, as in "Among Schoolchildren", he is momentarily tempted into this self-pitying nostalgia, he rapidly overcomes it by self-depreciating irony, and goes on to one of the most triumphant examples in literary history of the "integration of experience", the famous final apostrophe of that poem.

As we might expect, it is in his early poems that Yeats most nearly approximates the stock Romantic attitudes towards children. Even here, however, the stress is not so much on the more doubtful of the Romantic concepts—innocence, wisdom, religious sensibility—as on the more observable, provable features of childhood: its fragility and vulnerability. The first reference is in the first poem in the first section of *Collected Poems,* and it is to "the stammering schoolboy" who awkwardly reads aloud in class some story of heroic adventure. This first reference is characteristic and indicative: Yeats was always aware of the pressures which orthodox systems of education impose upon the child. The boy's stammer is an objective correlative which sums up all his nervousness, his shyness, his sense of being entangled in some world he never made; and the emphasis is not on the boy's inherent superiority to adults but on his sense of inferiority, even if it is implied that that sense of inferiority is baseless. (In a late poem, "A Dialogue of Self and Soul",

Yeats was to enshrine this same perception in the memorable phrase "the ignominy of boyhood".)

The next reference to childhood, however, is not so admirable, and is one of the few examples of Yeats' falling into the trap of Romantic exaggeration. The allusion occurs in that most awkward and ugly of all Yeats' poems, "Ephemera", and it reads "when the poor tired child, Passion, falls asleep". In the background of that line lie many of the clichés of Victorian poetry and fiction, those scenes in which pitiful children die or innocent children fall asleep while maternal tears cascade upon the pillowslip.

Another Victorian stereotype, that of the sensitive child who must escape from the harsh world of reality to some land of faery or Treasure Island of romance, occurs in "The Stolen Child", with its monotonous, sentimental refrain:

> Come away, O human child!
> To the waters and the wild
> With a faery, hand in hand,
> For the world's more full of weeping
> Than you can understand.

Even in this weak poem, however, the sentimentality is checked by irony: Yeats makes the faeries faintly ridiculous by having them whisper in the ears of "slumbering trout" to "Give them unquiet dreams", by having them lean from ferns "that drop their tears / over the young streams", and by having them foolishly congratulate themselves on the fact that "The solemn-eyed" child will

> ... hear no more the lowing
> Of the calves on the warm hillside
> Or the kettle on the hob
> Sing peace into his breast,
> Or see the brown mice bob
> Round and round the oatmeal-chest.

This implied endorsement of the pleasures of the real world, indeed, transposes the whole effect of the poem, and what began as a piece of sentimental escapism ends in an acceptance of familiar, domestic reality.

The Romantic concept of the spontaneous, happy child finds expression in "The Meditation of the Old Fisherman", but here again it is decisively modified. The old fisherman who sees the waves "dance by my feet like children at play" and dreams nostalgically of the days "When I was a boy with never a crack in my heart", is guilty of the falsification of experience, of deliberate self-delusion. But the poem is a dramatic utterance: it is the fisherman, not Yeats, who asserts that "the waves were more gay", the Junes warmer, the herring more plentiful, and the girls more beautiful in the halcyon days of his boyhood.

Yeats himself came closer to falsification in "The Ballad of Moll Magee", one of the many Romantic and Victorian poems dealing with the death of a child and the woes of its grief-stricken mother. Perhaps it was a consciousness of this fact that led Yeats to dismiss this poem, in a letter to John O'Leary, as a "mere experiment". Once again, however, romantic illusions are not allowed full play: the "little childer" to whom Moll tells her story are not romantic innocents but very real sadists—she has to begin and end her story by begging them not to throw stones at her!

In a rather similar fashion, Yeats manages to redeem "A Cradle Song" from the excesses of that popular nineteenth-century genre, the sentimental lullaby. Here, however, it is humour, rather than realism, which is the saving salt. The angels who stoop above the infant's bed are said to be doing so because "They weary of trooping / With the whimpering dead." Too charitably, perhaps, I take that as a bit of black humour—an attitude, however, to which Yeats himself leads some confirmation by the explicit humorous gaiety of the second stanza:

> God's laughing in Heaven
> To see you so good,
> The Sailing Seven
> Are gay with his mood.

After such comic relief, we are almost ready to swallow the unabashed sentimentality of the third and final stanza:

> I sigh that kiss you,
> For I must own
> That I shall miss you
> When you have grown.

There is a matter-of-factness about that stanza, a kind of honest platitudinousness, which does something to redeem it. We know it could be so much worse in, say, Coventry Patmore.

There is at least one instance, however, where Yeats is guilty of what Coveney calls the late nineteenth-century practice of drawing on "the general sympathy for childhood", or of what I. A. Richards might have called using the child merely to elicit a stock response. It occurs in one of Yeats' most flatulent poems, "The Lover Tells of the Rose in his Heart". There, declaring that "All things uncomely and broken, all things worn out and old" are "wronging your image that blossoms a rose in the deep of my heart", he suddenly, for no apparent reason except that the weeping child was a guaranteed source of facile emotion in the late Victorian period, brings in "The cry of a child by the roadway". The mature Yeats would never have allowed himself to indulge in such an unmotivated and unspecific allusion.

There are some other references to children in the early poems of Yeats, but they add nothing to what we have said of his attitudes. In these early poems we see Yeats accepting in their main outlines the Romantic and occasionally even Victorian attitudes towards children, but always modifying them to some extent and usually to a decisive extent. Irony, realism, and humour almost always are invoked, singly or in combination, to stop the poem short of the worst excesses of idealizing or sentimentalizing of childhood. In the poems of Yeats' maturity, the poems written after 1900, the relics of the Romantic or Victorian stereotypes are very rare indeed: there is a new honesty, a new realism, in both the content and style of his allusions to children. At the same time, the main ingredient of his attitude, his tender concern for childish fragility and vulnerability, persists and is indeed strengthened.

The first hint of the mature manner comes in that poem which in so many ways marks a turning-point in Yeats' poetic career, "Adam's Curse". It comes as a mere aside, when the "beautiful mild woman" replies:

> "To be born woman is to know—
> Although they do not talk of it at school—
> That we must labour to be beautiful."

The hint is not so much in what is said—although the reference to the obliviousness of orthodox education to the real conditions of human life reflects one of Yeats' deepest convictions, and points forward to "Among Schoolchildren"—as in the tone and manner of expression. The tone is no longer rhetorical, nostalgic, or sentimental: rather it is sarcastic, off-hand, mordant, and dry. The words are not richly sensuous nor in any sense ornamental—they are the words of ordinary speech, in the order and rhythm of speech. There is implied a whole effort to get away from conventional attitudes and opinions, and to see things as they really are. The mood is closer to Swift than to Tennyson.

This far more thoroughgoing realism, verging now towards bitterness as in the early poems it had sometimes come dangerously close to sentimentality, is found in "The Coming of Wisdom with Time". In this poem it is implied that, if childhood is indeed a time of relative happiness, its happiness is deceptive and treacherous:

> Though leaves are many, the root is one;
> Through all the lying days of my youth
> I swayed my leaves and flowers in the sun;
> Now I may wither into the truth.

We have here a strong premonition of the danger against which Yeats was to struggle—but struggle successfully—in all his late, great poems about childhood: the danger of exaggerating the tragic dimension of human experience, of indulging in easy cynicism.

The balance tips ominously towards facile cynicism in the pair of poems "To a Child Dancing in the Wind" and "Two Years Later". Here the innocence of the child is seen rather as ignorance: the vulnerable child can dance and tumble out her hair in spontaneous joy only because she does not recognize her own vulnerability and the power of the destructive forces which surround her. To accept life, to see the world as ultimately beneficent, is to indulge in dreams; the reality is suffering and the end is tragedy:

> O you will take whatever's offered
> And dream that all the world's a friend,
> Suffer as your mother suffered,
> Be as broken in end.

Yeats, however, recognized this danger of facile cynicism in one of the best stanzas of one of his best poems, "A Prayer for my Daughter":

> My mind, because the minds that I have loved,
> The sort of beauty that I have approved,
> Prosper but little, has dried up of late,
> Yet knows that to be choked with hate
> May well be of all evil chances chief.
> If there's no hatred in a mind
> Assault and battery of the wind
> Can never tear the linnet from the leaf.

This poem illustrates how Yeats did succeed in making his best poems about children a means to the integration of experience. His sense of the little girl's vulnerability, so powerfully expressed in the early references to a howling storm, the levelling wind, the screaming Atlantic gale, the flooded stream, the frenzied drum and "the murderous innocence of the sea", is complemented by his later affirmation of the values which can cushion her against the shocks of disaster: modest beauty, natural kindness, courtesy, self-reliance, custom, ceremony, and the "radical innocence" of the human soul. Here Yeats, in his emphasis upon order, discipline, and self-restraint, comes closer to the eighteenth-century conception of the child than to the Romantic conception: the child is seen as a delicate growth which needs the shelter of social and civilized values, rather than as a beautiful blossom which society will warp and wither.

If "A Prayer for my Daughter" illustrates the greater balance and profundity of the mature Yeats' treatment of the child, it also illustrates the advances in his mature style. The predominantly run-on lines of the first two stanzas create an effect of frightening speed; then the poem, as if by a supreme effort of will, a deliberate refusal to be stampeded into panic, slows down to a grave and dignified pace. The image of the wind, introduced in the first line, recurs several times in the first and second stanzas, in the "assault and battery of the wind" in the seventh stanza, in the "old bellows full of angry wind" in the eighth, in the "every windy quarter howl" in the ninth—and is conspicuous by its absence in the tenth and last, where the laurel tree of custom spreads its branches in a windless sky. Thus the wind, which in the first stanza was seen as all powerful and triumphantly destructive—what protection is there in a cradle-hood and coverlid against a wind that can level haystacks and roofs?—is gradually cut down, first, to the figure of an angry but impotent boxer or blustering petty criminal, next to the ridiculous form of an old bellows, then to a silly howler that can frighten no one, and finally is stilled altogether. Counterpointing the diminishing image of the wind is the steadily enlarging image of the tree: in the first stanza "Gregory's wood" is dismissed as "no obstacle" to the wind; in the second stanza the branches of the elm scream and dance in agony; in the sixth stanza the growing girl is seen as "a flourishing hidden tree" and as "some green laurel / Rooted in one dear perpetual place"; in the seventh stanza, the tree has become a safe refuge for the linnet, which the wind cannot dislodge; and in the final stanza the laurel tree, proudly spreading its branches, has defeated the wind entirely. The poem, like all Yeats' greatest poems, is a profoundly humanistic, life-affirming document. The wind, by the end of the poem, has come to symbolize all those evil forces which assault humanity, the tree to symbolize all the human values which staunchly withstand them; and there is no doubt which has triumphed.

"A Prayer for my Son" is at first glance less humanistic and more religious. Again an infant is being threatened by evil forces, but this time the forces are supernatural—"devilish things"—rather than natural, and, accordingly, supernatural powers are invoked to protect the child. "A strong ghost" is bidden to stand at the head of his bed, and Christ, the all-powerful God who has nevertheless known what it is to be a helpless infant, is asked to do the bidding. The religious figures of the poem, however, are very human persons, and the poem is at least as much a tribute to the fidelity of human love as a plea for divine intervention. Christ, "wailing upon a woman's knee", is said to have known "All that worst ignominy / Of flesh and bone", and His parents are deliberately referred to as "a woman and a man", who, when He was hunted by Herod's servants, protected Him "with human love."

This poem is a further instance of the tact and skill with which Yeats manages his material, so disposing and modulating it that it is saved from excess. The experience upon which the poem is based, detailed by Yeats on page 16 of the 1962 edition of *A Vision*, is, to say the least, bizarre, and to a sceptical mind plainly incredible:

> A little after my son's birth I came home to confront my wife with the statement "Michael is ill". A smell of burnt feathers had announced what she and the doctor had hidden. When regular communication was near its end and my work of study and arrangement begun, I was told that henceforth the Frustrators would attack my health and that of my children, and one afternoon, knowing from the smell of burnt feathers that one of my children would be ill within three hours, I felt before I could recover self-control the medieval helpless horror at witchcraft. I can discover no apparent difference between a natural and supernatural smell, except that the natural smell comes and goes gradually while the other is suddenly there and then as suddenly gone.

This does not seem a very promising basis for a tolerable twentieth-century poem, but Yeats brings it off. He does so by introducing into the strange episode so much of the familiar world. The references to the child turning in bed, to his morning meal, to the mother's very human need of sleep, to Christ's wailing upon His mother's knee, to Joseph and Mary hurrying like any anxious parents "through the smooth and rough"—these references anchor the poem in the ordinary world and give credibility and human relevance to an experience which we might otherwise reject as utterly fantastic.

Contributing to the same effect is the diction of the poem. Throughout, with one or two conspicuous exceptions to act as foils, Yeats uses the simplest, strongest, most familiar words. Think, for example, of what a subtle but fatal alteration of effect would have resulted from the use of "mighty" rather than "strong" as the adjective for the ghost, of "wail" rather than "cry", of "need of sleep" rather than "fill of sleep". Words like "fist", "devilish things", "simplest want", "knee", "flesh and bone", "servants", "a woman and a man" all humanize and domesticate the otherwise *outré* situation.

Indeed, the more closely one examines this poem the more one is impressed by its subtlety, ambiguity, and profundity. It is called a prayer, and apostrophizes Christ, but it ends by praising human love and by affirming that it was by the patient fidelity of his human parents that Christ himself was saved. It is, thus, a prayer that provides its own answer: we are felt with the clear implication that the child's strongest defence against whatever devilish things assail him is not any strong ghost nor supernatural agent but his own natural, human parents. "A Prayer for my Son" is only an apparent exception to Yeats' persistent humanism.

Equally humanistic in its effect is "The Dolls". Here again is a poem which far transcends the occasion (the rumoured pregnancy of a mistress) which is said to have prompted it. It is a satire on those who prefer the deadly perfection of dolls to the lively imperfection of children, and it is closely related to one of the themes of "Among Schoolchildren": that true meaning is to be found in organic growth rather than in static perfection. The dolls, because they do not decay with age (one of them, "being kept for show", has "lived" for many generations), and because they do not cry and defecate, think that they are superior to the human baby which their makers have suddenly produced in their midst: one of them calls the infant an insult, another calls it "a noisy and filthy thing" which will disgrace them. With a beautiful twist of irony, Yeats has the mother of the human child accept the view of the dolls, and humbly apologize to her husband for her fecundity: "My dear, my dear, O dear, / It was an accident." This, of course, suggests another of Yeats' persistent themes, that many good things come by chance, that wisdom is a butterfly and not a gloomy bird of prey.

This poem is so full of irony and ambiguity that it is odd that recent critics, so fond of these qualities in an age made tolerable only by ironic ambiguity of vision, have not paid more respectful attention to it. The proud dolls are "in the doll-maker's house": in other words, for all their pride they are only creatures of a creature, occupants of a house only on the sufferance of its rightful owners. Although they accuse the infant of being noisy, one of them bawls and the other "out-screams the whole shelf"; although the dolls accuse the child of filthiness, they are "kept for show" and thus owe any cleanliness they may claim to the efforts of those who keep them; although they feel superior to humanity, their proudest boast is that "There's not a *man* can report / Evil of this place"; and although they think they are so very knowing, they have no knowledge of the generation of children and think that the man and woman have merely *brought* the child here. The woman, instead of being proud of her capacity to generate true life, allows the dolls to convince her that her child is somehow disgraceful, and apologizes to her equally troubled husband. The relevance of all this, at a time when some people are ready to elevate the computer over the human brain, or the electronic media over the humanly imperfect book, scarcely needs pointing out. Nor do I need to describe in any detail how the poem illustrates the balanced nature of the mature Yeats' attitude to childhood: children *are* noisy and filthy, but they are also alive, and thus can grow as dolls can not.

If "The Dolls" has suffered undue neglect at the hands of the critics, "Among Schoolchildren" has suffered the opposite fate. So many essays in exegesis have been devoted to it that, if it were not so central to my theme, there would be a temptation to omit it altogether. Discussion, however, will be comparatively brief.

With all due deference to the insights of Cleanth Brooks, John Wain, Frank Kermode and Thomas Parkinson, I believe that the single most illuminating essay on this poem is "'Among Schoolchildren' and the Education of the Irish Spirit" by Donald T. Torchiana in the book *In*

Excited Reverie. By proving that Yeats was endorsing the system of education practised and promoted by Maria Montessori, Professor Torchiana has disposed of many misinterpretations of the poem, and has permitted us to see its structure in a new light.

John Wain (in *Interpretations*, 1955) asserts that "the poem breaks into two halves", that Yeats "abandons the circular technique; after the halfway mark, there is no recurrence of the school-room, the children, the nun, the personal situation." He concludes: "Instead of circling back on itself, the poem moves forward, in the form of a bridge, then suddenly stops with no opposite shore in sight. It is not a bridge after all but a pier. It leads nowhere; its purpose is to afford us, before we turn and retrace our steps, a bleak and chastening glimpse into the deep waters." Almost every clause in the above series can be factually refuted. What has led Mr. Wain astray, perhaps, is that he has too narrowly conceived the subject of the poem, which he begins his essay by declaring to be "the relationship or interpenetration of matter and spirit." If one looks for a straightforward analysis of such an abstract problem as that the poem may seem to break into two, or to lead nowhere.

The subject of "Among Schoolchildren" is what its title leads us to expect it will be: a series of observations, memories, and meditations of the poet on finding himself among a class of schoolchildren. The schoolroom, the nun, the children, the classwork, the singing and the "smiling public man" are there all the time; if we are in any danger of forgetting that, Yeats jogs our memory by mentioning or alluding to one or other or several of them at intervals throughout the poem. The schoolroom, for example, is described in the first stanza, is implied in the second by the "harsh reproof", is referred to in the "there" of the third stanza, is implied by the "old scarecrow" of the fourth and "that shape with sixty or more winters on its head" in the fifth, is suggested by the reference to Aristotle birching Alexander in the sixth and to the nuns and mothers in the seventh, and is quite clearly present by contrast in the references to labour and "blear-eyed wisdom out of midnight oil" in the eighth and last. It would be possible, but impossibly tiresome to do the same kind of analysis for all the major ingredients of that first stanza. The poem is very intricately integrated.

Its structure *is* circular, but circular in a somewhat unusual way. The first stanza is the hub of the wheel; the succeeding stanzas are spokes radiating from this hub; the connections between the stanzas from the rim of the wheel; the final stanza returns to the hub. The middle six stanzas of the poem do indeed fall into two linked sequences, but the poem does not break in half. Stanzas II to IV relate to the particular case of Maud Gonne, who was once a child like these but is now an ageing woman; stanzas V to VII generalize this problem of change and decay and refer it for possible solutions to theories of reincarnation, philosophy, and religion; but there is no abrupt break between stanzas IV and V, since the "comfortable kind of old scarecrows" of IV is obviously "that shape / With sixty or more winters on its head" of V.

There is not space in this essay for a detailed explication of "Among Schoolchildren", but its implications for Yeats' attitude towards children may be briefly summarized. That an orthodox and repressive educational system was destructive of childish joy and spontaneity was a commonplace of Romantic discussions of childhood, perhaps the most memorable expression of it being Blake's "The School Boy":

I love to rise in a summer morn,
When the birds sing on every tree:
The distant huntsman winds his horn,
And the skylark sings with me.
O! what sweet company!

But to go to school in a summer morn,
O! it drives all joy away,
Under a cruel eye outworn
The little ones spend the day
In sighing and dismay....

O! father and mother, if buds are nipp'd
And blossoms blown away...
How shall the summer arise in joy,
Or the summer fruits appear?

Yeats accepted this Romantic view, but instead of carrying it to the extreme of declaring, as Blake did, that "there is no use in education", he looked about for a form of education that would release and nourish the child's potentialities rather than inhibit them. His speeches to the Senate, and to the Irish Literary Society on November 30, 1925, make it clear that he saw the nearest approximation to such an ideal education in the modern Italian system as set forth by Montessori and Gentile. In Maria Montessori's book, *The Montessori Method*, there are many passages which suggest the final stanza of "Among Schoolchildren". Here are a few examples:

> If any educational act is to be efficacious, it will be only that which tends to help toward the complete unfolding of this life. To be thus helpful it is necessary rigorously to avoid the arrest of spontaneous movements and the imposition of arbitrary tasks.

> By education must be understood the active help given to the normal expansion of the life of the child. The child is a body which grows, and a soul which develops—these two forms, physiological and psychic, have one eternal font, life itself. We must neither mar nor stifle the mysterious powers which lie within these two forms of growth, but we must await from them the manifestations which we know will succeed one another.

> The educational conception of this age must be solely that of aiding the psychophysical development of the individual.

The whole of the Montessori method, in fact, is based on the premise that schoolwork—"labour"—can be joyful, "blossoming or dancing", as witness this description of a child learning to write:

> The child who wrote a word for the first time was full of excited joy. Indeed no one could escape from the noisy manifestations of the little one. He would call everyone to see, and if there were some who did not go, he ran to take hold of their clothes, forcing them to come and see. We all had to go and stand about the written work to admire the marvel, and to unite our exclamations of surprise with the joyous cries of the fortunate author.

Such are the ideas that underlie "Among Schoolchildren", which is primarily, although by no means exclusively, a poem about the education of children. Yeats begins the poem by describing, approvingly, an ideal form of education in a model school; then, realistically, he is struck with the realization that no system of education can save us from the process of ageing; he glances at theories of reincarnation, speculations of philosophers, and the consolations of religion, only to dismiss them as inadequate attempts to find permanence amidst flux; and then in the final triumphant stanza he accepts and glories in the fact of flux, seeing the cycle of spontaneous life itself as the one permanent and self-sufficing thing. Work becomes joy when it is performed voluntarily, spontaneously, and rhythmically; life becomes joyful when body and soul function in harmony; true beauty is a spontaneous development and not something to be desperately sought after; wisdom arises from our normal, free involvement with our environment rather than by other- or self-imposed discipline; human life is not a long slow descent from childish innocence to senile despair but a cycle like the life-cycle of a tree, with each segment of the cycle having its own rightness, its own function; we cannot abstract that which performs the cycle from the cycle itself, any more than we can have a true dance without a dancer or a dancer without a dance. "Among Schoolchildren" is a poem of humanistic affirmation, but it is an affirmation made only after all the negative factors have been looked at squarely and long.

Another facet of Yeats' humanistic affirmation which is involved with his treatment of children is his concern with the continuity of a human tradition. We have already glanced at this concern in reference to "A Prayer for my Daughter", but it is a quite frequent theme in his later poetry. In the introductory poem to *Responsibilities* he movingly regrets his own failure, up to that time, to produce offspring: "I have no child, I have nothing but a book, / Nothing but that to prove your blood and mine." But perhaps the most poignant and powerful passage on this matter occurs in the fourth section of his "Meditations in Time of Civil War". There he does not suggest, as the lines just quoted from *Responsibilities* may be felt to suggest, that the mere generation of children is a guarantee of continuity. Yeats' dominant attitude, for all his occasional descents into bleak despair, is affirmative, but it is by no means a facile affirmation:

> Having inherited a vigorous mind
> From my old fathers, I must nourish
>   dreams
> And leave a woman and a man behind
> As vigorous of mind, and yet it seems
> Life scarce can cast a fragrance on the
>   wind,
> Scarce spread a glory to the morning
>   beams,
> But the torn petals strew the garden plot;
> And there's but common greenness
>   after that.
>
> And what if my descendants lose the
>   flower
> Through natural declension of the soul,

Through too much business with the passing hour,
Through too much play or marriage with a fool?
May this laborious stair and this stark tower
Become a roofless rain that the owl
May build in the cracked masonry and cry
Her desolation to the desolate sky.

A similar realism is found in Yeats' reminiscences of his own boyhood. The reminiscences in his poetry are few, and he never indulges in the facile nostalgia which was so common an ingredient in Romantic and Victorian literature. Instead of idealizing his childhood associates or himself as a child, he gives us specific memories, portraits which show the warts and all. In "Under Saturn", for example, he writes:

… my horse's flanks are spurred
By childish memories of an old cross Pollexfen,
And of a Middleton, whose name you never heard,
And of a red-haired Yeats whose looks, although he died
Before my time, seem like a vivid memory.
You heard that labouring man who had served my
people. He said
Upon the open road, near to the Sligo quay—
No, no, not said, but cried it out—'You have come again,
And surely after twenty years it was time to come'.
I am thinking of a child's vow sworn in vain
Never to leave that valley his fathers called their home.

Instead of looking back to his childhood regretfully, as did so many of the Romantics, and using nostalgia as an evasion of adult responsibilities, Yeats in his sixties declares that he has still all the faculties he had as a boy: uses his own youth, in other words, not as a saddle but as a spur. In "The Towers" he declares:

Never had I more excited, passionate, fantastical
Imagination, nor an ear and eye
That more expected the impossible—
No, not in boyhood when with rod and fly,
Or the humbler worm, I climbed Ben Bulben's back

And had the livelong summer day to spend.

Rather than as a source of boasting, he is inclined to use memories of his boyhood as a means to humility, as in the self-depreciation of the middle stanza of "At Algeciras":

Often at evening when a boy
Would I carry to a friend—
Hoping more substantial joy
Did an older mind commend—
Not such as are in Newton's metaphor,
But actual shells of Ross's level shore.

This note of self-depreciation, balanced it is true with a certain measure of self-approbation, is also struck in "What Then?" the poem Yeats as an elderly man wrote for the boys of the high school he had attended. In its irony and ambiguity, the fine balance it strikes between humanistic affirmation and an awareness of the possible ultimate futility of all human effort, its realistic clearsightedness and yet its persistent refusal to be fully daunted, this poem makes a fitting conclusion for this essay:

His chosen comrades thought at school
He must grow a famous man;
He thought the same and lived by rule,
All his twenties crammed with toil,
'What then?' sang Plato's ghost. 'When then?'

Everything he wrote was read,
After certain years he won
Sufficient money for his need,
Friends that have been friends indeed;
'What then?' sang Plato's ghost. 'What then?'
All his happier dreams came true—
A small old house, wife, daughter, son,
Grounds where plum and cabbage grew,
Poets and Wits about him drew;
'What then?' sang Plato's ghost. 'When then?'

'The work is done;' grown old he thought,
'According to my boyish plan;
Let the fools rage, I swerved in naught,
Something to perfection brought';
But louder sang the ghost, 'What then?'

To sum up, as is proved by this and the other poems that have been quoted or alluded to, Yeats' attitude towards children was not rationalistic, or Puritan, or romantic, but profoundly humanistic and realistic. Aware of human strength, he was also aware of human weaknesses; aware of our reach for perfection, he was also aware of the limitations of our grasp of perfection when seen *sub specie oeternitatis.* He saw the child not as a species apart, but as one who shared the constant vulnerability and the occasional splendour of the whole human race.

Source: Desmond Pacey, "Children in the Poetry of Yeats," in *Dalhousie Review*, Vol. 50, No. 2, Summer 1970, pp. 233–48.

SOURCES

Allison, Jonathan, "Introduction," in *Poetry for Young People*, edited by Jonathon Allison and illustrated by Glenn Harrington, Sterling, 2002, p. 5.

Hall, James, and Martin Steinmann, eds., *The Permanence of Yeats*, Macmillan, 1950, p. 124.

Lynd, Robert, "Old and New Masters," in *W. B. Yeats: The Critical Heritage*, edited by A. Norman Jeffares, Routledge & Kegan Paul, 1977, p. 222; originally published in *Old and New Masters*, J. M. Dent & Sons, 1919.

Pethica, James, "Yeats, Folklore, and Irish Legend," in *The Cambridge Companion to W. B. Yeats*, edited by Marjorie Howes and John Kelly, Cambridge University Press, 2006, pp. 132, 133.

Philip, Neil, "Introduction," in *Fairy Tales of Ireland*, by William Butler Yeats, Delacorte Press, 1990, p. 10.

Reid, B. L., "William Butler Yeats," in *Dictionary of Literary Biography*, Vol. 19, *British Poets, 1880–1914*, edited by Donald E. Stanford, Gale Research, 1983, p. 3.

Rosenthal, M. L., *Running to Paradise: Yeats's Poetic Art*, Oxford University Press, 1997, p. 149.

"The Trooping Fairies: The Changelings," in *Irish Fairy and Folk Tales*, edited by William Butler Yeats, Barnes & Noble Books, 1993, p. 65.

Yeats, William Butler, *Prefaces and Introductions*, edited by William H. O'Donnell, Macmillan Press, 1988, pp. 8, 10, 12.

———, "The Stolen Child," in *The Collected Poems of W. B. Yeats*, edited by Richard J. Finneran, Scribner Paperback Poetry, 1996, pp. 18–19.

FURTHER READING

Brennan, Eilis, and Sandra Gillespie, *Nationalism and Unionism: From Union to Partition*, Cambridge University Press, 1996.

> One of the Perspective series of student texts, this book helps students to understand what shaped the culture and socio-economic structures of Ireland.

Brown, Terence, *The Life of W. B. Yeats*, Blackwell, 1999.

> This critical biography describes the poet's engagement with occultism and spiritualism, his pursuit of power through institutions, and his social concerns as an artist and citizen.

Foster, R. F., *W. B. Yeats: A Life*, Oxford University Press, 1997.

> In this comprehensive look at the private and public life of Yeats, including his political, personal, and literary associations, Foster draws upon previously unavailable documents to present new information. The book also provides illustrations and photographs.

Howes, Marjorie, and John Kelly, eds., *The Cambridge Companion to W. B. Yeats*, Cambridge University Press, 2006.

> This international collection of essays chronologically examines Yeats's poetry, drama, and prose in terms of themes, political and social influences, and spiritual quest. This compilation is suitable for first-time readers as well as researchers.

Jeffares, A. Norman, ed., *W. B. Yeats: The Critical Heritage*, Routledge & Kegan Paul, 1977.

> This book is a collection of over one hundred excerpts of criticism and reviews of Yeats's work, taken from books, journals, newspapers, and letters published during his lifetime.

Moody, T. W., and F. X. Martin, *The Course of Irish History*, 4th ed., Roberts Rinehart, 2002.

> A collection of twenty-one essays by leading historians that takes into account the role that the geography of Ireland has played in its history as well as the people and events. This work is a compressed and highly readable history of an ancient land.

This Is Just to Say

WILLIAM CARLOS WILLIAMS
1934

"This Is Just to Say," a slice-of-life narrative, was written by William Carlos Williams in 1934. The title segues into a brief note from the poet to his wife, telling her that he has eaten the plums that were in the refrigerator. The purpose of this notification is to apologize for eating them when he knew that she was probably saving them for breakfast. However, he cannot resist telling her how good they were. The topic is trivial and domestic, but it fits with Williams's belief that poetry should be found in everyday life rather than major events and should focus on an object—in this case, the plums. Typical of Williams's spare style, "This Is Just to Say" contains only twenty-eight words arranged into three quatrains. Nonetheless, it manages to provide a snapshot of a relationship and raises questions about forgiveness and being considerate. This poem was one of the poet's personal favorites and has been popular with readers. It is considered an excellent example of an imagist poem. "This Is Just to Say" can be found in various anthologies of American or imagist poetry, including the book *This Is Just to Say: Poems of Apology and Forgiveness,* in which children ages nine to twelve have written their own poems of apology and gotten back some charming replies. Of course, the poem is included in collections of Williams's poetry, such as *The Collected Poems of William Carlos Williams, Vol. 1: 1909–1939,* which can be found in many libraries and bookstores.

Williams Carlos Williams (Alfred Eisenstaedt / Time Life Pictures / Getty Images)

AUTHOR BIOGRAPHY

William Carlos Williams was born on September 17, 1883, in Rutherford, New Jersey, to an English father and a Puerto Rican mother. Williams's education was varied and cosmopolitan; he initially attended the Rutherford public schools, then was sent to schools in Geneva and Paris for two years. He finished his secondary schooling in New York City at Horace Mann. In 1902, he enrolled at the University of Pennsylvania, first in the School of Dentistry and then transferred to the School of Medicine. After graduation in 1906, he did internships at hospitals in New York City, then went to Leipzig, Germany, to study pediatrics. He also used his time in Europe to travel throughout France, the Netherlands, Spain, and England. In 1910, he returned to Rutherford and began a medical practice that would continue until 1951.

It was during his time in Pennsylvania, however, that Williams's literary life was ignited. He befriended writers Ezra Pound and Hilda Doolittle (called H. D.) and painter Charles Demuth; through their influence he became part of the imagist movement. His first book of poetry, *Poems*, was published in 1909. He published two more books in the next eight years and became involved with a group of avant-garde New York writers known as The Others, and this involvement made him a central figure in the modernist movement.

Although Williams continued to publish poems, plays, and novels regularly, his reputation was overshadowed by Pound and T. S. Eliot. Nonetheless, he was known as a writer's writer among noted authors of the day. In the 1930s, his poetry garnered some public attention, but it was not until 1946 that he became widely known as an important figure on the literary scene. It was then that he published *Paterson I*, the first of a five-part epic poem that focused on everyday American society and truly showcased Williams's unique perspective and style. In 1952, he was asked to be a consultant to the Library of Congress, but the offer was withdrawn because of accusations of communist affiliations. The honor was later restored, but not renewed for the following year.

Williams's later life was marked by literary recognition and failing health. In 1948, he suffered his first heart attack, followed by a series of strokes over the next seven years. The Library of Congress incident put him in a hospital to receive treatment for depression. He received numerous awards and honorary degrees through the years, including the National Book Award in 1950. Posthumously in 1963, he received the Pulitzer Prize for his *Pictures from Brueghel and Other Poems* and the Gold Medal for Poetry from the National Institute of Arts and Letters.

Williams was married to Florence (Flossie) Herman in 1912, and they had two sons, William Eric, born in 1912, and Paul Herman, born in 1914. Williams died on March 4, 1963, at his home in Rutherford.

POEM TEXT

> I have eaten
> the plums
> that were in
> the icebox
>
> and which   5
> you were probably
> saving
> for breakfast

Forgive me
they were delicious
so sweet
and so cold

10

MEDIA ADAPTATIONS

- A group of audio recordings can be found on the Internet at http://writing.upenn.edu/pennsound/x/Williams-WC.html. Accessible through this site are MP3 recordings of the readings of eighty-nine of Williams's poems. In addition, there are twenty-eight other recordings of readings, interviews, and commentary ranging from a few minutes to two hours in length. There are also five separate short recordings about "This Is Just to Say" specifically and further short recordings on a few other poems. All these audio recordings are also available at www.ubu.com/sound/wcw.html.

POEM SUMMARY

"This Is Just to Say" is written with the informality and brevity of a note left on a refrigerator. The title indicates that this is just a quick message, an FYI. There is no punctuation in the poem, as might be expected in a hastily scribbled note. This lack of punctuation contributes to the poem's ambiguity of tone and meaning. Also, only two words are capitalized: the first word of each of the two unpunctuated sentences, although the first word is "I" so it would have been capitalized anyway. Williams probably left out punctuation to make the direct address sound like natural speech, but used capitalization to still indicate sentence structure. The poem consists of three stanzas of four short lines each. No line is longer than three words, and of the twenty-eight words in the poem, twenty-one are one syllable.

Metrically, the poem exhibits no regularity of stress or of syllable count. Except for lines 2 and 4, each an iamb (a foot containing two syllables, one unstressed, then one stressed), and lines 8 and 9, each an amphibrach (a foot containing three syllables, one unstressed, one stressed, one unstressed), no two lines have the same metrical pattern. However, Williams did use the same metric pattern, the spondee (one unstressed syllable followed by two stressed syllables), in four strategic places: at the end of each stanza ("the icebox," "for breakfast," and "and so cold") and in the first line of the third stanza ("Forgive me"). This repeated pattern provides a poetic sound to the seemingly ordinary message and provides closure at the end of each stanza.

Williams said that it had to be a poem because it was metrically absolutely regular, but it is not. Perhaps he was referring to the fact that the three quatrains look alike; they have roughly the same physical shape. Thus, the reading of the poem is guided by the structure of the poem and the relationships established by the line breaks. The consonance of the letters *th* in lines 2, 3, 4, as well as the consonance of the letter *f* in lines 8 and 9, and the letter *s* in lines 10, 11 and 12 give rise to a natural rhythm when the poem is read aloud.

The focus throughout the poem is on the plums. The word "plum" as strategically placed at the end of the second line to draw attention to the subject and followed by the relative pronoun "that" to emphasize that it was the plums that were in the icebox. (Before the use of chemical coolants for refrigeration, food was placed in a refrigerator-like wooden or metal chest with an actual block of ice in a top compartment to keep it cold, thus, the icebox.) In the second stanza, the pronoun "which" refers back to the plums, whereas in the third stanza the pronoun "they" once again brings the attention back to the plums. There is a narrator and an intended reader, but the plums are the subject around which everything rotates: In the first stanza is the announcement that the plums have been eaten; in the second stanza, the plum-eater realizes that the plums were probably intended for the reader's breakfast; and in the third stanza, the narrator asks for forgiveness for his indulging himself, by eating the delicious, sweet, and cold plums.

Stanza 1

The first word, "I," establishes that this poem has a first person narrator. This is the stanza that has iambs in lines 2 and 4 and the *th* sound in lines 2, 3, and 4. By placing "eaten" and "plums" at the end of the first two lines, the reader is immediately notified of the subject of the poem, the transgression that has been committed. Putting "icebox" at the end of the stanza establishes the scene of the crime, so to speak, as occurring in the kitchen.

Stanza 2

The first and second stanzas are connected by the conjunction "and." In this stanza, there is only one iamb, in line 5, but there is an amphibrach in line 8. The narrator directly addresses the person to whom the note is written with the word "you" and acknowledges that the plums were probably intended for that person's breakfast, but the word "probably" leaves enough room for doubt and self-justification. Putting the word "saving" by itself on line 7, however, indicates that the narrator is aware enough of his wife's preferences that he can assume the plums were not meant for him. They were not in the icebox for general consumption but had been set aside by his wife to be eaten at breakfast.

Stanza 3

The *f* in the word "for" from line 8 of stanza two is repeated in line 9 of the third stanza to create a connection between the two stanzas despite the period at the end of line 8. Line 9 is the other amphibrach in the poem. The focus is momentarily shifted with the phrase "Forgive me," emphasized by its position alone on the first sentence of the third stanza. However, the focus quickly shifts back to the plums with a sensuous description enhance by the repeated use of the *s* sound. This stanza presents the twist in the message: The writer begs forgiveness for eating the plums but then goes on to describe how delicious they were.

THEMES

Transcendence

Transcendence refers to going from one state of existence to another. In this case, an everyday event is turned into an art form. Williams believed in finding poetry subjects among ordinary things, and it is possible that he disguised his poem as a note to his wife for the purpose of challenging the reader to transcend the note and move into the poem. The physical eating of the plums is transformed into an art form, poetry.

Indulgence and Forgiveness

"This Is Just to Say" tells a tiny story. It is a snippet of a narrative that allows the reader to glimpse a common household scene: one person looking into the icebox to see what is available for a snack. Since there is a suggestion that his wife was saving the plums for breakfast, the reader might assume that the person has come in late from work, perhaps after the wife has gone to bed. He has worked hard and is hungry. The plums would probably satisfy the immediate hunger, but the wife often enjoyed plums at breakfast. He does not want to deprive her of her treat, but there is nothing else that appeals to him. He knows she will understand, so he indulges himself and finds that the plums were indeed a satisfying choice.

The question that readers may ask is whether this is an innocent indulgence, like having a piece of cake despite being on a diet, or is this a mean-spirited action. Does the speaker describe the delicious nature of the plums to say that the flavor was worth the risk of offending his wife, or is he being spiteful. The issue of indulgence in the poem causes readers to weigh the severity of the offense, to reflect on how many times others have done something similar, and then to decide whether the speaker should be granted the forgiveness that he requests.

Forgiveness, then, is also an important theme of the poem. In the loving relationship of a couple who has been married for a long time, the wife might respond to the note with a grin and, at most, mild annoyance. Williams said (in an interview printed in *Massachusetts Review* that the poem resulted from an actual event and that his wife replied with a charming parody about food she had prepared for him. The title "This Is Just to Say" indicates a casual approach and an expectation of forgiveness from an understanding wife. He did not just eat the plums and walk off without comment. Rather, he cared enough to leave a note of explanation and apology.

All poetry is open to interpretation. Imagists did not allow emotion to enter a poem directly because they wanted to concentrate on the concrete subject. Williams held that there was space enough in the poem for readers to insert emotion. That means readers are free to project reactions onto the described action and plea for forgiveness. These reactions have a wide range. Some feel that the poem is indeed a love note.

TOPICS FOR FURTHER STUDY

- Write your own version of "This Is Just to Say," making an apology for some minor offense, yet explaining the temptation. Then send the poem to the person for whom the apology is intended and see what kind of response you get.

- For a number of years, Williams was a follower of the imagist movement but later became a leader of the modernist movement. Write a compare and contrast paper explaining the similarities and differences between the two movements in poetry.

- Williams went straight from prep school to the University of Pennsylvania in 1902 at age nineteen and graduated just four years later with a medical degree. Divide the class into several groups with each group researching medical education in a different time period; for example, 1875 to 1900; 1901 to 1925; 1926 to 1950, and so on. When did a bachelor's degree become required to attend medical school? How many years did it take to go to medical school? How long were internships and residencies? When did physicians stop making house calls? What could a doctor expect to earn? Each group should prepare a report to present to the class on the basic requirements.

- "This Is Just to Say" was written in 1934 in the middle of the Great Depression. One of the government programs created to put people back to work hired photographers to record scenes from this tragic period and artists to paint murals in post offices and other public buildings. Each student in the class should search the Internet and the library to find photographs from the Great Depression and copy one to show to the class. Look for pictures of the Dust Bowl, soup kitchen lines, and similar scenes. Alternatively, find out if there are any buildings in your town that still have artwork from a New Deal program and take a photograph of the art to show to the class. If there is a structure built by the Civilian Conservation Corps (CCC), it can also be the subject of a photograph.

- Williams won the Pulitzer Prize for Poetry in 1963. What is the Pulitzer? After whom was it named? How long have prizes been given? What categories of awards are there? Why is this prize important? As a class, look through the information that the teacher provides from the Internet or another source to answer this questions together. Then each student should pick a Pulitzer Prize winner from any time period in any eligible field and write a note-card description about that person and the work that earned the person the award. These cards can be used for a bulletin board display on the Pulitzer Prize.

Others see it as sad, as an expression of indifference toward another person's feelings.

Some critics have read into the poem a sexual theme. It might be that the plums are described as cold because the speaker thinks his wife or their relationship is cold. If he cannot have her sexually because she is cold, at least he can have her cold plums. However, that interpretation ignores the fact that the plums are sweet. Another view is that his confession about eating the plums might be his way of admitting that he is partaking of forbidden fruit elsewhere. Further, the description of deliciousness might mean that he found the extramarital activity too enjoyable to resist.

The theme could be about living in the moment while the plums are still so sweet, cold, and available. After all, why let a good opportunity pass when it is easier to ask for forgiveness than permission? The poem could be a statement

An early twentieth-century icebox, precursor to the refrigerator (© Underwood & Underwood / Corbis)

of the triumph of the physical over the spiritual. However, "This Is Just to Say" is a poem, and readers detect meaning according to their own understanding.

STYLE

Free verse

The most commonly used style of poetry in modern times is free verse. Using short, usually irregular line lengths and a controlled rhythm, free verse lacks the regular stress pattern or recurrent beat, metric feet, and rhyme of traditional verse. Nonetheless, it qualifies as poetry because of its pattern of imagery and sound, and the rhythmic effect gained from repetition of words and phrases with similar structures. Rhythm is also achieved through balance, variation of phrases, or phrases of about equal length. A poet using free verse may change the expected word order and thus increase the effect of pace, pause, and timing. Word associations such as assonance, alliteration, and internal rhyme are used to create the desired sound qualities. Of importance are the divisions within a poem—not just stanza divisions but divisions from one line to the next. Line length can also help to convey emphasis or create tension. For example, a series of long lines followed by one short line might signal a commentary on the preceding lines or the solution to a problem. Poets noted for their use of free verse are Walt Whitman, William Carlos Williams, T. S. Eliot, Ezra Pounds, and E. E. Cummings, among many others. Williams most likely used free verse because it enables open expression and lacks a prescribed form.

"This Is Just to Say" definitely qualifies as a free verse poem. It has no metrical regularity. Williams used short lines and short words of almost equal length to create a rhythm from the similar structures. It is as if he weighed each line to achieve balance. He also used repetition of sounds to create rhythm. The lack of punctuation until the end of the second stanza causes the reader to keep moving through the description of his domestic crime but then stop before the request for forgiveness. The first line "Forgive me" does not end with punctuation but flows into an explanation of how irresistible the plums were. This is the kind of suspension of expected sentence structure used in free verse to create an effect and amplify the message.

Simplicity

"This Is Just to Say" is often anthologized, probably because it has all the characteristics of Williams's style: free verse, an economy of words, and a simple idea presented sincerely, honestly, and directly. Williams compressed a poem to its core so that the reader could go straight to its essence. There is not as much figurative language as might be expected in a poem. Since the topic is plums, the sensory language of taste is naturally the dominant feature: eaten, delicious, sweet, and cold. Williams believed not only in concentrating on concrete subjects, on things, but also in paying attention to a particular subject at a particular place and time, because doing so could reveal universal truths. The particular subject in "This Is Just to Say" is the plums; the place and time is in the kitchen on a day when he has eaten the plums that his wife was probably saving for later. Readers are left to discover on their own the universal truths about indulgence and forgiveness.

The simplicity of this poem also depends on its construction. Form and content are always dependent on each other in poetry. Consider if

Williams had written his note in prose form, with conventional punctuation, as most people would. What turns these two sentences into a poem is the way the words are placed on the page and thus given an enhanced relationship to each other. Williams's choices of word and line length give the message a rhythm and tone. The explanation of the action is broken up into units of thought and thereby units of presentation. The arrangement of the words on paper looks simple, but behind it is the complexity of poetic technique and style.

HISTORICAL CONTEXT

Imagism

Imagism was a movement started by American and British poets around 1912. The name comes from the movement's interest in achieving clarity through the use of precise visual images as opposed to the vagueness that critics such as T. E. Hulme (1883–1917) found in romanticism. The principles of imagism were formulated by Ezra Pound and the circle of poets that included Hilda Doolittle (better known as H. D.), Richard Aldington, and F. S. Flint. In 1914, Pound turned to another type of poetry, but not before he introduced imagism to Williams who embraced the call for free verse, common language, exact rather than symbolic descriptions, and freedom of subject that he had been seeking. Imagists said that a new idea deserved a new cadence, so they did not use traditional rhythm patterns in their poetry. Imagism strove to be as concentrated on a subject as a painting or sculpture. The insistence on exact language precluded superfluous words; consequently, imagist poems tend to be short. Pound's famous poem "In a Station of the Metro" is only two lines long. However, this brevity does not necessarily mean simple; imagist poems are sometimes a challenge to understand.

After Pound, Amy Lowell led the imagist group, including John Gould Fletcher and Harriet Monroe. The American magazine *Poetry* and the British magazine *Egoist* published imagist poetry, and four imagist anthologies were published by 1917. The movement also influenced later poets such as Wallace Stevens, D. H. Lawrence, Marianne Moore, T. S. Eliot, and Conrad Aiken, all of whom were born in the 1880s and died well into the twentieth century.

Objectivism

Objectivism was a continuation of imagism, a further compression process that strove to eliminate foreign references, allusions, abstractions, and adjectives. Also rejected were long-respected poetic forms, such as the sonnet. The objectivist view was that such predetermined forms did not serve the purposes of modern poetry. However, objectivism added more thought and feeling to imagism and narrowed the focus on the sound of small, everyday words. Williams was a leader of this effort during the 1930s, and his poetry from this decade embraced life, growth, and change. Louis Zukofsky gave this style its name in 1931 when he was editing *Poetry* magazine and trying to find a label for a group of poets that included himself, Williams, Basil Bunting, Charles Reznikoff, and several others. The members of the group soon went their separate ways, but not without affecting the work of the Beat Generation of the 1950s and other groups through the 1970s. While few critics say objectivism ever made it to the status of a movement, Williams's work garnered more notice because of it.

The Great Depression

The Great Depression began with the stock market crash in October 1929. Many investors lost everything in the days and months that followed. By 1932, stocks had fallen to only 20 percent of their previous value, and many banks began closing because they could not meet the surge of withdrawals from their customers. The U.S. economy fractured as factories and stores closed, resulting in the highest unemployment rate in history. About 25 percent of the workforce was out of work. The U.S. financial collapse matched a global slump. World trade slowed as countries protected their industries with high tariffs. The crisis caused a number of countries to invade neighbors for their resources or seek new leadership. Japan invaded China, and in their desperation for change, the Germans elected Adolph Hitler. The aggressive behaviors of Japan and Germany precipitated World War II (1939–1945). Ironically, it was the war that brought the United States out of the economic depression with the heightened demand for production of war goods and foodstuffs for its allies.

Herbert Hoover, elected in 1928, was president of the United States when long-term economic problems finally exploded into financial disaster. In 1932, as the depression continued, Franklin Delano Roosevelt was elected president. He promised a New Deal for the American people. His administration changed the role of government,

COMPARE & CONTRAST

- **1934:** Because of the Great Depression, many urban families in the United States are able to obtain fruit only about once a month and then most likely from a government food allotment. For a household to have plums suggests its relative wealth.

  Today: Although there are still families on welfare for whom plums are a luxury, for most families plums are readily available in a supermarket. In fact, plums are the second most cultivated fruit, with apples the most cultivated.

- **1934:** The refrigerator is patented in 1914, and by 1944, approximately 85 percent of American households have a refrigerator. In 1934, the first laundromat, or washateria, opens at a business in Fort Worth, Texas. Both gas and electric stoves are available, but many rural families use coal or wood-burning stoves. The household washing machine does not have a spin cycle, so clothes have to be manually put through a wringer. Dryers are available only for commercial use, so most laundry is hung on a line to dry.

  Today: Although some elderly people may still refer to the refrigerator as an icebox, only refrigerators are in use. Modern kitchens have gas or electric stoves and a microwave oven. Washing machines are usually paired with a dryer, and both have a range of automatic cycles that can be programmed electronically.

giving federal programs the power to initiate massive public works programs that created jobs such as creating the Tennessee Valley Authority for flood control and the Civilian Conservation Corps for development of public facilities and national parks. The government also insured bank deposits, established the Social Security system, and provided food assistance.

Williams wrote "This Is Just to Say" in 1934, in the midst of the Depression. As a physician who had been in practice for twenty-four years, he saw the effects of this crisis on the families whom he served. From his unique position of close involvement with ordinary people and as a recorder of the common voice, he could write stories and poetry that reflected the lives of Americans. "This Is Just to Say" suggests the frugality typical of the 1930s, when food was measured out and saved and when eating food on impulse would have been frowned upon.

CRITICAL OVERVIEW

Much poetry elicits multiple interpretations. That is certainly the case with "This Is Just to Say." Critics continue to debate the simplicity versus the complexity of this poem, sometimes in the same breath.

In his book *William Carlos Williams and the American Poem*, Charles Doyle stated: "Many typical Williams poems are completely independent of paraphrase. Of these, perhaps best know is 'This Is Just to Say.'" Doyle added that this poem is often used to "illustrate the basic triviality of both Williams's method and material." However, in Doyle's view, critics are being too serious with that response because "Here the immediate, small occasion is light-hearted, even comic." Doyle admitted that there is much more to the poem than it might seem and judges it to be "a celebration of the physical life, rendered with stringent economy but with a high degree of essential 'vividness.'"

Charles Altieri chose "This Is Just to Say" for a lengthy analysis in his book *Act & Quality: A Theory of Literary Meaning and Humanistic Understanding*. Altieri stated there are three way to read the poem. The first way is to "read the note ironically" if only because critics see it as their job to look suspiciously for motives. In that case, the eating of the plums and the writing of the note can be seen as acts of aggression without confrontation. The plums are sexual surrogates,

Plums (Image copyright Paul Cowan, 2009. Used under license from Shutterstock.com)

as cold as the wife, and the apology is hollow. Also, "the title becomes an ironic undercutting of any ideal meaning in justice; just saying is always only saying."

According to Altieri, the second way to read the poem is as an "extremely intelligent and tactful form of apology." It is carefully crafted to play upon the wife's understanding nature with a justification for the temptation in the description of the plums. A third way to read the poem is to combine interpretations of irony and optimism because the words of the poem vacillate between hoping for understanding and the very human tendency to resent having to apologize. Altieri did not prefer one type of reading over another, but pointed out that there is a huge difference between reading "This Is Just to Say" as a poetic note and reading it is a poem about a note. In conclusion, Altieri explained that this poem "achieve[s] so much by so little explicit content" because Williams recognized "how fully performance relies upon and elicits the implicit grounds of grammatical competence which serve as the foundation for achievable and achieved meanings."

Williams's own judgment of the poem, a personal favorite, is reported by Neil Baldwin, in *To All Gentleness: William Carlos Williams, the Doctor-Poet*. Williams claimed that the poem started out as exactly what it seems—a note to his wife. After all, his philosophy of poetry was that poets can make into poetry whatever is actually in their own lives. That can be done because if the subject is, as Williams is quoted in Baldwin as saying, "'sufficiently authentic to our lives and touches us deeply enough with a certain amount of feeling, [it] is capable of being organized into a form which can be a poem.'" Baldwin added that Williams "never tired of repeating this important message to anyone, anywhere, who would listen."

CRITICISM

Lois Kerschen

Kerschen is an English instructor and freelance writer. In this essay, she shows how Williams's style and focus on American topics is reflected in "This Is Just to Say."

WHAT DO I READ NEXT?

- *Selected Poems* by Ezra Pound, published by New Directions Paperbacks in 1957, is an eclectic collection by this famous modernist contemporary of Williams, noted for his mastery of the musical qualities of the English language.
- The 1994 Penguin Classics paperback edition of *Complete Poems* by Marianne Moore, a contemporary and friend of Williams, covers sixty years of Moore's poetry and includes her own explanatory notes.
- *Selected Essays of William Carlos Williams*, a New Directions paperback published in 1969, is a collection of previously published and unpublished essays from various points in Williams's career that reveal his philosophies on the arts, politics, and history and help the reader to understand his poetry.
- *The Doctor Stories*, by William Carlos Williams and published by New Directions in 1984, is a group of short, vivid stories written about the poet's medical practice in pediatrics during the Depression. The stories describe some of the immigrant families of Patterson, New Jersey.
- Although Williams wrote "This Is Just to Say" as an imagist poem, by 1934 he was involved in the modernist movement. *The Cambridge Companion to Modernist Poetry* (2007), edited by Alex Davis and Lee M. Jenkins, offers an overview of the movement and its major authors, as well as an extended discussion about followers of modernism among poets in the Caribbean, Africa, and India.
- William Carlos Williams attempted in *In the American Grain* (New Directions Books, 1925) to analyze the founding stories about the United States and the nation's development.
- Williams resented the fame that T. S. Eliot gained with "The Waste Land" and disapproved of Eliot's poetic techniques and expatriate lifestyle. Example of Eliot's work can be found in *T. S. Eliot: The Waste Land & Other Poems* (2009).
- Christopher MacGowan's *Poetry for Young People: William Carlos Williams* (2003) presents thirty-two Williams poems with illustrations, helpful annotations, and a biography designed to introduce Williams to young readers.

William Carlos Williams felt strongly about how poetry should be written and the subjects it should address. One of his most admired imagist poems "This Is Just to Say" is a good example of his compressed style and use of common language. It describes an ordinary moment in the life a middle-class couple during the Great Depression.

The poem illustrates typical imagist style: It is written in free verse, and it says what it has to say with a minimum of words while focusing on one object. In just twenty-eight words, Williams describes what happened to some plums in his icebox, a single subject, a single place, in a particular moment. In skilled hands, the form of a poem and its subject work together to convey the message, and the message fits the form. Yet the decision to eat the plums generates questions about indulgence, forgiveness, and transcendence.

As a poet, Williams was attracted to imagism because of the physical nature of poetry, that is, the image presented by a poem, whether written or spoken, leaves a picture in the mind that outlasts the style and structure that the poet used. Anyone who has read "This Is Just to Say" carries away a mental picture of a person eating plums and writing a note. Therefore, the most important aspect of a poem is the thing it describes or presents. If only one quotation from Williams survives the ages, it will be the often repeated line from his poem "Patterson": "No ideas but in things." Williams illustrated his

> WILLIAMS TRUSTED HIS READERS TO FIND THEIR OWN SENSE OF IMPORTANCE IN THE RED WHEELBARROW, THE GREEN GLASS OF THE HOSPITAL, OR THE IRRESISTIBLE PLUMS AND THUS TO BE RELIEVED OF THE TASK OF TRYING TO EKE OUT SYMBOLS."

preference for a single subject with the belief that material for a poem can come from any object; even the simple act of eating plums is worthy of poetry.

This focus on the thing, on an object, ties Williams to reality, which is what he wanted. He did not believe that the imagination is merely a means to escape reality. He felt that poetry should move the world, not re-create it. Understanding that reality is matter and force, which science has proven to be indestructible, he did not try to change it but rather to select from reality in order to show it in new ways. That does not make a symbol out of the thing because truth can be found in the thing without investing another level of meaning. Williams trusted his readers to find their own sense of importance in the red wheelbarrow, the green glass of the hospital, or the irresistible plums and thus to be relieved of the task of trying to eke out symbols.

This direct path to the thing was connected to a sense of immediacy that Williams wanted to preserve in his poetry. Imagism facilitated that effort by eliminating unnecessary words, ignoring poetic conventions, and welcoming use of innovative rhythms that convey immediacy. "This Is Just to Say" exemplifies the here and now: the here is at the icebox, a particular place and one place only; eating the plums and jotting a note takes place in the now in just a few moments. The poem is not a life story; it is not the description of a drama that spans a period of days. The poem is a snapshot of the here and now.

Williams rejected rigidly order poetry. He wanted to drop the old rules and start using something new. That is why Williams disliked it when Ezra Pound and T. S. Eliot used foreign languages and alluded to classical works. If the reader did not understand the allusions, part of the message was lost, which made Williams wonder what good they did. Williams preferred to takes his subject and themes from ordinary, everyday things. Pound may have formulated imagist techniques, but Williams brought a freshness and directness to their application.

If poetry could come from any subject and had more clarity when it came from local conditions, then Williams felt his job was to find art in common speech and events, and from that starting point he and the readers could discover what is universal in the detail. Therefore, affirms Linda W. Wagner in *Reference Guide to American Literature*, "Williams wrote consistently in a mode based on the rhythms of the speaking voice, complete with idiomatic language, colloquial word choice, organic form and structure, and an intense interest in locale as both setting and subject." The expression, "this is just to say," starts his famous poem with an American idiom, a common phrase that indicates a simple message. The poem also uses the homely term "icebox" and sets the narrative in a local place—his own kitchen.

Native idioms, colloquial language, subjects that are local and ordinary—all these elements meant, of course, that Williams had to write about American culture and the experience he knew firsthand. He was naturally inclined to do so because he grew up as the son of an English father and a Puerto Rican mother, wanting to assimilate, to feel that he belonged in one place rather than in two. As Lisa Steinman explains in *Made in America*, "Specifically, he felt the need to argue that his life as a doctor in America and his daily contact with people who were neither literary nor avant-garde formed the best possible environment in which to develop a new poetry."

Williams's mission to mirror American speech became a lifelong endeavor. Not only was he trying to use appropriate language for his subjects, but he was also trying to demonstrate democracy through the material found in American thought and to put himself on an equal level with his readers. He used the material he knew: the lives of his patients, which he saw firsthand as he made house calls and which he treated with a deep sense of compassion and human understanding. His point was not to teach a lesson or attach a moral to a story, but to help his readers recognize beauty in the real world.

Imagism fit this American purpose. Imagism allowed Williams to describe Rutherford, New Jersey, in a style that fit American culture and did not lose its authenticity by depending upon old-style European forms and foreign diction. The use of American idiom, Williams believed, would energize poetic language, giving it a rawness that reflected the country's social and cultural mix. Many critics believe that Williams revitalized twentieth-century American poetry just as Whitman, a poet whom Williams admired, brought a new energy and uniquely American speech to poetry in the nineteenth century.

Williams felt that imagism allowed him to focus on a subject and to pick new subjects rather than those more typical of the past, which was, according to Christopher MacGowan in *American Writers: A Collection of Literary Biographies*, "too often contaminated with inherited ways of thinking that were not pertinent to current American needs." In a 1950 interview for the Rutherford Library (reprinted in the *Massachusetts Review* in 1973), an interview that, by the way, started with a reading of "This Is Just to Say" to test the recording equipment, Williams explained his motivations for using commonplace American speech and subjects. The first motive, of course, was to prove that any subject is worthy of being made into a poem "if it's sufficiently authentic to our lives and touches us deeply enough with a certain amount of feeling."

In addition, he used ordinary American speech in response to the British attitude that an American accent was unsuitable for reading poetry aloud, and nothing in the colonies could be important enough to be "put down in words and given a *form*." Williams objected to the idea that poetry had to sound like something from the ancient Greeks. He said: "you have to get used to the fact that in your own life, that which touches you" can be the stuff of poetry. Such stuff can be for the person one lives with, as he says, "the poor kid [who] had these things saved for supper and here you come along and raid it." With a laugh, in the interview, Williams adds: "Why it's practically a rape of the icebox!"

Williams's efforts helped to define the American voice and define American literature. The combination of natural cadences and inflections of American speech with subjects that are the fiber of American lives created a poetry that appealed to many readers. In the final analysis, many scholars find Williams to be one of the best and most influential American poets of the twentieth century, one whose style became an integral part of American literature.

Source: Lois Kerschen, Critical Essay on "This Is Just to Say," in *Poetry for Students*, Gale, Cengage Learning, 2010.

Melodie Monahan

Monahan has a Ph.D. in English and operates an editing service, The Inkwell Works. In the following essay, she explores how people handled food in their homes during the Great Depression, a discussion relevant to "This Is Just to Say."

William Carlos Williams wrote his poem "This Is Just to Say" in 1934, during the economic hard times of the Great Depression, which began in 1929 and continued until the early 1940s. The date of composition and the reference in the poem to the icebox and to the intention of saving food for a later meal hint at the social and economic times in which Williams, a pediatrician by profession, was writing. Some historical information about the Depression and about iceboxes and how families handled food during those hard years can enhance readers' appreciation of this poem.

The Great Depression is often said to have begun with the stock market crash in late October 1929. That crash was more like a chip in the porcelain of the U.S. economy because stocks dropped only about 12 percent between October 24 and October 29. That amount was enough to cause panic and escalating fear. By July 1932, however, stocks had lost 89 percent of their pre-October 1929 value; 25 percent of the U.S. workforce was jobless; and by March 1933, 5,000 U.S. banks had failed. Clearly through the four years following the crash, economic matters went from bad to unimaginably worse. In addition, in 1930, the weather across the Great Plains decided to exacerbate the national economic disaster. That year drought began in Arkansas and spread into Colorado, Kansas, Oklahoma, and New Mexico, creating the famed Dust Bowl that whipped topsoil off farmland and destroyed all hope for crops to grow and make it to market. Food became scarce. As money became extremely tight, prices fell, but that did not make available food more affordable since ordinary people did not have money for purchases. Ironically, as malnutrition grew among the general population and related physical problems spiked among families in which there was no employed worker, farmers often could not sell the products they carried to market. Franklin Delano Roosevelt was elected in 1932, and his New Deal went into effect as quickly as possible, but the positive effects of that massive government project were slow to reach ordinary families who were struggling to get by.

While so many were unemployed, Williams had plenty of work as a medical doctor, and likely some payment he collected came in the form of home-grown fruits and vegetables or services bartered for his medical care. He and his wife, and their two sons, lived in Rutherford, New Jersey, where Williams had a private medical practice. "This Is Just to Say" is set in a middle-class home, equipped with an icebox, containing fresh plums. The feeling one gets from the poem is of a frugal kitchen and thoughtful family members who typically handle their provisions prudently.

Harvesting pond ice was common throughout the nineteenth century and into the early decades of the twentieth century. Before the development of artificial coolants, ice was delivered to homes twice a week by horse-drawn cart. By the 1930s, delivery trucks were commonly used. People put order cards in their front windows telling the iceman what weight of ice block was needed, usually five, ten, or twenty pounds. The iceman came around to the back of the house carrying the block in giant ice tongs or pincers designed to dig into the slippery surface. He delivered the block to the icebox families often placed near the back door of their kitchens. The block of ice was placed in a top portion of the vertical chest so the cool air dropped over the food beside and below the ice. A tube directed water from the melting block to a pan in a drawer below the block or to a pan on the floor below the icebox. In some houses, the icebox was equipped with an opening at the back and was positioned in line with a chute that opened to the outside like a milk chute. In these instances, without entering the kitchen, the iceman could open the chute and slide the block directly into the icebox. Having an icebox in the early 1930s was not uncommon among city dwellers, in homes or apartments; however, by the late 1940s, electric refrigerators had replaced them.

Plums grow in most areas of the United States that have a good winter but without severely cold temperatures. So the plums alluded to in Williams's poems could have come from a nearby grocer, from a medical patient in payment for services, or from the backyard tree on a neighbor's property. Plums would be enjoyed fresh as the speaker in this poem reports, but at least as common in the 1930s would have been the practice of cooking plums to make fruit compote or jam. Canning was a common and economical method for food preservation, a practice of putting by for the winter months. In a time when commercially canned foods were both expensive and often poor quality, canning was a widespread household practice.

So when the speaker in the poem remarks that the plums were being saved for later, he hints at a number of realities of family life in the 1930s. Food *was* saved for later. It was stretched to feed more. Portions were measured and counted, and a frugal housewife calculated on how many servings she could get from a given amount of fresh food. Sharing and stretching food for more meals was economically necessary and practical. If there was more fruit than the family was expected to eat fresh, then it would be canned and served during the winter when such fruit, if it was available at all, would likely have been canned, costly, and of poor quality.

The speaker in Williams's poem justifies eating the fruit that he knows is being saved by explaining how delicious the plums are. The poem describes an extravagant and impulsive act: He opens the icebox, sees the cold plums, and eats them. This indulgence that overrides the practical and the cautionary deserves a formal apology. Such self-indulgence is a rarity, an extravagance, and perhaps only excused if the fruit is irresistible. In the United States in the early 2000s, despite the economic downturn, many middle-class family members habitually raid the refrigerator between meals. They come in their kitchens when it is not mealtime, and they feel entitled to grab whatever highly processed snacks are available, such as jam tarts warmed in a toaster or chicken nuggets ready to eat from the microwave in two minutes. American affluence is such that this kind of between-meal eating is taken for granted, and a mother who fails to keep the refrigerator well stocked with these expensive, dietetically inferior items is a likely target for criticism from her family members and in magazine and television advertising. Williams's poem is of a different time, a time of frugality, putting by, appreciation of fresh food, and courtesy to others. His poem "This Is Just to Say" is a window into a different era and a different way of handling food and eating it.

Source: Melodie Monahan, Critical Essay on "This Is Just to Say," in *Poetry for Students*, Gale, Cengage Learning, 2010.

SOURCES

Altieri, Charles, *Act & Quality: A Theory of Literary Meaning and Humanistic Understanding*, University of Massachusetts Press, 1981, pp. 162, 163, 165, and 175.

Baldwin, Neil, *To All Gentleness: William Carlos Williams, the Doctor-Poet*, Atheneum, 1984, p. 127.

Doyle, Charles, *William Carlos Williams and the American Poem*, St. Martin's Press, 1982, p. 55.

MacGowan, Christopher, "William Carlos Williams," in *American Writers: A Collection of Literary Biographies*, edited by A. Walton Litz and Molly Weigel, Charles Scribner's Sons, 1998.

Perkins, George, et al., eds. *The American Tradition in Literature*, 6th ed., Random House, 1985, p. 1337.

Sidman, Joyce, *This Is Just to Say: Poems of Apology and Forgiveness*, illustrated by Pamela Zagarenski, Houghton Mifflin Books for Children, 2007, p. 6.

Steinman, Lisa M., *Made in America: Science, Technology, and American Modernist Poets*, Yale University Press, 1987, p. 81.

Wagner, Linda W., "William Carlos Williams: Overview," in *Reference Guide to American Literature,*, 3rd ed., edited by Jim Kamp, St. James Press, 1994.

Wallace, Emily M., and William Carlos Williams, "An Interview with William Carlos Williams," in the *Massachusetts Review*, Vol. 1, No. 1, Winter 1973, pp. 140, 141, 142.

Williams, William Carlos, "Patterson," *The Collected Poems of William Carlos Williams, Vol. 1: 1909–1939*, edited by A. Walton Litz and Christopher MacGowan, New Directions, 1991, p. 263.

———, "This Is Just to Say," *The Collected Poems of William Carlos Williams, Vol. 1: 1909–1939*, edited by A. Walton Litz and Christopher MacGowan, New Directions, 1991, p. 372.

FURTHER READING

Breeden, David, *This Is Just to Say: Meditations on a Theme by William Carlos Williams*, Virtual Artists Collective, 2009.

> Breeden presents a series of meditations based on "This Is Just to Say," in which he contemplates sin, redemption, myth, language, symbols, and the consequences of actions.

Coles, Robert, and Thomas Roma, *House Calls with William Carlos Williams, M.D.*, powerHouse Books, 2008.

> This book contains a collection of photographs of subjects that inspired Williams in writing his poetry, and it compares his poetry to the composition of the photographs.

Rauchway, Eric, *The Great Depression and the New Deal: A Very Short Introduction*, Oxford University Press, 2008.

> The work provides a compact history with illustrations of the Great Depression and the successes and failures of the New Deal. This study provides a useful foundation for understanding major American policy changes that have affected government ever since the 1930s.

Williams, William Carlos, *The Autobiography of William Carlos Williams*, New Directions, 1967.

> In telling the story of his own life, Williams discusses his roles as a physician and poet and describes his literary friends, all in an open and warm manner.

To Althea, From Prison

RICHARD LOVELACE

1649

"To Althea, From Prison" was written in 1642 by Richard Lovelace while he was actually in prison. A prominent landowner and supporter of Charles I (1625–1649) during the English Civil Wars (1642–1646; 1648–1649), Lovelace presented a royalist petition to the opposition in Parliament and was incarcerated for seven weeks for his defiance. While in Gatehouse Prison, Lovelace wrote a poem addressed to Althea, but it is not known for certain if Althea was an imaginary person or a pseudonym for Lucy Sacheverell, a love interest of Lovelace. The theme of the poem is that the mind cannot be imprisoned like the body. The poem was not published until 1649, but it was previously distributed for several years among Lovelace's friends and inspired imitations as the days grew darker for the Royalists. The first and last stanzas were set to music by John Wilson, and the song was published in 1659 in the collection *Playford Songs or Ballads for Three Voices*. Although Lovelace did not pursue writing as a profession and did not achieve greatness as a poet, "To Althea, From Prison" can be found in most anthologies of British poetry because it contains two of the most famous lines in all of literature: "Stone walls do not a prison make / Nor iron bars a cage." Lovelace wrote some other notable poems that can be found in a collection of his work such as *Lucasta: The Poems of Richard Lovelace*, published in 2009 by W. Carew Hazlitt.

Richard Lovelace (The Library of Congress)

AUTHOR BIOGRAPHY

Richard Lovelace was born in Woolwich, Kent, in 1618, the eldest son of eight children born to Sir William and Anne Barne Lovelace. A prominent and distinguished landowner, Sir William was killed in 1627 while serving in the military. At age eleven, Richard was sent to Charterhouse School in London, and at age fifteen he was made a *Gentleman Wayter Extraordinary* to the king. He later enrolled at Gloucester Hall at the University of Oxford.

While at Oxford, Lovelace wrote a comedic play called *The Scholars*, which was performed in Oxford and London. At eighteen, he was granted a master of arts degree by King Charles I and Queen Henrietta Maria who, during a visit to Oxford, were struck by his witty charm and good looks. Lovelace then spent several months at Cambridge University before joining the military.

A fervent and loyal Royalist, Lovelace served in the Bishops' Wars in Scotland in 1639 and 1640 as an ensign and then captain. Afterward, Lovelace returned home to oversee his father's lands and assume his role as justice of the peace. Lovelace was an accomplished amateur painter and musician, and his poetry was another product of his gentlemanly life, in which an educated man was expected to dabble in literary pursuits. Some of his poems were set to music by friends, as was popular at the time, but writing was never his primary occupation.

Political and religious turmoil interrupted his time at home, and in 1641, Lovelace led a group of men who took an anti-Episcopal petition meant for the House of Commons and destroyed it. In 1642, he instead presented a pro-royalist petition on behalf of Kent to the House of Commons and was subsequently imprisoned in the Westminster Gatehouse from April 30 to June 21. It was during this confinement that he penned "To Althea, From Prison." Released on bail under the condition that he could not leave London without permission, he was thus prevented from joining the king's army in Ireland. Instead, he sold most of his land and used the money to buy horses and weapons for the Royalists during England's Civil War.

Lovelace then fought in Holland and France on behalf of Louis XIV. Wounded at Dunkirk in October 1646, he returned to England in 1647, but by this time Charles I had been captured. Nonetheless, Lovelace was again imprisoned for being a royalist leader, this time in Peterhouse Prison, from October 1648 to April 1649. While incarcerated, he prepared his first volume of poetry, *Lucasta*, and it was published upon his release. His financial circumstances in dire straits, he sold the remainder of his family land, including the manor house and its possessions, and spent the last of his days living in poverty and relying on the generosity of friends.

Lovelace died in London, about 1658, and was buried in Saint Bride's Church, which was destroyed during the Great Fire of London in 1666. In his memory, his brother published *Lucasta: Posthume Poems* in 1660.

POEM TEXT

> When Love with unconfinéd wings
> Hovers within my gates,
> And my divine Althea brings
> To whisper at the grates;
> When I lie tangled in her hair   5
> And fettered to her eye,
> The birds that wanton in the air
> Know no such liberty.
>
> When flowing cups run swiftly round
> With no allaying Thames,   10

Our careless heads with roses bound,
Our hearts with loyal flames;
When thirsty grief in wine we steep,
When healths and draughts go free—
Fishes that tipple in the deep   15
Know no such liberty.

When, like committed linnets, I
With shriller throat shall sing
The sweetness, mercy, majesty,
And glories of my King;   20
When I shall voice aloud how good
He is, how great should be,
Enlargéd winds, that curl the flood,
Know no such liberty.

Stone walls do not a prison make,   25
Nor iron bars a cage;
Minds innocent and quiet take
That for an hermitage;
If I have freedom in my love
And in my soul am free,   30
Angels alone, that soar above,
Enjoy such liberty.

MEDIA ADAPTATIONS

- "To Althea, From Prison" was set to music by the British folk group Fairport Convention and recorded on their 1973 album *Nine*.
- *81 Famous Poems* is a two-cassette sound recording, which includes "To Althea, From Prison." It was produced by Audio Partners in 1987.
- The folk group Three Pressed Men recorded "To Althea, From Prison" on their first album *Daddy Fox* (1998).

POEM SUMMARY

"To Althea, From Prison" is a lyric poem of four eight-line stanzas. The odd numbered lines contain eight syllables whereas the even numbered lines contain just six syllables, all in the unstressed/stressed iambic meter; in other words, Lovelace alternates lines between iambic tetrameter and iambic trimeter. The rhyme scheme is *ababcdcd* throughout. This balanced structure nonetheless gives a feeling of spontaneity because of colloquial, casual, and even surprising word choices. The single speaker uses simple, concrete diction. Lovelace uses conceits, that is, exaggerated comparisons, to convey the great freedom his mind provides while his body is not free; he contrasts his physical imprisonment with his superior moral and spiritual freedom.

Stanza 1

In line 1, the accent in "unconfinéd" indicates that the last syllable receives stress: un-con-fin-ed. This word begins the theme of freedom. In line 2 the word "gates" stands for the cell doors. Line 3 reports what the wings of love bring to his cell: his Althea, who, according to line 4, has come to whisper to him at the "grates" or bars of the cell. The prisoner's imagination lets Althea enter the cell where he can lie with her and exchange his prison chains for being locked in her gaze. The freedom to be with Althea in his mind is compared to the liberty of the gods who are "wanton," that is, playful. In at least six manuscript versions of the poem, Lovelace used "birds" instead of "gods," but for some reason the word was changed to "gods" when the poem was published. Birds might make more sense since the wantonness takes place in the air. Also, birds convey freedom as they soar, so the comparison to their liberty is fitting. However, in the poet's time, gods were imagined to be in the air, and they are free to do as they please, so a comparison to the liberty of the gods is appropriate as well.

Stanza 2

This stanza alludes to a work by the Roman poet Horace. In Ode 2.11, Horace asks a slave to temper his fiery wine with water from a passing stream, but the speaker wants "no allaying Thames." That is, he wants no water from the Thames River that flows through London to dilute his wine. Horace invites a friend to drink with him and have roses placed onto their hair like a garland, noting that wine dispels worries. Similarly, the speaker calls for "careless heads with roses bound." The Royalists, whose hearts burn with "loyal flames" are grieved by the opposition to the king and the hardships, such as prison, that they endure. The speaker, therefore, advocates allaying their "thirsty grief" by imbibing freely from the full "flowing" cups passed "swiftly round." Extreme circumstances

TOPICS FOR FURTHER STUDY

- Collect information about the concept of the *Renaissance man*, identifying features of his lifestyle and education. Then have a class discussion about whether it would be possible in modern times to be a Renaissance man.

- Divide the class into groups with each group choosing to research and represent a different member of the Sons of Ben, the literary group made up of followers of Ben Jonson. Each group can make a presentation about its selected author in which students present a short biography and list his most important works, then rank him in relation to his peers. Include a picture of the selected poets to be presented to classmates.

- Lovelace was imprisoned twice for political reasons. Study instances in modern times when people have been imprisoned or put under house arrest for opposition to the ruling party. Are there any current prime ministers or presidents who were once prisoners in their own country? Working individually, in pairs, or in groups according to teacher preference, research such situations in the last century and write a report on your famous prisoner. One suggestion is to begin looking among Nobel Peace Prize winners.

- It was rumored that the Althea in "To Althea, From Prison" was actually Lucy Sacheverell. As a project, find out more about Sacheverell and write a short play or short story telling the love story of Richard and Lucy and the reason they could not marry.

- It was common practice during the seventeenth century for the verses written by Cavaliers for the court to be set to music. "To Althea, From Prison" was set to music. Choose one of Lovelace's poems and compose a song for it in any style of music you wish, preferably in a current popular style or in an ethnic style of music.

---

demand extreme remedies; serious drinking is required to combat the serious punishment of prison. They drink toasts, or "healths," probably to each other and to the king. "Draughts" means drawing in through the mouth or down the throat, so the wine is being drunk as freely as the toasts are being given. All this revelry is compared to fish in the "deep," or deep blue seas, who "tipple" the ocean waters. To tipple means to drink alcoholic beverages continuously in small amounts, just as fish continuously process water through their gills. Consequently, just as fishes swim freely, the speaker and his friends engorge themselves in a different liquid medium and know even greater freedom because they know freedom of spirit.

Stanza 3

The "linnets" in line 1 are songbirds. They are "committed" as one is committed to an asylum or jail; therefore, they are caged songbirds. Like the linnet, the speaker refuses to be bound in song and spirit and will sing even louder, even "shriller" from his cell than the birds from their cage. The song he will sing will testify to his unvanquished fealty to the king; he will sing of the "sweetness, mercy, majesty, and glories" of the king. Lovelace's words will loudly praise the king's goodness and greatness, so loudly, in fact, that they will outdo winds so great that they can "curl the flood," that is, create waves on the water. As with "unconfinéd," "Enlargéd" receives a stress on the final syllable. Even these enlarged winds, perhaps of hurricane force, do not know the freedom to make noise like the speaker intends to make, at least in his mind, expressing his continued royalist allegiance.

Stanza 4

The simplicity and clarity of Lovelace's language makes the first two lines of this stanza memorable. Lovelace proclaims that a person's mind cannot be imprisoned by physical materials; freedom is a matter of attitude. In line 3, the speaker declares he is innocent of any wrongdoing, and those who are innocent and quiet, perhaps enjoying peace of mind, can therefore transform a prison into a hermitage. A hermitage is a place where people willingly go for solitude, a retreat where a person can concentrate on what really matters. Lovelace focuses on the speaker's love for Althea and the principles by which he lives. His love and his honor give him freedom. This stanza is the culmination of the speaker's message, that he will not be overwhelmed or controlled by others. Indeed, the freedom he feels in his love and in his soul is only matched by the freedom angels have.

THEMES

Freedom

As many prisoners of war have discovered, a person's body can be imprisoned, but the jailors can never imprison the mind. In the final analysis, freedom of the mind is all that really counts because imagination can take a person anywhere, even outside one's cell. Imagination can bring Althea to the speaker in Lovelace's poem. At first she is just whispering outside the bars of his cell, but then his imagination brings him into her arms, tangled in her hair, and gazing longingly into her eyes. The speaker's mind is free to imagine being with his friends at a party where the wine flows as plentifully as ocean water as it assuages the pain of royalist grief over the state of the kingdom. Lovelace was in prison for his loyalty to the king, but in his mind he was still free to sing the praises of the monarch, and he did so by writing this poem. Prison took away his physical freedom, but it could not limit his thoughts, his honor, his devotion, and his love. As the speaker states in the last stanza of "To Althea, From Prison," if his soul is free, then he still has the ultimate freedom, the only truly important freedom.

Stoicism, Honor, and Loyalty

Stoicism is a philosophy that originated in ancient Greece. It advocates self-control, reason, and fortitude so that destructive emotions can be avoided and happiness can be found in virtues such as honor and loyalty. A stoic person can remain serene even when sick, in danger, in exile, or in prison. Stoicism is achieved through an act of will that enables a person to endure hardships patiently. In writing "To Althea, From Prison," Lovelace proved that he could be a stoic. His imagination separated him from the negative aspects of his imprisonment. The poem's speaker is an honorable man, one who about love and loyalty, one who imagines despite being incarcerated because he believes his cause is right. The Royalists believed that it was both their duty and their great honor to serve the king. In the same spirit as a knight of medieval days, Lovelace placed honor above all, and at the end of his life, that is all he had left. He had pledged his life, his honor, and his riches to the king, and he made good on his pledge. Lovelace's loyalty is evident in the third stanza of "To Althea, From Prison" when the speaker defiantly praises the king.

Carpe Diem

The Latin saying *carpe diem* translates as *seize the day*. The recommendation is to live fully in the moment. Since the future is uncertain, live life to the fullest in the present. Lovelace uses this common Cavalier theme in "To Althea, From Prison." Incarceration assumes that one's enjoyment is postponed until the person is liberated, but the speaker in Lovelace's poem turns this bad time into a good one. By controlling his mental focus, he enjoys his love for Althea and the king's greatness. Through the freedom of his mental focus, he can maintain his values and loyalties. In this poem, the speaker seizes upon what is available to him to make his day bearable: the amazing ability of his imagination to make him feel free even when physically he is not free.

STYLE

Conceit

The Cavaliers, including Lovelace, were influenced by John Donne. They used the metaphysical conceit made fashionable by Donne. A metaphysical conceit is a figure of speech that creates an elaborate parallel between two objects or situations that seem to be unlike. One of Donne's best known conceits occurs in "A Valediction Forbidding Mourning," in which the poet compares the coordinated movements of the two feet of a circle-drawing compass to that of the relationship between his soul and the soul of his lady, that is, they work in unison, even when separated. In the first stanza of "To Althea, From Prison," the speaker in Lovelace's

An engraving by Le Maitre of a seventeenth-century prison in France (DeAgostini Picture Library | DeAgostini | Getty Images)

poem compares the freedom given to him by love to the liberty of the gods. In the second stanza, he compares the abundance of wine at his imaginary party to the amount of water in the ocean. In the third stanza, he compares the extent of his praises for the king to the wind that generates waves across flood waters. In the last stanza, he compares the freedom of his mind to the freedom of the angels.

Sprezzatura

The Renaissance man was defined by Baldassare Castiglione (1478–1529) in *Il Cortegiano* (*The Courtier*), published in Italy in 1528. The Renaissance man was a cultivated member of the royal court who was well-rounded in his intellectual and artistic education and in his physical training, including military skills. As a soldier and statesman, the Renaissance gentleman was expected to be an excellent athlete, a good conversationalist, and a subtle philosopher with literary and artistic pursuits. His relations with women were chivalrous and platonic. This multi-talented person acted in all these ways with ease, with the grace of what Castiglione called *sprezzatura*. This casual manner was expressed through the simple language used by the Cavalier poets, tending even to the colloquial. In "To Althea, From Prison," Lovelace wrote about "fishes that tipple," with "tipple" being a common euphemism for the act of drinking habitually. In the rest of the poem, the language is so simple that few words are more than two syllables.

HISTORICAL CONTEXT

The Cavalier Poets

The Cavalier literary movement flourished from 1625 to 1649 and was characterized by direct and colloquial language, individualism, lighthearted wit, elegant mannerisms, amorous and sometime erotic themes, and adherence to upper-class values. The word *cavalier* means *not too serious*. As aristocratic gentlemen, the Cavalier poets were expected to emulate the Renaissance man, that

COMPARE & CONTRAST

- **Mid-1600s:** Great Britain is controlled by the Puritans who have defeated Charles I then captured and executed him. Led briefly by Oliver Cromwell, this government eventually collapses, and the son of Charles I is crowned Charles II in 1660, an event later called the Restoration.

    Today: Great Britain (meaning England, Northern Ireland, Scotland, and Wales) is a constitutional monarchy with a royal family whose continuous line of succession dates from the tenth century.

- **Mid-1600s:** The Puritans, who call themselves Anabaptists, are a radical Protestant sect bent on removing remnants of Catholicism from the Church of England, including changing the Book of Common Prayer.

    Today: Radical Protestant sects, who identify themselves as fundamentalists or evangelicals, are active in politics, attempting to impose their beliefs on government and law.

- **Mid-1600s:** A young man can be granted a master's degree on order of the king and queen. Only members of the aristocracy attend college after receiving private tutoring at home.

    Today: Admissions policies at Oxford University are criticized for being elitist. Oxford University has stringent academic requirements that must be met before students are granted a degree.

---

is, be well-educated, talented in various sports and literary pursuits, conversant in Latin and Greek, witty, romantic, a soldier, and a chivalrous Christian. However, they were not deeply religious, did not ponder their immortal souls, and most definitely pursued earthly enjoyment. Their lifestyle forced their poetry to be only an cultivated hobby, not something they seriously sought to publish. Lovelace sought publication as a source of income, after he lost his wealth in service to the king.

Poetry served as an amusement to be shared with friends in court, as a way of saying thanks for a great party, as a means to celebrate a royal event, as a gift, or as a commemoration of a wedding or funeral. The Cavaliers also wrote plays that were performed at private gatherings because the theaters were closed during the rule of Oliver Cromwell. Naturally, these plays made many references to politics and religion.

Besides Lovelace, the chief Cavalier poets were Thomas Carew, Robert Herrick, and Sir John Suckling. Politically, the Cavaliers were Royalists who supported Charles I against Parliament and the Roundheads (Puritans) during the civil wars. Carew, Suckling, and Lovelace served in the King's army, while Herrick was an Anglican clergyman.

Since the Cavalier poets imitated Ben Jonson's elegant ease with language, they are sometimes referred to as the Sons of Ben or the Tribe of Ben. However, they also owed something to John Donne's intellectual conceits, that is, Donne's elaborate parallels between two dissimilar subjects. The work of Lovelace and Carew also shows the influence of Petrarch, or Francesco Petrarca, the fourteenth-century Italian scholar and poet. Petrarch's sonnets were admired and imitated throughout Europe during the Renaissance and became a model for lyrical poetry.

English Civil Wars

The English Civil Wars had their origin in the early seventeenth century during the reign of James I. A middle class had arisen among the gentry and merchants as a result of the tremendous growth of markets and trade under the Tudors, so by the time Elizabeth died in 1603 and her Scottish cousin took the throne, this expanding and anti-royalist class was ready for representation in Parliament. James, however, refused to compromise on religious questions with the Puritan majority in the Parliament, so it responded with reluctance to fund the king's endeavors. James closed Parliament in 1610, and the next fifteen years were ones of continuous contention between king and Parliament.

Matters did not improve with the ascent of Charles I as he and Parliament were in a power struggle. Charles dissolved the Parliament and attempted to rule by himself for eleven years. However, religious conflicts in Scotland led to the Bishops' Wars in 1639, in which Lovelace fought, and the king was compelled to call upon Parliament for financial aid in 1640. Charles I dissolved Parliament again in just three weeks, but the Scottish war was such a disaster that the king had to give in to his opposition. Parliament resumed and greatly strengthened its powers by law. Nonetheless, when rebellion broke out in Ireland, Parliament was too afraid of the king to authorize an army for him, fearing that he would use the army against Parliament members themselves. Further radical proposals by Puritans drove moderates to side with the king. Then, in 1642, the king tried to capture a Puritan leader, and civil war ensued.

Those supporting the king were called Royalists and were mostly Anglican and Catholic members of the upper class. Those supporting the Puritans were called Roundheads because of their bowl-shaped haircuts. The first war lasted until 1646 when the king surrendered to a type of house arrest with the Scots. However, the Scots delivered the king to Parliament in 1647. A dissonant portion of the army took the king away from Parliament, but he escaped from them and took refuge on the Isle of Wight. Negotiations brought some agreement, but uprisings in Wales, Kent, and Essex caused a second civil war that further split the opposition forces. The army under Oliver Cromwell took over Parliament, tried the king for treason, executed him in 1649, and set up a republic. Charles's son, later crowned Charles II, was recognized as king in parts of Ireland and Scotland, but he was forced to flee to the continent in 1651, and then the wars, also known as the Puritan Revolution, finally ended. The Cromwell Commonwealth lasted only eleven years. In 1660, Parliament invited Charles II to assume the English throne. Although many of the Puritan changes were revoked and Anglicanism was restored as the

A linnet (Image copyright David Dohnal, 2009. Used under license from Shutterstock.com)

state church, the climate was permanently changed, so in 1688, in a move called the Glorious Revolution, Parliament and the king reached an agreement for a separation of powers that has been the government structure in Great Britain ever since.

CRITICAL OVERVIEW

During his lifetime, Lovelace had a reputation as a gentleman poet, but that amateur status caused him to be excluded from a critique of major and minor contemporary poets written by Sir John Suckling, even though Suckling was a fellow Cavalier poet. Lovelace received mention in some late seventeenth-century literary critical works, but his name virtually disappeared until two of his poems, "To Lucasta, Going to the Warres" and "To Althea, From Prison" were published in a 1765 anthology. Attention continued to be sparse for many decades. *Gentleman's Magazine* published a critical appreciation in 1791 and 1792, and in 1817 and 1818 all of Lovelace's poetry was published by S. W. Singer, but with deletions of parts. Both *Lucasta* and *Lucasta: Posthume Poems* came out it 1864 in one volume, edited by W. Carew Hazlitt. Then, in 1884, A. E. Waite, using recently discovered documents, produced the best biographical material up to that point. In 1925, the definitive edition of Lovelace's poetry was published by C. H. Wilkinson, who thoroughly examined both Lovelace's life and works. Also that year, C. H. Hartmann published the only book-length study to that date of Lovelace's work, but it was flawed by presumptions about Lovelace's life and motives. The last full-length work on Lovelace was published in 1970 by Manfred Weidhorn. However, critical articles continue to be published; in fact, there was renewed interest in Lovelace in the second half of the twentieth century.

"To Althea, From Prison" remains Lovelace's most acclaimed poem, so there are a number of critical reviews specific to it. Raymond A. Anselment found that "Lovelace's indomitable, festive stoicism is a distinct and individualistic part of a historic moment." Anselment noted that such stoic "triumph of the mind over the body" is usually Christian, though Lovelace does not espouse specifically Christian themes. Rather, Lovelace "celebrates a stoicism consciously at odds with prevailing, religiously inspired transformations of prison's harshness."

Agnes Repplier in her 1891 book *Points of View* suggested that Lovelace took an impetuous nature into a stormy situation and the resulting imprisonment, as described in "To Althea, From Prison," reveals that "passion, made dignified by suffering, rewards with lavish hand the captive, happy with his chains." She further theorized that this poem is the perfect product of the "tempered delicacy" and "finer grain" of a "many-sided existence." Similarly, C. V. Wedgwood commented in *Poetry and Politics under the Stuarts* that the poem "arises directly from the political circumstances of the time in which it was written, but it transcends the temporary and lifts Lovelace to the immortals." Wedgwood added that this poem "simple and profound, limpid and musical ... has rightly become one of the most quoted verses in the whole of English literature." Echoing this sentiment that there is good reason for the inclusion of this poem in nearly every anthology of great British poetry, Robin Skelton emphasized in *Cavalier Poets* that

> MORE THAN A CAVALIER, LOVELACE WAS A RENAISSANCE MAN, HEARKENING BACK TO THE AGE OF KNIGHTHOOD AND CHIVALRY WHEN A GENTLEMAN PLEDGED HIS SERVICES TO WOMEN AND TO THE KING."

"We do not often get work with the controlled strength, the strong personal touch, and the gaiety and courage of 'To Althea, From Prison.'"

CRITICISM

Lois Kerschen

Kerschen is an educator and freelance writer. In this essay, she examines the role that the Cavalier played in the creation of "To Althea, From Prison."

As with all writers, Lovelace's style and technique were influenced by his education, by other poets, and by his times. As a member of the land-holding upper class, he had the best education available, studied literature, was expected to dabble in the fine arts, and was drawn into the religious and class wars of the Carolinian era in British history. A product of seventeenth-century aristocracy, Lovelace was also graced with exceptionally good looks, charm, wit, and a nobility of character. This last trait was supposed to be the mark of his breeding, but in reality it was often lacking in others of his rank. With Lovelace, however, his honor and loyalty were apparently sincere and were expressed in his masterpiece "To Althea, From Prison."

In the seventeenth century, a young boy of Lovelace's social status would have been provided private tutors at his family estate as the first level of his education. Then he would be sent to a fashionable boarding school, and at age fifteen or sixteen, the brightest male students were sent to one of England's two great universities, Oxford or Cambridge. In Lovelace's case, at eleven he went to Charterhouse School, which remains a premier preparatory school in the twenty-first century. By the age of fifteen, Lovelace was serving at court, and shortly thereafter,

WHAT DO I READ NEXT?

- *Poems of Thomas Carew*, edited by Arthur Vincent and published in 1972, presents the poetry of one of the best known of the Cavalier poets with an introduction about his life and works. With a reputation as a rascal and a writer of sexually risqué verses, Carew usually produced short, witty lines but also masques, translations of Psalms, and a widely acclaimed elegy on the death of John Donne.

- *Robert Herrick 1591–1674: Selected Poems*, edited and with an introduction by David Jesson-Dibley, was published in 1989. This collection illustrates why Herrick was one of the most talented of the Cavalier poets and a great songwriter who, although an Anglican priest, wrote sensual verses and advocated seizing the moment before youth passes away, evident in his famous line "Gather ye rosebuds while ye may."

- An overview of the English Renaissance and Cavalier poets is available in *Literary Criticism of Seventeenth-Century England*. This 2000 anthology, edited by Edward Taylor, surveys the tastes and practices of poets and essayists such as Ben Jonson, Francis Bacon, John Milton, George Herbert, and Andrew Marvell.

- *The Cavalier Poets: An Anthology*, edited by Thomas Crofts and published in 1996, contains more than 120 works of poets associated with the court of Charles I, including Herrick, Carew, Suckling, and Lovelace.

- *The Poems of Richard Lovelace: Lucasta, Etc.*, is a paperback edition from the Legacy Reprint Series that reproduces historical books, imperfections and all, in an effort to preserve culturally important literature. This edition is a copy of Lovelace's first volume of poetry, published by BiblioLife in 2009.

- *The Poems, Plays, and Other Remains of Sir John Suckling*, edited by William Carew Hazlitt in 1892, is available in paperback and hardback editions published in 2006 and 2007 by Kessinger. This two-volume work about the man most often associated poetically with Richard Lovelace includes biography, notes, and illustrations.

- *The Complete Odes and Epodes* of Horace, the Roman poet, published by Penguin Classics in 1983, is a good complement to the works of Lovelace because it is a sample of the type of literature that Lovelace would have studied and to which he alluded in his poetry.

- *The Boy Who Dared*, by Susan Campbell Bartoletti, a young adult novel published by Scholastic Press in 2008, is about a sixteen-year-old German boy who goes to prison for exposing the truth about his government by distributing anti-Nazi leaflets.

- *The Best Poems Ever: A Collection of Poetry's Greatest Verses* is a Scholastic Classics paperback published in 2002 for the young adult reader, which presents imaginative poems from different ethnicities around the world.

---

he enrolled at Oxford. After receiving a master's degree at Oxford, he spent a short time at Cambridge as well. In addition to learning to hunt and engage in sports, he was taught philosophy, science, literature, the fine arts, and several languages. He knew Greek and Latin and ancient Greek and Roman literature. In choosing Althea, a Greek name, Lovelace pays tribute to the classics and displays his education.

Lovelace would also have studied Horace, the leading Roman lyric poet during the time of Caesar Augustus. In "To Althea, From Prison," the first three lines are a variation of lines from an Horatian ode. Since Lovelace's audience would have had the same type of education, he could expect that his readers would instantly recognize the allusion and appreciate the way he incorporated Horace's call for garlands for their heads and wine to soothe their cares. Lovelace knew all the Cavaliers were thoroughly experienced in celebrating with wine, women, and song.

Lovelace is often called the best example of a Cavalier, so it is appropriate to compare him to the commonly accepted characteristics of this group, although it seems for every commonality there is a difference. Walter R. Davis, writing for the *Reference Guide to English Literature*, notes that the work of Lovelace shared with that of his fellow Cavaliers traits of wit and "metrical regularity, dilation of thought and image rather than compression, and care for the whole poem rather than strikingly original parts of it." However, Davis adds, Lovelace is distinguished from the rest by complexity of view, subtle tone, and "poetry of poise—distant, judicious, open to conflict." The metric regularity can be seen in the consistent meter in "To Althea, From Prison," the dilation of image in the extended conceit, and the quality of writing in the entire poem that has earned it the reputation of being Lovelace's finest. Nonetheless, it is just this superiority of quality that separates him from the other Cavaliers who may have had more consistency of quality throughout their poetry, but few achieved anything close to the complete package of poetic attributes found in "To Althea, From Prison."

In the centuries that followed him, Lovelace was never considered the best of the Cavalier poets because of the inconsistency of his work. Some of his poetry is amateurish, some is just good, while a few pieces, such as "To Althea, From Prison," have earned him a place in most anthologies of the greatest English poetry. His inconsistency may be explained by the fact that as a gentleman of the court he was expected to be sufficiently skilled to write poetry for entertainment, but nothing more. A gentleman pursued the arts as a hobby, but of course he did not need to do anything as mundane as to write for a living. Life was to be enjoyed, so a gentleman did not get too serious about anything, except perhaps his honor and duty to the king; he was supposed to have a light-hearted, cavalier attitude. Consequently, Lovelace gave some of his leisure time by writing trivial verse designed for amusement only. After the onset of the wars, Lovelace's leisure time diminished. He became a soldier, and in two decades of writing, he was able to produce only two volumes of poetry. However, when he had the time, as when he was in prison with nothing else to do but concentrate on his writing, he was capable of producing something as timeless and superior as "To Althea, From Prison."

Another explanation for his inconsistency may be that Lovelace attempted more types of poetry than the other Cavaliers. Jonathan F. S. Post, writing in *English Lyric Poetry: The Early Seventeenth Century*, explains that Lovelace had a versatility that made it appear as if he were "the least in control of his muse" among the Cavaliers. But the problem, Post suggests, may not have been a lack of mastery so much as a penchant for experimentation. The range of forms in his poetry may have had a negative effect on his reputation, but a different type of diversity had a positive effect, according to Harry Blemires in *A Short History of English Literature*: "Lovelace's work reveals a wide range of feelings rather than a set of postures" like that found sometimes in the works of other Cavaliers, especially Carew. Blemires thinks that when Lovelace was posing, he did so purposely and obviously in the manner of John Donne's mockeries.

Moreover, Lovelace could display a depth of emotion that was not typical of the Cavaliers. Blemires states that the Cavaliers had a "courtly polish which seems to distance tribulation—and such distancing of what might disturb with passion or anguish is a mark of Cavalier poetry in general." In other words, they were too cool to make commitments or to act as if they cared. When Lovelace wrote about fidelity and duty, however, he was serious and authentic. In some of Lovelace's light verses, he may have played with a lady's affections, but in "To Althea, From Prison," he describes a sense of being fettered or locked with his beloved's eyes—a symbol for the poet's permanent attachment to the woman to whom the poem is addressed. Also, he may have risen in scorn above the confinement of prison, but that was a scorn born of dignity, not aloofness.

Consistent with this evaluation of Lovelace's depth is the opinion that he was perhaps more sensuous than the other Cavaliers. The code of platonic love espoused in much poetry of the time is missing in the description of Althea's tangled hair. More than a Cavalier, Lovelace was a Renaissance man, hearkening back to the age of knighthood and chivalry when a gentleman pledged his services to women and to the king. Anselment suggests that in "To Althea, From Prison" honor and the prisoner's love for Althea are "either explicitly or implicitly synonymous with the King, and raising a cup to the monarch's health and being raised by the image of the beloved seem in the context of" the poem to be as one. It is this emotional complexity that makes "To Althea, From Prison" so extraordinary.

Robin Skelton, author of *Cavalier Poets* states that Lovelace's most Cavalier poems are the least like him. Rather, Lovelace is most himself, Skelton believes, when he could play with words "within the confines of a decorously frigid meter." This previously mentioned metric regularity, combined with such surprising word choices in as "no allaying Thames," "tipple," "committed linnets," and "shriller throat," makes for lively and interesting poetry that is of much higher quality than the usual amateur verses written for courtly entertainment. As Sharon Cadmon Seelig notes, Lovelace "places clause against clause, line against line, yet interrupts that balanced structure with the surprising word so that the result is a sense of grace, elegance, and control that never ceases to seem spontaneous." The effect is a musically balanced poem in which the beauty of his soul, often commented upon by friends and literary critics, could be seen in his expression of an idyllic theme of honor.

The Cavalier poets celebrated convivial drinking, if not outright drunkenness and debauchery. C. V. Wedgwood comments in his book *Poetry and Politics under the Stuarts*: "There had always been among the Cavaliers a strain of light-heartedness, a willingness to dismiss dull care and call for a drink." That was fun until they found themselves, as Royalists, on the losing side of the civil war. The disintegration of their playful camaraderie can be seen in the songs that they wrote and played as the Roundheads took control. For example, the poems in Lovelace's book *Lucasta* include some melancholy descriptions of their suffering and captivity in the 1640s. Among them, "To Althea, From Prison," written in 1642, established a popular trend with the Cavaliers as they, too, suffered similar fates. However, according to Wedgwood, "None of the imitations comes at all near to the beauty of the original, and the theme, as the years went by, was treated with increasing crudity."

In the final analysis, Lovelace was the epitome of a Cavalier in his lifestyle as a gentleman at court and gallant soldier, and in his appearance and behavior, but he was unlike the other

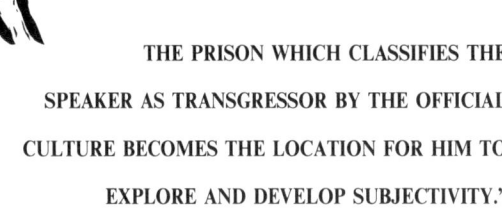

THE PRISON WHICH CLASSIFIES THE SPEAKER AS TRANSGRESSOR BY THE OFFICIAL CULTURE BECOMES THE LOCATION FOR HIM TO EXPLORE AND DEVELOP SUBJECTIVITY."

Cavalier poets when he wrote seriously. In those instances, he tried various forms, showed a depth of feeling, exhibited an honorable and brave spirit, and produced poems still worthy of study centuries later. These stellar poems may have been few in number, but given the skill in "To Althea, From Prison," Lovelace is likely be remembered for all time.

Source: Lois Kerschen, Critical Essay on "To Althea, From Prison," in *Poetry for Students*, Gale, Cengage Learning, 2010.

Bronwen Price

In the following essay, Price discusses the serious issues of subjectivity and agency in the Cavalier poet Richard Lovelace's prison poems.

Appearing for the first time in 1649, at the end of the Civil War, Lovelace's collection of poetry, *Lucasta*, represents the work of a committed royalist and faithful subject to the king. References to battle, prison, shattered loyalties and lost ideals resonate throughout the volume. The historical and political specificity of Lovelace's poetry has received much critical consideration. In an illuminating study of Lovelace's and Marvell's poetry, Leah Marcus draws attention to *Lucasta*'s continual recalling of Caroline iconography, particularly through its allusion to rural ritual and hermeticism, which were idealised by and incorporated within royalist doctrine by the *Book of Sports* and Stuart entertainments. Marcus sees *Lucasta* as 'a Cavalier paradigm, a treasury of political motifs' which 'repeatedly imbeds rituals and symbols of the vanished court in protected rural enclosures as a way of perpetuating vestiges of the culture that was lost'. In *Lucasta* the grove provides the emblem of both the palace and the Anglican church in prewar terms, whose values and rituals are recovered in private, sacred realms.

However, while the images of enclosures are a way of resurrecting and naturalising the

An engraving by Holler of the Tower of London, a prison, as viewed across the River Thames, c. 1680 (Edward Gooch | Hulton Archive | Getty Images)

royalist programme, Marcus also suggests that they signify retreat, stagnation and insularity; a failure to engage with the world outside them. Underlying the protected idyllic grove lies a sense of anxiety about the erosion of Royal power—'a self-doubt that had to be countered with various rituals of mastery', where the male royalist subject's 'self-worth' is re-established by his adoption of 'the role which the monarch had proved too weak to sustain'.

It is with some of the implications of this self-doubt, identified at the end of Marcus's analysis, that I would like to begin my examination of Lovelace. I will focus not on the pastoral verse with its rural sanctuaries, but on some exemplary, mainly lyric poems concerning the subject, its placements and its retreats into internal enclosures, poems which through their very form highlight the disjunction between loss and recuperation so fundamental to Lovelace's work. While Marcus's study is invaluable in its analysis of the specific political motifs of royalist poetry, I would like to argue that throughout Lovelace's work we encounter a crisis within the subject which goes beyond the immediate concerns and effects of the Civil War itself. Rather, the war symbolises a broader struggle within identification, signification and epistemology taking place during the Seventeenth Century, which in Lovelace's poetry centres around the precarious position of the subject and its status. Indeed, Lovelace's work constantly signals an incipient discourse of subjectivity and identity which contests with and fractures the mythic corporeal language of monarchic absolutism onto which the royalist subject attempts to cling. Within this struggle the position of the loyal subject is polarised into a series of dilemmas: where is the location of this subject without its centre of signification—the king—and how can it now articulate and define itself?

I

These questions and the complex problems they arouse are the issue of 'The Lady A. L. My Asylum in a great extremity', a significant poem which has rarely been discussed. The poem begins with a description of the moment in which Charles I was dethroned and beheaded. It then shifts from this public display to focus on the effect of the king's execution on his loyal subject, the speaker. This is followed by the enigmatic entry of the symbolic female figure, A. L., who rescues and recovers the speaker from desperation and death. The final part of the poem is devoted to thanking and praising her, with no further reference being made to the king:

"The Lady A. L. My Asylum in a great extremity."

With that delight the Royal Captiv's brought
Before the Throne, to breathe his farewell thought,
To tel his last tale, and so end with it;
Which gladly he esteemes a Benefit;
When the brave Victor at his great Soule dumbe
Findes something there, Fate cannot overcome,
Cals the chain'd Prince, and by his glory led,
First reaches him his Crowne, and then his Head;
Who ne're 'til now thinks himself slave and poor;
For though nought else, he had himselfe before;
He weepes at this faire chance, nor wil allow.
But that the Diadem doth brand his brow,
And under-rates himselfe below mankinde,
Who first had lost his Body, now his Minde.
With such a Joy came I to heare my Dombe,
And haste the preparation of my Tombe,
When like good Angels who have heav'nly charge
To steere and guide mans sudden giddy barge,
She snatcht me from the Rock I was upon,
And landed me at lifes Pavillion;
Where I thus wound out of th'immense Abysse,
Was straight set on a Pinnacle of Blisse.
Let me leape in againe! and by that Fall
Bring me to my first woe, so cancel all;
Ah's this a quitting of the debt you owe,
To Crush her and her goodness at one blow?
Defend me from so foule Impiety,
Would make Fiends grieve, & Furies weep to see ...
Where then thou bold instinct shal I begin
My endlesse taske? To thanke her were a sin
Great as not speake, and not to speake a blame
Beyond what's worst, such as doth want a Name;
So thou my All, poore Gratitude, ev'n thou
In this, wilt an unthankful Office do;
Or wilt I fling all at her feet I have?
My Life, my Love, my very Soule a Slave?
Tye my free Spirit onely unto her,
And yeeld up my Affection Prisoner?
Fond Thought in this thou teachest me to give
What first was hers, since by her breath I live;
And hast but show'd me how I may resigne
Possession of those things are none of mine.

The poem opens with the ceremonial spectacle of the king's execution, a moment which seems to mark both the instance and displacement of a pre-modern corporeal code of meaning. That theatre of sovereign power and vengeance which manifested the subjection of people within the monarchic frame, the public execution, is inverted to become the location where the king himself is displayed as the man condemned. In the monarch's final performance we apparently view the staging of his own subjection. As the corporeal body of the sovereign is offered as a spectacle, so it is disintegrated. As it is displayed, so it is negated. The player-king seems to take his final bow on the pre-modern stage, and as we observe we see the dissolution of the observed/observing omnipresent monarchic gaze.

This spectacle is indeed full of ambivalence. Although the text details each procedure leading to the king's execution in ritualistic terms, the apparent negation of his power is not clear-cut. Although physically subjected as 'Captiv', 'chain'd' and thinking himself 'slave and poor' (11.1–9), the king's 'great Soule', his immortal part, cannot be completely overcome (11.5–6). His kingliness continues as Christ remains God after the crucifixion. While losing his head, the king appears to lose himself (1.10) and so 'underrates himself below mankinde' (1.13), the diadem which 'doth brand his brow' (1.12) marks kingship both as his burden and inherent right, a sign which echoes Christ's crown of thorns. The ultimate act of apparent subjection is also perceived to be a release from earthly imprisonment, something to which the king looks forward with 'delight' (1.1) and 'Which gladly he esteemes a Benefit' (1.4).

As we arrive at the description of the execution, however, it becomes increasingly difficult to identify who is the agent of action. While 'the brave Victor' manifestly manages the ceremony of execution, he is, in the process, deprived of the power of language, made 'dumbe' (1.5) as if he were the victim. To behead the king involves bewilderment, a loss of control, for this seeming supreme act of power entails finding 'something there, Fate cannot overcome' and so to be by the king's 'glory led' (11.6–7). The text thus seems to cling desperately to the remnants of an absolutist ideology, figured in the body of the king, as it simultaneously describes the dissolution of that signifying system. With the loss of that supreme subject, God's lieutenant in whom all others are located and by whom all others are defined, there is some confusion as to whom pronouns refer (11.9 & 13). The king appears as both subject and object, a 'master-signifier' and debased slave, whose terms of power are intensified at the very moment in which they are emptied of meaning.

At this symbolic instance of crisis the text turns its attention in the second stanza to the speaker and the implications of the monarch's execution for him, the faithful subject of the former kingly frame. The speaker's reaction to his own immanent death resembles the king's response to his execution. With the splitting of the body in which his own intelligibility has been located, the speaker looks forward to his own death as a release (11.15–16). Yet, while the speaker's death seems to be bound up with the monarch's through his political and conceptual identification of himself as the king's subject, he also perceives the glint of a new epistemology in which he is already caught up. In this, the interior concerns of 'I' and 'my' are foregrounded and the drama of his own inner turmoil takes the place of and displaces the spectacular sovereign body. The speaker's emergence as an individual self thus appears a troubling prospect, one of desolation, vulnerability, placelessness and fear, an arrival at 'the Rock' after journeying on 'mans sudden giddy barge', at the living hell of 'th'immense Abysse' (11.18–21).

This moment of struggle within the speaker's status as a subject is, however, suddenly reprieved by the unexpected intervention of the woman at line 19. Her entry grants the speaker asylum from the division of subject-hood where self-assertion involves self-annihilation. She encompasses and eclipses the speaker's self, guaranteeing his continued existence by providing a restoration of the values which have been lost. The description of her ministrations is imbedded within a Christian discourse (11.17ff.) so that she appears as an agent of divine truth, where the sexual is embraced within the notion of religious salvation (11.21–22). In the woman the speaker thus finds another centre of meaning; as he is dispossessed of his self, so he becomes absorbed by and dependent on her. In this sense she appears to stand in for the king.

The terms in which the woman is perceived resonate with the ideals of the lost monarchy. The particular reference to her purity, 'Goodnes and Justice' (1.52) links her, for example, with the Roman goddess Astraea, a figure who formed an important part of Elizabeth I's iconography 'as the empress of the world, guardian of religion, patroness of peace, restorer of virtue', a role which parallels A. L.'s in this poem. In A. L. the speaker sees the possibility of retrieving the perfect circle, the halo which he asks to be given to her by 'some glistering ray / To Circle her' (11.40–41) appearing as a crown, an image which unites monarchy, divinity and nature.

In portraying A. L. as possessing monarchic and divine qualities, the speaker's praise of her resembles the motifs of romantic platonism, which, as Graham Parry has shown, were cultivated into 'a refined cult of love' by the Caroline court. Thus A. L. is elevated, idealised and idolised, while the speaker presents himself as humble and distant from her, contemplating her moral and spiritual beauty, discovering in her the heavenly beauty of God. Expressing A. L.'s true worth and offering her thanks is perceived as an impossibility, for she is the source of meaning and truth on earth. Moreover, she appears to incorporate the speaker as the monarch did before. Through her he seems able to relinquish his subjectivity, for his existence depends on her (1.94). She possesses his 'All', 'My Life, my

Love, my very Soule', 'my free Spirit', 'my Affection' (11.87ff.).

The poem therefore turns its attention from the spectacle of social and political schism to the recuperation of the figurative ideals of monarchic rule, united in the decorporealised frame of the courtly woman; from the debasement of sovereign government to the elevation of the woman's mythic power; from the grotesque disarticulation of the monarchic body to the sublime pronouncement of meaning and truth through the presence of A. L.; from the imprisonment and subjection of the monarch to the realisation and pleasure in confinement by the speaker to the woman. The king's 'last tale' (1.3) is renewed with the woman's 'owne Story' (1.61).

However, the poem reveals that the speaker cannot so easily abandon his newly-awakened subjectivity. With his fall into 'th'immense Abysse' comes a loss of innocence, the flickering knowledge of himself as a subject alone. In attempting to dissolve and transcend his subjectivity by presenting himself as embodied within the woman, by whom he is defined and identified, he comes to define the woman. She is an object to whom meaning is applied by the speaking subject. While A. L. appears to command control, it is the speaker who confers power on her. He is her author, constructing her signification. This ambivalence of the terms of power in the poem is heightened by the contradictory presentation of the woman. She is likened to divine immortal beings (11.37ff.) while also perceived to be subject to time and mortality (11.42–48). Even though the woman is regarded as possessing the speaker's 'All' and commanding his life (1.94), a 'leape' by the speaker back into 'th'immense Abysse' is viewed as capable of crushing her (11.23–26). And while the image of A. L.'s coronation appears as a symbolic restoration which reverses the ritualised dethronement of the opening stanza, it is the speaker who asks that A. L. be served and crowned (11.40–41) and who intends to perform this act of coronation with his 'Bayes' and 'Lawrels' of poetry (11.73–76). The ambivalence implied by the gender politics here signals the ambivalence of the terms of subject-hood which the poem apparently attempts to recuperate, as the disquieting spectres of loss and division displayed in the opening spectacle resurface within the very images of restoration.

It is, indeed, the speaker who ultimately emerges as the central focus of the poem, with the text appearing less concerned with the woman than with how the speaker can express himself adequately to give her due praise and thanks. Paradoxically, even as his subjectivity seems to dissolve, the speaker asserts himself as a writing subject, forging a split between himself and the textualised object, A. L. This is highlighted in the last lines in which the speaker claims that his 'All' is the woman's possession. His refusal of subject-hood appears so final that he seems to disown himself, referring to his 'bold Instinct', his 'Thought', his 'All' as 'thou' (11.83ff.). However, this distancing and objectifying of himself as he speaks also appears to reveal the glimmer of an emergent divided subject who retreats from its connection with the public spectacle of the opening stanza into the self-addressed interiorised monologue of the final lines.

II

'The Lady A. L.' seems to signal the awakening of a new discourse of subjectivity even as the poem attempts to repress it. The poem's efforts to retain the terms of meaning symbolically displaced with the beheading of the king paradoxically mark their very loss. These problems and ambivalences of the subject's status come still more to the surface in Lovelace's famous 'prison' poems. In 'To Lucasta. From Prison' it is the speaker who is presented as the condemned person, for with the decapitation of the king comes the sentencing of his loyal subjects, evicted from the inclusive royal anatomy even as it is dismembered. The speaker's punishment, however, is not exhibited in the public theatre of execution, but is hidden from view within the dark enclosed domain of the prison:

"To Lucasta, From Prison, An Epode."

I.

Long in thy Shackels, liberty,
I ask not from these walls, but thee;
Left for a while anothers Bride
To fancy all the world beside.

II.

Yet e're I doe begin to love,
See! How I all my objects prove;
Then my free Soule to that confine,
'Twere possible I might call mine.

III.

First I would be in love with *Peace*,
And her rich swelling breasts increase;
But how alas! how may that be,
Despising Earth, will she love me?

IV.

Faine would I be in love with *War,*
As my deare Just avenging star;
But War is lov'd so ev'ry where,
Ev'n He disdaines a Lodging here.

V.

Thee and thy wounds I would bemoane
Faire thorough-shot *Religion*,
But he lives only that kills thee,
And who so bindes thy hands, is free.

VI.

I would love a *Parliament*
As a maine Prop from Heav'n sent;
But ah! Who's he that would be wedded
To th'fairest body that's beheaded?

VII.

Next would I court my *Liberty*,
And then my Birth-right, *Property*;
But can that be, when it is knowne
There's nothing you can call your owne?

VIII.

A *Reformation* I would have,
As for our griefes a *Sov'raigne* salve;
That is, a cleansing of each wheele
Of State, that yet some rust doth feele;

IX.

But not a Reformation so,
As to reforme were to ore'throw;
Like Watches by unskilfull men
Disjoynted, and set ill againe.

X.

The *Publick Faith* I would adore,
But she is banke-rupt of her store;
Nor how to trust her can I see,
For she that couzens all, must me.

XI.

Since then none of these can be
Fit objects for my Love and me;
What then remaines, but th'only spring
Of all our loves and joyes? The KING.

XII.

He who being the whole Ball
Of Day on Earth, lends it to all;
When seeking to ecclipse his right,
Blinded, we stand in our owne light.

XIII.

And now an universall mist
Of Error is spread or'e each breast,
With such a fury edg'd, as is
Not found in th'inwards of th'Abysse.

XIV.

Oh from thy glorious starry Waine
Dispense on me one sacred Beame
To light me where I soone may see
How to serve you, and you trust me.

The poem opens by suggesting that it is not the physical walls of the prison which are the cause of the speaker's confinement, but his fidelity to 'Lucasta', a name which signifies chastity and which comes to represent the speaker's dutiful tie to the deposed king. However, although the poem is addressed to Lucasta, 'she' seems to disappear after line two when the text concentrates on surveying and assessing the various parts of the state's anatomy as alternative possible objects of desire. In prison the speaker thus apparently breaks free from his bond to 'Lucasta' and takes the liberty 'To fancy all the world beside' (1.4).

In surveying his potential partners the speaker removes attention from his own body and its sensations to the public anatomy of the social structure and so to his troubled soul, as he, the lonely subject, observes the object-body of the 'Politick World' from which he appears distant and isolated. Ironically, his observations contribute to the very process of dissection and division he reviles, as he fragments the body politic into a series of abstractions, disclosing each item to be in disarray. The speaker cuts up the social and political body at the same moment as he discovers it to be dismembered, the divided kingdom reflecting back on the newly-divided subject who perceives it. However, the speaker does not yet readily appear to take up the position of the autonomous sovereign subject who endeavours to master the objects of his gaze. While the speaker seems to be credited with the control of selection and appraisal, identification and classification, this power is clearly ambivalent, as the objects he surveys are presented as possessing agency themselves (stanzas III, IV & X). Further, the process of choosing and defining which apparently empowers the speaker with the claims of judgement and knowledge are problematised by his pursuit of an ideal in which he is not the agent of action and meaning, but subject to a sovereign.

This playing with the placing of subjection and agency, imprisonment and liberty, signified and signifier, pinpoints the dislocation and elusiveness of power and meaning in the poem as the signs which once possessed clear signification for the speaker are perceived to have lost their intelligibility. The text appears subject-centred as the speaker seems decentred from the world he regards. He asserts himself as 'I' in judging the social and political body, while the objects he surveys reveal him to be excluded, alienated, positioned as 'other' in prison, and this is underlined by the confusion of gender at line three where 'he' is 'Left for a while anothers Bride'. In listing and classifying the components of the social and political frame, the speaker finds them to be alien and defamiliarised. Those elements which comprised an integral part of the monarchic body are perceived to be in chaos and marked physically (stanzas V, VI & IX) as the criminal within absolutist monarchy was marked through torture for defiling the royal body. Thus, in seeking alternative love-objects to Lucasta/the monarchy, the speaker finds only repulsive mutilated forms, his own incarcerated body offering a distorted reflection of the unregulated grotesque figure of the anatomy he beholds.

Ultimately, as we might expect, the single desirable object of love is presented to be the lost king, who, as in 'The Lady A. L.', is associated with Christ-like qualities (11.43–46). The monarch appears as God's agent, rejection of whom is the cause of pride (11.47–48) which results in the fall of the present living hell (stanza XIII), while the love the speaker expresses for the monarch is devotional and prayer-like, as he turns from the dismembered, topsy-turvy, terrestrial social and political body to the sublime 'truth' radiated by the king's frame which is 'the whole Ball / Of Day on Earth' (11.45–46). In the royal body there is no division, in the king subject-hood disintegrates. When praising the monarch the speaker moves away from subject-based statements to the concerns of 'our', 'all' and 'we', which are incorporated within the king.

In the end, however, the speaker is still left with the problem of division from the sovereign. The absence and distance of the king from Earth is emphasised in the final stanza, where the king's 'glorious Starry Waine' is beyond the reach of the speaker who seeks 'one sacred Beame' (11.53–54). 'Thy' and 'you' are separate from 'I' and 'me'. The speaker's prison appears to be the inferno of 'Error', the dungeon of blindness on Earth, for he is left in isolation and darkness, his final questions of 'How to serve you, and you trust me' remaining unanswered.

The questions as to the speaker's status and to what extent and in what ways he is subject and subjected thus abound in the poem. As in 'The Lady A. L.', the very attempts to define himself as the king's subject still paradoxically identify the speaker's inauguration as a thinking, knowing, doubting subject exiled from the symbolic system of meaning of which he wishes to be a part. Like the asylum of 'The Lady A. L.', incarceration seems to signal the speaker's loss of a centre of meaning, marking him as both subject to the monarch and cut off from the signifying system the king represents as dismembered limb of the royal frame. Hence the prison polarises the ambivalence of the subject's status, standing as a sign both for his bond to the king and his isolation and alienation within the newly-formed bonds of subjectivity, by which the body is decentred and enslaved.

The problem of the terms in which the speaker may serve and show loyalty to the king from prison is again addressed in 'To Althea, From Prison', in which the text once more explores and plays with different notions of subjection and liberty. . . .

Here the speaker is portrayed as transcending the confines of the prison which, in the previous poem, defined his dislocation from the signifying system of absolutist monarchy. The text, however, is also marked by a sense of displacement, presenting a series of contrasting, apparently disconnected scenarios, which both pinpoint the speaker's 'liberty' and his fidelity to the king. As in 'To Lucasta. From Prison', the poem begins by identifying the speaker's tie to his lover, Althea, but then suddenly shifts in the second stanza to a scene of drinking and comradeship, denoting loyalty to the royal cause. This is followed by a further disjunction in tone when the speaker offers devotional praise to the king and the poem returns finally to the scene of prison which is now transformed into a spiritual sanctuary. This process of dislocation and transformation informs the terms within which the relationship between subjection and liberty are defined and redefined in the poem.

In the opening stanza it is the platonic ideal of spiritual love which is perceived as overcoming the speaker's physical confinement. His spiritual bond to Althea signifies his liberty to sublimate his material shackles. The 'unconfined wings' (1.1) of Cupid which bring him 'my divine *Althea*' (1.3) thus also appear as wings of victory able to surmount the gates of the prison and are recalled in the image of the angel which overrides terrestrial constraints in the conclusion of the poem.

In the second stanza the terms of subjection and liberty alter and are complicated further when we are presented with a sudden shift of scene and mood. As in 'To Lucasta', the woman disappears from the text after the opening, the claims of sexual fidelity prefiguring statements of loyalty to the monarch. The speaker turns from describing his triumphant personal love to presenting himself as part of a body of opinion expressing its commitment to the lost, conquered king. Here the love by which the speaker and his comrades are fettered is their love for the monarch, the crowns of roses which bind their heads replicating the king's crown (1.11). Their prison is not physical, but a dungeon of misery caused by the dissolution of the royal frame, from which they are now released; while the liberty with which they drink 'Healths and draughts' suppresses, rather than transcends their 'thirsty griefe' (11.13–14). The freedom the king's loyal subjects possess is therefore ambivalent, signifying an act of despair which enables them to 'lose their heads' so as to become 'carelesse' (1.11), an act which ironically recalls the decapitation of the king.

In the final stanzas the speaker's relationship to liberty and subjection is marked by a further readjustment. The displacement of the speaker's identification as faithful lover by his role as loyal comrade is now replaced by his affirmation of monastic devotion to the monarch by which he is able to surmount the crisis resulting from the king's dethronement. The speaker appears to find a way of answering the problem posed by 'To Lucasta' of how he may serve the king and enlist his trust. His physical imprisonment, which there had been viewed as a sign of his dislocation from the royal body, is metamorphosed here into a place where he can praise the king and recall him as the centre of meaning. The speaker seems to overcome despair, alienation and entrapment in subjecthood by perceiving the prison as an emblem of his loyalty and commitment to the king, a place which establishes him still as the sovereign's subject, as he uses it as a site of worship and dedication to the monarch, as a church to God.

In reinstating the king as Head, the speaker recovers his own head, which is converted from a 'carelesse' state of distress and drunkenness to one of carefulness, devoted to offering hymn-like praise to the monarch (stanza III). The speaker's mind is no longer a site of 'disease', anaesthetised through drink, but a healthy place, innocent and quiet', (1.27), able to transcend and transform its circumstances by thinking and feeling as it chooses. The 'Stone Walls' and 'Iron bars' (11.25–26), designating incarceration and subjection, are dissolved as they are perceived in terms of a different signifying system, reshaped into 'an Hermitage' (1.28). The prison is thus not viewed as a place of limitation and suppression, but rather one which expresses the speaker's devotion and within which he voices his commitments 'aloud' (1.21). The arena of punishment and political hardship is converted into an asylum, the enclosed sacred space found in 'The Lady A. L.' The speaker overcomes the domain of the conquered, ultimately appearing in a state of triumph and supremacy, as he sublimates terrestrial confines, concentrating on the concerns of the soul and so enjoys the liberty of angels that 'sore above' (1.31).

And yet, in seeking to reinstate the king as head and centre of meaning, the speaker paradoxically asserts the self. The prison which classifies the speaker as transgressor by the official culture becomes the location for him to explore and develop subjectivity ... and affirm his immersion within bourgeois epistemology. In identifying himself as the king's subject, the speaker ironically defines himself as an autonomous, thinking, knowing subject, commanding and manipulating the signification of the outer world from within. It is the condition of the mind and soul which is cited as being central to meaning and it is the speaker's perceptions which possess and produce 'reality', which 'take' (1.27) and 'make' (1.25) signification. The conversion of the speaker's surroundings from cell to hermitage, prison to asylum, is indeed a mark of the speaker's own conversion to a subject-based discourse in which he stands as the God-like centre of his own world. The thinking subject thus usurps the king as its own origin of meaning, positing itself as the centre of its statements, asserting itself as 'the author and guarantee of its own (subjective) truth'. The king no longer commands and articulates the speaker's status, rather he is subject to the speaker's word, who will 'sing' and 'voyce' (11.18 & 21) his greatness. The monarch is paradoxically dethroned by the newly-installed sovereign subject. The attempted annihilation of subjectivity ironically involves the affirmation of the bourgeois subject.

This transformation of the subject's position inaugurates with it a change in the terms of representation. Meaning is no longer focused in the spectacular body of the pre-modern signifying system, symbolised by the king. The corporeal now lies silenced, as the speaker distances himself from his body, forcing it out of the arena of signification. He identifies himself as mind and soul alone, like 'Angels', so supporting Descartes's claim 'that our soul is of a nature entirely independent of the body'. The speaker's 'liberty' is interiorised in the soul and mind, the internalised textualised pleasure of release overriding and ousting the sensations of the flesh. The speaker's apparent transcendence of the prison walls involves the creation of 'A Paradise within', where the confinement of the body is ultimately viewed as a positive measure, its regulation and discipline enabling the release and development of the free soul.

The creation of this 'Paradise within' is, however, inevitably troubled. The hermitage created by the speaker remains a cell, the affirmation of a healthy mind, 'innocent and quiet' (1.27), involves the uneasy restive knowledge that the body and its desires lie suppressed. While the speaker appears to translate the stone walls and iron bars which entrap him into a haven, this very process is a mark of the severed contorted subject, alienated from his body. The assertion of the 'free' soul entails the subject's censorship and denial of his body. The speaker's triumph over his physical prison indicates the triumph of the modern 'noncorporeal soul' which is now 'the prison of the body', marking the speaker's ultimate imprisonment within subjectivity, where his subjection is so profound that it is not exercised from without, but rather he censors himself from within.

III

In the poems I have discussed the speaker's uneasy inauguration into subjectivity is bound up in his desire to be incorporated within the mythic frame of the king. However, this crisis of the subject is further problematised and heightened by the elusive, but recurrent appearance of a woman in each poem—A. L., Lucasta, Althea. It is to this shadowy third figure, who surfaces most prominently in 'The Lady A. L.', that I would finally like to return.

In all three poems, the woman invariably represents or is associated with the idealised motifs and values of the lost monarchy. A. L. appears to stand in for the king, recuperating his role as centre of meaning for the speaker, while in the 'prison' poems Lucasta and Althea anticipate and become symbols of the speaker's fidelity to the sovereign. In each case the woman indicates a point of excess in the poems, as she is pivotal and yet peripheral to the main concern with retrieving the lost king and the plenary system of meaning for which he once stood as centre. As a site of excess her appearance, however, signals the very anxieties which the speaking subject of the poems tries to repress: the sense of absence and loss which underpins the conceptualisation of recuperation. She highlights the process of displacement and replacement we find in each poem. In 'The Lady A. L.' she takes the place of the beheaded king, in the 'prison' poems she herself is displaced by the speaker's overriding preoccupation with restoring the deposed monarch and becomes a sign of the subject's re-placed expression of loyalty within the interior realm of the mind.

In the late lyric 'In mine one Monument', a poem which appears in the posthumous 1659–1660 edition of *Lucasta* reference to the lost ideals of the royalist court is less obvious, as it appears that the subject himself is at the centre of the poem:

'Song'

1.

In mine one Monument I lye,
And in my Self am buried;
Sure the quick Lightning of her Eye
Melted my Soul ith' Scabberd, dead;
And now like some pale ghost I walk,
And with anothers Spirit talk.

2

Nor can her beams a heat convey
That may my frozen bosome warm,
Unless her Smiles have pow'r, as they
That a cross charm can countercharm;
But this is such a pleasing pain,
I'm loth to be alive again.

Images of enclosure, retreat and asylum, predominant in other poems, again resonate here, only in this poem they are not apparently represented in terms of a restored monarchic sanctuary in the mind, but as a 'Monument' in which 'I lye, / And in my Self am buried' (11.1–2). As Jonathan Sawday points out, the retreat into the self in this poem and others is bound up with allusions to self-dissolution. The released free soul of 'To Althea' is 'Melted' (1.4), the 'Paradise within' is envisaged as a corpse.

In the poem it is the female figure, this time unnamed, who again points to the paradoxes of this self-enclosed, self-annihilating subject. Significantly the poem's discourse of interiority is shot through with the familiar tropes of courtly love, in which the woman leads the male lover into a state of sublime subjection. In representing these ideals of the courtly convention the female figure once more indicates what is now marginal and other—values associated with the dissolved court—thus suggesting the poem's anachronism. The affirmation of the subject in the poem as interiorised, however, ironically allows him to engage in such nostalgic phantasies, in which the corporeal pleasure and pain of the courtly lover are recalled even as the body is put to rest, through the speaker's disembodied hankerings. The woman signals the *mise en abyme* around which these phantoms of courtly mythology gather, as a spectre of an ideology now relegated to the grave, the place in which the speaker yearns to be. She therefore indicates, as in the previous poems, the sense of loss and lack out of which the subject is conceived and from which desire emerges. The speaker's imagined subjection to the courtly woman is indeed underpinned by his subjection within subjectivity and the desire for his own displacement and dispossession (1.1), whereby he may be ghost-like, 'with anothers Spirit talk' and 'loth to be alive again' (11.5–6 & 12).

IV

Lovelace's poetry displays the splintering of the very grounds upon which Cavalier codes of values are based at the same moment as exemplifying them. While clinging on to the vestiges of chivalric and courtly symbols, Lovelace's work is invaded by an inaugural language of identity which must displace the realm of meanings which it seeks to restore. The subjection the loyal subject of Lovelace's poetry must face is the understanding of himself alone, at the brink of modern subjectivity, where the once plenary anatomy of the king is emptied of its former signification.

In each poem I have discussed it is significantly a female figure with whom these lost meanings and values are associated. Each woman to a greater or lesser extent represents the ideals of pre-modern monarchy, but re-presents those ideals in the modern sense of 'standing in for' them. The woman therefore becomes the site of lost presence in the text. Both there and not there, included and excluded, she pinpoints an abyss—the absent centre of the poems—for in re-presenting the values the speaker seeks to reprieve, she simultaneously identifies them as an empty space prefiguring the sense of loss, difference and desire upon which the incipient language of subjectivity is poised. It is around this absent presence of woman that the question of the crisis of meaning, identity, subject and knowledge is brought into play. In this sense, woman is the location of what is troublesome in the poetry. Standing at the intersection of meanings, she opens up a gap in the terms of signification which lie at the surface of the poems, those of subject, subjection and subjectivity.

Source: Bronwen Price, "'Th' inwards of th' Abysse': Questions of the Subject in Lovelace's Poetry," in *English*, Vol. 43, No. 176, Summer 1994, pp. 117–37.

Bruce King

In the following essay, King argues that Lovelace's work is not in keeping with standard Cavalier poetry. It is not of a confident and carefree nature but rather is more serious and about attitudes of mind.

One purpose of rhetoric is to lie. Poetic affirmations should be regarded with suspicion, especially if the poet is not religious or mystical. Consider "To Althea, From Prison." Every school child knows the poem, and knows that it represents the gay, confident, debonair Cavalier spirit. But does it? Isn't our concept of the Cavalier spirit partly Restoration propaganda and partly a nineteenth-century romanticization derived from Scott? For that matter is Lovelace's tone really so confident? "Stone walls doe not a Prison make, / Nor I'ron bars a Cage." This might sound like a confident affirmation to someone with an ear for Victorian music; by Caroline standards it sounds a little strained. "Althea" is not about chivalry or public virtues, it is about states of mind ("And in my soule am free"). Its idealism might be considered as a strategy for denying the effect of physical surroundings upon the mind. The poem's affirmation is really a turning inward, a process that is common to many of Lovelace's poems. "The

EVEN THE FAIREST DAY MAY LEAD TO RUIN."

Vintage to the Dungeon" might be a blueprint for the strategy of "Althea."

I

Sing out pent Soules, sing cheerefully!
Care Shackles you in Liberty,
Mirth frees you in Captivity:
Would you double fetters adde?
Else why so sadde?

Chorus

Besides your pinion'd armes you'l finde
Griefe too can manakell the minde.

II

Live then Pris'ners uncontrol'd;
Drinke oth' strong, the Rich, the Old,
Till wine too hath your Wits in hold;
Then if still your Jollitie,
And Throats are free;

Chorus

Tryumph in your Bonds and Paines,
And daunce to th' Musick of your Chaines

"The Vintage" is not a simple drinking song; as in "Althea" the theme is deceptive. It says sing, affirm, drink, do anything to fight off the effects of imprisonment upon the mind.

Lovelace's power derives not from a simple chivalric code but from a complex awareness that his ideals offer protection against reality. The best poems acknowledge the actual world, while trying out idealistic postures in reply. The ideals offered in "Althea," "The Grasse-hopper," and "To Lucasta, Going to the Warres" might be described as defensive masks. The lesser poems are more completely disillusioned and do not offer any protection, or do so crudely. In "To Lucasta from Prison, An Epode" Lovelace lists his grievances against life. Here, and also in "Mock Song," the awkward wit is more painful than relieving. Tensions accumulate and are not discharged. How, Lovelace asks, can peace love him, if it despises the earth. "War is lov'd so ev'ry where." Parliament is "beheaded," property is insecure; and ever since Parliament began borrowing money on it "Publick Faith" has become a mockery: "For she that couzens all, must me." A religious reform might be desirable,

But not a Reformation so,
As to reforme were to ore'throw;
Likes Watches by unskilfull men
Disjoynted, and set ill againe.

Here is Lovelace's image of his time:

And now an universall mist
Of Error is spread or'e each breast,
With such a fury edg'd, as is
Not found in th' inwards of th' Abysse.

With the world out of joint Lovelace's defense against total demoralization is a purposefully blind trust in monarchy and honor. He appears to have been aware that while ideals are without power in the world, they may be psychologically necessary. The snail is one of his favorite images: "Wise Emblem of our Politick World, / Sage Snayl, within thine own self curl'd." The snail's self-containment is an example of how to keep one's values during times of evil and disorder:

But banisht, I admire his fate
Since neither Ostracisme of State,
Nor a perpetual exile,
Can force this Virtue change his Soyl;
And wheresoever he doth go,
He wanders with his Country too.
("**Another**")

Lovelace's poems often record a feeling of exile.

When reality makes demands upon people, vague public values are often used to cover resulting conflicts. The famous song "To Lucasta, Going to the Warres" mocks while affirming soldierly values. The surprising wit of its middle stanza represents a discharge of psychic tension. The rhetoric of courtship provides pivotal words ("chase," "imbrace," "mistresse") upon which to introduce, and then by mockery to master, the pressures of reality:

True; a new Mistress now I chase,
The first Foe in the Field;
And with a stronger Faith imbrace
A Sword, a Horse, a Shield.

Lovelace's confidence is a not very consistently worn mask, the purpose of which is to ward off reality. Honor represents a tension of will, the snail's ability to remain true to itself in exile; but demoralization lies behind the affirmations, waiting for a relaxation of will, a moment of slackness.

While his values may seem quixotic and arbitrarily imposed upon disintegrating forms of society, without such a blind affirmation of honor Lovelace's sentiments become crude. In a "Saraband" ("Nay, prethee Dear") there is a coarsening of touch:

> See all the World how 't staggers,
> More ugly drunk then we,
> As if far gone in daggers,
> And blood it seem'd to be.

The carefree Cavalier attitude suddenly appears as a desperate reaction to brutal reality. The withdrawal and the turning to drink become gross sensuality:

> Now, is there such a Trifle
> As Honour, the fools Gyant?
> What is there left to rifle,
> When Wine makes all parts plyant?
> Let others Glory follow,
> In their false riches wallow,
> And with their grief be merry;
> Leave me but Love and Sherry.

If the subject of "Saraband" bears obvious similarities to other Cavalier libertine poems, the tone is coarser and more aggressive. Carew's libertinism has a strategic value in the battle of the sexes; but Lovelace's libertinism lacks balance and suggests a total disillusionment with experience. It has none of the allure of libertinism that Milton warns against in *Comus*. It is a libertinism that results rather from hatred of life than love of the senses.

The pressure of reality must have been very great upon Lovelace. It comes into his poems unexpectedly, often breaking their mood, but creating the necessary tension that raises his best work above that of most Caroline lyricists. It is not surprising that many poems in the posthumous edition of 1659 are distrustful, violent, even paranoiac in reaction to society. The natural world becomes filled with emblems of a distasteful reality. "A Fly caught in a Cobweb" is described as "Small type of great ones, that do hum, / Within this whole World's narrow Room." The snail becomes a "Wise Emblem of our Politick World." The Ant represents the new order ("For thy example is become our Law"), which is seen as uselessly striving against devouring fate. The law of the animal world is also the law of man. Because life is insecure, deferment of pleasure is pointless:

> Thue we unthrifty thrive within Earths
>   Tomb,
> For some more rav'nous and ambitious
>   Jaw:
> The *Grain* in th' *Ants,* the *Ants* in the
>   *Pies* womb,
> The *Pie* in th' *Hawks,* the *Hawks* ith'
>   *Eagles* maw:
> So scattering to hord 'gainst a long Day,
> Thinking to save all, we cast all away.
> (**"The Ant"**)

This is a truth about Lovelace which is often missed: he is not untouched by the sceptical or cynical; indeed, his more affirmative poems are examples of a disillusioned mind trying to hang on to something, anything, in a world where it can find no resting place, no secure perch. Nor is the cynicism merely political. The disillusioned streak in Lovelace's poetry is not a matter of party or commitment. The distrust is deeper, and it affects the antennae of his sensibility, changing the way he feels the world. References to imprisonment and images of dungeons are common to his poetry, often occurring in such unexpected places as the opening lines of "The Triumphs of Philamore and Amoret," and of "Night," an otherwise innocent poem ("Night! loathed Jaylor of the lock'd up Sun").

Miss Wedgwood suggests that after the death of Charles I the Cavalier poets lost their spirit of gallantry and that disintegration set in. She speaks of a rotting away of the cause. Lovelace's "Advice" to his brother illustrates a deeper insecurity, however, than merely having been vanquished. The insecurity is spiritual and physical as well as political. There is a generalized distrust of the world. The poem begins with Lovelace warning his brother to avoid sea voyages; all activity leads to disaster:

> ... dream, dream still,
> Lull'd in *Dione's* cradle, dream, untill
> Horrour awake your sense, and you
>   now find
> Your self a bubled pastime for the
>   Wind,
> And in loose *Thetis* blankets torn and tost;
> *Frank* to undo thy self why art at cost.

If the sea is dangerous, land is no better; inactivity also leads to disaster. The image for this insecurity is metaphysical in the best sense; it finds a correspondence between a particular idea and the nature of the world:

> Nor be too confident, fix'd on the shore,
> For even that too borrows from the
>   store

Of her rich Neighbour, since, now wisest
   know,
(And this to *Galileo's* judgment ow)
The palsie Earth it self is every jot
As frail, inconstant, waveing as that
   blot
We lay upon the Deep; . . .

The poem is an uneven, confused, but surprising performance. Its scepticism is intense. All things on earth will be "Turn'd to that Antick confus'd state they were." There is no way out of such a condition. The "golden mean" has "wrongs entail'd upon't." Stoic indifference should be a means to neutralize pain: "A breast of proof defies all Shocks of Fate, / Fears in the best, hopes in the worser state!" but the poem's conclusion suggests Lovelace's inability to anaesthetize the turmoil of reality:

Draw all your Sails in quickly, though
   no storm
Threaten your ruine with a sad alarm;
For tell me how they differ, tell me pray,
A cloudly tempest, and a too fair day.

This is distrust of optimism with a vengeance.

If we were to compare Lovelace's "Advice" to his brother with Dryden's poem to his *Honor'd Kinsman*, we would see two radically different reactions by Royalists to revolution. Whereas Dryden speaks of retirement as a means of achieving happiness "Unvex'd with anxious cares, and void of strife," Lovelace advocates a desperate withdrawal from reality. Whereas Dryden's poem is a prescription for happiness and future reward, Lovelace's poem is meant to neutralize hope. Dryden's aim is to praise a constructive, decent style of life, Lovelace's is to avoid harm. But, amazingly, Lovelace's poem is *meant* to be optimistic. Its tone is occasionally even jaunty, and it contains several passages to the effect that life cannot always be so bad as it is now; but no sooner does Lovelace say this than he warns against hope. Even the fairest day may lead to ruin. The poet's theme of cautionary balance is strongly in conflict with his insecure and fearful attitude.

With "Going to the Warres" and "Althea," "The Grasse-hopper" is central to any interpretation of Lovelace. But it is a poem in which the poet's attitude and the conventions of his theme need to be separated. "The Grasse-hopper" belongs to the mid-seventeenth-century tradition of poetry of solitude and retirement: a tradition usually associated with disappointed Royalists, but which might well include Marvell and others who, though perhaps not Royalists, found rural retreat a comfort, whether in fact or symbolically, from the confusions of the Civil War and the resulting chaos. I think Professor D. C. Allen is right when he writes of the grasshopper as Cavalier and poet. Lovelace's mind does seem to channel political pressures into traditional images, "The Ant," "The Grasse-hopper"'s companion piece, is an image of husbandry and puritanism: "thy example is become our Law." Singing insects are poets of whom the Ant is an enemy:

And thou almighty foe, lay by thy sting,
Whilst thy unpay'd Musicians, Crickets,
   sing.

"The Grasse-hopper" is not, however, limited to despair at the Royalist defeat. Rather than political events it is nature as revealed in images of time and seasons that is the destroyer of man's happiness. The moral is almost medieval. The material world is subject to change and decay; all things are mutable. Earthly joys are insecure.

I do not think that Lovelace is using traditional images of mutability to express a change in the political climate. The images are metaphors of something fundamental rather than topical. They express a similar insecurity before the temporal world to that expressed in Lovelace's "Advice" to his brother. Lovelace does not complain. He has already adopted a psychological attitude to defend himself against reality. Man is a fool not to have expected the worst:

But ah the Sickle! Golden Eares are
   Cropt;
Ceres and *Bacchus* bid good night;
Sharpe frosty fingers all your Flowr's
   have topt,
And what sithes spar'd, Winds shave off
   quite.
Poore verdant foole! and now green Ice!
   thy Joys
Large and as lasting, as thy Peirch of
   Grasse,
Bid us lay in 'gainst Winter, Raine, and
   poize
Their flouds, with an o'reflowing glasse.

These images are recalled at the end of the poem where the unpleasantness of the actual world, as represented by the political situation and the winter season, will be ignored and replaced by a subjective reality.

The conclusion of "The Grasse-hopper" involves a strategy for dealing with reality. The poem has long since stopped being about insects. But what is the central subject of the poem and what is Lovelace's solution to the problem it raises? If the poem has primarily been about defeated Royalists then its conclusion affirms the primacy of personal relationships during a period of public confusion. The structure of the poem, however, argues against such an interpretation. After the two movements describing the joys and fate of the grasshopper we are seemingly offered drink and friendship as consolations for life. However, to see conviviality as Lovelace's reply to reality would be to miss the point. It would replace one set of external props with another, and would make nonsense of the poem's final stanza:

> Thus richer then untempted Kings are we,
> That asking nothing, nothing need:
> Though Lord of all what Seas imbrace; yet he
> That wants himselfe, is poore indeed.

The prominence given to friendship in the final stanzas is deceptive. Lovelace, like Marvell and other mid-seventeenth-century poets, tends to give more prominence to examples and less to development of theme than we usually expect. It is almost the style of the period, and it is sometimes confusing. Perhaps that is why Geoffrey Walton claims "'The Grasshopper' is an invitation to conviviality of which the insect is supposed to set an example;" if Professor Walton were right, the fate of the insect would be sufficient argument against accepting the invitation. While the grasshopper is normally a symbol of light-heartedness, it is used here as an example of the false joys of the external world and therefore of the vanity of human wishes. The poem's theme is neither politics nor conviviality, but attitudes of mind; its final defense against reality is rather stoical fortitude and lack of desire than friendship. To be "untempted" by any hope is to ask nothing and is one way to cope with a mutable world. The attitudes that Lovelace creates are striking, but they are, finally, defenses against demoralization.

Source: Bruce King, "Green Ice and a Breast of Proof," in *College English*, Vol. 26, No. 7, April 1965, pp. 511–15.

SOURCES

Anselment, Raymond A., "'Stone Walls' and 'Iron Bars': Richard Lovelace and the Conventions of Seventeenth-Century Prison Literature," in *Renaissance and Reformation*, Vol. 17, No. 1, Winter 1993, pp. 15–34.

Blemires, Harry, *A Short History of English Literature*, Routledge, 1984, p. 104.

Davis, Walter R., "Richard Lovelace: Overview," in *Reference Guide to English Literature*, 2nd ed., edited by D. L. Kirkpatrick, St. James Press, 1991.

Lovelace, Richard, "To Althea, From Prison," in *Richard Lovelace: Selected Poems*, edited with an introduction and notes by Gerald Hammond, Flyfield Books, 1987, p. 41.

Post, Jonathan F. S., *English Lyric Poetry: The Early Seventeenth Century*, Routledge, 1999, p. 127.

Repplier, Agnes, *Points of View*, Houghton Mifflin, 1891, p. 41.

Seelig, Sharon Cadmon, "Richard Lovelace," in *Dictionary of Literary Biography*, Vol. 131, *Seventeenth-Century British Nondramatic Poets, Third Series*, edited by M. Thomas Hester, Gale Research, 1993, p. 3.

Skelton, Robin, "The Cavalier Poets," in *British Writers*, Vol. 2, edited by Ian Scott-Kilvert, Charles Scribner's Sons, 1979.

Wedgwood, C. V., *Poetry and Politics under the Stuarts*, Cambridge University Press, 1960, pp. 105–106.

FURTHER READING

Corns, Thomas N., ed., *The Cambridge Companion to English Poetry, Donne to Marvell*, Cambridge University Press, 1993.
> This easy-to-read collection of essays provides studies on Donne, Jonson, Herrick, Herbert, Carew, Suckling, Lovelace, Milton, Crashaw, Vaughan, and Marvell as well as the political and social context in which they wrote.

Gaunt, Peter, *The English Civil Wars: 1642–1651*, Osprey, 2003.
> Gaunt examines the causes and consequences of the Roundhead and Royalist conflict, including the effect on civilians, biographies of important figures, and the national, regional, and local perspectives on the wars.

Glancy, Ruth, "Freedom and Captivity," in *Thematic Guide to British Poetry*, Greenwood Press, 2002, pp. 89–92.
> This short article discusses "To Althea, From Prison" and other poems with the theme of freedom. Poets include Thomas Chatterton, Shelley, Byron, Emily Brontë, Oscar Wilde, and John Barbour.

Wilkinson, C. H., ed. *The Poems of Richard Lovelace*, 2 vols., Oxford University Press, 1925, 1930.
> Considered the definitive collection of Lovelace's poetry, this two-volume edition also provides information about the poet's life.

Up-Hill

CHRISTINA GEORGINA ROSSETTI

1861

Christina Rossetti composed "Up-Hill" on June 29, 1858, but the poem was not published until February 1861, when it appeared in *Macmillan's Magazine*. Rossetti also included "Up-Hill" in her most critically acclaimed collection of poetry, *Goblin Market and Other Poems*, published in 1862. "Up-Hill" is a sixteen-line lyrical poem, written in iambic meter. The poem is a dialogue consisting of a series of questions and answers, which present an extended metaphor on the mortal journey to heaven. Much of Rossetti's poetry incorporates Christian themes, and this is especially true of "Up-Hill," in which a doubting and unsure questioner is reassured that after death, she will find her reward in heaven. "Up-Hill" appeared in *The Complete Poems of Christina Rossetti*, volume 1, published in 1979 and in *Goblin Market and Other Poems* (1995), a facsimile edition of the 1865 text.

AUTHOR BIOGRAPHY

Born in 1830 in London, England, Christina Rossetti was the youngest of four children born to Gabriele Rossetti and Frances Polidori. Rossetti was, perhaps, destined to be a poet. Her father was an Italian poet and Dante scholar, who emigrated from Italy to London in 1824, where he became the chairman of the Department of Italian Studies at King's College. Rossetti was

Christina Georgina Rossetti (© *Bettmann / Corbis*)

educated at home by her mother, who had been a governess before marriage. Rossetti's early education emphasized religious texts, which her mother often read aloud to the children. In a household where poetry was such an important part of her father's career, it is understandable that reading and writing poetry was an important part of Rossetti's childhood education. She wrote her first poem, "To My Mother on her Birthday," when she was eleven. The Rossettis became advocates of the Oxford Movement during the 1840s. Also known as the Tractarians, members were either Anglican High Church or Puritans. This religious belief was an important lifelong influence on Rossetti's writing.

In 1843, Rossetti's father became too ill to continue working, and her mother return to work as a governess. One of Rossetti's sisters also began working, as did one of her brothers. Rossetti became a companion to her father, who was now blind. In 1845, Rossetti suffered some sort of collapse, whether physical or mental is not known. In spite of her illness, she continued to compose poetry, and by age sixteen, Rossetti had written more than fifty poems. A collection of thirty-nine of these early poems was published privately by her maternal grandfather in 1847, as *Verses*. When Rossetti was seventeen, two of her poems were accepted for publication by *The Athenaeum*, a prestigious literary periodical. She also had several poems published in *The Germ*, a literary journal published by the Pre-Raphaelite Brotherhood, a group of poets organized by Rossetti's brother, Dante Gabriel Rossetti.

In 1848, Rossetti accepted a marriage proposal from James Collinson, a Roman Catholic, who converted to Anglicanism before Rossetti agreed to marry him; however, the engagement ended in 1850 when Collinson returned to the Roman Catholic Church. That same year, Rossetti wrote a novella, loosely based on her own romantic misadventure, called *Maude: A Story for Girls*, which was not published until 1897. The family suffered financially after Rossetti's father died in 1854. Her older brother, William, became the sole support of the family. During the 1850s and early 1860s, several of Rossetti's poems were published in anthologies and literary magazines. Macmillan, an important literary press in England, published Rossetti's first collection of poetry, *Goblin Market and Other Poems* in 1862. This collection was followed by *The Prince's Progress and Other Poems* in 1866. Rossetti also wrote short stories, many of which were published as a collection, *Commonplace and Other Stories*, in 1870. *A Pageant and Other Poems*, another poetry collection, was published the following year. That same year, Rossetti was diagnosed with Graves' disease, and thereafter, she became more reclusive. However, she continued to write. Rossetti also developed breast cancer. She had a mastectomy in 1892, which was thought to be successful, but the cancer remained, and her last year was one of failing health and often severe pain. Rossetti died in London on December 29, 1894, of breast cancer. Two years after her death, a final collection of poetry, *New Poems* was published by Rossetti's brother, Dante Gabriel.

POEM TEXT

Does the road wind up-hill all the way?
Yes, to the very end.
Will the day's journey take the whole long day?
From morn to night, my friend.

But is there for the night a resting-place?   5
A roof for when the slow dark hours begin.
May not the darkness hide it from my face?

You cannot miss that inn.

Shall I meet other wayfarers at night?
Those who have gone before.   10
Then must I knock, or call when 'ust in sight?
They will not keep you standing at that door.

Shall I find comfort, travel-sore and weak?
Of labor you shall find the sum.
Will there be beds for me and all who seek?   15
Yea, beds for all who come.

POEM SUMMARY

Lines 1–2

The first two lines of "Up-Hill" establish the formula the rest of the poem follows. The first line of each pairing is a question, and the second line provides a response. Line one begins with a simple query about whether the road goes up-hill the entire way. The up-hill road is a metaphor for the lifelong journey that Christians endure as they move through life and prepare for death and an eventual place in heaven. When the first speaker asks if the road is up-hill all the way, the tone is one of apprehension and perhaps some weariness and expresses a hope that the journey will not be an arduous one. The response, however, from the second speaker, makes it clear that the entire trip is up-hill. The implication is that the journey will not be an easy one. Speaker two does not state her reply as a way to discourage the questioner; instead, she speaks as one who seeks to reassure but who is honest about the difficulties that lay ahead.

Lines 3–4

The speaker's second question further establishes that she is not yet resolved to a difficult journey. She still seeks reassurance that the journey will be an easy one, and thus she asks if the journey will take all day. Speaker one uses the word "long" to suggest her concerns that the journey may be too lengthy and difficult to undertake. This second question begins an important theme in the poem, that of day and night. The day is the journey through life, and the night is the eventual rest from life's travails. Although the first speaker refers to a day's journey, a day is not a short period of time in this poem. The day's journey is a lifetime spent journeying uphill. The second speaker responds with a simple statement that the journey will take all day, from "morn to night." As she answers, the second speaker retains her very matter-of-fact tone. She does not gloss

MEDIA ADAPTATIONS

- There is no media adaptation of "Up-Hill," but one of Rossetti's other poems, "Who Has Seen the Wind," is included on the CD *Growing Up with the Classics: A Children's Treasury of Piano Music Classics & Favorite Poems* (1998), composed and performed by Julia Muench Lakhani for Classic Productions.

over the difficulty ahead. Moreover, the difficulty is not better or worse for the questioner than for any other traveler.

Lines 5–6

In her third question, speaker one asks about accommodations along her journey. She asks if there will be a resting place for the night and is reassured by speaker two that she will find shelter from the darkness. This represents the Christian belief that God brings light into the world. The eternal rest in death will not a sheltered one. When the "slow dark hours begin" the speaker will find herself sheltered under the protective roof of God's making. This response is intended to offer comfort to the speaker and put her mind at rest, as she continues uphill on this difficult journey.

Lines 7–8

Speaker one is not easily soothed, however, and so she asks in her fourth question if the darkness might disguise her resting place and keep it hidden from her view. This question makes clear that the first speaker fears she may not be comforted for her efforts. This fourth question implies her fear that she might miss her destination. In response, the second speaker continues her efforts to ease the first speaker's fears. Speaker two affirms that the resting place, now referred to as an "inn," is impossible to miss. Although the speaker is only suggesting the possibility, it seems certain that the inn will be aglow with lights, so brilliant that the weary traveler cannot possibly miss it.

Lines 9–10

For her fifth question, the traveler asks if there are other travelers, who will rest at the inn, where she is to rest. Speaker one does not ask if there are other travelers on the day portion of the journey, the actual journey through life, but she asks if there will be other travelers at night taking shelter at the inn. The implication is that the journey is a solitary one. Each man and woman undertakes the journey to heaven alone, but once there, each person can expect to find other people who have also made the journey on their own. These are the ones, who have "gone before."

Lines 11–12

For her sixth question, the first speaker asks if she is to announce her arrival as she nears the inn. This question again conveys concern. Although the second speaker has answered her questions calmly and patiently, the first speaker is still doubtful and perhaps even anxious. She worries that she will arrive and be unable to enter. She does not ask if the door will be locked to her, but the question suggests that may be her underlying fear. Once again the second speaker offers a calm and clear answer: The door will readily open. The traveler will not be left on the threshold unsure if she will be admitted. The door will open immediately to allow her to enter.

Lines 13–14

In her seventh question, the speaker asks if she will find comfort when she arrives weakened from her journey. Again, the second speaker offers reassuring words. There will be rest for the weary traveler, and there will be many to share her labors and ease her burdens. These are the "sum" of the many hands, who wait in the inn to lift the burdens from the traveler's shoulders and offer her the help often denied to her along the mortal path.

Lines 15–16

The final question presents the crux of the traveler's concerns. She asks if there will be a bed for her and for "all who seek" shelter at the inn. She is asking if there is, indeed, salvation for those who undertake the difficult journey. The second speaker's response offers assurances of beds for all whose journey ends at the inn. The journey is toward death and comfort beyond in heaven. When the journey is completed, there will be plenty of time to rest, many hands ready to relieve burdens, and a final resting place, where the weary and weakened can finally be restored.

THEMES

Day and Night: Life and Death

Day and night together present an important theme in "Up-Hill," that of a journey and an arrival. The day portion is the journey through life, which can be both difficult and lengthy. In contrast, the night represents the time of arrival and restorative rest. The day's journey does not refer to a twenty-four-hour period but rather a lifespan of relentless effort and difficulty. The second speaker responds as one who has already completed the journey. This speaker affirms that the journey will take all day, from morning to night, and that both day and night are necessary. The reward of eternal rest comes only after a lifetime of hard work.

Journey

The journey is equated with the lifespan, and the journey is only finished when a person dies. Mortals begins their journeys at birth and continue until they die; only then does the journey end. In "Up-Hill," the journey is undertaken by speaker one, who is daunted by the length of the trip and the fact that there are no easier places along the way. Speaker two is more knowledgeable about the journey's outcome. She describes the reward that the traveler is certain to receive at the end of the journey. Although there are experiences to be endured during the journey through life, such as illness and loss, which makes the journey an uphill challenge, at the end of the journey is the promised reward for having undertaken the trip.

Patient Suffering

During much of Christian history, and certainly through the period in which Rossetti is writing, patient suffering was viewed as a Christian virtue. Patience is a virtue that leads to greater faith in God. The Book of Job is the ultimate model of patient suffering, in which the sufferer endures much but is ultimately rewarded. Job does not have Rossetti's New Testament faith in a final judgment before Christ, but he believes that God can restore him and reward him for his suffering if he remains faithful and devout. In "Up-Hill," Rossetti's second speaker urges patient suffering. The journey to heaven's reward is difficult, but the reward is the rest at the end, when the traveler reaches the "inn" of heaven.

TOPICS FOR FURTHER STUDY

- One of the best ways to learn about poetic form is to write poetry. "Up-Hill" is an example of religious poetry. Using Rossetti's poem as a guide, write at least one or two poems that imitate both her style, language use, and content. When you have completed your poems, write a brief evaluation of your work, comparing it to Rossetti's poem. In your written critique of your poems, consider what you learned about the difficulty of writing poetry on religious themes.

- Rossetti lived in Victorian England, the same place that serves as a setting for most of Charles Dickens's dark and often pessimistic novels. Read one of Dickens's novels and write an essay in which you discuss what he says about the difficulty of life in Victorian England. In writing your essay be sure to consider what Rossetti is saying about the rewards that await the sojourner and believer. What does Dickens imply about the devout believers in the world of his novels?

- Artists are often inspired by poets. Spend some time looking through art books in the library and try to locate a picture or illustration that you feel best illustrates the journey in Rossetti's poem. You might consider different images of heaven or the final journey to heaven as possible topics. Then, in an essay, compare the art that you have selected to "Up-Hill," noting similarities and the differences between these two works.

- Research the life of any least one of the following nineteenth century female poets, who were contemporaries of Rossetti: Emily Brontë, Elizabeth Barrett Browning, Elizabeth Siddal, or George Eliot (Mary Ann Evans). Write a research paper in which you discuss how this poet's life, her experiences, and her religious beliefs are expressed in at least two of her poems.

- Do some research on Anglicanism. Prepare an oral presentation in which you describe the main tenets of this religion and how they are suggested in Rossetti's poem, "Up-Hill."

- With two or three other classmates, create a group presentation in which you report on what it was like to live in Victorian England. Divide the work by assigning different tasks to each member of the group. Good group presentations involve multimedia, so take the time to prepare graphs, timelines, and handouts that will help your classmates follow the presentation. Be sure to prepare a bibliography of your sources.

- The best way to understand poetry is to read it aloud, and yet very few readers make an effort to read poetry aloud. With a friend, read "Up-Hill" aloud as a two-part dialogue, and then read it aloud to an audience of friends or classmates. Ask two of your friends to read the poem aloud and listen to their voices, noting the inflections of tone as they read aloud to you. What do you discover about the poem in each of these readings? Consider if the poem changes with these subsequent readings and what you learn about poetry, and write a one-page essay in which you discuss your observations.

STYLE

Allegory

In poetry, an allegory is an extended metaphor in which objects in the poem are provided meaning outside the narrative. In "Up-Hill," the day-long journey that takes a lifetime represents the whole of a person's experiences during the person's life. The object in an allegory also has meaning beyond its name. Thus the inn is not simply a literal roadside hotel but the spiritual home for the human soul. Allegory can be confused with

An uphill path through the forest (Image copyright Zsolt, Biczo, 2009. Used under license from Shutterstock.com)

symbol. In symbol one word stands for another word, such as *water*, which in a Christian context may represent *rebirth*. By contrast, allegory tells a two-level story, the literal and the metaphoric. The explicit allegorical storyline is parallel to and made to represent another storyline; in this case the up-hill journey is parallel to the mortal life that concludes after death in heaven.

Dialogue

A dialogue is a conversation between two or more people. In "Up-Hill," Rossetti presents a dialogue between two speakers, one fearful and doubtful and the other assured and all-knowing. The question-and-answer dialogue between these two speakers develops the poem's purpose of assuaging skepticism with faith. Thus, Rossetti uses a question-and-answer format to advance an idea. In this case, the dialogue serves to reassure her readers that their struggle and suffering will come to an end one day, and they will find rest.

Ballad Meter

In a traditional ballad, the rhythm is four eight-syllable lines, alternating with three six-syllable lines. In "Up-Hill," Rossetti uses a variation of this form. Rossetti alternates meter in "Up-Hill" to emphasize the differences between the speakers. Thus the meter itself helps to reveal the meaning in this poem. The questions tend to include iambs (unstressed/stressed) with trochee (stressed/unstressed) and dactyls (stressed/unstressed/unstressed), whereas the answers tend to be in regular iambic (unstressed/stressed). Thus, the words in the questions seem to trip over themselves with a sense of urgency, whereas the answers are simple assurances underscored by regular iambic beat. The meter Rossetti uses reinforces the speakers' positions (both in terms of faith and in terms of the journey). The doubting questioner is undertaking the journey (it lies ahead), but the faithful answerer has completed the journey and thus knows its outcome.

Tenor and Vehicle

Tenor and vehicle, terms first used by I. A. Richards in *Principles of Literary Criticism* (1924), describe the two parts of a metaphor. The tenor is the subject and the vehicle is the object used for comparison. The vehicle presents an image that makes it easier to visualize or understand the subject of comparison, the tenor. In "Up-Hill," the road that goes uphill in front of the person who undertakes a journey on foot (the vehicle) is compared to the arduous effort a person expends in day-to-day labors and difficulties (the tenor). Readers can visualize a road that slants uphill; everyone knows that one that slants downhill is easier to walk. The tenor is the less easily grasped idea that life takes a lot of work; it takes sustained effort. Also, no one can take steps for another person; individuals take their own steps and carry their own load.

HISTORICAL CONTEXT

Victorian London

London was England's literary and artistic center. Since the eighteenth century, the coffeehouses and literary salons had served as meeting places for writers and artists. Newspapers and journal publishers were based in London, which encouraged writers to congregate in the city. However, there was much more to living in London than the proximity of great literary figures. In 1800, the

COMPARE & CONTRAST

- **1860s:** In 1859, Charles Darwin and Alfred Russel Wallace deliver a joint paper on their evolutionary theory of natural selection before the members of the Linnean Society in London. Darwin's *On the Origins of Species* is published in November 1859.

  Today: Darwin's theory of natural selection is rejected by people who read the Bible as literal truth.

- **1860s:** In 1861, more than three million people live in London, making it the largest and one of the most crowded cities in the world.

  Today: One of the most densely populated cities is Mumbai, India, with more than thirteen million people. Like 1860s London, Mumbai suffers from overcrowding and poverty.

- **1860s:** In 1863, the first section of the London Underground opens between Paddington and Farmington, providing the first underground transportation system in the world.

  Today: In Guangzhou, China, construction is underway on what is being called one of the largest and most technologically advanced subway systems in the world.

- **1860s:** In 1865, the Transatlantic cable is completed, allowing telegraph communication between Europe and the United States for the first time. An earlier 1858 attempt had failed within weeks of completion.

  Today: Global communication by telephone and Internet is no longer dependent on cable, but on wireless technology facilitated by satellites orbiting above the Earth.

---

population in London was estimated to be about one million, but by 1880, that population had grown to an estimated 4.5 million. That spectacular growth resulted in some spectacular problems as well. Overcrowding was one of the largest problems, which was partly caused by the Enclosure Acts that forced peasants off the land and into the urban center in search of work. Another cause was the new railroads, which quickly and easily brought many people from rural areas into the city.

The city streets were unpaved and filthy, invariably filled with the manure of the thousands of horses used as the principle means of transportation. Street cleaners were unable to keep up with the manure. In addition, cattle were driven through the streets until the mid-nineteenth century, adding animal waste and stench. Cattle were slaughtered by the hundreds at the slaughter centers in Whitechapel and Smithfield, both in London. Hundreds of carcasses hanging outside added to the air pollution, insects, and blood runoff, which slid ankle-deep in some streets down to the Thames River.

In nineteenth-century London, coal and chimney pots were used for heating homes, turning the air black, inside and out. The soot clung to the buildings and to the people and their clothing as travelers moved from one part of the city to the next. The streets were dirt, and when it rained, the streets were mud several inches deep. Raw sewage and human waste flowed in ditches along roads in poor districts and from these places into the Thames, which flows through the center of London. The city was noisy, filled with the sounds of street vendors, but it was also dangerous. Pickpockets, prostitutes, beggars, and drunks filled the streets. In *Little Dorrit*, Dickens describes the rain in London as dirty and foul-smelling. Londoners drank the water from the Thames, into which their sewage flowed. Contaminated drinking water caused diseases, such as cholera. In 1858, the stench from the Thames was so severe that government came to a halt, when Parliament was unable to continue meeting. This is the

A painting of a roadside inn, 1872 (© *Photo Art Collection (PAC) | Alamy*)

London in which Rossetti was writing "Up-Hill." Life was difficult, there was much suffering, and death was believed to bring welcome relief.

Pre-Raphaelitism

The term *Pre-Raphaelite* refers to both art and literature. Rossetti's brother, Dante Gabriel, was one of the founders of the Pre-Raphaelite Brotherhood, which began in 1848. Members of this movement hoped to influence art and literature by making it reflect the new modern age. One goal was to refocus art on nature and simple devotion. Dante Gabriel Rossetti thought had art had changed after 1500 and was no longer relevant. To reach this goal of modernization, artists and writers rejected conventional ideas about the construction of their works. In poetry, this movement promoted pictorial elements and symbolic realism. Emerging from Pre-Raphaelitism in the late 1850s was Aesthetic Pre-Raphaelitism, the second stage of the movement. The Aesthetics focused on philosophy and beauty. Although no women were members of the Pre-Raphaelite Brotherhood, Christina Rossetti was very much an informal part of this organization, and it was an important influence on her poetry.

CRITICAL OVERVIEW

Unlike many other early poets, Rossetti's poetry has never been out of fashion. Her work has continued to be published and enjoyed by readers, since their first publication during her lifetime. One way to judge the uniqueness and importance of her work can be found in reviews of *Goblin Market and Other Poems*. Many poetry collections are never reviewed, but when in 1862 when Rossetti's collection, *Goblin Market and Other Poems* was published, two literary magazines reviewed it, Rossetti's first book of poetry. In an anonymous review for the *Saturday Review*, the writer begins by noting that "Rossetti's poetical power is most undeniable." After noting Rossetti's many talents, including her "very good musical ear, great strength and clearness of language," the reviewer states that the poet's imagination is equally notable. The compliments continue as the writer points out that some of Rossetti's poems in *Goblin Market and Other Poems* are as picturesque and pure in quality as "any modern poem that can be named." The reviewer credits Rossetti's achievement to hard work and a talent for "saying the right thing" in the "best and shortest way."

"Up-Hill" is only one of more than sixty poems included in *Goblin Market and Other Poems*, and yet it earns special recognition in this review. In focusing on this poem, the reviewer for *Saturday Review* notes "Up-Hill"'s many strengths, which reflect Rossetti's many talents as a poet. Of special mention is the strength of her "symbolic expression." This is especially evident in "Up-Hill," which is described as "one of the most perfect little pieces in this volume." According to the reviewer, this poem conveys an important message but does not say "more than is needed" on a topic, about which most writers say far too much.

In the anonymous review written for *Athenaeum*, the reviewer is also a fan of Rossetti's poetry. Although slightly more reserved in this review of *Goblin Market and Other Poems*, the writer does point out the poetry's many strengths, including that these poems "express both in essence and form the individuality of the writer." According to this writer, Rossetti's poems are a welcome change from "the laboured and skilful, but not original, verse" written by other poets in recent years. According to this reviewer, many of the poems in Rossetti's *Goblin Market and Other Poems* are rich in symbolism, "without the stiffness of set allegory," although this reviewer does did not like all of the poems in this collection, they all display "imagination and beauty which are both undeniable and unborrowed." Readers in the decades to follow established that both of Rossetti's 1862 reviewers quickly grasped the significance of this volume of poetry and its power to endure.

CRITICISM

Sheri Metzger Karmiol

Karmiol teaches literature and drama at The University of New Mexico, where she is a lecturer in the University Honors Program. In this essay, she discusses Rossetti's use of extended metaphor in "Up-Hill."

WHAT DO I READ NEXT?

- Oxford World's Classics has published *Poems and Prose* (2008) by Rossetti. This edition contains the poet's most distinctive work and the strongest, according to her critics.
- *Christina Rossetti: Passion & Devastation* (1999) is an illustrated anthology of Rossetti's poetry, intended for young adult readers.
- All of Rossetti's prose is included in *Prose Works of Christina Rossetti: Four Volumes* (2004).
- *Elizabeth Barrett Browning: Selected Poems*, published by Bloomsbury in 1992, provides an excellent introduction to the work of the most successful of Rossetti's contemporary female poets.
- *From the Garden to the Street: Three Hundred Years of Poetry for Children* (1997), edited by Morag Styles, is a collection of children's poetry, intended for middle-school readers.
- Jan Marsh's biography, *Christina Rossetti: A Writer's Life* (1994, reissued by Viking in 1995), relies upon Rossetti's letters and those of her family. This biography provides a thorough study of the poet's life.
- Charles Dickens's novel, *Oliver Twist* (serialized in 1837–1839 and reissued by Penguin in 1985), captures life on the streets of Victorian London and provides a glimpse into the London Rossetti knew.
- *Universal Verse: Poetry for Children* (2006), compiled by Edgardo Zaghini and Deborah Hallford, contains poems from around the world and from earlier and contemporary writers.

No study of Rossetti's poetry would be complete without a discussion of her use of metaphor in "Up-Hill." Metaphors are familiar to many

> ROSSETTI MAKES THE UNSEEN TENOR OF LIFE BEYOND THE GRAVE CLEAR BY COMPARING IT TO THE ARRIVAL AT A COMFORTABLE INN AFTER A LONG ARDUOUS JOURNEY."

people in Judeo-Christian cultures, since the Bible provides abundant examples of metaphors, especially in the Parables; however, metaphors are also found in classical literature. Homer used extended metaphors in his epic narratives, and in the *Poetics*, Aristotle discusses four kinds of metaphor. In the centuries preceding Rossetti, poets relied on metaphor to hint at layers of meaning in their poetry. In "Up-Hill," Rossetti uses metaphor to make visible, the invisible—the journey to heaven, which is usually expressed in religious terms as an idea and not a physical journey.

To understand Rossetti's extended metaphor in "Up-Hill," it is important to understand the tradition of metaphor use in poetry. An early mention of metaphor as a poetic device is found in Aristotle. In his *Poetics* (c. 335 B.C.), Aristotle defines metaphor as "the application of a strange term either transferred from the genus and applied to the species or from the species and applied to the genus, or from one species to another or else by analogy." In other words, a metaphor compares one object with another. However, the actual use of metaphor predates Aristotle.

The Old Testament provides many examples of metaphors. One occurs in Genesis, where God creates the Garden of Eden and is described as a gardener (Genesis 2:7-8). The Old Testament also contains several examples of an extended metaphor in poetry, such as that found in Isaiah 5:1-7. In these verses the prophet Isaiah sings a song honoring God's vineyard, which he planted "on a very fertile hill" and planted with "choice vines." The vineyard is Jerusalem, as the prophet makes clear when he addresses the people of Jerusalem as "Inhabitants of Jerusalem" (Isaiah 5:3). In these verses, Isaiah laments that God's vineyard did "yield wild grapes" from the good grapes he planted. In verse 7, Isaiah clarifies the metaphor when he explains that "the vineyard of the Lord of hosts is the house of Israel, and the men of Judah are his pleasant planting."

Although there are many examples of metaphor in the Old Testament, the extended poetic metaphor in Isaiah, in which the Jews are described as grapes in God's vineyard is crucial to understanding the cycle of apostasy in the Old Testament, in which the Jews alternatively abandon their religious observance and then recommit to God. This cycle of apostasy in Isaiah captures the difficult journey demanded of those who have religious belief. While Isaiah might simply have stated that the men of Judah have disappointed God, the extended metaphor explains all of God's hope and hard work and the level of disappointment he feels in the failure of his plantings to turn out as expected. Any gardener can easily understand the metaphor of a garden failure.

Biblical metaphor helps believers understand what is unknown and unseen by illustrating ideas with what is known. Rossetti's poem is like a parable. Parables are brief stories easily recognized from ordinary life, which can be used to teach ethical and moral lessons. Rossetti does the same thing with poetry. When the questioner in "Up-Hill" reveals her anxiety about the difficult journey ahead, the responder creates a parable-like story to offer comfort. The journey through life is still filled with hardships, as speaker two explains, but there is a light at the end of the journey to lead the weary traveler to the inn and an opportunity for a well-deserved rest. Heaven might not be easily visualized, but a well-lighted inn and comfortable bed are images that people understand.

While a metaphor is a one-to-one relationship between two different objects, an extended metaphor sustains a comparison by presenting related pairs of correspondences. Such an extended comparison is also called a conceit. An extended comparison using the words *like* or *as* in epic is called an epic simile. These occur frequently in Homer's long narrative poem, *Odyssey*. One example of an epic simile occurs in Book 8 (ll. 522–524), when Demodokos sings of Achilles and Odysseus at Troy. As Odysseus listens to descriptions of the many deaths that have occurred, "a tear from under his eyelids wet his cheek, / As a woman weeps embracing her beloved husband / Who has fallen before his own city and his own people." Homer uses this simile to convey that Odysseus grieves as intensely as a widow would as she embraces her slain husband on a battlefield. Another example occurs in Book 10 (ll. 408–414), when Odysseus is reunited with his men after Circe turns them back from swine into men:

> I found my trusty companions on the swift ship,
> Lamenting piteously, shedding large tears.
> As when calves of the fields all skip around together
> In front of the drove of cows that are coming into the dung yard
> When they are filled up on grass, and the pens no longer
> Hold them, but they run in throngs around their mothers,
> Lowing on and on, so did the men act when their eyes saw me.

This extended simile describes the excitement that Odysseus's men feel when at last they are reunited with their leader. The common farm image of calves so excited that they dance around their mothers, anticipating that they will soon be fed, is easily understood by agrarian people; it is a vehicle or device for dramatizing and thus explaining the mood of the men when they see Odysseus. Homer's epic similes explain what his readers may not be able to imagine, using familiar scenes they are likely to know firsthand. Thus, the unknown more complicated subject is explained by being compared to a common, well-known subject readers are likely to understand.

John Milton used epic similes in *Paradise Lost*. One of the first epic similes in *Paradise Lost* occurs in Book 1 (ll. 201–208), Satan is compared to a titan or leviathan that waged war against Jove at Mount Olympus. The juxtaposition in this example helps the reader understand the imposing power of Satan and establishes the danger he poses. In Book 4 (ll. 183–187), Satan's sneaking into Eden is compared to something Milton's readers would understand: a wolf seeking prey that easily leaps over a fence:

> As when a prowling Wolf,
> Whom hunger drives to seek new haunt for prey
> Watching where Shepherds pen their Flocks at eve
> In hurdl'd Cotes amid the field secure,
> Leaps o'er the fence with ease into the Fold.

The fence that the shepherd relies upon is not sufficient to keep the wolf from the flock. Nor does a gate protect the Garden of Eden from Satan. A second vehicle occurs in this extended comparison when Milton compares Satan to a thief who finding the front door locked sneaks around and enters the house through an unlocked window in the back. The Garden of Eden is secure at its main gates, but like the wolf who seeks his prey or the thief who finds an unsecured way in, Satan easily leaps over an unguarded wall and enters the prelapsarian Garden of Eden. The wolf going after sheep and the thief breaking into a house to rob are subjects readers recognize from their own world. Readers know that someone who intends to do wrong can outsmart a prudent person. To describe the invisible (how Satan could penetrate God's perfect creation, Eden), the poet says the same way a wolf or thief steals despite the vigilance of the owner.

To explain the incomparable and incomprehensible rest people receive at the end of their lives, according to Christian belief, Rossetti uses several familiar phrases and images as vehicles. Nowhere in "Up-Hill" does the poet identify the journey as toward heaven. The meaning is implied. The poem's meaning emerges through the use of pairs of corresponding ideas. For instance, the journey that takes an entire day, from "morn to night" refers to the journey through life. The roof that shelters the weary traveler at night is the shelter that heaven provides when the mortal journey ends at death. When the traveler expresses concern that she might somehow miss the resting place, she is reassured that she "cannot miss that inn," since the inn is death, and every life ends in death. Also the traveler is reassured that at the end of the journey, she will meet "other wayfarers" who have "gone before." A common Christian idea is that when people die they are reunited with loved ones who predeceased them. Christian belief asserts that upon death the devout traveler will find a welcome shelter with God. Believers will not be kept "standing at the door." Instead of weariness, there will be "beds for all who come." In "Up-Hill," Rossetti makes the unseen tenor of life beyond the grave clear by comparing it to the arrival at a comfortable inn after a long arduous journey.

Through an extended metaphor, Rossetti makes the unknown known, the invisible visible. In the sustained comparison to something known, the poet helps readers imagine what Christians believe lies beyond the physical world and beyond the end of human life.

Source: Sheri Metzger Karmiol, Critical Essay on "Up-Hill," in *Poetry for Students*, Gale, Cengage Learning, 2010.

Harriet Devine

Devine has a Ph.D. in English literature and is emeritus professor in English literature at Edge Hill College, Lancashire, United Kingdom. In the following essay, she explains how "Up-Hill" reflects the Christian beliefs of the poet Christina Rossetti.

To understand how Christina Rossetti's "Up-Hill" would have been understood by Victorian readers, it is necessary to know something of the religious beliefs of its author. Christina Rossetti was a committed Christian, and indeed even at a period when most of the population of England held to some form of Christian belief, she was notable for her extreme religious devotion. Her early years had partly prepared her for this commitment: Regular attendance at the nearby Anglican church was an accepted weekly ritual for the Rossetti family as it was for all middle-class families during the Victorian period. Rossetti's English-born mother, Frances Rossetti, had been raised as a Protestant, while her father, Gabriele, born in Italy, was, nominally at least, a Roman Catholic. This conflicting religious background of her parents does not seem to have caused any problems, probably because Gabriele was not particularly devoted to his religion. The four children, of whom Rossetti was the youngest, had a typical middle-class Church of England upbringing.

Children in those days were given books of nursery poems that explicitly set out to instruct them in morality: the dangers of idleness ("Satan finds some mischief still / For idle hands to do," as the eighteenth-century lyric by Isaac Watts, quoted by Jan Marsh in *Christina Rossetti: A Literary Biography*, famously put it); the need to control one's temper and suppress passionate desires; the duty of kindness and compassion to the poor and needy; and the dangers of vanity. Frances also had a picture book of illustrated stories from the Bible to which the children were introduced when they were very young, and Rossetti was given her own Bible at the age of six.

> THE POEM OFFERS COMFORT TO ANY GOOD CHRISTIAN WHO IS ANXIOUS ABOUT WHAT HAPPENS AFTER DEATH."

One of the lessons she would have learned very early was that, however much sorrow and pain human beings experience in their lives, as long as they follow the teachings of Christ, they will be fully rewarded by joy and fulfillment in heaven. This idea, fundamental to Christian thought, lies at the basis of "Up-Hill."

Rossetti was evidently drawn to religion from an early age, and one of the first poems she is known to have written was a short hymn "to the God who reigns on high." But in her teenage years, she became seriously devout, and she remained so throughout her life. Her sustained devotion was undoubtedly owed, in part at least, to the new form of Christian dogma that attracted her mother in the 1840s. Known as the High Church revival, or Tractarianism (after the series of religious pamphlets, or tracts, published by its founders), this movement adopted practices formerly confined to Roman Catholicism, such as confession, the use of incense and religious icons, and the setting up of religious orders in which women could devote themselves entirely to religious life. Tractarianism evidently provided Rossetti with the spiritual sustenance she craved, and she remained a loyal member of the High Church until her death. One result of this commitment was the considerable number of religious poems she composed throughout her writing life and which appeared in all her published volumes. In the first (1862) edition of *Goblin Market*, for example, the last section of the book contains eighteen short poems under the subheading "Devotional Pieces." These poems have explicitly Christian themes, as the titles indicate: "The Love of Christ which Passeth Knowledge," "A Better Resurrection," and "Advent," among others. Though "Up-Hill" does not appear in this section of the book, it is clearly underpinned by Rossetti's Christian beliefs. In fact, it has sometimes been set to music and has appeared in Christian hymn books. Though the language is simple, the meaning of the poem is not as straightforward as it might appear.

Obviously the poem consists of a conversation, or question-and-answer session, about a journey. The question-and-answer structure of the poem is a form that Rossetti probably imitated from the great seventeenth-century Christian poet George Herbert (1593–1633), whose poems she had loved and admired since childhood. But it is left to the reader of the poem to decide the identities of the two speakers. The questioner is evidently a pilgrim of sorts, one who is setting out on a long and difficult journey and feeling decidedly apprehensive about what the final destination will be. It is less easy to determine the identity of the answerer, although it is evident that the person speaks from a position of knowledge and wisdom. Some readers have taken this speaker to be God, or Christ, while others believe the speaker to represent a soul that has already undertaken the journey and so speaks from a position of knowledge. Yet another interpretation is that the two speakers represent two aspects of a single person, the questioning side of ordinary human doubts and fears and the answers that religious instruction puts forward.

Once the poem is read as an extended metaphor (a figure of speech that expresses an idea through the image of another object), the basic ideas are plain enough. If the poem is viewed in a Christian context, the journey can be seen to represent the frequently difficult and painful struggle of human life. Such seems to be the implication of the road winding "up-hill all the way," which suggests that it will be a tiring way to travel. The fact that the road winds upwards also implies the idea, which is brought out later in the poem, that there is a higher goal to be reached, its attainment comparable to the relief and satisfaction experienced by anyone who has climbed a mountain and finally reaches the summit. That there is to be no rest or relief from suffering along the way seems to be implied by the fact that this challenging journey will last "the whole long day," since here the "day" clearly represents life and "night" stands for death, the ultimate and inescapable end of all human beings.

In the second stanza, the questioner is eager to be reassured that at the end of the journey, when night falls, there will be a place to rest, and when told that there is indeed "a roof," worries that it will be hidden by the darkness. One way of reading the poem in a Christian context is that the "inn," which cannot be missed, stands for Heaven, that afterlife plane of existence where God dwells for all eternity and into which all good Christian souls hope finally to be received. Those souls are the "other wayfarers" who have preceded the questioner on the journey. That the traveler is sure of finding a place in the inn (or the soul a place in Heaven) is confirmed by the reply to the anxious question in the third stanza about the necessity of calling or knocking on arrival: "They will not keep you standing at that door." In an actual inn, "they" would presumably be the owners or the servants employed as doorkeepers; it is up to the reader here to decide who the metaphorical equivalent is, though traditionally it is St. Peter who keeps the keys to the gates of Heaven and decides who is to be admitted. This point immediately highlights the problem with this interpretation of the poem. Tractarian Christians do not believe that everyone is automatically assured of a place in Heaven. They hold that each soul is to be judged for the deeds of the person's mortal life, and if they are found to be sinful, they will be denied entrance to Heaven and will, indeed, be banished to Hell for all eternity.

There is, in fact, a suggestion or hint of this idea in the first two lines of the final stanza. The pilgrim, knowing how exhausting and debilitating the journey will have been, asks if "comfort" will be found there. "Of labour you shall find the sum," replies the answerer. "Labour" is work, or the deeds and activities of a person's life, and the "sum" is the total, the final reckoning. So this line could be read as meaning that the sum total of a person's life work must be judged to have been satisfactory; otherwise, that person will not be able to gain admission. Such a reading is the predictable Christian interpretation of the lines. The word "labour" suggests that the poet may have been thinking of the famous passage from the Bible in which Jesus says: "Come unto me, all ye that labour and are heavy laden, and I will give you rest" (Matthew 11:28). This passage could indeed be the starting point for the whole poem. But, as Jesus goes on to say, it is necessary to learn from his example the qualities of meekness and lowliness (Matthew 11:29). The implication seems to be that if individuals fail to measure up to this Christly standard, they may not be granted the eternal rest promised to the meek and lowly. Instead, as Jesus suggests in

Matthew 7:14, they will be punished by eternal damnation in Hell.

However, the idea that not all people will be automatically admitted into the inn, or, metaphorically, into Heaven, is apparently contradicted by the final two lines of the poem. The questioner, still anxious, wants to be reassured that there will indeed be a bed for anyone who arrives at the door, and the answer, in the last line, is unequivocal: "Yea, beds for all who come." This line has led some readers to wonder if, after all, the poem goes against one of the most fundamental teachings of among Christian faiths, that only the deserving will gain a place in Heaven. But taking this point is to ignore the basic premise of the poem, which is that the pilgrim has only arrived at the inn after a long, weary, and troublesome journey and so is, indeed, in Jesus' words, one who has laboured and is heavy laden (Matthew 11:28). The up-hill struggle undertaken by the pilgrim thus surely parallels the difficult, and seldom-taken, path that Jesus referred to when he said "strait [i.e. small] *is* the gate, and narrow *is* the way, which leadeth unto life, and few there be that find it" (Matthew 7:14). Thus, the poem offers comfort to any good Christian who is anxious about what will happen after death (as the questioner/pilgrim obviously is) and does so by reestablishing that fundamental Christian belief that, however much people suffer in their lives, they will find their reward in Heaven.

Through the late twentieth century and into the early 2000s, it became unfashionable to interpret Rossetti's poetry through the lens of her Christian devotion. But it seems clear that this is how her contemporary readers would have read "Up-Hill," and probably accounts, in part at least, for the poem's immediate and enduring popularity.

Source: Harriet Devine, Critical Essay on "Up-Hill," in *Poetry for Students*, Gale, Cengage Learning, 2010.

SOURCES

"Aesthetic Pre-Raphaelitism," http://www.victorianweb.org/painting/prb/3.html (accessed July 6, 2009).

Aristotle, *The Poetics*, translated and edited by Stephen Halliwell, Lobe Classical Library, Harvard University Press, 1995, p. 105.

Cody, David, "A Brief History of London," in *The Victorian Web: Literature, History, and Culture in the Age of Victoria*, http://www.victorianweb.org/history/hist4.html (accessed July 6, 2009).

Cookson, Gillian, "The Transatlantic Cable," http://www.history-magazine.com/cable.html (accessed July 6, 2009).

"Darwin, Wallace, and the Linnean Society," *Linnean Society of London*, http://www.linnean.org/index.php?id=378 (accessed July 6, 2009).

DeRoche, Joseph, "Preface on Poetry," in *Heath Introduction to Poetry*, D. C. Heath, 1992, pp. 16–17.

Everett, Glenn, "Christina Rossetti," *The Victorian Web: Literature, History, and Culture in the Age of Victoria*, http://www.victorianweb.org/authors/crossetti/index.html (accessed July 2, 2009).

Fabb, Nigel, and Morris Halle, "Metrical Complexity in Christina Rossetti's Verse," in *College Literature*, Vol. 33, No. 2, Spring 2006, 91–112.

Holman, Hugh C., and William Harmon, *A Handbook to Literature*, 11th ed., Pearson Prentice Hall, 2009, pp. 14–15, 159, 202, 343–44, 434, 547.

Holy Bible, CollinsBible, 1994, pp. 9, 14.

Homer, *Odyssey*, translated and edited by Albert Cook, Norton, 1993, pp. 90, 112–13.

Marsh, Jan, *Christina Rossetti: A Literary Biography*, Jonathan Cape, 1994, p. 11.

———, *Christina Rossetti: A Writer's Life*, Viking, 1995.

Masci, David, "Darwin and His Theory of Evolution," *The Pew Forum on Religion and Public Life*, February 4, 2009, http://pewforum.org/docs/?DocID=397 (accessed July 6, 2009).

May, Herbert G, and Bruce M. Metzger, *The New Oxford Annotated Bible with the Apocrypha*, Oxford University Press, 1977, pp. 3–4, 828.

Milton, John, *Complete Poems and Major Prose*, edited by Merit Y. Hughes, Odyssey Press, 1957, pp. 216, 282.

Moses, Carole, "Homer's *Odyssey*," in *Explicator*, Vol. 63, No. 3, Spring, 2006, 130–31.

Review of *Goblin Market and Other Poems*, in *Athenaeum*, No. 1800, April 26, 1862, pp. 557, 558.

Review of *Goblin Market and Other Poems*, in *Saturday Review*, Vol. 13, No. 343, May 24, 1862, p. 595.

Rossetti, Christina, "Up-Hill," in *The Complete Poems of Christina Rossetti: A Variorum Edition*, Vol. 1, edited by R. W. Crump, Louisiana State University Press, 1979, pp. 65–66.

Shaffner, T. P., "How the Atlantic Cable Is Worked," *Debow's Review, Agricultural, Commercial, Industrial Progress and Resources*, Vol. 5, No. 8, August 1868, pp. 734–38.

FURTHER READING

Ash, Russell, *Dante Gabriel Rossetti*, Pavilion, 1997.
Dante Gabriel was the most notable of Rossetti's brothers, both as a poet and as a painter. This book contains a critical discussion of his work and reproductions of forty of Rossetti's paintings.

Barringer, Tim, *Reading the Pre-Raphaelites*, Yale University Press, 1999.
This art book is an illustrated history of the artists of the Pre-Raphaelite period.

Faught, C. Brad, *The Oxford Movement: A Thematic History of the Tractarians and Their Times*, Pennsylvania State University, 2004.
This book is a comprehensive look at the religious movement that was most influential in Rossetti's life and poetry.

Gouldstone, Timothy, *The Rise and Decline of Anglican Idealism in the Nineteenth Century* Palgrave, 2005.
Gouldstone examines the interaction between science and religious faith during the nineteenth century. The author also discusses the influence of philosophical idealism on nineteenth-century writers.

Murray, John, *Murray's Modern London 1860: A Visitor's Guide* (Facsimile), Old House Books, reissued 2003.
Murray provides a walking tour of Rossetti's London, as she would have known it.

Nead, Lynda, *Victorian Babylon: People, Streets, and Images in Nineteenth-Century London*, Yale University Press, 2005.
This well-researched interdisciplinary study of Victorian London explains the city as Rossetti would have experienced it during her life.

Scheinberg, Cynthia, *Women's Poetry and Religion in Victorian England: Jewish Identity and Christian Culture*, Cambridge University Press, 2002.
This text is an examination of female poets in nineteenth-century England, including Rossetti and Browning, at a time when religion was an important part of their identity. The author examines poetry, religious studies, and feminist literary criticism.

The Waking

THEODORE ROETHKE
1953

"The Waking" is by American poet Theodore Roethke (pronounced RET-kee). The poem was first published in 1953 in the volume of the same title, *The Waking: Poems 1933–1953*. It is available in *The Collected Poems of Theodore Roethke* (1974) and *Theodore Roethke: Selected Poems* (2005).

Roethke is one of the most notable of American poets who were writing from the 1940s to the 1960s. He belongs in the romantic and transcendentalist tradition of literature, and "The Waking" might be understood as a poem of spiritual awakening in which the speaker describes his insights into life and how to live well. He describes an approach to understanding based on feeling and intuition, honoring the sacred element in life and savoring each moment of it, accepting the reality of things without argument or protest. The poem is written in the form of a villanelle, a complex poetic form that relies on only two rhymes and utilizes two lines as refrains.

"The Waking" is notable not only as one of the best of modern villanelles but also because it gives an introduction to Roethke's main themes, which involve the quest to understand the nature of the self and its connection to the cosmos as a whole.

AUTHOR BIOGRAPHY

Theodore Roethke was born on May 25, 1908, in Saginaw, Michigan, the son of Otto and Helen

Theodore Roethke (The Library of Congress)

Roethke. His father and uncle owned a large greenhouse, and Roethke grew up with a deep knowledge of various plants and flowers that would later inform his poetry. His father died of cancer in 1923, when Roethke was fourteen; his uncle committed suicide in the same year.

In 1925, Roethke entered the University of Michigan, and he graduated in 1929. He pursued graduate study in English at Harvard University from 1930 to 1931, and at this time he first discovered his gift for poetry, encouraged by established poet and faculty member Robert Hillyer. In 1931, Roethke began to teach English and coach the tennis team at Lafayette College in Easton, Pennsylvania. It was at Lafayette that Roethke first established his reputation as an outstanding teacher, a quality he was known for throughout the rest of his life.

Leaving Lafayette in 1935, Roethke taught at Michigan State College at Lansing (later Michigan State University). In the fall, Roethke was hospitalized for mental illness, and his teaching contract was not renewed for the following year. Over the years, Roethke's manic-depressive illness would result in further hospitalizations. In 1936, Roethke resumed his academic career, teaching at Pennsylvania State University, where he remained until 1943. It was during this period that Roethke became friends with the poet W. H. Auden and published his first volume of poems, *Open House* (1941), to favorable reviews. In 1943, he took a leave of absence from Pennsylvania State to teach at Bennington College in Vermont. He won a Guggenheim Fellowship in 1945, was hospitalized again for mental illness in 1946, and in 1947 began teaching at the University of Washington in Seattle, a position he retained until his death.

Roethke's second volume of poetry, *The Lost Son and Other Poems*, was published in 1948, and his third book, *Praise to the End!* followed in 1951. By then Roethke was established as one of the leading American poets of the day. He was awarded another Guggenheim Fellowship in 1950, *Poetry* magazine's Levinson Prize in 1951, and grants from the Ford Foundation and the National Institute of Arts and Letters in 1952.

In 1953, Roethke married Beatrice O'Connell. This was also the year that *The Waking: Poems 1933–1953* was published. This collection included "The Waking." The book won the Pulitzer Prize in 1954. In 1955, Roethke was awarded a Fulbright Lectureship and taught in Italy. Two years later, in 1957, Roethke published *Words for the Wind*, which was awarded the Bollingen Prize, the National Book Award, and the Edna St. Vincent Millay Prize.

On August 1, 1963, Roethke died of a heart attack while visiting friends at Bainbridge Island, Washington. His final collection of poems, *The Far Field*, was published posthumously and received the National Book Award in 1964.

POEM SUMMARY

Stanza 1

"The Waking" consists of six three-line stanzas. In the first stanza, the first-person speaker begins with a paradox (an apparently contradictory statement). He states that he is waking up, only to sleep. He wakes up slowly. This line cannot be understood at a literal level. It may be that that sleep is a metaphor for death, and as

MEDIA ADAPTATIONS

- The Poetry Foundation has preserved archival recordings from the 1950s of Theodore Roethke reading "The Waking" and several other poems. These can be heard online at *Poetry Archive*, available at http://www.poetryarchive.org/poetryarchive/singlePoet.do?poetId=7169 (accessed October 11, 2009).

- *Theodore Roethke: Essential American Poets* presents the 1950s recordings of Roethke reading at the YMHA Poetry Center, in New York City.

the poet wakes he knows that he is one day closer to his own death, so he is determined to savor each day. In line 2, the speaker states that he is unafraid of whatever destiny awaits him. In line 3, he states that he learns about life simply by living it.

Stanza 2

Like the previous stanza, this stanza begins with a paradox regarding how humans think. The speaker is referring to an intuitive form of knowing rather than knowledge derived from the rational thinking process. In line 2, he senses with his hearing the liveliness of his entire being; he does not think about it in an intellectual kind of way. Line 3 is an exact repetition of the first line of the first stanza. It conveys the sense that the speaker is relishing and savoring his life, awake to whatever experience it may bring.

Stanza 3

In this stanza something new enters the poem. The speaker up to this point has been musing about his life and about life in general. Now, in line 1, he directly addresses an unnamed person. This person is one of many to whom the speaker feels close, but he does not know which one it is. He may be referring to people he has known who are now dead, but whose presence he still feels.

In line 2 he asks for God's blessings, perhaps for the earth in which the dead lie. The capitalization of the word *Ground* suggests also that the speaker may be referring to something more than the earth itself; perhaps he means the deepest levels of life, the basis of human essence. In the second half of line 2, the speaker resolves to respect both the person whose presence he senses, as well as life itself, by walking carefully, without making noise or fuss. Line 3 repeats exactly the last line of stanza one. It reemphasizes how the speaker is committed to learning about life as he lives it, and he may also be referring to his final destination, which as for everyone is death.

Stanza 4

This stanza begins with a reference to a tree that is, perhaps, suddenly seen in a shaft of light, perhaps in a moment of mystical illumination. However, the fact that the word *Tree* is capitalized suggests that the reference may be to more than an actual tree. It may also be a reference to the Tree of Life described in the book of Genesis, set in the middle of the Garden of Eden. In the second part of the first line, the speaker suggests that no one knows how the process of light illuminating the tree works. It is a mystery. In the second line, the image is of a worm ascending a stair; perhaps this image suggests that everything, even the lowest forms in creation, are engaged in a spiritual ascent from lower to higher orders of being. This stanza ends with a repetition of the first line of stanza one, which is also the last line of stanza two.

Stanza 5

In this stanza the speaker addresses someone directly. This person may be the one referred to in the previous stanza, or the speaker may be referring to the reader, and by implication, to everyone. The speaker suggests indirectly that life has a purpose for all, so the advice he gives is to enjoy it with a positive attitude. The last line repeats, with a variation, the last lines of stanzas one and three.

Stanza 6

This stanza, like stanzas one and two, begins with a paradox. The speaker is referring perhaps to the thoughts he has been expressing, which keep him from being complacent and help him to understand life, and this understanding provides him with an anchor in life. He feels that he knows what he is talking about. Line 2 is difficult to explicate, but the sense may be that life is transient; nothing lasts forever, and death is always near. It might, however, mean something different: the notion that it is hard to live in the present moment, the *now*, since the present is always slipping away and yet is always close at hand. The poem ends with a repetition of the two lines that have appeared as refrains throughout. The effect is to reinforce the meaning of the poem: The speaker savors life, learning from it as much as he can, as he continues on the path that must inevitably lead to death.

THEMES

Intuitive Knowledge

The speaker celebrates the marvel of being alive, and he seeks to experience it as fully and as joyfully as possible. He wants to understand life, but he makes it clear that life cannot be understood merely by using the rational mind. The purpose and direction of life has to be grasped with an intuitive rather than rational mode of knowing. Intuition is a kind of sixth sense, an instinct almost. It is different from reason, which is a process involving a chain of thoughts in which something is worked out or thought through. In contrast, intuition is immediate; it comes from some mysterious place in the mind that is beyond ordinary thought. An intuition is more like a feeling, and in this poem, feeling is presented as superior to thinking, as the first line of the second stanza shows quite explicitly.

Throughout the poem, the speaker senses what he has to do and how he has to live simply by doing it. It is not as if he can have all his questions answered before he does anything. The question he poses in the first line of the second stanza suggests that trying to think things through is a waste of time. He must feel life in all its dynamic fullness with his senses. It appears that his intention is to go through life feeling each moment, trying not to get bogged down by unanswerable questions, but just experiencing fully what this thing called life is. No one, he implies in another question (in the first line of stanza four), can really explain how life works. Be content to just experience it, without thinking or trying to puzzle it out, the speaker seems to be saying; go beyond the mind, which will continue to ask questions to which there are

TOPICS FOR FURTHER STUDY

- Study the form of the villanelle, read some examples, and write a villanelle of your own. Remember that the two lines that make up the refrains must be strong ones that express the poem's theme and also serve as effective conclusions.

- Read "The Right Thing," another villanelle by Roethke. It can be found in his *Collected Poems*. Write an essay in which you compare and contrast this poem with "The Waking." What themes do the two poems have in common? How do they differ? How does Roethke vary the villanelle form in "The Right Thing"?

- Using PowerPoint or similar program, give a class presentation in which you explain the structure of the villanelle and read two or three examples of the form. Comment on any variation in the form that the poems contain.

- Memorize "The Waking" and recite it to your class. After the recitation talk about what you learned about the poem through learning it by heart and reciting it that you did not notice when you read it silently. What does that tell you about poetry as a literary form?

- Consult *Lifelines: A Poetry Anthology Patterned on the Stages of Life* (Dutton Juvenile, 1994), an anthology compiled by Leonard M. Marcus with young adult readers in mind. The anthology is divided into different stages of life, including childhood, adolescence, middle age, and old age. Select one or two poems that you like and which express themes that might be similar to "The Waking" or serve as a contrast to it. Then write an essay about your findings.

no known answers, and grasp truth intuitively. Using intuition to live, rather than always trying to puzzle everything out, the speaker suggests, is to put one in touch and in harmony with the

A man waking slowly (Image copyright Nosha, 2009. Used under license from Shutterstock.com)

purpose of nature (as suggested in stanza five), and this depends on trust. It is not as if people can be supplied with a map of their individual journey in life or have everything explained to them before they start. Individuals learn about life by living it, bolstered by an intuitive faith—although the speaker avoids using the word faith, perhaps because he does not want to align his thoughts with any particular religious idea or doctrine. He really just wants to cultivate this trusting attitude to life, using feeling and intuition, to help him live more in the moment, without thinking about the past or worrying about the future.

The Sacredness of Life

Although this is not an overtly religious poem, it does convey the sense that life is sacred. Life has a higher purpose. There is a God (as stanza three, line 3 establishes), and the whole of life, from the lowest forms of life to the highest, must be understood as a continual spiritual ascent. This can be deduced from line 2 in stanza four. Everything in life is evolving in an upward spiral, which suggests that for this speaker, all of creation must be respected and honored for being a part of that grand process of spiritual growth.

The higher aspect of life hinted at might be understood as another order of being, beyond what everyday sense perception might be able to detect, that humans can trust in and aspire to. This higher order is suggested by the capitalization of the words "Ground," "Tree," and "Nature." The capitalization of the first of these words suggests a metaphysical dimension to life. The reference is not only to the earth itself but also, perhaps, to the deepest aspect of the human spirit, soul, or being. A theologian might refer, for example, to "the ground of our being," meaning the most fundamental level of the human self that rests in God or is close to God. The unusual capitalization of the word "Tree," and the fact that is directly linked to light, also suggests a spiritual dimension to life, although this interpretation can only be stated tentatively, since the speaker does not elaborate on what he means. There may here be a reference to the Tree of Life in the Garden of Eden, in which case this tree may symbolically represent a fruitful life blessed by the light of God, although, the speaker suggests, there is no way in which this truth can be fully grasped by human reason.

The fact that the poet chooses to capitalize the word "Nature" in stanza five suggests that he attaches some special meaning to it. Nature seen in this light seems to suggest some higher purpose to life that nature enacts and pushes forward. Life is not meaningless or random. The speaker appears to believe that what he or anyone should do is simply accept that nature has a purpose and so move through life enjoying what life offers, savoring its beauty with an attitude of trust.

STYLE

Villanelle

The poem is in the form of a villanelle. The villanelle is a complex poetic form that originated in France. It consists of five tercets (three-line stanzas) followed by one four-line stanza. There are only two rhymes throughout the villanelle. This is the first rhyme: in each tercet, line 1 rhymes with line 3. In the final stanza, lines 1, 2, and 4 rhyme. This is the second rhyme: The second lines of each of the tercets, as well as the second line of the final stanza, rhyme. The rhyme scheme can be represented as *aba aba aba aba aba abaa*. The villanelle also contains two refrains. A refrain is a phrase or sentence that is repeated, usually at the end of a stanza. In the first refrain in the villanelle, line 1 is repeated exactly to form line 6 (the last line of the second tercet), line 12 (the last line of the fourth tercet), and line 18 (the third line of the final stanza). For the second refrain, line 3 is repeated to form line 9 (the last line of the third tercet), line 15 (the last line of the fifth tercet), and line 19 (the last line of the poem). "The Waking" is a slightly irregular villanelle since the second refrain is slightly varied. Lines 9 and 15 are almost but not quite the same as line 1. In line 15, for example, an extra word has been added. Roethke also makes use of imperfect rhyme (sometimes called *partial* or *near rhyme*). In imperfect rhymes, the vowel sounds may be approximate. Examples occur in lines 1 and 3 of the third, fourth, and fifth tercet. Also, in the rhymes for the second line of each tercet and final stanza, the first two tercets contain a perfect rhyme, but the third tercet contains a partial rhyme. Lines 2 of tercets 4 and 5 are perfect rhymes of the word that formed only a partial rhyme in the third tercet, and then in line 2 of the final stanza, the rhyme is a perfect rhyme of line 2 of tercets 1 and 2 but an imperfect one of the second lines of tercets 4 and 5.

Although "The Waking" has serious themes that might not be thought of as simple, the use of the villanelle form conveys the feeling the poet wishes to express, of walking lightly through life.

Paradox

M. H. Abrams, in *A Glossary of Literary Terms*, defines paradox as "a statement which seems on its face to be self-contradictory or absurd, yet turns out to make good sense." There are three paradoxes in this poem. The first occurs in the first phrase in the first line, which also forms part of the refrain, and which makes no sense at the literal level. Perhaps the poet is referring to putting the questioning, intellectual side of his mind into the background—putting it to sleep, that is—and living in a more instinctive, intuitive way, with a quiet mind. The reference might also be to the inevitability of death, a possibility that is perhaps strengthened by the second line of the first stanza.

The second paradox occurs in the first sentence of the second tercet. Thought and feeling are normally considered as two different things; the paradox here elevates feeling to the point where it not only replaces thought but becomes it. A feeling is also a thought.

The third paradox occurs in the first sentence of the final stanza. Something that is moving about in an erratic kind of way is not usually thought of as being stable or reliable. The presence of the paradox forces the reader to consider in what ways the speaker's attitude to life in general is paradoxical, and what this might mean in practice.

Alliteration

Alliteration refers to the repetition of consonants, usually at the beginning of a word. Roethke uses alliteration to create another layer of poetic effects, in addition to rhyme, meter, and refrain. Alliteration can be found in the repetition of the *s* sound in the first line, of the *f* sound in tercet 1, line 2, of the *g* sound in the first line of the third tercet, and the *w* sound of the second line of the fourth tercet.

Iambic Pentameter

The poem is written in iambic pentameter, one of the most common meters in English poetry. An iamb is a poetic foot in which an unstressed syllable is followed by a stressed syllable. (A foot, in English poetic meter, consists of two or three syllables, one strongly stressed syllable and one lightly stressed syllable or one strong stress and two lighter ones.) Pentameter refers to five feet per line.

Almost all the lines in this poem are iambic. However, the poet does vary the meter in certain places. Line 2 of the third tercet begins with a spondee, which is a foot in which both syllables are equally heavily stressed. The unexpected emphasis on the first syllable, which in an iambic foot would not be stressed, brings the reader's attention to the fact that a new element in the poem, the deity, has been introduced into the poem.

Another metrical variation occurs in the first lines of the fourth and fifth tercet, both of which begin with a trochaic foot. A trochee is the opposite of an iamb; it consists of a stressed syllable followed by an unstressed syllable. The first words in these tercets, therefore, stand out strongly, since what the reader hears is not what he or she is expecting, given the predominance of iambic feet in the poem. The variation stands out against the expected metrical base.

HISTORICAL CONTEXT

American Poetry in the 1950s

In the late-1940s, immediately after World War II, the most well-established American poets were T. S. Eliot (who published *Four Quartets* collectively in 1943), Wallace Stevens, William Carlos Williams, Marianne Moore, and Robert Frost. Ezra Pound was also a prominent figure. These writers were modernists, a literary movement that began in the early 1900s as a revolt against traditional forms and gathered force in the wake of the dislocation of Western society following World War I.

During the same immediate postwar period, a number of poets sometimes referred to as the middle generation of twentieth-century American poets began to publish for the first time. These were poets mostly born between 1900 and 1920 who had grown up reading the works of the modernists. For example, John Berryman published *The Dispossessed* in 1948; Robert Lowell published *Lord Weary Castle* (1946), and Elizabeth Bishop's *North & South* appeared in 1946. Roethke was also a member of this generation of poets, and he published one of his most acclaimed books *The Lost Son and Other Poems* in 1948. Other influential poets of this period, Randall Jarrell, Karl Shapiro, and Delmore Schwartz, had begun publishing in the 1930s or early 1940s and remained active after the war.

During the 1950s, the poets of the middle generation established themselves as the leading poets of the day, although they did not develop any new movement for poetry, even though the heyday of modernism was long past. According to James E. B. Breslin, in *Columbia Literary History of the United States*, these poets were intimidated by the high status of their literary predecessors, and this, together with "economic prosperity, and social and political conservatism combined to create the bland literary hegemony of the fifties. In literature ... the basic procedures had already been invented." However, during the 1950s and into the 1960s, there was an infusion of new energy into the literary scene. This took the form of movements outside the poetic mainstream, such as the Beat poets, who included Allen Ginsberg and Gary Snyder. The publication of Ginsberg's turbulent, visionary *Howl! and Other Poems* in 1956 was a major event in the history of post-World War II American poetry. Also influential were the Black Mountain poets, named as such because Charles Olsen, the founder of this school, taught at Black Mountain College in North Carolina. Olson's influential manifesto *Projective Verse* was published in 1950. Robert Creeley and Denise Levertov were two prominent poets associated with this movement.

In addition to these movements, some poets of the middle generation, including Lowell, Berryman, and Roethke, as well as younger poets such as Sylvia Plath and Anne Sexton, produced verse that is sometimes called *confessional*. In these poems, the poets reveal the most painful aspects of their personal lives, including traumatic events such as divorce and mental illness. As Richard Ruland and Malcolm Bradbury put it in *From Puritanism to Postmodernism: A History of American Literature*, such poetry embodied "widespread exploitation of the poet's psychological life, a driven willingness to reveal innermost experience for the sake of art—and for the sake too, no doubt, of mental balance and survival."

COMPARE & CONTRAST

- **1950s:** Several well-known poets, including Sylvia Plath ("Mad Girl's Love Song" and "Denouement") and Dylan Thomas ("Do Not Go Gentle into that Good Night") write villanelles.

   Today: Contemporary poets Donald Justice, Paul Muldoon, Seamus Heaney, and David Shapiro all write villanelles. Harvey Stanbrough's villanelle, "Roses" appears in his *Beyond the Masks* (2005), and Peter Cole's villanelle, "Improvisation on Lines by Isaac the Blind" appears in his *Things on Which I've Stumbled* (2008).

- **1950s:** Continuing a development that began after World War II, many poets, including Roethke, are employed by universities to teach literature and creative writing. They are, therefore, able to support themselves without having to accept jobs unrelated to poetry or writing. Poets become part of the academic establishment rather than living on the margins of society or being employed in another profession.

   Today: Many of the leading American poets are employed by universities, but poetry also flourishes outside the academy. Poetry slams are popular, in which poets read their work and the audience judges which poem is the best. The emphasis is on performance, and the successful poems are those that can be easily understood on first hearing.

- **1950s:** Most established poets write in conventional poetic poems, using rhyme and meter, but experimentation is also in the air, and free verse becomes popular.

   Today: Free verse is the dominant poetic form, but the New Formalists of the 1980s and 1990s have created a continuing interest in formal, traditional verse.

CRITICAL OVERVIEW

Since "The Waking" was the title poem in a collection that won the Pulitzer Prize, it is not surprising that most critics, when they discuss Roethke's work, make some comment on this poem. Randall Stiffler, in *Theodore Roethke: The Poet and His Critics*, called it "one of the finest renditions in the twentieth century of the complex poetic form, the villanelle." Regarding the poem as one of Roethke's "most successful unions of form and content," Karl Malkoff, in *Theodore Roethke: An Introduction to the Poetry*, commented, "The poem's slow, steady rhythms support its meaning; the end-stopped lines, miraculously avoiding monotony, convey the sense of step-by-step movement." For Richard Allen Blessing, in *Theodore Roethke's Dynamic Vision*, "The Waking" "is an attempt to present through energetic thrusts and turns of the language that 'always' which is Now and which falls away before a man can touch it with hand or word." Jay Parini, in *Theodore Roethke: An American Romantic*, views the poem as an example of the romantic dialectic. He also comments on the technical aspects of the poem, referring to the "two brilliant refrain lines." He continues:

> Each stanza ... takes the refrain lines and slightly alters or extends their meaning. Indeed, the form itself dictates a tentative approach toward experience, for each refrain line, end stopped and seemingly final in its expression, is abruptly given a new color by its successive contexts.

CRITICISM

Bryan Aubrey

Aubrey holds a Ph.D. in English. In this essay, he discusses "The Waking" in terms of its connections to the romantic tradition in literature.

Theodore Roethke's "The Waking" is a complex poem, not easy to explicate, that packs

An earthworm (Image copyright Dark Raptor, 2009. Used under license from Shutterstock.com)

a lot of meaning into its nineteen lines. It is, in sum, a poem of spiritual awakening. There is a longing in this poem for knowing how to live in a right manner, in harmony with the great sweep of nature, living in a state of freedom, moment to moment, confident that the direction of life is always in favor of expanding consciousness and spiritual growth. The speaker professes a confidence that he has mastered this way of living, which he accomplishes through feeling and intuition rather than the reasoning intellect.

Given these themes, "The Waking" is a poem that places Roethke firmly in the tradition of romanticism. The major romantic poets in England in the late-eighteenth and early nineteenth century, as well as their successors, the transcendentalists in the United States, sought to restore a lost sense of unity between the individual self and the world. For the most part, they believed in a transcendent reality, beyond the limitations of space and time, to which all life aspired. Ralph Waldo Emerson described this reality as the Over-Soul, which he defined in his essay of that title:

that Unity, that Over-Soul, within which every man's particular being is contained and made one with all other. . . . within man is the soul of the whole; the wise silence; the universal beauty, to which every part and particle is equally related; the eternal ONE. And this deep power in which we exist, and whose beatitude is all accessible to us, is not only self-sufficing and perfect in every hour, but the act of seeing and the thing seen, the seer and the spectacle, the subject and the object, are one.

Emerson here summarizes the essence of the romantic philosophy: the reaching for the infinite, the belief, often grounded in direct experience, in the unity between the individual self and the larger, cosmic self. Understood in this light, the goal of the romantics was to overcome the alienation and isolation of the individual by reuniting with nature, which was understood as the dynamic flow of infinite life expressing itself in finite form.

This was the framework in which Roethke worked also, seeking as his poetic career developed a way of expressing this transcendent philosophy of life in his own way, using his own terms.

THE SPEAKER REACHES FOR A LIFE LIVED IN THE MOMENT, IN WHAT MYSTICS AND VISIONARIES SOMETIMES REFER TO AS THE ETERNAL NOW, WHICH IS BEYOND TIME AND SPACE, HIDDEN WITHIN EVERY MOMENT."

Although it did not reach its fullest expression until his final collection, *The Far Field*, published posthumously in 1964, the romantic spirit of Roethke's enterprise can be readily discerned in "The Waking" in several aspects: its emphasis on feeling rather than thought, intuition rather than analytic reason; its embrace of opposites; its interest in higher states of consciousness, and the consequent desire to live in the moment, in the Now in which eternity may be found.

Roethke, a teacher of literature as well as a poet, knew the work of the English romantics extremely well, and it was those poets who placed such importance on feeling as opposed to thought. William Wordsworth famously described poetry, in his preface to *Lyrical Ballads* in 1802, as the "spontaneous overflow of powerful feelings." In feelings, the romantics believed, lay a more authentic kind of experience, closer to the needs and desires of the human heart than could be attained by the analytic intellect. Reason, for the romantics, could only dissect, discriminating one object from another; it could perceive differences but not the underlying unity of things. John Keats, one of the second generation of the English romantics, declared in one of his letters, "I have never yet been able to perceive how any thing can be known for truth by consequitive reasoning," and he longed for "a Life of Sensations rather than of Thoughts!" This is exactly what the speaker in "The Waking" expresses at the beginning of the second tercet. Feeling, this tercet suggests, is a profound way of knowing; indeed, as the second part of the line implies, it can provide all the knowledge needed in life. Interestingly, Roethke himself commented directly on the meaning of this line in his essay "On 'Identity'":

> [The line] is a description of the metaphysical poet who thinks with his body: an idea for him can be as real as the smell of a flower or a blow on the head. And those so lucky as to bring their whole sensory equipment to bear on the process of thought grow faster, jump more frequently from one plateau to another more often.

This description suggests a way of gaining immediate, vital knowledge through feeling and sense experience, a kind of intuitive grasp of things through the body that bypasses the intellect and helps to create that elusive sense of unity with the environment. The second line of that second tercet in "The Waking" is a poetic expression of what the experience Roethke describes in prose actually feels like; it is a lively animation of the entire being. Essentially, it wakes a person up.

For many of the romantics, their distinctive sense of the unity of all things came about through an embrace of the totality of life, including all opposites, what Blake called "contraries": "Without Contraries is no progression," he wrote in *The Marriage of Heaven and Hell*. The idea is that all life consists of opposing forces that interact in a kind of dynamic polarity. Grasping these polarities rather than accepting one and rejecting the other leads to an apprehension of the wholeness of life, the knowledge that the polarities are just different manifestations of the one eternal consciousness. In the third, fourth, and fifth tercets of "The Waking," a process similar to this dialectic is presented. The third tercet shows awareness of the reality of death and presents it, paradoxically, as a living presence, something to be honored. The next tercet describes the opposite pole of existence, a heightened awareness of life. The poet may well be presenting an experience he actually had in which he perceived a tree illumined and transfigured by a kind of transcendent light that appeared to give it a holy significance. Perhaps this is why the word is capitalized, to suggest that it seemed at that time to belong to another dimension of life. Roethke claimed to have had many mystical experiences, some of which may have resembled this. He wrote in "On 'Identity'" of the feeling of "'oneness,' [that] is ... the first stage in mystical illumination ... the sense that all is one and one is all," adding that "This experience has come to me so many times, in so many varying circumstances, that I cannot suspect its validity." He also noted in the same essay that on occasion, a person can see an inanimate being or object so intensely, the perceiver becomes a part of what he perceives. When that happens, says, Roethke, "you are by way of

WHAT DO I READ NEXT?

- For those who find the villanelle an attractive poetic form, *Compass Card: One Hundred Villanelles* (2000), by George Emery, is a must read. Emery's skill with the form shows how varied and flexible it can be in the hands of a master craftsman.
- One of the finest post-World War II American poets was Elizabeth Bishop. Her poem, "One Art," first published in 1976, is a well known and much admired modern villanelle. It can be found in Bishop's *The Complete Poems: 1927–1979* (1984).
- American poet Edwin Arlington Robinson (1869–1935) wrote in traditional poetic forms, and his "The House on the Hill," first published in 1894, is an early example of the villanelle. It is also a good example of Robinson's interest in sad and gloomy topics. The poem can be found in *Robinson: Poems* (2007), in the Everyman Library Pocket Poets series or online at the Website maintained by the Academy of American poets.
- *The Glass House: The Life of Theodore Roethke* (1991), by Roethke's friend and colleague Allan Seager, is the first biography of Roethke. The book does not present an in-depth discussion of Roethke's poetry, but it does delve into how Roethke made himself into a poet and promoted his own work, always seeking recognition. Seager also gives detailed accounts of the progress of Roethke's mental illness.
- *English Romantic Poetry: An Anthology* (1996), edited by Stanley Applebaum, is a selection of 123 poems by the six major English romantic poets: William Blake, William Wordsworth, Samuel Taylor Coleridge, John Keats, Percy Bysshe Shelley, and Lord Byron. Most of the major short poems by these poets are included, along with excerpts from longer ones. As a whole, the anthology gives any reader an understanding of the romantic tradition to which Roethke was drawn.
- *Black Nature: Four Centuries of African American Nature Poetry* (2009), edited by Camille T. Dungy, consists of 180 poems by 23 African American poets, including such well-known figures as Phillis Wheatley, Rita Dove, Gwendolyn Brooks, Robert Hayden, and Melvin B. Tolson as well as newer voices, including Douglas Kearney, Major Jackson, and Janice Harrington. This book will interest anyone who enjoys reading nature poetry and understanding the contribution made to it by African Americans.
- *Be a Poet!* (2007), by Nancy Bogen, is a textbook about how to write poetry, written in brief chapters, each of which focuses on a different poetic technique. The author gives many examples from noted poets. The book was a finalist for a number of awards for young adult nonfiction.

---

getting somewhere: knowing you will break from self-involvement." Something of this heightened perception and the liberation it may bring is apparent in that rather cryptic fourth tercet, which is reminiscent of Wordsworth and Blake in moments when they saw the world, or aspects of it, lit up by transcendental light. Wordsworth describes exactly this in the first stanza of his famous "Ode: Intimations of Immortality":

There was a time, when meadow, grove, and stream
The earth, and every common sight,
To me did seem
Apparelled in celestial light,
The glory and the freshness of a dream.

Wordsworth refers to a time in childhood; as he grew older he became less and less capable of seeing the world in this heightened, illuminated

A tree in the forest lit by a sunbeam (Image copyright Kevin D. Walsh, 2009. Used under license from Shutterstock.com)

way, and in the fourth stanza of the ode he vividly describes this loss, focusing in the first line on one tree in particular:

> —But there's a Tree, of many, one,
> A single Field which I have looked
>   upon,
> Both of them speak of something that is
>   gone:
> The Pansy at my feet
> Doth the same tale repeat:
> Whither is fled the visionary gleam?
> Where is it now, the glory and the
>   dream?

Did Roethke, about 150 years later, pick up the fallen torch of Wordsworth and see that tree, illumined by the "gleam" that the long-ago poet once knew? Certainly, the heightened awareness of the tree and the status accorded to it—significantly, the word is capitalized in "The Waking"—immediately leads into the speaker's declaration, expressed in symbolic terms, that the entire universe, from the worm on up, is part of a dynamic, evolving spiritual consciousness.

The fifth tercet presents the results of the dialectic between life and death that takes place in the third and fourth tercets. The synthesis that results gives the speaker a kind of freedom to go forth in life, transfigured by the knowledge of nature's higher purposes. Again, as with the word "Tree," the capitalization of the word "Nature" is significant.

The romantic underpinnings of this poem are again apparent in line 2 of the final stanza, in which the speaker reaches for a life lived in the moment, in what mystics and visionaries sometimes refer to as the eternal Now, which is beyond time and space, hidden within every moment. It is part of that other dimension of life that the speaker has been driving at throughout the poem. William Blake wrote often of this moment, notably in the following quotation from his poem *Milton*, in which Satan represents, in Blake's symbolic universe, reason, the analytic intellect, which as "The Waking" also makes clear, cannot perceive such a moment:

> There is a Moment in each Day that Satan cannot find,
> Nor can his Watch Fiends find it; but the Industrious find
> This Moment & it multiply, & when it once is found
> It renovates every Moment of the Day if rightly placed.

Roethke knew Blake's work intimately, and this passage is very close to Roethke's meaning in the last stanzas of "The Waking"—a poem that trips along so lightly, as befits its villanelle form, but carries a great weight of meaning for those who are willing to puzzle it out.

Source: Bryan Aubrey, Critical Essay on "The Waking," in *Poetry for Students*, Gale, Cengage Learning, 2010.

John Montague

In the following essay, Montague recounts spending time with Theodore Roethke and gives biographical information about the poet.

Shortly after my first, slim volume, *Forms of Exile*, appeared in 1958, I got a very friendly note from Theodore Roethke, "with the admiration of an old party." His response was probably prompted by our mutual friend, the painter Morris Graves, but it was pleasant all the same for a novice to receive. I was twenty-nine, but poets grew up more slowly in those thorny days; the garden was wild and difficult.

I already knew and admired Roethke's work, with its strong lyric thrust, so unusual in contemporary American poetry: had Dylan Thomas not asked to meet him on one of his wearing lecture tours? I had begun to read Roethke when I was a teaching assistant at Berkeley, in a department that was academically strong but not awash with enthusiasm for poetry. For nourishment I listened to Kenneth Rexroth fulminating on Sunday mornings on KPFA, the local intellectual radio station, but Robert Duncan and Jack Spicer were on the East Coast, and Ginsberg had not yet slouched toward the Bay Area to be reborn. Even Snyder was away, either in rural Japan, at sea, or in a Zen monastery.

Roethke's plangent music brought me back to the traditional lyric, but with a post-Freudian lilt—Yeats in the speakeasy. As in "My Papa's Waltz":

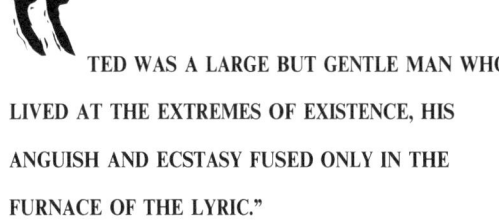

" TED WAS A LARGE BUT GENTLE MAN WHO LIVED AT THE EXTREMES OF EXISTENCE, HIS ANGUISH AND ECSTASY FUSED ONLY IN THE FURNACE OF THE LYRIC."

> The whiskey on your breath
> Could make a small boy dizzy;
> But I hung on like death:
> Such waltzing was not easy.

Was I moved by memories of my own father in Rodney Street, Brooklyn? I seemed to see the callused hand of a hard-worked man, hear the scraping of a fiddle, perhaps my Uncle John or Eddie Montague playing as the drunks were tossed down the tenement stairs and the women wrung their hands:

> We romped until the pans
> Slid from the kitchen shelf;
> My mother's countenance
> Could not unfrown itself.
> The hand that held my wrist
> Was battered on one knuckle;
> At every step you missed
> My right ear scraped a buckle.

Was a gangster called Garland shot in our kitchen? Had my father really been found, out cold, in the morgue, his forehead creased from a car accident? What I remembered more than anything else, beyond the roar of the El and the confusions of the period, was his caress:

> You beat time on my head
> With a palm caked hard by dirt,
> Then waltzed me off to bed
> Still clinging to your shirt.

And like myself, Roethke had known the spell of childless old women, "[t]hese nurses of nobody else ... [who] plotted for more than themselves." I could be back in my restoring Garvaghy home with my aunts when I read lingering lines like these from "Frau Bauman, Frau Schmidt, and Frau Schwartze":

> ... they picked me up, a spindly kid,
> Pinching and poking my thin ribs
> Till I lay in their laps, laughing,
> Weak as a whiffet;

Now, when I'm alone and cold in my
   bed,
They still hover over me,
These ancient leathery crones ...

But it was not all simple child's-eye memories of growth in a green place; Saginaw, Michigan, or Garvaghy, County Tyrone. I had bought a copy of the Pulitzer Prize-winning *The Waking* (1953), with a brooding portrait of the beetle-browed poet on the cover. Already a beat of madness could be heard in the slow, ominous lines of the title poem, a villanelle, frightening in its fierce control:

We think by feeling. What is there to
   know?
I hear my being dance from ear to ear.
I wake to sleep, and take my waking
   slow.

Here was a book by a poet determined to go the whole hog, a book dense with physical memories of the soiling of childhood, full of little comforting cries and invocations against the dark powers, and seeking aid and example from the greatest, from Dante to Wordsworth:

Dante attained the purgatorial hill,
Trembled at hidden virtue without flaw,
Shook with a mighty power beyond his
   will,—
Did Beatrice deny what Dante saw?

("Four for Sir John Davies")

Seeking indeed that cosmic dance of unity glimpsed by Sir John Davies and celebrated by Yeats as his supreme symbol—was it still possible in our time? "Is that dance slowing in the mind of man/That made him think the universe could hum?"

By the time his *Words for the Wind* came out in England in 1958, I was newly married and back working in Dublin. I loved the disgusting little songs for children because, though he never had any, Roethke could enter immediately into their natural naughtiness, unfulfilled by laundered Mother Goose rhymes. Perhaps "The Cow" had special meaning for me because I had tried to learn how to milk in our warm, wood-stalled byre and been slapped across the face for my lack of skill by the tail of an urgent, fecund mother.

There Once was a Cow with a Double
   Udder.
When I think of it now, I just have to
   Shudder!

She was too much for One, you can bet
   your Life:
She had to be Milked by a Man and his
   Wife.

But the volume's new note was a sequence of love poems, lyrical with delight but again with a Yeatsian undertow. Trying to live through similar experiences myself, I was troubled by these poems' heavily literary references going all the way back to Tudor times, the lovesick pursuits of Thomas Wyatt and Philip Sidney, so closely woven that though the lines extolled love, I could not catch sight of a flesh-and-blood beloved through the thicket of words. I did not believe, any more than Joyce Kilmer, that my love was "sweeter than a tree," but I could recognize the obsession, and the need to fulfill oneself with another, the greatest adventure possible to us in this life:

I kiss her moving mouth,
Her swart hilarious skin;
She breaks my breath in half;
She frolicks like a beast;
And I dance round and round,
A fond and foolish man,
And see and suffer myself
In another being, at last.

("Words for the Wind")

From Morris Graves and his friend Richard, I learned that Roethke had married a beautiful young woman called Beatrice O'Connell, of Irish background, presumably, although she was a Bennington girl from Virginia. For Morris and Richard, he was the Poet, a larger-than-life-size figure, balanced on the edge of excess. So I was not surprised when I received a wild piece, "The Old Florist's Lament," a Yeatsian ballad about Roethke's Prussian father, sent from some nursing home on February 19, 1959. With neighbors like Brendan Behan and Patrick Kavanagh, I was ready for anything in the line of eccentricity, but I was taken aback by the vehemence of this "Slight Song in Dubious Taste":

Who but a Prussian hog could know,
Or a sleek Polish ham,
Stettin's a place so cold and wet,
Pork keeps in good supply.
A cold-eyed, drunken Prussian man
Taught Jews new ways to die.

In the summer of 1960 I had a further note from Roethke, announcing his arrival in Ireland with his beloved, Beatrice. He was not staying at

Morris Graves's lordly Woodtown Manor but in a small private hotel, which boded well for his Dublin visit because it placed him in the center of a Dublin just beginning to come alive again, with architects, poets, and painters—a circle of gaiety into which he was quickly drawn. Michael Scott, our leading architect, who redesigned the Abbey Theatre, threw a big party for him, where Roethke distinguished himself by approaching a lady from both ends of her dress, a vigorous salutation not altogether common in Ireland. She took it in good part, since her husband was engaged in a less dramatic version of the same approach across the room. But there was another side to Roethke than these antics of a roaring boy.

It was a red-letter day when he came round to see me in our basement flat in Herbert Street. Released from Bord Fáilte, the Irish Tourist Board, I was working on my second book, *Poisoned Lands*, and copies of many of the poems were spread across our only table. He had brought some of the beautiful nature meditations that would form part of his "North American Sequence," lamentations leavened suddenly by exultation, the long, moody line of Whitman a movement more natural to his ebullient American self, taking over from Yeats:

> On the Bullhead, in the Dakotas, where the eagles eat well,
> In the country of few lakes, in the tall buffalo grass at the base of the clay buttes,
> In the summer heat, I can smell the dead buffalo,
> The stench of their damp fur drying in the sun,
> The buffalo chips drying.
> Old men should be explorers?
> I'll be an Indian.
> Ogalala?
> Iroquois.

It was heady stuff, of a kind I was not really used to in Ireland: a young and a veteran poet exchanging verses across a table. Though I had many friendly acquaintances among Irish writers, writing itself, like lovemaking, was a private occupation, and craft was rarely discussed in the way Roethke did, praising the four-beat lines in some of my newer poems, and my attempted use of a refrain. I remember also that quite a few adverbs went to the wall. It was my first experience since the Iowa workshop of this workmanlike approach to the process of poetry ... yet in Iowa I had not been lucky enough to be taught by a master. I was so pleased that I suggested we should go together to visit Mrs. Yeats.

When I made the suggestion, I was ignoring some storm signals. After our session in Herbert Street, Roethke produced a hip flask from his back pocket, the contents of which cascaded down his throat after he anxiously warned me not to tell Beatrice. I had nothing against drink, in fact was in favor of it, at the right time, as relaxation in good company. But Ted's application to it had begun to seem reckless and lacking in ceremony. I suggested that we should repair to a pub and have a few celebratory and companionable pints, but he was afraid Beatrice would not like that, though I proposed we ask her to join us in, let's say, Phil Ryan's in Baggot Street, where Liam Miller might drop in on his way home from the Dolmen Press. Roethke had already met the bearded Miller, and they had taken to each other mightily, but he seemed still afraid of the easy exposure of a pub, serious talking with glasses in hand and maybe a song in the background (that attitude would change, however, when he got to Inishbofin Island).

Meanwhile he was distracted by my wife's return from work, and that good Frenchwoman was politely startled by the way in which, with little ado, Roethke managed to pay manual homage to her bottom; in other words, to grab her ass. I hustled him up the stairs and pointed him home, toward Leeson Street and his waiting Beatrice.

We met next afternoon at the top of Dawson Street, outside a florist's. The idea, of course, was Ted's, since even the writing Irish were not literate in the language of flowers. But for Mrs. Yeats only the best would do, and when the shopgirl produced a conventional bouquet, her offering was greeted with not-so-friendly roars of disparagement.

"When I say flowers," Roethke growled, "I mean real flowers, not limp, dead stalks ready for the garbage. Christ Jesus, I was reared in a greenhouse!"

The assistant cowered, and I cowered with her.

"I'm going to see a lady, a great lady, a specialist in spooks! Have you ever heard of the poet Yeats and his wife, George?"

The poor girl was clearly not a great scholar of poetry, so I interposed on her behalf. "We are going to see an old friend of mine, the poet's widow. Perhaps we could see some roses?"

"Yeah! Roses! Let's see some roses!" roared Roethke from behind me. "Real roses, not these dying, crumpled things! Bring me your best! I know everything there is to know about roses."

Indeed he did, and would celebrate them in that wonderful poem, "The Rose":

And I think of roses, roses,
White and red, in the wide six-hundred-foot greenhouses,
And my father standing astride the cement benches,
Lifting me high over the four-foot stems, the Mrs. Russells, and his own elaborate hybrids,
And how those flowerheads seemed to flow toward me, to beckon me, only a child, out of myself.

The manager was called, and the matter was settled only when he and Roethke descended into the bowels of the shop to choose a basket of flowers, mainly roses. Ted seemed mollified, but he was still fussing as we hovered on the pavement outside.

"Do you think we got it right, John? Is there anything else she might like, besides flowers?" And then the leading question, "Does Mrs. Yeats drink?"

He swayed anxiously on the footpath like an outsize Red Riding Hood, swinging his basket of flowers. He was nervous as a kitten, or a swain on a first date, and badly in need of fortification, which I thought it better not to seek out; Mrs. Yeats had said she wasn't feeling her best, and the idea of the two of us turning up late and bombed on her doorstep did not appeal to me. When I assured him that she did take a drop, he was relieved, but he was less happy when I directed him to a fashionable shop, Smiths of the Green, to buy a bottle of Bristol Cream.

"Sherry! Good God, she drinks sherry! I don't know anyone that drinks stuff like that! That's for old ladies!" (Which, of course, she was.)

We hailed a taxi by the Traitors' Arch and left for Rathmines, the basket between us with the nozzle of the bottle protruding among the flowers like a gangster's gat. But when we reached the gate and steps to her late-Georgian house, Roethke was still in a tizzy; all those years of studying Yeats were fizzing in him like champagne.

"Is this her house? Did Yeats ever live here himself?"

As the bell rang and rang in the depths of the house, Ted became more agitated, taking out the bottle to swing in his left hand while he held the flowers in the right. Finally I heard Mrs. Yeats shuffling toward the door, which opened slowly, all the more because the carpet had got curled into it.

"Hello, John," said George Yeats, bending to smooth the rug with her left hand. The wait was too much for the tense Roethke, who now shot out his right hand in greeting.

"Mrs. Yeats, I brought you some flowers!" he bellowed, whereupon she straightened her back, scattering most of them across the floor.

"Hmph!" she said, a cross between a hoot of dismay and a cry of astonishment, and turned to disappear in the direction of the kitchen.

"What's wrong? What's happened?" cried Ted, as we gathered the scattered flowers. "Is she coming back? Did we upset her?"

When she returned she was carrying a vase, and she began to beam with pleasure as Roethke tidied the flowers into it.

"Roses! How nice of you. Poor Willy's favorite flower, the only ones he could recognize. He was nearly color-blind, you know."

As we helped her select a spot for them in the sitting room, she explained that she was not feeling well and could not guide us through the library. Sensing a companion in misery, Roethke detailed his own health problems, and soon they were discussing cures for arthritis and the relationship between rheumatism and climate, the Pacific Northwest being nearly as rainy as Ireland. He offered to rub her back as she stretched on a couch, but she accepted a glass of sherry instead. Soon they were at ease, gossiping about critics and poetic contemporaries. One English poet-critic who had bored her got short shrift.

"He keeps sending me his absurd books. As a critic he may have some place in a university, but as a poet he is intolerable!"

Her vehemence delighted Roethke. "I've been thinking of the right word for that fella for years. And intolerable hits the nail right on the head. He's dry as a bone in the desert."

It was clear they had taken to each other, and I left to wander into the library. In due course I was joined there by a (for once) totally contented Roethke. I showed him some of the mystical notebooks with designs elaborate as geometry or higher algebra, and he was boyishly impressed. He had simmered down to a thoughtful quietness, his best mood, as when we were looking together at the poems. We said good-bye to Mrs. Yeats, who was nearly asleep; Ted tucked the rug around her with great tenderness.

Instead of going home, I brought him to a large, comfortable public house in Rathmines that I sometimes frequented on my way to and from the library. I ordered a fine, slowly drawn pint of Guinness, but before it had arrived with its priestlike collar of froth, Roethke had already sunk two large whiskeys and called for a third. It seemed a good time to be serious. I asked why he drank in the haphazard way he did and said I found it hard to reconcile the two Roethkes, the sensitive poet and the other, the roaring boy whose heart somehow did not seem in it. He hunched his large shoulders, and his domed head glistened with nervous sweat.

"I drink like this," he said, "because I'm afraid of death. It's all I seem to think about."

The dark mood eventually passed, and by the time I brought him back to his hotel he was ready to berate Beatrice for not being a medium. In a few days they would leave to see Richard Murphy on Inishbofin Island, where I planned to catch up with them; but by the time I got there, Roethke was in Ballinasloe Hospital. On Inishbofin he had discovered the company of drinkers and pub singers; there was little else to do on the island for long periods. But something about that Ireland was dangerous for the euphoric side of his temperament; songs like "Gob Music" were nearly in as bad taste as "The Old Florist's Lament":

> Indeed I saw a shimmering lake
> Of slime and shining spit,
> And I kneeled down and did partake
> A bit of the likes of it.
> And it reminded me—But Oh!
> I'll keep my big mouth shut.

In three years Roethke would be dead; the marvelous poems he showed me would be published posthumously. The travail of that generation of American poets is now well documented. The loneliness of the poetic vocation is a constant, exacerbated by the indifference of that vast country, but there is always some context in Ireland, however rough and residual. That is perhaps what Roethke glimpsed in Dublin and Inishbofin; Ireland may be the last place in the English-speaking world where the title "poet" has some authority, and Ted would have loved to participate in such a community. His melancholy "Saginaw Song" describes the constricting gentility of his midwestern background:

> In Saginaw, in Saginaw,
> There's never a household fart,
> For if it did occur,
> It would blow the place apart,—

whereas he dreamt himself a beloved bard, performing before an admiring audience:

> O, I'm the genius of the world,—
> Of that you can be sure,
> But alas, alack, and me achin' back,
> I'm often a drunken boor;
> But when I die—and that won't be
>   soon—
> I'll sing with dear Tom Moore,
> With that lovely man, Tom Moore.

There was, too, a pattern of drinking during that period. Few from Ireland can afford to cast a stone, but there was a madness to the martini mystique. In its way it was as primitive a ritual as proving masculinity through the consumption of pints in the student pubs of Dublin. But it was more dangerous because less passive: the object was to stimulate the brain cells, dissolve the inhibitions rather than ease them. And there were the fantasies hard liquor feeds: Roethke's father was a strict German, not a wild drunk, and his son probably had not run with gangsters: "A place I surely did like to go / Was the underbelly of Cicero . . ." ("Song for the Squeeze-Box").

American poets have found shelter in the academy, but there is something artificial in this arrangement, like seeking sanctuary during the medieval plagues: what about real life, as they say. French poets like André Frenaud and Eugène Guillevic earned their livings as civil servants, and there is a long tradition of poets in the diplomatic service, such as Pablo Neruda and Octavio Paz from Latin America, Paul Claudel and Saint-John Perse from France, and Denis Devlin from Ireland. Besides, English departments are often hostile and uncomprehending; however scholarly a poetic interloper may be, they find it hard to take him or her seriously unless the poet bears and wears the insignia of serious scholarship, as T. S. Eliot did. Creative writing classes have eased this artificial division between creator and explicator, but Roethke was a pioneer in those early days of the poetry workshop, and he still believed in being a scholar of the poetic tradition.

Both Robert Lowell and Roethke had massive personal problems into which it would be presumptuous to pry. Ted was a large but gentle man who lived at the extremes of existence, his anguish and ecstasy fused only in the furnace of the lyric. He tried to play the athlete as well as the poet, a two-fisted drinker who identified with the minute and the helpless, as in his delicate poem "The Meadow Mouse":

> But this morning the shoe-box house on the back porch is empty.
> Where has he gone, my meadow mouse,
> My thumb of a child that nuzzled in my palm?—
> To run under the hawk's wing,
> Under the eye of the great owl watching from the elm-tree,
> To live by courtesy of the shrike, the snake, the tom-cat.
> I think of the nestling fallen into the deep grass,
> The turtle gasping in the dusty rubble of the highway,
> The paralytic stunned in the tub, and the water rising,—
> All things innocent, hapless, forsaken.

Above all there was that fierce competitiveness, the need to be number one, that raged throughout that generation like a virus, as if poetry were a form of prize fighting and they were all vying to be heavyweight champion. Fame is the spur, indeed, but one should not rowel pegasus. Lowell was among the chief culprits, with his power mania: when Berryman was completing (I almost wrote competing) the *Dream Songs* in Dublin, Lowell wrote to him, saying that his Irish poems—which are not his best—made Berryman "the best Irish poet since Yeats." Willful lines he was later to use about Heaney, though there is no evidence that he had ever bothered to read Austin Clarke, Kavanagh, even Thomas Kinsella and myself, or indeed any contemporary Irish poetry in either language, before he put the skunk among the pigeons.

Meanwhile Roethke, on the far Pacific coast, had done his homework. His notes to me were garnished with generous postscripts: "Say hello to Kavanagh"; or, more surprisingly (because he had published so little), "Give my best to [Padraic] Fallon." His class notes showed that he had introduced his students to contemporary Irish poetry, and according to his biographer, Allan Seager, "Even in London, Ted had not fallen into a literary circle he liked better." I believe he glimpsed in Ireland a community where he might have prospered, but it was too late, and it only drove him mad again. Later in the decade, John Berryman would arrive to live and work for a longer period against the same backdrop. My last communication from Roethke was a sad, small, Blakeian lyric of travail wrought into a healing sweetness. It was on a small card, surprisingly tinseled with stars:

> In a hand like a bowl
> Danced my own soul,
> Small as an elf,
> All by itself.

Source: John Montague, "Gentle Giant," in *Southern Review*, Vol. 32, Summer 1996, pp. 561–71.

SOURCES

Abrams, M. H., *A Glossary of Literary Terms*, 4th ed., Holt, Rinehart, and Winston, 1981, p. 127.

Blake, William, *The Marriage of Heaven and Hell*, in *Blake: Complete Writings*, edited by Geoffrey Keynes, Oxford University Press, 1974, p. 149.

———, *Milton*, in *Blake: Complete Writings*, edited by Geoffrey Keynes, Oxford University Press, 1974, p. 526.

Blessing, Richard Allen, *Theodore Roethke's Dynamic Vision*, Indiana University Press, 1974, p. 23.

Breslin, James E. B., "Poetry," in *Columbia Literary History of the United States*, edited by Martha Banta, Terence Martin, et al., Columbia University Press, 1988, p. 1082.

Emerson, Ralph Waldo, "The Over-Soul," in *Emerson's Essays*, J. M. Dent, 1955, p. 150.

Keats, John, *Letters of John Keats*, edited by Robert Gittings, Oxford University Press, 1970, p. 37.

Malkoff, Karl, *Theodore Roethke: An Introduction to the Poetry*, Columbia University Press, 1966, pp. 122–23.

Parini, Jay, *Theodore Roethke: An American Romantic*, University of Massachusetts Press, 1979, pp. 143–44.

Roethke, Theodore, "On 'Identity'," in *On the Poet and His Craft: Selected Prose of Theodore Roethke*, edited with an introduction by Ralph J. Mills Jr., University of Washington Press, 1974, pp. 25, 26, 27.

———, "The Waking," in *The Collected Poems of Theodore Roethke*, Anchor Books, 1975, p. 104.

Ruland, Richard, and Malcolm Bradbury, *From Puritanism to Postmodernism: A History of American Literature*, Viking, 1991, p. 407.

Stiffler, Randall, *Theodore Roethke: The Poet and His Critics*, American Library Association, 1986, p. 119.

Wolff, George, *Theodore Roethke*, Twayne's United States Author Series No. 390, Twayne, 1981.

Wordsworth, William, "Ode: Intimations of Immortality from Recollections of Early Childhood," in *The Norton Anthology of English Literature*, Vol. 2, 5th ed., edited by M. H. Abrams, Norton, 1986, pp. 209–210.

———, Preface, in *Lyrical Ballads: Wordsworth and Coleridge*, edited with introduction, notes and appendices by R. L. Brett and A. R. Jones, Methuen, 1968, p. 266.

FURTHER READING

Abrams, M. H., *Natural Supernaturalism: Tradition and Revolution in Romantic Literature*, Norton, 1971.

> This classic study of romanticism is one of the best books ever to appear on the subject. Abrams deals mostly with poetry and philosophy in England and Germany, showing what romantic writers had in common in themes and style. The book provides a context for understanding the tradition in which Roethke placed himself.

Balakian, Peter, *Theodore Roethke's Far Fields: The Evolution of His Poetry*, Louisiana State University Press, 1989.

> This book focuses on Roethke's development as a poet. Balakian finds in Roethke's work both continuity and evolution. Balakian also discusses Roethke's position and importance in modern poetry.

Bowers, Neal, *Theodore Roethke: The Journey from I to Otherwise*, University of Missouri Press, 1982.

> The premise of this book is that Roethke's mental illness was instrumental in giving him mystical experience. His illness, which had peaks and troughs in terms of his mood, helped him to understand that there is another level of reality than is normally perceived. This awareness formed the basis of Roethke's search for identity.

Kalaidjian, Walter B., *Understanding Theodore Roethke*, University of South Carolina Press, 1987.

> This book is written for students and general readers. It presents a clear overview of Roethke's life and work, devoting a chapter to each of Roethke's book. There is also an annotated bibliography.

Women

ALICE WALKER

1973

Alice Walker's poem "Women" was written in 1970 and first published in her second volume of poetry *Revolutionary Petunias & Other Poems* (1973), in a chapter titled "In These Dissenting Times." "Women" celebrates the African American women of earlier generations, those who struggled and made sacrifices and whose efforts benefited the women of Walker's generation. Walker uses "Women" to honor the women of her mother's generation and to remind her readers that a woman's success is also measured by the hard work of her ancestors. This poem is Walker's attempt to keep alive the memories of these earlier women, as an inspiration to later generations. "Women" is a twenty-six-line, free verse poem, with short lines consisting of only one to five words and no punctuation until the concluding line, when the one-sentence poem ends with a period. "Women" was included in Walker's 1974 essay, "In Search of Our Mothers' Gardens," which was later included in a collection of her essays, *In Search of Our Mothers' Gardens: Womanist Prose*, published in 1983. Walker also included the poem in *Her Blue Body Everything We Know; Earthling Poems, 1965–1990 Complete*, published in 1991.

AUTHOR BIOGRAPHY

Alice Walker was born in Eatonton, Georgia, on February 9, 1944. She was the youngest of eight

Alice Walker (AP Images)

children born to Winnie Lee Walker and Minnie Tallulah Grant Walker. Walker's parents were sharecroppers, and while the family was poor, Walker describes her childhood as happy until a BB gun accident at age eight, when Walker was accidentally shot in the right eye by one of her brothers. The damage caused a scar and resulted in significant teasing at school, causing Walker to be withdrawn and to isolate herself from family and friends. The scar tissue was finally removed when she was fourteen. Walker attended Spelman College in Atlanta, Georgia, but transferred to Sarah Lawrence College in 1964, graduating in 1966. The following year she married civil rights attorney, Melvyn Rosenman Leventhal. In 1968, her first collection of poetry, *Once*, was published, and Walker took a position as writer-in-residence at Jackson State College. Her only child, her daughter Rebecca, was born in 1969. In 1970, Walker became a writer-in-residence at Tougaloo College, was awarded a Radcliffe Institute Fellowship, and published her first novel, *The Third Life of Grange Copeland*.

In 1972, Walker became a lecturer at Wesley College and at the University of Massachusetts, Boston. Her second book of poetry, *Revolutionary Petunias & Other Poems*, published in 1973, received a National Book Award nomination and the Lillian Smith Award from the Southern Regional Council. After publishing her first collection of short stories, *In Love & Trouble: Stories of Black Women* in 1973, Walker agreed to become the editor of *Ms.* magazine. Walker and her husband were divorced in 1976, and two years later, she moved to California. Another volume of poetry, *Good-night, Willie Lee, I'll See You in the Morning*, was published in 1979, as was *I Love Myself When I am Laughing ... And Then Again When I am Looking Mean and Impressive: A Zora Neale Hurston Reader*, an anthology devoted to the work of Hurston. Walker's anthology rescued Hurston from literary obscurity and secured for her a well-deserved place in feminist and African American literary studies.

Walker is probably best known for her 1982 novel, *The Color Purple*, for which she received a National Book Award and the Pulitzer Prize in Fiction in 1983, the first female African American writer to receive this award. In 1983, a collection of non-fiction essays, *In Search of Our Mothers' Gardens: Womanist Prose*, offered Walker the opportunity to comment on a variety of subjects, including race and the African American literary tradition. She created Wild Trees Press in 1984 to provide African American writers with a more accessible avenue for publishing their work; however, Walker did not quit writing once she turned to publishing.

Another poetry collection *Horses Make a Landscape Look More Beautiful* was published in 1984. In the 1988 collection *Living by the Word: Essays*, she addressed many issues connected to the reception of *The Color Purple*, which had been criticized for perpetuating stereotypes of African American men as wife beaters. Collected poems appeared in *Her Blue Body Everything We Know: Earthling Poems, 1965–1990* (1991). In 1993, Walker collaborated with Pratibha Parmer to co-produce a documentary film and companion book, *Warrior Marks*, about female circumcision ritual. In 1994, Walker changed her middle name to Tallulah-Kate, to honor her mother and paternal grandmother. In 1997, Walker was honored by the American Humanist Association as Humanist

MEDIA ADAPTATIONS

- Stephen Spielberg's 1985 film *The Color Purple* is based on Walker's novel. Starring Whoopi Goldberg and Oprah Winfrey, *The Color Purple* was nominated for eleven Academy Awards but received none.

of the Year. Her *Collected Poems* appeared in 2005. As of 2009, Walker had published nine books of poetry, twelve novels, several short story and essay collections, as well as children's books. Walker has been a poet, novelist, essayist, short story writer, editor, publisher, and social activist. As of 2009, she lived in California.

POEM SUMMARY

Lines 1–8

The opening lines reveal that Walker is singling out the women of her mother's generation for tribute. The poet describes the women's physical characteristics first. These women were strong and had deep, full voices. They were determined and tough. They walked with self-assurance, and they used their fists, not just their hands. They were willing to fight for what they wanted. In these first eight lines, Walker presents a picture of stout, indomitable women. If they have doubts, they do not reveal them. The women of her mother's generation accomplished what needed to be done. They beat down doors where they met resistance; they did not retreat from challenges. When needed to demand action, their hands were quick to form fists.

Lines 9–11

Walker honors the domestic work these women did in order to support their daughters. They laundered, starched, and ironed white shirts. Many of the women of her mother's generation worked as domestics, cleaning homes and ironing the shirts of those who employed them. These mothers worked hard for their children and were prepared to take on any kind of work to meet their children's needs. The suggestion is also that the women were as stiff and starched as the shirts they ironed. They are sturdy and resolute. White shirts also suggest affluence, which is the promise of education and career opportunities not previously available to African Americans. These mothers prepared their children for a world that did not yet exist; they saw the possibility of a better future.

Lines 12–18

The women of Walker's mother's generation had militant power. These mothers with rags tied on their heads led armies across dangerous terrain in their determination to create a better world for their children. Walker mentions mine fields and booby-traps, in order to suggest that the women confronted hidden danger and risks they could not anticipate. These women were survivors; they managed to persist and carry on despite the traps set for them.

Lines 19–26

In the final eight lines Walker focuses on education. She mentions books and desks, the symbols of schooling, which also signifies greater opportunities. These mothers knew that demanding a better education for their sons and daughters would give them the possibility of a better life. The women of Walker's mother's generation understood how important it was for their children to achieve an education equal to that provided to white children. Lines 19 through 21 refer specifically to the demands that African American parents made for better schools, textbooks, and teachers equal to those employed in white schools.

Walker ends the poem by commenting that these mothers knew that education would be the key to a better life. They knew the value of education, even though they, themselves, were not educated. These women knew their children must be able to read, even though they were unable to read. Walker makes their illiteracy clear when she observes that they could not read a page of what they demanded their children be able to read. "Women" is a tribute to the mothers who had the foresight and courage to demand opportunities for their descendents, perhaps because these women knew what it was to live without them.

TOPICS FOR FURTHER STUDY

- Nikki Giovanni writes many poems for young people. Read one of Giovanni's poems and consider how her poem differs in tone and content from Walker's poem. You might consider either "Revolutionary Dreams," or "nikki-rosa," from *Ego-Tripping and Other Poems for Young People* (1973). Prepare an evaluation of the differences that you noted and present your findings as an oral report to your classmates.

- Walker's poem was composed in the early 1970s. Research the economic and social status of African Americans in the 1960s and 1970s. Prepare an oral report in which you discuss the experiences of African Americans during this period and the role of the civil rights movement on providing greater educational and employment opportunities for African Americans. Include a brief PowerPoint presentation to accompany your oral report.

- Take the first line of Walker's poem and use it as the first line of your own poem. Write a poem of at least twenty-five lines by continuing this new first line to whatever conclusion fits your own experiences with struggle or fighting for an opportunity. Write a brief paragraph to attach to your poem, in which you evaluate what your poem says about your life story.

- Research the education and career opportunities facing African American female adults in the 1950s and 1970s. Find statistics in these two areas for each groups. Identify if possible differences between women living in the rural South and those living in urban areas of the North during these two decades. Write an essay that uses this research to explain differences between the speaker in Walker's poem and the women of the previous generation who are described in it.

- Spend some time looking through art books and select a picture or illustration that you feel best illustrates the hard working women depicted in Walker's poem. You might consider images of women working as domestic servants as possible topics. Then, in an essay, compare the art that you have selected to "Women," noting both the similarities and the differences between these two images.

- Much modern poetry reflects the poet's experiences. Study the biography and two poems by a female poet who is a contemporary of Walker. Write a research paper in which you discuss how this poet's life, her experiences, and her view of women are reflected in at least two of her poems. Choose one of the following: Maya Angelou, Gwendolyn Brooks, Sonia Sanchez, Shirley Geok-Lin Lim, or Sharon Olds.

- Walker's poem is a reminder of the changes that the civil rights movement brought to African Americans. With two or three classmates, create a group presentation in which you report on the civil rights movement of the second half of the twentieth century. Divide the work by assigning different chores to each member of the group. Prepare a handouts for your classmates, which includes a bibliography of your sources.

THEMES

Education

In the last half of "Women," Walker focuses on the importance of education. She mentions books and desks as two things her mother's contemporaries did not have and wanted for their children. These mothers valued education, perhaps even more because they were not educated themselves. They were willing to work

The first integrated class at School 99 in Baltimore, MD (© *Bettmann / Corbis*)

hard to secure an education for their children, although they had not read even a page of the textbooks they envisioned their children might someday study. These women were prepared to knock down closed doors that barred their way. Education was so important that they were willing to spend their days ironing starched white shirts; they were willing to fight explicit and covert opposition because they understood that an education offered a way to escape poverty and have opportunities for better employment.

Social Change

Social change does not occur without sacrifice, and Walker clearly understands how much the women of her mother's generation had to sacrifice in their efforts to change the world for the next generation. These women were not afraid to challenge the idea of separate-but-equal public education. Their goal was to make sure that their children had the same opportunities as white children. These women were willing to persist in their own work because they had the hope their children would have better work to do.

STYLE

Free Verse

Free verse is poetry that does not comply with the structure, rhyme, or meter of established poetic forms. Free verse liberates the poet from the restrictions of a particular meter and rhyme scheme. Free verse is often associated with modern poetry, and Walker's poem is an example of it. There is no prescribed pattern of rhyme or meter to "Women." The irregular line breaks fit the content of the poem. Walker does not adhere to any conventional pattern of meter; nor is there any stanza division in this poem. Walker uses free verse because it allows her certain choices in fitting the form of her poem to its content.

Imagery

Imagery is the collection of word pictures in a literary work. Images are conveyed through the physical senses; they depict the real world in concrete rather than abstract terms. Images deliver sensory cues and help readers visualize or comprehend what the poet wants to say in physical terms. Thus, imagery conveys meaning by connecting the idea of the poem to sensory experience. For instance in "Women," Walker describes the women as stout, with husky voices, and working hands that can form fists. The risks these women take in seeking equal education for their children are likened to stepping across a field with mines buried in it or scrambling across a ditch that has been booby trapped. The battlefield images convey how tricky and dangerous such social protest can be.

Modern Poetry

In the twentieth century, much poetry and fiction departed from literary traditions followed in the nineteenth century. Modern writers deliberately broke from pre-World War I literary conventions. They attempted to create a new world by challenging people's perceptions and assumptions. Walker's poem stands as a challenge to historically respected class and racial inequality. It takes persistent, hard-working, clever, and courageous ordinary domestic servants and equates them and their influence to generals who lead armies. It remarks on equality in public education which has become institutionalized because certain ordinary people insisted on it at great personal expense. Once the literary form of an elite, poetry as Walker writes it pays tribute to common workers who were dedicated to changing the world for the better.

Parallelism

Parallelism is a grammatical arrangement, which creates balance and emphasis. "Women" is a sentence with parallel parts. The phrases beginning with the word "how" are parallel. Arranged this way the subjects of these phrases have a cumulative effect: the women beat down doors, led armies, knew what their daughters must know. The cumulative arrangement suggests that the knowing is more important than the work of pushing through barriers and leading masses in social protest. The knowing is what matters most; without that, the other two actions are not possible. The poem also has sets of parallel nouns, which when juxtaposed are understood in a fresh way. The beating down of doors is paired with ironing shirts. The meaning seems to be that the acts of aggression are as courageous but no more courageous than the daily work of ironing that makes a living and provides for a family. Similarly, the dramatic traversing mine-filled fields and getting across ditches is rewarded with the seemingly mundane arrival at books and desks. Again, the arrangement makes the reader think. The great battlefield effort is justly rewarded in the discovery an education offers. The grammar fits and underscores the poem's meaning.

HISTORICAL CONTEXT

African American Education

In 1954, the United States Supreme Court ruled that segregation was unconstitutional. The ruling, however, had little effect on the segregated American South, where discrimination and racial inequality continued for much of the next twenty years. Efforts to integrate public schools often resulted in vehement opposition from white school and government officials. In September 1957, after Governor Orval Faubus sent state troopers to prevent African American students from enrolling at Little Rock High School, President Dwight Eisenhower sent one thousand federal troops to enforce school desegregation in Arkansas. After federal troops arrived, nine African American children were escorted into the high school and began taking classes.

In another example, during September 1962, an African American student enrolled for classes at the University of Mississippi, but when he attempted to enter the campus, state troopers sent by Governor Ross Barnett blocked the student's way to the campus. President John F. Kennedy responded by sending federal marshals to escort the African American student to class. A riot ensued, and an angry white mob stormed the campus. Three people were killed and more than fifty were injured.

Although the Supreme Court ruling took place in 1954, schools in Alabama were not integrated until 1963. Twenty years after the 1954 ruling, violent clashes with police over enforced busing

COMPARE & CONTRAST

- **1960–1970s:** In April 1968, Dr. Martin Luther King Jr. is assassinated in Memphis, Tennessee. His death leads to riots in 167 cities and at many college campuses.

   Today: The third Monday of every January is set aside as a federal holiday to honor the work of Dr. King, who dedicated his life to nonviolent resistance as a way to bring about social change.

- **1960–1970s:** Shirley Chisholm is the first African American woman to be elected to the U.S. Congress. She is a candidate for the United States presidency as a Democrat in 1972 and wins 152 delegates before withdrawing from the race.

   Today: A total of 12 African American women serve in the 111th Congress in 2009. In all, women hold only 16.8 percent of congressional seats in 2009.

- **1960–1970s:** In April 1971, the Supreme Court issues a decision in *Swann v. Charlotte-Mecklenburg Board of Education* that unanimously upholds school busing to achieve desegregation of public schools.

   Today: In 2007, the Supreme Court rules against busing programs, stating in cases regarding Seattle, Washington, and Louisville, Kentucky, that race cannot be used in determining which schools students attend.

- **1960–1970s:** The black aesthetic movement is an effort to create a populist art to be identified with African American culture by African American publishers, theater groups, and literature. This movement asserts that African American experiences, as depicted in art and literature, are different from the experience of other racial and ethnic groups.

   Today: Although the black aesthetic movement ended soon after it began, it has two legacies. College courses focus on the proponents of the black aesthetic movement and the literature that traces it origins to it. Also, the works of such writers as Alice Walker, Toni Morrison, and Maya Angelou appeal to readers of all ethnic and racial groups.

- **1960–70s:** In October 1972, Michael Jackson and the Jackson Five have the number one song in the United States.

   Today: Michael Jackson dies in 2009. His death results in a media frenzy on television and the Internet.

---

closed schools in Boston, thus proving that it was easier to legislate integration than to act on it.

Racism and African American Women's Lives

In 1964, President Lyndon Johnson signed the Civil Rights Act, which prohibits racial discrimination by voting registrars and in employment, public facilities, places of public accommodation, union membership, and federally funded programs. Although the idea of civil rights had momentum, the implementation to make it a reality was difficult. Passage of the new law led to riots in Harlem and to deaths in Mississippi when African Americans attempted to register to vote, all within months of the passage of the Civil Rights Act. In 1965, the Voting Rights Act was passed by Congress, but legislation alone was not enough to end the disenfranchisement of African Americans. African American frustration over poverty, poor housing, and unemployment led to race riots in Los Angeles in 1965. In the following three years, there were urban riots in Cleveland, Chicago, Atlanta, Detroit, and more than 125 other U.S. cities. Although the riots eventually ended, racial segregation in housing did not. During the 1970s, African Americans were much more likely than whites to live in inner city ghettos where schools lacked funding and jobs were limited. Racial segregation in housing reinforced

Daisy Bates stands with students in front of her home in Little Rock, Arkansas, September 1957. Bates was the advisor of nine African American teens who attempted to enroll in Little Rock High School, beginning the movement toward desegregation. (Thomas D. McAvoy / Time & Life Pictures / Getty Images)

poor education and employment opportunities for African Americans of all ages.

Although discrimination was a problem for African American men, it was an even more significant a problem for African American women. Economic studies of the 1970s show that for every dollar a white man earned, an African American man earned seventy cents, a white woman earned fifty-eight cents, and an African American woman earned fifty cents. African American activism, which Walker's poem celebrates, helped to dismantled racial segregation, but in spite of the legislative changes, poverty among African Americans did not end. Social class stratification was linked to a lack of employment, much of which was the result of the poor education African American children received. African American women were often limited to jobs that were part-time, poorly paid, and without job security or benefits. As more jobs moved to suburban areas or overseas, employment for African American women, many of whom lived in urban neighborhoods, became even less available. As a result, for many women, employment was limited to service or domestic work.

CRITICAL OVERVIEW

Although Walker may be best known to many readers as the author of *The Color Purple*, she was an accomplished poet long before the publication of her Pulitzer Prize-winning novel. When *Revolutionary Petunias & Other Poems* was published in 1973, it was reviewed widely, which is unusual for poetry. That Walker received so much attention indicates her reputation as an accomplished poet was already established. Many of the reviews emphasized her role as a southern African American poet who is able to successfully depict her roots and her community. For instance, in a review for *Black World*, Mary Helen Washington noted that Walker is "heir" to the traditions of the "southern Black woman writer." Walker uses that knowledge so that a reader "leaves her work understanding not only the southern Black experience a little better but also understanding better the nature of the Black experience as a whole." Washington compared Walker's work favorably to that of Richard Wright, whose novel *Black Boy* is considered a classic of African American literature. Washington also noted that the poems in the first section of *Revolutionary Petunias & Other Poems* honor the past as though it were "Alice Walker's own sacred ritual" to bring forth "traditions that are solid and unifying because they are shared." The heritage of the southern African American writer in Walker's poetry was also cited by Gwendolyn Davis in her review for *New South*. Like Washington, Davis mentioned the significance of the opening section of Walker's collection of poetry, how it "pays tribute to hardy black elders and the enduring lifestyle" of their past. Davis pointed out that Walker accomplishes more than just honoring her roots as a southern poet. According to Davis, Walker is capable of creating lyrical poetry in which the reader can find "a delicate declaration that love, beauty, truth and other romantic ideals can exist amidst turmoil." Walker's poems, Davis suggested, can celebrate not only the individual but also "the emotional experience of a people."

The review of *Revolutionary Petunias & Other Poems* by poet Jerry W. Ward emphasized Walker's celebration of her roots. In his review for *College Language Association Journal*, Ward lamented that Walker has not received more critical attention because her poems are "hopeful strategies for recapturing one's humanity" and thus deserve more critical acclaim. He pointed out that Walker uses her "black southern roots" to provide her poetry with the "definition and tone of Afro-American writing." In honoring their African American heritage, poets such as Walker pay homage to their past and create a cultural legacy for the future. Ward also observed that Walker creates "poems of extraordinary grace, wisdom, and strength," all of which was predicted in her first volume of poetry, *Once*.

CRITICISM

Sheri Metzger Karmiol

Karmiol teaches literature and drama at The University of New Mexico, where she is a lecturer in the University Honors Program. In this essay, she

WHAT DO I READ NEXT?

- *Absolute Trust in the Goodness of the Earth* (2003) is Walker's sixth collection of poetry. These poems, written after September 11, 2001, celebrate nature and love and are a protest against war.

- Walker's first collection of short stories, *In Love & Trouble: Stories of Black Women* (1973), focuses on the lives of African American women living in the American South.

- *The Color Purple* (1982) is Walker's Pulitzer Prize-winning epistolary novel about a poor African American woman and how she survives racism and incest.

- *I Love Myself When I am Laughing ... And Then Again When I am Looking Mean and Impressive: A Zora Neale Hurston Reader* (1978), which was edited by Walker, presents a collection of work by Hurston, the early twentieth-century African American author.

- Nikki Giovanni's *Grand Mothers: Poems, Reminiscences, and Short Stories About the Keepers of Our Traditions* (1996) is intended for adolescent readers. Giovanni presents stories by and about grandmothers, including stories from Asian and African writers and stories from the Civil War.

- Maya Angelou's autobiography *I Know Why the Caged Bird Sings* (1969) includes an indictment of the separate and grossly unequal public school system available to white and black children in Stamps, Arkansas, during the late 1930s and 1940s.

- *The Best Short Stories by Black Writers, 1899–1967: The Class Anthology* (1969) contains stories selected by Langston Hughes and written by notable African American writers of the twentieth century.

- Alice Walker maintains a Website (http://www.alicewalkersgarden.com), which contains biographical information, as well as photos, a blog, and a list of her upcoming appearances.

discusses Walker's emphasis on memory as a way to change women's lives in the poem "Women."

"Women" celebrates the African American women of earlier generations, those mothers and grandmothers, who struggled, who sacrificed, and whose efforts benefited the women of Walker's generation. The women in Walker's poem do not allow the past to govern their lives. The poem acknowledges the changes these women worked so hard to create. These women wanted to change the world and dreamed they would be able to do so, if only they persevered. It is their triumph that Walker acknowledges.

Walker's poem is framed by her own experiences. In her poem, she honors the women of her mother's generation and reminds readers that a woman's success is determined in part by the hard work of her ancestors. In her essay, "Lest We Forget: An Open Letter to My Sisters Who Are Brave," Walker asserts that African American women, collectively, have the ability to "become the Goddess of the Three Directions." What she means is that they can assess where they are now, where they have been, and what the future holds for them. The women described in Walker's poem were able to look back and see that their present was no better than their past and that their children's future would be no different than their past if they did not insist on necessary changes.

In this essay, Walker recalls her own struggles at school. She describes how the school that her parents and neighbors built for their children was burned by whites who did not want African American children to be educated. Instead, Walker and her siblings walked five miles to school, while white children rode buses to a nearby school. She also recounts how her parents worked hard to create a school from discarded army barracks. Their books were those "cast off" from the white schools "that we were not, as black children, permitted to enter." African American children were also not allowed to use the town library, and thus, Walker was an adult before she knew libraries existed. This is the educational world that the women in Walker's poem struggled to change and that Walker, herself, experienced.

In a 1973 interview, Walker told John O'Brien that she is "committed to exploring the oppressions, the insanities, the loyalties, and the triumphs of black women." Walker finds their stories compelling. These women have survived in the face of oppression and indignity. Their survival, according to Walker, makes African American women "the most fascinating creations in the world." She also comments on the lives of African American women in her essay "In Search of Our Mothers' Gardens," where she discusses the artistic talent that her mother and other women had but were unable to express. Here, Walker pays homage to her own mother, whose efforts to create beauty for her family required hours of effort each morning both before she left to work in the fields and each evening after she returned. Walker writes that her mother "handed down respect for the possibilities," as well as the determination to make the possibilities real. Walker writes that in the post-Reconstruction South, African American women "dreamed dreams that no one knew—not even themselves." They dreamed of things they did not understand, these grandmothers and mothers, and "they waited for a day when the unknown thing that was in them would be made known."

Walker learned from her mother that the opportunity for change exists. All that is needed is the ability to visualize change. The wisdom and foresight of the women of her mother's generation who knew the promise of what they might one day have but had not yet experienced for themselves are described with appreciation in Walker's poem. These women knew what they must do to reverse decades of oppression during which they had no education themselves and were not free. Their wisdom is also described in "In Search of Our Mothers' Gardens." Walker stresses the importance of recording her mother's stories and states that the stories of the mothers "must be recorded," lest they be forgotten. "Women" works to keep the memories of African American women alive, as an inspiration to African American women who follow. In recalling the achievements of these mothers and grandmothers, Walker is guaranteeing that their experiences "have not perished in the wilderness." Instead, they continue to inspire young women and to encourage them to create their own change.

In her review of *Revolutionary Petunias & Other Poems*, Mary Helen Washington notes that the poems in the first section of the book, entitled "In These Dissenting Times ... Surrounding Ground and Autobiography," are intended to honor the past, as though it was

"Alice Walker's own sacred ritual" to pay "tribute to those who have made her." Certainly this is what she has done in the poem "Women," which is in the first section of the collection.

Walker also intends her poem to celebrate the lives and dreams of all African American women. Hanna Nowak suggests in her essay "Poetry Celebrating Life" that "Walker is concerned with the historical experiences of black people and her own participation in them." Walker moves beyond her own experience in order to acknowledge that it was the contributions and dreams of many women that made her who she grew up to be. According to Nowak, Walker blends both her private life and experiences with those of a larger, more public group of African American women. As a result, African American life in the South and Walker's own participation in that life are merged in her poetry, with the personal representing the public. As Nowak points out, Walker treats her own experiences "as representative of the collective history of the American South." Thus, a poem about her mother becomes a poem about all African American mothers. The efforts that the parents made to build a school for their children and find books and desks for that school become in "Women" the story of how all African American mothers were inspired to build schools and find books and desks. Clearly, Walker sees herself as part of the larger group of strong women who struggle to improve the world, and she realizes "that she is part of a tradition of women who have tried to assert themselves." This linking of past and present, ancestor and self, defines the poet and the poet's work.

Remembering and honoring the women who changed the world is crucial to Walker. She writes in "Lest We Forget: An Open Letter to My Sisters Who Are Brave" that her own nieces do not seem to remember the past and the changes these earlier women helped to create. Walker's poem corrects this amnesia. Nowak states that "with her celebration of black life, the South, the spirit of community and, most of all, of black womanhood," Walker locates herself within the tradition of African American writers, for whom African American womanhood is an important subject. Walker's poem is more than a celebration of the past and a tribute to African American women; it is a reminder to all women of color that they can change the

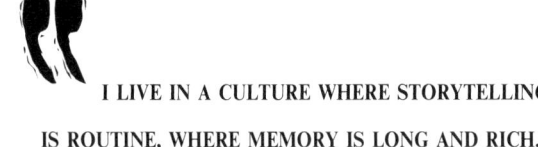

I LIVE IN A CULTURE WHERE STORYTELLING IS ROUTINE, WHERE MEMORY IS LONG AND RICH."

world, if only they refuse to accept the inequalities they face in the present.

Source: Sheri Metzger Karmiol, Critical Essay on "Women," in *Poetry for Students*, Gale, Cengage Learning, 2010.

William R. Ferris

In the following essay, Ferris presents a series of excerpts from recordings of Alice Walker as she reflected on a variety of subjects.

My friendship with Alice Walker began in the fall of 1970 when I taught in the English department of Jackson State University in Jackson, Mississippi. At that time Alice lived in Jackson and had just finished her manuscript of *The Third Life of Grange Copeland*. She shared with me encouraging comments that Ernest Gaines had written about the manuscript. During that time Alice also published her impressive volume of poetry *Revolutionary Petunias* and did an important interview with Eudora Welty that was published in the *Harvard Advocate*.

When I taught at Yale in the mid-seventies, Alice visited the campus and gave a moving seminar with faculty and students. Our lives crossed again when I served as a consultant on her film *The Color Purple*. When I worked at the University of Mississippi's Center for the Study of Southern Culture, Alice wrote me that she was coming for a visit. We arranged a reading and book party for her at Square Books in Oxford and a tour of the Blues Archive at the University of Mississippi during that visit in the mid-1990s. We also met in my home, where I recorded these reflections about Alice's work as a writer and her love for the blues.

ON WOMEN'S LIVES

If you think of the early stories, it's true that the women did badly, but it's because they belong to the generation of my mother and grandmother, when they were suspended because they had nowhere to go. All of them couldn't be Bessie Smith or Billie Holiday, so they ended up doing all kinds of destructive things. Most of that generation didn't have any fame or glory. But notice that all of those women are much older then I am. They exist in an historical place that is removed from my generation of women. It's not until *The Third Life of Grange Copeland* that I got my generation of people. It starts so far back because I wanted to have a really good understanding of the historical progression. I wrote about those women in *In Search of Our Mothers' Gardens.* The women who have not had anything have been, almost of necessity, self-destructive. They've just been driven insane. And the ones who have managed have been the ones who could focus their enormous energies on art forms that where not necessarily recognized as art forms—on quilting, on flowers, on making things. It's a very human need, to make things, to create. To think that women didn't need that—that by having a baby you fulfill your whole function—is and demeaning.

ON ENCOUNTERING ZORA NEALE HURSTON

When I was in Mississippi, there was a woman named—what was her name?—someone who had read *Their Eyes Were Watching God,* and we were talking about it, and she loved it. And I got it, and I read it, and I loved it. That was when I connected really with Zora. The oddest thing is that in that same anthology that Langston Hughes did—where he put "To Hell with Dying"—there's a story by Zora. But at that time I was so convinced that only men wrote literature that I had to read, that I read that anthology without really noticing. It's terrible, but I think it's true. Then I read *Their Eyes Were Watching God,* and it was to much my culture. I had never read a book that was so true to my specific southern black culture, full of music, full of humor, full of just—not righteousness—craziness. People living their lives, people having good times, people fussing and fighting. At the same time, as with my mother and father, they are absolutely rooted in the earth, in earth life. People in *Their Eyes Were Watching God* are really pagan. They are not bamboozled by religion as it is taught in the South. They are always poking fun at the hypocrisy. And the passages that are so incredible are, of course, when they drop a bean in the soil, and up comes this food. The Indians, too, the way they knew a storm was coming. They started leaving. The animals knew, they started moving. Only people were hesitating. Most of the people were not as connected. They had already gotten two or three steps removed from what is the natural rhythm of the earth, so they didn't know and so they had to sit there, be scared, and pray to the sky god, watching the sky god.

Now this is an aspect that I rarely see reflected in any review. Basically, it carries forward my sense of the transformation that many people have to go through to shed what is a deadening sky-god religion, whatever it is, in order to come back to their rootedness in nature as the source of divinity. That is why *The Color Purple* really is a book about learning to believe in your own god or goddess or divinity or whatever is sacred to you. It's not about what other people are telling you. You get rid of the Charlton Heston-type God, you get rid of Yahweh, you get rid of all these people that, while you are worshipping; try to convince you that you are nothing, and you begin instead to be a child of what you actually are, a child of—you are a child of the earth. That is why, at the end, Celie understands that if God is anything, God is everything. And so the birds, the trees she sees—she makes a long list of all these things. That is what this book is primarily about. It's about understanding that people may well need to have religions in order to further their social programs and their political agendas or even their spiritual desires, but essentially what is divine is in front of you all the time. You cannot separate yourself even from the earth. I was thinking that if you understand that, you lose all fear of dying. You may be grass, you may be a cow, but you'll always be here, in fact even if they shoot you. I was thinking, what would they do to me to really punish me for being an earth lover? I mean they could shoot me to another planet, but because I'm made of earth, I could never leave. That is my home, that is what I am. I love this feeling of always being at home and always being with what is sacred to me, what is divine to me. It was a gift from my mother without her knowing because, before she died, she became a Jehovah's Witness, and part of those people's belief is that if your own child is not also a Witness, you don't speak to the child. Isn't it amazing? Imagine having that as your guiding light.

Because my work is grounded spirituality rather than in politics, I am able to follow my intuition and my sense of being one with other people much more easily than I ever thought possible. When I write as I have done about these African children who are mutilated, I can do so without getting bogged down in all the cultural baggage and the political resistance of various African governments and African people. I really understand what they are saying. Some people have to do studies to know these things, but they have proved that things hurt if you hurt them. If you put a monkey in a cage and put electric shocks on one side and not on the other, they will try to stay on the side away from the shocks. So, if you can believe those children feel pain, and if you think that is not right, then you try to change that. My point is that there is a lot of opposition to people wanting to alleviate suffering by people who have a vested interest in continuing it, because it's their means of ruling, literally controlling.

ON CIVIL RIGHTS LEADERS

I have this theory, and I wrote a poem about it, that Martin Luther King, had he lived, would have become a violent revolutionary rather than a nonviolent one simply because he would have perceived that he had met an object, specifically, this country, that is not going to be changed nonviolently. I think his dedication was so intense that he would have tried other strategies. In the poem, I talk about his love in front and his necessary fist behind. I also mention that people who are crucified should decide not to be crucified—that they should do as much as they can, but then they should know when to stop, that they're much more valuable farming, or raising tulips somewhere, than they are dead—if they would only understand that.

A good example is Bob Moses, who was in Mississippi in the early sixties and who was rapidly becoming a legend. He was with SNCC (Student Nonviolent Coordinating Committee), and he was just wonderful because he knew how to go into a community and let people lead him rather than trying to tell the people what they needed. He would listen to what they wanted done and then he would try to help them do it, which is the true revolutionary way. But then the people started saying that this man was their Moses because they make these quick religious connections, and he decided he didn't want to be their Moses; he wanted to disappear. So he changed his name, took his mother's name, and he just walked away. The last time I heard anything about him, he was teaching school in Tanzania. I think that's brilliant. That's exactly what people should do.

After King's speech against the war in Vietnam, it would have been so lovely if he had known somehow. He had all these premonitions, but he was so into the propelling force of history, where you have to go right to the end and be shot. He never considered not listening to all the things telling him that the end was coming. He knew the end was coming. But wouldn't it have been terrific if after the speech "On the Mountain Top," he had gone back to Atlanta, said, "Coretta, get the children, we're gonna go to California. Let somebody else lead. I've had it." He was tired. Or think about Malcolm. Malcolm could have started a little farm in Detroit and been ready to come back another time.

If people think that's taking the easy way out, well, to hell with people. I think the symbols are wrong. I think the symbols have always been wrong. I think that the worship of death is really stupid; to hound people until they feel they have to be shot is just sick. We got to a point when people were saying, "Well, now it's time for King to be assassinated for him to be any good." Now that's sick. Here's a man who had given every ounce of his energy, absolutely everything he had. And there we were just saying, "Well, he's screwed up in Chicago; he can't reach people in Harlem. The only thing left for him to do is to stand there and be shot." I've thought about it constantly. I would like for people to think they can have more than one life and that there are more ways to be committed than to give your absolute life's blood. Going to teach in Tanzania or Harlem or Mississippi, that's a commitment. I would love to have had Malcolm or Martin Luther King teach my child.

But the culture doesn't deserve those good people if violence is the only thing that will move them. If people are going to sit back in front of the television set and only be moved because you're dying, they don't deserve you. I think the culture is sick. The thing to do is to think of ways not to give in to the culture, to affirm what you believe to be stronger and more important. Great importance is attached to an assassination, as if people will rise up and great changes will happen. But that doesn't happen. People can forget overnight.

Flannery O'Connor said that anybody who's outlived her childhood has enough material to last her the rest of her life. I draw heavily on my childhood and what I knew and what I saw and felt. But after *Meridian* I have slowly moved away from that. I'm creating situations and characters that are really much removed from what I knew as a child.

I was very much into my community, but at the same time I had this sense of almost always knowing, I was observing it. Even with things like my father's funeral I was very aware that, on one level, my father was dead and therefore that meant great, weighty stuff. But I was also very observant about everybody's reaction to everything and remembered with great alertness everything that was said.

I will always draw on my background because it was so rich, and I always recognized it as being rich. I really have liked it. Richard Wright, for example, found very little in his childhood to like and admire, and he often felt it was barren; I feel just the opposite. When I go back to Eatonton, Georgia, I get these new reverberations of things, new enlightenment; I understand on a deeper level. That will probably always be somewhere in the work. But *Meridian* was set almost equally in New York and Mississippi, and I think that means something. In my own life I have had the kind of mobility that has taken me not just all over the South but all over the country.

I would not have missed having a child. It was tough going at times, but I think children connect us to the natural world and the natural processes of life in a way that you can't really grasp. In the long labor and the sheer pain involved I felt like I was connected to women wherever they are and whatever condition they are in, in a way that I had never felt. It was a bonding with my mother, with her mother, with my great grandmother. I understood as never before what it was like for women and what it is still like for women all over the world.

I thought about my mother. Finally, they gave me what they call a saddle block so that I didn't have all the pain at the end, but you know she had eight children, and I remember her saying that the pain increased with each child, didn't diminish. They claim it diminishes, and she claimed that she had forgotten it, but I don't think so. So, I felt like, with Rebecca, I was given this information, this knowledge, and I think it just made me more humble in the face of what women go through in order to populate the earth. They provide all the workers, they provide all the teachers, and they provide the labor force that keeps everything moving. Which is why I think there should be a moratorium on birth until the planet has gotten back into a shape that really can sustain a high quality of life. I just don't see the point of everybody continuing to have children, even one. I mean I think that one is good, but I think it's really very thoughtless for people to continue to populate an overpopulated earth when they haven't attended to the earth so they can keep sustaining this.

ON REVISION IN HER WORK

There is much revision in my novels. I started *The Third Life of Grange Copeland* at MacDowell, a writer's colony in New Hampshire, and I worked on it through several winter months. Three years later, when I finished it, I had changed everything except one line, and then I changed that line. I have four or five complete drafts of that novel. Since *Meridian* was written in a different way—not chronological—I revised the sections a great deal. Do you know that I had a great fight with my editor because the original jacket was of a little black girl who looked exactly like a cockroach wearing a dress. They tried to sneak that cover over on me. We had this huge fight and I made them change it. Nevertheless, the novels take a lot of revision. They don't really write themselves, but a lot of them are just somehow formed. I might work on the dialogue to make it sharper.

The ideas for the novels come from wanting to understand something. With *Grange* I wanted to understand what happened in family life over a period of years. And I wanted to understand the concept of self-hatred and family hatred, the kind of destructive thing that Brownfield exemplified. I wanted to understand Brownfield and also to understand people who could be Brownfield but were not. I wanted to know what made the difference. Everything starts from wanting to understand something, whether it's a person or just an event. For instance, the scenes in *Grange* when Brownfield notices that whenever a white man comes around, Grange's behavior changes completely—those scenes come from living in a culture that produces that kind of reaction. I have seen people change their behavior because there are white people around them. My father's behavior changed. He just lived in a culture that was intent on destroying him, so he built up defenses of various sorts.

In *Meridian* I started out being really concerned about some of the things that people did to each other in the sixties in the name of change, in the name of revolution. I wanted to see what qualities we were giving up in exchange for other qualities. Somehow part of it really understands the questions, not just understands the answers. Sometimes when you start, you just have the vaguest notion of where you're going, and you don't even know what things are important to work with. This has nothing to do with that, but it may show you what I mean. My regret is that Langston Hughes died before I knew what to ask him.

I live in a culture where storytelling is routine, where memory is long and rich. I was born into this huge family where everybody told stories, and it was my function to make some sense out of all of it to write it down and present it. It's not just me knowing; it's what they've let me know.

ON LITERARY INFLUENCES

In college I loved Camus. He was just a beautiful man. I [also] really love the Russian writers. I'm a moralist. I'm very concerned about moral questions, and I have definite feelings about what is right and what is not. Russian writers have a kind of essential passion, and they can engage in that kind of questioning of the universe and of human interactions. They really care. I like that. I don't like writers who don't care. I think writers should care desperately. I just discovered the poetry of Anna Akhmatova. She's typical of the Russians in that she has passion and political sensibility. The Russians live completely in their world on every level. There is no worrying about how their political involvement will be perceived. This poem is called "The Last Toast":

> I drink to our ruined house,
> to the dolor of my life,
> to our loneliness together,
> and to you, I raise my glass.
> To lying lips, that have betrayed us,
> to dead, cold, pitiless eyes,
> and to the hard realities that the world is
>   brutal and coarse,
> that God, in fact, has not saved us.

Isn't that terrific? I think that is so true. God hasn't saved us. I really thought for so long that God had saved black people. I thought that we were really saved. However, we're not.

Victor Hugo was another influence. He was also a moralist and very compassionate and big. I like really big writers who have scope and who see things in a distance. I love Flannery O'Connor, but it was very upsetting when I read in some of her correspondence that she referred to black people as "nigger." The Brontës were influential. *Jane Eyre* was one of my favorite books. I loved that sense of life intensity that you see in Mr. Rochester. I love writers who make you feel the cold when it's a cold, gray day. There are people who influence you. And there are people you discover later on, and you know that you're on the same wavelength and that you would give anything to have had them earlier. That's where Tillie Olsen comes in, that's where Zora comes in, that's actually where Toomer comes in. I didn't read *Cane* until 1967, and I didn't read Zora until the seventies.

I wanted to play the piano, and I think I would have been good at it. But piano lessons were fifty cents, and I tried very hard, but I couldn't raise it every week. Then I wanted to draw, but I wasn't that good. I think writing was just all that was left. I became really interested because of my oldest sister, Molly, who left Eatonton when I was an infant. There was no high school for black people, so she had to go away. She's twelve years older than I am. When she was thirteen, she left to go to Macon High School. And she was a great reader. I was an infant, but she would come back, especially after she went off to college. She went off to Morris Brown in Atlanta, and when she came home in the summers, she would read to us. She would tell us stories. She introduced us to a new kind of aesthetic. My mother was Cherokee, and she had that real Indian belief that basically you let things live where they grow. When you grow them, you don't cut them; you just let them be. But my sister, who actually looks very much like my mothers' grandmother, very Cherokee looking, had gone to school. She knew that there were people who actually cut flowers and brought them into the house. This was a different way of looking at things.

My father and mother, even though they went through the fifth grade and the fourth grade respectively, loved education, really worshipped education. They were that generation of black people who would do anything to educate their child, and so they let my sister go because they wanted her to be educated. They read to us, things like the newspaper. Whenever books were thrown out by any white person they worked for, they were happy to have them, bring them back, and they would read to us. So we always had books in the house. I think that was unusual because many people like my parents did not have books around, or they did not appreciate them enough to take them out of the trash when someone was throwing them out. But my parents worshipped reading. They thought it was just the greatest thing. Of course, by the time I was the sixth or seventh child, they were rather exhausted, and that's where my sister came in. She came back for the summers, and she would read. You know the song "God Bless Mother Africa"? When I was six or seven years old, my sister taught me that song. It's incredible. The ANC [African National Congress] was around then, trying to teach people what was going on in South Africa. She was obviously very moved by the struggle, and she learned that song, and she taught it to me. Those are the kinds of things that influenced me a lot.

I also had great teachers in the sense that they loved my family and me. They knew my family, they cared about me. I wasn't just another little face. My mother had to take me to the fields, and I would trail along behind her as she chopped cotton, or I'd fall asleep out at the edge of the field where she couldn't really look after me because she had to work. When I was four I went to school, and my first grade teacher, who is still alive, gave me books for my birthday and gave me my first clothing.

When I was eight or nine or ten, I was writing, and I kept a notebook because my life has had its trials. I learned very early that this was a way to deal with pain and isolation. I also had brothers. They were very brutal in some of their ways, any they were brought up not to be gentle with animals or younger siblings. I learned that you could put things on paper, but a safer method was actually to just keep them in your head. So I have kept until very recently the habit of writing very long and complex works in my mind before I write them because I always feel that's the safe way.

ON THE SOUTHERN LABEL

I don't consider myself a southern writer. I think I'm dealing with regions inside people. The people are in the South, but I really just leave that up to other people to decide. If people can only understand the work by placing it in a context, that's fine. But I'm really trying to understand people and how they get to be the way they are. The region is the heart and the mind, not the section.

There are many reasons I am still not at ease with the southern label. Part of it is that any kind of label limits. It tends to make what you're dealing with seem localized, when in fact your main focus is to find out why people act the way they do. Wherever people are, that's where you are. Also, when you think of southern writers, you think of white southern writers. I don't really have any interest in integrating southern writers. On the other hand, how can I possibly ever not be considered a southern writer since I am a southerner and since I write?

ON ZORA AND AUTOBIOGRAPHY

The only time I know of that an autobiography did not work was Zora Hurston's autobiography. An autobiography is very difficult to write. It's the hardest writing if it's going to mean something, and if it's going to be honest. The hardest thing in the world is to write down what you really think, what you're really feeling. The tendency is that you're thinking, "I am a rotten person," but by the time you get it down on the paper, it's, "Well, I'm not so rotten." Zora suffered from that.

She also had to placate this "godmother" of hers. This woman financed Zora's expeditions into the South to do folklore. She gave money to almost all the [Harlem] Renaissance people, including Langston Hughes. She really thought that black people were these wonderful, exotic primitives and that she could read their minds. She thought she could read Zora's mind. Zora would have a party with her friends and would say, "Let me call Godmother." So at five o'clock in the morning, Zora would gather her friends around and call Godmother. Zora would say, "Godmother?" and Godmother would say, "Yes, Zora?" "Godmother, do you know what I'm thinking now?" And Godmother would say, "OH yes, you're thinking this or that." And Zora would have a big laugh. It was really hokey and a sad example of how, in order to get work done, people have to do so many terrible things.

This godmother would not allow Zora to publish certain things that she wrote until her godmother said she could. Her work was really controlled. In addition to her writing, Zora made films. They were on children's games, the Mardi Gras, and on some of the conjurers whom she met in New Orleans. Among the things that she learned from these voodoo doctors and conjurers was how to kill. She became a converted soul.

I don't know the nature of her relationship to Van Vechten, but supposedly she placed a spell on him, albeit probably playfully. The problem with rich and poor is that the poor person can never forget that the rich person is rich. And no matter how hard one may try, it's impossible to forget that they have more than they need and you don't have enough. There was a lot of that in Van Vechten and Zora's relationship, although she kept saying, "I love you and it's not because I need anything. I mean, please don't think I'm asking for money." And she wasn't. It's just that he happened to be so bloody rich, and she happened to be so bloody poor. It's really hard to love people who have had all the advantages that you don't have. It's very difficult, and I can say that with a great deal of experience. Even with much effort, I still find it difficult to love people who control, who have everything. And it's so sad because no matter what they do, the feeling remains. They can be ever so wonderful, and yet this barrier rises like a ghost.

ON BELIEVING IN VOODOO

I believe in voodoo as much as I believe in any other religion. It works for the people who need it to work, and there are probably some definite medicinal qualities the people use. In Haiti, for example, the thing that Hurston discovered about the Zombies is that they know this secret that they brought from Guinea, which apparently puts a part of the brain to sleep and allows people to appear to die. But they're not really dead. They can be brought back, and they can be put to work, to just work and do nothing else. But the part of the brain that controls memory and speech and everything else is gone. I think that's entirely possible. I don't see why it couldn't be. All of these things can probably be explained. Zora talked about the way people would collect dirt from graveyards to use to destroy people. It's in *Tell My Horse*. What she discovered after taking some of this dirt to a chemist was that it's full of disease and germs. So if you went to the grave of someone who died of smallpox and took the dirt, it keeps its potency up to twenty years or so, and you could actually give a horrible disease to someone.

With my own mother I understand new layers of meaning in our relationship. She was devoutly Christian and went to the church regularly as a mother of the church for most of my life when I lived at home. Yet behind that, I think she was the most sincere worshipper of nature. I know that because I am also. And I know that what's different about the way that I relate to nature and to the earth is that I don't feel compelled to put a Christian face on what is essentially a pagan mark. So I just love the earth and love nature, worship it, and think of it as my source of life and any kind of life. I know there is a galaxy and a cosmos, but I think that if there is a divine intelligence that orders everything, it's too much for me to comprehend. So I'm happy to just love what I can feel. And I feel. And this I think was true of my mother in the sense that she had absolute faith in nature. But if you had asked her that, she would not have necessarily understood what you meant. But she did because I have seen her visit a house, and if there was a sprig of anything lying that had broken off of any plant, she would take it home, stick it in any little bit of soil, and would have absolute certainty that it would do well, and it did. That was her way. I grew up with a woman who was so connected to life and so much in sync with the source of all that there is. It was just wonderful watching her exist in the world, and this was true even though we were poor and we had to deal with people who hated us or couldn't really see us. There's no doubt in my mind that my mother was a great, great spirit, and I actually think of her as a goddess ...

I love B. B. because he loves women. They can be mean, they can be bitchy, they can be carrying on, but you can tell he really loves them. He's full of love, I would like to be the literary B. B. King. There's something about him that has remained true and has remained genuine. He seems to be authentic. Average people respond immediately to what he is and what he says, and I like that. That is the best kind of acceptance.

The blues can be very disturbing actually. I love it, and I love some songs much more than others, some musicians more than others, but what's truly disturbing is how frequently when women are singing they are telling about abusive relationships. I'm struck by that time and time again. And then of course it makes me think about all the stories those women were trying to hint at that they were not able to say. You know, I remember once, Quincy [Jones] was talking, and he laughed and said, "You know, Celie is the blues." And that's so true, because if Celie were singing, she would be like Mamie

[Smith], Bessie [Smith], and Ma Rainey, all of whom were abused. Those women were abused by men. I always feel so deeply when I listen to them, and then I think about how people took it for granted that your man would be this way. Of course you'll be abused. And so they weren't really heard, and they got used to it, actually dancing to this. It was like a spiral that was not going up but going down. People sing about this and then expect it in relationships. It was self-perpetuating. I doubt if any of these people had relationships that nourished them. They had relationships, instead, that prompted cries of anguish that were then used to entertain. The people who were entertained modeled themselves on what they were hearing, and it was just a very bad cycle.

What I love about the blues, of course, is the music and the honesty with which the people were trying to sing about what was actually happening. I hate the kind of music that was popular back then, and is popular now, where no matter what is happening, it is a kind of la, la, la, la, all sweetness and light, and you can hear that phoniness in their voices. You would not want to go across the street with those people because they are totally dishonest about their emotions. They don't know what emotions they were feeling. They are very unauthentic, but with the blues you feel like you are hearing authentic feeling and that people are struggling to find joy in life. I mean, look at Bessie. She's got all the vitality in the world. She is connected to the source, and she knows it. And the world, the rest of the world, is really trying to tell her that she's not anybody big, and there's all these little ways that this is done. Your hair has to be straight if it's kinky, and you must wear powder, do something to your nose, whatever. All of those things are really designed to try to convince you that you are not what life and poetry are about. But Bessie used all of that power she had to affirm constantly that, "Absolutely, I'm what this is all about. I mean, I don't care what you are doing. I know what I am doing, I am here."

I know what the earth says. Life in earth says, Be like me. I mean, I grow bananas, I grow strawberries, I have trees dropping nuts all the time, I have waterfalls. I mean the earth says constantly, I am not a poor person. The earth says, I have everything. And so do we. That is one of the reasons, on a whole other level, why people who do have everything are constantly robbed of it. You know, it's like people come up on something that's just magnificent, and they just can't stop until they've stripped it and killed it. This is what's happening to the earth itself. And we are no different; we're the same. There's no such thing as mankind or peoplekind having the earth. I mean, please, have a little humility before all of this. Before all of this. Just one little red clover—you can't make that. So, we live in paradise.

Source: William R. Ferris, "Alice Walker: 'I Know What the Earth Says,'" in *Southern Cultures*, Vol. 10, No. 1, Spring 2004, pp. 5–24.

SOURCES

"Alice Walker's Garden," http://www.alicewalkersgarden.com (accessed August 3, 2009).

"Black Arts Movement," http://aalbc.com/authors/blackartsmovement.htm (accessed July 16, 2009).

Collins, Patricia Hill, *Black Feminist Thought*, 2nd ed., Routledge, 2000, pp. 58–61.

Courtenay-Thompson, Fiona, and Kate Phelps, eds., *The 20th Century Year by Year*, Barnes & Noble Press, 1998, pp. 202, 228, 237, 249, 266.

Davis, Gwendolyn, Review of *Revolutionary Petunias & Other Poems*, in *New South*, Vol. 28, Winter 1973, pp. 62–63.

"Divided Court Rejects School Diversity Plans," June 28, 2007, http://www.cnn.com/2007/LAW/06/28/scotus.race/index.html (accessed July 16, 2009).

Glennon, Lorraine, ed., "The World in 1970," in *The Twentieth Century*, JG Press, 1999, p. 509.

Harmon, William, and Hugh Holman, *A Handbook to Literature*, 11th ed., Pearson Prentice Hall, 2008, pp. 8–9, 241, 285, 350–52, 399, 540.

Jennings, Peter, and Todd Brewster, "Years of Doubt 1969–1981," in *The Century*, Doubleday, 1998, pp. 444–45.

Jones, Nicholas A., and James S. Jackson, "The Demographic Profile of African Americans, 1970 to 2000–01," in *Black Collegian*, 2005, http://www.black-collegian.com/issues/30thAnn/demographic2001-30th.shtml (accessed July 19, 2009).

Nowak, Hanna, "Poetry Celebrating Life," in *Alice Walker: Critical Perspectives, Past and Present*, edited by Henry Louis Gates Jr. and K. A. Appiah, Amistad, 1993, pp. 180, 181, 182, 187; originally published in *A Salzburg Miscellany: English and American Studies, 1964–1984*, Institut für Anglistik und Amerikanistik, Universität Salzburg, 1984.

Swann v. Charlotte-Mecklenburg Board of Education, North Carolina History Project, http://www.northcarolinahistory.org/encyclopedia/296/entry (accessed July 16, 2009).

Walker, Alice, "In Search of Our Mothers' Gardens," in *In Search of Our Mothers' Gardens: Womanist Prose*, Harcourt Brace Jovanovich, 1983, pp. 231–43.

———, "Lest We Forget: An Open Letter to My Sisters Who Are Brave," in *Meridians: Feminism, Race, Transnationalism*, Vol. 9, No. 1, 2009, pp. 183–88.

———, "Women," in *Revolutionary Petunias & Other Poems*, Harcourt Brace Jovanovich, 1973, p. 5.

Walker, Alice, and John O'Brien, "Alice Walker: An Interview," in *Alice Walker: Critical Perspectives, Past and Present*, edited by Henry Louis Gates Jr. and K. A. Appiah, Amistad, 1993, p. 331; originally published in *Interviews with Black Writers*, edited by John O'Brien, Norton, 1973.

Ward, Jerry W., Review of *Revolutionary Petunias & Other Poems*, in *College Language Association Journal*, Vol. 17, No. 1, September 1973, pp. 127, 128.

Washington, Mary Helen, Review of *Revolutionary Petunias & Other Poems*, in *Black World*, Vol. 22, No. 11, September 1973, pp. 51, 52.

"Women in the U.S. Congress 2009," *Center for American Women and Politics*, http://www.cawp.rutgers.edu/fast_facts/levels_of_office/documents/cong.pdf (accessed July 16, 2009).

FURTHER READING

Bolden, Tonya, *The Book of African American Women: 150 Crusaders, Creators, and Uplifters*, Adams Media, 2004.

This collection of brief biographies begins with the 1619 biography of a slave brought to the Jamestown colony. Bolden includes biographies of famous women and also those of women who made significant contributions to African American history and culture without ever becoming famous.

Franklin, John Hope, and Alfred A. Moss Jr., *From Slavery to Freedom: A History of African Americans*, Knopf, 2000.

Franklin and Moss present a history of African American life in the United States. The authors begin with the origins of slavery, describing the sale and kidnap of Africans in Africa and leading up to the civil rights movement of the last half of the twentieth century. Maps, charts, and many illustrations are included.

Gates, Henry Louis, Jr., and K. A. Appiah, eds., *Alice Walker: Critical Perspectives, Past and Present*, Amistad Press, 1993.

These collected reviews and essays focus on Walker's writing. In the preface, Gates emphasizes Walker's connection to African American women writers of the past, especially Zora Neale Hurston.

Gates, Henry Louis, Jr., and Cornell West, *The African-American Century: How Black Americans Have Shaped Our Country*, Free Press, 2002.

Gates and West provide the stories of 100 important African Americans who have changed the United States. The content is divided into decades, with ten biographies for each decade.

Higginbotham, A. Leon, Jr., et al., *Race-ing Justice, En-Gendering Power: Essays on Anita Hill, Clarence Thomas, and the Construction of Social Reality*, Pantheon, 1992.

Toni Morrison wrote the introduction to these nineteen essays, which deal with various topics, including African American identity, civil rights, equality, and the public perception of race and gender equality. The essays explore important ideas about equality for African American women and illustrate the extent to which race and equality in the United States remain complicated subjects for discussion.

Lazo, Caroline, *Alice Walker: Freedom Writer*, Lerner, 2000.

This biography of Walker is intended for children, grades eight and up. The author includes many photographs of Walker. This book is highly complimentary and is not a critical study of Walker.

Medearis, Angela Shelf, *The African American Kitchen: Cooking from Our Heritage*, Plume, 1997.

More than a list of favorite recipes, this cookbook is an exploration of African American culinary heritage and family history and the function that cooking plays in women's lives.

Mondale, Sarah, ed., *School: The Story of American Public Education*, Beacon Press, 2002.

Mondale describes education in the United States from 1770 to 2000. She also explores the experiences of different racial, ethnic, and religious groups in the American school system, as it evolved over time.

Muir, Kenneth, *Kids Explore America's African American Heritage*, Avalon Travel, 1996.

Designed for children, ages nine to twelve, this book explores African American culture through literature, music, crafts, food, and the history of civil rights.

Patton, Sharon F., *African-American Art*, Oxford University Press, 1998.

This book describes the artistic achievements of African Americans and includes art from the 1800s and 1900s created by both slaves and free persons.

Prigoff, James, and Robin J. Dunitz, *Walls of Heritage: African American Murals*, Pomegranate Communications, 2000.

This book reproduces 200 murals painted by African American artists. In addition to the murals, the authors include artist biographies and descriptions supplied by the artists.

Sniderman, Paul M., and Thomas Piazza, *Black Pride and Black Prejudice*, Princeton University Press, 2004.

The authors provide a provocative look at race relations in the United States. The focus is on how African Americans view themselves and how they think they are viewed by other groups. Topics include black pride, black intolerance, and racism.

West, Cornell, *Race Matters*, Vintage, 1994.
These personal essays explore a number of issues that are important to African Americans, including affirmative action, African American leadership, and the legacy of Malcolm X.

White, Evelyn C., *Alice Walker: A Life*, Norton, 2005.
White relies upon many of Walker's interviews to construct this biography, which also includes excerpts from many of Walker's published works.

Glossary of Literary Terms

A

Abstract: Used as a noun, the term refers to a short summary or outline of a longer work. As an adjective applied to writing or literary works, abstract refers to words or phrases that name things not knowable through the five senses.

Accent: The emphasis or stress placed on a syllable in poetry. Traditional poetry commonly uses patterns of accented and unaccented syllables (known as feet) that create distinct rhythms. Much modern poetry uses less formal arrangements that create a sense of freedom and spontaneity.

Aestheticism: A literary and artistic movement of the nineteenth century. Followers of the movement believed that art should not be mixed with social, political, or moral teaching. The statement "art for art's sake" is a good summary of aestheticism. The movement had its roots in France, but it gained widespread importance in England in the last half of the nineteenth century, where it helped change the Victorian practice of including moral lessons in literature.

Affective Fallacy: An error in judging the merits or faults of a work of literature. The "error" results from stressing the importance of the work's effect upon the reader—that is, how it makes a reader "feel" emotionally, what it does as a literary work—instead of stressing its inner qualities as a created object, or what it "is."

Age of Johnson: The period in English literature between 1750 and 1798, named after the most prominent literary figure of the age, Samuel Johnson. Works written during this time are noted for their emphasis on "sensibility," or emotional quality. These works formed a transition between the rational works of the Age of Reason, or Neoclassical period, and the emphasis on individual feelings and responses of the Romantic period.

Age of Reason: See *Neoclassicism*

Age of Sensibility: See *Age of Johnson*

Agrarians: A group of Southern American writers of the 1930s and 1940s who fostered an economic and cultural program for the South based on agriculture, in opposition to the industrial society of the North. The term can refer to any group that promotes the value of farm life and agricultural society.

Alexandrine Meter: See *Meter*

Allegory: A narrative technique in which characters representing things or abstract ideas are used to convey a message or teach a lesson. Allegory is typically used to teach moral, ethical, or religious lessons but is sometimes used for satiric or political purposes.

Alliteration: A poetic device where the first consonant sounds or any vowel sounds in words or syllables are repeated.

Allusion: A reference to a familiar literary or historical person or event, used to make an idea more easily understood.

Amerind Literature: The writing and oral traditions of Native Americans. Native American literature was originally passed on by word of mouth, so it consisted largely of stories and events that were easily memorized. Amerind prose is often rhythmic like poetry because it was recited to the beat of a ceremonial drum.

Analogy: A comparison of two things made to explain something unfamiliar through its similarities to something familiar, or to prove one point based on the acceptedness of another. Similes and metaphors are types of analogies.

Anapest: See *Foot*

Angry Young Men: A group of British writers of the 1950s whose work expressed bitterness and disillusionment with society. Common to their work is an anti-hero who rebels against a corrupt social order and strives for personal integrity.

Anthropomorphism: The presentation of animals or objects in human shape or with human characteristics. The term is derived from the Greek word for "human form."

Antimasque: See *Masque*

Antithesis: The antithesis of something is its direct opposite. In literature, the use of antithesis as a figure of speech results in two statements that show a contrast through the balancing of two opposite ideas. Technically, it is the second portion of the statement that is defined as the "antithesis"; the first portion is the "thesis."

Apocrypha: Writings tentatively attributed to an author but not proven or universally accepted to be their works. The term was originally applied to certain books of the Bible that were not considered inspired and so were not included in the "sacred canon."

Apollonian and Dionysian: The two impulses believed to guide authors of dramatic tragedy. The Apollonian impulse is named after Apollo, the Greek god of light and beauty and the symbol of intellectual order. The Dionysian impulse is named after Dionysus, the Greek god of wine and the symbol of the unrestrained forces of nature. The Apollonian impulse is to create a rational, harmonious world, while the Dionysian is to express the irrational forces of personality.

Apostrophe: A statement, question, or request addressed to an inanimate object or concept or to a nonexistent or absent person.

Archetype: The word archetype is commonly used to describe an original pattern or model from which all other things of the same kind are made. This term was introduced to literary criticism from the psychology of Carl Jung. It expresses Jung's theory that behind every person's "unconscious," or repressed memories of the past, lies the "collective unconscious" of the human race: memories of the countless typical experiences of our ancestors. These memories are said to prompt illogical associations that trigger powerful emotions in the reader. Often, the emotional process is primitive, even primordial. Archetypes are the literary images that grow out of the "collective unconscious." They appear in literature as incidents and plots that repeat basic patterns of life. They may also appear as stereotyped characters.

Argument: The argument of a work is the author's subject matter or principal idea.

Art for Art's Sake: See *Aestheticism*

Assonance: The repetition of similar vowel sounds in poetry.

Audience: The people for whom a piece of literature is written. Authors usually write with a certain audience in mind, for example, children, members of a religious or ethnic group, or colleagues in a professional field. The term "audience" also applies to the people who gather to see or hear any performance, including plays, poetry readings, speeches, and concerts.

Automatic Writing: Writing carried out without a preconceived plan in an effort to capture every random thought. Authors who engage in automatic writing typically do not revise their work, preferring instead to preserve the revealed truth and beauty of spontaneous expression.

Avant-garde: A French term meaning "vanguard." It is used in literary criticism to describe new writing that rejects traditional approaches to literature in favor of innovations in style or content.

B

Ballad: A short poem that tells a simple story and has a repeated refrain. Ballads were originally intended to be sung. Early ballads, known as folk ballads, were passed down through generations, so their authors are often unknown. Later ballads composed by known authors are called literary ballads.

Baroque: A term used in literary criticism to describe literature that is complex or ornate in style or diction. Baroque works typically express tension, anxiety, and violent emotion. The term "Baroque Age" designates a period in Western European literature beginning in the late sixteenth century and ending about one hundred years later. Works of this period often mirror the qualities of works more generally associated with the label "baroque" and sometimes feature elaborate conceits.

Baroque Age: See *Baroque*

Baroque Period: See *Baroque*

Beat Generation: See *Beat Movement*

Beat Movement: A period featuring a group of American poets and novelists of the 1950s and 1960s—including Jack Kerouac, Allen Ginsberg, Gregory Corso, William S. Burroughs, and Lawrence Ferlinghetti—who rejected established social and literary values. Using such techniques as stream of consciousness writing and jazz-influenced free verse and focusing on unusual or abnormal states of mind—generated by religious ecstasy or the use of drugs—the Beat writers aimed to create works that were unconventional in both form and subject matter.

Beat Poets: See *Beat Movement*

Beats, The: See *Beat Movement*

Belles- lettres: A French term meaning "fine letters" or "beautiful writing." It is often used as a synonym for literature, typically referring to imaginative and artistic rather than scientific or expository writing. Current usage sometimes restricts the meaning to light or humorous writing and appreciative essays about literature.

Black Aesthetic Movement: A period of artistic and literary development among African Americans in the 1960s and early 1970s. This was the first major African-American artistic movement since the Harlem Renaissance and was closely paralleled by the civil rights and black power movements. The black aesthetic writers attempted to produce works of art that would be meaningful to the black masses. Key figures in black aesthetics included one of its founders, poet and playwright Amiri Baraka, formerly known as LeRoi Jones; poet and essayist Haki R. Madhubuti, formerly Don L. Lee; poet and playwright Sonia Sanchez; and dramatist Ed Bullins.

Black Arts Movement: See *Black Aesthetic Movement*

Black Comedy: See *Black Humor*

Black Humor: Writing that places grotesque elements side by side with humorous ones in an attempt to shock the reader, forcing him or her to laugh at the horrifying reality of a disordered world.

Black Mountain School: Black Mountain College and three of its instructors—Robert Creeley, Robert Duncan, and Charles Olson—were all influential in projective verse, so poets working in projective verse are now referred as members of the Black Mountain school.

Blank Verse: Loosely, any unrhymed poetry, but more generally, unrhymed iambic pentameter verse (composed of lines of five two-syllable feet with the first syllable accented, the second unaccented). Blank verse has been used by poets since the Renaissance for its flexibility and its graceful, dignified tone.

Bloomsbury Group: A group of English writers, artists, and intellectuals who held informal artistic and philosophical discussions in Bloomsbury, a district of London, from around 1907 to the early 1930s. The Bloomsbury Group held no uniform philosophical beliefs but did commonly express an aversion to moral prudery and a desire for greater social tolerance.

Bon Mot: A French term meaning "good word." A *bon mot* is a witty remark or clever observation.

Breath Verse: See *Projective Verse*

Burlesque: Any literary work that uses exaggeration to make its subject appear ridiculous, either by treating a trivial subject with profound seriousness or by treating a dignified subject frivolously. The word "burlesque" may also be used as an adjective, as in "burlesque show," to mean "striptease act."

C

Cadence: The natural rhythm of language caused by the alternation of accented and unaccented syllables. Much modern poetry—notably free verse—deliberately manipulates cadence to create complex rhythmic effects.

Caesura: A pause in a line of poetry, usually occurring near the middle. It typically corresponds to a break in the natural rhythm or sense of the line but is sometimes shifted to create special meanings or rhythmic effects.

Canzone: A short Italian or Provencal lyric poem, commonly about love and often set to music. The *canzone* has no set form but typically contains five or six stanzas made up of seven to twenty lines of eleven syllables each. A shorter, five- to ten-line "envoy," or concluding stanza, completes the poem.

Carpe Diem: A Latin term meaning "seize the day." This is a traditional theme of poetry, especially lyrics. A *carpe diem* poem advises the reader or the person it addresses to live for today and enjoy the pleasures of the moment.

Catharsis: The release or purging of unwanted emotions—specifically fear and pity—brought about by exposure to art. The term was first used by the Greek philosopher Aristotle in his *Poetics* to refer to the desired effect of tragedy on spectators.

Celtic Renaissance: A period of Irish literary and cultural history at the end of the nineteenth century. Followers of the movement aimed to create a romantic vision of Celtic myth and legend. The most significant works of the Celtic Renaissance typically present a dreamy, unreal world, usually in reaction against the reality of contemporary problems.

Celtic Twilight: See *Celtic Renaissance*

Character: Broadly speaking, a person in a literary work. The actions of characters are what constitute the plot of a story, novel, or poem. There are numerous types of characters, ranging from simple, stereotypical figures to intricate, multifaceted ones. In the techniques of anthropomorphism and personification, animals—and even places or things—can assume aspects of character. "Characterization" is the process by which an author creates vivid, believable characters in a work of art. This may be done in a variety of ways, including (1) direct description of the character by the narrator; (2) the direct presentation of the speech, thoughts, or actions of the character; and (3) the responses of other characters to the character. The term "character" also refers to a form originated by the ancient Greek writer Theophrastus that later became popular in the seventeenth and eighteenth centuries. It is a short essay or sketch of a person who prominently displays a specific attribute or quality, such as miserliness or ambition.

Characterization: See *Character*

Classical: In its strictest definition in literary criticism, classicism refers to works of ancient Greek or Roman literature. The term may also be used to describe a literary work of recognized importance (a "classic") from any time period or literature that exhibits the traits of classicism.

Classicism: A term used in literary criticism to describe critical doctrines that have their roots in ancient Greek and Roman literature, philosophy, and art. Works associated with classicism typically exhibit restraint on the part of the author, unity of design and purpose, clarity, simplicity, logical organization, and respect for tradition.

Colloquialism: A word, phrase, or form of pronunciation that is acceptable in casual conversation but not in formal, written communication. It is considered more acceptable than slang.

Complaint: A lyric poem, popular in the Renaissance, in which the speaker expresses sorrow about his or her condition. Typically, the speaker's sadness is caused by an unresponsive lover, but some complaints cite other sources of unhappiness, such as poverty or fate.

Conceit: A clever and fanciful metaphor, usually expressed through elaborate and extended comparison, that presents a striking parallel between two seemingly dissimilar things—for example, elaborately comparing a beautiful woman to an object like a garden or the sun. The conceit was a popular device throughout the Elizabethan Age and Baroque Age and was the principal technique of the seventeenth-century English metaphysical poets. This usage of the word conceit is unrelated to the best-known definition of conceit as an arrogant attitude or behavior.

Concrete: Concrete is the opposite of abstract, and refers to a thing that actually exists or a description that allows the reader to experience an object or concept with the senses.

Concrete Poetry: Poetry in which visual elements play a large part in the poetic effect. Punctuation marks, letters, or words are arranged on a page to form a visual design: a cross, for example, or a bumblebee.

Confessional Poetry: A form of poetry in which the poet reveals very personal, intimate, sometimes shocking information about himself or herself.

Connotation: The impression that a word gives beyond its defined meaning. Connotations may be universally understood or may be significant only to a certain group.

Consonance: Consonance occurs in poetry when words appearing at the ends of two or more verses have similar final consonant sounds but have final vowel sounds that differ, as with "stuff" and "off."

Convention: Any widely accepted literary device, style, or form.

Corrido: A Mexican ballad.

Couplet: Two lines of poetry with the same rhyme and meter, often expressing a complete and self-contained thought.

Criticism: The systematic study and evaluation of literary works, usually based on a specific method or set of principles. An important part of literary studies since ancient times, the practice of criticism has given rise to numerous theories, methods, and "schools," sometimes producing conflicting, even contradictory, interpretations of literature in general as well as of individual works. Even such basic issues as what constitutes a poem or a novel have been the subject of much criticism over the centuries.

D

Dactyl: See *Foot*

Dadaism: A protest movement in art and literature founded by Tristan Tzara in 1916. Followers of the movement expressed their outrage at the destruction brought about by World War I by revolting against numerous forms of social convention. The Dadaists presented works marked by calculated madness and flamboyant nonsense. They stressed total freedom of expression, commonly through primitive displays of emotion and illogical, often senseless, poetry. The movement ended shortly after the war, when it was replaced by surrealism.

Decadent: See *Decadents*

Decadents: The followers of a nineteenth-century literary movement that had its beginnings in French aestheticism. Decadent literature displays a fascination with perverse and morbid states; a search for novelty and sensation—the "new thrill"; a preoccupation with mysticism; and a belief in the senselessness of human existence. The movement is closely associated with the doctrine Art for Art's Sake. The term "decadence" is sometimes used to denote a decline in the quality of art or literature following a period of greatness.

Deconstruction: A method of literary criticism developed by Jacques Derrida and characterized by multiple conflicting interpretations of a given work. Deconstructionists consider the impact of the language of a work and suggest that the true meaning of the work is not necessarily the meaning that the author intended.

Deduction: The process of reaching a conclusion through reasoning from general premises to a specific premise.

Denotation: The definition of a word, apart from the impressions or feelings it creates in the reader.

Diction: The selection and arrangement of words in a literary work. Either or both may vary depending on the desired effect. There are four general types of diction: "formal," used in scholarly or lofty writing; "informal," used in relaxed but educated conversation; "colloquial," used in everyday speech; and "slang," containing newly coined words and other terms not accepted in formal usage.

Didactic: A term used to describe works of literature that aim to teach some moral, religious, political, or practical lesson. Although didactic elements are often found in artistically pleasing works, the term "didactic" usually refers to literature in which the message is more important than the form. The term may also be used to criticize a work that the critic finds "overly didactic," that is, heavy-handed in its delivery of a lesson.

Dimeter: See *Meter*

Dionysian: See *Apollonian and Dionysian*

Discordia concours: A Latin phrase meaning "discord in harmony." The term was coined by the eighteenth-century English writer Samuel Johnson to describe "a combination of dissimilar images or discovery of occult resemblances in things apparently unlike." Johnson created the expression by reversing a phrase by the Latin poet Horace.

Dissonance: A combination of harsh or jarring sounds, especially in poetry. Although such combinations may be accidental, poets sometimes intentionally make them to achieve particular effects. Dissonance is also sometimes used to refer to close but not identical rhymes. When this is the case, the word functions as a synonym for consonance.

Double Entendre: A corruption of a French phrase meaning "double meaning." The term is used to indicate a word or phrase that is deliberately ambiguous, especially when one of the meanings is risque or improper.

Draft: Any preliminary version of a written work. An author may write dozens of drafts which are revised to form the final work, or he or she may write only one, with few or no revisions.

Dramatic Monologue: See *Monologue*

Dramatic Poetry: Any lyric work that employs elements of drama such as dialogue, conflict, or characterization, but excluding works that are intended for stage presentation.

Dream Allegory: See *Dream Vision*

Dream Vision: A literary convention, chiefly of the Middle Ages. In a dream vision a story is presented as a literal dream of the narrator. This device was commonly used to teach moral and religious lessons.

E

Eclogue: In classical literature, a poem featuring rural themes and structured as a dialogue among shepherds. Eclogues often took specific poetic forms, such as elegies or love poems. Some were written as the soliloquy of a shepherd. In later centuries, "eclogue" came to refer to any poem that was in the pastoral tradition or that had a dialogue or monologue structure.

Edwardian: Describes cultural conventions identified with the period of the reign of Edward VII of England (1901-1910). Writers of the Edwardian Age typically displayed a strong reaction against the propriety and conservatism of the Victorian Age. Their work often exhibits distrust of authority in religion, politics, and art and expresses strong doubts about the soundness of conventional values.

Edwardian Age: See *Edwardian*

Electra Complex: A daughter's amorous obsession with her father.

Elegy: A lyric poem that laments the death of a person or the eventual death of all people. In a conventional elegy, set in a classical world, the poet and subject are spoken of as shepherds. In modern criticism, the word elegy is often used to refer to a poem that is melancholy or mournfully contemplative.

Elizabethan Age: A period of great economic growth, religious controversy, and nationalism closely associated with the reign of Elizabeth I of England (1558-1603). The Elizabethan Age is considered a part of the general renaissance—that is, the flowering of arts and literature—that took place in Europe during the fourteenth through sixteenth centuries. The era is considered the golden age of English literature. The most important dramas in English and a great deal of lyric poetry were produced during this period, and modern English criticism began around this time.

Empathy: A sense of shared experience, including emotional and physical feelings, with someone or something other than oneself. Empathy is often used to describe the response of a reader to a literary character.

English Sonnet: See *Sonnet*

Enjambment: The running over of the sense and structure of a line of verse or a couplet into the following verse or couplet.

Enlightenment, The: An eighteenth-century philosophical movement. It began in France but had a wide impact throughout Europe and America. Thinkers of the Enlightenment valued reason and believed that both the individual and society could achieve a state of perfection. Corresponding to this essentially humanist vision was a resistance to religious authority.

Epic: A long narrative poem about the adventures of a hero of great historic or legendary importance. The setting is vast and the action is often given cosmic significance through the intervention of supernatural forces such as gods, angels, or demons. Epics are typically written in a classical style of grand simplicity with elaborate metaphors and allusions that enhance the symbolic importance of a hero's adventures.

Epic Simile: See *Homeric Simile*

Epigram: A saying that makes the speaker's point quickly and concisely.

Epilogue: A concluding statement or section of a literary work. In dramas, particularly those of the seventeenth and eighteenth centuries, the epilogue is a closing speech, often in verse, delivered by an actor at the end of a play and spoken directly to the audience.

Epiphany: A sudden revelation of truth inspired by a seemingly trivial incident.

Epitaph: An inscription on a tomb or tombstone, or a verse written on the occasion of a person's death. Epitaphs may be serious or humorous.

Epithalamion: A song or poem written to honor and commemorate a marriage ceremony.

Epithalamium: See *Epithalamion*

Epithet: A word or phrase, often disparaging or abusive, that expresses a character trait of someone or something.

Erziehungsroman: See *Bildungsroman*

Essay: A prose composition with a focused subject of discussion. The term was coined by Michel de Montaigne to describe his 1580 collection of brief, informal reflections on himself and on various topics relating to human nature. An essay can also be a long, systematic discourse.

Existentialism: A predominantly twentieth-century philosophy concerned with the nature and perception of human existence. There are two major strains of existentialist thought: atheistic and Christian. Followers of atheistic existentialism believe that the individual is alone in a godless universe and that the basic human condition is one of suffering and loneliness. Nevertheless, because there are no fixed values, individuals can create their own characters—indeed, they can shape themselves—through the exercise of free will. The atheistic strain culminates in and is popularly associated with the works of Jean-Paul Sartre. The Christian existentialists, on the other hand, believe that only in God may people find freedom from life's anguish. The two strains hold certain beliefs in common: that existence cannot be fully understood or described through empirical effort; that anguish is a universal element of life; that individuals must bear responsibility for their actions; and that there is no common standard of behavior or perception for religious and ethical matters.

Expatriates: See *Expatriatism*

Expatriatism: The practice of leaving one's country to live for an extended period in another country.

Exposition: Writing intended to explain the nature of an idea, thing, or theme. Expository writing is often combined with description, narration, or argument. In dramatic writing, the exposition is the introductory material which presents the characters, setting, and tone of the play.

Expressionism: An indistinct literary term, originally used to describe an early twentieth-century school of German painting. The term applies to almost any mode of unconventional, highly subjective writing that distorts reality in some way.

Extended Monologue: See *Monologue*

F

Feet: See *Foot*

Feminine Rhyme: See *Rhyme*

Fiction: Any story that is the product of imagination rather than a documentation of fact. Characters and events in such narratives may be based in real life but their ultimate form and configuration is a creation of the author.

Figurative Language: A technique in writing in which the author temporarily interrupts the order, construction, or meaning of the writing for a particular effect. This interruption takes the form of one or more figures of speech such as hyperbole, irony, or simile. Figurative language is the opposite of literal language, in which every word is truthful, accurate, and free of exaggeration or embellishment.

Figures of Speech: Writing that differs from customary conventions for construction, meaning, order, or significance for the purpose of a special meaning or effect. There are two major types of figures of speech: rhetorical figures, which do not make changes in the meaning of the words, and tropes, which do.

Fin de siecle: A French term meaning "end of the century." The term is used to denote the last decade of the nineteenth century, a transition period when writers and other artists abandoned old conventions and looked for new techniques and objectives.

First Person: See *Point of View*

Folk Ballad: See *Ballad*

Folklore: Traditions and myths preserved in a culture or group of people. Typically, these are passed on by word of mouth in various forms—such as legends, songs, and proverbs—or preserved in customs and ceremonies. This term was first used by W. J. Thoms in 1846.

Folktale: A story originating in oral tradition. Folktales fall into a variety of categories, including legends, ghost stories, fairy tales, fables, and anecdotes based on historical figures and events.

Foot: The smallest unit of rhythm in a line of poetry. In English-language poetry, a foot is typically one accented syllable combined with one or two unaccented syllables.

Form: The pattern or construction of a work which identifies its genre and distinguishes it from other genres.

Formalism: In literary criticism, the belief that literature should follow prescribed rules of construction, such as those that govern the sonnet form.

Fourteener Meter: See *Meter*

Free Verse: Poetry that lacks regular metrical and rhyme patterns but that tries to capture the cadences of everyday speech. The form allows a poet to exploit a variety of rhythmical effects within a single poem.

Futurism: A flamboyant literary and artistic movement that developed in France, Italy, and Russia from 1908 through the 1920s. Futurist theater and poetry abandoned traditional literary forms. In their place, followers of the movement attempted to achieve total freedom of expression through bizarre imagery and deformed or newly invented words. The Futurists were self-consciously modern artists who attempted to incorporate the appearances and sounds of modern life into their work.

G

Genre: A category of literary work. In critical theory, genre may refer to both the content of a given work—tragedy, comedy, pastoral—and to its form, such as poetry, novel, or drama.

Genteel Tradition: A term coined by critic George Santayana to describe the literary practice of certain late nineteenth- century American writers, especially New Englanders. Followers of the Genteel Tradition emphasized conventionality in social, religious, moral, and literary standards.

Georgian Age: See *Georgian Poets*

Georgian Period: See *Georgian Poets*

Georgian Poets: A loose grouping of English poets during the years 1912-1922. The Georgians reacted against certain literary schools and practices, especially Victorian wordiness, turn-of-the-century aestheticism, and contemporary urban realism. In their place, the Georgians embraced the nineteenth-century poetic practices of William Wordsworth and the other Lake Poets.

Georgic: A poem about farming and the farmer's way of life, named from Virgil's *Georgics*.

Gilded Age: A period in American history during the 1870s characterized by political corruption and materialism. A number of important novels of social and political criticism were written during this time.

Gothic: See *Gothicism*

Gothicism: In literary criticism, works characterized by a taste for the medieval or morbidly attractive. A gothic novel prominently features elements of horror, the supernatural, gloom, and violence: clanking chains, terror, charnel houses, ghosts, medieval castles, and mysteriously slamming doors. The term "gothic novel" is also applied to novels that lack elements of the traditional Gothic setting but that create a similar atmosphere of terror or dread.

Graveyard School: A group of eighteenth-century English poets who wrote long, picturesque meditations on death. Their works were designed to cause the reader to ponder immortality.

Great Chain of Being: The belief that all things and creatures in nature are organized in a hierarchy from inanimate objects at the bottom to God at the top. This system of belief was popular in the seventeenth and eighteenth centuries.

Grotesque: In literary criticism, the subject matter of a work or a style of expression characterized by exaggeration, deformity, freakishness, and disorder. The grotesque often includes an element of comic absurdity.

H

Haiku: The shortest form of Japanese poetry, constructed in three lines of five, seven, and five syllables respectively. The message of a *haiku* poem usually centers on some aspect of spirituality and provokes an emotional response in the reader.

Half Rhyme: See *Consonance*

Harlem Renaissance: The Harlem Renaissance of the 1920s is generally considered the first significant movement of black writers and artists in the United States. During this period, new and established black writers published more fiction and poetry than ever before, the first influential black literary journals were established, and black authors and artists received their first widespread recognition and serious critical appraisal. Among the major writers associated with this period are Claude McKay, Jean Toomer, Countee Cullen, Langston Hughes, Arna Bontemps, Nella Larsen, and Zora Neale Hurston.

Hellenism: Imitation of ancient Greek thought or styles. Also, an approach to life that focuses on the growth and development of the intellect. "Hellenism" is sometimes used to refer to the belief that reason can be applied to examine all human experience.

Heptameter: See *Meter*

Hero/Heroine: The principal sympathetic character (male or female) in a literary work. Heroes and heroines typically exhibit admirable traits: idealism, courage, and integrity, for example.

Heroic Couplet: A rhyming couplet written in iambic pentameter (a verse with five iambic feet).

Heroic Line: The meter and length of a line of verse in epic or heroic poetry. This varies by language and time period.

Heroine: See *Hero/Heroine*

Hexameter: See *Meter*

Historical Criticism: The study of a work based on its impact on the world of the time period in which it was written.

Hokku: See *Haiku*

Holocaust: See *Holocaust Literature*

Holocaust Literature: Literature influenced by or written about the Holocaust of World War II. Such literature includes true stories of survival in concentration camps, escape, and life after the war, as well as fictional works and poetry.

Homeric Simile: An elaborate, detailed comparison written as a simile many lines in length.

Horatian Satire: See *Satire*

Humanism: A philosophy that places faith in the dignity of humankind and rejects the medieval perception of the individual as a weak, fallen creature. "Humanists" typically believe in the perfectibility of human nature and view reason and education as the means to that end.

Humors: Mentions of the humors refer to the ancient Greek theory that a person's health and personality were determined by the balance of four basic fluids in the body: blood, phlegm, yellow bile, and black bile. A dominance of any fluid would cause extremes in behavior. An excess of blood created a sanguine person who was joyful, aggressive, and passionate; a phlegmatic person was shy, fearful, and sluggish; too much yellow bile led to a choleric temperament characterized by impatience, anger, bitterness, and stubbornness; and excessive black bile created melancholy, a state of laziness, gluttony, and lack of motivation.

Humours: See *Humors*

Hyperbole: In literary criticism, deliberate exaggeration used to achieve an effect.

I

Iamb: See *Foot*

Idiom: A word construction or verbal expression closely associated with a given language.

Image: A concrete representation of an object or sensory experience. Typically, such a representation helps evoke the feelings associated with the object or experience itself. Images are either "literal" or "figurative." Literal images are especially concrete and involve little or no extension of the obvious meaning of the words used to express them. Figurative images do not follow the literal meaning of the words exactly. Images in literature are usually visual, but the term "image" can also refer to the representation of any sensory experience.

Imagery: The array of images in a literary work. Also, figurative language.

Imagism: An English and American poetry movement that flourished between 1908 and 1917. The Imagists used precise, clearly presented images in their works. They also used common, everyday speech and aimed for conciseness, concrete imagery, and the creation of new rhythms.

In medias res: A Latin term meaning "in the middle of things." It refers to the technique of beginning a story at its midpoint and then using various flashback devices to reveal previous action.

Induction: The process of reaching a conclusion by reasoning from specific premises to form a general premise. Also, an introductory portion of a work of literature, especially a play.

Intentional Fallacy: The belief that judgments of a literary work based solely on an author's stated or implied intentions are false and misleading. Critics who believe in the concept of the intentional fallacy typically argue that the work itself is sufficient matter for interpretation, even though they may concede that an author's statement of purpose can be useful.

Interior Monologue: A narrative technique in which characters' thoughts are revealed in a way that appears to be uncontrolled by the author. The interior monologue typically aims to reveal the inner self of a character. It portrays emotional experiences as they occur at both a conscious and unconscious level. Images are often used to represent sensations or emotions.

Internal Rhyme: Rhyme that occurs within a single line of verse.

Irish Literary Renaissance: A late nineteenth- and early twentieth-century movement in Irish literature. Members of the movement aimed to reduce the influence of British culture in Ireland and create an Irish national literature.

Irony: In literary criticism, the effect of language in which the intended meaning is the opposite of what is stated.

Italian Sonnet: See *Sonnet*

J

Jacobean Age: The period of the reign of James I of England (1603-1625). The early literature of this period reflected the worldview of the Elizabethan Age, but a darker, more cynical attitude steadily grew in the art and literature of the Jacobean Age. This was an important time for English drama and poetry.

Jargon: Language that is used or understood only by a select group of people. Jargon may refer to terminology used in a certain profession, such as computer jargon, or it may refer to any nonsensical language that is not understood by most people.

Journalism: Writing intended for publication in a newspaper or magazine, or for broadcast on a radio or television program featuring news, sports, entertainment, or other timely material.

K

Knickerbocker Group: A somewhat indistinct group of New York writers of the first half of the nineteenth century. Members of the group were linked only by location and a common theme: New York life.

Kunstlerroman: See *Bildungsroman*

L

Lais: See *Lay*

Lake Poets: See *Lake School*

Lake School: These poets all lived in the Lake District of England at the turn of the nineteenth century. As a group, they followed no single "school" of thought or literary practice, although their works were uniformly disparaged by the *Edinburgh Review*.

Lay: A song or simple narrative poem. The form originated in medieval France. Early French *lais* were often based on the Celtic legends and other tales sung by Breton minstrels—thus the name of the "Breton lay." In fourteenth-century England, the term "lay" was used to describe short narratives written in imitation of the Breton lays.

Leitmotiv: See *Motif*

Literal Language: An author uses literal language when he or she writes without exaggerating or embellishing the subject matter and without any tools of figurative language.

Literary Ballad: See *Ballad*

Literature: Literature is broadly defined as any written or spoken material, but the term most often refers to creative works.

Lost Generation: A term first used by Gertrude Stein to describe the post-World War I generation of American writers: men and women haunted by a sense of betrayal and emptiness brought about by the destructiveness of the war.

Lyric Poetry: A poem expressing the subjective feelings and personal emotions of the poet. Such poetry is melodic, since it was originally accompanied by a lyre in recitals. Most Western poetry in the twentieth century may be classified as lyrical.

M

Mannerism: Exaggerated, artificial adherence to a literary manner or style. Also, a popular style of the visual arts of late sixteenth-century Europe that was marked by elongation of the human form and by intentional spatial distortion. Literary works that are self-consciously high-toned and artistic are often said to be "mannered."

Masculine Rhyme: See *Rhyme*

Measure: The foot, verse, or time sequence used in a literary work, especially a poem. Measure is often used somewhat incorrectly as a synonym for meter.

Metaphor: A figure of speech that expresses an idea through the image of another object. Metaphors suggest the essence of the first object by identifying it with certain qualities of the second object.

Metaphysical Conceit: See *Conceit*

Metaphysical Poetry: The body of poetry produced by a group of seventeenth-century English writers called the "Metaphysical Poets." The group includes John Donne and Andrew Marvell. The Metaphysical Poets made use of everyday speech, intellectual analysis, and unique imagery. They aimed to portray the ordinary conflicts and contradictions of life. Their poems often took the form of an argument, and many of them emphasize physical and religious love as well as the fleeting nature of life. Elaborate conceits are typical in metaphysical poetry.

Metaphysical Poets: See *Metaphysical Poetry*

Meter: In literary criticism, the repetition of sound patterns that creates a rhythm in poetry. The patterns are based on the number of syllables and the presence and absence of accents. The unit of rhythm in a line is called a foot. Types of meter are classified according to the number of feet in a line. These are the standard English lines: Monometer, one foot; Dimeter, two feet; Trimeter, three feet; Tetrameter, four feet; Pentameter, five feet; Hexameter, six feet (also called the Alexandrine); Heptameter, seven feet (also called the "Fourteener" when the feet are iambic).

Modernism: Modern literary practices. Also, the principles of a literary school that lasted from roughly the beginning of the twentieth century until the end of World War II. Modernism is defined by its rejection of the literary conventions of the nineteenth century and by its opposition to conventional morality, taste, traditions, and economic values.

Monologue: A composition, written or oral, by a single individual. More specifically, a speech given by a single individual in a drama or other public entertainment. It has no set length, although it is usually several or more lines long.

Monometer: See *Meter*

Mood: The prevailing emotions of a work or of the author in his or her creation of the work. The mood of a work is not always what might be expected based on its subject matter.

Motif: A theme, character type, image, metaphor, or other verbal element that recurs throughout a single work of literature or occurs in a number of different works over a period of time.

Motiv: See *Motif*

Muckrakers: An early twentieth-century group of American writers. Typically, their works exposed the wrongdoings of big business and government in the United States.

Muses: Nine Greek mythological goddesses, the daughters of Zeus and Mnemosyne (Memory). Each muse patronized a specific area of the liberal arts and sciences. Calliope presided over epic poetry, Clio over history, Erato over love poetry, Euterpe over music or lyric poetry, Melpomene over tragedy, Polyhymnia over hymns to the gods, Terpsichore over dance, Thalia over comedy, and Urania over astronomy. Poets and writers traditionally made appeals to the Muses for inspiration in their work.

Myth: An anonymous tale emerging from the traditional beliefs of a culture or social unit. Myths use supernatural explanations for natural phenomena. They may also explain cosmic issues like creation and death. Collections of myths, known as mythologies, are common to all cultures and nations, but the best-known myths belong to the Norse, Roman, and Greek mythologies.

N

Narration: The telling of a series of events, real or invented. A narration may be either a simple narrative, in which the events are recounted chronologically, or a narrative with a plot, in which the account is given in a style reflecting the author's artistic concept of the story. Narration is sometimes used as a synonym for "storyline."

Narrative: A verse or prose accounting of an event or sequence of events, real or invented. The term is also used as an adjective in the sense "method of narration." For example, in literary criticism, the expression "narrative technique" usually refers to the way the author structures and presents his or her story.

Narrative Poetry: A nondramatic poem in which the author tells a story. Such poems may be of any length or level of complexity.

Narrator: The teller of a story. The narrator may be the author or a character in the story through whom the author speaks.

Naturalism: A literary movement of the late nineteenth and early twentieth centuries. The movement's major theorist, French novelist Emile Zola, envisioned a type of fiction that would examine human life with the objectivity of scientific inquiry. The Naturalists typically viewed human beings as either the products of "biological determinism," ruled by hereditary instincts and engaged in an endless struggle for survival, or as the products of "socioeconomic determinism," ruled by social and economic forces beyond their control. In their works, the Naturalists generally ignored the highest levels of society and focused on degradation: poverty, alcoholism, prostitution, insanity, and disease.

Negritude: A literary movement based on the concept of a shared cultural bond on the part of black Africans, wherever they may be in the world. It traces its origins to the former French colonies of Africa and the Caribbean. Negritude poets, novelists, and essayists generally stress four points in their writings: One, black alienation from traditional African culture can lead to feelings of inferiority. Two, European colonialism and Western education should be resisted. Three, black Africans should seek to affirm and define their own identity. Four, African culture can and should be reclaimed. Many Negritude writers also claim that blacks can make unique contributions to the world, based on a heightened appreciation of nature, rhythm, and human emotions—aspects of life they say are not so highly valued in the materialistic and rationalistic West.

Negro Renaissance: See *Harlem Renaissance*

Neoclassical Period: See *Neoclassicism*

Neoclassicism: In literary criticism, this term refers to the revival of the attitudes and styles of expression of classical literature. It is generally used to describe a period in European history beginning in the late seventeenth century and lasting until about 1800. In its purest form, Neoclassicism marked a return to order, proportion, restraint, logic, accuracy, and decorum. In England, where Neoclassicism perhaps was most popular, it reflected the influence of seventeenth-century French writers, especially dramatists. Neoclassical writers typically reacted against the intensity and enthusiasm of the Renaissance period. They wrote works that appealed to the intellect, using elevated language and classical literary forms such as satire and the ode. Neoclassical works were often governed by the classical goal of instruction.

Neoclassicists: See *Neoclassicism*

New Criticism: A movement in literary criticism, dating from the late 1920s, that stressed close textual analysis in the interpretation of works of literature. The New Critics saw little merit in historical and biographical analysis. Rather, they aimed to examine the text alone, free from the question of how external events—biographical or otherwise—may have helped shape it.

New Journalism: A type of writing in which the journalist presents factual information in a form usually used in fiction. New journalism emphasizes description, narration, and character development to bring readers closer to the human element of the story, and is often used in personality profiles and in-depth feature articles. It is not compatible with "straight" or "hard" newswriting, which is generally composed in a brief, fact-based style.

New Journalists: See *New Journalism*

New Negro Movement: See *Harlem Renaissance*

Noble Savage: The idea that primitive man is noble and good but becomes evil and corrupted as he becomes civilized. The concept of the noble savage originated in the Renaissance period but is more closely identified with such later writers as Jean-Jacques Rousseau and Aphra Behn.

O

Objective Correlative: An outward set of objects, a situation, or a chain of events corresponding to an inward experience and evoking this experience in the reader. The term frequently appears in modern criticism in discussions of authors' intended effects on the emotional responses of readers.

Objectivity: A quality in writing characterized by the absence of the author's opinion or feeling about the subject matter. Objectivity is an important factor in criticism.

Occasional Verse: poetry written on the occasion of a significant historical or personal event. *Vers de societe* is sometimes called occasional verse although it is of a less serious nature.

Octave: A poem or stanza composed of eight lines. The term octave most often represents the first eight lines of a Petrarchan sonnet.

Ode: Name given to an extended lyric poem characterized by exalted emotion and dignified style. An ode usually concerns a single, serious theme. Most odes, but not all, are addressed to an object or individual. Odes are distinguished from other lyric poetic forms by their complex rhythmic and stanzaic patterns.

Oedipus Complex: A son's amorous obsession with his mother. The phrase is derived from the story of the ancient Theban hero Oedipus, who unknowingly killed his father and married his mother.

Omniscience: See *Point of View*

Onomatopoeia: The use of words whose sounds express or suggest their meaning. In its simplest sense, onomatopoeia may be represented by words that mimic the sounds they denote such as "hiss" or "meow." At a more subtle level, the pattern and rhythm of sounds and rhymes of a line or poem may be onomatopoeic.

Oral Tradition: See *Oral Transmission*

Oral Transmission: A process by which songs, ballads, folklore, and other material are transmitted by word of mouth. The tradition of oral transmission predates the written record systems of literate society. Oral transmission preserves material sometimes over generations, although often with variations. Memory plays a large part in the recitation and preservation of orally transmitted material.

Ottava Rima: An eight-line stanza of poetry composed in iambic pentameter (a five-foot line in which each foot consists of an unaccented syllable followed by an accented syllable), following the abababcc rhyme scheme.

Oxymoron: A phrase combining two contradictory terms. Oxymorons may be intentional or unintentional.

P

Pantheism: The idea that all things are both a manifestation or revelation of God and a part of God at the same time. Pantheism was a common attitude in the early societies of Egypt, India, and Greece—the term derives from the Greek *pan* meaning "all" and *theos* meaning "deity." It later became a significant part of the Christian faith.

Parable: A story intended to teach a moral lesson or answer an ethical question.

Paradox: A statement that appears illogical or contradictory at first, but may actually point to an underlying truth.

Parallelism: A method of comparison of two ideas in which each is developed in the same grammatical structure.

Parnassianism: A mid nineteenth-century movement in French literature. Followers of the movement stressed adherence to well-defined artistic forms as a reaction against the often chaotic expression of the artist's ego that dominated the work of the Romantics. The Parnassians also rejected the moral, ethical, and social themes exhibited in the works of French Romantics such as Victor Hugo. The aesthetic doctrines of the Parnassians strongly influenced the later symbolist and decadent movements.

Parody: In literary criticism, this term refers to an imitation of a serious literary work or the signature style of a particular author in a ridiculous manner. A typical parody adopts the style of the original and applies it to an inappropriate subject for humorous effect. Parody is a form of satire and could be considered the literary equivalent of a caricature or cartoon.

Pastoral: A term derived from the Latin word "pastor," meaning shepherd. A pastoral is a literary composition on a rural theme. The conventions of the pastoral were originated by the third-century Greek poet Theocritus, who wrote about the experiences, love affairs, and pastimes of Sicilian shepherds. In a pastoral, characters and language of a courtly nature are often placed in a simple setting. The term pastoral is also used to classify dramas, elegies, and lyrics that exhibit the use of country settings and shepherd characters.

Pathetic Fallacy: A term coined by English critic John Ruskin to identify writing that falsely endows nonhuman things with human intentions and feelings, such as "angry clouds" and "sad trees."

Pen Name: See *Pseudonym*

Pentameter: See *Meter*

Persona: A Latin term meaning "mask." *Personae* are the characters in a fictional work of literature. The *persona* generally functions as a mask through which the author tells a story in a voice other than his or her own. A *persona* is usually either a character in a story who acts as a narrator or an "implied author," a voice created by the author to act as the narrator for himself or herself.

Personae: See *Persona*

Personal Point of View: See *Point of View*

Personification: A figure of speech that gives human qualities to abstract ideas, animals, and inanimate objects.

Petrarchan Sonnet: See *Sonnet*

Phenomenology: A method of literary criticism based on the belief that things have no existence outside of human consciousness or awareness. Proponents of this theory believe that art is a process that takes place in the mind of the observer as he or she contemplates an object rather than a quality of the object itself.

Plagiarism: Claiming another person's written material as one's own. Plagiarism can take the form of direct, word-for-word copying or the theft of the substance or idea of the work.

Platonic Criticism: A form of criticism that stresses an artistic work's usefulness as an agent of social engineering rather than any quality or value of the work itself.

Platonism: The embracing of the doctrines of the philosopher Plato, popular among the poets of the Renaissance and the Romantic period. Platonism is more flexible than Aristotelian Criticism and places more emphasis on the supernatural and unknown aspects of life.

Plot: In literary criticism, this term refers to the pattern of events in a narrative or drama. In its simplest sense, the plot guides the author in composing the work and helps the reader follow the work. Typically, plots exhibit causality and unity and have a beginning, a middle, and an end. Sometimes, however, a plot may consist of a series of disconnected events, in which case it is known as an "episodic plot."

Poem: In its broadest sense, a composition utilizing rhyme, meter, concrete detail, and expressive language to create a literary experience with emotional and aesthetic appeal.

Poet: An author who writes poetry or verse. The term is also used to refer to an artist or writer who has an exceptional gift for expression, imagination, and energy in the making of art in any form.

Poete maudit: A term derived from Paul Verlaine's *Les poetes maudits* (*The Accursed Poets*), a collection of essays on the French symbolist writers Stephane Mallarme, Arthur Rimbaud, and Tristan Corbiere. In the sense intended by Verlaine, the poet is "accursed" for choosing to explore extremes of human experience outside of middle-class society.

Poetic Fallacy: See *Pathetic Fallacy*

Poetic Justice: An outcome in a literary work, not necessarily a poem, in which the good are rewarded and the evil are punished, especially in ways that particularly fit their virtues or crimes.

Poetic License: Distortions of fact and literary convention made by a writer—not always a poet—for the sake of the effect gained. Poetic license is closely related to the concept of "artistic freedom."

Poetics: This term has two closely related meanings. It denotes (1) an aesthetic theory in literary criticism about the essence of poetry or (2) rules prescribing the proper methods, content, style, or diction of poetry. The term poetics may also refer to theories about literature in general, not just poetry.

Poetry: In its broadest sense, writing that aims to present ideas and evoke an emotional experience in the reader through the use of meter, imagery, connotative and concrete words, and a carefully constructed structure based on rhythmic patterns. Poetry typically relies on words and expressions that have several layers of meaning. It also makes use of the effects of regular rhythm on the ear and may make a strong appeal to the senses through the use of imagery.

Point of View: The narrative perspective from which a literary work is presented to the reader. There are four traditional points of view. The "third person omniscient" gives the reader a "godlike" perspective, unrestricted by time or place, from which to see actions and look into the minds of characters. This allows the author to comment openly on characters and events in the work. The "third person" point of view presents the events of the story from outside of any single character's perception, much like the omniscient point of view, but the reader must understand the action as it takes place and without any special insight into characters' minds or motivations. The "first person" or "personal" point of view relates events as they are perceived by a single character. The main character "tells" the story and may offer opinions about the action and characters which differ from those of the author. Much less common than omniscient, third person, and first person is the "second person" point of view, wherein the author tells the story as if it is happening to the reader.

Polemic: A work in which the author takes a stand on a controversial subject, such as abortion or religion. Such works are often extremely argumentative or provocative.

Pornography: Writing intended to provoke feelings of lust in the reader. Such works are often condemned by critics and teachers, but those which can be shown to have literary value are viewed less harshly.

Post-Aesthetic Movement: An artistic response made by African Americans to the black aesthetic movement of the 1960s and early '70s. Writers since that time have adopted a somewhat different tone in their work, with less emphasis placed on the disparity between black and white in the United States. In the words of post-aesthetic authors such as Toni Morrison, John Edgar Wideman, and Kristin Hunter, African Americans are portrayed as looking inward for answers to their own questions, rather than always looking to the outside world.

Postmodernism: Writing from the 1960s forward characterized by experimentation and continuing to apply some of the fundamentals of modernism, which included existentialism and alienation. Postmodernists have gone a step further in the rejection of tradition begun with the modernists by also rejecting traditional forms, preferring the anti-novel over the novel and the anti-hero over the hero.

Pre-Raphaelites: A circle of writers and artists in mid nineteenth-century England. Valuing the pre-Renaissance artistic qualities of religious symbolism, lavish pictorialism, and natural sensuousness, the Pre-Raphaelites cultivated a sense of mystery and melancholy that influenced later writers associated with the Symbolist and Decadent movements.

Primitivism: The belief that primitive peoples were nobler and less flawed than civilized peoples because they had not been subjected to the tainting influence of society.

Projective Verse: A form of free verse in which the poet's breathing pattern determines the lines of the poem. Poets who advocate projective verse are against all formal structures in writing, including meter and form.

Prologue: An introductory section of a literary work. It often contains information establishing the situation of the characters or presents information about the setting, time period, or action. In drama, the prologue is spoken by a chorus or by one of the principal characters.

Prose: A literary medium that attempts to mirror the language of everyday speech. It is distinguished from poetry by its use of unmetered, unrhymed language consisting of logically related sentences. Prose is usually grouped into paragraphs that form a cohesive whole such as an essay or a novel.

Prosopopoeia: See *Personification*

Protagonist: The central character of a story who serves as a focus for its themes and incidents and as the principal rationale for its development. The protagonist is sometimes referred to in discussions of modern literature as the hero or anti-hero.

Proverb: A brief, sage saying that expresses a truth about life in a striking manner.

Pseudonym: A name assumed by a writer, most often intended to prevent his or her identification as the author of a work. Two or more authors may work together under one pseudonym, or an author may use a different name for each genre he or she publishes in. Some publishing companies maintain "house pseudonyms," under which any number of authors may write installations in a series. Some authors also choose a pseudonym over their real names the way an actor may use a stage name.

Pun: A play on words that have similar sounds but different meanings.

Pure Poetry: poetry written without instructional intent or moral purpose that aims only to please a reader by its imagery or musical flow. The term pure poetry is used as the antonym of the term "didacticism."

Q

Quatrain: A four-line stanza of a poem or an entire poem consisting of four lines.

R

Realism: A nineteenth-century European literary movement that sought to portray familiar characters, situations, and settings in a realistic manner. This was done primarily by using an objective narrative point of view and through the buildup of accurate detail. The standard for success of any realistic work depends on how faithfully it transfers common experience into fictional forms. The realistic method may be altered or extended, as in stream of consciousness writing, to record highly subjective experience.

Refrain: A phrase repeated at intervals throughout a poem. A refrain may appear at the end of each stanza or at less regular intervals. It may be altered slightly at each appearance.

Renaissance: The period in European history that marked the end of the Middle Ages. It began in Italy in the late fourteenth century. In broad terms, it is usually seen as spanning the fourteenth, fifteenth, and sixteenth centuries, although it did not reach Great Britain, for example, until the 1480s or so. The Renaissance saw an awakening in almost every sphere of human activity, especially science, philosophy, and the arts. The period is best defined by the emergence of a general philosophy that emphasized the importance of the intellect, the individual, and world affairs. It contrasts strongly with the medieval worldview, characterized by the dominant concerns of faith, the social collective, and spiritual salvation.

Repartee: Conversation featuring snappy retorts and witticisms.

Restoration: See *Restoration Age*

Restoration Age: A period in English literature beginning with the crowning of Charles II in 1660 and running to about 1700. The era, which was characterized by a reaction against Puritanism, was the first great age of the comedy of manners. The finest literature of the era is typically witty and urbane, and often lewd.

Rhetoric: In literary criticism, this term denotes the art of ethical persuasion. In its strictest sense, rhetoric adheres to various principles developed since classical times for arranging facts and ideas in a clear, persuasive, appealing manner. The term is also used to refer to effective prose in general and theories of or methods for composing effective prose.

Rhetorical Question: A question intended to provoke thought, but not an expressed answer, in the reader. It is most commonly used in oratory and other persuasive genres.

Rhyme: When used as a noun in literary criticism, this term generally refers to a poem in which words sound identical or very similar and appear in parallel positions in two or more lines. Rhymes are classified into different types according to where they fall in a line or stanza or according to the degree of similarity they exhibit in their spellings and sounds. Some major types of rhyme are "masculine" rhyme, "feminine" rhyme, and "triple" rhyme. In a masculine rhyme, the rhyming sound falls in a single accented syllable, as with "heat" and "eat." Feminine rhyme is a rhyme of two syllables, one stressed and one unstressed, as with "merry" and "tarry." Triple rhyme matches the sound of the accented syllable and the two unaccented syllables that follow: "narrative" and "declarative."

Rhyme Royal: A stanza of seven lines composed in iambic pentameter and rhymed *ababbcc*. The name is said to be a tribute to King James I of Scotland, who made much use of the form in his poetry.

Rhyme Scheme: See *Rhyme*

Rhythm: A regular pattern of sound, time intervals, or events occurring in writing, most often and most discernably in poetry. Regular, reliable rhythm is known to be soothing to humans, while interrupted, unpredictable, or rapidly changing rhythm is disturbing. These effects are known to authors, who use them to produce a desired reaction in the reader.

Rococo: A style of European architecture that flourished in the eighteenth century, especially in France. The most notable features of *rococo* are its extensive use of ornamentation and its themes of lightness, gaiety, and intimacy. In literary criticism, the term is often used disparagingly to refer to a decadent or over-ornamental style.

Romance: A broad term, usually denoting a narrative with exotic, exaggerated, often idealized characters, scenes, and themes.

Romantic Age: See *Romanticism*

Romanticism: This term has two widely accepted meanings. In historical criticism, it refers to a European intellectual and artistic movement of the late eighteenth and early nineteenth centuries that sought greater freedom of personal expression than that allowed by the strict rules of literary form and logic of the eighteenth-century neoclassicists. The Romantics preferred emotional and imaginative expression to rational analysis. They considered the individual to be at the center of all experience and so placed him or her at the center of their art. The Romantics believed that the creative imagination reveals nobler truths—unique feelings and attitudes—than those that could be discovered by logic or by scientific examination. Both the natural world and the state of childhood were important sources for revelations of "eternal truths." "Romanticism" is also used as a general term to refer to a type of sensibility found in all periods of literary history and usually considered to be in opposition to the principles of classicism. In this sense, Romanticism signifies any work or philosophy in which the exotic or dreamlike figure strongly, or that is devoted to individualistic expression, self-analysis, or a pursuit of a higher realm of knowledge than can be discovered by human reason.

Romantics: See *Romanticism*

Russian Symbolism: A Russian poetic movement, derived from French symbolism, that flourished between 1894 and 1910. While some Russian Symbolists continued in the French tradition, stressing aestheticism and the importance of suggestion above didactic intent, others saw their craft as a form of mystical worship, and themselves as mediators between the supernatural and the mundane.

S

Satire: A work that uses ridicule, humor, and wit to criticize and provoke change in human nature and institutions. There are two major types of satire: "formal" or "direct" satire speaks directly to the reader or to a character in the work; "indirect" satire relies upon the ridiculous behavior of its characters to make its point. Formal satire is further divided into two manners: the "Horatian," which ridicules gently, and the "Juvenalian," which derides its subjects harshly and bitterly.

Scansion: The analysis or "scanning" of a poem to determine its meter and often its rhyme scheme. The most common system of scansion uses accents (slanted lines drawn above syllables) to show stressed syllables, breves (curved lines drawn above syllables) to show unstressed syllables, and vertical lines to separate each foot.

Second Person: See *Point of View*

Semiotics: The study of how literary forms and conventions affect the meaning of language.

Sestet: Any six-line poem or stanza.

Setting: The time, place, and culture in which the action of a narrative takes place. The elements of setting may include geographic location, characters' physical and mental environments, prevailing cultural attitudes, or the historical time in which the action takes place.

Shakespearean Sonnet: See *Sonnet*

Signifying Monkey: A popular trickster figure in black folklore, with hundreds of tales about this character documented since the 19th century.

Simile: A comparison, usually using "like" or "as," of two essentially dissimilar things, as in "coffee as cold as ice" or "He sounded like a broken record."

Slang: A type of informal verbal communication that is generally unacceptable for formal writing. Slang words and phrases are often colorful exaggerations used to emphasize the speaker's point; they may also be shortened versions of an often-used word or phrase.

Slant Rhyme: See *Consonance*

Slave Narrative: Autobiographical accounts of American slave life as told by escaped slaves. These works first appeared during the abolition movement of the 1830s through the 1850s.

Social Realism: See *Socialist Realism*

Socialist Realism: The Socialist Realism school of literary theory was proposed by Maxim Gorky and established as a dogma by the first Soviet Congress of Writers. It demanded adherence to a communist worldview in works of literature. Its doctrines required an objective viewpoint comprehensible to the working classes and themes of social struggle featuring strong proletarian heroes.

Soliloquy: A monologue in a drama used to give the audience information and to develop the speaker's character. It is typically a projection of the speaker's innermost thoughts. Usually delivered while the speaker is alone on stage, a soliloquy is intended to present an illusion of unspoken reflection.

Sonnet: A fourteen-line poem, usually composed in iambic pentameter, employing one of several rhyme schemes. There are three major types of sonnets, upon which all other variations of the form are based: the "Petrarchan" or "Italian" sonnet, the "Shakespearean" or "English" sonnet, and the "Spenserian" sonnet. A Petrarchan sonnet consists of an octave rhymed *abbaabba* and a "sestet" rhymed either *cdecde, cdccdc,* or *cdedce*. The octave poses a question or problem, relates a narrative, or puts forth a proposition; the sestet presents a solution to the problem, comments upon the narrative, or applies the proposition put forth in the octave. The Shakespearean sonnet is divided into three quatrains and a couplet rhymed *abab cdcd efef gg*. The couplet provides an epigrammatic comment on the narrative or problem put forth in the quatrains. The Spenserian sonnet uses three quatrains and a couplet like the Shakespearean, but links their three rhyme schemes in this way: *abab bcbc cdcd ee*. The Spenserian sonnet develops its theme in two parts like the Petrarchan, its final six lines resolving a problem, analyzing a narrative, or applying a proposition put forth in its first eight lines.

Spenserian Sonnet: See *Sonnet*

Spenserian Stanza: A nine-line stanza having eight verses in iambic pentameter, its ninth verse in iambic hexameter, and the rhyme scheme ababbcbcc.

Spondee: In poetry meter, a foot consisting of two long or stressed syllables occurring together. This form is quite rare in English verse, and is usually composed of two monosyllabic words.

Sprung Rhythm: Versification using a specific number of accented syllables per line but disregarding the number of unaccented syllables that fall in each line, producing an irregular rhythm in the poem.

Stanza: A subdivision of a poem consisting of lines grouped together, often in recurring patterns of rhyme, line length, and meter. Stanzas may also serve as units of thought in a poem much like paragraphs in prose.

Stereotype: A stereotype was originally the name for a duplication made during the printing process; this led to its modern definition as a person or thing that is (or is assumed to be) the same as all others of its type.

Stream of Consciousness: A narrative technique for rendering the inward experience of a character. This technique is designed to give the impression of an ever-changing series of thoughts, emotions, images, and memories in the spontaneous and seemingly illogical order that they occur in life.

Structuralism: A twentieth-century movement in literary criticism that examines how literary texts arrive at their meanings, rather than the meanings themselves. There are two major types of structuralist analysis: one examines the way patterns of linguistic structures unify a specific text and emphasize certain elements of that text, and the other interprets the way literary forms and conventions affect the meaning of language itself.

Structure: The form taken by a piece of literature. The structure may be made obvious for ease of understanding, as in nonfiction works, or may obscured for artistic purposes, as in some poetry or seemingly "unstructured" prose.

Sturm und Drang: A German term meaning "storm and stress." It refers to a German literary movement of the 1770s and 1780s that reacted against the order and rationalism of the enlightenment, focusing instead on the intense experience of extraordinary individuals.

Style: A writer's distinctive manner of arranging words to suit his or her ideas and purpose in writing. The unique imprint of the author's personality upon his or her writing, style is the product of an author's way of arranging ideas and his or her use of diction, different sentence structures, rhythm, figures of speech, rhetorical principles, and other elements of composition.

Subject: The person, event, or theme at the center of a work of literature. A work may have one or more subjects of each type, with shorter works tending to have fewer and longer works tending to have more.

Subjectivity: Writing that expresses the author's personal feelings about his subject, and which may or may not include factual information about the subject.

Surrealism: A term introduced to criticism by Guillaume Apollinaire and later adopted by Andre Breton. It refers to a French literary and artistic movement founded in the 1920s. The Surrealists sought to express unconscious thoughts and feelings in their works. The best-known technique used for achieving this aim was automatic writing—transcriptions of spontaneous outpourings from the unconscious. The Surrealists proposed to unify the contrary levels of conscious and unconscious, dream and reality, objectivity and subjectivity into a new level of "super-realism."

Suspense: A literary device in which the author maintains the audience's attention through the buildup of events, the outcome of which will soon be revealed.

Syllogism: A method of presenting a logical argument. In its most basic form, the syllogism consists of a major premise, a minor premise, and a conclusion.

Symbol: Something that suggests or stands for something else without losing its original identity. In literature, symbols combine their literal meaning with the suggestion of an abstract concept. Literary symbols are of two types: those that carry complex associations of meaning no matter what their contexts, and those that derive their suggestive meaning from their functions in specific literary works.

Symbolism: This term has two widely accepted meanings. In historical criticism, it denotes an early modernist literary movement initiated in France during the nineteenth century that reacted against the prevailing standards of realism. Writers in this movement aimed to evoke, indirectly and symbolically, an order of being beyond the material world of the five senses. Poetic expression of personal emotion figured strongly in the movement, typically by means of a private set of symbols uniquely identifiable with the individual poet. The principal aim of the Symbolists was to express in words the highly complex feelings that grew out of everyday contact with the world. In a broader sense, the term "symbolism" refers to the use of one object to represent another.

Symbolist: See *Symbolism*

Symbolist Movement: See *Symbolism*

Sympathetic Fallacy: See *Affective Fallacy*

T

Tanka: A form of Japanese poetry similar to *haiku*. A *tanka* is five lines long, with the lines containing five, seven, five, seven, and seven syllables respectively.

Terza Rima: A three-line stanza form in poetry in which the rhymes are made on the last word of each line in the following manner: the first and third lines of the first stanza, then the second line of the first stanza and the first and third lines of the second stanza, and so on with the middle line of any stanza rhyming with the first and third lines of the following stanza.

Tetrameter: See *Meter*

Textual Criticism: A branch of literary criticism that seeks to establish the authoritative text of a literary work. Textual critics typically compare all known manuscripts or printings of a single work in order to assess the meanings of differences and revisions. This procedure allows them to arrive at a definitive version that (supposedly) corresponds to the author's original intention.

Theme: The main point of a work of literature. The term is used interchangeably with thesis.

Thesis: A thesis is both an essay and the point argued in the essay. Thesis novels and thesis plays share the quality of containing a thesis which is supported through the action of the story.

Third Person: See *Point of View*

Tone: The author's attitude toward his or her audience may be deduced from the tone of the work. A formal tone may create distance or convey politeness, while an informal tone may encourage a friendly, intimate, or intrusive feeling in the reader. The author's attitude toward his or her subject matter may also be deduced from the tone of the words he or she uses in discussing it.

Tragedy: A drama in prose or poetry about a noble, courageous hero of excellent character who, because of some tragic character flaw or *hamartia*, brings ruin upon him- or herself. Tragedy treats its subjects in a dignified and serious manner, using poetic language to help evoke pity and fear and bring about catharsis, a purging of these emotions. The tragic form was practiced extensively by the ancient Greeks. In the Middle Ages, when classical works were virtually unknown, tragedy came to denote any works about the fall of persons from exalted to low conditions due to any reason: fate, vice, weakness, etc. According to the classical definition of tragedy, such works present the "pathetic"—that which evokes pity—rather than the tragic. The classical form of tragedy was revived in the sixteenth century; it flourished especially on the Elizabethan stage. In modern times, dramatists have attempted to adapt the form to the needs of modern society by drawing their heroes from the ranks of ordinary men and women and defining the nobility of these heroes in terms of spirit rather than exalted social standing.

Tragic Flaw: In a tragedy, the quality within the hero or heroine which leads to his or her downfall.

Transcendentalism: An American philosophical and religious movement, based in New England from around 1835 until the Civil War. Transcendentalism was a form of American romanticism that had its roots abroad in the works of Thomas Carlyle, Samuel Coleridge, and Johann Wolfgang von Goethe. The Transcendentalists stressed the importance of intuition and subjective experience in communication with God. They rejected religious dogma and texts in favor of mysticism and scientific naturalism. They pursued truths that lie beyond the "colorless" realms perceived by reason and the senses and were active social reformers in public education, women's rights, and the abolition of slavery.

Trickster: A character or figure common in Native American and African literature who uses his ingenuity to defeat enemies and escape difficult situations. Tricksters are most often animals, such as the spider, hare, or coyote, although they may take the form of humans as well.

Trimeter: See *Meter*

Triple Rhyme: See *Rhyme*

Trochee: See *Foot*

U

Understatement: See *Irony*

Unities: Strict rules of dramatic structure, formulated by Italian and French critics of the Renaissance and based loosely on the principles of drama discussed by Aristotle in his *Poetics*.

Foremost among these rules were the three unities of action, time, and place that compelled a dramatist to: (1) construct a single plot with a beginning, middle, and end that details the causal relationships of action and character; (2) restrict the action to the events of a single day; and (3) limit the scene to a single place or city. The unities were observed faithfully by continental European writers until the Romantic Age, but they were never regularly observed in English drama. Modern dramatists are typically more concerned with a unity of impression or emotional effect than with any of the classical unities.

Urban Realism: A branch of realist writing that attempts to accurately reflect the often harsh facts of modern urban existence.

Utopia: A fictional perfect place, such as "paradise" or "heaven."

Utopian: See *Utopia*

Utopianism: See *Utopia*

V

Verisimilitude: Literally, the appearance of truth. In literary criticism, the term refers to aspects of a work of literature that seem true to the reader.

Vers de societe: See *Occasional Verse*

Vers libre: See *Free Verse*

Verse: A line of metered language, a line of a poem, or any work written in verse.

Versification: The writing of verse. Versification may also refer to the meter, rhyme, and other mechanical components of a poem.

Victorian: Refers broadly to the reign of Queen Victoria of England (1837-1901) and to anything with qualities typical of that era. For example, the qualities of smug narrowmindedness, bourgeois materialism, faith in social progress, and priggish morality are often considered Victorian. This stereotype is contradicted by such dramatic intellectual developments as the theories of Charles Darwin, Karl Marx, and Sigmund Freud (which stirred strong debates in England) and the critical attitudes of serious Victorian writers like Charles Dickens and George Eliot. In literature, the Victorian Period was the great age of the English novel, and the latter part of the era saw the rise of movements such as decadence and symbolism.

Victorian Age: See *Victorian*

Victorian Period: See *Victorian*

W

Weltanschauung: A German term referring to a person's worldview or philosophy.

Weltschmerz: A German term meaning "world pain." It describes a sense of anguish about the nature of existence, usually associated with a melancholy, pessimistic attitude.

Z

Zarzuela: A type of Spanish operetta.

Zeitgeist: A German term meaning "spirit of the time." It refers to the moral and intellectual trends of a given era.

Cumulative Author/Title Index

A

A Pièd (McElroy): V3
Accounting (Alegría): V21
Ackerman, Diane
   On Location in the Loire Valley: V19
Acosta, Teresa Palomo
   My Mother Pieced Quilts: V12
Addonizio, Kim
   Knowledge: V25
Address to the Angels (Kumin): V18
After Apple Picking (Frost): V32
The Afterlife (Collins): V18
An African Elegy (Duncan): V13
After Raphael (Brock-Broido): V26
Ah, Are You Digging on My Grave? (Hardy): V4
Ai
   Reunions with a Ghost: V16
Aiken, Conrad
   The Room: V24
Air for Mercury (Hillman): V20
Akhmatova, Anna
   Everything is Plundered: V32
   Midnight Verses: V18
   Requiem: V27
Alabama Centennial (Madgett): V10
The Alchemy of Day (Hébert): V20
Alegría, Claribel
   Accounting: V21
Alexander, Elizabeth
   The Toni Morrison Dreams: V22
All I Was Doing Was Breathing (Mirabai): V24
All It Takes (Phillips): V23
Allegory (Bang): V23
Always (Apollinaire): V24

America, America (Youssef): V29
American Poetry (Simpson): V7
Amichai, Yehuda
   Not like a Cypress: V24
Ammons, A. R.
   The City Limits: V19
Anasazi (Snyder): V9
An Ancient Gesture (Millay): V31
And What If I Spoke of Despair (Bass): V19
Angelou, Maya
   Harlem Hopscotch: V2
   On the Pulse of Morning: V3
   Woman Work: V33
Angle of Geese (Momaday): V2
Annabel Lee (Poe): V9
Anniversary (Harjo): V15
Anonymous
   Barbara Allan: V7
   Go Down, Moses: V11
   Lord Randal: V6
   The Seafarer: V8
   Sir Patrick Spens: V4
   Swing Low Sweet Chariot: V1
Anorexic (Boland): V12
Another Night in the Ruins (Kinnell): V26
Answers to Letters (Tranströmer): V21
An Anthem (Sanchez): V26
Any Human to Another (Cullen): V3
anyone lived in a pretty how town (cummings): V30
Apollinaire, Guillaume
   Always: V24
Apple sauce for Eve (Piercy): V22
Archaic Torso of Apollo (Rilke): V27

Arnold, Matthew
   Dover Beach: V2
Ars Poetica (MacLeish): V5
The Arsenal at Springfield (Longfellow): V17
The Art of the Novel (Sajé): V23
Art Thou the Thing I Wanted (Fulton): V25
An Arundel Tomb (Larkin): V12
Arvio, Sarah
   Memory: V21
As I Walked Out One Evening (Auden): V4
Ashbery, John
   Paradoxes and Oxymorons: V11
   Self-Portrait in a Convex Mirror: V28
Astonishment (Szymborska): V15
At the Bomb Testing Site (Stafford): V8
At the Cancer Clinic (Kooser): V24
An Attempt at Jealousy (Tsvetaeva): V29
Atwood, Margaret
   Siren Song: V7
Auden, W. H.
   As I Walked Out One Evening: V4
   Funeral Blues: V10
   Musée des Beaux Arts: V1
   September 1, 1939: V27
   The Unknown Citizen: V3
Aurora Leigh (Browning): V23
Auto Wreck (Shapiro): V3
Autobiographia Literaria (O'Hara): V34
Autumn Begins in Martins Ferry, Ohio (Wright): V8

B

Babii Yar (Yevtushenko): V29
Baggott, Julianna
   What the Poets Could Have Been: V26
Ballad of Birmingham (Randall): V5
Ballad of Orange and Grape (Rukeyser): V10
Bang, Mary Jo
   Allegory: V23
Baraka, Amiri
   In Memory of Radio: V9
Barbara Allan (Anonymous): V7
Barbarese, J. T.
   Walk Your Body Down: V26
Barbie Doll (Piercy): V9
Barot, Rick
   Bonnard's Garden: V25
Barrett, Elizabeth
   Sonnet 43: V2
The Base Stealer (Francis): V12
Bashō, Matsuo
   Falling Upon Earth: V2
   The Moon Glows the Same: V7
   Temple Bells Die Out: V18
Bass, Ellen
   And What If I Spoke of Despair: V19
Baudelaire, Charles
   Hymn to Beauty: V21
The Bean Eaters (Brooks): V2
Because I Could Not Stop for Death (Dickinson): V2
Bedtime Story (MacBeth): V8
Behn, Robin
   Ten Years after Your Deliberate Drowning: V21
Bell, Marvin
   View: V25
La Belle Dame sans Merci (Keats): V17
The Bells (Poe): V3
Beowulf (Wilbur): V11
Berry, Wendell
   The Peace of Wild Things: V30
Berryman, John
   Dream Song 29: V27
Beware: Do Not Read This Poem (Reed): V6
Beware of Ruins (Hope): V8
Bialosky, Jill
   Seven Seeds: V19
Bidart, Frank
   Curse: V26
Bidwell Ghost (Erdrich): V14
Biele, Joelle
   Rapture: V21
Birch Canoe (Revard): V5
Birches (Frost): V13
Birney, Earle
   Vancouver Lights: V8
A Birthday (Rossetti): V10
Bishop, Elizabeth
   Brazil, January 1, 1502: V6
   Filling Station: V12
   The Fish: V31
   The Man-Moth: V27
The Black Heralds (Vallejo): V26
A Black Man Talks of Reaping (Bontemps): V32
The Black Snake (Oliver): V31
Black Zodiac (Wright): V10
Blackberrying (Plath): V15
Blake, William
   The Fly: V34
   The Lamb: V12
   A Poison Tree: V24
   The Tyger: V2
A Blessing (Wright): V7
"Blighters" (Sassoon): V28
Blood Oranges (Mueller): V13
The Blue Rim of Memory (Levertov): V17
Blumenthal, Michael
   Inventors: V7
Bly, Robert
   Come with Me: V6
   Driving to Town Late to Mail a Letter: V17
Bogan, Louise
   Words for Departure: V21
Boland, Eavan
   Anorexic: V12
   It's a Woman's World: V22
   Outside History: V31
Bonnard's Garden (Barot): V25
Bontemps, Arna
   A Black Man Talks of Reaping: V32
Borges and I (Borges): V27
Borges, Jorge Luis
   Borges and I: V27
The Boy (Hacker): V19
Bradstreet, Anne
   To My Dear and Loving Husband: V6
   Upon the Burning of Our House, July 10th, 1666: V33
Brazil, January 1, 1502 (Bishop): V6
The Bridegroom (Pushkin): V34
Bright Star! Would I Were Steadfast as Thou Art (Keats): V9
Brock-Broido, Lucie
   After Raphael: V26
The Bronze Horseman (Pushkin): V28
Brontë, Emily
   Old Stoic: V33
Brooke, Rupert
   The Soldier: V7
Brooks, Gwendolyn
   The Bean Eaters: V2
   The Explorer: V32
   The Sonnet-Ballad: V1
   Strong Men, Riding Horses: V4
   We Real Cool: V6
Brouwer, Joel
   Last Request: V14
Brown, Fleda
   The Women Who Loved Elvis All Their Lives: V28
Browning, Elizabeth Barrett
   Aurora Leigh: V23
   Sonnet 43: V2
   Sonnet XXIX: V16
Browning, Robert
   My Last Duchess: V1
   Porphyria's Lover: V15
Bryant, William Cullen
   Thanatopsis: V30
Bukowski, Charles
   The Tragedy of the Leaves: V28
Burns, Robert
   A Red, Red Rose: V8
Business (Cruz): V16
The Bustle in a House (Dickinson): V10
But Perhaps God Needs the Longing (Sachs): V20
Butcher Shop (Simic): V7
Byrne, Elena Karina
   In Particular: V20
Byron, Lord
   The Destruction of Sennacherib: V1
   She Walks in Beauty: V14
   When We Two Parted: V29

C

The Canterbury Tales (Chaucer): V14
Cargoes (Masefield): V5
Carroll, Lewis
   Jabberwocky: V11
   The Walrus and the Carpenter: V30
Carruth, Hayden
   I, I, I: V26
Carson, Anne
   New Rule: V18
Carson, Ciaran
   The War Correspondent: V26
Carver, Raymond
   The Cobweb: V17
Casey at the Bat (Thayer): V5
Castillo, Ana
   While I Was Gone a War Began: V21
Cavafy, C. P.
   Ithaka: V19
Cavalry Crossing a Ford (Whitman): V13
Celan, Paul
   Late and Deep: V21

The Centaur (Swenson): V30
Cervantes, Lorna Dee
   Freeway 280: V30
The Chambered Nautilus (Holmes): V24
The Charge of the Light Brigade (Tennyson): V1
Chaucer, Geoffrey
   The Canterbury Tales: V14
Chicago (Sandburg): V3
Childhood (Rilke): V19
Chin, Marilyn
   How I Got That Name: V28
Chocolates (Simpson): V11
Chorale (Young): V25
Christ Climbed Down (Ferlinghetti): V28
The Cinnamon Peeler (Ondaatje): V19
Cisneros, Sandra
   Once Again I Prove the Theory of Relativity: V19
The City Limits (Ammons): V19
Clampitt, Amy
   Iola, Kansas: V27
Classic Ballroom Dances (Simic): V33
Clifton, Lucille
   Climbing: V14
   homage to my hips: V29
   Miss Rosie: V1
Climbing (Clifton): V14
The Cobweb (Carver): V17
Coleridge, Samuel Taylor
   Kubla Khan: V5
   The Rime of the Ancient Mariner: V4
Colibrí (Espada): V16
Collins, Billy
   The Afterlife: V18
Come with Me (Bly): V6
The Constellation Orion (Kooser): V8
Concord Hymn (Emerson): V4
The Conquerors (McGinley): V13
Conscientious Objector (Millay): V34
The Continuous Life (Strand): V18
Conversation with a Stone (Szymborska): V27
Cool Tombs (Sandburg): V6
Cooper, Jane
   Rent: V25
The Cossacks (Pastan): V25
The Country Without a Post Office (Shahid Ali): V18
Courage (Sexton): V14
The Courage That My Mother Had (Millay): V3
Crane, Stephen
   War Is Kind: V9
The Creation (Johnson): V1
Creeley, Robert
   Fading Light: V21
The Cremation of Sam McGee (Service): V10
The Crime Was in Granada (Machado): V23
Cruz, Victor Hernandez
   Business: V16
Cullen, Countee
   Any Human to Another: V3
cummings, e. e.
   anyone lived in a pretty how town: V30
   i was sitting in mcsorley's: V13
   l(a: V1
   maggie and milly and molly and may: V12
   old age sticks: V3
   since feeling is first: V34
   somewhere i have never travelled,gladly beyond: V19
Curse (Bidart): V26
The Czar's Last Christmas Letter. A Barn in the Urals (Dubie): V12

D

Daddy (Plath): V28
The Darkling Thrush (Hardy): V18
Darwin in 1881 (Schnackenberg): V13
Daughter-Mother-Maya-Seeta (Vazirani): V25
Dawe, Bruce
   Drifters: V10
Daylights (Warren): V13
Dear Reader (Tate): V10
The Death of the Ball Turret Gunner (Jarrell): V2
The Death of the Hired Man (Frost): V4
Death Sentences (Lazić): V22
Deep Woods (Nemerov): V14
Dennis, Carl
   The God Who Loves You: V20
The Destruction of Sennacherib (Byron): V1
Dickey, James
   The Heaven of Animals: V6
   The Hospital Window: V11
Dickinson, Emily
   Because I Could Not Stop for Death: V2
   The Bustle in a House: V10
   "Hope" Is the Thing with Feathers: V3
   I Died for Beauty: V28
   I felt a Funeral, in my Brain: V13
   I Heard a Fly Buzz—When I Died—: V5
   Much Madness Is Divinest Sense: V16
   My Life Closed Twice Before Its Close: V8
   A Narrow Fellow in the Grass: V11
   The Soul Selects Her Own Society: V1
   Success Is Counted Sweetest: V32
   There's a Certain Slant of Light: V6
   This Is My Letter to the World: V4
Digging (Heaney): V5
Divakaruni, Chitra Banerjee
   My Mother Combs My Hair: V34
Diving into the Wreck (Rich): V29
Dobyns, Stephen
   It's like This: V23
Do Not Go Gentle into that Good Night (Thomas): V1
Donne, John
   Holy Sonnet 10: V2
   A Valediction: Forbidding Mourning: V11
Doty, Mark
   The Wings: V28
Dove, Rita
   Geometry: V15
   This Life: V1
Dover Beach (Arnold): V2
Dream Song 29 (Berryman): V27
Dream Variations (Hughes): V15
Drifters (Dawe): V10
A Drink of Water (Heaney): V8
Drinking Alone Beneath the Moon (Po): V20
Driving to Town Late to Mail a Letter (Bly): V17
Drought Year (Wright): V8
The Drunken Boat (Rimbaud): V28
Dubie, Norman
   The Czar's Last Christmas Letter. A Barn in the Urals: V12
Du Bois, W. E. B.
   The Song of the Smoke: V13
Duffy, Carol Ann
   Originally: V25
Dugan, Alan
   How We Heard the Name: V10
Dulce et Decorum Est (Owen): V10
Dunbar, Paul Laurence
   Sympathy: V33
Duncan, Robert
   An African Elegy: V13
Dunn, Stephen
   The Reverse Side: V21
Duration (Paz): V18

E

The Eagle (Tennyson): V11
Early in the Morning (Lee): V17
Easter 1916 (Yeats): V5
Eating Poetry (Strand): V9
Ego-Tripping (Giovanni): V28
Elegy for My Father, Who is Not Dead (Hudgins): V14
Elegy Written in a Country Churchyard (Gray): V9

An Elementary School Classroom in a Slum (Spender): V23
Elena (Mora): V33
Eliot, T. S.
   The Hollow Men: V33
   Journey of the Magi: V7
   The Love Song of J. Alfred Prufrock: V1
   The Waste Land: V20
Emerson, Claudia
   My Grandmother's Plot in the Family Cemetery: V27
Emerson, Ralph Waldo
   Concord Hymn: V4
   The Rhodora: V17
   The Snow-Storm: V34
Erdrich, Louise
   Bidwell Ghost: V14
Espada, Martín
   Colibrí: V16
   We Live by What We See at Night: V13
Ethics (Pastan): V8
Everything is Plundered (Akhmatova): V32
The Exhibit (Mueller): V9
The Explorer (Brooks): V32

F

Facing It (Komunyakaa): V5
Fading Light (Creeley): V21
Falling Upon Earth (Bashō): V2
A Far Cry from Africa (Walcott): V6
A Farewell to English (Hartnett): V10
Farrokhzaad, Faroogh
   A Rebirth: V21
Fenton, James
   The Milkfish Gatherers: V11
Ferlinghetti, Lawrence
   Christ Climbed Down: V28
Fern Hill (Thomas): V3
Fiddler Crab (Jacobsen): V23
Fifteen (Stafford): V2
Filling Station (Bishop): V12
Finch, Anne
   A Nocturnal Reverie: V30
Fire and Ice (Frost): V7
The Fish (Bishop): V31
The Fish (Moore): V14
The Fly (Blake): V34
Follower (Heaney): V30
For a New Citizen of These United States (Lee): V15
For An Assyrian Frieze (Viereck): V9
For Jean Vincent D'abbadie, Baron St.-Castin (Nowlan): V12
For Jennifer, 6, on the Teton (Hugo): V17
For the Sake of Strangers (Laux): V24
For the Union Dead (Lowell): V7
For the White poets who would be Indian (Rose): V13
The Force That Through the Green Fuse Drives the Flower (Thomas): V8
Forché, Carolyn
   The Garden Shukkei-en: V18
The Forest (Stewart): V22
Four Mountain Wolves (Silko): V9
Fragment 2 (Sappho): V31
Francis, Robert
   The Base Stealer: V12
Fraser, Kathleen
   Poem in Which My Legs Are Accepted: V29
Freeway 280 (Cervantes): V30
From the Rising of the Sun (Milosz): V29
Frost, Robert
   After Apple Picking: V32
   Birches: V13
   The Death of the Hired Man: V4
   Fire and Ice: V7
   Mending Wall: V5
   Nothing Gold Can Stay: V3
   Out, Out—: V10
   The Road Not Taken: V2
   Stopping by Woods on a Snowy Evening: V1
   The Wood-Pile: V6
Fu, Tu
   Jade Flower Palace: V32
Fully Empowered (Neruda): V33
Fulton, Alice
   Art Thou the Thing I Wanted: V25
Funeral Blues (Auden): V10

G

Gacela of the Dark Death (García Lorca): V20
Gallagher, Tess
   I Stop Writing the Poem: V16
García Lorca, Federico
   Gacela of the Dark Death: V20
   Lament for Ignacio Sánchez Mejías: V31
The Garden Shukkei-en (Forché): V18
Geometry (Dove): V15
Ghazal (Spires): V21
Ginsberg, Allen
   Howl: V29
   A Supermarket in California: V5
Gioia, Dana
   The Litany: V24
Giovanni, Nikki
   Ego-Tripping: V28
   Knoxville, Tennessee: V17
Glück, Louise
   The Gold Lily: V5
   The Mystery: V15
Go Down, Moses (Anonymous): V11
Goblin Market (Rossetti): V27
The God Who Loves You (Dennis): V20
The Gold Lily (Glück): V5
Good Night, Willie Lee, I'll See You in the Morning (Walker): V30
Goodison, Lorna
   The River Mumma Wants Out: V25
A Grafted Tongue (Montague): V12
Graham, Jorie
   The Hiding Place: V10
   Mind: V17
Grandmother (Mort): V34
Gray, Thomas
   Elegy Written in a Country Churchyard: V9
The Greatest Grandeur (Rogers): V18
Gregg, Linda
   A Thirst Against: V20
Grennan, Eamon
   Station: V21
Grudnow (Pastan): V32
Gunn, Thom
   The Missing: V9

H

H.D.
   Helen: V6
   Sea Rose: V28
Hacker, Marilyn
   The Boy: V19
Hahn, Kimiko
   Pine: V23
Hall, Donald
   Names of Horses: V8
HaNagid, Shmuel
   Two Eclipses: V33
Hanging Fire (Lorde): V32
Hardy, Thomas
   Ah, Are You Digging on My Grave?: V4
   The Darkling Thrush: V18
   The Man He Killed: V3
Harjo, Joy
   Anniversary: V15
   Remember: V32
Harlem (Hughes): V1
Harlem Hopscotch (Angelou): V2
Hartnett, Michael
   A Farewell to English: V10
Hashimoto, Sharon
   What I Would Ask My Husband's Dead Father: V22
Having a Coke with You (O'Hara): V12
Having it Out with Melancholy (Kenyon): V17
Hawk Roosting (Hughes): V4
Hayden, Robert
   Runagate Runagate: V31
   Those Winter Sundays: V1

Heaney, Seamus
   Digging: V5
   A Drink of Water: V8
   Follower: V30
   Midnight: V2
   The Singer's House: V17
Heart's Needle (Snodgrass): V29
The Heaven of Animals (Dickey): V6
Hébert, Anne
   The Alchemy of Day: V20
Hecht, Anthony
   "More Light! More Light!": V6
The Heights of Macchu Picchu (Neruda): V28
Hejinian, Lyn
   Yet we insist that life is full of happy chance: V27
Helen (H.D.): V6
Herbert, George
   Virtue: V25
Herbert, Zbigniew
   Why The Classics: V22
Herrick, Robert
   The Night Piece: To Julia: V29
   To the Virgins, to Make Much of Time: V13
The Hiding Place (Graham): V10
High Windows (Larkin): V3
The Highwayman (Noyes): V4
Hillman, Brenda
   Air for Mercury: V20
The Hippopotamus (Nash): V31
Hirsch, Edward
   Omen: V22
Hirshfield, Jane
   Three Times My Life Has Opened: V16
His Speed and Strength (Ostriker): V19
Hoagland, Tony
   Social Life: V19
The Hollow Men (Eliot): V33
Holmes, Oliver Wendell
   The Chambered Nautilus: V24
   Old Ironsides: V9
Holy Sonnet 10 (Donne): V2
homage to my hips (Clifton): V29
Hongo, Garrett
   The Legend: V25
   What For: V33
Hope, A. D.
   Beware of Ruins: V8
Hope Is a Tattered Flag (Sandburg): V12
"Hope" Is the Thing with Feathers (Dickinson): V3
Hopkins, Gerard Manley
   Pied Beauty: V26
The Horizons of Rooms (Merwin): V15
The Horses (Hughes): V32
The Hospital Window (Dickey): V11

Housman, A. E.
   To an Athlete Dying Young: V7
   When I Was One-and-Twenty: V4
How I Got That Name (Chin): V28
How We Heard the Name (Dugan): V10
Howe, Marie
   What Belongs to Us: V15
Howl (Ginsberg): V29
Hudgins, Andrew
   Elegy for My Father, Who is Not Dead: V14
Hugh Selwyn Mauberley (Pound): V16
Hughes, Langston
   Dream Variations: V15
   I, Too: V30
   Harlem: V1
   Mother to Son: V3
   The Negro Speaks of Rivers: V10
   Theme for English B: V6
Hughes, Ted
   Hawk Roosting: V4
   The Horses: V32
   Perfect Light: V19
Hugo, Richard
   For Jennifer, 6, on the Teton: V17
Hum (Lauterbach): V25
Hunger in New York City (Ortiz): V4
Huong, Ho Xuan
   Spring-Watching Pavilion: V18
Hurt Hawks (Jeffers): V3
Huswifery (Taylor): V31
Hymn to Aphrodite (Sappho): V20
Hymn to Beauty (Baudelaire): V21

I

I Died for Beauty (Dickinson): V28
I felt a Funeral, in my Brain (Dickinson): V13
I Go Back to May 1937 (Olds): V17
I Hear America Singing (Whitman): V3
I Heard a Fly Buzz—When I Died— (Dickinson): V5
I, I, I (Carruth): V26
I Stop Writing the Poem (Gallagher): V16
I, Too (Hughes): V30
I Wandered Lonely as a Cloud (Wordsworth): V33
i was sitting in mcsorley's (cummings): V13
The Idea of Order at Key West (Stevens): V13
If (Kipling): V22
In a Station of the Metro (Pound): V2
In Flanders Fields (McCrae): V5
In Memory of Radio (Baraka): V9
In Particular (Byrne): V20

In Response to Executive Order 9066: All Americans of Japanese Descent Must Report to Relocation Centers (Okita): V32
In the Land of Shinar (Levertov): V7
In the Suburbs (Simpson): V14
Incident in a Rose Garden (Justice): V14
Inventors (Blumentha): V7
Iola, Kansas (Clampitt): V27
An Irish Airman Foresees His Death (Yeats): V1
Island of the Three Marias (Ríos): V11
Ithaka (Cavafy): V19
It's a Woman's World (Boland): V22
It's like This (Dobyns): V23

J

Jabberwocky (Carroll): V11
Jacobsen, Josephine
   Fiddler Crab: V23
Jade Flower Palace (Fu): V32
Jarrell, Randall
   The Death of the Ball Turret Gunner: V2
   Losses: V31
Jazz Fantasia (Sandburg): V33
Jeffers, Robinson
   Hurt Hawks: V3
   Shine Perishing Republic: V4
Johnson, James Weldon
   The Creation: V1
Jonson, Ben
   On My First Son: V33
   Song: To Celia: V23
Journey of the Magi (Eliot): V7
Justice, Donald
   Incident in a Rose Garden: V14

K

Keats, John
   La Belle Dame sans Merci : V17
   Bright Star! Would I Were Steadfast as Thou Art: V9
   Ode on a Grecian Urn : V1
   Ode to a Nightingale: V3
   On the Grasshopper and the Cricket: V32
   When I Have Fears that I May Cease to Be: V2
Kelly, Brigit Pegeen
   The Satyr's Heart: V22
Kenyon, Jane
   Having it Out with Melancholy: V17
   "Trouble with Math in a One-Room Country School": V9
Kilroy: (Viereck): V14
Kim, Sue (Suji) Kwock
   Monologue for an Onion: V24

Kindness (Nye): V24
King James Bible
   Psalm 8: V9
   Psalm 23: V4
Kinnell, Galway
   Another Night in the Ruins: V26
   Saint Francis and the Sow: V9
Kipling, Rudyard
   If: V22
Kizer, Carolyn
   To an Unknown Poet: V18
Knowledge (Addonizio): V25
Knoxville, Tennessee (Giovanni): V17
Koch, Kenneth
   Paradiso: V20
Komunyakaa, Yusef
   Facing It: V5
   Ode to a Drum: V20
   Slam, Dunk, & Hook: V30
Kooser, Ted
   At the Cancer Clinic: V24
   The Constellation Orion: V8
Kubla Khan (Coleridge): V5
Kumin, Maxine
   Address to the Angels: V18
Kunitz, Stanley
   The War Against the Trees: V11
Kyger, Joanne
   September: V23

L

l(a (cummings): V1
The Lady of Shalott (Tennyson): V15
Lake (Warren): V23
The Lake Isle of Innisfree (Yeats): V15
The Lamb (Blake): V12
Lament for Ignacio Sánchez Mejías (Lorca): V31
Lament for the Dorsets (Purdy): V5
Landscape with Tractor (Taylor): V10
Lanier, Sidney
   Song of the Chattahoochee: V14
Larkin, Philip
   An Arundel Tomb: V12
   High Windows: V3
   Toads: V4
The Last Question (Parker): V18
Last Request (Brouwer): V14
Late and Deep (Celan): V21
Lauterbach, Ann
   Hum: V25
Laux, Dorianne
   For the Sake of Strangers: V24
Lawrence, D. H.
   Piano: V6
Layton, Irving
   A Tall Man Executes a Jig: V12
Lazić, Radmila
   Death Sentences: V22

Leda and the Swan (Yeats): V13
Lee, Li-Young
   Early in the Morning: V17
   For a New Citizen of These United States: V15
   The Weight of Sweetness: V11
The Legend (Hongo): V25
Lepidopterology (Svenbro): V23
Levertov, Denise
   The Blue Rim of Memory: V17
   In the Land of Shinar: V7
   A Tree Telling of Orpheus: V31
Leviathan (Merwin): V5
Levine, Philip
   Starlight: V8
Lim, Shirley Geok-lin
   Pantoun for Chinese Women: V29
Lineage (Walker): V31
The Litany (Gioia): V24
Longfellow, Henry Wadsworth
   The Arsenal at Springfield: V17
   Paul Revere's Ride: V2
   A Psalm of Life: V7
   The Wreck of the Hesperus: V31
Lord Randal (Anonymous): V6
Lorde, Audre
   Hanging Fire: V32
   What My Child Learns of the Sea: V16
Losses (Jarrell): V31
Lost in Translation (Merrill): V23
Lost Sister (Song): V5
The Lotus Flowers (Voigt): V33
Love Calls Us to the Things of This World (Wilbur): V29
The Love Song of J. Alfred Prufrock (Eliot): V1
Lovelace, Richard
   To Althea, From Prison: V34
   To Lucasta, Going to the Wars: V32
Lowell, Amy
   The Taxi: V30
Lowell, Robert
   For the Union Dead: V7
   The Quaker Graveyard in Nantucket: V6
Loy, Mina
   Moreover, the Moon: V20

M

MacBeth, George
   Bedtime Story: V8
Machado, Antonio
   The Crime Was in Granada: V23
MacLeish, Archibald
   Ars Poetica: V5
Madgett, Naomi Long
   Alabama Centennial: V10
maggie and milly and molly and may (cummings): V12
Malroux, Claire
   Morning Walk: V21

The Man He Killed (Hardy): V3
The Man-Moth (Bishop): V27
Marlowe, Christopher
   The Passionate Shepherd to His Love: V22
A Martian Sends a Postcard Home (Raine): V7
Marvell, Andrew
   To His Coy Mistress: V5
Masefield, John
   Cargoes: V5
Mastectomy (Ostriker): V26
Maternity (Swir): V21
Matsuo Bashō
   Falling Upon Earth: V2
   The Moon Glows the Same: V7
   Temple Bells Die Out: V18
Maxwell, Glyn
   The Nerve: V23
McCrae, John
   In Flanders Fields: V5
McElroy, Colleen
   A Pièd: V3
McGinley, Phyllis
   The Conquerors: V13
   Reactionary Essay on Applied Science: V9
McHugh, Heather
   Three To's and an Oi: V24
McKay, Claude
   The Tropics in New York: V4
Meeting the British (Muldoon): V7
Memoir (Van Duyn): V20
Memory (Arvio): V21
Mending Wall (Frost): V5
Merlin Enthralled (Wilbur): V16
Merriam, Eve
   Onomatopoeia: V6
Merrill, James
   Lost in Translation: V23
Merwin, W. S.
   The Horizons of Rooms: V15
   Leviathan: V5
Metamorphoses (Ovid): V22
Midnight (Heaney): V2
Midnight Verses (Akhmatova): V18
Midsummer, Tobago (Walcott): V34
The Milkfish Gatherers (Fenton): V11
Millay, Edna St. Vincent
   An Ancient Gesture: V31
   Conscientious Objector: V34
   The Courage That My Mother Had: V3
   Wild Swans: V17
Milosz, Czeslaw
   From the Rising of the Sun: V29
   Song of a Citizen: V16
Milton, John
   [On His Blindness] Sonnet 16: V3
   On His Having Arrived at the Age of Twenty-Three: V17
Mind (Graham): V17

Mirabai
  All I Was Doing Was Breathing: V24
Mirror (Plath): V1
Miss Rosie (Clifton): V1
The Missing (Gunn): V9
Momaday, N. Scott
  Angle of Geese: V2
  To a Child Running With Outstretched Arms in Canyon de Chelly: V11
Monologue for an Onion (Kim): V24
Montague, John
  A Grafted Tongue: V12
Montale, Eugenio
  On the Threshold: V22
The Moon Glows the Same (Bashō): V7
Moore, Marianne
  The Fish: V14
  Poetry: V17
Mora, Pat
  Elena: V33
"More Light! More Light!" (Hecht): V6
Moreover, the Moon (Loy): V20
Morning Walk (Malroux): V21
Mort, Valzhyna
  Grandmother: V34
Mother to Son (Hughes): V3
Much Madness Is Divinest Sense (Dickinson): V16
Muldoon, Paul
  Meeting the British: V7
  Pineapples and Pomegranates: V22
Mueller, Lisel
  Blood Oranges: V13
  The Exhibit: V9
Musée des Beaux Arts (Auden): V1
Mushrooms (Plath): V33
Music Lessons (Oliver): V8
Muske-Dukes, Carol
  Our Side: V24
My Father's Song (Ortiz): V16
My Grandmother's Plot in the Family Cemetery (Emerson): V27
My Last Duchess (Browning): V1
My Life Closed Twice Before Its Close (Dickinson): V8
My Mother Combs My Hair (Divakaruni): V34
My Mother Pieced Quilts (Acosta): V12
My Papa's Waltz (Roethke): V3
The Mystery (Glück): V15

N

Names of Horses (Hall): V8
A Narrow Fellow in the Grass (Dickinson): V11

Nash, Ogden
  The Hippopotamus: V31
Native Guard (Trethewey): V29
The Negro Speaks of Rivers (Hughes): V10
Nemerov, Howard
  Deep Woods: V14
  The Phoenix: V10
Neruda, Pablo
  Fully Empowered: V33
  The Heights of Macchu Picchu: V28
  Tonight I Can Write: V11
The Nerve (Maxwell): V23
New Rule (Carson): V18
The Night Piece: To Julia (Herrick): V29
A Nocturnal Reverie (Finch): V30
A Noiseless Patient Spider (Whitman): V31
Not like a Cypress (Amichai): V24
Not Waving but Drowning (Smith): V3
Nothing Gold Can Stay (Frost): V3
Nowlan, Alden
  For Jean Vincent D'abbadie, Baron St.-Castin: V12
Noyes, Alfred
  The Highwayman: V4
Nye, Naomi Shihab
  Kindness: V24
  Shoulders: V33
The Nymph's Reply to the Shepherd (Raleigh): V14

O

O Captain! My Captain! (Whitman): V2
Ode on a Grecian Urn (Keats): V1
Ode to a Drum (Komunyakaa): V20
Ode to a Nightingale (Keats): V3
Ode to the West Wind (Shelley): V2
O'Hara, Frank
  Autobiographia Literaria: V34
  Having a Coke with You: V12
  Why I Am Not a Painter: V8
Okita, Dwight
  In Response to Executive Order 9066: All Americans of Japanese Descent Must Report to Relocation Centers: V32
old age sticks (cummings): V3
Old Ironsides (Holmes): V9
Olds, Sharon
  I Go Back to May 1937: V17
Old Stoic (Brontë): V33
Oliver, Mary
  The Black Snake: V31
  Music Lessons: V8
  Wild Geese: V15
Omen (Hirsch): V22
On Being Brought from Africa to America (Wheatley): V29

On Freedom's Ground (Wilbur): V12
[On His Blindness] Sonnet 16 (Milton): V3
On His Having Arrived at the Age of Twenty-Three (Milton): V17
On Location in the Loire Valley (Ackerman): V19
On My First Son (Jonson): V33
On the Grasshopper and the Cricket (Keats): V32
On the Pulse of Morning (Angelou): V3
On the Threshold (Montale): V22
Once Again I Prove the Theory of Relativity (Cisneros): V19
Ondaatje, Michael
  The Cinnamon Peeler: V19
  To a Sad Daughter: V8
One Is One (Ponsot): V24
One of the Smallest (Stern): V26
Onomatopoeia (Merriam): V6
Oranges (Soto): V30
Ordinary Words (Stone): V19
Originally (Duffy): V25
Ortiz, Simon
  Hunger in New York City: V4
  My Father's Song: V16
Ostriker, Alicia
  His Speed and Strength: V19
  Mastectomy: V26
Our Side (Muske-Dukes): V24
Out, Out— (Frost): V10
Outside History (Boland): V31
Overture to a Dance of Locomotives (Williams): V11
Ovid, (Naso, Publius Ovidius)
  Metamorphoses: V22
Owen, Wilfred
  Dulce et Decorum Est: V10
Oysters (Sexton): V4
Ozymandias (Shelley): V27

P

Pantoun for Chinese Women (Lim): V29
Paradiso (Koch): V20
Paradoxes and Oxymorons (Ashbery): V11
Parker, Dorothy
  The Last Question: V18
The Passionate Shepherd to His Love (Marlowe): V22
Pastan, Linda
  The Cossacks: V25
  Ethics: V8
  Grudnow: V32
Paul Revere's Ride (Longfellow): V2
Pavese, Cesare
  Two Poems for T.: V20
Paz, Octavio
  Duration: V18
  Sunstone: V30

The Peace of Wild Things (Berry): V30
Perfect Light (Hughes): V19
Phillips, Carl
   All It Takes: V23
The Phoenix (Nemerov): V10
Piano (Lawrence): V6
Pied Beauty (Hopkins): V26
Piercy, Marge
   Apple sauce for Eve: V22
   Barbie Doll: V9
   To Be of Use: V32
Pine (Hahn): V23
Pineapples and Pomegranates (Muldoon): V22
Pinsky, Robert
   Song of Reasons: V18
Plath, Sylvia
   Blackberrying: V15
   Daddy: V28
   Mirror: V1
   Mushrooms: V33
A Psalm of Life (Longfellow): V7
Po, Li
   Drinking Alone Beneath the Moon: V20
Poe, Edgar Allan
   Annabel Lee: V9
   The Bells: V3
   The Raven: V1
Poem in Which My Legs Are Accepted (Fraser): V29
Poetry (Moore): V17
A Poison Tree (Blake): V24
Ponsot, Marie
   One Is One: V24
Pope, Alexander
   The Rape of the Lock: V12
Porphyria's Lover (Browning): V15
Portrait of a Couple at Century's End (Santos): V24
Possibilities (Szymborska): V34
Pound, Ezra
   Hugh Selwyn Mauberley: V16
   In a Station of the Metro: V2
   The River-Merchant's Wife: A Letter: V8
Practice (Voigt): V23
Proem (Tennyson): V19
Psalm 8 (King James Bible): V9
Psalm 23 (King James Bible): V4
Purdy, Al
   Lament for the Dorsets: V5
   Wilderness Gothic: V12
Pushkin, Alexander
   The Bridegroom: V34
   The Bronze Horseman: V28

Q

The Quaker Graveyard in Nantucket (Lowell): V6
Queen-Ann's-Lace (Williams): V6

R

Raine, Craig
   A Martian Sends a Postcard Home: V7
Raleigh, Walter, Sir
   The Nymph's Reply to the Shepherd: V14
Ramanujan, A. K.
   Waterfalls in a Bank: V27
Randall, Dudley
   Ballad of Birmingham: V5
The Rape of the Lock (Pope): V12
Rapture (Biele): V21
The Raven (Poe): V1
Reactionary Essay on Applied Science (McGinley): V9
A Rebirth (Farrokhzaad): V21
A Red, Red Rose (Burns): V8
The Red Wheelbarrow (Williams): V1
Reed, Ishmael
   Beware: Do Not Read This Poem: V6
Remember (Harjo): V32
Remember (Rossetti): V14
Rent (Cooper): V25
Requiem (Akhmatova): V27
Reunions with a Ghost (Ai): V16
Revard, Carter
   Birch Canoe: V5
The Reverse Side (Dunn): V21
The Rhodora (Emerson): V17
Rich, Adrienne
   Diving into the Wreck: V29
   Rusted Legacy: V15
Richard Cory (Robinson): V4
Rilke, Rainer Maria
   Archaic Torso of Apollo: V27
   Childhood: V19
Rimbaud, Arthur
   The Drunken Boat: V28
The Rime of the Ancient Mariner (Coleridge): V4
Rios, Alberto
   Island of the Three Marias: V11
The River-Merchant's Wife: A Letter (Pound): V8
The River Mumma Wants Out (Goodison): V25
The Road Not Taken (Frost): V2
Robinson, E. A.
   Richard Cory: V4
Roethke, Theodore
   My Papa's Waltz: V3
   The Waking: V34
Rogers, Pattiann
   The Greatest Grandeur: V18
The Room (Aiken): V24
Rose, Wendy
   For the White poets who would be Indian: V13
Rossetti, Christina
   A Birthday: V10
   Goblin Market: V27
   Remember: V14
   Up-Hill: V34
Ruefle, Mary
   Sentimental Education: V26
Rukeyser, Muriel
   Ballad of Orange and Grape: V10
   St. Roach: V29
Runagate Runagate (Hayden): V31
Russian Letter (Yau): V26
Rusted Legacy (Rich): V15

S

Sachs, Nelly
   But Perhaps God Needs the Longing: V20
Sailing to Byzantium (Yeats): V2
Saint Francis and the Sow (Kinnell): V9
Sajé, Natasha
   The Art of the Novel: V23
Salter, Mary Jo
   Trompe l'Oeil: V22
Sanchez, Sonia
   An Anthem: V26
Sandburg, Carl
   Chicago: V3
   Cool Tombs: V6
   Hope Is a Tattered Flag: V12
   Jazz Fantasia: V33
Santos, Sherod
   Portrait of a Couple at Century's End: V24
Sappho
   Fragment 2: V31
   Hymn to Aphrodite: V20
Sassoon, Siegfried
   "Blighters": V28
A Satirical Elegy on the Death of a Late Famous General (Swift): V27
The Satyr's Heart (Kelly): V22
Schnackenberg, Gjertrud
   Darwin in 1881: V13
   Supernatural Love: V25
Sea Rose (H.D.): V28
The Seafarer (Anonymous): V8
The Second Coming (Yeats): V7
Seeing You (Valentine): V24
Self-Portrait (Zagajewski): V25
Self-Portrait in a Convex Mirror (Ashbery): V28
Sentimental Education (Ruefle): V26
September (Kyger): V23
September 1, 1939 (Auden): V27
Service, Robert W.
   The Cremation of Sam McGee: V10
Seven Seeds (Bialosky): V19

Sexton, Anne
    Courage: V14
    Oysters: V4
    Young: V30
Shahid Ali, Agha
    The Country Without a Post Office: V18
Shakespeare, William
    Sonnet 18: V2
    Sonnet 19: V9
    Sonnet 29: V8
    Sonnet 30: V4
    Sonnet 55: V5
    Sonnet 116: V3
    Sonnet 130: V1
Shapiro, Karl
    Auto Wreck: V3
She Walks in Beauty (Byron): V14
Shelley, Percy Bysshe
    Ode to the West Wind: V2
    Ozymandias: V27
    To a Sky-Lark: V32
Shine, Perishing Republic (Jeffers): V4
Shoulders (Nye): V33
Sidney, Philip
    Ye Goatherd Gods: V30
Silko, Leslie Marmon
    Four Mountain Wolves: V9
    Story from Bear Country: V16
Simic, Charles
    Butcher Shop: V7
    Classic Ballroom Dances: V33
Simpson, Louis
    American Poetry: V7
    Chocolates: V11
    In the Suburbs: V14
since feeling is first (Cummings): V34
The Singer's House (Heaney): V17
Sir Patrick Spens (Anonymous): V4
Siren Song (Atwood): V7
60 (Tagore): V18
Slam, Dunk, & Hook (Komunyakaa): V30
Small Town with One Road (Soto): V7
Smart and Final Iris (Tate): V15
Smith, Stevie
    Not Waving but Drowning: V3
Snodgrass, W. D.
    Heart's Needle: V29
The Snow-Storm (Emerson): V34
Snyder, Gary
    Anasazi: V9
    True Night: V19
Social Life (Hoagland): V19
The Soldier (Brooke): V7
Some People Like Poetry (Szymborska): V31
somewhere i have never travelled,gladly beyond (cummings): V19

Song, Cathy
    Lost Sister: V5
Song of a Citizen (Milosz): V16
Song of Reasons (Pinsky): V18
Song of the Chattahoochee (Lanier): V14
The Song of the Smoke (Du Bois): V13
Song: To Celia (Jonson): V23
Sonnet 16 [On His Blindness] (Milton): V3
Sonnet 18 (Shakespeare): V2
Sonnet 19 (Shakespeare): V9
Sonnet 29 (Shakespeare): V8
Sonnet 30 (Shakespeare): V4
Sonnet XXIX (Browning): V16
Sonnet 43 (Browning): V2
Sonnet 55 (Shakespeare): V5
Sonnet 75 (Spenser): V32
Sonnet 116 (Shakespeare): V3
Sonnet 130 (Shakespeare): V1
The Sonnet-Ballad (Brooks): V1
Soto, Gary
    Oranges: V30
    Small Town with One Road: V7
The Soul Selects Her Own Society (Dickinson): V1
Southbound on the Freeway (Swenson): V16
Soyinka, Wole
    Telephone Conversation: V27
Spender, Stephen
    An Elementary School Classroom in a Slum: V23
Spenser, Edmund
    Sonnet 75: V32
Spires, Elizabeth
    Ghazal: V21
Spring-Watching Pavilion (Huong): V18
St. Roach (Rukeyser): V29
Stafford, William
    At the Bomb Testing Site: V8
    Fifteen: V2
    Ways to Live: V16
Starlight (Levine): V8
Station (Grennan): V21
Stern, Gerald
    One of the Smallest: V26
Stevens, Wallace
    The Idea of Order at Key West: V13
    Sunday Morning: V16
Stewart, Susan
    The Forest: V22
The Stolen Child (Yeats): V34
Stone, Ruth
    Ordinary Words: V19
Stopping by Woods on a Snowy Evening (Frost): V1
Storm Ending (Toomer): V31
Story from Bear Country (Silko): V16

Strand, Mark
    The Continuous Life: V18
    Eating Poetry: V9
Strong Men, Riding Horses (Brooks): V4
Success Is Counted Sweetest (Dickinson): V32
Sunday Morning (Stevens): V16
Sunstone (Paz): V30
A Supermarket in California (Ginsberg): V5
Supernatural Love (Schnackenberg): V25
Svenbro, Jesper
    Lepidopterology: V23
Swenson, May
    The Centaur: V30
    Southbound on the Freeway: V16
Swift, Jonathan
    A Satirical Elegy on the Death of a Late Famous General: V27
Swing Low Sweet Chariot (Anonymous): V1
Swir, Anna
    Maternity: V21
Sympathy (Dunbar): V33
Szymborska, Wisława
    Astonishment: V15
    Conversation with a Stone: V27
    Possibilities: V34
    Some People Like Poetry: V31

T

Tagore, Rabindranath
    60: V18
A Tall Man Executes a Jig (Layton): V12
Tate, James
    Dear Reader: V10
    Smart and Final Iris: V15
The Taxi (Lowell): V30
Taylor, Edward
    Huswifery: V31
Taylor, Henry
    Landscape with Tractor: V10
Tears, Idle Tears (Tennyson): V4
Teasdale, Sara
    There Will Come Soft Rains: V14
Telephone Conversation (Soyinka): V27
Temple Bells Die Out (Bashō): V18
Ten Years after Your Deliberate Drowning (Behn): V21
Tennyson, Alfred, Lord
    The Charge of the Light Brigade: V1
    The Eagle: V11
    The Lady of Shalott: V15
    Proem: V19
    Tears, Idle Tears: V4
    Ulysses: V2

Thanatopsis (Bryant): V30
Thayer, Ernest Lawrence
  Casey at the Bat: V5
Theme for English B (Hughes): V6
There's a Certain Slant of Light (Dickinson): V6
There Will Come Soft Rains (Teasdale): V14
A Thirst Against (Gregg): V20
This Is Just to Say (Williams): V34
This Life (Dove): V1
Thomas, Dylan
  Do Not Go Gentle into that Good Night: V1
  Fern Hill: V3
  The Force That Through the Green Fuse Drives the Flower: V8
Those Winter Sundays (Hayden): V1
Three Times My Life Has Opened (Hirshfield): V16
Three To's and an Oi (McHugh): V24
Tintern Abbey (Wordsworth): V2
To a Child Running With Outstretched Arms in Canyon de Chelly (Momaday): V11
To a Sad Daughter (Ondaatje): V8
To a Sky-Lark (Shelley): V32
To Althea, From Prison (Lovelace): V34
To an Athlete Dying Young (Housman): V7
To an Unknown Poet (Kizer): V18
To Be of Use (Piercy): V32
To His Coy Mistress (Marvell): V5
To His Excellency General Washington (Wheatley): V13
To Lucasta, Going to the Wars (Lovelace): V32
To My Dear and Loving Husband (Bradstreet): V6
To the Virgins, to Make Much of Time (Herrick): V13
Toads (Larkin): V4
Tonight I Can Write (Neruda): V11
The Toni Morrison Dreams (Alexander): V22
Toomer, Jean
  Storm Ending: V31
The Tragedy of the Leaves (Bukowski): V28
Tranströmer, Tomas
  Answers to Letters: V21
A Tree Telling of Orpheus (Levertov): V31
Trethewey, Natasha
  Native Guard: V29
Trompe l'Oeil (Salter): V22
The Tropics in New York (McKay): V4
True Night (Snyder): V19
Tsvetaeva, Marina
  An Attempt at Jealousy: V29

Two Eclipses (HaNagid): V33
Two Poems for T. (Pavese): V20
The Tyger (Blake): V2

U
Ulysses (Tennyson): V2
Ungaretti, Giuseppe
  Variations on Nothing: V20
The Unknown Citizen (Auden): V3
Up-Hill (Rossetti): V34
Upon the Burning of Our House, July 10th, 1666 (Bradstreet): V33

V
A Valediction: Forbidding Mourning (Donne): V11
Valentine, Jean
  Seeing You: V24
Vallejo, César
  The Black Heralds: V26
Van Duyn, Mona
  Memoir: V20
Vancouver Lights (Birney): V8
Variations on Nothing (Ungaretti): V20
Vazirani, Reetika
  Daughter-Mother-Maya-Seeta: V25
Viereck, Peter
  For An Assyrian Frieze: V9
  Kilroy: V14
View (Bell): V25
Virtue (Herbert): V25
Voigt, Ellen Bryant
  The Lotus Flowers: V33
  Practice: V23

W
Walcott, Derek
  A Far Cry from Africa: V6
  Midsummer, Tobago: V34
Waldner, Liz
  Witness: V26
Walker, Alice
  Good Night, Willie Lee, I'll See You in the Morning: V30
  Women: V34
Walker, Margaret
  Lineage: V31
Walk Your Body Down (Barbarese): V26
The Walrus and the Carpenter (Carroll): V30
The Waking (Roethke): V34
The War Against the Trees (Kunitz): V11
The War Correspondent (Carson): V26
War Is Kind (Crane): V9
Warren, Rosanna
  Daylights: V13
  Lake: V23

The Waste Land (Eliot): V20
Waterfalls in a Bank (Ramanujan): V27
Ways to Live (Stafford): V16
We Live by What We See at Night (Espada): V13
We Real Cool (Brooks): V6
The Weight of Sweetness (Lee): V11
What Belongs to Us (Howe): V15
What For (Hongo): V33
What I Would Ask My Husband's Dead Father (Hashimoto): V22
What My Child Learns of the Sea (Lorde): V16
What the Poets Could Have Been (Baggott): V26
Wheatley, Phillis
  On Being Brought from Africa to America: V29
  To His Excellency General Washington: V13
When I Have Fears That I May Cease to Be (Keats): V2
When I Heard the Learn'd Astronomer (Whitman): V22
When I Was One-and-Twenty (Housman): V4
When We Two Parted (Byron): V29
While I Was Gone a War Began (Castillo): V21
Whitman, Walt
  Cavalry Crossing a Ford: V13
  I Hear America Singing: V3
  A Noiseless Patient Spider: V31
  O Captain! My Captain!: V2
  When I Heard the Learn'd Astronomer: V22
Whoso List to Hunt (Wyatt): V25
Why I Am Not a Painter (O'Hara): V8
Why The Classics (Herbert): V22
Wilbur, Richard
  Beowulf: V11
  Love Calls Us to the Things of This World: V29
  Merlin Enthralled: V16
  On Freedom's Ground: V12
Wild Geese (Oliver): V15
Wild Swans (Millay): V17
Wilderness Gothic (Purdy): V12
Williams, William Carlos
  Overture to a Dance of Locomotives: V11
  Queen-Ann's-Lace: V6
  The Red Wheelbarrow: V1
  This Is Just to Say: V34
The Wings (Doty): V28
Witness (Waldner): V26
Woman Work (Angelou): V33
Women (Walker): V34
The Women Who Loved Elvis All Their Lives (Brown): V28

The Wood-Pile (Frost): V6
Words for Departure (Bogan): V21
Wordsworth, William
   I Wandered Lonely as a Cloud: V33
   Lines Composed a Few Miles above Tintern Abbey: V2
The Wreck of the Hesperus (Longfellow): V31
Wright, Charles
   Black Zodiac: V10
Wright, James
   A Blessing: V7
   Autumn Begins in Martins Ferry, Ohio: V8
Wright, Judith
   Drought Year: V8
Wyatt, Thomas
   Whoso List to Hunt: V25

Y

Yau, John
   Russian Letter: V26
Yeats, William Butler
   Easter 1916: V5
   An Irish Airman Foresees His Death: V1
   The Lake Isle of Innisfree: V15
   Leda and the Swan: V13
   Sailing to Byzantium: V2
   The Second Coming: V7
   The Stolen Child: V34
Ye Goatherd Gods (Sidney): V30
Yet we insist that life is full of happy chance (Hejinian): V27
Yevtushenko, Yevgeny
   Babii Yar: V29
Young (Sexton): V30
Young, Kevin
   Chorale: V25
Youssef, Saadi
   America, America: V29

Z

Zagajewski, Adam
   Self-Portrait: V25

Cumulative Nationality/Ethnicity Index

Acoma Pueblo
Ortiz, Simon
  Hunger in New York City: V4
  My Father's Song: V16

African American
Ai
  Reunions with a Ghost: V16
Angelou, Maya
  Harlem Hopscotch: V2
  On the Pulse of Morning: V3
  Woman Work: V33
Baraka, Amiri
  In Memory of Radio: V9
Bontemps, Arna
  A Black Man Talks of Reaping: V32
Brooks, Gwendolyn
  The Bean Eaters: V2
  The Explorer: V32
  The Sonnet-Ballad: V1
  Strong Men, Riding Horses: V4
  We Real Cool: V6
Clifton, Lucille
  Climbing: V14
  homage to my hips: V29
  Miss Rosie: V1
Cullen, Countee
  Any Human to Another: V3
Dove, Rita
  Geometry: V15
  This Life: V1
Dunbar, Paul Laurence
  Sympathy: V33
Giovanni, Nikki
  Ego-Tripping: V28
  Knoxville, Tennessee: V17

Hayden, Robert
  Runagate Runagate: V31
  Those Winter Sundays: V1
Hughes, Langston
  Dream Variations: V15
  Harlem: V1
  I, Too: V30
  Mother to Son: V3
  The Negro Speaks of Rivers: V10
  Theme for English B: V6
Johnson, James Weldon
  The Creation: V1
Komunyakaa, Yusef
  Facing It: V5
  Ode to a Drum: V20
  Slam, Dunk, & Hook: V30
Lorde, Audre
  Hanging Fire: V32
  What My Child Learns of the Sea: V16
Madgett, Naomi Long
  Alabama Centennial: V10
McElroy, Colleen
  A Pièd: V3
Phillips, Carl
  All It Takes: V23
Randall, Dudley
  Ballad of Birmingham: V5
Reed, Ishmael
  Beware: Do Not Read This Poem: V6
Sanchez, Sonia
  An Anthem: V26
Toomer, Jean
  Storm Ending: V31
Trethewey, Natasha
  Native Guard: V29

Walker, Alice
  Good Night, Willie Lee, I'll See You in the Morning: V30
  Women: V34
Walker, Margaret
  Lineage: V31
Wheatley, Phillis
  On Being Brought from Africa to America: V29
  To His Excellency General Washington: V13

American
Ackerman, Diane
  On Location in the Loire Valley: V19
Acosta, Teresa Palomo
  My Mother Pieced Quilts: V12
Addonizio, Kim
  Knowledge: V25
Ai
  Reunions with a Ghost: V16
Aiken, Conrad
  The Room: V24
Alegría, Claribel
  Accounting: V21
Alexander, Elizabeth
  The Toni Morrison Dreams: V22
Ammons, A. R.
  The City Limits: V19
Angelou, Maya
  Harlem Hopscotch: V2
  On the Pulse of Morning: V3
  Woman Work: V33
Ashbery, John
  Paradoxes and Oxymorons: V11
  Self-Portrait in a Convex Mirror: V28

Cumulative Nationality/Ethnicity Index

Arvio, Sarah
   Memory: V21
Auden, W. H.
   As I Walked Out One Evening: V4
   Funeral Blues: V10
   Musée des Beaux Arts: V1
   September 1, 1939: V27
   The Unknown Citizen: V3
Baggott, Julianna
   What the Poets Could Have Been: V26
Bang, Mary Jo
   Allegory: V23
Barbarese, J. T.
   Walk Your Body Down: V26
Barot, Rick
   Bonnard's Garden: V25
Bass, Ellen
   And What If I Spoke of Despair: V19
Behn, Robin
   Ten Years after Your Deliberate Drowning: V21
Bell, Marvin
   View: V25
Berry, Wendell
   The Peace of Wild Things: V30
Berryman, John
   Dream Song 29: V27
Bialosky, Jill
   Seven Seeds: V19
Bidart, Frank
   Curse: V26
Biele, Joelle
   Rapture: V21
Bishop, Elizabeth
   Brazil, January 1, 1502: V6
   Filling Station: V12
   The Fish: V31
   The Man-Moth: V27
Blumenthal, Michael
   Inventors: V7
Bly, Robert
   Come with Me: V6
   Driving to Town Late to Mail a Letter: V17
Bogan, Louise
   Words for Departure: V21
Bontemps, Arna
   A Black Man Talks of Reaping: V32
Bradstreet, Anne
   To My Dear and Loving Husband: V6
   Upon the Burning of Our House, July 10th, 1666: V33
Brock-Broido, Lucie
   After Raphael: V26
Brooks, Gwendolyn
   The Bean Eaters: V2
   The Explorer: V32
   The Sonnet-Ballad: V1
   Strong Men, Riding Horses: V4
   We Real Cool: V6
Brouwer, Joel
   Last Request: V14
Bryant, William Cullen
   Thanatopsis: V30
Bukowski, Charles
   The Tragedy of the Leaves: V28
Byrne, Elena Karina
   In Particular: V20
Carruth, Hayden
   I, I, I: V26
Carver, Raymond
   The Cobweb: V17
Castillo, Ana
   While I Was Gone a War Began: V21
Cervantes, Lorna Dee
   Freeway 280: V30
Chin, Marilyn
   How I Got That Name: V28
Cisneros, Sandra
   Once Again I Prove the Theory of Relativity: V19
Clampitt, Amy
   Iola, Kansas: V27
Clifton, Lucille
   Climbing: V14
   homage to my hips: V29
   Miss Rosie: V1
Collins, Billy
   The Afterlife: V18
Cooper, Jane
   Rent: V25
Crane, Stephen
   War Is Kind: V9
Creeley, Robert
   Fading Light: V21
Cruz, Victor Hernandez
   Business: V16
Cullen, Countee
   Any Human to Another: V3
cummings, e. e.
   anyone lived in a pretty how town: V30
   i was sitting in mcsorley's: V13
   l(a: V1
   maggie and milly and molly and may: V12
   old age sticks: V3
   since feeling is first: V34
   somewhere i have never travelled,gladly beyond: V19
Dennis, Carl
   The God Who Loves You: V20
Dickey, James
   The Heaven of Animals: V6
   The Hospital Window: V11
Dickinson, Emily
   Because I Could Not Stop for Death: V2
   The Bustle in a House: V10
   "Hope" Is the Thing with Feathers: V3
   I Died for Beauty: V28
   I felt a Funeral, in my Brain: V13
   I Heard a Fly Buzz—When I Died—: V5
   Much Madness Is Divinest Sense: V16
   My Life Closed Twice Before Its Close: V8
   A Narrow Fellow in the Grass: V11
   The Soul Selects Her Own Society: V1
   Success Is Counted Sweetest: V32
   There's a Certain Slant of Light: V6
   This Is My Letter to the World: V4
Divakaruni, Chitra Banerjee
   My Mother Combs My Hair: V34
Dobyns, Stephen
   It's like This: V23
Dove, Rita
   Geometry: V15
   This Life: V1
Dubie, Norman
   The Czar's Last Christmas Letter. A Barn in the Urals: V12
Du Bois, W. E. B.
   The Song of the Smoke: V13
Dugan, Alan
   How We Heard the Name: V10
Dunbar, Paul Laurence
   Sympathy: V33
Duncan, Robert
   An African Elegy: V13
Dunn, Stephen
   The Reverse Side: V21
Eliot, T. S.
   The Hollow Men: V33
   Journey of the Magi: V7
   The Love Song of J. Alfred Prufrock: V1
Emerson, Claudia
   My Grandmother's Plot in the Family Cemetery: V27
Emerson, Ralph Waldo
   Concord Hymn: V4
   The Rhodora: V17
   The Snow-Storm: V34
Erdrich, Louise
   Bidwell Ghost: V14
Espada, Martín
   Colibrí: V16
   We Live by What We See at Night: V13
Ferlinghetti, Lawrence
   Christ Climbed Down: V28
Forché, Carolyn
   The Garden Shukkei-En: V18
Francis, Robert
   The Base Stealer: V12
Fraser, Kathleen
   Poem in Which My Legs Are Accepted: V29

Frost, Robert
   After Apple Picking: V32
   Birches: V13
   The Death of the Hired Man: V4
   Fire and Ice: V7
   Mending Wall: V5
   Nothing Gold Can Stay: V3
   Out, Out—: V10
   The Road Not Taken: V2
   Stopping by Woods on a Snowy Evening: V1
   The Wood-Pile: V6
Fulton, Alice
   Art Thou the Thing I Wanted: V25
Gallagher, Tess
   I Stop Writing the Poem: V16
Ginsberg, Allen
   Howl: V29
   A Supermarket in California: V5
Gioia, Dana
   The Litany: V24
Giovanni, Nikki
   Ego-Tripping: V28
   Knoxville, Tennessee: V17
Glück, Louise
   The Gold Lily: V5
   The Mystery: V15
Graham, Jorie
   The Hiding Place: V10
   Mind: V17
Gregg, Linda
   A Thirst Against: V20
Gunn, Thom
   The Missing: V9
H.D.
   Helen: V6
   Sea Rose: V28
Hacker, Marilyn
   The Boy: V19
Hahn, Kimiko
   Pine: V23
Hall, Donald
   Names of Horses: V8
Harjo, Joy
   Anniversary: V15
   Remember: V32
Hashimoto, Sharon
   What I Would Ask My Husband's Dead Father: V22
Hayden, Robert
   Runagate Runagate: V31
   Those Winter Sundays: V1
Hecht, Anthony
   "More Light! More Light!": V6
Hejinian, Lyn
   Yet we insist that life is full of happy chance: V27
Hillman, Brenda
   Air for Mercury: V20
Hirsch, Edward
   Omen: V22

Hirshfield, Jane
   Three Times My Life Has Opened: V16
Hoagland, Tony
   Social Life: V19
Holmes, Oliver Wendell
   The Chambered Nautilus: V24
   Old Ironsides: V9
Hongo, Garrett
   The Legend: V25
   What For: V33
Howe, Marie
   What Belongs to Us: V15
Hudgins, Andrew
   Elegy for My Father, Who is Not Dead: V14
Hughes, Langston
   Dream Variations: V15
   Harlem: V1
   I, Too: V30
   Mother to Son: V3
   The Negro Speaks of Rivers: V10
   Theme for English B: V6
Hugo, Richard
   For Jennifer, 6, on the Teton: V17
Jarrell, Randall
   The Death of the Ball Turret Gunner: V2
   Losses: V31
Jeffers, Robinson
   Hurt Hawks: V3
   Shine, Perishing Republic: V4
Johnson, James Weldon
   The Creation: V1
Justice, Donald
   Incident in a Rose Garden: V14
Kelly, Brigit Pegeen
   The Satyr's Heart: V22
Kenyon, Jane
   Having it Out with Melancholy: V17
   "Trouble with Math in a One-Room Country School": V9
Kim, Sue (Suji) Kwock
   Monologue for an Onion: V24
Kinnell, Galway
   Another Night in the Ruins: V26
   Saint Francis and the Sow: V9
Kizer, Carolyn
   To An Unknown Poet: V18
Koch, Kenneth
   Paradiso: V20
Komunyakaa, Yusef
   Facing It: V5
   Ode to a Drum: V20
   Slam, Dunk, & Hook: V30
Kooser, Ted
   At the Cancer Clinic: V24
   The Constellation Orion: V8
Kumin, Maxine
   Address to the Angels: V18
Kunitz, Stanley
   The War Against the Trees: V11

Kyger, Joanne
   September: V23
Lanier, Sidney
   Song of the Chattahoochee: V14
Lauterbach, Ann
   Hum: V25
Laux, Dorianne
   For the Sake of Strangers: V24
Lee, Li-Young
   Early in the Morning: V17
   For a New Citizen of These United States: V15
   The Weight of Sweetness: V11
Levertov, Denise
   The Blue Rim of Memory: V17
   In the Land of Shinar: V7
   A Tree Telling of Orpheus: V31
Levine, Philip
   Starlight: V8
Lim, Shirley Geok-lin
   Pantoun for Chinese Women: V29
Longfellow, Henry Wadsworth
   The Arsenal at Springfield: V17
   Paul Revere's Ride: V2
   A Psalm of Life: V7
   The Wreck of the Hesperus: V31
Lorde, Audre
   Hanging Fire: V32
   What My Child Learns of the Sea: V16
Lowell, Amy
   The Taxi: V30
Lowell, Robert
   For the Union Dead: V7
   The Quaker Graveyard in Nantucket: V6
Loy, Mina
   Moreover, the Moon: V20
MacLeish, Archibald
   Ars Poetica: V5
Madgett, Naomi Long
   Alabama Centennial: V10
McElroy, Colleen
   A Pièd: V3
McGinley, Phyllis
   The Conquerors: V13
   Reactionary Essay on Applied Science: V9
McHugh, Heather
   Three To's and an Oi: V24
McKay, Claude
   The Tropics in New York: V4
Merriam, Eve
   Onomatopoeia: V6
Merrill, James
   Lost in Translation: V23
Merwin, W. S.
   The Horizons of Rooms: V15
   Leviathan: V5
Millay, Edna St. Vincent
   An Ancient Gesture: V31
   Conscientious Objector: V34

*The Courage that My Mother
    Had:* V3
Wild Swans: V17
Momaday, N. Scott
    Angle of Geese: V2
    *To a Child Running With
        Outstretched Arms in Canyon de
        Chelly:* V11
Montague, John
    A Grafted Tongue: V12
Moore, Marianne
    The Fish: V14
    Poetry: V17
Mora, Pat
    Elena: V33
Mueller, Lisel
    The Exhibit: V9
Muske-Dukes, Carol
    Our Side: V24
Nash, Ogden
    The Hippopotamus: V31
Nemerov, Howard
    Deep Woods: V14
    The Phoenix: V10
Nye, Naomi Shihab
    Kindness: V24
    Shoulders: V33
O'Hara, Frank
    Autobiographia Literaria: V34
    Having a Coke with You: V12
    Why I Am Not a Painter: V8
Olds, Sharon
    I Go Back to May 1937: V17
Oliver, Mary
    The Black Snake: V31
    Music Lessons: V8
    Wild Geese: V15
Ortiz, Simon
    Hunger in New York City: V4
    My Father's Song: V16
Ostriker, Alicia
    His Speed and Strength: V19
    Mastectomy: V26
Okita, Dwight
    *In Response to Executive Order
        9066: All Americans of Japanese
        Descent Must Report to
        Relocation Centers:* V32
Parker, Dorothy
    The Last Question: V18
Pastan, Linda
    The Cossacks: V25
    Ethics: V8
    Grudnow: V32
Phillips, Carl
    All It Takes: V23
Piercy, Marge
    Apple sauce for Eve: V22
    Barbie Doll: V9
    To Be of Use: V32
Pinsky, Robert
    Song of Reasons: V18

Plath, Sylvia
    Blackberrying: V15
    Daddy: V28
    Mirror: V1
    Mushrooms: V33
Poe, Edgar Allan
    Annabel Lee: V9
    The Bells: V3
    The Raven: V1
Ponsot, Marie
    One Is One: V24
Pound, Ezra
    Hugh Selwyn Mauberley: V16
    In a Station of the Metro: V2
    *The River-Merchant's Wife: A
        Letter:* V8
Randall, Dudley
    Ballad of Birmingham: V5
Reed, Ishmael
    Beware: Do Not Read This Poem:
        V6
Revard, Carter
    Birch Canoe: V5
Rich, Adrienne
    Diving into the Wreck: V29
    Rusted Legacy: V15
Ríos, Alberto
    Island of the Three Marias: V11
Robinson, E. A.
    Richard Cory: V4
Roethke, Theodore
    My Papa's Waltz: V3
    The Waking: V34
Rogers, Pattiann
    The Greatest Grandeur: V18
Rose, Wendy
    *For the White poets who would be
        Indian:* V13
Ruefle, Mary
    Sentimental Education: V26
Rukeyser, Muriel
    Ballad of Orange and Grape: V10
    St. Roach: V29
Salter, Mary Jo
    Trompe l'Oeil: V22
Sanchez, Sonia
    An Anthem: V26
Sandburg, Carl
    Chicago: V3
    Cool Tombs: V6
    Jazz Fantasia: V33
    Hope Is a Tattered Flag: V12
Santos, Sherod
    *Portrait of a Couple at Century's
        End:* V24
Schnackenberg, Gjertrud
    Darwin in 1881: V13
    Supernatural Love: V25
Sexton, Anne
    Courage: V14
    Oysters: V4
    Young: V30

Shapiro, Karl
    Auto Wreck: V3
Silko, Leslie Marmon
    Four Mountain Wolves: V9
    Story from Bear Country: V16
Simic, Charles
    Butcher Shop: V7
Simpson, Louis
    American Poetry: V7
    Chocolates: V11
    In the Suburbs: V14
Snodgrass, W. D.
    Heart's Needle: V29
Snyder, Gary
    Anasazi: V9
    True Night: V19
Song, Cathy
    Lost Sister: V5
Soto, Gary
    Oranges: V30
    Small Town with One Road: V7
Spires, Elizabeth
    Ghazal: V21
Stafford, William
    At the Bomb Testing Site: V8
    Fifteen: V2
    Ways to Live: V16
Stern, Gerald
    One of the Smallest: V26
Stevens, Wallace
    The Idea of Order at Key West:
        V13
    Sunday Morning: V16
Stewart, Susan
    The Forest: V22
Stone, Ruth
    Ordinary Words: V19
Strand, Mark
    The Continuous Life: V18
Swenson, May
    The Centaur: V30
    Southbound on the Freeway: V16
Tate, James
    Dear Reader: V10
    Smart and Final Iris: V15
Taylor, Edward
    Huswifery: V31
Taylor, Henry
    Landscape with Tractor: V10
Teasdale, Sara
    There Will Come Soft Rains:
        V14
Thayer, Ernest Lawrence
    Casey at the Bat: V5
Toomer, Jean
    Storm Ending: V31
Trethewey, Natasha
    Native Guard: V29
Valentine, Jean
    Seeing You: V24
Van Duyn, Mona
    Memoir: V20

Vazirani, Reetika
   Daughter-Mother-Maya-Seeta: V25
Viereck, Peter
   For An Assyrian Frieze: V9
   Kilroy: V14
Voigt, Ellen Bryant
   The Lotus Flowers: V33
   Practice: V23
Waldner, Liz
   Witness: V26
Walker, Alice
   Good Night, Willie Lee, I'll See You in the Morning: V30
   Women: V34
Walker, Margaret
   Lineage: V31
Warren, Rosanna
   Daylights: V13
   Lake: V23
Wheatley, Phillis
   On Being Brought from Africa to America: V29
   To His Excellency General Washington: V13
Whitman, Walt
   Cavalry Crossing a Ford: V13
   I Hear America Singing: V3
   A Noiseless Patient Spider: V31
   O Captain! My Captain!: V2
   When I Heard the Learn'd Astronomer: V22
Wilbur, Richard
   Beowulf: V11
   Love Calls Us to the Things of This World: V29
   Merlin Enthralled: V16
   On Freedom's Ground: V12
Williams, William Carlos
   Overture to a Dance of Locomotives: V11
   Queen-Ann's-Lace: V6
   The Red Wheelbarrow: V1
   This Is Just to Say: V34
Wright, Charles
   Black Zodiac: V10
Wright, James
   A Blessing: V7
   Autumn Begins in Martins Ferry, Ohio: V8
Yau, John
   Russian Letter: V26
Young, Kevin
   Chorale: V25

Argentinian

Borges, Jorge Luis
   Borges and I: V27

Arab American

Nye, Naomi Shihab
   Kindness: V24
   Shoulders: V33

Asian American

Chin, Marilyn
   How I Got That Name: V28
Hahn, Kimiko
   Pine: V23
Hashimoto, Sharon
   What I Would Ask My Husband's Dead Father: V22
Hongo, Garrett
   The Legend: V25
   What For: V33
Kim, Sue (Suji) Kwok
   Monologue for an Onion: V24
Lim, Shirley Geok-lin
   Pantoun for Chinese Women: V29
Okita, Dwight
   In Response to Executive Order 9066: All Americans of Japanese Descent Must Report to Relocation Centers: V32
Yau, John
   Russian Letter: V26

Australian

Dawe, Bruce
   Drifters: V10
Hope, A. D.
   Beware of Ruins: V8
Wright, Judith
   Drought Year: V8

Belarusian

Mort, Valzhyna
   Grandmother: V34

Canadian

Atwood, Margaret
   Siren Song: V7
Birney, Earle
   Vancouver Lights: V8
Carson, Anne
   New Rule: V18
Hébert, Anne
   The Alchemy of Day: V20
Jacobsen, Josephine
   Fiddler Crab: V23
Layton, Irving
   A Tall Man Executes a Jig: V12
McCrae, John
   In Flanders Fields: V5
Nowlan, Alden
   For Jean Vincent D'abbadie, Baron St.-Castin: V12
Ondaatje, Michael
   The Cinnamon Peeler: V19
   To a Sad Daughter: V8
Purdy, Al
   Lament for the Dorsets: V5
   Wilderness Gothic: V12
Service, Robert W.
   The Cremation of Sam McGee: V10
Strand, Mark
   Eating Poetry: V9

Chilean

Neruda, Pablo
   Fully Empowered: V33
   The Heights of Macchu Picchu: V28
   Tonight I Can Write: V11

Chinese

Chin, Marilyn
   How I Got That Name: V28
Fu, Tu
   Jade Flower Palace: V32
Po, Li
   Drinking Alone Beneath the Moon: V20

Egyptian

Cavafy, C. P.
   Ithaka: V19

English

Alleyn, Ellen
   A Birthday: V10
Arnold, Matthew
   Dover Beach: V2
Auden, W. H.
   As I Walked Out One Evening: V4
   Funeral Blues: V10
   Musée des Beaux Arts: V1
   September 1, 1939: V27
   The Unknown Citizen: V3
Blake, William
   The Fly: V34
   The Lamb: V12
   A Poison Tree: V24
   The Tyger: V2
Bradstreet, Anne
   To My Dear and Loving Husband: V6
   Upon the Burning of Our House, July 10th, 1666: V33
Brontë, Emily
   Old Stoic: V33
Brooke, Rupert
   The Soldier: V7
Browning, Elizabeth Barrett
   Aurora Leigh: V23
   Sonnet XXIX: V16
   Sonnet 43: V2
Browning, Robert
   My Last Duchess: V1
   Porphyria's Lover: V15
Byron, Lord
   The Destruction of Sennacherib: V1
   She Walks in Beauty: V14
   When We Two Parted: V29

Carroll, Lewis
   Jabberwocky: V11
   The Walrus and the Carpenter: V30
Chaucer, Geoffrey
   The Canterbury Tales: V14
Coleridge, Samuel Taylor
   Kubla Khan: V5
   The Rime of the Ancient Mariner: V4
Donne, John
   Holy Sonnet 10: V2
   A Valediction: Forbidding Mourning: V11
   The Waste Land: V20
Eliot, T. S.
   The Hollow Men: V33
   Journey of the Magi: V7
   The Love Song of J. Alfred Prufrock: V1
Fenton, James
   The Milkfish Gatherers: V11
Finch, Anne
   A Nocturnal Reverie: V30
Gray, Thomas
   Elegy Written in a Country Churchyard: V9
Gunn, Thom
   The Missing: V9
Hardy, Thomas
   Ah, Are You Digging on My Grave?: V4
   The Darkling Thrush: V18
   The Man He Killed: V3
Herbert, George
   Virtue: V25
Herrick, Robert
   The Night Piece: To Julia: V29
   To the Virgins, to Make Much of Time: V13
Hopkins, Gerard Manley
   Pied Beauty: V26
Housman, A. E.
   To an Athlete Dying Young: V7
   When I Was One-and-Twenty: V4
Hughes, Ted
   Hawk Roosting: V4
   The Horses: V32
   Perfect Light: V19
Jonson, Ben
   On My First Son: V33
   Song: To Celia: V23
Keats, John
   La Belle Dame sans Merci: V17
   Bright Star! Would I Were Steadfast as Thou Art: V9
   Ode on a Grecian Urn: V1
   Ode to a Nightingale: V3
   On the Grasshopper and the Cricket: V32
   When I Have Fears that I May Cease to Be: V2

Kipling, Rudyard
   If: V22
Larkin, Philip
   An Arundel Tomb: V12
   High Windows: V3
   Toads: V4
Lawrence, D. H.
   Piano: V6
Levertov, Denise
   The Blue Rim of Memory: V17
   In the Land of Shinar: V7
   A Tree Telling of Orpheus: V31
Lovelace, Richard
   To Althea, From Prison: V34
   To Lucasta, Going to the Wars: V32
Loy, Mina
   Moreover, the Moon: V20
Marlowe, Christopher
   The Passionate Shepherd to His Love: V22
Marvell, Andrew
   To His Coy Mistress: V5
Masefield, John
   Cargoes: V5
Maxwell, Glyn
   The Nerve: V23
Milton, John
   [On His Blindness] Sonnet 16: V3
   On His Having Arrived at the Age of Twenty-Three: V17
Noyes, Alfred
   The Highwayman: V4
Owen, Wilfred
   Dulce et Decorum Est: V10
Pope, Alexander
   The Rape of the Lock: V12
Raine, Craig
   A Martian Sends a Postcard Home: V7
Raleigh, Walter, Sir
   The Nymph's Reply to the Shepherd: V14
Rossetti, Christina
   A Birthday: V10
   Goblin Market: V27
   Remember: V14
   Up-Hill: V34
Sassoon, Siegfried
   "Blighters": V28
Service, Robert W.
   The Cremation of Sam McGee: V10
Shakespeare, William
   Sonnet 18: V2
   Sonnet 19: V9
   Sonnet 29: V8
   Sonnet 30: V4
   Sonnet 55: V5
   Sonnet 116: V3
   Sonnet 130: V1
Shelley, Percy Bysshe
   Ode to the West Wind: V2
   Ozymandias: V27
   To a Sky-Lark: V32

Sidney, Philip
   Ye Goatherd Gods: V30
   Ozymandias: V27
Smith, Stevie
   Not Waving but Drowning: V3
Spender, Stephen
   An Elementary School Classroom in a Slum: V23
Spenser, Edmund
   Sonnet 75: V32
Swift, Jonathan
   A Satirical Elegy on the Death of a Late Famous General: V27
Taylor, Edward
   Huswifery: V31
Taylor, Henry
   Landscape with Tractor: V10
Tennyson, Alfred, Lord
   The Charge of the Light Brigade: V1
   The Eagle: V11
   The Lady of Shalott: V15
   Proem: V19
   Tears, Idle Tears: V4
   Ulysses: V2
Williams, William Carlos
   Overture to a Dance of Locomotives: V11
   Queen-Ann's-Lace: V6
   The Red Wheelbarrow: V1
   This Is Just to Say: V34
Wordsworth, William
   I Wandered Lonely as a Cloud: V33
   Lines Composed a Few Miles above Tintern Abbey: V2
Wyatt, Thomas
   Whoso List to Hunt: V25

French

Apollinaire, Guillaume
   Always: V24
Baudelaire, Charles
   Hymn to Beauty: V21
Malroux, Claire
   Morning Walk: V21
Rimbaud, Arthur
   The Drunken Boat: V28

German

Amichai, Yehuda
   Not like a Cypress: V24
Blumenthal, Michael
   Inventors: V7
Erdrich, Louise
   Bidwell Ghost: V14
Mueller, Lisel
   Blood Oranges: V13
   The Exhibit: V9
Rilke, Rainer Maria
   Archaic Torso of Apollo: V27
   Childhood: V19

Roethke, Theodore
    My Papa's Waltz: V3
    The Waking: V34
Sachs, Nelly
    But Perhaps God Needs the Longing: V20
Sajé, Natasha
    The Art of the Novel: V23

Ghanaian

Du Bois, W. E. B.
    The Song of the Smoke: V13

Greek

Cavafy, C. P.
    Ithaka: V19
Sappho
    Fragment 2: V31
    Hymn to Aphrodite: V20

Hispanic American

Castillo, Ana
    While I Was Gone a War Began: V21
Cervantes, Lorna Dee
    Freeway 280: V30
Cruz, Victor Hernandez
    Business: V16
Espada, Martín
    Colibrí: V16
Mora, Pat
    Elena: V33
Williams, William Carlos
    Overture to a Dance of Locomotives: V11
    Queen-Ann's-Lace: V6
    The Red Wheelbarrow: V1
    This Is Just to Say: V34

Indian

Divakaruni, Chitra Banerjee
    My Mother Combs My Hair: V34
Mirabai
    All I Was Doing Was Breathing: V24
Ramanujan, A. K.
    Waterfalls in a Bank: V27
Shahid Ali, Agha
    Country Without a Post Office: V18
Tagore, Rabindranath
    60: V18
Vazirani, Reetika
    Daughter-Mother-Maya-Seeta: V25

Indonesian

Lee, Li-Young
    Early in the Morning: V17
    For a New Citizen of These United States: V15
    The Weight of Sweetness: V11

Iranian

Farrokhzaad, Faroogh
    A Rebirth: V21

Iraqi

Youssef, Saadi
    America, America: V29

Irish

Boland, Eavan
    Anorexic: V12
    It's a Woman's World: V22
    Outside History: V31
Carson, Ciaran
    The War Correspondent: V26
Grennan, Eamon
    Station: V21
Hartnett, Michael
    A Farewell to English: V10
Heaney, Seamus
    Digging: V5
    A Drink of Water: V8
    Follower: V30
    Midnight: V2
    The Singer's House: V17
Muldoon, Paul
    Meeting the British: V7
    Pineapples and Pomegranates: V22
Swift, Jonathan
    A Satirical Elegy on the Death of a Late Famous General: V27
Yeats, William Butler
    Easter 1916: V5
    An Irish Airman Foresees His Death: V1
    The Lake Isle of Innisfree: V15
    Leda and the Swan: V13
    Sailing to Byzantium: V2
    The Second Coming: V7
    The Stolen Child: V34

Israeli

Amichai, Yehuda
    Not like a Cypress: V24

Italian

Apollinaire, Guillaume
    Always: V24
Montale, Eugenio
    On the Threshold: V22
Pavese, Cesare
    Two Poems for T.: V20
Ungaretti, Giuseppe
    Variations on Nothing: V20

Jamaican

Goodison, Lorna
    The River Mumma Wants Out: V25
McKay, Claude
    The Tropics in New York: V4

Simpson, Louis
    In the Suburbs: V14

Japanese

Ai
    Reunions with a Ghost: V16
Bashō, Matsuo
    Falling Upon Earth: V2
    The Moon Glows the Same: V7
    Temple Bells Die Out: V18

Jewish

Bell, Marvin
    View: V25
Blumenthal, Michael
    Inventors: V7
Espada, Martín
    Colibrí: V16
    We Live by What We See at Night: V13
HaNagid, Shmuel
    Two Eclipses: V33
Hirsch, Edward
    Omen: V22
Pastan, Linda
    The Cossacks: V25
    Ethics: V8
    Grudnow: V32
Piercy, Marge
    Apple sauce for Eve: V22
    Barbie Doll: V9
    To Be of Use: V32
Sachs, Nelly
    But Perhaps God Needs the Longing: V20
Shapiro, Karl
    Auto Wreck: V3
Stern, Gerald
    One of the Smallest: V26

Kiowa

Momaday, N. Scott
    Angle of Geese: V2
    To a Child Running With Outstretched Arms in Canyon de Chelly: V11

Lithuanian

Milosz, Czeslaw
    From the Rising of the Sun: V29
    Song of a Citizen: V16

Malaysian

Lim, Shirley Geok-lin
    Pantoun for Chinese Women: V29

Mexican

Paz, Octavio
    Duration: V18
    Sunstone: V30

Soto, Gary
  Oranges: V30
  Small Town with One Road: V7

Native American
Ai
  Reunions with a Ghost: V16
Erdrich, Louise
  Bidwell Ghost: V14
Harjo, Joy
  Anniversary: V15
  Remember: V32
Momaday, N. Scott
  Angle of Geese: V2
  To a Child Running With Outstretched Arms in Canyon de Chelly: V11
Ortiz, Simon
  Hunger in New York City: V4
  My Father's Song: V16
Revard, Carter
  Birch Canoe: V5
Rose, Wendy
  For the White poets who would be Indian: V13
Silko, Leslie Marmon
  Four Mountain Wolves: V9
  Story from Bear Country: V16

Nigerian
Soyinka, Wole
  Telephone Conversation: V27

Osage
Revard, Carter
  Birch Canoe: V5

Peruvian
Vallejo, César
  The Black Heralds: V26

Philippine
Barot, Rick
  Bonnard's Garden: V25

Polish
Herbert, Zbigniew
  Why The Classics: V22
Milosz, Czeslaw
  From the Rising of the Sun: V29
  Song of a Citizen: V16
Swir, Anna
  Maternity: V21
Szymborska, Wisława
  Astonishment: V15
  Conversation with a Stone: V27
  Possibilities: V34
  Some People Like Poetry: V31
Zagajewski, Adam
  Self-Portrait: V25

Roman
Ovid (Naso, Publius Ovidius)
  Metamorphoses: V22

Romanian
Celan, Paul
  Late and Deep: V21

Russian
Akhmatova, Anna
  Everything is Plundered: V32
  Midnight Verses: V18
  Requiem: V27
Merriam, Eve
  Onomatopoeia: V6
Pushkin, Alexander
  The Bridegroom: V34
  The Bronze Horseman: V28
Shapiro, Karl
  Auto Wreck: V3
Tsvetaeva, Marina
  An Attempt at Jealousy: V29
Yevtushenko, Yevgeny
  Babii Yar: V29

St. Lucian
Walcott, Derek
  A Far Cry from Africa: V6
  Midsummer, Tobago: V34

Scottish
Burns, Robert
  A Red, Red Rose: V8
Duffy, Carol Ann
  Originally: V25
MacBeth, George
  Bedtime Story: V8

Senegalese
Wheatley, Phillis
  On Being Brought from Africa to America: V29
  To His Excellency General Washington: V13

Serbian
Lazić, Radmila
  Death Sentences: V22

Spanish
García Lorca, Federico
  Gacela of the Dark Death: V20
  Lament for Ignacio Sánchez Mejías: V31
HaNagid, Shmuel
  Two Eclipses: V33
Machado, Antonio
  The Crime Was in Granada: V23
Williams, William Carlos
  The Red Wheelbarrow: V1

Sri Lankan
Ondaatje, Michael
  The Cinnamon Peeler: V19
  To a Sad Daughter: V8

Swedish
Sandburg, Carl
  Chicago: V3
  Cool Tombs: V6
  Jazz Fantasia: V33
  Hope Is a Tattered Flag: V12
Svenbro, Jesper
  Lepidopterology: V23
Tranströmer, Tomas
  Answers to Letters: V21

Vietnamese
Huong, Ho Xuan
  Spring-Watching Pavilion: V18
Thomas, Dylan
  Do Not Go Gentle into that Good Night: V1
  Fern Hill: V3
  The Force That Through the Green Fuse Drives the Flower: V8

Yugoslavian
Lazić, Radmila
  Death Sentences: V22
Simic, Charles
  Classic Ballroom Dances: V33

Subject/Theme Index

A

African American culture
   The Bridegroom:, 38–42
   Women:, 318–319, 321–322
African American history
   Conscientious Objector:, 47, 51
   Women:, 317–319
Aging
   Grandmother:, 97–98
Allegories
   Up-Hill:, 282–283
Alliteration
   Conscientious Objector:, 49–50
   The Waking:, 298
American Asian culture
   My Mother Combs My Hair:, 136–137
American culture. *See also:* Great Depression
   since feeling is first:, 176, 178
   This is Just to Say:, 246, 248–252
American literature
   The Waking:, 299–300
Animals
   Autobiographia Literaria:, 5–6, 8
   Conscientious Objector:, 47
Archetype
   Autobiographia Literaria:, 7
Art
   Autobiographia Literaria:, 5, 13–14, 21–23
   Midsummer, Tobago:, 125–129
   The Snow-Storm:, 197–198
   The Stolen Child:, 222–223
   Up-Hill:, 285
Asian American culture
   My Mother Combs My Hair:, 136

Asian culture
   Up-Hill:, 284

B

Ballads
   Up-Hill:, 283
British culture
   To Althea, From Prison:, 261–264, 273–277
   The Fly:, 76
British history. *See also:* English history
   To Althea, From Prison:, 259–260
Brotherhood of man
   Conscientious Objector:, 49

C

Caribbean culture
   Midsummer, Tobago:, 118, 121–125
Caribbean history
   Midsummer, Tobago:, 112, 116–118
Carpe diem
   To Althea, From Prison:, 257
   since feeling is first:, 179–181
Cavalier
   To Althea, From Prison:, 258–259, 261–264, 273–277
Character
   Grandmother:, 96–97
Childhood
   Autobiographia Literaria:, 8
   The Stolen Child:, 230–238
Communism. *See also:* Soviet Union
   Grandmother:, 99–100

Possibilities:, 153–154
Conceit
   To Althea, From Prison:, 257–258
Confessional poetry
   Autobiographia Literaria:, 10–12
Conflict
   Conscientious Objector:, 51
Contrasts
   Possibilities:, 152–153, 167–170
Crime
   The Bridegroom:, 34
   The Stolen Child:, 223

D

Death. *See also:* Wars
   Conscientious Objector:, 49
   The Fly:, 70, 72
   Up-Hill:, 281
Dialogue
   The Bridegroom:, 33
   Up-Hill:, 283
Dreams
   The Bridegroom:, 31, 34

E

Education
   Women:, 315–316, 317–318
18th Century
   The Fly:, 76–77
English history
   Up-Hill:, 283–285
Engraving
   The Fly:, 69, 75, 76
Enlightenment (Cultural movement)
   The Bridegroom:, 33

Subject/Theme Index

Environmentalism
  The Snow-Storm:, 200
Experience
  Grandmother:, 96–97

F

Fairy tales
  The Bridegroom:, 25, 34, 36–38
Family
  Grandmother:, 96
Fear
  The Bridegroom:, 30
Feminism
  My Mother Combs My Hair:, 135
  since feeling is first:, 174, 178
Folk culture
  The Stolen Child:, 220, 224–228
Free verse
  Conscientious Objector:, 50
  Midsummer, Tobago:, 116
  This is Just to Say:, 244
  Women:, 316–317
Freedom
  To Althea, From Prison:, 257

G

German history
  Conscientious Objector:, 50–52
God
  Grandmother:, 98
Great Depression
  Conscientious Objector:, 50
  This is Just to Say:, 243, 245–246, 250–252

H

Honor
  To Althea, From Prison:, 257
Hyperbole
  Autobiographia Literaria:, 6–7

I

Iambic pentameter
  The Waking:, 298–299
Identity
  Grandmother:, 96–97
Ideology
  Possibilities:, 156–158, 167–170
Imagery (Literature). *See also:* Metaphors; Similes
  Grandmother:, 101–104
  Midsummer, Tobago:, 116
  My Mother Combs My Hair:, 135, 138–141
  The Stolen Child:, 221–222
  Women:, 317
Imagination
  The Fly:, 72–73
Imagism
  since feeling is first:, 175, 177
  This is Just to Say:, 242, 245

Immigrant life
  The Snow-Storm:, 200
Indian culture
  My Mother Combs My Hair:, 133–135, 136–137
  Up-Hill:, 284
Indian history
  My Mother Combs My Hair:, 136
Individualism
  since feeling is first:, 175
Indulgence
  This is Just to Say:, 242–244
Interpretation
  The Fly:, 82–89, 89–91
Intuition
  The Waking:, 296–297
Irish culture
  The Stolen Child:, 222, 223, 224–228, 229
Irish history
  The Stolen Child:, 222, 228
Irish nationalsim
  The Stolen Child:, 222
Irony
  My Mother Combs My Hair:, 135, 140

J

Journeys (philosophy)
  Up-Hill:, 281

L

Lethargy
  Midsummer, Tobago:, 115
Life (Philosophy)
  since feeling is first:, 173–175
  The Waking:, 297–298
Lists
  Possibilities:, 153
Loneliness
  Autobiographia Literaria:, 4–5, 16
  The Stolen Child:, 221
Loss (Psychology)
  The Stolen Child:, 221
Lost Generation
  since feeling is first:, 176–177
Loyalty
  To Althea, From Prison:, 257
Lyceum movement
  The Snow-Storm:, 201–202
Lyric poetry
  Conscientious Objector:, 64–66
  The Fly:, 74

M

Marriage
  The Bridegroom:, 32–33, 34
  My Mother Combs My Hair:, 131, 133–135, 136–137
Memory
  Women:, 321–322

Metaphors. *See also:* Allegories
  Autobiographia Literaria:, 22
  Grandmother:, 99
  Up-Hill:, 283, 286–289
Modernism (Literature). *See also:* Imagism; Lost Generation
  Autobiographia Literaria:, 7, 13
  since feeling is first:, 175–176
  The Waking:, 299
Modernization
  Women:, 317
Morality
  Midsummer, Tobago:, 115
Mortality. *See also:* Death
  The Fly:, 70, 72
Music
  The Stolen Child:, 222

N

Narrative poetry
  The Bridegroom:, 33
Nationalism
  The Stolen Child:, 222
Nature. *See also:* Transcendentalism
  Autobiographia Literaria:, 5–6
  Midsummer, Tobago:, 115
  My Mother Combs My Hair:, 135, 138–141
  since feeling is first:, 185–192
  The Snow-Storm:, 197
Nazism
  Conscientious Objector:, 50–52
New York School of Poets
  Autobiographia Literaria:, 8–9
1920s (Decade)
  since feeling is first:, 176, 178
1930s (Decade)
  Conscientious Objector:, 51
  This is Just to Say:, 246
1950s (Decade)
  Autobiographia Literaria:, 8
  The Waking:, 299–300
1960s (Decade)
  Women:, 318
1970s (Decade)
  Midsummer, Tobago:, 118
  Women:, 318
1980s (Decade)
  Possibilities:, 154
1990s (Decade)
  My Mother Combs My Hair:, 136
19th century
  The Bridegroom:, 34
  The Snow-Storm:, 200
  The Stolen Child:, 223
  Up-Hill:, 284

O

Objectivism
  This is Just to Say:, 245

P

Pacifism
  Conscientious Objector:, 53–55
Paradoxes
  Grandmother:, 98
  The Waking:, 298
Parallelism
  Women:, 317
Patriarchy
  The Bridegroom:, 31–32
Personification
  Conscientious Objector:, 50
  Grandmother:, 98–99
  The Snow-Storm:, 198–199
Philosophy
  The Snow-Storm:, 205–210
Point of view (Literature)
  Autobiographia Literaria:, 8
Polish culture
  Possibilities:, 153–155, 160
Polish history
  Possibilities:, 154, 156, 163
Politics
  Conscientious Objector:, 55–64
  The Fly:, 76
  Possibilities:, 154
Postmodernism
  Autobiographia Literaria:, 7–8
Pre-Raphaelites
  The Stolen Child:, 222–223
  Up-Hill:, 285
Psychology
  Autobiographia Literaria:, 8

R

Racism
  Women:, 318–319
Religious beliefs
  Grandmother:, 98
  The Stolen Child:, 223
  Up-Hill:, 281, 284, 289–291
Religious history
  The Snow-Storm:, 200
Repetition
  Possibilities:, 153
Resistance
  Conscientious Objector:, 49, 53–55
Revolutions
  Grandmother:, 99–100

Rhythm
  The Waking:, 298–299
Romanticism
  The Bridegroom:, 33–34
  The Fly:, 75
  The Waking:, 300–305
Russian history. *See also:* Soviet Union
  The Bridegroom:, 35

S

17th Century
  To Althea, From Prison:, 258–260
Sexuality
  since feeling is first:, 178
Silence
  since feeling is first:, 181–185
Similes
  The Fly:, 75
  Grandmother:, 99
  My Mother Combs My Hair:, 133, 139
Simplicity
  This is Just to Say:, 244–245
Social change
  Women:, 316
Solidarity Movement
  Grandmother:, 99–100
  Possibilities:, 154–155
Sound
  The Stolen Child:, 222
Soviet Union
  The Bridegroom:, 38–42
  Grandmother:, 94, 99, 99–100, 101, 108
  Possibilities:, 154–155
Spirituality
  The Waking:, 297–298
Sprezzatura
  To Althea, From Prison:, 258
Stanzas
  The Bridegroom:, 33
Stoicism
  To Althea, From Prison:, 257
Suffering
  Up-Hill:, 281
Supernatural
  The Stolen Child:, 219–220

Symbolism
  The Stolen Child:, 223

T

Technology
  Up-Hill:, 284
Threats
  The Stolen Child:, 220
Time
  Midsummer, Tobago:, 115–116, 119–121
Transcendence
  This is Just to Say:, 242
Transcendentalism
  since feeling is first:, 178
  The Snow-Storm:, 194, 199–201, 203–205
Translation
  Possibilities:, 166–167

V

Vanity
  Autobiographia Literaria:, 6, 12
Victorian period literature, 1832-1901
  Up-Hill:, 283–285
Villanelle
  The Waking:, 298, 300

W

Wars
  Autobiographia Literaria:, 7
  Conscientious Objector:, 46–47
  This is Just to Say:, 245
Western culture
  My Mother Combs My Hair:, 133–135
Women. *See also:* Feminism
  To Althea, From Prison:, 264–273
  My Mother Combs My Hair:, 136, 141–144
  Women:, 318–319, 321–322
World War I, 1914-1918
  Autobiographia Literaria:, 7
  Conscientious Objector:, 47
World War II, 1939-1945
  This is Just to Say:, 245

Cumulative Index of First Lines

A

A brackish reach of shoal off Madaket,— (The Quaker Graveyard in Nantucket) V6:158

"A cold coming we had of it (Journey of the Magi) V7:110

A few minutes ago, I stepped onto the deck (The Cobweb) V17:50

A gentle spring evening arrives (Spring-Watching Pavilion) V18:198

A line in long array where they wind betwixt green islands, (Cavalry Crossing a Ford) V13:50

A narrow Fellow in the grass (A Narrow Fellow in the Grass) V11:127

A noiseless patient spider, (A Noiseless Patient Spider) V31:190–91

A pine box for me. I mean it. (Last Request) V14: 231

A poem should be palpable and mute (Ars Poetica) V5:2

A stone from the depths that has witnessed the seas drying up (Song of a Citizen) V16:125

A tourist came in from Orbitville, (Southbound on the Freeway) V16:158

A wind is ruffling the tawny pelt (A Far Cry from Africa) V6:60

a woman precedes me up the long rope, (Climbing) V14:113

About me the night moonless wimples the mountains (Vancouver Lights) V8:245

About suffering they were never wrong (Musée des Beaux Arts) V1:148

Across Roblin Lake, two shores away, (Wilderness Gothic) V12:241

After the double party (Air for Mercury) V20:2–3

After the party ends another party begins (Social Life) V19:251

After you finish your work (Ballad of Orange and Grape) V10:17

Again I've returned to this country (The Country Without a Post Office) V18:64

"Ah, are you digging on my grave (Ah, Are You Digging on My Grave?) V4:2

All Greece hates (Helen) V6:92

All my existence is a dark sign a dark (A Rebirth) V21:193–194

All night long the hockey pictures (To a Sad Daughter) V8:230

All over Genoa (Trompe l'Oeil) V22:216

All winter your brute shoulders strained against collars, padding (Names of Horses) V8:141

Also Ulysses once—that other war. (Kilroy) V14:213

Always (Always) V24:15

Among the blossoms, a single jar of wine. (Drinking Alone Beneath the Moon) V20:59–60

Anasazi (Anasazi) V9:2

"And do we remember our living lives?" (Memory) V21:156

And God stepped out on space (The Creation) V1:19

And what if I spoke of despair—who doesn't (And What If I Spoke of Despair) V19:2

Animal bones and some mossy tent rings (Lament for the Dorsets) V5:190

Announced by all the trumpets of the sky, (The Snow-Storm) V34:195

Any force— (All It Takes) V23:15

April is the cruellest month, breeding (The Waste Land) V20:248–252

As I perceive (The Gold Lily) V5:127

As I walked out one evening (As I Walked Out One Evening) V4:15

As I was going down impassive Rivers, (The Drunken Boat) V28:83

As in an illuminated page, whose busy edges (Bonnard's Garden) V25:33

As virtuous men pass mildly away (A Valediction: Forbidding Mourning) V11:201

As you set out for Ithaka (Ithaka) V19:114

At five in the afternoon. (Lament for Ignacio Sánchez Mejías) V31:128–30

At noon in the desert a panting lizard (At the Bomb Testing Site) V8:2

Cumulative Index of First Lines

At six I lived for spells: (What For) V33:266
Ay, tear her tattered ensign down! (Old Ironsides) V9:172

B

Back then, before we came (On Freedom's Ground) V12:186
Bananas ripe and green, and ginger-root (The Tropics in New York) V4:255
Be happy if the wind inside the orchard (On the Threshold) V22:128
Because I could not stop for Death— (Because I Could Not Stop for Death) V2:27
Before the indifferent beak could let her drop? (Leda and the Swan) V13:182
Before you know what kindness really is (Kindness) V24:84–85
Below long pine winds, a stream twists. (Jade Flower Palace) V32:145
Bent double, like old beggars under slacks, (Dulce et Decorum Est) V10:109
Between my finger and my thumb (Digging) V5:70
Beware of ruins: they have a treacherous charm (Beware of Ruins) V8:43
Bright star! would I were steadfast as thou art— (Bright Star! Would I Were Steadfast as Thou Art) V9:44
But perhaps God needs the longing, wherever else should it dwell, (But Perhaps God Needs the Longing) V20:41
By the rude bridge that arched the flood (Concord Hymn) V4:30
By way of a vanished bridge we cross this river (The Garden Shukkei-en) V18:107

C

Cassandra's kind of crying was (Three To's and an Oi) V24:264
Celestial choir! enthron'd in realms of light, (To His Excellency General Washington) V13:212
Come with me into those things that have felt his despair for so long— (Come with Me) V6:31
Complacencies of the peignoir, and late (Sunday Morning) V16:189
Composed in the Tower, before his execution ("More Light! More Light!") V6:119

D

Darkened by time, the masters, like our memories, mix (Black Zodiac) V10:46
Dear Sirs: (In Response to Executive Order 9066: All Americans of Japanese Descent Must Report to Relocation Centers) V32:129
Death, be not proud, though some have called thee (Holy Sonnet 10) V2:103
Devouring Time, blunt thou the lion's paws (Sonnet 19) V9:210
Disoriented, the newly dead try to turn back, (Our Side) V24:177
Do not go gentle into that good night (Do Not Go Gentle into that Good Night) V1:51
Do not weep, maiden, for war is kind (War Is Kind) V9:252
Does the road wind up-hill all the way? (Up-Hill) V34:279
Don Arturo says: (Business) V16:2
Drink to me only with thine eyes, (Song: To Celia) V23:270–271
(Dumb, (A Grafted Tongue) V12:92

E

Each day the shadow swings (In the Land of Shinar) V7:83
Each morning the man rises from bed because the invisible (It's like This) V23:138–139
Each night she waits by the road (Bidwell Ghost) V14:2
Even when you know what people are capable of, (Knowledge) V25:113
Everything has been plundered, betrayed, sold out, (Everything Is Plundered) V32:113

F

Face of the skies (Moreover, the Moon) V20:153
Falling upon earth (Falling Upon Earth) V2:64
Farewell, thou child of my right hand, and joy; (On My First Son) V33:166
Far far from gusty waves these children's faces. (An Elementary School Classroom in a Slum) V23:88–89
Fast breaks. Lay ups. With Mercury's (Slam, Dunk, & Hook) V30:176–177
First, the self. Then, the observing self. (I, I, I) V26:97
Five years have past; five summers, with the length (Tintern Abbey) V2:249
Flesh is heretic. (Anorexic) V12:2
For a long time the butterfly held a prominent place in psychology (Lepidopterology) V23:171–172
For Jews, the Cossacks are always coming. (The Cossacks) V25:70
For three years, out of key with his time, (Hugh Selwyn Mauberley) V16:26
Forgive me for thinking I saw (For a New Citizen of These United States) V15:55
From my mother's sleep I fell into the State (The Death of the Ball Turret Gunner) V2:41
From the air to the air, like an empty net, (The Heights of Macchu Picchu) V28:137

G

Gardener: Sir, I encountered Death (Incident in a Rose Garden) V14:190
Gather ye Rose-buds while ye may, (To the Virgins, to Make Much of Time) V13:226
Gazelle, I killed you (Ode to a Drum) V20:172–173
Glory be to God for dappled things— (Pied Beauty) V26:161
Go down, Moses (Go Down, Moses) V11:42
God save America, (America, America) V29:2
Grandmothers who wring the necks (Classic Ballroom Dances) V33:3
Gray mist wolf (Four Mountain Wolves) V9:131

H

"Had he and I but met (The Man He Killed) V3:167
Had we but world enough, and time (To His Coy Mistress) V5:276
Hail to thee, blithe Spirit! (To a Sky-Lark) V32:251
Half a league, half a league (The Charge of the Light Brigade) V1:2
Having a Coke with You (Having a Coke with You) V12:105
He clasps the crag with crooked hands (The Eagle) V11:30
He was found by the Bureau of Statistics to be (The Unknown Citizen) V3:302
He was seen, surrounded by rifles, (The Crime Was in Granada) V23:55–56

Hear the sledges with the bells— (The Bells) V3:46
Heart, you bully, you punk, I'm wrecked, I'm shocked (One Is One) V24:158
Her body is not so white as (Queen-Ann's-Lace) V6:179
Her eyes the glow-worm lend thee; (The Night Piece: To Julia) V29:206
Her eyes were coins of porter and her West (A Farewell to English) V10:126
Here, above, (The Man-Moth) V27:135
Here they are. The soft eyes open (The Heaven of Animals) V6:75
His Grace! impossible! what dead! (A Satirical Elegy on the Death of a Late Famous General) V27:216
His speed and strength, which is the strength of ten (His Speed and Strength) V19:96
Hog Butcher for the World (Chicago) V3:61
Hold fast to dreams (Dream Variations) V15:42
Hope is a tattered flag and a dream out of time. (Hope is a Tattered Flag) V12:120
"Hope" is the thing with feathers— ("Hope" Is the Thing with Feathers) V3:123
How do I love thee? Let me count the ways (Sonnet 43) V2:236
How is your life with the other one, (An Attempt at Jealousy) V29:23
How shall we adorn (Angle of Geese) V2:2
How soon hath Time, the subtle thief of youth, (On His Having Arrived at the Age of Twenty-Three) V17:159
How would it be if you took yourself off (Landscape with Tractor) V10:182
Hunger crawls into you (Hunger in New York City) V4:79

I

I am fourteen (Hanging Fire) V32:93
I am not a painter, I am a poet (Why I Am Not a Painter) V8:258
I am silver and exact. I have no preconceptions (Mirror) V1:116
I am the Smoke King (The Song of the Smoke) V13:196
I am trying to pry open your casket (Dear Reader) V10:85
I became a creature of light (The Mystery) V15:137
I cannot love the Brothers Wright (Reactionary Essay on Applied Science) V9:199
I caught a tremendous fish (The Fish) V31:44
I died for Beauty—but was scarce (I Died for Beauty) V28:174
I don't mean to make you cry. (Monologue for an Onion) V24:120–121
I felt a Funeral, in my Brain, (I felt a Funeral in my Brain) V13:137
I gave birth to life. (Maternity) V21:142–143
I have eaten (This Is Just to Say) V34:240
I have just come down from my father (The Hospital Window) V11:58
I have met them at close of day (Easter 1916) V5:91
I have sown beside all waters in my day. (A Black Man Talks of Reaping) V32:20
I haven't the heart to say (To an Unknown Poet) V18:221
I hear America singing, the varied carols I hear (I Hear America Singing) V3:152
I heard a Fly buzz—when I died— (I Heard a Fly Buzz— When I Died—) V5:140
I know that I shall meet my fate (An Irish Airman Foresees His Death) V1:76
I know what the caged bird feels, alas! (Sympathy) V33:203
I leant upon a coppice gate (The Darkling Thrush) V18:74
I lie down on my side in the moist grass (Omen) v22:107
I looked in my heart while the wild swans went over. (Wild Swans) V17:221
I met a traveller from an antique land (Ozymandias) V27:173
I prove a theorem and the house expands: (Geometry) V15:68
I saw that a star had broken its rope (Witness) V26:285
I see them standing at the formal gates of their colleges, (I go Back to May 1937) V17:112
I shall die, but that is all that I shall do for Death. (Conscientious Objector) V34:46
I shook your hand before I went. (Mastectomy) V26:122
I sit in one of the dives (September 1, 1939) V27:234
I sit in the top of the wood, my eyes closed (Hawk Roosting) V4:55
I thought, as I wiped my eyes on the corner of my apron: (An Ancient Gesture) V31:3
I thought wearing an evergreen dress (Pine) V23:223–224
I, too, sing America. (I, Too) V30:99
I wandered lonely as a cloud (I Wandered Lonely as a Cloud) V33:71
I was angry with my friend; (A Poison Tree) V24:195–196
I was born in the congo (Ego-Tripping) V28:112
I was born too late and I am much too old, (Death Sentences) V22:23
I was born under the mudbank (Seeing You) V24:244–245
I was sitting in mcsorley's. outside it was New York and beautifully snowing. (i was sitting in mcsorley's) V13:151
I will arise and go now, and go to Innisfree, (The Lake Isle of Innisfree) V15:121
If all the world and love were young, (The Nymph's Reply to the Shepard) V14:241
If ever two were one, then surely we (To My Dear and Loving Husband) V6:228
If every time their minds drifted, (What the Poets Could Have Been) V26:261
If I should die, think only this of me (The Soldier) V7:218
If you can keep your head when all about you (If) V22:54–55
If you want my apartment, sleep in it (Rent) V25:164
I'm delighted to see you (The Constellation Orion) V8:53
"Imagine being the first to say: *surveillance*," (Inventors) V7:97
Impatient for home, (Portrait of a Couple at Century's End) V24:214–215
In 1790 a woman could die by falling (The Art of the Novel) V23:29
In 1936, a child (Blood Oranges) V13:34
In a while they rose and went out aimlessly riding, (Merlin Enthralled) V16:72
In China (Lost Sister) V5:216
In ethics class so many years ago (Ethics) V8:88
In Flanders fields the poppies blow (In Flanders Fields) V5:155

In India in their lives they happen (Ways to Live) V16:228
In May, when sea-winds pierced our solitudes, (The Rhodora) V17:191
In such a night, when every louder wind (A Nocturnal Reverie) V30:119–120
In the bottom drawer of my desk... (Answers to Letters) V21:30–31
In the evening (Another Night in the Ruins) V26:12
In the groves of Africa from their natural wonder (An African Elegy) V13:3
In the Shreve High football stadium (Autumn Begins in Martins Ferry, Ohio) V8:17
In the sixty-eight years (Accounting) V21:2–3
In Xanadu did Kubla Khan (Kubla Khan) V5:172
Ink runs from the corners of my mouth (Eating Poetry) V9:60
Is it the boy in me who's looking out (The Boy) V19:14
It is a cold and snowy night. The main street is deserted. (Driving to Town Late to Mail a Letter) V17:63
It is an ancient Mariner (The Rime of the Ancient Mariner) V4:127
It is in the small things we see it. (Courage) V14:125
It is said, the past (Russian Letter) V26:181
It little profits that an idle king (Ulysses) V2:278
It looked extremely rocky for the Mudville nine that day (Casey at the Bat) V5:57
It must be troubling for the god who loves you (The God Who Loves You) V20:88
It seems vainglorious and proud (The Conquerors) V13:67
It starts with a low rumbling, white static, (Rapture) V21:181
It was in and about the Martinmas time (Barbara Allan) V7:10
It was many and many a year ago (Annabel Lee) V9:14
It was not dying: everybody died. (Losses) V31:167–68
It was the schooner Hesperus, (The Wreck of the Hesperus) V31:317
Its quick soft silver bell beating, beating (Auto Wreck) V3:31
I've got the children to tend (Woman Work) V33:289
I've known rivers; (The Negro Speaks of Rivers) V10:197

J

Januaries, Nature greets our eyes (Brazil, January 1, 1502) V6:15
Just off the highway to Rochester, Minnesota (A Blessing) V7:24
just once (For the White poets who would be Indian) V13:112

L

l(a (l(a) V1:85
Las casitas near the gray cannery, (Freeway 280) V30:62
Leave Crete and come to me now, to that holy temple, (Fragment 2) V31:63
Legs! (Poem in Which My Legs Are Accepted) V29:262
Let me not to the marriage of true minds (Sonnet 116) V3:288
Let us console you. (Allegory) V23:2–3
Listen, my children, and you shall hear (Paul Revere's Ride) V2:178
Little Fly, (The Fly) V34:70
Little Lamb, who made thee? (The Lamb) V12:134
Long long ago when the world was a wild place (Bedtime Story) V8:32

M

Made of the first gray light (One of the Smallest) V26:141
maggie and milly and molly and may (maggie & milly & molly & may) V12:149
Mary sat musing on the lamp-flame at the table (The Death of the Hired Man) V4:42
May breath for a dead moment cease as jerking your (Curse) V26:75
Men with picked voices chant the names (Overture to a Dance of Locomotives) V11:143
Morning and evening (Goblin Market) V27:92
"Mother dear, may I go downtown (Ballad of Birmingham) V5:17
Much Madness is divinest Sense— (Much Madness is Divinest Sense) V16:86
My black face fades (Facing It) V5:109
My father stands in the warm evening (Starlight) V8:213
My friend, are you sleeping? (Two Eclipses) V33:220
my grandmother (Grandmother) V34:95
My grandmothers were strong. (Lineage) V31:145–46
My heart aches, and a drowsy numbness pains (Ode to a Nightingale) V3:228
My heart is like a singing bird (A Birthday) V10:33
My life closed twice before its close— (My Life Closed Twice Before Its Close) V8:127
My long two-pointed ladder's sticking through a tree (After Apple Picking) V32:3
My mistress' eyes are nothing like the sun (Sonnet 130) V1:247
My uncle in East Germany (The Exhibit) V9:107

N

Nature's first green is gold (Nothing Gold Can Stay) V3:203
No easy thing to bear, the weight of sweetness (The Weight of Sweetness) V11:230
No monument stands over Babii Yar. (Babii Yar) V29:38
Nobody heard him, the dead man (Not Waving but Drowning) V3:216
Not like a cypress, (Not like a Cypress) V24:135
Not marble nor the gilded monuments (Sonnet 55) V5:246
Not the memorized phone numbers. (What Belongs to Us) V15:196
Now as I was young and easy under the apple boughs (Fern Hill) V3:92
Now as I watch the progress of the plague (The Missing) V9:158
Now I rest my head on the satyr's carved chest, (The Satyr's Heart) V22:187
Now one might catch it see it (Fading Light) V21:49

O

O Captain! my Captain, our fearful trip is done (O Captain! My Captain!) V2:146
O Lord our Lord, how excellent is thy name in all the earth! who hast set thy glory above the heavens (Psalm 8) V9:182
O my Luve's like a red, red rose (A Red, Red Rose) V8:152
O what can ail thee, knight-at-arms, (La Belle Dame sans Merci) V17:18
"O where ha' you been, Lord Randal, my son? (Lord Randal) V6:105

Cumulative Index of First Lines

O wild West Wind, thou breath of Autumn's being (Ode to the West Wind) V2:163
Oh, but it is dirty! (Filling Station) V12:57
old age sticks (old age sticks) V3:246
On a shore washed by desolate waves, *he* stood, (The Bronze Horseman) V28:27
On either side the river lie (The Lady of Shalott) V15:95
On the seashore of endless worlds children meet. The infinite (60) V18:3
Once some people were visiting Chekhov (Chocolates) V11:17
Once upon a midnight dreary, while I pondered, weak and weary (The Raven) V1:200
One day I'll lift the telephone (Elegy for My Father, Who Is Not Dead) V14:154
One day I wrote her name upon the strand, (Sonnet 75) V32:215
One foot down, then hop! It's hot (Harlem Hopscotch) V2:93
one shoe on the roadway presents (A Piéd) V3:16
Our vision is our voice (An Anthem) V26:34
Out of the hills of Habersham, (Song of the Chattahoochee) V14:283
Out walking in the frozen swamp one gray day (The Wood-Pile) V6:251
Oysters we ate (Oysters) V4:91

P

Pentagon code (Smart and Final Iris) V15:183
Poised between going on and back, pulled (The Base Stealer) V12:30

Q

Quinquireme of Nineveh from distant Ophir (Cargoes) V5:44
Quite difficult, belief. (Chorale) V25:51

R

Recognition in the body (In Particular) V20:125
Red men embraced my body's whiteness (Birch Canoe) V5:31
Remember me when I am gone away (Remember) V14:255
Remember the sky you were born under, (Remember) V32:185
Riches I hold in light esteem, (Old Stoic) V33:143

S

Shall I compare thee to a Summer's day? (Sonnet 18) V2:222
She came every morning to draw water (A Drink of Water) V8:66
She reads, of course, what he's doing, shaking Nixon's hand, (The Women Who Loved Elvis All Their Lives) V28:273
She sang beyond the genius of the sea. (The Idea of Order at Key West) V13:164
She walks in beauty, like the night (She Walks in Beauty) V14:268
She was my grandfather's second wife. Coming late (My Grandmother's Plot in the Family Cemetery) V27:154
Side by side, their faces blurred, (An Arundel Tomb) V12:17
since feeling is first (since feeling is first) V34:172
Since the professional wars— (Midnight) V2:130
Since then, I work at night. (Ten Years after Your Deliberate Drowning) V21:240
S'io credesse che mia risposta fosse (The Love Song of J. Alfred Prufrock) V1:97
Sky black (Duration) V18:93
Sleepless as Prospero back in his bedroom (Darwin in 1881) V13:83
so much depends (The Red Wheelbarrow) V1:219
So the man spread his blanket on the field (A Tall Man Executes a Jig) V12:228
So the sky wounded you, jagged at the heart, (Daylights) V13:101
Softly, in the dark, a woman is singing to me (Piano) V6:145
Some say it's in the reptilian dance (The Greatest Grandeur) V18:119
Some say the world will end in fire (Fire and Ice) V7:57
Something there is that doesn't love a wall (Mending Wall) V5:231
Sometimes walking late at night (Butcher Shop) V7:43
Sometimes, a lion with a prophet's beard (For An Assyrian Frieze) V9:120
Sometimes, in the middle of the lesson (Music Lessons) V8:117
somewhere i have never travelled,gladly beyond (somewhere i have never travelled,gladly beyond) V19:265
South of the bridge on Seventeenth (Fifteen) V2:78
Stop all the clocks, cut off the telephone, (Funeral Blues) V10:139
Strong Men, riding horses. In the West (Strong Men, Riding Horses) V4:209
Such places are too still for history, (Deep Woods) V14:138
Sundays too my father got up early (Those Winter Sundays) V1:300
Sweet day, so cool, so calm, so bright, (Virtue) V25:263
Swing low sweet chariot (Swing Low Sweet Chariot) V1:283

T

Take heart, monsieur, four-fifths of this province (For Jean Vincent D'abbadie, Baron St.-Castin) V12:78
Take sheds and stalls from Billingsgate, (The War Correspondent) V26:235
Tears, idle tears, I know not what they mean (Tears, Idle Tears) V4:220
Tell me not, in mournful numbers (A Psalm of Life) V7:165
Tell me not, Sweet, I am unkind, (To Lucasta, Going to the Wars) V32:291
Temple bells die out. (Temple Bells Die Out) V18:210
That is no country for old men. The young (Sailing to Byzantium) V2:207
That negligible bit of sand which slides (Variations on Nothing) V20:234
That time of drought the embered air (Drought Year) V8:78
That's my last Duchess painted on the wall (My Last Duchess) V1:165
The apparition of these faces in the crowd (In a Station of the Metro) V2:116
The Assyrian came down like the wolf on the fold (The Destruction of Sennacherib) V1:38
The bored child at the auction (The Wings) V28:242
The broken pillar of the wing jags from the clotted shoulder (Hurt Hawks) V3:138
The bud (Saint Francis and the Sow) V9:222
The Bustle in a House (The Bustle in a House) V10:62

The buzz saw snarled and rattled in the yard (Out, Out—) V10:212
The couple on the left of me (Walk Your Body Down) V26:219
The courage that my mother had (The Courage that My Mother Had) V3:79
The Curfew tolls the knell of parting day (Elegy Written in a Country Churchyard) V9:73
The fiddler crab fiddles, glides and dithers, (Fiddler Crab) V23:111–112
The force that through the green fuse drives the flower (The Force That Through the Green Fuse Drives the Flower) V8:101
The grasses are light brown (September) V23:258–259
The green lamp flares on the table (This Life) V1:293
The house is crammed: tier beyond tier they grin ("Blighters") V28:3
The ills I sorrow at (Any Human to Another) V3:2
The instructor said (Theme for English B) V6:194
The king sits in Dumferling toune (Sir Patrick Spens) V4:177
The land was overmuch like scenery (Beowulf) V11:2
The last time I saw it was 1968. (The Hiding Place) V10:152
The Lord is my shepherd; I shall not want (Psalm 23) V4:103
The man who sold his lawn to standard oil (The War Against the Trees) V11:215
The moon glows the same (The Moon Glows the Same) V7:152
The old South Boston Aquarium stands (For the Union Dead) V7:67
The others bent their heads and started in ("Trouble with Math in a One-Room Country School") V9:238
The pale nuns of St. Joseph are here (Island of Three Marias) V11:79
The Phoenix comes of flame and dust (The Phoenix) V10:226
The plants of the lake (Two Poems for T.) V20:218
The poetry of earth is never dead: (On the Grasshopper and the Cricket) V32:161
The rain set early in to-night: (Porphyria's Lover) V15:151
The river brought down (How We Heard the Name) V10:167
The room is full (My Mother Combs My Hair) V34:132
The rusty spigot (Onomatopoeia) V6:133
The sea is calm tonight (Dover Beach) V2:52
The sea sounds insincere (The Milkfish Gatherers) V11:111
The slow overture of rain, (Mind) V17:145
The Soul selects her own Society— (The Soul Selects Her Own Society) V1:259
The summer that I was ten— (The Centaur) V30:20
"The sun was shining on the sea, (The Walrus and the Carpenter) V30:258–259
The surface of the pond was mostly green— (The Lotus Flowers) V33:107
The time you won your town the race (To an Athlete Dying Young) V7:230
The way sorrow enters the bone (The Blue Rim of Memory) V17:38
The whiskey on your breath (My Papa's Waltz) V3:191
The white ocean in which birds swim (Morning Walk) V21:167
The wind was a torrent of darkness among the gusty trees (The Highwayman) V4:66
The windows were open and the morning air was, by the smell of lilac and some darker flowering shrub, filled with the brown and chirping trills of birds. (Yet we insist that life is full of happy chance) V27:291
There are blows in life, so hard … I just don't know! (The Black Heralds) V26:47
There are strange things done in the midnight sun (The Cremation of Sam McGee) V10:75
There have been rooms for such a short time (The Horizons of Rooms) V15:79
There is a hunger for order, (A Thirst Against) V20:205
There is no way not to be excited (Paradiso) V20:190–191
There is the one song everyone (Siren Song) V7:196
There will come soft rains and the smell of the ground, (There Will Come Soft Rains) V14:301
There you are, in all your innocence, (Perfect Light) V19:187
There's a Certain Slant of Light (There's a Certain Slant of Light) V6:211
There's no way out. (In the Suburbs) V14:201
These open years, the river (For Jennifer, 6, on the Teton) V17:86
These unprepossessing sunsets (Art Thou the Thing I Wanted) V25:2–3
They eat beans mostly, this old yellow pair (The Bean Eaters) V2:16
They said, "Wait." Well, I waited. (Alabama Centennial) V10:2
They say a child with two mouths is no good. (Pantoun for Chinese Women) V29:241
they were just meant as covers (My Mother Pieced Quilts) V12:169
This girlchild was: born as usual (Barbie Doll) V9:33
This is a litany of lost things, (The Litany) V24:101–102
This is my letter to the World (This Is My Letter to the World) V4:233
This is the Arsenal. From floor to ceiling, (The Arsenal at Springfield) V17:2
This is the black sea-brute bulling through wave-wrack (Leviathan) V5:203
This is the ship of pearl, which, poets feign, (The Chambered Nautilus) V24:52–53
This poem is concerned with language on a very plain level (Paradoxes and Oxymorons) V11:162
This tale is true, and mine. It tells (The Seafarer) V8:177
Thou still unravish'd bride of quietness (Ode on a Grecian Urn) V1:179
Three days Natasha'd been astray, (The Bridegroom) V34:26
Three times my life has opened. (Three Times My Life Has Opened) V16:213
Time in school drags along with so much worry, (Childhood) V19:29
to fold the clothes. No matter who lives (I Stop Writing the Poem) V16:58
To him who in the love of Nature holds (Thanatopsis) V30:232–233
To replay errors (Daughter-Mother-Maya-Seeta) V25:83

To weep unbidden, to wake (Practice) V23:240
Toni Morrison despises (The Toni Morrison Dreams) V22:202–203
Tonight I can write the saddest lines (Tonight I Can Write) V11:187
tonite, *thriller* was (Beware: Do Not Read This Poem) V6:3
Truth be told, I do not want to forget (Native Guard) V29:183
Turning and turning in the widening gyre (The Second Coming) V7:179
'Twas brillig, and the slithy toves (Jabberwocky) V11:91
'Twas mercy brought me from my pagan land, (On Being Brought from Africa to America) V29:223
Two roads diverged in a yellow wood (The Road Not Taken) V2:195
Tyger! Tyger! burning bright (The Tyger) V2:263

W

wade (The Fish) V14:171
Wanting to say things, (My Father's Song) V16:102
We are saying goodbye (Station) V21:226–227
We came from our own country in a red room (Originally) V25:146–147
We cannot know his legendary head (Archaic Torso of Apollo) V27:3
We could be here. This is the valley (Small Town with One Road) V7:207
We met the British in the dead of winter (Meeting the British) V7:138
We real cool. We (We Real Cool) V6:242
Well, son, I'll tell you (Mother to Son) V3:178
What dire offense from amorous causes springs, (The Rape of the Lock) V12:202
What happens to a dream deferred? (Harlem) V1:63
What of the neighborhood homes awash (The Continuous Life) V18:51

What thoughts I have of you tonight, Walt Whitman, for I walked down the sidestreets under the trees with a headache self-conscious looking at the full moon (A Supermarket in California) V5:261
Whatever it is, it must have (American Poetry) V7:2
When Abraham Lincoln was shoveled into the tombs, he forgot the copperheads, and the assassin... in the dust, in the cool tombs (Cool Tombs) V6:45
When despair for the world grows in me (The Peace of Wild Things) V30:159
When he spoke of where he came from, (Grudnow) V32:73
When I consider how my light is spent ([On His Blindness] Sonnet 16) V3:262
When I go away from you (The Taxi) V30:211–212
When I have fears that I may cease to be (When I Have Fears that I May Cease to Be) V2:295
When I heard the learn'd astronomer, (When I Heard the Learn'd Astronomer) V22:244
When I see a couple of kids (High Windows) V3:108
When I see birches bend to left and right (Birches) V13:14
When I was a child (Autobiographia Literaria) V34:2
When I was born, you waited (Having it Out with Melancholy) V17:98
When I was one-and-twenty (When I Was One-and-Twenty) V4:268
When I watch you (Miss Rosie) V1:133
When Love with confinéd wings (To Althea, From Prison) V34:254
When the mountains of Puerto Rico (We Live by What We See at Night) V13:240
When the world was created wasn't it like this? (Anniversary) V15:2
When they said *Carrickfergus* I could hear (The Singer's House) V17:205
When we two parted (When We Two Parted) V29:297
When you consider the radiance, that it does not withhold (The City Limits) V19:78

When you look through the window in Sag Harbor and see (View) V25:246–247
When, in disgrace with Fortune and men's eyes (Sonnet 29) V8:198
Whenever Richard Cory went down town (Richard Cory) V4:116
Where dips the rocky highland (The Stolen Child) V34:216
While I was gone a war began. (While I Was Gone a War Began) V21:253–254
While my hair was still cut straight across my forehead (The River-Merchant's Wife: A Letter) V8:164
While the long grain is softening (Early in the Morning) V17:75
While this America settles in the mould of its vulgarity, heavily thickening to empire (Shine, Perishing Republic) V4:161
While you are preparing for sleep, brushing your teeth, (The Afterlife) V18:39
Who has ever stopped to think of the divinity of Lamont Cranston? (In Memory of Radio) V9:144
Whose woods these are I think I know (Stopping by Woods on a Snowy Evening) V1:272
Whoso list to hunt: I know where is an hind. (Whoso List to Hunt) V25:286
Why should I let the toad *work* (Toads) V4:244

Y

You are small and intense (To a Child Running With Outstretched Arms in Canyon de Chelly) V11:173
You can't hear? Everything here is changing. (The River Mumma Wants Out) V25:191
You do not have to be good. (Wild Geese) V15:207
You should lie down now and remember the forest, (The Forest) V22:36–37
You stood thigh-deep in water and green light glanced (Lake) V23:158
You were never told, Mother, how old Illya was drunk (The Czar's Last Christmas Letter) V12:44

Cumulative Index of Last Lines

A

... a capital T in the endless mass of the text. (Answers to Letters) V21:30–31
a fleck of foam. (Accounting) V21:2–3
A heart that will one day beat you to death. (Monologue for an Onion) V24:120–121
A heart whose love is innocent! (She Walks in Beauty) V14:268
a man then suddenly stops running (Island of Three Marias) V11:80
A perfect evening! (Temple Bells Die Out) V18:210
a space in the lives of their friends (Beware: Do Not Read This Poem) V6:3
A sudden blow: the great wings beating still (Leda and the Swan) V13:181
A terrible beauty is born (Easter 1916) V5:91
About him, and lies down to pleasant dreams. (Thanatopsis) V30:232–233
About my big, new, automatically defrosting refrigerator with the built-in electric eye (Reactionary Essay on Applied Science) V9:199
about the tall mounds of termites. (Song of a Citizen) V16:126
Across the expedient and wicked stones (Auto Wreck) V3:31
affirming its brilliant and dizzying love. (Lepidopterology) V23:171

Ah, dear father, graybeard, lonely old courage-teacher, what America did you have when Charon quit poling his ferry and you got out on a smoking bank and stood watching the boat disappear on the black waters of Lethe? (A Supermarket in California) V5:261
All losses are restored and sorrows end (Sonnet 30) V4:192
Amen. Amen (The Creation) V1:20
Anasazi (Anasazi) V9:3
and a vase of wild flowers. (The War Correspondent) V26:239
and all beyond saving by children (Ethics) V8:88
and all the richer for it. (Mind) V17:146
And all we need of hell (My Life Closed Twice Before Its Close) V8:127
And, being heard, doesn't vanish in the dark. (Variations on Nothing) V20:234
and changed, back to the class ("Trouble with Math in a One-Room Country School") V9:238
and chant him a blessing, a sutra. (What For) V33:267
And covered up—our names— (I Died for Beauty) V28:174
And dances with the daffodils. (I Wandered Lonely as a Cloud) V33:71

And death i think is no parenthesis (since feeling is first) V34:172
And Death shall be no more: Death, thou shalt die (Holy Sonnet 10) V2:103
and destruction. (Allegory) V23:2–3
And drunk the milk of Paradise (Kubla Khan) V5:172
and fear lit by the breadth of such calmly turns to praise. (The City Limits) V19:78
And Finished knowing—then— (I Felt a Funeral in My Brain) V13:137
And gallop terribly against each other's bodies (Autumn Begins in Martins Ferry, Ohio) V8:17
and go back. (For the White poets who would be Indian) V13:112
And handled with a Chain—(Much Madness is Divinest Sense) V16:86
And has not begun to grow a manly smile. (Deep Woods) V14:139
And his own Word (The Phoenix) V10:226
And I am Nicholas. (The Czar's Last Christmas Letter) V12:45
And I let the fish go. (The Fish) V31:44
And I was unaware. (The Darkling Thrush) V18:74
And in the suburbs Can't sat down and cried. (Kilroy) V14:213
And it's been years. (Anniversary) V15:3
and joy may come, and make its test of us. (One Is One) V24:158

and leaving essence to the inner eye. (Memory) V21:156
And life for me ain't been no crystal stair (Mother to Son) V3:179
And like a thunderbolt he falls (The Eagle) V11:30
And makes me end where I begun (A Valediction: Forbidding Mourning) V11:202
And 'midst the stars inscribe Belinda's name. (The Rape of the Lock) V12:209
And miles to go before I sleep (Stopping by Woods on a Snowy Evening) V1:272
and my father saying things. (My Father's Song) V16:102
And no birds sing. (La Belle Dame sans Merci) V17:18
And not waving but drowning (Not Waving but Drowning) V3:216
And oh, 'tis true, 'tis true (When I Was One-and-Twenty) V4:268
And reach for your scalping knife. (For Jean Vincent D'abbadie, Baron St.-Castin) V12:78
and retreating, always retreating, behind it (Brazil, January 1, 1502) V6:16
And settled upon his eyes in a black soot ("More Light! More Light!") V6:120
And shuts his eyes. (Darwin in 1881) V13: 84
and so cold (This Is Just to Say) V34:241
And so live ever—or else swoon to death (Bright Star! Would I Were Steadfast as Thou Art) V9:44
and strange and loud was the dingoes' cry (Drought Year) V8:78
and stride out. (Courage) V14:126
and sweat and fat and greed. (Anorexic) V12:3
And that has made all the difference (The Road Not Taken) V2:195
And the deep river ran on (As I Walked Out One Evening) V4:16
And the midnight message of Paul Revere (Paul Revere's Ride) V2:180
And the mome raths outgrabe (Jabberwocky) V11:91
And the Salvation Army singing God loves us.... (Hopeis a Tattered Flag) V12:120
And therewith ends my story. (The Bridegroom) V34:28

and these the last verses that I write for her (Tonight I Can Write) V11:187
and thickly wooded country; the moon. (The Art of the Novel) V23:29
And those roads in South Dakota that feel around in the darkness... (Come with Me) V6:31
and to know she will stay in the field till you die? (Landscape with Tractor) V10:183
and two blankets embroidered with smallpox (Meeting the British) V7:138
and waving, shouting, *Welcome back*. (Elegy for My Father, Who Is Not Dead) V14:154
And—which is more—you'll be a Man, my son! (If) V22:54–55
and whose skin is made dusky by stars. (September) V23:258–259
And wild for to hold, though I seem tame.' (Whoso List to Hunt) V25:286
And would suffice (Fire and Ice) V7:57
And yet God has not said a word! (Porphyria's Lover) V15:151
and you spread un the thin halo of night mist. (Ways to Live) V16:229
And Zero at the Bone— (A Narrow Fellow in the Grass) V11:127
(answer with a tower of birds) (Duration) V18:93
Around us already perhaps future moons, suns and stars blaze in a fiery wreath. (But Perhaps God Needs the Longing) V20:41
aspired to become lighter than air (Blood Oranges) V13:34
As any She belied with false compare (Sonnet 130) V1:248
As ever in my great Task-Master's eye. (On His Having Arrived at the Age of Twenty-Three) V17:160
As far as Cho-fu-Sa (The River-Merchant's Wife: A Letter) V8:165
as it has disappeared. (The Wings) V28:244
As the contagion of those molten eyes (For An Assyrian Frieze) V9:120
As they lean over the beans in their rented back room that is full of beads and receipts and dolls and clothes, tobacco crumbs, vases and fringes (The Bean Eaters) V2:16

as we crossed the field, I told her. (The Centaur) V30:20
As what he loves may never like too much. (On My First Son) V33:166
at home in the fish's fallen heaven (Birch Canoe) V5:31
away, pedaling hard, rocket and pilot. (His Speed and Strength) V19:96

B

Back to the play of constant give and change (The Missing) V9:158
Beautiful & dangerous. (Slam, Dunk, & Hook) V30:176–177
Before it was quite unsheathed from reality (Hurt Hawks) V3:138
before we're even able to name them. (Station) V21:226–227
behind us and all our shining ambivalent love airborne there before us. (Our Side) V24:177
Black like me. (Dream Variations) V15:42
Bless me (Hunger in New York City) V4:79
bombs scandalizing the sanctity of night. (While I Was Gone a War Began) V21:253–254
But, baby, where are you?" (Ballad of Birmingham) V5:17
But be (Ars Poetica) V5:3
But for centuries we have longed for it. (Everything Is Plundered) V32:34
but it works every time (Siren Song) V7:196
but the truth is, it is, lost to us now. (The Forest) V22:36–37
But there is no joy in Mudville— mighty Casey has "Struck Out." (Casey at the Bat) V5:58
But we hold our course, and the wind is with us. (On Freedom's Ground) V12:187
by a beeswax candle pooling beside their dinnerware. (Portrait of a Couple at Century's End) V24:214–215
by good fortune (The Horizons of Rooms) V15:80

C

Calls through the valleys of Hall. (Song of the Chattahoochee) V14:284
chickens (The Red Wheelbarrow) V1:219
clear water dashes (Onomatopoeia) V6:133

Cumulative Index of Last Lines

Columbia. (Kindness) V24:84–85
come to life and burn? (Bidwell Ghost) V14:2
Comin' for to carry me home (Swing Low Sweet Chariot) V1:284
cool as from underground springs and pure enough to drink. (The Man-Moth) V27:135
crossed the water. (All It Takes) V23:15

D

Dare frame thy fearful symmetry? (The Tyger) V2:263
"Dead," was all he answered (The Death of the Hired Man) V4:44
deep in the deepest one, tributaries burn. (For Jennifer, 6, on the Teton) V17:86
Delicate, delicate, delicate, delicate—now! (The Base Stealer) V12:30
Die soon (We Real Cool) V6:242
Do what you are going to do, I will tell about it. (I go Back to May 1937) V17:113
down from the sky (Russian Letter) V26:181
Down in the flood of remembrance, I weep like a child for the past (Piano) V6:145
Downward to darkness, on extended wings. (Sunday Morning) V16:190
Driving around, I will waste more time. (Driving to Town Late to Mail a Letter) V17:63
dry wells that fill so easily now (The Exhibit) V9:107
dust rises in many myriads of grains. (Not like a Cypress) V24:135
dusty as miners, into the restored volumes. (Bonnard's Garden) V25:33

E

endless worlds is the great meeting of children. (60) V18:3
Enjoy such liberty. (To Althea, From Prison) V34:255
Eternal, unchanging creator of earth. Amen (The Seafarer) V8:178
Eternity of your arms around my neck. (Death Sentences) V22:23
even as it vanishes—were not our life. (The Litany) V24:101–102
ever finds anything more of immortality. (Jade Flower Palace) V32:145
every branch traced with the ghost writing of snow. (The Afterlife) V18:39

F

fall upon us, the dwellers in shadow (In the Land of Shinar) V7:84
Fallen cold and dead (O Captain! My Captain!) V2:147
filled, never. (The Greatest Grandeur) V18:119
Firewood, iron-ware, and cheap tin trays (Cargoes) V5:44
Fled is that music:—Do I wake or sleep? (Ode to a Nightingale) V3:229
For I'm sick at the heart, and I fain wad lie down." (Lord Randal) V6:105
For nothing now can ever come to any good. (Funeral Blues) V10:139
For the love of God they buried his cold corpse. (The Bronze Horseman) V28:31
For the world's more full of weeping than he can understand. (The Stolen Child) V34:217
forget me as fast as you can. (Last Request) V14:231
from one kiss (A Rebirth) V21:193–194

G

garish for a while and burned. (One of the Smallest) V26:142
going where? Where? (Childhood) V19:29

H

Had anything been wrong, we should certainly have heard (The Unknown Citizen) V3:303
Had somewhere to get to and sailed calmly on (Mus,e des Beaux Arts) V1:148
half eaten by the moon. (Dear Reader) V10:85
hand over hungry hand. (Climbing) V14:113
Happen on a red tongue (Small Town with One Road) V7:207
hard as mine with another man? (An Attempt at Jealousy) V29:24
Has no more need of, and I have (The Courage that My Mother Had) V3:80
Has set me softly down beside you. The Poem is you (Paradoxes and Oxymorons) V11:162
Hath melted like snow in the glance of the Lord! (The Destruction of Sennacherib) V1:39
He rose the morrow morn (The Rime of the Ancient Mariner) V4:132
He says again, "Good fences make good neighbors." (Mending Wall) V5:232
He writes down something that he crosses out. (The Boy) V19:14
here; passion will save you. (Air for Mercury) V20:2–3
History theirs whose languages is the sun. (An Elementary School Classroom in a Slum) V23:88–89
How at my sheet goes the same crooked worm (The Force That Through the Green Fuse Drives the Flower) V8:101
How can I turn from Africa and live? (A Far Cry from Africa) V6:61
How sad then is even the marvelous! (An Africian Elegy) V13:4

I

I am a true Russian! (Babii Yar) V29:38
I am black. (The Song of the Smoke) V13:197
I am going to keep things like this (Hawk Roosting) V4:55
I am not brave at all (Strong Men, Riding Horses) V4:209
I could not see to see— (I Heard a Fly Buzz—When I Died—) V5:140
I cremated Sam McGee (The Cremation of Sam McGee) V10:76
I didn't want to put them down. (And What If I Spoke of Despair) V19:2
I have just come down from my father (The Hospital Window) V11:58
I hear it in the deep heart's core. (The Lake Isle of Innisfree) V15:121
I know why the caged bird sings! (Sympathy) V33:203
I never writ, nor no man ever loved (Sonnet 116) V3:288
I rest in the grace of the world, and am free. (The Peace of Wild Things) V30:159
I romp with joy in the bookish dark (Eating Poetry) V9:61
I see Mike's painting, called SARDINES (Why I Am Not a Painter) V8:259
I shall but love thee better after death (Sonnet 43) V2:236

I should be glad of another death (Journey of the Magi) V7:110
I stand up (Miss Rosie) V1:133
I stood there, fifteen (Fifteen) V2:78
I take it you are he? (Incident in a Rose Garden) V14:191
I, too, am America. (I, Too) V30:99
I turned aside and bowed my head and wept (The Tropics in New York) V4:255
If Winter comes, can Spring be far behind? (Ode to the West Wind) V2:163
I'll be gone from here. (The Cobweb) V17:51
I'll dig with it (Digging) V5:71
Imagine! (Autobiographia Literaria) V34:2
In a convulsive misery (The Milkfish Gatherers) V11:112
In balance with this life, this death (An Irish Airman Foresees His Death) V1:76
in earth's gasp, ocean's yawn. (Lake) V23:158
In Flanders fields (In Flanders Fields) V5:155
In ghostlier demarcations, keener sounds. (The Idea of Order at Key West) V13:164
In hearts at peace, under an English heaven (The Soldier) V7:218
In her tomb by the side of the sea (Annabel Lee) V9:14
in the family of things. (Wild Geese) V15:208
in the grit gray light of day. (Daylights) V13:102
In the rear-view mirrors of the passing cars (The War Against the Trees) V11:216
In these Chicago avenues. (A Thirst Against) V20:205
in this bastion of culture. (To an Unknown Poet) V18:221
in your unsteady, opening hand. (What the Poets Could Have Been) V26:262
iness (l(a) V1:85
Into blossom (A Blessing) V7:24
Is Come, my love is come to me. (A Birthday) V10:34
is love—that's all. (Two Poems for T.) V20:218
is safe is what you said. (Practice) V23:240
is still warm (Lament for the Dorsets) V5:191
It asked a crumb—of Me ("Hope" Is the Thing with Feathers) V3:123
It had no mirrors. I no longer needed mirrors. (I, I, I) V26:97
It is our god. (Fiddler Crab) V23:111–112
it is the bell to awaken God that we've heard ringing. (The Garden Shukkei-en) V18:107
it over my face and mouth. (An Anthem) V26:34
It rains as I write this. Mad heart, be brave. (The Country Without a Post Office) V18:64
It was your resting place." (Ah, Are You Digging on My Grave?) V4:2
it's always ourselves we find in the sea (maggie & milly & molly & may) V12:150
its bright, unequivocal eye. (Having it Out with Melancholy) V17:99
It's the fall through wind lifting white leaves. (Rapture) V21:181
its youth. The sea grows old in it. (The Fish) V14:172

J

Judge tenderly—of Me (This Is My Letter to the World) V4:233
Just imagine it (Inventors) V7:97

K

kisses you (Grandmother) V34:95

L

Laughing the stormy, husky, brawling laughter of Youth, half-naked, sweating, proud to be Hog Butcher, Tool Maker, Stacker of Wheat, Player with Railroads and Freight Handler to the Nation (Chicago) V3:61
Learn to labor and to wait (A Psalm of Life) V7:165
Leashed in my throat (Midnight) V2:131
Leaving thine outgrown shell by life's un-resting sea (The Chambered Nautilus) V24:52–53
Let my people go (Go Down, Moses) V11:43
Let the water come. (America, America) V29:4
life, our life and its forgetting. (For a New Citizen of These United States) V15:55
Life to Victory (Always) V24:15
like a bird in the sky … (Ego-Tripping) V28:113
like a shadow or a friend. *Colombia.* (Kindness) V24:84–85
Like Stone— (The Soul Selects Her Own Society) V1:259
Little Lamb, God bless thee. (The Lamb) V12:135
Look'd up in perfect silence at the stars. (When I Heard the Learn'd Astronomer) V22:244
love (The Toni Morrison Dreams) V22:202–203
Loved I not Honour more. (To Lucasta, Going to the Wars) V32:291
Luck was rid of its clover. (Yet we insist that life is full of happy chance) V27:292

M

'Make a wish, Tom, make a wish.' (Drifters) V10: 98
make it seem to change (The Moon Glows the Same) V7:152
May be refined, and join the angelic train. (On Being Brought from Africa to America) V29:223
may your mercy be near. (Two Eclipses) V33:221
midnight-oiled in the metric laws? (A Farewell to English) V10:126
Monkey business (Business) V16:2
More dear, both for themselves and for thy sake! (Tintern Abbey) V2:250
My foe outstretchd beneath the tree. (A Poison Tree) V24:195–196
My love shall in my verse ever live young (Sonnet 19) V9:211
My soul has grown deep like the rivers. (The Negro Speaks of Rivers) V10:198
My soul I'll pour into thee. (The Night Piece: To Julia) V29:206

N

never to waken in that world again (Starlight) V8:213
newness comes into the world (Daughter-Mother-Maya-Seeta) V25:83
Nirvana is here, nine times out of ten. (Spring-Watching Pavilion) V18:198
No, she's brushing a boy's hair (Facing It) V5:110
no—tell them *no*—(The Hiding Place) V10:153
Noble six hundred! (The Charge of the Light Brigade) V1:3
nobody,not even the rain,has such small hands (somewhere i have never travelled,gladly beyond) V19:265

Nor swim under the terrible eyes of prison ships. (The Drunken Boat) V28:84
Not a roof but a field of stars. (Rent) V25:164
not be seeing you, for you have no insurance. (The River Mumma Wants Out) V25:191
Not even the blisters. Look. (What Belongs to Us) V15:196
Not of itself, but thee. (Song: To Celia) V23:270–271
Nothing, and is nowhere, and is endless (High Windows) V3:108
Nothing gold can stay (Nothing Gold Can Stay) V3:203
Now! (Alabama Centennial) V10:2
nursing the tough skin of figs (This Life) V1:293

O

O Death in Life, the days that are no more! (Tears, Idle Tears) V4:220
O Lord our Lord, how excellent is thy name in all the earth! (Psalm 8) V9:182
O Roger, Mackerel, Riley, Ned, Nellie, Chester, Lady Ghost (Names of Horses) V8:142
o, walk your body down, don't let it go it alone. (Walk Your Body Down) V26:219
Of all our joys, this must be the deepest. (Drinking Alone Beneath the Moon) V20:59–60
of blood and ignorance. (Art Thou the Thing I Wanted) V25:2–3
of gentleness (To a Sad Daughter) V8:231
of love's austere and lonely offices? (Those Winter Sundays) V1:300
of peaches (The Weight of Sweetness) V11:230
Of the camellia (Falling Upon Earth) V2:64
Of the Creator. And he waits for the world to begin (Leviathan) V5:204
of our festivities (Fragment 2) V31:63
Of what is past, or passing, or to come (Sailing to Byzantium) V2:207
Oh that was the garden of abundance, seeing you. (Seeing You) V24:244–245
Old Ryan, not yours (The Constellation Orion) V8:53
On rainy Monday nights of an eternal November. (Classic Ballroom Dances) V33:3
On the dark distant flurry (Angle of Geese) V2:2
on the frosty autumn air. (The Cossacks) V25:70
On the look of Death— (There's a Certain Slant of Light) V6:212
On the reef of Norman s Woe! (The Wreck of the Hesperus) V31:317
On your head like a crown (Any Human to Another) V3:2
One could do worse that be a swinger of birches. (Birches) V13:15
"Only the Lonely," trying his best to sound like Elvis. (The Women Who Loved Elvis All Their Lives) V28:274
or a loose seed. (Freeway 280) V30:62
Or does it explode? (Harlem) V1:63
Or help to half-a-crown." (The Man He Killed) V3:167
Or if I die. (The Fly) V34:70
Or just some human sleep. (After Apple Picking) V32:3
or last time, we look. (In Particular) V20:125
or last time, we look. (In Particular) V20:125
Or might not have lain dormant forever. (Mastectomy) V26:123
or nothing (Queen-Ann's-Lace) V6:179
Or pleasures, seldom reached, again pursued. (A Nocturnal Reverie) V30:119–120
or the one red leaf the snow releases in March. (ThreeTimes My Life Has Opened) V16:213
ORANGE forever. (Ballad of Orange and Grape) V10:18
our every corpuscle become an elf. (Moreover, the Moon) V20:153
Our love shall live, and later life renew." (Sonnet 75) V32:215
outside. (it was New York and beautifully, snowing... (i was sitting in mcsorley's) V13:152
owing old (old age sticks) V3:246

P

patient in mind remembers the time. (Fading Light) V21:49
Penelope, who really cried. (An Ancient Gesture) V31:3
Perhaps he will fall. (Wilderness Gothic) V12:242
Petals on a wet, black bough (In a Station of the Metro) V2:116
Plaiting a dark red love-knot into her long black hair (The Highwayman) V4:68
Powerless, I drown. (Maternity) V21:142–143
Práise him. (Pied Beauty) V26:161
Pro patria mori. (Dulce et Decorum Est) V10:110

R

Rage, rage against the dying of the light (Do Not Go Gentle into that Good Night) V1:51
Raise it again, man. We still believe what we hear. (The Singer's House) V17:206
Remember. (Remember) V32:185
Remember the Giver fading off the lip (A Drink of Water) V8:66
Ride me. (Witness) V26:285
rise & walk away like a panther. (Ode to a Drum) V20:172–173
Rises toward her day after day, like a terrible fish (Mirror) V1:116

S

Shall be lifted—nevermore! (The Raven) V1:202
Shall you be overcome. (Conscientious Objector) V34:46
Shantih shantih shantih (The Waste Land) V20:248–252
share my shivering bed. (Chorale) V25:51
she'd miss me. (In Response to Executive Order 9066: All Americans of Japanese Descent Must Report to Relocation Centers) V32:129
Show an affirming flame. (September 1, 1939) V27:235
Shuddering with rain, coming down around me. (Omen) V22:107
Simply melted into the perfect light. (Perfect Light) V19:187
Singing of him what they could understand (Beowulf) V11:3
Singing with open mouths their strong melodious songs (I Hear America Singing) V3:152
Sister, one of those who never married. (My Grandmother's Plot in the Family Cemetery) V27:155
Sleep, fly, rest: even the sea dies! (Lament for Ignacio Sánchez Mejías) V31:128–30
slides by on grease (For the Union Dead) V7:67
Slouches towards Bethlehem to be born? (The Second Coming) V7:179
so like the smaller stars we rowed among. (The Lotus Flowers) V33:108

So long lives this, and this gives life to thee (Sonnet 18) V2:222
So prick my skin. (Pine) V23:223–224
Somebody loves us all. (Filling Station) V12:57
Speak through my words and my blood. (The Heights of Macchu Picchu) V28:141
spill darker kissmarks on that dark. (Ten Years after Your Deliberate Drowning) V21:240
Stand still, yet we will make him run (To His Coy Mistress) V5:277
startled into eternity (Four Mountain Wolves) V9:132
Still clinging to your shirt (My Papa's Waltz) V3:192
Stood up, coiled above his head, transforming all. (A Tall Man Executes a Jig) V12:229
strangers ask. *Originally?* And I hesitate. (Originally) V25:146–147
Surely goodness and mercy shall follow me all the days of my life: and I will dwell in the house of the Lord for ever (Psalm 23) V4:103
syllables of an old order. (A Grafted Tongue) V12:93

T

Take any streetful of people buying clothes and groceries, cheering a hero or throwing confetti and blowing tin horns... tell me if the lovers are losers... tell me if any get more than the lovers... in the dust... in the cool tombs (Cool Tombs) V6:46
Than from everything else life promised that you could do? (Paradiso) V20:190–191
Than that you should remember and be sad. (Remember) V14:255
that does not see you. You must change your life. (Archaic Torso of Apollo) V27:3
that might have been sweet in Grudnow. (Grudnow) V32:74
That then I scorn to change my state with Kings (Sonnet 29) V8:198
that there is more to know, that one day you will know it. (Knowledge) V25:113
That when we live no more, we may live ever (To My Dear and Loving Husband) V6:228
That's the word. (Black Zodiac) V10:47

the bigger it gets. (Smart and Final Iris) V15:183
The bosom of his Father and his God (Elegy Written in a Country Churchyard) V9:74
the bow toward torrents of *veyz mir.* (Three To's and an Oi) V24:264
The crime was in Granada, his Granada. (The Crime Was in Granada) V23:55–56
The dance is sure (Overture to a Dance of Locomotives) V11:143
The eyes turn topaz. (Hugh Selwyn Mauberley) V16:30
the flames? (Another Night in the Ruins) V26:13
The frolic architecture of the snow. (The Snow-Storm) V34:196
The garland briefer than a girl's (To an Athlete Dying Young) V7:230
The Grasshopper's among some grassy hills. (On the Grasshopper and the Cricket) V32:161
The guidon flags flutter gayly in the wind. (Cavalry Crossing a Ford) V13:50
The hands gripped hard on the desert (At the Bomb Testing Site) V8:3
The holy melodies of love arise. (The Arsenal at Springfield) V17:3
the knife at the throat, the death in the metronome (Music Lessons) V8:117
The Lady of Shalott." (The Lady of Shalott) V15:97
The lightning and the gale! (Old Ironsides) V9:172
The lone and level sands stretch far away. (Ozymandias) V27:173
the long, perfect loveliness of sow (Saint Francis and the Sow) V9:222
The Lord survives the rainbow of His will (The Quaker Graveyard in Nantucket) V6:159
The man I was when I was part of it (Beware of Ruins) V8:43
the quilts sing on (My Mother Pieced Quilts) V12:169
The red rose and the brier (Barbara Allan) V7:11
The self-same Power that brought me there brought you. (The Rhodora) V17:191
The shaft we raise to them and thee (Concord Hymn) V4:30
the skin of another, what I have made is a curse. (Curse) V26:75

The sky became a still and woven blue. (Merlin Enthralled) V16:73
The spirit of this place (To a Child Running With Outstretched Arms in Canyon de Chelly) V11:173
The town again, trailing your legs and crying! (Wild Swans) V17:221
the unremitting space of your rebellion (Lost Sister) V5:217
The woman won (Oysters) V4:91
The world should listen then—as I am listening now. (To a Sky-Lark) V32:252
their dinnerware. (Portrait of a Couple at Century's End) V24:214–215
their guts or their brains? (Southbound on the Freeway) V16:158
Then chiefly lives. (Virtue) V25:263
There are blows in life, so hard... I just don't know! (The Black Heralds) V26:47
There is the trap that catches noblest spirits, that caught—they say— God, when he walked on earth (Shine, Perishing Republic) V4:162
there was light (Vancouver Lights) V8:246
They also serve who only stand and wait." ([On His Blindness] Sonnet 16) V3:262
They are going to some point true and unproven. (Geometry) V15:68
They have not sown, and feed on bitter fruit. (A Black Man Talks of Reaping) V32:21
They rise, they walk again (The Heaven of Animals) V6:76
They say a child with two mouths is no good. (Pantoun for Chinese Women) V29:242
They think I lost. I think I won (Harlem Hopscotch) V2:93
They'd eaten every one." (The Walrus and the Carpenter) V30:258–259
This is my page for English B (Theme for English B) V6:194
This Love (In Memory of Radio) V9:145
Tho' it were ten thousand mile! (A Red, Red Rose) V8:152
Though I sang in my chains like the sea (Fern Hill) V3:92

Till human voices wake us, and we drown (The Love Song of J. Alfred Prufrock) V1:99
Till Love and Fame to nothingness do sink (When I Have Fears that I May Cease to Be) V2:295
Till the gossamer thread you fling catch somewhere, O my soul. (A Noiseless Patient Spider) V31:190–91
To every woman a happy ending (Barbie Doll) V9:33
to glow at midnight. (The Blue Rim of Memory) V17:39
to its owner or what horror has befallen the other shoe (A Pied) V3:16
To live with thee and be thy love. (The Nymph's Reply to the Shepherd) V14:241
To mock the riddled corpses round Bapaume. ("Blighters") V28:3
To strengthen whilst one stands." (Goblin Market) V27:96
To strive, to seek, to find, and not to yield (Ulysses) V2:279
To the moaning and the groaning of the bells (The Bells) V3:47
To the temple, singing. (In the Suburbs) V14:201
To wound myself upon the sharp edges of the night? (The Taxi) V30:211–212
torn from a wedding brocade. (My Mother Combs My Hair) V34:133
Turned to that dirt from whence he sprung. (A Satirical Elegy on the Death of a Late Famous General) V27:216

U

Undeniable selves, into your days, and beyond. (The Continuous Life) V18:51
until at last I lift you up and wrap you within me. (It's like This) V23:138–139
Until Eternity. (The Bustle in a House) V10:62
unusual conservation (Chocolates) V11:17
Uttering cries that are almost human (American Poetry) V7:2

W

War is kind (War Is Kind) V9:253
watching to see how it's done. (I Stop Writing the Poem) V16:58
water. (Poem in Which My Legs Are Accepted) V29:262
We are satisfied, if you are; but why did I die? (Losses) V31:167–68
we tread upon, forgetting. Truth be told. (Native Guard) V29:185
Went home and put a bullet through his head (Richard Cory) V4:117
Were not the one dead, turned to their affairs. (Out, Out—) V10:213
Were toward Eternity— (Because I Could Not Stop for Death) V2:27
What will survive of us is love. (An Arundel Tomb) V12:18
When I died they washed me out of the turret with a hose (The Death of the Ball Turret Gunner) V2:41
when they untie them in the evening. (Early in the Morning) V17:75
when you are at a party. (Social Life) V19:251
When you have both (Toads) V4:244
Where deep in the night I hear a voice (Butcher Shop) V7:43
Where ignorant armies clash by night (Dover Beach) V2:52
Which Claus of Innsbruck cast in bronze for me! (My Last Duchess) V1:166
Which for all you know is the life you've chosen. (The God Who Loves You) V20:88
which is not going to go wasted on me which is why I'm telling you about it (Having a Coke with You) V12:106
which only looks like an *l*, and is silent. (Trompe l'Oeil) V22:216
white ash amid funereal cypresses (Helen) V6:92
Who are you and what is your purpose? (The Mystery) V15:138
Why am I not as they? (Lineage) V31:145–46
Wi' the Scots lords at his feit (Sir Patrick Spens) V4:177
Will always be ready to bless the day (Morning Walk) V21:167
will be easy, my rancor less bitter... (On the Threshold) V22:128
Will hear of as a god." (How we Heard the Name) V10:167
Wind, like the dodo's (Bedtime Story) V8:33
windowpanes. (View) V25:246–247
With courage to endure! (Old Stoic) V33:144
With gold unfading, WASHINGTON! be thine. (To His Excellency General Washington) V13:213
with my eyes closed. (We Live by What We See at Night) V13:240
With silence and tears. (When We Two Parted) V29:297
with the door closed. (Hanging Fire) V32:93
With the slow smokeless burning of decay (The Wood-Pile) V6:252
With what they had to go on. (The Conquerors) V13:67
Without cease or doubt sew the sweet sad earth. (The Satyr's Heart) V22:187
Would scarcely know that we were gone. (There Will Come Soft Rains) V14:301

Y

Ye know on earth, and all ye need to know (Ode on a Grecian Urn) V1:180
Yea, beds for all who come. (Up-Hill) V34:280
You live in this, and dwell in lovers' eyes (Sonnet 55) V5:246
You may for ever tarry. (To the Virgins, to Make Much of Time) V13:226
you who raised me? (The Gold Lily) V5:127
You're all that I can call my own. (Woman Work) V33:289
you'll have understood by then what these Ithakas mean. (Ithaka) V19:114

For Reference
Not to be taken from this room

LINCC